How to Use the Maps in *Twentieth-Century World History*, Fourth Edition

Here are some basic map concepts that will help you to get the most out of the maps in this textbook.

- Always look at the scale, which allows you to determine the distance in miles or kilometers between locations on the map.

- Examine the legend carefully. It explains the colors and symbols used on the map.

- Note the locations of mountains, rivers, oceans, and other geographic features, and consider how these would affect such human activities as agriculture, commerce, travel, and warfare.

- Read the map caption thoroughly. It provides important information, sometimes not covered in the text itself, and poses a thought question to encourage you to think beyond the mere appearance of the map and make connections across chapters, regions, and concepts.

- Several "spot maps" appear in each chapter, to allow you to view in detail smaller areas that may not be apparent in larger maps. For example, a spot map in Chapter 15 lets you zoom in on Iraq.

- Many of the text's maps also carry a globe icon, which indicates that they or similar maps appear in interactive form at http://worldrc.wadsworth.com/

FOURTH EDITION

TWENTIETH-CENTURY
WORLD HISTORY

WILLIAM J. DUIKER

The Pennsylvania State University

WADSWORTH
CENGAGE Learning

Australia • Brazil • Japan • Korea • Mexico • Singapore • Spain • United Kingdom • United States

**Twentieth-Century World History,
Fourth Edition**
William J. Duiker

Publisher: Clark Baxter

History Editor: Ashley Dodge

Senior Development Editor: Sue Gleason

Editorial Assistant: Ashley Spicer

Development Project Manager:
Lee McCracken

Executive Marketing Manager: Janise Fry

Marketing Assistant: Teresa Jessen

Marketing Communications Manager:
Tami Strang

Project Manager, Editorial Production:
Katy German

Creative Director: Rob Hugel

Art Director: Maria Epes

Print Buyer: Nora Massuda

Permissions Editor: Roberta Broyer

Production Service: John Orr

Photo Researcher: Image Quest

Copy Editor: Pat Lewis

Cover Designer: Marsha Cohen

Compositor: International Typesetting
and Composition

Cover Image: © Jon Hicks/Corbis

For product information and technology assistance, contact us at
Cengage Learning Customer & Sales Support, 1-800-354-9706
For permission to use material from this text or product, submit all requests online at **cengage.com/permissions**
Further permissions questions can be e-mailed to
permissionrequest@cengage.com

Library of Congress Control Number: 2006936431

ISBN-13: 978-0-495-09592-7

ISBN-10: 0-495-09592-3

Wadsworth
25 Thomson Place
Boston, MA 02210
USA

Cengage Learning is a leading provider of customized learning solutions with office locations around the globe, including Singapore, the United Kingdom, Australia, Mexico, Brazil, and Japan. Locate your local office at:
www.cengage.com/global

Cengage Learning products are represented in Canada by Nelson Education, Ltd.

To learn more about Wadsworth, visit **www.cengage.com/wadsworth**

Purchase any of our products at your local college store or at our preferred online store
www.ichapters.com

Printed in the United States of America
4 5 6 7 10 09 08

ABOUT THE AUTHOR

WILLIAM J. DUIKER is liberal arts professor emeritus of East Asian studies at The Pennsylvania State University. A former U.S. diplomat with service in Taiwan, South Vietnam, and Washington, D.C., he received his doctorate in Far Eastern history from Georgetown University in 1968, where his dissertation dealt with the Chinese educator and reformer Cai Yuanpei. At Penn State, he has written extensively on the history of Vietnam and modern China, including the widely acclaimed *The Communist Road to Power in Vietnam* (revised edition, Westview Press, 1996), which was selected for a Choice Outstanding Academic Book Award in 1982–1983 and 1996–1997. Other recent books are *China and Vietnam: The Roots of Conflict* (Berkley, 1987), *Sacred War: Nationalism and Revolution in a Divided Vietnam* (McGraw-Hill, 1995), and *Ho Chi Minh: A Life* (Hyperion, 2000). While his research specialization is in the field of nationalism and Asian revolutions, his intellectual interests are considerably more diverse. He has traveled widely and has taught courses on the History of Communism and Non-Western Civilizations at Penn State, where he was awarded a Faculty Scholar Medal for Outstanding Achievement in the spring of 1996.

To Kirsten and Zachary,
as you face the challenges of the new century
W.J.D.

Brief Contents

DETAILED CONTENTS

PART III
ACROSS THE IDEOLOGICAL DIVIDE   139

7 EAST AND WEST IN THE GRIP OF THE COLD WAR   140

8 THE UNITED STATES, CANADA, AND LATIN AMERICA   160

9 BRAVE NEW WORLD: THE RISE AND FALL OF COMMUNISM IN THE SOVIET UNION AND EASTERN EUROPE   181

DOCUMENTS

MAPS

PREFACE

THE TWENTIETH CENTURY was an era of paradox. When it began, Western civilization was a patchwork of squabbling states that bestrode the world like a colossus. As the century came to an end, the West was prosperous and increasingly united, yet there were signs global economic and political hegemony was beginning to shift to the East. The era of Western dominance had come to an end. It had been an age marked by war and revolution but also by rapid industrial growth and widespread economic prosperity, a time of growing interdependence but also of burgeoning ethnic and national consciousness, a period that witnessed the rising power of science but also fervent religiosity and growing doubts about the impact of technology on the human experience.

Twentieth-Century World History attempts to chronicle the key events in this revolutionary century while seeking to throw light on some of the underlying issues that shaped the times. Did the beginning of a new millennium mark the end of the long period of Western dominance? If so, will recent decades of European and American superiority be followed by a "Pacific century" with economic and political power shifting to the nations of eastern Asia? Will the end of the Cold War lead to a "new world order" marked by global cooperation, or are we on the verge of an unstable era of ethnic and national conflict? Why was a time of unparalleled prosperity and technological advance accompanied by deep pockets of poverty and widespread doubts about the role of government and the capabilities of human reason? Although this book does not promise final answers to such questions, it can provide a framework for analysis and a better understanding of some of the salient issues of modern times.

A number of decisions must be made by any author sufficiently foolhardy to seek to encompass in a single volume the history of a turbulent century. First in importance is whether to present the topic as an integrated whole or to focus on individual cultures and societies. The world that we live in today is in many respects an interdependent one in terms of economics as well as culture and communications, a reality that is often expressed by the familiar phrase "global village." At the same time, the process of globalization is by no means complete, as ethnic, religious, and regional differences continue to exist and to shape the course of our times. The tenacity of these differences is reflected not only in the rise of internecine conflicts in such divergent areas as Africa, South Asia, and eastern Europe but also in the emergence in recent years of such regional organizations as the African Union, the Association for the Southeast Asian Nations, and the European Economic Community. Political leaders in various parts of the world speak routinely (if sometimes wistfully) of "Arab unity," the "African road to socialism," and the "Confucian path to economic development."

The issue has practical implications. College students today are all too often not well informed about the distinctive character of civilizations such as China, India, and sub-Saharan Africa. Without sufficient exposure to the historical evolution of such societies, students will assume all too readily that the peoples in these countries have had historical experiences similar to their own and respond to various stimuli in a similar fashion to those living in western Europe or the United States. If it is a mistake to ignore the forces that link us together, it is equally erroneous to underestimate the factors that continue to divide us and to differentiate us into a world of diverse peoples.

My response to this challenge has been to seek a balance between a global and a regional approach. The opening chapters focus on issues that have a global impact, such as the Industrial Revolution, the era of imperialism, and the two world wars. Later chapters center on individual regions of the world, while singling out contrasts and comparisons that link them to the broader world community. The book is divided into five parts. The first four parts are each followed by a short section labeled "Reflection," which attempts to link events in a broad comparative and global framework. The chapter in the fifth and final part examines some of the common problems of our time—including environmental pollution, the population explosion, and spiritual malaise—and takes a cautious look into the future to explore how such issues will evolve in the twenty-first century.

Another issue that requires attention is the balance of the treatment of Western civilization and its counterparts in Asia and Africa. The modern world is often viewed essentially as the history of Europe and the Western Hemisphere, with other regions treated as appendages of the industrial countries. It is certainly true that much of the twentieth century was dominated by events in Europe and North America, and in recognition of this fact, the opening chapters focus primarily on issues related to the rise of the West, including the Industrial Revolution and the age of imperialism. In recent decades, however, other parts of the world have assumed greater importance, thus restoring a global balance that had existed prior to the scientific and technological revolution that transformed the West in the eighteenth and nineteenth centuries. Later chapters examine this phenomenon, according to regions such as Africa, Asia, and Latin America the importance that they merit today.

One final feature of the book merits brief mention here. Many textbooks on world history tend to simplify the content of history courses by emphasizing an intellectual or political perspective or, most recently, a social perspective, often at the expense of providing sufficient details in a chronological framework. This approach can be confusing to students whose high school social studies programs have often neglected a systematic study of world history. I have attempted to write a well-balanced work in which political, economic, social, and cultural history have been integrated into a chronologically ordered synthesis. In my judgment, a strong narrative, linking key issues in a broad interpretive framework, is still the most effective way to present the story of the past to young minds.

To supplement the text, I have included a number of boxed documents that illustrate key issues within each chapter. Extensive maps and illustrations, each positioned at the appropriate place in the chapter, serve to deepen the reader's understanding of the text. "Spot maps" provide details not visible in the larger maps, have been added. An annotated bibliography at the end of the book reviews the most recent literature on each period while referring also to some of the older "classical" works in the field.

The following supplements are available for instructors' use:

- **ExamView**—ExamView computerized testing allows users to create, deliver, and customize tests and study guides (both print and online) in minutes.

- **Transparency Acetates for World History**—includes over one hundred full-color maps from the text and other sources.

- **Book Companion Website** (academic.cengage.com/history/duiker)—provides chapter-by-chapter resources for this textbook for both instructors and students, as well as access to the Wadsworth History Resource Center. Text-specific content for students includes interactive maps, interactive timelines, tutorial quizzes, glossary, hyperlinks, InfoTrac® exercises, and Internet activities. Instructors also have access to the Instructor's Manual, lesson plans, and PowerPoint slides (access code required). From the home page, instructors and students can access many selections, such as an Internet Guide for History, a career center, simulations, movie activities, the World History image bank, and links to a wealth of primary-source documents.

I would like to express my appreciation to the reviewers who have read individual chapters and provided me with useful suggestions for improvement: Elizabeth Clark, West Texas A&M University; Sandi Cooper, College of Staten Island; Richard Grossman, De Paul University; James Harrison, Siena College; Mary Louise Loe, James Madison University; Jotham Parsons, Duquesne University; Roger Ransom, University of California, Riverside; Barbara Reeves-Ellington, Siena College; E. Timothy Smith, Barry University; Stuart Smyth, State University of New York, Albany; Gregory Vitarbo, Meredith College.

Jackson Spielvogel, who is coauthor of our textbook *World History* (now in its fifth edition), has been kind enough to permit me to use some of his sections in that book for the purposes of writing this one. Several of my other colleagues at Penn State—including Kumkum Chatterjee, On-cho Ng, and Arthur F. Goldschmidt—have provided me with valuable assistance in understanding parts of the world that are beyond my own area of concentration. To Clark Baxter, whose unfailing good humor, patience, and sage advice have so often eased the trauma of textbook publishing, I offer my heartfelt thanks. I am also grateful to Sue Gleason and Katy German of Wadsworth Publishing, and to Amy Guastello, for their assistance in bringing this project to fruition, and to John Orr of Orr Book Services for production. For this edition, ImageQuest has been helpful in obtaining images for this book.

Finally, I am eternally grateful to my wife, Yvonne V. Duiker, Ph.D. Her research and her written contributions on art, architecture, literature, and music have added sparkle to this book. Her presence at my side has added immeasurable sparkle to my life.

William J. Duiker
The Pennsylvania State University

NEW WORLD IN THE MAKING

SHEFFIELD SMOKE.
From a Drawing by A. MORROW.

*Sheffield became one of England's greatest manufacturing
cities during the nineteenth century*

1

THE RISE OF INDUSTRIAL SOCIETY IN THE WEST

*T*HE TWENTIETH CENTURY was a turbulent era, marked by two violent global conflicts, a bitter ideological struggle between two dominant world powers, explosive developments in the realm of science, and dramatic social change. When it began, the vast majority of the world's peoples lived on farms, and the horse was still the most common means of transportation. As it ended, human beings had trod on the moon and lived in a world increasingly defined by urban sprawl and modern technology.

What had happened to bring about these momentous changes? Although a world as complex as ours cannot be assigned a single cause, a good candidate for consideration is the Industrial Revolution, which began on the British Isles at the end of the eighteenth century and spread steadily throughout the world during the next two hundred years. The Industrial Revolution was unquestionably one of the most important factors in laying the foundation of the modern world. It not only transformed the economic means of production and distribution, but also altered the political systems, the social institutions and values, and the intellectual and cultural life of all the societies that it touched. The impact has been not only massive but controversial as well. Where proponents have alluded to the enormous material and technological benefits that industrialization has brought in its wake, critics have pointed out the high costs involved, from growing economic inequality to the dehumanization of everyday life. Already in the nineteenth century, German philosopher Karl Marx charged that factory labor had reduced workers to a mere "appendage of the machine," and the English writer Charles Dickens described in his novels an urban environment of factories, smoke, and ashes that seemed an apparition from Dante's Hell. ◆

The Industrial Revolution in Great Britain

Why the Industrial Revolution broke out in Great Britain rather than in another part of the world has been a subject for debate among historians for many decades. A number of factors certainly contributed to the rapid transformation of eighteenth-century British society from a predominantly agricultural to an industrial and commercial economy. First, improvements in agriculture during the eighteenth century had led to a significant increase in food production. British agriculture could now feed more people at lower prices with less labor; even ordinary British families no longer had to use most of their income to buy food, giving them the potential to purchase manufactured goods. At the same time, a rapid growth of population in the second half of the eighteenth century provided a pool of surplus labor for the new factories of the emerging British industrial sector.

A second factor was the rapid increase in national wealth. Two centuries of expanding trade had provided Britain with a ready supply of capital for investment in the new industrial machines and the factories that were required to house them. In addition to profits from trade, Britain possessed an effective central bank and well-developed, flexible credit facilities. Many early factory owners were merchants and entrepreneurs who had profited from the eighteenth-century cottage industry. The country also possessed what might today be described as a "modernization elite"—individuals who were interested in making profits if the opportunity presented itself. In that objective, they were generally supported by the government.

Third, Britain was richly supplied with important mineral resources, such as coal and iron ore, needed in the

Sheffield Smoke. The Industrial Revolution changed the physical landscape of every society that went through the experience, and sometimes in dramatic ways. Nowhere was this more true than in Great Britain, where coal mining and railroads transformed the Midlands from a region of farms and wooded hills into a barren land pockmarked with factories belching fire and black smoke. Shown here is a view of the city of Sheffield, a onetime farming center that became one of England's greatest manufacturing cities during the nineteenth century.

SHEFFIELD SMOKE.
From a Drawing by A. MORROW.

© Hulton Getty/Getty Images

manufacturing process. Britain was also a small country, and the relatively short distances made transportation facilities readily accessible. In addition to nature's provision of abundant rivers, from the mid-seventeenth century onward, both private and public investment poured into the construction of new roads, bridges, and canals. By 1780, roads, rivers, and canals linked the major industrial centers of the north, the Midlands, London, and the Atlantic coast.

Finally, foreign markets gave British industrialists a ready outlet for their manufactured goods. British exports quadrupled between 1660 and 1760. In the course of its eighteenth-century wars and conquests (see Chapter 2), Great Britain had developed a vast colonial empire at the expense of its leading continental rivals, the Dutch Republic and France. These territories provided domestic manufacturing with a source of cheap raw materials not available in the British Isles.[1]

During the last decades of the century, technological innovations, including the flying shuttle, the spinning jenny, and the power loom, led to a significant increase in production. The cotton textile industry achieved even greater heights of productivity with the invention of the steam engine, which proved invaluable to Britain's Industrial Revolution. The steam engine was a tireless source of power and depended for fuel on a substance—namely, coal—that seemed then to be available in unlimited quantities. The success of the steam engine increased the demand for coal and led to an expansion in coal production. In turn, new processes using coal furthered the development of an iron industry, the production of machinery, and the invention of the railroad.

The Spread of the Industrial Revolution

By the turn of the nineteenth century, industrialization had begun to spread to the continent of Europe, where it took a different path than had been followed in Great Britain (see Map 1.1). Governments on the Continent were accustomed to playing a major role in economic affairs and continued to do so as the Industrial Revolution got under way, subsidizing inventors, providing incentives to factory owners, and improving the transportation network. By 1850, a network of iron rails had spread across much of western and central Europe, while water routes were improved by the deepening and widening of rivers and canals.

Across the Atlantic Ocean, the United States experienced the first stages of its industrial revolution in the first half of the nineteenth century. In 1800, America was still a predominantly agrarian society, as six out of every seven workers were farmers. Sixty years later, only half of all workers were farmers, yet the total population had grown from 5 to 30 million people, larger than Great Britain itself.

The initial application of machinery to production was accomplished by borrowing from Great Britain. Soon, however, Americans began to equal or surpass British technical inventions. The Harpers Ferry arsenal, for example, built muskets with interchangeable parts. Because all the individual parts of a musket were identical (for example, all triggers were the same), the final product could be put together quickly and easily; this innovation enabled Americans to avoid the more costly system in which skilled craftsmen fitted together individual parts made separately. The so-called American system reduced costs and revolutionized production by saving labor, an important consideration in a society that had few skilled artisans.

Unlike Britain, the United States was a large country. The lack of a good system of internal transportation seemed to limit American economic development by making the transport of goods prohibitively expensive. This difficulty was gradually remedied, however. Thousands of miles of roads and canals were built linking east and west.

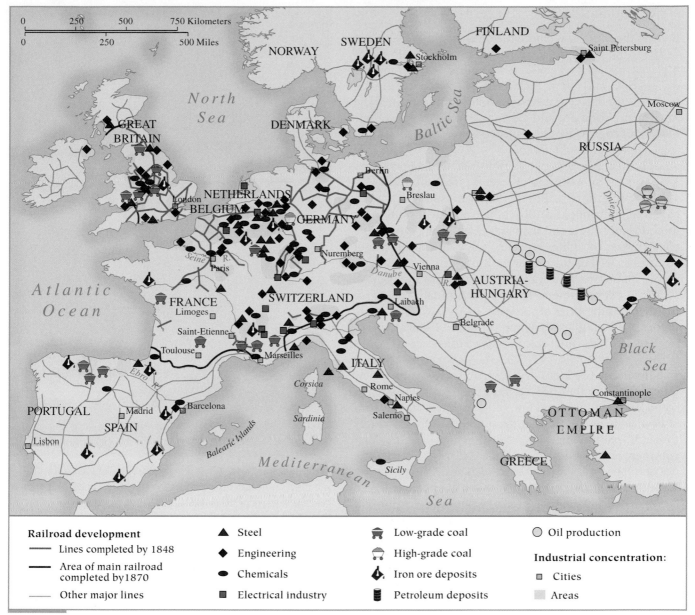

MAP 1.1 The Industrial Regions of Europe at the end of the Nineteenth Century. By the end of the nineteenth century, the Industrial Revolution—in steelmaking, electricity, petroleum, and chemicals—had spurred substantial economic growth and prosperity in western and central Europe; it also sparked economic and political competition between Great Britain and Germany. ❓ What parts of Europe not industrialized in 1850 had become industrialized in the ensuing decades?

🌐 View an animated version of this map or related maps at the World History Resource Center, at worldrc.wadsworth.com/.

The steamboat facilitated transportation on the Great Lakes, Atlantic coastal waters, and rivers. Most important of all in the development of an American transportation system was the railroad. Beginning with 100 miles in 1830, more than 27,000 miles of railroad track were laid in the next thirty years. This transportation revolution turned the United States into a single massive market for the manufactured goods of the Northeast, the early center of American industrialization, and by 1860, the United States was well on its way to being an industrial nation.

New Products and New Patterns

During the fifty years before the outbreak of World War I in 1914, the Western world witnessed a dynamic age of material prosperity. Thanks to new industries, new sources of energy, and new technological achievements, a second stage of the Industrial Revolution transformed the human environment and led people to believe that their material progress would improve world conditions and solve all human problems.

The first major change in industrial development after 1870 was the substitution of steel for iron. Steel, an alloy stronger and more malleable than iron, soon became an essential component of the Industrial Revolution. New methods for rolling and shaping steel made it useful in the construction of lighter, smaller, and faster machines and engines as well as for railways, shipbuilding, and armaments. It also paved the way for the building of the first skyscrapers, a development that would eventually transform the shape of the cities of the West. In 1860, Great Britain, France, Germany, and Belgium produced 125,000 tons of steel; by 1913, the total was 32 million tons.

The Invention of Electricity Electricity was a major new form of energy that proved to be of great value since it could be easily converted into other forms of energy, such as heat, light, and motion, and moved relatively effortlessly through space by means of transmitting wires. The first commercially practical generators of electric current were not developed until the 1870s. By 1910, hydroelectric power stations and coal-fired steam-generating plants enabled entire districts to be tied into a single power distribution system that provided a common source of power for homes, shops, and industrial enterprises.

Electricity spawned a whole series of new products. The invention of the incandescent filament lamp opened homes and cities to illumination by electric lights. A revolution in communications ensued when Alexander Graham Bell invented the telephone in 1876 and Guglielmo Marconi sent the first radio waves across the Atlantic in 1901. Although most electricity was initially used for lighting, it was eventually put to use in transportation. By the 1880s, streetcars and subways had appeared in major European cities. Electricity also transformed the factory. Conveyor belts, cranes, machines, and machine tools could all be powered by electricity and located anywhere.

The Internal Combustion Engine The development of the internal combustion engine had a similar effect. The processing of liquid fuels—petroleum and its distilled derivatives—made possible the widespread use of the internal combustion engine as a source of power in transportation. An oil-fired engine was made in 1897, and by

The Colossus of Paris. When it was completed for the Paris World's Fair in 1889, the Eiffel Tower became, at 1,056 feet, the tallest man-made monument in the world. The colossus, which seemed to be rising from the shadows of the city's feudal past like some new technological giant, symbolized the triumph of the Industrial Revolution and machine-age capitalism, proclaiming the dawn of a new era possessing endless possibilities and power. Constructed of wrought iron and comprising more than 2.5 million rivet holes, the structure was completed in two years and was paid for entirely by the builder himself, the engineer Gustave Eiffel. From the outset, the monument was wildly popular. Nearly two million people lined up at the fair to visit this gravity-defying marvel.

1902, the Hamburg-Amerika Line had switched from coal to oil on its new ocean liners. By the beginning of the twentieth century, some naval fleets had been converted to oil burners as well.

The internal combustion engine gave rise to the automobile and the airplane. In 1900, world production stood at 9,000 cars; by 1906, Americans had overtaken the initial lead of the French. It was an American, Henry Ford, who revolutionized the automotive industry with the mass production of the Model T. By 1916, Ford's factories were producing 735,000 cars a year. In the meantime, air transportation had emerged with the Zeppelin airship in 1900. In 1903, at Kitty Hawk, North Carolina, the Wright brothers made the first flight in a fixed-wing plane powered by a gasoline engine. World War I stimulated the aircraft industry, and in1919 the first regular passenger air service was established.

Trade and Manufacturing The growth of industrial production depended on the development of markets for the sale of manufactured goods. Competition for foreign markets was keen, and by 1870, European countries were increasingly compelled to focus on promoting domestic demand. Between 1850 and 1900, real wages increased in Britain by two-thirds and in Germany by one-third. A decline in the cost of food combined with lower prices for manufactured goods because of reduced production and transportation costs made it easier for Europeans to buy consumer products. In the cities, new methods for retail distribution—in particular, the department store— were used to expand sales of a whole new range of consumer goods made possible by the development of the steel and electric industries. The desire to own sewing machines,

clocks, bicycles, electric lights, and typewriters generated a new consumer ethic that has since become a crucial part of the modern economy.

Meanwhile, increased competition for foreign markets and the growing importance of domestic demand led to a reaction against the free trade that had characterized the European economy between 1820 and 1870. By the 1870s, Europeans were returning to the practice of tariff protection in order to guarantee domestic markets for the products of their own industries. At the same time, cartels were being formed to decrease competition internally. In a cartel, independent enterprises worked together to control prices and fix production quotas, thereby restraining the kind of competition that led to reduced prices. Cartels were especially strong in Germany, where banks moved to protect their investments by eliminating the "anarchy of competition." Founded in 1893, the Rhenish-Westphalian Coal Syndicate controlled 98 percent of Germany's coal production by 1904.

The formation of cartels was paralleled by a move toward ever-larger manufacturing plants, especially in the iron and steel, machinery, heavy electric equipment, and chemical industries. This growth in the size of industrial plants led to pressure for greater efficiency in factory production at the same time that competition led to demands for greater economy. The result was a desire to streamline or rationalize production as much as possible. The development of precision tools enabled manufacturers to produce interchangeable parts, which in turn led to the creation of the assembly line for production. In the second half of the nineteenth century, it was primarily used in manufacturing nonmilitary goods, such as sewing machines, typewriters, bicycles, and finally, automobiles.

The First Department Store. In the middle of the nineteenth century, a new way to promote the sale of manufactured goods first appeared in Europe—the department store. First of its kind was *Au Bon marché*, founded by the onetime traveling salesman Aristide Boucicaut in 1872. The store offered a number of innovations, including free entry, mail-order sales, and home delivery. It also contained a cafeteria and a rest area for its employees. Rebuilt as shown here in 1910, the store remains popular with Parisian shoppers today.

By 1900, much of western and central Europe had entered a new era, characterized by rising industrial production and material prosperity. Another part of Europe, however, the backward and little industrialized area to the south and east, consisting of southern Italy, most of Austria-Hungary, Spain, Portugal, the Balkan kingdoms, and Russia, was still largely agricultural and relegated by industrial countries to the function of providing food and raw materials. The presence of Romanian oil, Greek olive oil, and Serbian pigs and prunes in western Europe served as reminders of an economic division of Europe that continued well into the twentieth century.

Toward a World Economy

The economic developments of the late nineteenth century, combined with the transportation revolution that saw the growth of marine transport and railroads, fostered a true world economy. By 1900, Europeans were receiving beef and wool from Argentina and Australia, coffee from Brazil, nitrates from Chile, iron ore from Algeria, and sugar from Java. European capital was also invested abroad to develop railways, mines, electric power plants, and banks. High rates of return provided plenty of incentive. Of course, foreign countries also provided markets for the surplus manufactured goods of Europe. With its capital, industries, and military might, Europe dominated the world economy by the beginning of the nineteenth century.

Trade among various regions of the world, of course, had taken place for centuries. As early as the first millennium C.E., China and the Roman Empire had exchanged goods through intermediaries on both the maritime route across the Indian Ocean and over the famous Silk Road through the parched deserts of Central Asia. Trade across the Eurasian supercontinent increased with the rise of the Arab empire in the Middle East in the ninth century and then reached a peak during the thirteenth and fourteenth centuries, when the Mongol Empire stretched from the shores of the Pacific to the borders of eastern Europe. Trade routes also snaked across the Sahara to central and western Africa and along the eastern coast from the Red Sea to the island of Madagascar.

Not until the sixteenth century, however, was a truly global economy created, a product of the circumnavigation of the globe by the Portuguese adventurer Ferdinand Magellan and the voyages of exploration that followed. With the establishment of contacts between the Old World and the societies in the Western Hemisphere, trade now literally spanned the globe. New crops from the Americas, such as corn, potatoes, and manioc, entered the world market and changed eating habits and social patterns as far away as China. Tobacco from the Americas and coffee and tea from the Orient became the new craze in affluent circles in Europe and the Middle East.

In the view of some contemporary historians, it was this process that enabled a resurgent Europe to launch the economic and technological advances that led to the Industrial Revolution. According to historian Immanuel Wallerstein, one of the leading proponents of this theory, the age of exploration led to the creation of a new "world system" characterized by the emergence of global trade networks dominated by the rising force of European capitalism. This commercial revolution, in fact, operated much to the advantage of the European countries. Profits from the spice trade with eastern Asia, along with gold and silver from the Americas, flowed into state treasuries and the pockets of private traders in London, Paris, and Amsterdam. The wealth and power of Europe increased rapidly during this period, thus laying the groundwork for the economic revolution of the nineteenth century.

The Structure of Mass Society

The new world created by the Industrial Revolution led to the emergence of a mass society by the end of the nineteenth century. A mass society meant new forms of expression for the lower classes as they benefited from the extension of voting rights, an improved standard of living, and compulsory elementary education. But there was a price to pay. Urbanization and rapid population growth led to overcrowding in the burgeoning cities and increasing public health problems. The development of expanded means of communication resulted in the emergence of new organizations that sought to manipulate and control the population for their own purposes. A mass press, for example, swayed popular opinion by flamboyant journalistic practices.

As the number and size of cities continued to mushroom, governments by the 1880s came to the reluctant conclusion that private enterprise could not solve the housing crisis. In 1890, a British housing law empowered local town councils to construct cheap housing for the working classes. London and Liverpool were the first communities to take advantage of their new powers. Similar activity had been set in motion in Germany by 1900. Everywhere, however, these lukewarm measures failed to do much to meet the real housing needs of the working classes. Nevertheless, the need for planning had been recognized, and in the 1920s, municipal governments moved into housing construction on a large scale. In housing, as in so many other areas of life in the late nineteenth and early twentieth centuries, the liberal principle that the government that governs least governs best (discussed later in this chapter) had proved untrue. More and more, governments were stepping into areas of activity that they would never have touched earlier.

Social Structures

At the top of European society stood a wealthy elite, constituting only 5 percent of the population but controlling between 30 and 40 percent of its wealth. This privileged minority was an amalgamation of the traditional landed aristocracy that had dominated European society for centuries and the emerging upper middle class, sometimes called the bourgeoisie. In the course of the nineteenth century, aristocrats coalesced with the most successful industrialists, bankers, and merchants to form a new elite.

Increasingly, aristocrats and plutocrats fused as the latter purchased landed estates to join the aristocrats in the pleasures of country living while the aristocrats bought lavish town houses for part-time urban life. Common bonds were also created when the sons of wealthy bourgeois families were admitted to the elite schools dominated by the children of the aristocracy. This educated elite assumed leadership roles in the government and the armed forces. Marriage also served to unite the two groups. Daughters of tycoons gained titles, and aristocratic heirs gained new sources of cash. When the American heiress Consuelo Vanderbilt married the duke of Marlborough, the new duchess brought £2 million (approximately $10 million) to her husband.

A New Middle Class Below the upper class was a middle level of the bourgeoisie that included professionals in law, medicine, and the civil service as well as moderately well-to-do industrialists and merchants. The industrial expansion of the nineteenth century also added new vocations to Western society such as business managers, office workers, engineers, architects, accountants, and chemists, who formed professional associations as the symbols of their newfound importance. At the lower end of the middle class were the small shopkeepers, traders, manufacturers, and prosperous peasants. Their chief preoccupation was the provision of goods and services for the classes above them.

The moderately prosperous and successful members of this new mass society shared a certain style of life, one whose values tended to dominate much of nineteenth-century society. They were especially active in preaching their worldview to their children and to the upper and lower classes of their society. This was especially evident in Victorian Britain, often considered a model of middle-class society. It was the European middle classes who accepted and promulgated the importance of progress and science. They believed in hard work, which they viewed as the primary human good, open to everyone and guaranteed to have positive results. They also believed in the good conduct associated with traditional Christian morality.

Such values were often scorned at the time by members of the economic and intellectual elite, and in later years, it became commonplace for observers to mock the Victorian era—the years of the long reign of Queen Victoria (r. 1837–1901) in Great Britain—for its vulgar materialism, its cultural philistinism, and its conformist values. As the historian Peter Gay has recently shown, however, this harsh portrayal of the "bourgeois" character of the age distorts the reality of an era of complexity and contradiction, with diverse forces interacting to lay the foundations of the modern world.[2]

The Working Class The working classes constituted almost 80 percent of the population of Europe. In rural areas, many of these people were landholding peasants, agricultural laborers, and sharecroppers, especially in eastern Europe. Only about 10 percent of the British population worked in agriculture, however; in Germany, the figure was 25 percent.

There was no homogeneous urban working class. At the top were skilled artisans in such traditional handicraft trades as cabinetmaking, printing, and jewelry making. The Industrial Revolution, however, also brought new entrants into the group of highly skilled workers, including machine-tool specialists, shipbuilders, and metalworkers. Many skilled workers attempted to pattern themselves after the middle class by seeking good housing and educating their children.

Semiskilled laborers, including such people as carpenters, bricklayers, and many factory workers, earned wages that were about two-thirds of those of highly skilled workers (see the box on p. 10). At the bottom of the hierarchy stood the largest group of workers, the unskilled laborers. They included day laborers, who worked irregularly for very low wages, and large numbers of domestic servants. One of every seven employed persons in Great Britain in 1900 was a domestic servant.

Urban workers did experience a betterment in the material conditions of their lives after 1870. A rise in real wages, accompanied by a decline in many consumer costs, especially in the 1880s and 1890s, made it possible for workers to buy more than just food and housing. Workers' budgets now included money for more clothes and even leisure at the same time that strikes and labor agitation were winning ten-hour days and Saturday afternoons off. The combination of more income and more free time produced whole new patterns of mass leisure.

Among the least attractive aspects of the era, however, was the widespread practice of child labor. Working conditions for underage workers were often abysmal. According to a report commissioned in 1832 to inquire into the conditions for child factory workers in Great Britain, children as young as six years of age began work before dawn. Those who were drowsy or fell asleep were tapped

DISCIPLINE IN THE NEW FACTORIES

Workers in the new factories of the Industrial Revolution had been accustomed to a lifestyle free of overseers. Unlike the cottage industry, where home-based workers spun thread and wove cloth in their own rhythm and time, the factories demanded a new, rigorous discipline geared to the requirements and operating hours of the machines. This selection is taken from a set of rules for a factory in Berlin in 1844. They were typical of company rules everywhere the factory system had been established.

How many of these regulations do you believe would be acceptable to employers and employees in today's labor market? Why or Why not?

Factory Rules, Foundry and Engineering Works, Royal Overseas Trading Company

In every large works, and in the coordination of any large number of workmen, good order and harmony must be looked upon as the fundamentals of success, and therefore the following rules shall be strictly observed.

1. The normal working day begins at all seasons at 6 A.M. precisely and ends, after the usual break of half an hour for breakfast, an hour for dinner, and half an hour for tea, at 7 P.M., and it shall be strictly observed. . . .

2. Workers arriving 2 minutes late shall lose half an hour's wages; whoever is more than 2 minutes late may not start work until after the next break, or at least shall lose his wages until then. Any disputes about the correct time shall be settled by the clock mounted above the gatekeeper's lodge. . . .

3. No workman, whether employed by time or piece, may leave before the end of the working day, without having first received permission from the overseer and having given his name to the gatekeeper. Omission of these two actions shall lead to a fine of ten silver groschen payable to the sick fund.

4. Repeated irregular arrival at work shall lead to dismissal. This shall also apply to those who are found idling by an official or overseer, and refused to obey their order to resume work. . . .

6. No worker may leave his place of work otherwise than for reasons connected with his work.

7. All conversation with fellow-workers is prohibited; if any worker requires information about his work, he must turn to the overseer, or to the particular fellow-worker designated for the purpose.

8. Smoking in the workshops or in the yard is prohibited during working hours; anyone caught smoking shall be fined five silver groschen for the sick fund for every such offense. . . .

10. Natural functions must be performed at the appropriate places, and whoever is found soiling walls, fences, squares, etc., and similarly, whoever is found washing his face and hands in the workshop and not in the places assigned for the purpose, shall be fined five silver groschen for the sick fund. . . .

12. It goes without saying that all overseers and officials of the firm shall be obeyed without question, and shall be treated with due deference. Disobedience will be punished by dismissal.

13. Immediate dismissal shall also be the fate of anyone found drunk in any of the workshops. . . .

14. Every workman is obliged to report to his superiors any acts of dishonesty or embezzlement on the part of his fellow workmen. If he omits to do so, and it is shown after subsequent discovery of a misdemeanor that he knew about it at the time, he shall be liable to be taken to court as an accessory after the fact and the wage due to him shall be retained as punishment.

SOURCE: From *Documents of European Economic History* by Sidney Pollard and Colin Holmes (New York: St. Martin's Press, 1968) Copyright © 1968 by S. Pollard and C. Holmes.

on the head, doused with cold water, strapped to a chair, or flogged with a stick.

Changing Roles for Women

The position of women during the Industrial Revolution was also changing. During much of the nineteenth century, many women adhered to the ideal of femininity popularized by writers and poets. Tennyson's poem *The Princess* expressed it well:

Man for the field and woman for the hearth:
Man for the sword and for the needle she:
Man with the head and woman with the heart:
Man to command and woman to obey;
All else confusion.

The reality was somewhat different. Under the impact of the Industrial Revolution, which created a wide variety of service and white-collar jobs, women began to accept employment as clerks, typists, secretaries, and salesclerks.

ESCAPING THE DOLL'S HOUSE

Although a majority of women probably followed the nineteenth-century middle-class ideal of women as keepers of the household and nurturers of husband and children, an increasing number of women fought for the rights of women. This selection is taken from Act III Henrik Ibsen's *A Doll House* (1879), in which the character Nora Palmer declares her independence from her husband's control over her life.

Why is Nora dissatisfied with her life in the "Doll's House"? What is her husband's response?

Henrik Ibsen, *A Doll's House*

NORA: (*Pause*) Does anything strike you as we sit here?

HELMER: What should strike me?

NORA: We've been married eight years: does it not strike you that this is the first time we two, you and I, man and wife, have talked together seriously?

HELMER: Seriously? What do you mean, seriously?

NORA: For eight whole years, and more—ever since the day we first met—we have never exchanged one serious word about serious things. . . .

HELMER: Why, my dearest Nora, what have you to do with serious things?

NORA: There we have it! You have never understood me. I've had great injustice done to me, Torvald; first by father, then by you.

HELMER: What! Your father and me? We, who have loved you more than all the world?

NORA: (*Shaking her head*): You have never loved me. You just found it amusing to think you were in love with me.

HELMER: Nora! What a thing to say!

NORA: Yes, it's true, Torvald. When I was living at home with father, he told me his opinions and mine were the same. If I had different opinions, I said nothing about them, because he would not have liked it. He used to call me his doll-child and played with me as I played with my dolls. Then I came to live in your house.

HELMER: What a way to speak of our marriage!

NORA (*Undisturbed*): I mean that I passed from father's hands into yours. You arranged everything to your taste and I got the same tastes as you; or pretended to—I don't know which—both, perhaps: sometimes one, sometimes the other. When I look back on it now, I seem to have been living here like a beggar, on hand-outs. I lived by performing tricks for you, Torvald. But that was how you wanted it. You and father have done me a great wrong. It is your fault that my life has come to naught.

HELMER: Why, Nora, how unreasonable and ungrateful! Haven't you been happy here?

NORA: No, never. I thought I was, but I never was.

HELMER: Not—not happy! . . .

NORA: I must stand quite alone if I am ever to know myself and my surroundings; so I cannot stay with you.

HELMER: Nora! Nora!

NORA: I am going at once. I daresay [my friend] Christina will take me in for tonight.

HELMER: You are mad! I shall not allow it! I forbid it!

NORA: It's no use your forbidding me anything now. I shall take with me only what belongs to me; from you I will accept nothing, either now or later.

HELMER: This is madness!

NORA: Tomorrow I shall go home—I mean to what was my home. It will be easier for me to find a job there.

HELMER: Oh, in your blind inexperience—

NORA: I must try to gain experience, Torvald.

HELMER: Forsake your home, your husband, your children! And you don't consider what the world will say.

NORA: I can't pay attention to that. I only know that I must do it.

HELMER: This is monstrous! Can you forsake your holiest duties?

NORA: What do you consider my holiest duties?

HELMER: Need I tell you that? Your duties to your husband and children.

NORA: I have other duties equally sacred.

HELMER: Impossible! What do you mean?

NORA: My duties toward myself.

HELMER: Before all else you are a wife and a mother.

NORA: That I no longer believe. Before all else I believe I am a human being, just as much as you are—or at least that I should try to become one. I know that most people agree with you, Torvald, and that they say so in books. But I can no longer be satisfied with what most people say and what is in books. I must think things out for myself and try to get clear about them.

SOURCE: From Wesley D. Camp, *Roots of Western Civilization.* Copyright © 1988 McGraw-Hill Companies.

Compulsory education opened the door to new opportunities in the medical and teaching professions. In some countries in western Europe, women's legal rights increased. Still, most women remained confined to their traditional roles of homemaking and child rearing. The less fortunate were still compelled to undertake marginal work at home as domestic servants or as pieceworkers in sweatshops.

Many of these improvements occurred as the result of the rise of Europe's first feminist movement. The movement had its origins in the social upheaval of the French Revolution, when some women advocated equality for women based on the doctrine of natural rights. In the 1830s, a number of women in the United States and Europe sought improvements for women by focusing on family and marriage law to strengthen the property rights of wives and enhance their ability to secure a divorce (see the box on p. 11). Later in the century, attention shifted to the issue of equal political rights. Many feminists believed that the right to vote was the key to all other reforms to improve the position of women.

The British women's movement was the most vocal and active in Europe, but it was divided over tactics. Moderates believed that women must demonstrate that they would use political power responsibly if they wanted Parliament to grant them the right to vote. Another group, however, favored a more radical approach. Emmeline Pankhurst (1858–1928) and her daughters, Christabel and Sylvia, in 1903 founded the Women's Social and Political Union, which enrolled mostly middle- and upper-class women. Pankhurst's organization realized the value of the media and used unusual publicity stunts to call attention to its insistence on winning women the right to vote and other demands. Its members pelted government officials with eggs, chained themselves to lampposts, smashed the windows of department stores on fashionable shopping streets, burned railroad cars, and went on hunger strikes in jail.

Before World War I, demands for women's rights were being heard throughout Europe and the United States, although only in Norway and some American states as well as in Australia and New Zealand did women actually receive the right to vote before 1914. It would take the dramatic upheaval of World War I before male-dominated governments capitulated on this basic issue.

Reaction and Revolution: The Decline of the Old Order

While the Industrial Revolution shook the economic and social foundations of European society, similar revolutionary developments were reshaping the political map of the Continent. These developments were the product of a variety of factors, including not only the Industrial Revolution itself but also the Renaissance, the Enlightenment, and the French Revolution at the end of the eighteenth century. The influence of these new forces resulted in a redefinition of political conditions in Europe. The conservative order—based on the principle of hereditary monarchy and the existence of great multinational states such as Russia, the Habsburg Empire, and the Ottoman Empire—had emerged intact from the defeat of Napoleon Bonaparte at the Battle of Waterloo in 1815, but by mid-century, it had come under attack along a wide front. Arrayed against the conservative forces was a set of new political ideas that began to come into their own in the first half of the nineteenth century and continue to affect the entire world today.

Liberalism and Nationalism

One of these new political ideas was liberalism. Liberalism owed much to the Enlightenment of the eighteenth century and the American and French Revolutions that erupted at the end of that century, all of which proclaimed the autonomy of the individual against the power of the state. Opinions diverged among people classified as liberals—many of them members of the emerging middle class—but all began with a common denominator, a conviction that in both economic and political terms, people should be as free from restraint as possible. Economic liberalism, also known as classical economics, was based on the tenet of laissez-faire—the belief that the state should not interfere in the free play of natural economic forces, especially supply and demand. Political liberalism was based on the concept of a constitutional monarchy or constitutional state, with limits on the powers of government and a written charter to protect the basic civil rights of the people. Nineteenth-century liberals, however, were not democrats in the modern sense. Although they held that people were entitled to equal civil rights, the right to vote and to hold office would be open only to men who met certain property qualifications.

Nationalism was an even more powerful ideology for change in the nineteenth century. The idea arose out of an awareness of being part of a community that had common institutions, traditions, language, and customs. In some cases, that sense of identity was based on shared ethnic or linguistic characteristics. In others, it was a consequence of a common commitment to a particular religion or culture. Such a community came to be called a "nation," and the primary political loyalty of individuals would be to this "nation" rather than, as was the case in much of Europe at that time, to a dynasty or a city-state or some other political unit. Nationalism did not become a popular force for change until the French Revolution, when the concept arose that governments should coincide with nationalities. Thus, a divided people such as the Germans wanted national unity in a German nation-state with one central government. Subject peoples, such as the Czechs and the Hungarians, wanted national self-determination, or the right to establish their own autonomy rather than be subject to a German minority in a multinational state such as the Habsburg Empire.

Liberalism and nationalism began to exert an impact on the European political scene in the 1830s, when a revolt led by reformist forces installed a constitutional monarchy in France, and nationalist uprisings, often given active support by liberal forces, took place in Belgium (which was then attached to the Dutch Republic), in Italy, and in Poland (then part of the Russian Empire). Only the Belgians were successful, as Russian forces crushed the Poles' attempt to liberate themselves from foreign domination, while Austrian troops intervened to uphold reactionary governments in a number of Italian states.

In the spring of 1848, a new series of uprisings against established authority broke out in several countries in central and western Europe. The most effective was in France, where an uprising centered in Paris overthrew the so-called bourgeois monarchy of King Louis Philippe and briefly brought to power a new republic composed of an alliance of workers, intellectuals, and progressive representatives of the urban middle class.

The Unification of Germany and Italy

Within a few months, however, it became clear that optimism about the imminence of a new order in Europe had not been justified. In France, the shaky alliance between workers and the urban bourgeoisie was ruptured when workers' groups and their representatives in the government began to demand extensive social reforms to provide guaranteed benefits to the poor. Moderates, frightened by rising political tensions in Paris, resisted such demands. Facing the specter of class war, the French nation drew back and welcomed the rise to power of Louis Napoleon, a nephew of the great Napoleon Bonaparte. Within three years, he declared himself Emperor Napoleon III. Elsewhere in Europe—in Germany, in the Habsburg Empire, and in Italy—popular uprisings failed to unseat autocratic monarchs and destroy the existing political order.

But the rising force of nationalism was not to be quenched. Italy, long divided into separate kingdoms, was finally united in the early 1860s. Germany followed a few years later. Unfortunately, the rise of nation-states in central Europe did not herald the onset of liberal principles or greater stability. To the contrary, it inaugurated a period of heightened tensions as an increasingly aggressive Germany began to dominate the politics of Europe. In 1870, German Prime Minister Otto von Bismarck (1815–1898) provoked a war with France. After the latter's defeat, a new German Empire was declared in the Hall of Mirrors at the Palace of Versailles, just outside Paris.

Many German liberals were initially delighted at the unification of their country after centuries of division. But they were soon to discover that the new German Empire would not usher in a new era of peace and freedom. Under Prussian leadership, the new state quickly proclaimed the superiority of authoritarian and militaristic values and abandoned the principles of liberalism and constitutional government. Nationalism had become a two-edged sword, as advocates of a greater Germany began to exert an impact on domestic politics.

Liberal principles made similarly little headway elsewhere in central and eastern Europe. After the transformation of the Habsburg Empire into the dual monarchy of Austria-Hungary in 1867, the Austrian part received a constitution that theoretically recognized the equality of the nationalities and established a parliamentary system with the principle of ministerial responsibility.

But the problem of reconciling the interests of the various nationalities remained a difficult one. The German minority that governed Austria felt increasingly threatened by the Czechs, Poles, and other Slavic groups within the empire. The granting of universal male suffrage in 1907 served only to exacerbate the problem when nationalities that had played no role in the government now agitated in the parliament for autonomy. This led prime ministers after 1900 to ignore the parliament and rely increasingly on imperial emergency decrees to govern. On the eve of World War I, the Austro-Hungarian Empire was far from solving its minorities problem. (See Map 1.2 on p. 14.)

Roots of Revolution in Russia

To the east, in the vast Russian Empire, neither the Industrial Revolution nor the European Enlightenment had exerted much impact. At the beginning of the nineteenth century, Russia was overwhelmingly rural, agricultural, and autocratic. The Russian tsar was still regarded as a divine-right monarch with unlimited power, although the physical extent of the empire made the claim impracticable. For centuries, Russian farmers had groaned under the yoke of an oppressive system that tied the peasant to poverty conditions and the legal status of a serf under the authority of his manor lord. An enlightened tsar, Alexander II (r. 1855–1881), had emancipated the serfs in 1861, but under conditions that left most Russian peasants still poor and with little hope for social or economic betterment. In desperation, the Russian peasants periodically lashed out at their oppressors in sporadic rebellions, but all such uprisings were quelled with brutal efficiency by the tsarist regime.

In western Europe, as we have seen, it was the urban bourgeoisie that took the lead in the struggle for change.

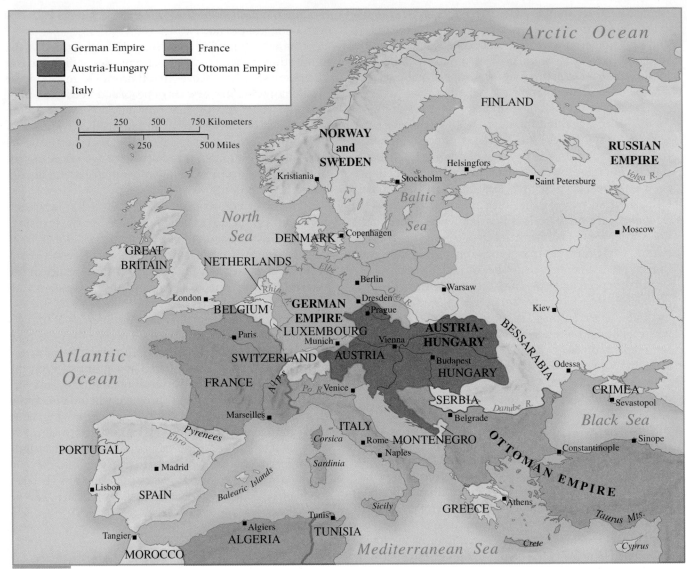

MAP 1.2 **Europe in 1871.** German unification in 1871 upset the balance of power that had prevailed in Europe for more than half a century and eventually led to a restructuring of European alliances. By 1907, Europe was divided into two opposing camps: the Triple Entente of Great Britain, Russia, and France and the Triple Alliance of Germany, Austria-Hungary, and Italy. ❓ Which of the countries identified on this map could be described as multinational empires? 🌐 **View an animated version of this map or related maps at the World History Resource Center, at** worldrc.wadsworth.com/.

In preindustrial Russia, the middle class was still small in size and lacking in self-confidence. A few, however, had traveled to the West and were determined to import Western values and institutions into the backward Russian environment. At mid-century, a few progressive intellectuals went out to the villages to arouse their rural brethren to the need for change. Known as *narodniks* (from the Russian term *narod,* for "people" or "nation"), they sought

to energize the peasantry as a force for the transformation of Russian society. Although many saw the answer to Russian problems in the western European model, others insisted on the uniqueness of the Russian experience and sought to bring about a revitalization of the country on the basis of the communal traditions of the native village.

For the most part, such efforts achieved little. The Russian peasant was resistant to change and suspicious of outsiders. In desperation, some radicals turned to terrorism in the hope that assassinations of public officials would spark tsarist repression, thus demonstrating the brutality of the system and galvanizing popular anger. Chief among such groups was the Narodnaya Volya ("the People's Will"), a terrorist organization that carried out the assassination of Tsar Alexander II in 1881.

The assassination of Alexander II convinced his son and successor, Alexander III (r. 1881–1894), that reform had been a mistake, and he quickly returned to the repressive measures of earlier tsars. When Alexander III died, his weak son and successor, Nicholas II (r. 1894–1917), began his rule armed with his father's conviction that the absolute power of the tsars should be preserved.

But it was too late, for conditions were changing. Although industrialization came late to Russia, it progressed rapidly after 1890, especially with the assistance of foreign investment capital. By 1900, Russia had become the fourth largest producer of steel, behind the United States, Germany, and Great Britain. At the same time, Russia was turning out half of the world's production of oil. Conditions for the working class, however, were abysmal, and opposition to the tsarist regime from workers, peasants, and intellectuals finally exploded into revolt in 1905. Facing an exhausting war with Japan in Asia (see Chapter 3), Tsar Nicholas reluctantly granted civil liberties and agreed to create a legislative assembly, the Duma, elected directly by a broad franchise. But real constitutional monarchy proved short-lived. By 1907, the tsar had curtailed the power of the Duma and fell back on the army and the bureaucracy to rule Russia.

The Ottoman Empire and Nationalism in the Balkans

Like the Austro-Hungarian Empire, the Ottoman Empire was threatened by the rising nationalist aspirations of its subject peoples. Beginning in the fourteenth century, the Ottoman Turks had expanded from their base in the Anatolian peninsula into the Balkans, southern Russia, and along the northern coast of Africa. Soon they controlled the entire eastern half of the Mediterranean Sea. But by the nineteenth century, despite state reform programs designed to modernize the empire, increasing nationalism and intervention of the European powers in Ottoman affairs challenged the legitimacy of the Ottoman state.

Gradually, the emotional appeal of nationhood began to make inroads among the various ethnic and linguistic groups in southeastern Europe. In the course of the nineteenth century, the Balkan provinces of the Ottoman Empire began to gain their freedom, although the intense rivalry in the region between Austria-Hungary and

Russia complicated the process. Serbia had already received a large degree of autonomy in 1829, although it remained a province of the Ottoman Empire until 1878. Greece became an independent kingdom in 1830 after a successful revolt. By the Treaty of Adrianople in 1829, Russia received a protectorate over the principalities of Moldavia and Wallachia, but was forced to give them up after the Crimean War. In 1861, they were merged into the state of Romania. Not until Russia's defeat of the Ottoman Empire in 1878, however, was Romania recognized as completely independent, along with Serbia at the same time. Although freed from Turkish rule, Montenegro was placed under an Austrian protectorate, and Bulgaria achieved autonomous status under Russian protection. The other Balkan territories of Bosnia and Herzegovina were placed under Austrian protection; Austria could occupy but not annex them. Despite these gains, the force of Balkan nationalism was by no means stilled.

Meanwhile, other parts of the empire began to break away from central control. In Egypt, the ambitious governor Muhammad Ali declared the region's autonomy from Ottoman rule and initiated a series of reforms designed to promote economic growth and government efficiency. During the 1830s, he sought to improve agricultural production and reform the educational system, and he imported machinery and technicians from Europe to carry out the first industrial revolution on African soil. In the end, however, the effort failed, partly because Egypt's manufactures could not compete with those of Europe and also because much of the profit from the export of cash crops went into the hands of conservative landlords.

Measures to promote industrialization elsewhere in the empire had even less success. By mid-century, a small industrial sector, built with equipment imported from Europe, took shape, and a modern system of transport and communications began to make its appearance. By the end of the century, however, the results were meager.

Liberalism Triumphant

In western Europe and North America, liberal principles experienced a better fate. By 1871, Great Britain had a functioning two-party parliamentary system. For fifty years, the Liberals and Conservatives alternated in power at regular intervals. Both were dominated by a coalition of aristocratic landowners frequently involved in industrial and financial activities and upper-middle-class businessmen. And each competed with the other in supporting legislation that expanded the right to vote. Reform acts in 1867 and 1884 greatly expanded the number of adult males who could vote, and by the end of World War I, all males over twenty-one and women over thirty had that right.

The growth of trade unions and the emergence in 1900 of the Labour Party, which dedicated itself to workers' interests, put pressure on the Liberals, who promoted a program of social welfare to seek the support of the workers. The National Insurance Act of 1911 provided benefits for workers in case of sickness or unemployment, to be paid for by compulsory contributions from workers, employers, and the state. Additional legislation provided a small pension for those over seventy and compensation for those injured in accidents at work.

A similar process was under way in France, where the overthrow of Napoleon III's Second Empire in 1870 led to the creation of a republican form of government. France failed, however, to develop a strong parliamentary system on the British two-party model because the existence of a dozen political parties forced the premier to depend on a coalition of parties to stay in power. The Third Republic was notorious for its changes of government. Between 1875 and 1914, there were no fewer than fifty cabinet changes; during the same period, the British had eleven. Nevertheless, the government's moderation gradually encouraged more and more middle-class and peasant support, and by 1914, the Third Republic commanded the loyalty of most French people.

By 1870, Italy had emerged as a geographically united state with pretensions to great-power status. But sectional differences (a poverty-stricken south and an industrializing north) weakened any sense of community. Chronic turmoil between labor and industry undermined the social fabric. The Italian government was unable to deal effectively with these problems because of the extensive corruption among government officials and the lack of stability created by ever-changing government coalitions. Abroad, Italy's pretensions to great-power status proved equally hollow when Italy became the first European power to lose a war to an African state, Ethiopia, a humiliation that later led to the costly (but successful) attempt to compensate by conquering Libya in 1911 and 1912.

The United States and Canada

Between 1860 and World War I, the United States made the shift from an agrarian to a mighty industrial nation. American heavy industry stood unchallenged in 1900. In that year, the Carnegie Steel Company alone produced more steel than Great Britain's entire steel industry. Industrialization also led to urbanization. While established cities, such as New York, Philadelphia, and Boston, grew even larger, other moderate-size cities, such as Pittsburgh, grew by leaps and bounds because of industrialization and the arrival of millions of immigrants from eastern Europe. Whereas 20 percent of Americans lived in cities in 1860, more than 40 percent did in 1900.

By 1900, the United States had become the world's richest nation and greatest industrial power. Yet serious questions remained about the quality of American life. In 1890, the richest 9 percent of Americans owned an incredible 71 percent of all the wealth. Labor unrest over unsafe working conditions, strict work discipline, and periodic cycles of devastating unemployment led workers to organize. By the turn of the twentieth century, one national organization, the American Federation of Labor, emerged as labor's dominant voice. Its lack of real power, however, is reflected in its membership figures: in 1900, it constituted but 8.4 percent of the American industrial labor force. And part of the U.S. labor force remained almost entirely disenfranchised. Although the victory of the North in the Civil War led to the abolition of slavery, political, economic, and social opportunities for the African American population remained limited, and racist attitudes were widespread.

During the so-called Progressive Era after 1900, the reform of many features of American life became a primary issue. At the state level, reforming governors sought to achieve clean government by introducing elements of direct democracy, such as direct primaries for selecting nominees for public office. State governments also enacted economic and social legislation, including laws that governed hours, wages, and working conditions, especially for women and children. The realization that state laws were ineffective in dealing with nationwide problems, however, led to a progressive movement at the national level.

National progressivism was evident in the administrations of Theodore Roosevelt and Woodrow Wilson. Under Roosevelt (1901–1909), the Meat Inspection Act and Pure Food and Drug Act provided for a limited degree of federal regulation of corrupt industrial practices. Roosevelt's expressed principle, "We draw the line against misconduct, not against wealth," guaranteed that public protection would have to be within limits tolerable to big corporations. Wilson (1913–1921) was responsible for the creation of a graduated federal income tax and the Federal Reserve System, which gave the federal government a role in important economic decisions formerly made by bankers. Like many European nations, the United States was moving into policies that extended the functions of the state.

Canada, too, faced problems of national unity between 1870 and 1914. At the beginning of 1870, the Dominion of Canada had only four provinces: Quebec, Ontario, Nova Scotia, and New Brunswick. With the addition of two more provinces in 1871—Manitoba and British Columbia—the Dominion now extended from the Atlantic Ocean to the Pacific. But real unity was difficult to achieve because of the distrust between the English-speaking and French-speaking peoples of Canada. Fortunately for Canada,

Sir Wilfrid Laurier, who became the first French Canadian prime minister in 1896, was able to reconcile Canada's two major groups and resolve the issue of separate schools for French Canadians. Laurier's administration also witnessed increased industrialization and successfully encouraged immigrants from central and eastern Europe to help populate Canada's vast territories.

Tradition and Change in Latin America

In the three centuries following the arrival of Christopher Columbus in the Western Hemisphere in 1492, Latin America fell increasingly into the European orbit. Portugal dominated Brazil, and Spain formed a vast empire that included most of the remainder of South America as well as Central America. Almost from the beginning, it was a multicultural society composed of European settlers, indigenous American Indians, immigrants from Asia, and black slaves brought from Africa to work on the sugar plantations and in other menial occupations. Intermarriage among the three groups resulted in the creation of a diverse population with a less rigid view of race than was the case in North America. Latin American culture, as well, reflected a rich mixture of Iberian, Asian, African, and Native American themes.

The Emergence of Independent States
Until the beginning of the nineteenth century, the various Latin American societies were ruled by colonial officials appointed by monarchical governments in Europe. An additional instrument of control was the Catholic church, which undertook a major effort to Christianize the indigenous peoples and transform them into docile and loyal subjects of the Portuguese and Spanish Empires. By 1800, however, local elites, mostly descendants of Europeans who had become permanent inhabitants of the Western Hemisphere, became increasingly affected by the spirit of nationalism that had emerged after the Napoleonic era in Europe. During the first quarter of the nineteenth century, under great leaders like Simón Bolívar of Venezuela and José de Saint Martín of Argentina, they launched a series of revolts that led to the eviction of the monarchical regimes and the formation of independent states from Argentina and Chile in the south to Mexico in Central America.

One of the goals of the independence movement had been to free the economies of Latin America from European control and to exploit the riches of the continent for local benefit. In fact, however, political independence did not lead to a new era of prosperity for the people of Latin America. Most of the powerful elites in the region earned their wealth from the land and had few incentives to learn from the Industrial Revolution. As a result, the previous trade pattern persisted, with Latin America exporting raw materials and foodstuffs (wheat and sugar) as well as tobacco and hides in exchange for manufactured goods from Europe and the United States.

Problems of Economic Dependence
With economic growth came a boom in foreign investment. Between 1870 and 1913, British investments—mostly in railroads, mining, and public utilities—grew from £85 million to £757 million, which constituted two-thirds of all foreign investment in Latin America. By the end of the century, the U.S. economic presence began to increase dramatically. As Latin Americans struggled to create more balanced economies after 1900, they concentrated on increasing industrialization, especially by building textile, food-processing, and construction materials factories.

Nevertheless, the growth of the Latin American economy came largely from the export of raw materials, and economic modernization in Latin America simply added to the growing dependence of the region on the capitalist nations of the West. Modernization was basically a surface feature of Latin American society; past patterns still largely prevailed. Rural elites dominated their estates and their rural workers. Although slavery was abolished by 1888, former slaves and their descendants were still at the bottom of society. The Native Americans remained poverty-stricken, debt servitude was still a way of life, and the region remained economically dependent on foreigners. Despite its economic growth, Latin America was still sorely underdeveloped.

The surface prosperity that resulted from the emergence of an export economy had both social and political repercussions. One result socially was the modernization of the elites, who grew determined to pursue their vision of modern progress. Large landowners increasingly sought ways to rationalize their production methods to make greater profits. As a result, cattle ranchers in Argentina and coffee barons in Brazil became more aggressive entrepreneurs.

Another result of the new prosperity was the growth of a small but increasingly visible middle class—lawyers, merchants, shopkeepers, businessmen, school-teachers, professors, bureaucrats, and military officers. Living mainly in the cities, these people sought education and decent incomes and increasingly considered the United States to be the model to emulate, especially in regard to industrialization and education.

As Latin American export economies boomed, the working class expanded, which in turn led to the growth of labor unions, especially after 1914. Radical unions often advocated the use of the general strike as an instrument for change. By and large, however, the governing elites succeeded in stifling the political influence of the working class by restricting the right to vote. The need for industrial labor also led Latin American countries to encourage European immigrants. Between 1880 and 1914, three million Europeans, primarily Italians and Spaniards, settled in Argentina. More than 100,000 Europeans, mostly Italian, Portuguese, and Spanish, arrived in Brazil each year between 1891 and 1900.

Social and Political Changes As in Europe and the United States, industrialization led to urbanization, evident in both the emergence of new cities and the rapid growth of old ones. Buenos Aires (the "Paris of South America") had 750,000 inhabitants by 1900 and two million by 1914—one-fourth of Argentina's population. By that time, urban dwellers made up 53 percent of Argentina's population overall. Brazil and Chile also witnessed a dramatic increase in the number of urban dwellers.

Latin America also experienced a political transformation after 1870. Large landowners began to take a more direct interest in national politics, sometimes expressed by a direct involvement in governing. In Argentina and Chile, for example, landholding elites controlled the governments, and although they produced constitutions similar to those of the United States and European countries, they were careful to ensure their power by regulating voting rights.

In some countries, large landowners made use of dictators to maintain the interests of the ruling elite. Porfirio Díaz, who ruled Mexico from 1876 to 1910, established a conservative, centralized government with the support of the army, foreign capitalists, large landowners, and the Catholic church, all of whom benefited from their alliance. But there were forces for change in Mexico that sought to precipitate a true social revolution.

The Rise of the Socialist Movement

One of the less desirable consequences of the Industrial Revolution was the yawning disparity in the distribution of wealth. If industrialization brought increasing affluence to an emerging middle class, to millions of others it brought grinding hardship in the form of low-paying jobs in mines or factories characterized by long working hours under squalid conditions. The underlying cause was clear: because of the rapid population growth taking place in most industrializing societies in Europe, factory owners remained largely free to hire labor on their own terms, based on market forces.

Beginning in the last decades of the eighteenth century, radical groups, inspired by the egalitarian ideals of the French Revolution, began to seek the means to rectify the problem. Some found the answer in intellectual schemes that envisaged a classless society based on the elimination of private property. Others prepared for an armed revolt to overthrow the ruling order and create a new society controlled by the working masses. Still others began to form trade unions to fight for improved working conditions and reasonable wages. Only one group sought to combine all of these factors into a comprehensive program to destroy the governing forces and create a new egalitarian society based on the concept of "scientific socialism." The founder of that movement was Karl Marx, a German Jew who had abandoned an academic career in philosophy to take up radical political activities in Paris.

The Rise of Marxism

Marxism made its first appearance in 1847 with the publication of a short treatise, *The Communist Manifesto,* written by Karl Marx (1818–1883) and his close collaborator, Friedrich Engels (1820–1895). In the *Manifesto,* the two authors predicted the outbreak of a massive uprising that would overthrow the existing ruling class and bring to power a new revolutionary regime based on their ideas (see the box on p. 19).

When revolutions broke out all over Europe in the eventful year of 1848, Marx and Engels eagerly but mistakenly predicted that the uprisings would spread throughout Europe and lead to a new revolutionary regime led by workers, dispossessed bourgeois, and communists. When that did not occur, Marx belatedly concluded that urban merchants and peasants were too conservative to support the workers and would oppose revolution once their own immediate economic demands were satisfied. As for the worker movement itself, it was clearly still too weak to seize power and could not expect to achieve its own objectives until the workers had become politically more sophisticated and better organized. In effect, revolution would not take place in western Europe until capitalism had "ripened," leading to a concentration of capital in the hands of a wealthy minority and an "epidemic of overproduction" because of inadequate purchasing power by the impoverished lower classes. Then a large and increasingly alienated proletariat could drive the capitalists from power and bring about a classless utopia.

For the remainder of his life, Marx acted out the logic of these conclusions. From his base in London, he undertook a massive study of the dynamics of the capitalist system, a project that resulted in the publication of the first volume of his most famous work, *Das Kapital* ("Capital"), in 1869. In the meantime, he attempted to prepare for the future revolution by organizing the scattered radical parties throughout Europe into a cohesive revolutionary movement, called the International Workingmen's Association (usually known today as the First International), that would be ready to rouse the workers to action when the opportunity came.

THE CLASSLESS SOCIETY

*I*n *The Communist Manifesto*, Karl Marx and Friedrich Engels predicted the creation of a classless society as the end product of the struggle between the bourgeoisie and the proletariat. In this selection, they discuss the steps by which that classless society would be reached.

How did Marx and Engels define the proletariat? The bourgeoisie? Why did Marxists come to believe that this distinction was paramount for understanding history? For shaping the future?

Karl Marx and Friedrich Engels, *The Communist Manifesto*

We have seen . . ., that the first step in the revolution by the working class is to raise the proletariat to the position of ruling class. . . . The proletariat will use its political supremacy to wrest, by degrees, all capital from the bourgeoisie, to centralize all instruments of production in the hands of the State, i.e., of the proletariat organized as the ruling class; and to increase the total of productive forces as rapidly as possible.

Of course, in the beginning, this cannot be effected except by means of despotic inroads on the rights of property, and on the conditions of bourgeois production; by means of measures, therefore, which appear economically insufficient and untenable, but which, in the course of the movement, outstrip themselves, necessitate further inroads upon the old social order, and are unavoidable as a means of entirely revolutionizing the mode of production.

These measures will of course be different in different countries.

Nevertheless, in the most advanced countries, the following will be pretty generally applicable:

1. Abolition of property in land and application of all rents of land to public purposes.
2. A heavy progressive or graduated income tax.
3. Abolition of all right of inheritance. . . .
5. Centralization of credit in the hands of the State, by means of a national bank with State capital and an exclusive monopoly.
6. Centralization of the means of communication and transport in the hands of the State.
7. Extension of factories and instruments of production owned by the State. . . .
8. Equal liability of all to labor. Establishment of industrial armies, especially for agriculture.
9. Combination of agriculture with manufacturing industries; gradual abolition of the distinction between town and country, by a more equable distribution of the population over the country.
10. Free education for all children in public schools. Abolition of children's factory labor in its present form. . . .

When, in the course of development, class distinctions have disappeared, and all production has been concentrated in the whole nation, the public power will lose its political character. Political power, properly so called, is merely the organized power of one class for oppressing another. If the proletariat during its contest with the bourgeoisie is compelled, by the force of circumstances, to organize itself as a class, if, by means of a revolution, it makes itself the ruling class, and, as such, sweeps away by force the old conditions of production, then it will, along with these conditions, have swept away the conditions for the existence of class antagonisms and of classes generally, and will thereby have abolished its own supremacy as a class.

In place of the old bourgeois society, with its classes and class antagonisms, we shall have an association, in which the free development of each is the condition for the free development of all.

SOURCE: From Karl Marx and Friedrich Engels, *The Communist Manifesto*.

Unity was short-lived. Although all members of the First International shared a common distaste for the capitalist system, some preferred to reform it from within (many of the labor groups from Great Britain), whereas others were convinced that only violent insurrection would suffice to destroy the existing ruling class (Karl Marx and the anarchists around Russian revolutionary Mikhail Bakunin). Even the radicals could not agree. Marx believed that revolution could not succeed without a core of committed communists to organize and lead the masses; Bakunin contended that the general insurrection should be a spontaneous uprising from below. In 1871, the First International disintegrated.

Capitalism in Transition

While Marx was grappling with the problems of preparing for the coming revolution, European society was undergoing significant changes. The advanced capitalist states such as Great Britain, France, and the Low Countries (Belgium, Luxembourg, and the Netherlands) were gradually evolving into mature, politically stable societies in which Marx's dire predictions were not being borne out. His forecast of periodic economic crises was correct enough, but his warnings of concentration of capital and the impoverishment of labor were somewhat wide of the mark, as capitalist societies began to eliminate or at least reduce some of the more flagrant inequities apparent in the early stages of capitalist development. These reforms occurred because workers and their representatives had begun to use the democratic political process to their own advantage, organizing labor unions and political parties to improve working conditions and enhance the role of workers in the political system. Many of these political parties were led by Marxists, who were learning that in the absence of a social revolution to bring the masses to power, the capitalist democratic system could be reformed from within to improve the working and living conditions of its constituents. In 1889, after Marx's death, several such parties (often labeled "social democratic" parties) formed the Second International, dominated by reformist elements committed to achieving socialism within the bounds of the Western parliamentary system.

Marx had also underestimated the degree to which nationalism would appeal to workers in most European countries. Marx had viewed nation and culture as false idols diverting the interests of the oppressed from their true concern, the struggle against the ruling class. In his view, the proletariat would throw off its chains and unite in the sacred cause of "internationalist" world revolution. In reality, workers joined peasants and urban merchants in defending the cause of the nation against its foreign enemies. A generation later, French workers would die in the trenches defending France from workers across the German border.

A historian of the late nineteenth century might have been forgiven for predicting that Marxism, as a revolutionary ideology, was dead. To the east, however, in the vast plains and steppes of central Russia, it was about to be reborn (see Chapter 4).

Toward the Modern Consciousness: Intellectual and Cultural Developments

The physical changes that were taking place in societies exposed to the Industrial Revolution were accompanied by an equally significant transformation in the arena of culture. Before 1914, most Westerners continued to believe in the values and ideals that had been generated by the impact of the Scientific Revolution and the Enlightenment. The ability of human beings to improve themselves and achieve a better society seemed to be well demonstrated by a rising standard of living, urban improvements, and mass education. Between 1870 and 1914, however, a dramatic transformation in the realm of ideas and culture challenged many of these assumptions. A new view of the physical universe, alternative views of human nature, and radically innovative forms of literary and artistic expression shattered old beliefs and opened the way to a modern consciousness. Although the real impact of many of these ideas was not felt until after World War I, they served to provoke a sense of confusion and anxiety before 1914 that would become even more pronounced after the war.

Developments in the Sciences: The Emergence of a New Physics

A prime example of this development took place in the realm of physics. Throughout much of the nineteenth century, Westerners adhered to the mechanical conception of the universe postulated by the classical physics of Isaac Newton. In this perspective, the universe was a giant machine in which time, space, and matter were objective realities that existed independently of the parties observing them. Matter was thought to be composed of indivisible, solid material bodies called atoms.

But these views began to be questioned at the end of the nineteenth century. Some scientists had discovered that certain elements such as radium and polonium spontaneously gave off rays or radiation that apparently came from within the atom itself. Atoms were therefore not hard material bodies but small worlds containing such subatomic particles as electrons and protons that behaved in a seemingly random and inexplicable fashion. Inquiry into the disintegrative process within atoms became a central theme of the new physics.

Building on this work, in 1900, a Berlin physicist, Max Planck (1858–1947), rejected the belief that a heated body radiates energy in a steady stream but maintained instead that it did so discontinuously, in irregular packets of energy that he called "quanta." The quantum theory raised fundamental questions about the subatomic realm of the atom. By 1900, the old view of atoms as the basic building blocks of the material world was being seriously questioned, and Newtonian physics was in trouble.

Albert Einstein (1879–1955), a German-born patent officer working in Switzerland, pushed these new theories of thermodynamics into new terrain. In 1905, Einstein published a paper setting forth his theory of relativity. According to relativity theory, space and time are not absolute but relative to the observer, and both are interwoven into what Einstein called a four-dimensional space-time continuum. Neither space nor time has an existence independent of human experience. Moreover, matter and energy reflect the relativity of time and space. Einstein concluded that matter was nothing but another form of energy. His epochal formula $E = mc^2$—each particle of matter is equivalent to its mass times the square of the velocity of light—was the key theory explaining the vast energies contained within the atom. It led to the atomic age.

THE THEORY OF EVOLUTION

Darwin published his theory of organic evolution in 1859, followed twelve years later by *The Descent of Man*, in which he argued that human beings, like other animals, evolved from lower forms of life. The theory provoked a firestorm of criticism, especially from the clergy. One critic described Darwin's theory as a "brutal philosophy—to wit, there is no God, and the ape is our Adam."

What evidence does the author cite to defend his theory of evolution? What is the essence of the theory?

Charles Darwin, *The Descent of Man*

The main conclusion here arrived at, and now held by many naturalists, who are well competent to form a sound judgment, is that man is descended from some less highly organized form. The grounds upon which this conclusion rests will never be shaken, for the close similarity between man and the lower animals in embryonic development, as well as in innumerable points of structure and constitution, both of high and of the most trifling importance,—the rudiments which he retains, and the abnormal reversions to which he is occasionally liable,—are facts which cannot be disputed. They have long been known, but until recently they told us nothing with respect to the origin of man. Now when viewed by the light of our knowledge of the whole organic world, their meaning is unmistakable. The great principle of evolution stands up clear and firm, when these groups of facts are considered in connection with others, such as the mutual affinities of the members of the same group, their geographical distribution in past and present times, and their geological succession. It is incredible that all these facts should speak falsely. He who is not content to look, like a savage, at the phenomena of nature as disconnected, cannot any longer believe that man is the work of a separate act of creation. He will be forced to admit that the close resemblance of the embryo of man to that, for instance, of a dog—the construction of his skull, limbs and whole frame on the same plan with that of other mammals, independently of the uses to which the parts may be put—the occasional reappearance of various structures, for instance of several muscles, which man does not normally possess . . .—and a crowd of analogous facts—all point in the plainest manner to the conclusion that man is the co-descendant with other mammals of a common progenitor. . . .

Man may be excused for feeling some pride at having risen, though not through his own exertions, to the very summit of the organic scale; and the fact of his having thus risen, instead of having been aboriginally placed there, may give him hope for a still higher destiny in the distant future. But we are not here concerned with hopes or fears, only with the truth as far as our reason permits us to discover it; and I have given the evidence to the best of my ability. We must, however, acknowledge, as it seems to me, that man with all his noble qualities, with sympathy which feels for the most debased, with benevolence which extends not only to other men but to the humblest living creature, with his god-like intellect which has penetrated into the movements and constitution of the solar system—with all these exalted power—Man still bears in his bodily frame the indelible stamp of his lowly origin.

SOURCE: From Charles Darwin, *The Descent of Man* (New York: Appleton, 1876), pp. 606–607, 619.

Charles Darwin and the Theory of Evolution

Equally dramatic changes took place in the biological sciences, where the British scientist Charles Darwin (1809–1882) stunned the world in 1859 with the publication of his book *The Origin of Species*. Drawing from evidence obtained during a scientific expedition to the Galapagos Islands, Darwin concluded that plants and animals were not the product of divine creation but evolved over time from earlier and simpler forms of life through a process of natural selection. In the universal struggle for existence, only the fittest species survived. Later, Darwin provoked even more controversy by applying his theory of evolution to human beings (see the box above).

Sigmund Freud and the Emergence of Psychoanalysis

Although poets and mystics had revealed a world of unconscious and irrational behavior, many scientifically oriented intellectuals under the impact of Enlightenment thought continued to believe that human beings responded to conscious motives in a rational fashion. But at the end of the nineteenth century, Viennese doctor Sigmund Freud (1856–1939) put forth a series of theories that undermined optimism about the rational nature of the human mind. Freud's thought, like the new physics, added to the uncertainties of the age. His major ideas were published in 1900 in *The Interpretation of Dreams*, which laid the basic foundation for what came to be known as psychoanalysis.

According to Freud, human behavior is strongly determined by the unconscious—former experiences and inner drives of which people are largely oblivious. To explore the contents of the unconscious, Freud relied not only on hypnosis but also on dreams, which were dressed in an elaborate code that needed to be deciphered if the contents were to be properly understood.

Why do some experiences whose influence persists in controlling an individual's life remain unconscious? According to Freud, repression is a process by which unsettling experiences are blotted from conscious awareness but still continue to influence behavior because they have become part of the unconscious. To explain how repression works, Freud elaborated an intricate theory of the inner life of human beings.

Although Freud's theory has had numerous critics, his insistence that a human being's inner life is a battleground of contending forces undermined the prevailing belief in the power of reason and opened a new era of psychoanalysis, by which a psychotherapist seeks to assist a patient in probing deep into memory to retrace the chain of repression back to its childhood origins, thus bringing about a resolution of the inner psychic conflict. Belief in the primacy of rational thought over the emotions would never be the same.

Literature and the Arts: The Culture of Modernity

The revolution in physics and psychology was paralleled by similar changes in literature and the arts. Throughout much of the late nineteenth century, literature was dominated by Naturalism. Naturalists accepted the material world as real and believed that literature should be realistic. By addressing social problems, writers could contribute to an objective understanding of the world.

The novels of the French writer Émile Zola (1840–1902) provide a good example of Naturalism. Against a backdrop of the urban slums and coalfields of northern France, Zola showed how alcoholism and different environments affected people's lives. The materialistic science of his age had an important influence on Zola. He had read Darwin's *Origin of Species* and had been impressed by its emphasis on the struggle for survival and the importance of environment and heredity.

By the beginning of the twentieth century, however, the belief that the task of literature was to represent "reality" had lost much of its meaning. By that time, the new psychology and the new physics had made it evident that many people were not sure what constituted reality anyway. The same was true in the realm of art, where in the late nineteenth century, painters were beginning to respond to ongoing investigations into the nature of optics and human perception by experimenting with radical new techniques to represent the multiplicity of reality. The changes that such cultural innovators produced have since been called Modernism.

The first to embark on the challenge were the Impressionists. Originating in France in the 1870s, they rejected indoor painting and preferred to go out to the countryside to paint nature directly. As Camille Pissarro (1830–1903), one of the movement's founders, expressed it: "Don't proceed according to rules and principles, but paint what you observe and feel. Paint generously and unhesitatingly, for it is best not to lose the first impression." The most influential of the Impressionists was Claude Monet (1840–1926), who painted several series of canvases on the same object—such as haystacks, Rouen Cathedral, and water lilies in the garden of his house on the Seine River—in the hope of breaking down the essential lines, planes, colors, and shadows of what the eye observed. His paintings that deal with the interplay of light and reflection on a water surface are considered to be among the wonders of modern painting.

The growth of photography gave artists another reason to reject visual realism. Invented in the 1830s, photography became popular and widespread after George Eastman created the first Kodak camera for the mass market in 1888. What was the point of an artist's doing what the camera did better? Unlike the camera, which could only mirror reality, artists could *create* reality. As in literature, so also in modern art, individual consciousness became the source of meaning. Between the beginning of the new century and the outbreak of World War I in 1914, this search for individual expression produced a great variety of painting schools—including Expressionism and Cubism—that would have a significant impact on the world of art for decades to come.

In Expressionism, the artist employed an exaggerated use of colors and distorted shapes to achieve emotional expression. Painters such as the Dutchman Vincent Van Gogh (1853–1890) and the Norwegian Edvard Munch (1863–1944) were interested not in capturing the optical play of light on a landscape but in projecting their inner selves onto the hostile universe around them. Who cannot be affected by the intensity of Van Gogh's dazzling sunflowers or by the ominous swirling stars above a church steeple in his *Starry Night* (1890)?

Another important artist obsessed with finding a new way to portray reality was the French painter Paul Cézanne (1839–1906). Scorning the photographic duplication of a landscape, he sought to isolate the pulsating structure beneath the surface. During the last years of his life, he produced several paintings of Mont Saint Victoire, located near Aix-en-Provence in the south of France. Although each canvas differed in perspective, composition, and color, they all reflect the same technique of reducing the landscape

Les Demoiselles d'Avignon. In this 1907 painting, Pablo Picasso presents reality from several perspectives simultaneously, using geometric shapes to replace traditional forms, forcing the viewer to re-create reality in his or her own mind. Picasso had intended the painting to call attention to the problem of venereal disease, as the five women represent prostitutes on display. Some critics have pointed to the influence of African art, and in particular the African mask, in the painting, which Cubists saw as a means of distorting reality and expressing the underlying role of violence in human existence.

to virtual geometric slabs of color to represent the interconnection of trees, earth, tiled roofs, mountain, and sky.

Following Cézanne was the Spaniard Pablo Picasso (1881–1973), one of the giants of twentieth-century painting. Settling in Paris in 1904, he and the French artist Georges Braque (1882–1963) collaborated in founding Cubism, the first truly radical approach in representing visual reality. To the Cubist, any perception of an object was a composite of simultaneous and different perspectives.

Modernism in the arts also revolutionized architecture and architectural practices. A new principle known as functionalism motivated this revolution by maintaining that buildings, like the products of machines, should be "functional" or useful, fulfilling the purpose for which they were constructed. Art and engineering were to be unified, and all unnecessary ornamentation was to be stripped away.

The United States was a leader in these pioneering architectural designs. Unprecedented urban growth and the absence of restrictive architectural traditions allowed for new building methods, especially in the relatively new city of Chicago. The Chicago school of the 1890s, led by Louis H. Sullivan (1856–1924), used reinforced concrete, steel frames, electric elevators, and sheet glass to build skyscrapers virtually free of external ornamentation. One of Sullivan's most successful pupils was Frank Lloyd Wright (1867–1959), who became known for innovative designs in domestic architecture. Wright's private houses, built chiefly for wealthy patrons, featured geometric structures with long lines, overhanging roofs, and severe planes of brick and stone. The interiors were open spaces and included cathedral ceilings and built-in furniture and lighting features. Wright pioneered the modern American house.

At the beginning of the twentieth century, developments in music paralleled those in painting. Expressionism in music was a Russian creation, the product of composer Igor Stravinsky (1882–1971) and the Ballet Russe, the dance company of Sergei Diaghilev (1872–1929). Together they revolutionized the world of music with Stravinsky's ballet *The Rite of Spring.* When it was performed in Paris in 1913, the savage and primitive sounds and beats of the music and dance caused a near riot among an audience outraged at its audacity.

By the end of the nineteenth century, then, traditional forms of literary, artistic, and musical expression were in a state of rapid retreat. Freed from conventional tastes and responding to the intellectual and social revolution that was getting under way throughout the Western world, painters, writers, composers, and architects launched a variety of radical new ideas that would revolutionize Western culture in coming decades.

CONCLUSION

𝒟URING THE COURSE OF THE NINETEENTH century, Western society underwent a number of dramatic changes. Countries that were predominantly agricultural in 1750 had by 1900 been transformed into essentially industrial and urban societies. The amount of material goods available to consumers had increased manyfold, and machines were rapidly replacing labor-intensive methods of production and distribution. The social changes were equally striking. Human beings were becoming more mobile and enjoyed more creature comforts than at any time since the Roman Empire. A mass society, based on the principles of universal education, limited government, and an expanding franchise, was in the process of creation.

The Industrial Revolution had thus vastly expanded the horizons and the potential of the human race. It had also broken down many walls of aristocratic privilege and opened the door to a new era based on merit. Yet the costs had been high. The distribution of wealth was as unequal as ever, and working and living conditions for millions of Europeans had deteriorated. The psychological impact of such rapid changes had also produced feelings of anger, frustration, and alienation on the part of many who lived through them. With the old certainties of religion and science now increasingly under challenge, many faced the future with doubt or foreboding.

Meanwhile, along the borders of Europe—in Russia, in the Balkans, and in the vast Ottoman Empire—the Industrial Revolution had not yet made an impact or was just getting under way. Old autocracies found themselves under increasing pressure from ethnic minorities and other discontented subjects but continued to resist pressure for reform. As the world prepared to enter a new century, the stage was set for dramatic change.

TIMELINE

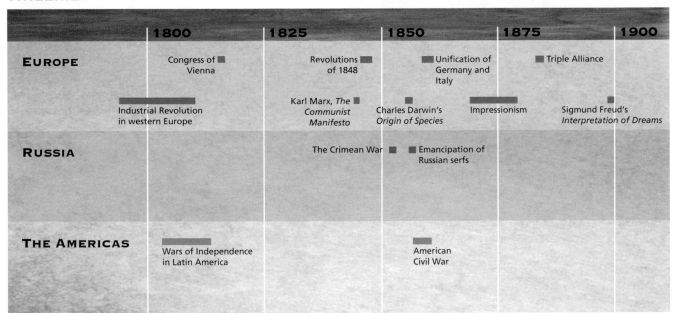

	1800	1825	1850	1875	1900
EUROPE	Congress of Vienna	Revolutions of 1848	Unification of Germany and Italy	Triple Alliance	
	Industrial Revolution in western Europe	Karl Marx, *The Communist Manifesto*	Charles Darwin's *Origin of Species*	Impressionism	Sigmund Freud's *Interpretation of Dreams*
RUSSIA			The Crimean War Emancipation of Russian serfs		
THE AMERICAS	Wars of Independence in Latin America		American Civil War		

CHAPTER NOTES

1. For an argument that coal and the benefits of overseas empire were key factors in the British head start to industrialization, see Kenneth Pomeranz, *The Great Divergence: China, Europe, and the Making of the Modern World Economy* (Princeton, 2000).
2. See Peter Gay, *Pleasure Wars: The Bourgeois Experience: Victoria to Freud* (New York, 1998).

2

THE HIGH TIDE OF IMPERIALISM: AFRICA AND ASIA IN AN ERA OF WESTERN DOMINANCE

𝓘N 1877, THE YOUNG BRITISH EMPIRE builder Cecil Rhodes drew up his last will and testament. He bequeathed his fortune, achieved as a diamond magnate in South Africa, to two of his close friends and acquaintances. He also instructed them to use the inheritance to form a secret society with the aim of bringing about "the extension of British rule throughout the world, the perfecting of a system of emigration from the United Kingdom . . . especially the occupation of the whole continent of Africa, the Holy Land, the valley of the Euphrates, the Islands of Cyprus and Candia [Crete], the whole of South America . . . the ultimate recovery of the United States as an integral part of the British Empire . . . [and] finally the foundation of so great a power to hereafter render wars impossible and promote the best interests of humanity." [1] A fervent supporter of the British imperial vision, Rhodes actively promoted the extension of British rule throughout the continent of Africa until his untimely death in 1902. ◆

The Spread of Colonial Rule

Preposterous as his ideas seem to us today, they serve as a graphic reminder of the hubris that characterized the worldview of Rhodes and many of his contemporaries during the age of imperialism, as well as the complex union of moral concern and vaulting ambition that motivated their actions on the world stage. During the nineteenth and early twentieth centuries, Western colonialism spread throughout much of the non-Western world. Spurred by the demands of the Industrial Revolution, a few powerful states—notably Great Britain, France, Germany, Russia, and the United States—competed avariciously for consumer markets and raw materials for their expanding economies. By the end of the nineteenth century, virtually all of the traditional societies in Asia and Africa were under direct or indirect colonial rule.

The Myth of European Superiority

To many Western observers at the time, the ease of the European conquest provided a clear affirmation of the innate superiority of Western civilization to its counterparts elsewhere in the world. Influenced by the popular theory of social Darwinism, which applied Charles Darwin's theory of natural selection to the evolution of human societies (see Chapter 1 and "The Philosophy of Colonialism" later in this chapter), historians in Europe and the United States began to view world history essentially as the story of the inexorable rise of the West, from the glories of ancient Greece to the emergence of modern Europe after the Enlightenment and the Industrial Revolution. The extension of Western influence to Africa and Asia, a process that began with the arrival of European fleets in the Indian Ocean in the early sixteenth century, was thus a reflection of Western cultural superiority and represented a necessary step in bringing civilization to the peoples of that area.

The truth, however, was quite different, for Western global hegemony was a relatively recent phenomenon. Prior to the age of Christopher Columbus, Europe was only an isolated appendage of a much larger world system of states stretching from the Atlantic Ocean to the Pacific. The center of gravity in this trade network was not in Europe or even in the Mediterranean Sea but much farther to the east, in the Persian Gulf and in Central Asia. The most sophisticated and technologically advanced region in the world was not Europe but China, whose proud history could be traced back several thousand years to the rise of the first Chinese state in the Yellow River valley. As for the transcontinental trade network that linked Europe with the nations of the Middle East, South Asia, and the Pacific basin, it had not been created by Portuguese and Spanish navigators but, had already developed under the Arab empire, with its capital in Baghdad. Later the Mongols took control of the land trade routes during their conquest of much of the Eurasian continent in the thirteenth and fourteenth centuries. During the long centuries of Arabic and Mongolian hegemony, the caravan routes and sea lanes stretching across the Eurasian continent and the Indian Ocean between China, Africa, and Europe carried not only commercial goods but also ideas and inventions such as the compass, printing, Arabic numerals, and gunpowder. Inventions such as these, many of them originating in China or India, would later play a major role in the emergence of Europe as a major player on the world's stage. Only in the sixteenth century, with the onset of the Age of Exploration, did Europe become important in the process. For the next three centuries, the ships of several European nations crossed the seas in quest of the spices, silks, precious metals, and porcelains of the Orient.

In a few cases, Europeans engaged in military conquest as a means of seeking their objective. They were aided by technological advances in shipbuilding and weaponry that gave them a distinct advantage over their rivals. During the eighteenth century, the islands of the Indonesian archipelago were gradually brought under Dutch colonial rule, and the British inexorably extended their political hegemony over the South Asian subcontinent. Spain, Portugal, and later other nations of western Europe divided up the Americas into separate colonial territories. For the most part, however, European nations were satisfied to trade with their Asian and African counterparts from coastal enclaves that they had established along the trade routes that threaded across the seas from the ports along the Atlantic and the Mediterranean Sea to their far-off destinations.

The Advent of Western Imperialism

In the nineteenth century, a new phase of Western expansion into Asia and Africa began. Whereas European aims in the East before 1800 could be summed up in the Portuguese explorer Vasco da Gama's famous phrase "Christians and spices," in the early nineteenth century, a new relationship took shape: European nations began to view Asian and African societies as a source of industrial raw materials and a market for Western manufactured goods. No longer were Western gold and silver exchanged for cloves, pepper, tea, silk, and porcelain. Now the prodigious output of European factories was sent to Africa and Asia in return for oil, tin, rubber, and the other resources needed to fuel the Western industrial machine.

The Impact of the Industrial Revolution The reason for this change, of course, was the Industrial Revolution. Now industrializing countries in the West needed vital raw materials that were not available at home as well as a reliable market for the goods produced in their factories. The latter factor became increasingly crucial as capitalist societies began to discover that their home markets could not always absorb domestic output. When consumer demand lagged, economic depression threatened.

As Western economic expansion into Asia and Africa gathered strength during the last quarter of the nineteenth century, it became fashionable to call the process imperialism. Although the term *imperialism* has many meanings, in this instance it referred to the efforts of capitalist states in the West to seize markets, cheap raw materials, and lucrative sources for the investment of capital in the countries beyond Western civilization. In this interpretation, the primary motives behind the Western expansion were economic. The best-known promoter of this view was the British political economist John A. Hobson, who published a major analysis, *Imperialism: A Study,* in 1902. In this influential book, Hobson maintained that modern imperialism was a direct consequence of the modern industrial economy. In his view, the industrialized states of the West often produced more goods than could be absorbed by the domestic market and thus had to export their manufactures to make a profit.

The issue was not simply an economic one, however, since economic concerns were inevitably tinged with political ones and with questions of national grandeur and moral purpose as well. In nineteenth-century Europe, economic wealth, national status, and political power went hand in hand with the possession of a colonial empire, at least in the minds of observers at the time. To global strategists of the day, colonies brought tangible benefits in the world of balance-of-power politics as well as economic profits, and many nations became involved in the pursuit of colonies as much to gain advantage over their rivals as to acquire territory for its own sake.

The relationship between colonialism and national survival was expressed directly in a speech by the French politician Jules Ferry in 1885. A policy of "containment or abstinence," he warned, would set France on "the broad road to decadence" and initiate its decline into a "third- or fourth-rate power." British imperialists agreed. To Cecil Rhodes, the extraction of material wealth from the colonies was only a secondary matter. "My ruling purpose," he remarked, "is the extension of the British Empire." [2] That British Empire, on which (as the saying went) "the sun never set," was the envy of its rivals and was viewed as the primary source of British global dominance during the latter half of the nineteenth century.

The Tactics With the change in European motives for colonization came a corresponding shift in tactics. Earlier, when their economic interests were more limited, European states had generally been satisfied to deal with existing independent states rather than attempt to establish direct control over vast territories. There had been exceptions where state power at the local level was on the point of collapse (as in India), where European economic interests were especially intense (as in Latin America and the East Indies), or where there was no centralized authority (as in North America and the Philippines). But for the most part, the Western presence in Asia and Africa had been limited to controlling the regional trade network and establishing a few footholds where the foreigners could carry on trade and missionary activity.

After 1800, the demands of industrialization in Europe created a new set of dynamics. Maintaining access to industrial raw materials, such as oil and rubber, and setting up reliable markets for European manufactured products required more extensive control over colonial territories. As competition for colonies increased, the colonial powers sought to solidify their hold over their territories to protect them from attack by their rivals. During the last two decades of the nineteenth century, the quest for colonies became a scramble as all the major European states, now joined by the United States and Japan, engaged in a global land grab. In many cases, economic interests were secondary to security concerns or national prestige. In Africa, for example, the British engaged in a struggle with their rivals to protect their interests in the Suez Canal and the Red Sea. In Southeast Asia, the United States seized the Philippines from Spain at least partly to keep them out of the hands of the Japanese, and the French took over Indochina for fear that it would otherwise be occupied by Germany, Japan, or the United States.

By 1900, virtually all the societies of Africa and Asia were either under full colonial rule or, as in the case of China and the Ottoman Empire, on the point of virtual collapse. Only a handful of states, such as Japan in East Asia, Thailand in Southeast Asia, Afghanistan and Iran in the Middle East, and mountainous Ethiopia in East Africa, managed to escape internal disintegration or political subjection to colonial rule. As the twentieth century began, European hegemony over the ancient civilizations of Asia and Africa seemed complete.

The Colonial System

Once they had control of most of the world, what did the colonial powers do with it? As we have seen, their primary objective was to exploit the natural resources of the subject areas and to open up markets for manufactured goods and capital investment from the mother country. In some cases, that goal could be realized in cooperation with local political elites, whose loyalty could be earned (or purchased) by economic rewards or by confirming them in their positions of authority and status in a new colonial setting. Sometimes, however, this policy, known as "indirect rule," was not feasible because local leaders refused to cooperate with their colonial masters or even actively resisted the foreign conquest. In such cases, the local elites were removed from power and replaced with a new set of officials recruited from the mother country.

The distinction between direct and indirect rule was not always clearly drawn, and many colonial powers vacillated between the two approaches, sometimes in the same colonial territory. The decision often had fateful consequences for the peoples involved. Where colonial powers encountered resistance and were forced to overthrow local political elites, they often adopted policies designed to eradicate the source of resistance and destroy the traditional culture. Such policies often had corrosive effects on the indigenous societies and provoked resentment that not only marked the colonial relationship but even affected relations after the restoration of national independence. The bitter struggles after World War II in Algeria, the Dutch East Indies, and Vietnam can be ascribed in part to that phenomenon.

The Philosophy of Colonialism

To justify their conquests, the colonial powers appealed, in part, to the time-honored maxim of "might makes right." In a manner reminiscent of the Western attitude toward the oil reserves in the Persian Gulf today, the European powers viewed industrial resources as vital to national survival and security and felt that no moral justification was needed for any action to protect access to them. By the end of the nineteenth century, that attitude received pseudoscientific validity from the concept of social Darwinism, which maintained that only societies that moved aggressively to adapt to changing circumstances would survive and prosper in a world governed by the Darwinist law of "survival of the fittest."

The White Man's Burden Some people, however, were uncomfortable with such a brutal view of the law of nature and sought a moral justification that appeared to benefit the victim. Here again, social Darwinism pointed the way: since human societies, like living organisms, must adapt to survive, the advanced nations of the West were obliged to assist the backward peoples of Asia and Africa so that they, too, could adjust to the challenges of the modern world. Few expressed this view as graphically as the English poet Rudyard Kipling, who called on the Anglo-Saxon peoples (in particular, the United States) to take up the "white man's burden" in Asia (see the box on p. 29).

Buttressed by such comforting theories, humane souls in Western countries could ignore the brutal aspects of the colonial process and persuade themselves that in the long run, the results would be beneficial to both sides. Some, like their antecedents in the sixteenth and seventeenth centuries, saw the issue primarily in religious terms. During the nineteenth century, Christian missionaries by the thousands went to Asia and Africa to bring the gospel to the "heathen masses." To others, the objective was the more secular one of bringing the benefits of Western democracy and capitalism to the tradition-ridden societies of the Orient. Either way, sensitive Western minds could console themselves with the belief that their governments were bringing civilization to the primitive peoples of the world. If commercial profit and national prestige happened to be by-products of that effort, so much the better. Few were as effective at making the case as the French colonial official Albert Sarraut. Conceding that colonialism was originally an "act of force" taken for material profit, he declared that the end result would be a "better life on this planet" for conqueror and conquered alike.

But what about the possibility that historically and culturally, the societies of Asia and Africa were fundamentally different from those of the West and could not, or would not, be persuaded to transform themselves along Western lines? After all, even Kipling had remarked that "East is East and West is West, and ne'er the twain shall meet." Was the human condition universal, in which case the Asian and African peoples could be transformed, in the quaint American phrase for the subject Filipinos, into "little brown Americans"? Or were human beings so shaped by their history and geographic environment that their civilizations would inevitably remain distinctive from those of the West?

If so, a policy of cultural transformation could not be expected to succeed.

Assimilation and Association In fact, colonial theory never decided this issue one way or the other. The French, who were most inclined to philosophize about the problem, adopted the terms *assimilation* (which implied an effort to transform colonial societies in the Western image) and *association* (collaborating with local elites while leaving local traditions alone) to describe the two alternatives and then proceeded to vacillate between them. French policy in Indochina, for example, began as one of association but switched to assimilation under pressure from liberal elements who felt that colonial powers owed a debt to their subject peoples. But assimilation aroused resentment among the local population, many of whom opposed the destruction of their native traditions.

Most colonial powers were not as inclined to debate the theory of colonialism as the French were. The United States, in formulating a colonial policy for the Philippines, adopted a strategy of assimilation in theory but was not quick to put it into practice. The British refused to entertain the possibility of assimilation and generally treated their subject peoples as culturally and racially distinctive (as Queen Victoria declared in 1858, her government disclaimed "the right and desire to impose Our conditions on Our subjects"). Although some observers have ascribed this attitude to a sense of racial superiority, not all agree. In his recent book *Ornamentalism: How the British Saw Their Empire,* the historian David Cannadine argues that the British simply attempted to replicate their own hierarchical system, based on the institutions of monarchy and aristocracy, and apply it to the peoples of the empire.

India Under the British Raj

The first of the major Asian civilizations to fall victim to European predatory activities was India. European traders had first arrived along the coast of India during the early sixteenth century, at a time when the country was ruled by the Mughals, a Muslim dynasty from Central Asia that governed a nation consisting primarily of people of the Hindu faith. During the next two centuries, several European countries established enclaves along the coast to carry on mercantile activities with the local population. By 1800, however, the Mughals were in decline, and the British—now established as the major European power in the region—used a combination of modern firepower and guile to consolidate their control over the subcontinent, expanding from their base areas along the coast into the interior. Some territories were taken over directly by the privately run East India Company, which at that time was given

WHITE MAN'S BURDEN, BLACK MAN'S SORROW

*O*ne of the justifications for modern imperialism was the notion that the allegedly "more advanced" white peoples had the moral responsibility to raise ignorant native peoples to a higher level of civilization. Few captured this notion better than the British poet Rudyard Kipling (1865–1936) in his famous poem *The White Man's Burden.* His appeal, directed to the United States, became one of the most famous sets of verses in the English-speaking world.

That sense of moral responsibility, however, was often misplaced or, even worse, laced with hypocrisy. All too often, the consequences of imperial rule were detrimental to everyone living under colonial authority. Few observers described the destructive effects of Western imperialism on the African people as well as Edmund Morel, a British journalist whose book *The Black Man's Burden* pointed out some of the more harmful aspects of colonialism in the Belgian Congo.

According to Kipling, why should Western nations take up the "white man's burden," as indicated in this poem? What was the "black man's burden," in the eyes of Edmund Morel?

Rudyard Kipling, *The White Man's Burden*

Take up the White Man's burden—
Send forth the best ye breed—
Go bind your sons to exile
To serve your captives' need;
To wait in heavy harness,
On fluttered folk and wild—
Your new-caught sullen peoples,
Half-devil and half-child.

Take up the White Man's burden—
In patience to abide,
To veil the threat of terror
And check the show of pride;
By open speech and simple,
An hundred times made plain
To seek another's profit,
And work another's gain.

Take up the White Man's burden—
The savage wars of peace—
Fill full the mouth of Famine
And bid the sickness cease;
And when your goal is nearest
The end for others sought,
Watch Sloth and heathen Folly
Bring all your hopes to nought.

Edmund Morel, *The Black Man's Burden*

It is [the Africans] who carry the "Black man's burden." They have not withered away before the white man's occupation. Indeed . . . Africa has ultimately absorbed within itself every Caucasian and, for that matter, every Semitic invader, too. In hewing out for himself a fixed abode in Africa, the white man has massacred the African in heaps. The African has survived, and it is well for the white settlers that he has. . . .

What the partial occupation of his soil by the white man has failed to do; what the mapping out of European political "spheres of influence" has failed to do; what the Maxim and the rifle, the slave gang, labour in the bowels of the earth and the lash, have failed to do; what imported measles, smallpox and syphilis have failed to do; whatever the overseas slave trade failed to do; the power of modern capitalistic exploitation, assisted by modern engines of destruction, may yet succeed in accomplishing.

For from the evils of the latter, scientifically applied and enforced, there is no escape for the African. Its destructive effects are not spasmodic; they are permanent. In its permanence resides its fatal consequences. It kills not the body merely, but the soul. It breaks the spirit. It attacks the African at every turn, from every point of vantage. It wrecks his polity, uproots him from the land, invades his family life, destroys his natural pursuits and occupations, claims his whole time, enslaves him in his own home.

SOURCES: From Rudyard Kipling, "The White Man's Burden," *McClure's Magazine* 12 (Feb. 1899). Edmund Morel, *The Black Man's Burden* (New York: Metro Books, 1972).

authority to administer Asian territories under British occupation, while others were ruled indirectly through their local maharajas (see Map. 2.1 on p. 30). British rule extended northward as far as present-day Afghanistan, where British fears of Russian expansionism led to a lengthy imperialist rivalry that was popularly labeled "the Great Game."

British governance brought order and stability to a society that had recently been wracked by civil war, as various regions of India, notably in the south, had begun to break away from central rule. Overall, however, the Mughal era had been a time of relative peace and prosperity for India. Although industrial development was still in its infancy, commerce and manufacturing flourished. Foreign trade, in particular, thrived as Indian goods, notably textiles, tropical food products, spices, and precious stones, were exported in exchange for gold and silver. Much of the foreign commerce was handled by Arab traders, since many Indians, like their Mughal rulers, did not care for travel

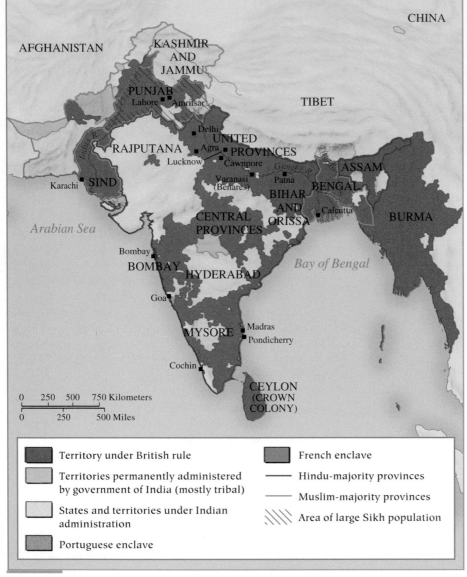

MAP 2.1 **India Under British Rule, 1805–1931.** This map shows the different forms of rule that the British applied in India under their control. ❓ Where were the major cities of the subcontinent located, and under whose rule did they fall? 🌐 **View an animated version of this map or related maps at the World History Resource Center, at** worldrc.wadsworth.com/.

Map legend:
- Territory under British rule
- Territories permanently administered by government of India (mostly tribal)
- States and territories under Indian administration
- Portuguese enclave
- French enclave
- Hindu-majority provinces
- Muslim-majority provinces
- Area of large Sikh population

was given to education. Through the efforts of the British administrator and historian Lord Macaulay, a new school system was established to train the children of Indian elites, and the British civil service examination was introduced (see the box on p. 31).

British rule also brought an end to some of the more inhumane aspects of Indian tradition. The practice of *sati* (cremation of a widow on her husband's funeral pyre) was outlawed, and widows were legally permitted to remarry. The British also attempted to put an end to the brigandage (known as *thuggee,* which gave rise to the English word *thug*) that had plagued travelers in India since time immemorial. Railroads, the telegraph, and the postal service were introduced to India shortly after they appeared in Great Britain. A new penal code based on the British model was adopted, and health and sanitation conditions were improved.

Agricultural Reforms But the Indian people paid dearly for the peace and stability brought by the British raj (from the Indian *raja,* or prince). Perhaps the most flagrant cost was economic. In rural areas, the British adopted the existing *zamindar* system, according to which local landlords were authorized to collect taxes from peasants and turn the taxes over to the government. The British mistakenly anticipated that by continuing the system, they would not only facilitate the collection of agricultural taxes but also create a landed gentry that could, as in Britain itself, become the conservative foundation of imperial rule. But the local gentry took advantage of their authority to increase taxes and force the less fortunate peasants to become tenants or lose their land entirely. When rural unrest threatened, the government passed legislation protecting farmers against eviction and unreasonable rent increases, but this measure had little effect outside the southern provinces, where it was originally enacted.

by sea. Internal trade, however, was dominated by large merchant castes, who were also active in banking and handicrafts. Although Indian peasants were required to pay heavy taxes, the system was applied fairly, and when drought struck, taxes were often reduced or even suspended altogether.

The Nature of British Rule

British rule in India led to a relatively honest and efficient government that in many respects operated to the benefit of the average Indian. For example, heightened attention

INDIAN IN BLOOD, ENGLISH IN TASTE AND INTELLECT

Thomas Babington Macaulay (1800–1859) was named a member of the Supreme Council of India in the early 1830s. In that capacity, he was responsible for drawing up a new educational policy for British subjects in the area. In his *Minute on Education,* he considered the claims of English and various local languages to become the vehicle for educational training and decided in favor of the former. It is better, he argued, to teach Indian elites about Western civilization so as " to form a class who may be interpreters between us and the millions whom we govern; a class of persons, Indian in blood and color, but English in taste, in opinions, in morals, and in intellect." Later Macaulay became a prominent historian.

How does the author of this document justify the teaching of the English language in India? How might a critic respond?

Thomas Babington Macaulay, *Minute on Education*

We have a fund to be employed as government shall direct for the intellectual improvement of the people of this country. The simple question is, what is the most useful way of employing it?

All parties seem to be agreed on one point, that the dialects commonly spoken among the natives of this part of India contain neither literary or scientific information, and are moreover so poor and rude that, until they are enriched from some other quarter, it will not be easy to translate any valuable work into them. . . .

What, then, shall the language [of education] be? One half of the Committee maintain that it should be the English. The other half strongly recommend the Arabic and Sanskrit. The whole question seems to me to be, what language is the best worth knowing?

I have no knowledge of either Sanskrit or Arabic—I have done what I could to form a correct estimate of their value. I have read translations of the most celebrated Arabic and Sanskrit works. I have conversed both here and at home with men distinguished by their proficiency in the Eastern tongues. I am quite ready to take the Oriental learning at the valuation of the Orientalists themselves. I have never found one among them who could deny that a single shelf of a good European library was worth the whole native literature of India and Arabia. . . .

It is, I believe, no exaggeration to say that all the historical information which has been collected from all the books written in the Sanskrit language is less valuable than what may be found in the most paltry abridgments used at preparatory schools in England.

SOURCE: Michael Edwards, *A History of India: From the Earliest Times to the Present Day* (London: Thames & Hudson, 1961), pp. 261–265.

Manufacturing British colonialism was also remiss in bringing modern science and technology to India. Some limited forms of industrialization took place, notably in the manufacturing of textiles and rope. The first textile mill opened in 1856; seventy years later, there were eighty mills in the city of Bombay alone. Nevertheless, the lack of local capital and the advantages given to British imports prevented the emergence of other vital new commercial and manufacturing operations, and the introduction of British textiles put thousands of Bengali women out of work and severely damaged the village textile industry.

Foreign rule also had an effect on the psyche of the Indian people. Although many British colonial officials sincerely tried to improve the lot of the people under their charge, the government made few efforts to introduce democratic institutions and values to the Indian people. Moreover, British arrogance and contempt for native traditions cut deeply into the pride of many Indians, especially those of high caste who were accustomed to a position of superior status in India. Educated Indians trained in the Anglo-Indian school system for a career in the civil service, as well as Eurasians born to mixed marriages, rightfully wondered where their true cultural loyalties lay. This cultural collision is poignantly described in the novel *A Passage to India* by the British writer E. M. Forster, which relates the story of a visiting Englishwoman who becomes interested in the Indian way of life, much to the dismay of the local European community.

The Colonial Takeover of Southeast Asia

Southeast Asia had been one of the first destinations for European adventurers en route to the East. For centuries the region had been an active participant in the trade network extending from the Pacific Ocean to the Middle East and beyond. Lured by the riches of the Spice Islands (at the eastern end of present-day Indonesia), European adventurers sailed to the area in the early sixteenth century in the hope of seizing control of the spice trade from Arab and Indian merchants. A century later, the trade was fast

An English Nabob in Colonial India.
When the British took over India in the late eighteenth and nineteenth centuries, many Indians began to imitate European customs for prestige or social advancement. Sometimes, however, the cultural influence went the other way. Here an English nabob, as European residents in the colonies were often called, apes the manner of an Indian aristocrat, complete with harem and hookah, the Indian water pipe. The paintings on the wall, however, are in the European style.

becoming a monopoly of the Dutch, whose sturdy ships and ample supply of capital gave them a significant advantage over their rivals.

In 1800, only two societies in Southeast Asia were under effective colonial rule: the Spanish Philippines and the Dutch East Indies. The British had been driven out of the Spice Islands trade by the Dutch in the seventeenth century and possessed only a small enclave on the southern coast of the island of Sumatra and some territory on the Malayan peninsula. The French had actively engaged in trade with states on the Asian mainland, but their activity in the area was eventually reduced to a small missionary effort run by the Society for Foreign Missions. The only legacy of Portuguese expansion in the region was the possession of half of the small island of Timor.

The Imposition of Colonial Rule

During the second half of the nineteenth century, however, European interest in Southeast Asia grew rapidly, and by 1900, virtually the entire area was under colonial rule (see Map 2.2). The process began after the end of the Napoleonic Wars, when the British, by agreement with the Dutch, abandoned their claims to territorial possessions in the East Indies in return for a free hand in the Malayan peninsula. In 1819, the colonial administrator Stamford Raffles founded a new British colony on a small island at the tip of the peninsula. Called Singapore ("City of the Lion"), it had previously been used by Malay pirates to raid ships passing through the Strait of Malacca. When the invention of steam power

enabled merchant ships to save time and distance by passing through the strait rather than sailing with the westerlies across the southern Indian Ocean, Singapore became a major stopping point for traffic to and from China and other commercial centers in the region. In the meantime, the British had sought and received the right to trade with the kingdom of Burma. A few decades later, the British took over the entire country and placed it under the colonial administration in India.

The British advance into Burma was watched nervously in Paris, where French geopoliticians were ever anxious about British operations in Asia and Africa. The French still maintained a clandestine missionary organization in Vietnam despite harsh persecution by the local authorities, who viewed Christianity as a threat to internal stability. In 1857, the French government decided to force the Vietnamese to accept French protection to prevent the British from obtaining a monopoly of trade in South China. A naval attack launched a year later was not a total success, but the French eventually forced the Vietnamese court to cede territories in the Mekong River delta. A generation later, French rule was extended over the remainder of the country. By the end of the century, French seizure of neighboring Cambodia and Laos had led to the creation of the French-ruled Indochinese Union.

With the French conquest of Indochina, Thailand was the only remaining independent state on the Southeast Asian mainland. During the last quarter of the century, British and French rivalry threatened to place the Thai, too, under colonial rule. But under the astute leadership of two

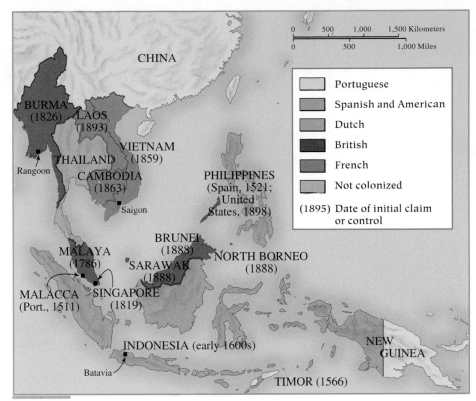

MAP 2.2 Colonial Southeast Asia. European colonial rule spread into Southeast Asia between the sixteenth century and the end of the nineteenth. ❓ What was the significance of Malacca? 🌐 **View an animated version of this map or related maps at the World History Resource Center, at** worldrc.wadsworth.com/.

Pearl Harbor into a naval station in 1887, American settlers gained control of the sugar industry on the islands. When Hawaiian natives tried to reassert their authority, the U.S. Marines were brought in to "protect" American lives. Hawaii was annexed by the United States in 1898 during the era of American nationalistic fervor generated by the Spanish-American War, which broke out after an explosion damaged a U.S. battleship anchored at Havana on the Spanish-held island of Cuba.

The defeat of Spain encouraged Americans to extend their empire by acquiring Puerto Rico, Guam, and the Philippine Islands. President William McKinley agonized over the fate of the latter but ultimately decided that the moral thing to do was to turn the islands into an American colony to prevent them from falling into the hands of the Japanese. In fact, the Americans (like the Spanish before them) found the islands convenient as a jumping-off point for the China trade (see Chapter 3).

remarkable rulers, King Mongkut (familiar to millions in the West as the king in *The King and I*) and his son King Chulalongkorn, the Thai sought to introduce Western learning and maintain relations with the major European powers without undermining internal stability or inviting an imperialist attack. In 1896, the British and the French agreed to preserve Thailand as an independent buffer zone between their possessions in Southeast Asia.

The final piece of the colonial edifice in Southeast Asia was put in place in 1898, when U.S. naval forces under Commodore George Dewey defeated the Spanish fleet in Manila Bay. Since gaining independence in the late eighteenth century, the United States had always considered itself to be an anticolonialist nation, and in 1823 President James Monroe enunciated the so-called Monroe Doctrine, warning European powers to refrain from restoring their colonial presence in the Western Hemisphere. But by the end of the century, many Americans believed that the United States was itself ready to expand abroad. The Pacific islands were the scene of great-power competition and witnessed the entry of the United States on the imperialist stage. Eastern Samoa became the first important American colony; the Hawaiian Islands were the next to fall. Soon after Americans had made

Not all Filipinos were pleased to be placed under U.S. tutelage. Led by Emilio Aguinaldo, guerrilla forces fought bitterly against U.S. troops to establish their independence from both Spain and the United States. But America's first war against guerrillas in Asia was a success, and the resistance collapsed in 1901. President McKinley had his stepping-stone to the rich markets of China.

Colonial Regimes in Southeast Asia

In Southeast Asia, economic profit was the immediate and primary aim of the colonial enterprise. For that purpose, colonial powers tried wherever possible to work with local elites to facilitate the exploitation of natural resources. Indirect rule reduced the cost of training European administrators and had a less corrosive impact on the local culture.

Colonial Administration In the Dutch East Indies, for example, officials of the Dutch East India Company (VOC) entrusted local administration to the indigenous landed aristocracy, known as the *priyayi*. The *priyayi* maintained law and order and collected taxes in return for a payment from the VOC (see the box on p. 34). The British followed

THE EFFECTS OF DUTCH COLONIALISM IN JAVA

E. Douwes Dekker was a Dutch colonial official who served in the East Indies for nearly twenty years. In 1860, he published a critique of the Dutch colonial system that had an impact in the Netherlands similar to that of Harriet Beecher Stowe's Uncle Tom's Cabin *in the United States. In the following excerpt from his book* Max Havelaar, or Coffee Auctions of the Dutch Trading Company, *Dekker described the system as it was applied on the island of Java, in the Indonesian archipelago.*

According to the author, what was the impact of Dutch policies on the lives of Javanese peasants? Why is he critical of such policies?

E. Douwes Dekker, *Max Havelaar*

The Javanese is by nature a husbandman; the ground whereon he is born, which gives much for little labor, allures him to it, and, above all things, he devotes his whole heart and soul to the cultivating of his rice fields, in which he is very clever. He grows up in the midst of his sawahs [rice fields] . . . ; when still very young, he accompanies his father to the field, where he helps him in his labor with plow and spade, in construction dams and drains to irrigate his fields; he counts his years by harvests; he estimates time by the color of the blades in his field; he is at home amongst the companions who cut paddy with him; he chooses his wife amongst the girls of the dessah [village], who every evening tread the rice with joyous songs. The possession of a few buffaloes for plowing is the ideal of his dreams. The cultivation of rice is in Java what the vintage is in the Rhine provinces and the south of France. But there came foreigners from the West, who made themselves masters of the country. They wished to profit by the fertility of the soil, and ordered the native to devote a part of his time and labor to the cultivation of other things which should produce higher profits in the markets of Europe. To persuade the lower orders to do so, they had only to follow a very simple policy. The Javanese obeys his chiefs; to win the chiefs, it was only necessary to give them a part of the gain,–and success was complete.

To be convinced of the success of that policy we need only consider the immense quantity of Javanese products sold in Holland; and we shall also be convinced of its injustice, for, if anybody should ask if the husbandman himself gets a reward in proportion to that quantity, then I must give a negative answer. The Government compels him to cultivate certain products on his ground; it punishes him if he sells what he has produced to any purchaser but itself; and it fixes the price actually paid. The expenses of transport to Europe through a privileged trading company are high; the money paid to the chiefs for encouragement increases the prime cost; and because the entire trade must produce profit, that profit cannot be got in any other way than by paying the Javanese just enough to keep him from starving, which would lessen the producing power of the nation.

SOURCE: *The World of Southeast Asia: Selected Historical Readings,* Harry J. Benda and John A. Larkin, eds. Copyright © 1967 by Harper & Row, Publishers. Used with permission of the author.

---

a similar practice in Malaya. While establishing direct rule over areas of crucial importance, such as the commercial centers of Singapore and Malacca and the island of Penang, the British signed agreements with local Muslim rulers to maintain princely power in the interior of the peninsula.

In some instances, however, local resistance to the colonial conquest made such a policy impossible. In Burma, faced with staunch opposition from the monarchy and other traditionalist forces, the British abolished the monarchy and administered the country directly through their colonial government in India. In Indochina, the French used both direct and indirect means. They imposed direct rule on the southern provinces in the Mekong delta, which had been ceded to France as a colony after the first war in 1858–1860. The northern parts of the country, seized in the 1880s, were governed as a protectorate, with the emperor retaining titular authority from his palace in Hué. The French adopted a similar policy in Cambodia and Laos, where local rulers were left in charge with French advisers to counsel them. Even the Dutch were eventually forced into a more direct approach. When the development of plantation agriculture and the extraction of oil in Sumatra made effective exploitation of local resources more complicated, they dispensed with indirect rule and tightened their administrative control over the archipelago.

Whatever method was used, colonial regimes in Southeast Asia, as elsewhere, were slow to create democratic institutions. The first legislative councils and assemblies were composed almost exclusively of European residents in the colonies. The first representatives from the indigenous population were wealthy and conservative in their political views. When Southeast Asians began to complain, colonial officials gradually and reluctantly began to broaden the franchise, but even such liberal thinkers as Albert Sarraut advised patience in awaiting the full benefits of colonial policy. "I will treat you like my younger brothers," he promised, "but do not forget that I am the older brother. I will slowly give you the dignity of humanity."[3]

Economic Development

Colonial powers were equally reluctant to shoulder the "white man's burden" in the area of economic development. As we have seen, their primary goals were to secure a source of cheap raw materials and to maintain markets for manufactured goods. So colonial policy concentrated on the export of raw materials—teakwood from Burma; rubber and tin from Malaya; spices, tea, coffee, and palm oil from the East Indies; and sugar and copra from the Philippines.

In some Southeast Asian colonial societies, a measure of industrial development did take place to meet the needs of the European population and local elites. Major manufacturing cities, including Rangoon in lower Burma, Batavia on the island of Java, and Saigon in French Indochina, grew rapidly. Although the local middle class benefited in various ways from the Western presence, most industrial and commercial establishments were owned and managed by Europeans or, in some cases, by Indian or Chinese merchants who had long been active in the area. In Saigon, for example, even the manufacture of *nuoc mam*, the traditional Vietnamese fish sauce, was under Chinese ownership. Most urban residents were coolies (laborers), factory workers, or rickshaw drivers or eked out a living in family shops as they had during the traditional era.

Rural Policies

Despite the growth of an urban economy, the vast majority of people in the colonial societies continued to farm the land. Many continued to live by subsistence agriculture, but the colonial policy of emphasizing cash crops for export also led to the creation of a form of plantation agriculture in which peasants were recruited to work as wage laborers on rubber and tea plantations owned by Europeans. To maintain a competitive edge, the plantation owners kept the wages of their workers at the poverty level. Many plantation workers were "shanghaied" (the English term originated from the practice of recruiting laborers, often from the docks and streets of Shanghai, by the use of force, alcohol, drugs, or other unscrupulous means) to work on plantations, where conditions were often so inhumane that thousands died. High taxes, enacted by colonial governments to pay for administrative costs or improvements in the local infrastructure, were a heavy burden for poor peasants.

The situation was made even more difficult by the steady growth of the population. Peasants in Asia had always had large families on the assumption that a high proportion of their children would die in infancy. But improved sanitation and medical treatment resulted in lower rates of infant mortality and a staggering increase in population. The population of the island of Java, for example, increased from about a million in the precolonial era to about 40 million at the end of the nineteenth century. Under these conditions, the rural areas could no longer support the growing populations, and many young people fled to the cities to seek jobs in factories or shops. The migratory pattern gave rise to squatter settlements in the suburbs of the major cities.

Imperialism in the Balance

As in India, colonial rule did bring some benefits to Southeast Asia. It led to the beginnings

The Esplanade. After occupying the island of Singapore early in the nineteenth century, the British turned what was once a pirate lair located at the entrance to the Strait of Malacca into one of the most important commercial seaports in Asia. By the end of the century, Singapore was home to a rich mixture of peoples, both European and Asian. This painting by a British artist in the 1890s graphically displays the multiracial character of the colony as strollers, rickshaw drivers, and lamplighters share space along the Esplanade, in Singapore harbor. Almost all colonial port cities became a melting pot of peoples from various parts of the world. Many of the immigrants served as merchants, urban laborers, and craftsmen in the new imperial marketplace.

of a modern economic infrastructure, and development of an export market helped create an entrepreneurial class in rural areas. On the outer islands of the Dutch East Indies (such as Borneo and Sumatra), for example, small growers of rubber, palm oil, coffee, tea, and spices began to share in the profits of the colonial enterprise.

A balanced assessment of the colonial legacy in Southeast Asia must take into account that the early stages of industrialization are difficult in any society. Even in western Europe, industrialization led to the creation of an impoverished and powerless proletariat, urban slums, and displaced peasants driven from the land. In much of Europe, however, the bulk of the population eventually enjoyed better material conditions as the profits from manufacturing and plantation agriculture were reinvested in the national economy and gave rise to increased consumer demand. In contrast, in Southeast Asia, most of the profits were repatriated to the colonial mother country, while displaced peasants fleeing to cities such as Rangoon, Batavia, and Saigon found little opportunity for employment. Many were left with seasonal employment, with one foot on the farm and one in the factory. The old world was being destroyed, and the new had yet to be born.

Empire Building in Africa

The last of the equatorial regions of the world to be placed under European colonial rule was the continent of Africa. European navigators had first established contacts with Africans south of the Sahara during the late fifteenth century, when Portuguese fleets sailed down the Atlantic coast on their way to the Indian Ocean. During the next three centuries, Europeans established port facilities along the coasts of East and West Africa to facilitate their trade with areas farther to the east and to engage in limited commercial relations with African societies. Eventually, the slave trade took on predominant importance, and several million unfortunate Africans were loaded onto slave ships destined for the Americas. For a variety of reasons, however, Europeans made little effort to penetrate the vast continent and were generally content to deal with African intermediaries along the coast to maintain their trading relationship. The Western psyche developed a deeply ingrained image of "darkest Africa"—a continent without a history, its people living out their days bereft of any cultural contact with the outside world.

Africa Before the Europeans

As with most generalizations, there was a glimmer of truth in the Western image of sub-Saharan Africa as a region outside the mainstream of civilization on the Eurasian landmass.

Although Africa was the original seedbed of humankind and the site of much of its early evolutionary experience, the desiccation of the Sahara during the fourth and third millennia B.C.E. had erected a major obstacle to communications between the peoples south of the desert and societies elsewhere in the world. The barrier was never total, however. From ancient times, caravans crossed the Sahara from the Niger River basin to the shores of the Mediterranean carrying gold and other tropical products in exchange for salt, textile goods, and other manufactured articles from the north. By the seventh century C.E., several prosperous trading societies, whose renown reached as far as medieval Europe and the Middle East, had begun to arise in the savanna belt in West Africa. In the baggage of merchants came not only commercial goods but also the religion and culture of Islam.

Farther to the east, the Sahara posed no obstacle to communication beyond the seas. The long eastern coast of the African continent had played a role in the trade network of the Indian Ocean since the time of the pharaohs along the Nile. Ships from India, the Persian Gulf, and as far away as China made regular visits to the East African ports of Kilwa, Malindi, and Sofala, bringing textiles, metal goods, and luxury articles in return for gold, ivory, and various tropical products from Africa. With the settlement of Arab traders along the eastern coast, the entire region developed a new synthetic culture (known as Swahili) combining elements of Arabic and indigenous cultures. Although the Portuguese briefly seized or destroyed most of the trading ports along the eastern coast, by the eighteenth century the Europeans had been driven out and local authority was restored.

The Growing European Presence in West Africa

By the beginning of the nineteenth century, the slave trade was in a state of decline. One reason was the growing sense of outrage in Europe over the purchase, sale, and exploitation of human beings. Traffic in slaves by Dutch merchants effectively came to an end in 1795 and by Danes in 1803. A few years later, the slave trade was declared illegal in both Great Britain and the United States. The British began to apply pressure on other nations to follow suit, and most did so after the end of the Napoleonic Wars in 1815, leaving only Portugal and Spain as practitioners of the trade south of the equator. Meanwhile, the demand for slaves began to decline in the Western Hemisphere, and by the 1880s, slavery had been abolished in all major countries of the world.

The decline of the slave trade in the Atlantic during the first half of the nineteenth century, however, did not lead to an overall reduction in the European presence in West Africa. To the contrary, European interest in what was sometimes called "legitimate trade" in natural resources increased. Exports of peanuts, timber, hides, and palm oil increased substantially during the first decades of the century, and imports of textile goods and other manufactured products also rose.

Stimulated by growing commercial interests in the area, European governments began to push for a more permanent presence along the coast. During the first decades of the nineteenth century, the British established settlements along the Gold Coast (present-day Ghana) and in Sierra Leone, where they attempted to set up agricultural plantations for freed slaves who had returned from the Western Hemisphere or had been liberated by British ships while en route to the Americas. A similar haven for ex-slaves was developed with the assistance of the United States in Liberia. The French occupied the area around the Senegal River near Cape Verde, where they attempted to develop peanut plantations.

The growing European presence in West Africa led to tensions with African governments in the area. British efforts to increase trade with Ashanti, in the area of the present-day state of Ghana, led to conflict in the 1820s, but British influence in the area intensified in later decades. Most African states, especially those with a fairly high degree of political integration, were able to maintain their independence from this creeping European encroachment, called "informal empire" by some historians, but eventually, the British stepped in and annexed the Ashanti kingdom as the first British colony of the Gold Coast in 1874. At about the same time, the British extended an informal protectorate over warring tribal groups in the Niger delta.

Imperialist Shadow over the Nile

A similar process was under way in the Nile valley. Ever since the voyages of the Portuguese explorers at the close of the fifteenth century, European trade with the East had been carried on almost exclusively by the route around the Cape of Good Hope at the southern tip of Africa. But from the outset, there was some interest in shortening the route by digging a canal east of Cairo, where only a low, swampy isthmus separated the Mediterranean from the Red Sea. The Ottoman Turks, who controlled the area, had considered constructing a canal in the sixteenth century, but nothing was accomplished until 1854, when the French entrepreneur Ferdinand de Lesseps signed a contract to begin construction of the canal. The completed project brought little immediate benefit to Egypt, however, which under the vigorous rule of the Ottoman official

Muhammad Ali was attempting to adopt reforms on the European model. The costs of construction imposed a major debt on the Egyptian government and forced a growing level of dependence on foreign financial support. When an army revolt against growing foreign influence broke out in 1881, the British stepped in to protect their investment (they had bought Egypt's canal company shares in 1875) and set up an informal protectorate that would last until World War I.

The weakening of Turkish rule in the Nile valley had a parallel farther to the west, where autonomous regions had begun to emerge under local viceroys in Tripoli, Tunis, and Algiers. In 1830, the French, on the pretext of reducing the threat of piracy to European shipping in the Mediterranean, seized the area surrounding Algiers and annexed it to the kingdom of France. By the mid-1850s, more than 150,000 Europeans had settled in the fertile region adjacent to the coast, though Berber resistance continued in the desert to the south. In 1881, the French imposed a protectorate on neighboring Tunisia. Only Tripoli and Cyrenaica (Ottoman provinces that make up modern-day Libya) remained under Turkish rule until the Italians took them in 1911–1912.

The Scramble for Africa

At the beginning of the 1880s, most of Africa was still independent. European rule was still limited to the fringes of the continent, and a few areas, such as Egypt, lower Nigeria, Senegal, and Mozambique, were under various forms of loose protectorate. But the trends were ominous, as the pace of European penetration was accelerating and the constraints that had limited European rapaciousness were fast disappearing.

The scramble began in the mid-1880s, when several European states engaged in what today would be called a feeding frenzy to seize a piece of African territory before the carcass had been picked clean. By 1900, virtually all of the continent had been placed under one form or another of European rule (see Map 2.3 on p. 39). The British had consolidated their authority over the Nile valley and seized additional territories in East Africa. The French retaliated by advancing eastward from Senegal into the central Sahara, where they eventually came eyeball to eyeball with the British in the Nile valley. They also occupied the island of Madagascar and other coastal territories in West and Central Africa. In between, the Germans claimed the hinterland opposite Zanzibar, as well as coastal strips in West and Southwest Africa

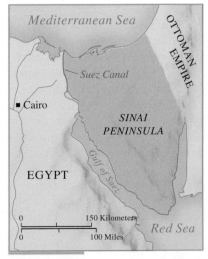

The Suez Canal

The Opening of the Suez Canal. The Suez Canal, which connected the Mediterranean and the Red Sea for the first time, was constructed under the direction of the French promoter Ferdinand de Lesseps. Still in use today, the canal is Egypt's greatest revenue producer. This sketch shows the ceremonial passage of the first ships through the canal upon its completion in 1869.

north of the Cape, and King Leopold II of Belgium claimed the Congo.

The Motives What had happened to spark the sudden imperialist hysteria that brought an end to African independence? Economic interests in the narrow sense were not at stake as they had been in South and Southeast Asia: the level of trade between Europe and Africa was simply not sufficient to justify the risks and the expense of conquest. Clearly, one factor was the growing rivalry among imperialist powers. European leaders might be provoked into an imperialist takeover not by economic considerations but by the fear that another state might do so, leaving them at a disadvantage.

Another consideration might be called the "missionary factor," as European missionary interests lobbied with their governments for a colonial takeover to facilitate their efforts to convert the African population to Christianity. In fact, considerable moral complacency was inherent in the process. The concept of the "white man's burden" persuaded many that it was in the interests of the African people to be introduced more rapidly to the benefits of Western civilization. Even the highly respected Scottish missionary David Livingstone had become convinced that missionary work and economic development had to go hand in hand, pleading to his fellow Europeans to introduce the "three Cs" (Christianity, commerce, and civilization) to the continent. How much easier such a task would be if African peoples were under benevolent European rule!

There were more prosaic reasons as well. Advances in Western technology and European superiority in firearms made it easier than ever for a small European force to defeat superior numbers. Furthermore, life expectancy for Europeans living in Africa had improved. With the discovery that quinine (extracted from the bark of the cinchona tree) could provide partial immunity from the ravages of malaria, the mortality rate for Europeans living in Africa dropped dramatically in the 1840s. By the end of the century, European residents in tropical Africa faced only slightly higher risks of death by disease than individuals living in Europe.

The Berlin Conference As rivalry among the competing powers heated up, a conference was convened at Berlin in 1884 to avert war and reduce tensions among European nations competing for the spoils of Africa. It proved reasonably successful at achieving the first objective but less so at the second. During the next few years, African territories were annexed without provoking a major confrontation between Western powers, but in the late 1890s, Britain and France reached the brink of conflict at Fashoda, a small town on the Nile River in the Sudan. The French had been advancing eastward across the Sahara with the transparent objective of controlling the regions around the upper Nile. In 1898, British and Egyptian troops seized the Sudan and then marched southward to head off the French. After a tense face-off between units of the two European countries at Fashoda, the French government backed down, and British authority over the area was secured. Except for Djibouti, a tiny portion of the Somali coast, the French were restricted to equatorial Africa.

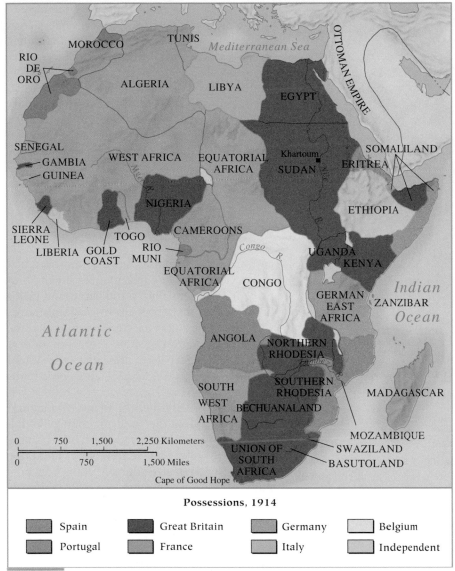

MAP 2.3 **Africa in 1914.** By the beginning of 1900, virtually all of Africa was under some form of European rule. The territorial divisions established by colonial powers on the continent of Africa on the eve of World War I are shown here. ❓ Which European countries possessed the most colonies in Africa? Why did Ethiopia remain independent? 🌐 **View an animated version of this map or related maps at the World History Resource Center, at** worldrc.wadsworth.com/.

Map legend — **Possessions, 1914**:
- Spain
- Portugal
- Great Britain
- France
- Germany
- Italy
- Belgium
- Independent

Bantus, Boers, and British in South Africa

Nowhere in Africa did the European presence grow more rapidly than in the south. During the eighteenth century, Dutch settlers from the Cape Colony began to migrate eastward into territory inhabited by local Khoisan- and Bantu-speaking peoples entering the area from the north. Internecine warfare among the Bantus had largely depopulated the region, facilitating occupation of the land by the Boers, the Afrikaans-speaking farmers descended from the

original Dutch settlers in the seventeenth century. But in the early nineteenth century, a Bantu people called the Zulus, under a talented ruler named Shaka, counterattacked, setting off a series of wars between the Europeans and the Zulus. Eventually, Shaka was overthrown, and the Boers continued their advance northeastward during the so-called Great Trek of the mid-1830s (see Map 2.4 on p. 40). By 1865, the total European population of the area had risen to nearly 200,000 people.

The Boers' eastward migration was provoked in part by the British seizure of the Cape from the Dutch during the Napoleonic Wars. The British government was generally more sympathetic to the rights of the local African population than were the Afrikaners, many of whom saw white superiority as ordained by God and fled from British rule to control their own destiny. Eventually, the Boers formed their own independent republics, the Orange Free State and the South African Republic (usually known as Transvaal). Much of the African population in these areas was confined to reserves.

The Boer War The discovery of gold and diamonds in the Transvaal complicated the situation. Clashes between the Afrikaner population and foreign (mainly British) miners and developers led to an attempt by Cecil Rhodes, prime minister of the Cape Colony and a prominent entrepreneur in the area, to subvert the Transvaal and bring it under British rule. In 1899, the so-called Boer War broke out between Britain and the Transvaal, which was backed by the Orange Free State. Guerrilla resistance by the Boers was fierce, but the vastly superior forces of the British were able to prevail by 1902. To compensate the defeated Afrikaner population for the loss of independence, the British government agreed that only whites would vote in the now essentially self-governing colony. The Boers were placated, but the brutalities committed during the war (the British introduced an institution later to be known as the concentration camp)

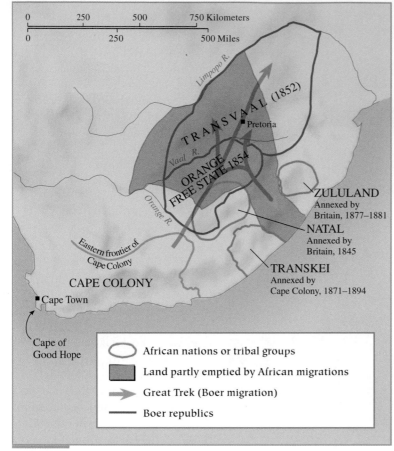

MAP 2.4 The Struggle for Southern Africa. Shown here is the expansion of European settlers from the Cape Colony into adjacent areas of southern Africa in the nineteenth century. The arrows indicate the routes taken by Afrikaans-speaking Boers. ❓ Who were the Boers, and why did they migrate eastward?

🌐 View an animated version of this map or related maps at the World History Resource Center, at worldrc.wadsworth.com/.

created bitterness on both sides that continued to fester for decades.

Colonialism in Africa

As we have seen, European economic interests were more limited in Africa than elsewhere. With economic concerns relatively limited except for isolated areas, such as gold mines in the Transvaal and copper deposits in the Belgian Congo, interest in Africa declined, and most European governments settled down to govern their new territories with the least effort and expense possible. In many cases, this meant a form of indirect rule reminiscent of the British approach to the princely states in the Indian peninsula. The British, with their tradition of decentralized government at home, were especially prone to adopt this approach.

Indirect Rule Nigeria offers a typical example of British indirect rule. British officials operated at the central level, but local authority was assigned to native chiefs, with British district officers serving as intermediaries with the central administration. Where a local aristocracy did not exist, the British assigned administrative responsibility to clan heads from communities in the vicinity. The local authorities were expected to maintain law and order and to collect taxes from the native population. As a general rule, indigenous customs were left undisturbed; a dual legal system was instituted that applied African laws to Africans and European laws to foreigners.

One advantage of such an administrative system was that it did not severely disrupt local customs and institutions. In fact, however, it had several undesirable consequences. In the first place, it was essentially a fraud because all major decisions were made by the British administrators while the native authorities served primarily as the means of enforcing decisions. Moreover, indirect rule served to perpetuate the autocratic system that often existed prior to colonial takeover. It was official policy to inculcate respect for authority in areas under British rule, and there was a natural tendency to view the local aristocracy as the African equivalent of the traditional British ruling class. Such a policy provided few opportunities for ambitious and talented young Africans from outside the traditional elite and thus sowed the seeds for class tensions after the restoration of independence in the twentieth century.

The situation was somewhat different in East Africa, especially in Kenya, which had a relatively large European population attracted by the temperate climate in the central highlands. The local government had encouraged Europeans to migrate to the area as a means of promoting economic development and encouraging financial self-sufficiency. To attract them, fertile farmlands in the central highlands were reserved for European settlement while, as in South Africa, specified reserve lands were set aside for Africans. The presence of a privileged European minority had an impact on Kenya's political development. The European settlers actively sought self-government and dominion status similar to that granted to such former British possessions as Canada and Australia. The British government, however, was not willing to run the risk of provoking racial tensions with the African majority and agreed only to establish separate government organs for the European and African populations.

The situation in South Africa, of course, was unique, not only because of the high percentage of European settlers

Revere the Conquering Heroes.
European colonial officials were quick to place themselves at the top of the political and social hierarchy in their conquered territories. Here British officials accept the submission of the Ashanti king and queen, according to African custom, in 1896.

but also because of the division between English-speaking and Afrikaner elements within the European population. In 1910, the British agreed to the creation of the independent Union of South Africa, which combined the old Cape Colony and Natal with the two Boer republics. The new union adopted a representative government, but only for the European population, while the African reserves of Basutoland (now Lesotho), Bechuanaland (now Botswana), and Swaziland were subordinated directly to the crown. The union was now free to manage its own domestic affairs and possessed considerable autonomy in foreign relations. Remaining areas south of the Zambezi River, eventually divided into the territories of Northern and Southern Rhodesia, were also placed under British rule. British immigration into Southern Rhodesia was extensive, and in 1922, after a popular referendum, it became a crown colony.

Direct Rule Most other European nations governed their African possessions through a form of direct rule. The prototype was the French system, which reflected the centralized administrative system introduced in France by Napoleon. As in the British colonies, at the top of the pyramid was a French official, usually known as a governor-general, who was appointed from Paris and governed with the aid of a bureaucracy in the capital city. At the provincial level, French commissioners were assigned to deal with local administrators, but the latter were required to be conversant in French and could be transferred to a new position at the needs of the central government.

The French ideal was to assimilate their African subjects into French culture rather than preserving their native traditions. Africans were eligible to run for office and to serve in the French National Assembly, and a few were appointed to high positions in the colonial administration. Such policies reflected the relative absence of racist attitudes in French society, as well as the French conviction of the superiority of Gallic culture and their revolutionary belief in the universality of human nature.

After World War I, European colonial policy in Africa entered a new and more formal phase. The colonial administrative network extended into outlying areas, where it was represented by a district official and defended by a small native army under European command. Colonial governments paid more attention to improving social services, including education, medicine, sanitation, and communications. The colonial system was now viewed more formally as a moral and social responsibility, a "sacred trust" to be maintained by the civilized countries until the Africans became capable of self-government. Governments placed more emphasis on economic development and the exploitation of natural resources to provide the colonies with the means of achieving self-sufficiency. More Africans were now serving in colonial administrations, though relatively few were in positions of responsibility. At the same time, race consciousness probably increased during this period. Segregated clubs, schools, and churches were established as more European officials brought their wives and began to raise families in the colonies.

Women in Colonial Africa

Colonial rule had a mixed impact on the rights and status of women in Africa. Sexual relationships changed profoundly during the colonial era, sometimes in ways that could justly be described as beneficial. Colonial governments attempted to put an end to forced marriage, bodily mutilation such as clitoridectomy, and polygamy. Missionaries introduced women to Western education and encouraged them to organize to defend their interests.

But the colonial system had some unfavorable consequences as well. African women had traditionally benefited from the prestige of matrilineal systems and were empowered by their traditional role as the primary agricultural producers in their community. Under colonialism, European settlers not only took the best land for themselves but also, in introducing new agricultural techniques, tended to deal exclusively with males, encouraging the latter to develop lucrative cash crops, while women were restricted to traditional farming methods. Whereas African men applied chemical fertilizer to the fields, women continued to use manure. While men began to use bicycles, and eventually trucks, to transport goods, women still carried their goods on their heads, a practice that continues today. In British colonies, Victorian attitudes of female subordination led to restrictions on women's freedom, and positions in government that they had formerly held were now closed to them.

CONCLUSION

By THE EARLY TWENTIETH CENTURY, virtually all of Africa and a good part of South and Southeast Asia were under some form of colonial rule. With the advent of the age of imperialism, a global economy was finally established, and the domination of Western civilization over those of Africa and Asia appeared to be complete.

Defenders of colonialism argue that the system was a necessary if sometimes painful stage in the evolution of human societies. Although its immediate consequences were admittedly sometimes unfortunate, Western imperialism was ultimately beneficial to colonial powers and subjects alike because it created the conditions for global economic development and the universal application of democratic institutions. Critics, however, charge that the Western colonial powers were driven by an insatiable lust for profits. They dismiss the Western civilizing mission as a fig leaf to cover naked greed and reject the notion that imperialism played a salutary role in hastening the adjustment of traditional societies to the demands of industrial civilization. Rather, it locked them in what many social scientists today describe as a "dependency relationship" with their colonial masters. "Why is Africa (or for that matter Latin America and much of Asia) so poor?" asked one recent Western critique of imperialism. "The answer is very brief: we have made it poor." [4]

Between these two irreconcilable views, where does the truth lie? It is difficult to provide a simple answer to this question, as the colonial record varied from country to country. In some cases, the colonial experience was probably beneficial in introducing Western technology, values, and democratic institutions into traditional societies. In other cases, as with the plantation system, the results were clearly destructive. As its defenders are quick to point out, colonialism often laid the foundation for preindustrial societies to play an active and rewarding role in the global economic marketplace. If, as the historian William McNeill believes, the introduction of new technology through cross-cultural encounters is the driving force of change in world history, then Western imperialism, whatever its faults, served a useful purpose in opening the door to such change.

Still, the critics have a point. Although colonialism did introduce the peoples of Asia and Africa to new technology and the expanding economic marketplace, it was unnecessarily brutal in its application and all too often failed to realize the exalted claims and objectives of its promoters. Existing economic networks—often potentially valuable as a foundation for later economic development—were ruthlessly swept aside in the interests of providing markets for Western manufactured goods. Potential sources of native industrialization were nipped in the bud to avoid competition for factories in Amsterdam, London, Pittsburgh, or Manchester. Training in Western democratic ideals and practices was ignored out of fear that the recipients might use them as weapons against the ruling authorities.

The fundamental weakness of colonialism, then, was that it was ultimately based on the self-interests of the citizens of the colonial powers. Where those interests collided with the needs of the colonial peoples, the former always triumphed. Much the same might be said about earlier periods in history, when Assyrians, Arabs, Mongols, and Chinese turned their conquests to their own profit. Where modern imperialism differed was in its tendency to clothe naked self-interest in the cloak of moral obligation. However sincerely the David Livingstones, Albert Sarrauts, and William McKinleys of the world were convinced of the rightness of their civilizing mission, the ultimate result was to deprive the colonial peoples of the right to make their own choices about their destiny.

In one area of Asia, the spreading tide of imperialism did not result in the establishment of formal Western colonial control. In East Asia, the traditional societies of China and Japan were buffeted by the winds of Western expansionism during the nineteenth century but successfully resisted foreign conquest. In the next chapter, we will see how they managed this and how they fared in their encounter with the West.

TIMELINE

	1800	1820	1840	1860	1880	1900
AFRICA	Slave trade declared illegal in Great Britain	French seize Algeria		Completion of Suez Canal	Berlin Conference on Africa	Boer War
ASIA		Stamford Raffles founds Singapore	British rail network opened in northern India	French attack Vietnam / French and British agree to neutralize Thailand		Spanish-American War

CHAPTER NOTES

1. J. G. Lockhart and C. M. Woodehouse, *Rhodes: The Colossus of Southern Africa* (New York 1953), pp. 69–70.
2. The quotations are from Henry Braunschwig, *French Colonialism, 1871–1914* (London, 1961), p. 80.
3. Quoted in Louis Roubaud, *Vietnam: La Tragédie Indochinoise* (Paris, 1926), p. 80.
4. Quoted in Tony Smith, *The Pattern of Imperialism: The United States, Great Britain, and the Late-Industrial World Since 1815* (Cambridge, England, 1981), p. 81.

WORLD HISTORY
RESOURCE CENTER

Visit the *Twentieth-Century World History* Book Companion website for resources specific to this textbook:

academic.cengage.com/history/duiker

The Wadsworth World History Resource Center at worldrc.wadsworth.com/ offers a variety of tools to help you succeed in this course, including access to quizzes; images; documents; interactive simulations, maps, and timelines; movie explorations; and a wealth of other sources.

3

SHADOWS OVER THE PACIFIC: EAST ASIA UNDER CHALLENGE

IN AUGUST 1793, a British ambassadorial mission led by Lord Macartney arrived at the North Chinese port of Dagu and embarked on the road to Beijing. His caravan, which included six hundred cases filled with presents for the emperor, bore flags and banners provided by the Chinese that proclaimed in Chinese characters "Ambassador bearing tribute from the country of England." Upon his arrival in the capital, Macartney refused his hosts' demand that he perform the kowtow, a traditional symbol of submission to the emperor. Eventually, the dispute over protocol was resolved with a compromise: Macartney agreed to bend on one knee, a courtesy that he displayed to his own sovereign.

In other respects, however, the mission was a failure, for China rejected the British request for an increase in trade between the two countries, and Macartney left Beijing in October with nothing to show for his efforts. It would not be until half a century later that the ruling Qing dynasty—at the point of a gun—agreed to the British demand for an expansion of commercial ties.

Historians have often viewed the failure of the Macartney mission as a reflection of the disdain of Chinese rulers toward their counterparts in other countries and their serene confidence in the superiority of Chinese civilization in a world inhabited by barbarians. But in retrospect, it is clear that the imperial concern over the aggressive behavior of the European barbarians was justified, for in the decades immediately following the abortive Macartney mission to Beijing, China faced a growing challenge from the escalating power and ambitions of the West. Backed by European guns, European merchants and missionaries pressed insistently for the right to carry out their activities in China and the neighboring islands of Japan. Despite their initial reluctance, the Chinese and Japanese governments were eventually forced to open their doors to the foreigners, whose presence and threat to the local way of life escalated rapidly during the final years of the century. ◇

China at Its Apex

In 1800, the Qing or Manchu dynasty (1644–1911) appeared to be at the height of its power. The Manchus, a seminomadic people whose original homeland was north of the Great Wall, had invaded North China in the mid-seventeenth century and conquered the tottering Ming dynasty in 1644. Under the rule of two great emperors, Kangxi (1661–1722) and Qianlong (1736–1795), China had then experienced a long period of peace and prosperity. Its borders were secure, and its culture and intellectual achievements were the envy of the world. Its rulers, hidden behind the walls of the Forbidden City in Beijing, had every reason to describe their patrimony as the Central Kingdom, China's historical name for itself. But a little over a century later, humiliated and harassed by the black ships and big guns of the Western powers, the Qing dynasty, the last in a series that had endured for more than two thousand years, collapsed in the dust (see Map 3.1).

Changeless China?

Historians once assumed that the primary reason for the rapid decline and fall of the Manchu dynasty was the intense pressure applied to a proud but somewhat complacent traditional society by the modern West. There is indeed some truth in that allegation. On the surface, China had long appeared to be an unchanging society patterned after the Confucian vision of a Golden Age in the remote past. This, in fact, was the image presented by China's rulers, who referred constantly to tradition as a model for imperial institutions and cultural values. That tradition was based firmly on a set of principles that were identified with the ancient philosopher Confucius (551–479 B.C.E.) and emphasized such qualities as obedience, hard work, rule by merit,

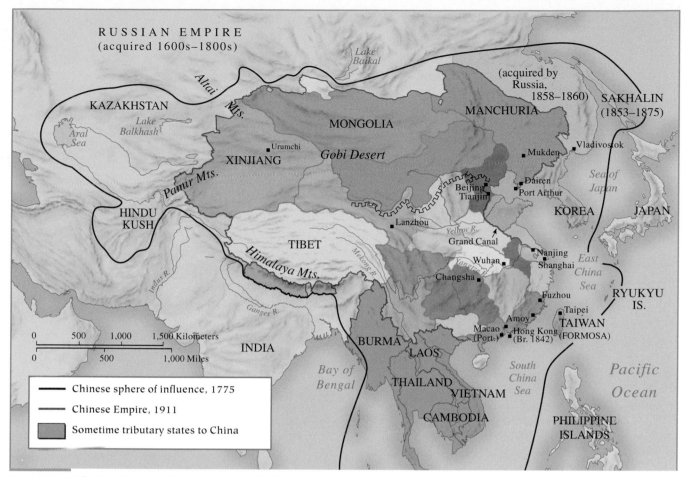

MAP 3.1 The Qing Empire. Shown here is the Qing Empire at the height of its power in the late eighteenth century, together with its shrunken boundaries at the moment of its dissolution in 1911.

❓ Where are China's tributary states on the map? 🌐 **View an animated version of this map or related maps at the World History Resource Center, at** worldrc.wadsworth.com/.

and the subordination of the individual to the interests of the community. Such principles, which had emerged out of the conditions of a continental society based on agriculture as the primary source of national wealth, had formed the basis for Chinese political and social institutions and values since the early years of the great Han dynasty in the second century B.C.E.

When European ships first began to arrive off the coast of China in the sixteenth and seventeenth centuries, they brought with them revolutionary new ideas and values that were strikingly at variance with those of imperial China. China's rulers soon came to recognize the nature of the threat represented by European missionaries and merchants and attempted to expel the former while restricting the latter to a limited presence in the southern coastal city of Canton. For the next two centuries, China was, at least in intent, an essentially closed society (see the box on p. 46).

It was the hope of influential figures at the imperial court in Beijing that by expelling the barbarians, they could protect the purity of Chinese civilization from the virus of foreign ideas. Their effort to freeze time was fruitless, however, for in reality, Chinese society was already beginning to change under their feet—and changing rather rapidly. Although few observers may have been aware of it at the time, by the beginning of the Manchu era in the seventeenth century, Confucian precepts were becoming increasingly irrelevant in a society that was becoming ever more complex.

Changes in Rural Areas Nowhere was change more evident than in the economic sector. During the early modern period, China was still a predominantly agricultural society, as it had been throughout recorded history. Nearly 85 percent of the people were farmers. In the south, the main

THE TRIBUTE SYSTEM IN ACTION

*I*n 1793, the British emissary Lord Macartney visited the Qing Empire to request the opening of formal diplomatic and trading relations between his country and China. Emperor Qianlong's reply, addressed to King George III of Britain, illustrates how the imperial court in Beijing viewed the world. King George could not have been pleased. The document provides a good example of the complacency with which the Celestial Empire viewed the world beyond its borders.

What reasons does the emperor give for refusing Macartney's request to have a permanent British ambassador in Beijing? How does the tribute system differ from the principles of international relations as practiced in the West?

A Decree of Emperor Qianlong

An Imperial Edict to the King of England: You, O King, are so inclined toward our civilization that you have sent a special envoy across the seas to bring to our Court your memorial of congratulations on the occasion of my birthday and to present your native products as an expression of your thoughtfulness. On perusing your memorial, so simply worded and sincerely conceived, I am impressed by your genuine respectfulness and friendliness and greatly pleased.

As to the request made in your memorial, O King, to send one of your nationals to stay at the Celestial Court to take care of your country's trade with China, this is not in harmony with the state system of our dynasty and will definitely not be permitted. Traditionally people of the European nations who wished to render some service under the Celestial Court have been permitted to come to the capital. But after their arrival they are obliged to wear Chinese court costumes, are placed in a certain residence, and are never allowed to return to their own countries. This is the established rule of the Celestial Dynasty with which presumably you, O King, are familiar. Now you, O King, wish to send one of your nationals to live in the capital, but he is not like the Europeans who come to Peking [Beijing] as Chinese employees, live there, and never return home again, nor can he be allowed to go and come and maintain any correspondence. This is indeed a useless undertaking.

Moreover the territory under the control of the Celestial Court is very large and wide. There are well-established regulations governing tributary envoys from the outer states to Peking, giving them provisions (of food and traveling expenses) by our post-houses and limiting their going and coming. There has never been a precedent for letting them do whatever they like. Now if you, O King, wish to have a representative in Peking, his language will be unintelligible and his dress different from the regulations; there is no place to accommodate him. . . .

The Celestial Court has pacified and possessed the territory within the four seas. Its sole aim is to do its utmost to achieve good government and to manage political affairs, attaching no value to strange jewels and precious objects. The various articles presented by you, O King, this time are accepted by my special order to the office in charge of such functions in consideration of the offerings having come from a long distance with sincere good wishes. As a matter of fact, the virtue and prestige of the Celestial Dynasty having spread far and wide, the kings of the myriad nations come by land and sea with all sorts of precious things. Consequently there is nothing we lack, as your principal envoy and others have themselves observed. We have never set much store on strange or ingenious objects, nor do we need any more of your country's manufactures. . . .

SOURCE: Reprinted by permission of the publisher from *China's Response to the West: A Documentary Survey, 1839–1923*, by Ssu-yu Teng and John King Fairbank, pp. 19, Cambridge, Mass.: Harvard University Press, copyright © 1954, 1979 by the President and Fellows of Harvard College, copyright renewed 1982 by Ssu-yu Teng and John King Fairbank.

---

crop was rice; in the north, it was wheat or dry crops. But even though China had few urban centers, the population was beginning to increase rapidly. Thanks to a long era of peace and stability, the introduction of new crops from the Americas, and the cultivation of new, fast-ripening strains of rice, the Chinese population doubled between the time of the early Qing and the end of the eighteenth century. And it continued to grow during the nineteenth century, reaching the unprecedented level of 400 million by 1900.

Of course, this population increase meant much greater pressure on the land, smaller farms, and an ever-thinner margin of safety in case of climatic disaster. The imperial court had attempted to deal with the problem by a variety of means—most notably by preventing the concentration of land in the hands of wealthy landowners—but by the end of the eighteenth century, almost all the land that could be irrigated was already under cultivation, and the problems of rural hunger and landlessness became increasingly serious. Not surprisingly, economic hardship quickly translated into rural unrest.

Seeds of Industrialization Another change that took place during the early modern period in China was the steady growth of manufacturing and commerce. Trade and manufacturing had existed in China since early times, but they had been limited by a number of factors, including social prejudice, official restrictions, and state monopolies on mining and on the production of such commodities as alcohol and salt. Now, taking advantage of the long era of peace and prosperity, merchants and manufacturers began to expand their operations beyond their immediate provinces. Trade in silk, metal and wood products, porcelain, cotton goods, and cash crops such as cotton and tobacco developed rapidly, and commercial networks began to operate on a regional and sometimes even a national basis.

With the expansion of trade came an extension of commercial contacts and guild organizations nationwide. Merchants began establishing guilds in cities and market towns throughout the country to provide legal protection, an opportunity to do business, and food and lodging for merchants from particular provinces. Foreign trade also expanded, with Chinese merchants, mainly from the coastal provinces of the south, setting up extensive contacts with countries in Southeast Asia. In many instances, the contacts in Southeast Asia were themselves Chinese who had settled in the area during the seventeenth and eighteenth centuries.

Some historians have suggested that this rise in industrial and commercial activity would, under other circumstances, have led to an indigenous industrial revolution and the emergence of a capitalist society such as that taking shape in Europe. The significance of these changes should not be exaggerated, however. In fact, there were some key differences between China and western Europe that would have impeded the emergence of capitalism in China. In the first place, although industrial production in China was on the rise, it was still based almost entirely on traditional methods of production. China had no uniform system of weights and measures, and the banking system was still primitive by European standards. The use of paper money, invented by the Chinese centuries earlier, had essentially been abandoned. There were few paved roads, and the Grand Canal, long the most efficient means of carrying goods between the north and the south, was silting up. As a result, merchants had to rely more and more on the coastal route, where they faced increasing competition from foreign shipping.

There were other, more deep-seated differences as well. The bourgeois class in China was not as independent as its European counterpart. Reflecting an ancient preference for agriculture over manufacturing and trade, the state levied heavy taxes on manufacturing and commerce while attempting to keep agricultural taxes low. Such attitudes were still shared by key groups in the population. Although much money could be made in commerce, most merchants who accumulated wealth used it to buy their way into the ranks of the landed gentry. The most that can

really be said, then, is that during the Qing dynasty, China was beginning to undergo major economic and social changes that might have led, in due time, to the emergence of an industrialized society.

Traditional China in Decline

When Western pressure on the Manchu Empire began to increase during the early nineteenth century, it served to exacerbate the existing strains in Chinese society. By 1800, the trade relationship that restricted Western merchants to a small commercial outlet at Canton was no longer acceptable to the British, who chafed at the growing trade imbalance resulting from a growing appetite for Chinese tea. Their solution was opium. A product more addictive than tea, opium was grown under company sponsorship in northeastern India and then shipped directly to the Chinese market. Soon demand for the product in South China became insatiable, despite an official prohibition on its use. Bullion now flowed out of the Chinese imperial treasury into the pockets of British merchants and officials.

Opium and Rebellion

When the Chinese attempted to prohibit the opium trade, the British declared war. The Opium War lasted three years (1839–1842) and graphically demonstrated the superiority of British firepower and military tactics to those of the Chinese. China sued for peace and, in the Treaty of Nanjing, agreed to open five coastal ports to British trade, limit tariffs on imported British goods, grant extraterritorial rights to British citizens in China, and pay a substantial indemnity to cover the British costs of the war. Beijing also agreed to cede the island of Hong Kong (dismissed by a senior British official as a "barren rock") to Great Britain. Nothing was said in the treaty about the opium trade.

Although the Opium War has traditionally been considered the beginning of modern Chinese history, it is unlikely that many Chinese at the time would have seen it that way. This was not the first time that a ruling dynasty had been forced to make concessions to foreigners, and the opening of five coastal ports to the British hardly constituted a serious threat to the security of the empire. Although a few concerned Chinese argued that the court should learn more about European civilization to find the secret of British success, others contended that China had nothing to learn from the barbarians and that borrowing foreign ways would undercut the purity of Confucian civilization.

The Opium War. The Opium War, waged between China and Great Britain between 1839 and 1842, was China's first conflict with a European power. Lacking modern military technology, the Chinese suffered a humiliating defeat. In this painting, heavily armed British steamships destroy unwieldy Chinese junks along the Chinese coast. China's humiliation at sea was a legacy of its rulers' lack of interest in maritime matters since the middle of the fifteenth century, when Chinese junks were among the most advanced sailing ships in the world.

National Maritime Museum, London

The Taiping Rebellion

The Manchus attempted to deal with the problem in the traditional way of playing the foreigners off against each other. Concessions granted to the British were offered to other Western nations, including the United States, and soon thriving foreign concession areas were operating in treaty ports along the southern Chinese coast from Canton in the south to Shanghai, a bustling new port on a tributary of the Yangtze, in the center.

In the meantime, the Qing court's failure to deal with pressing internal economic problems led to a major peasant revolt that shook the foundations of the empire. On the surface, the so-called Taiping Rebellion owed something to the Western incursion; the leader of the uprising, Hong Xiuquan, a failed candidate for the civil service examination, was a Christian convert who viewed himself as a younger brother of Jesus Christ and hoped to establish what he referred to as a "Heavenly Kingdom of Supreme Peace" in China. Its ranks swelled by impoverished peasants and other discontented elements throughout the southern provinces, the Taiping Rebellion swept northward, seizing the Yangtze River port of Nanjing in March 1853. The revolt continued for ten more years but gradually lost momentum, and in 1864, the Qing, though weakened, retook Nanjing

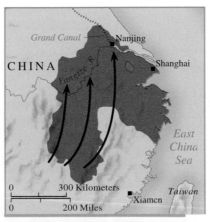

Area Under Taiping Rebellion Control

and destroyed the remnants of the rebel force. The rebellion had cost the lives of millions of Chinese.

One reason for the dynasty's failure to deal effectively with internal unrest was its continuing difficulties with the Western imperialists. In 1856, the British and the French, still smarting from trade restrictions and limitations on their missionary activities, launched a new series of attacks against China and seized the capital of Beijing in 1860. In the ensuing Treaty of Tianjin, the Qing agreed to humiliating new concessions: legalization of the opium trade, the opening of additional ports to foreign trade, and cession of the peninsula of Kowloon (opposite the island of Hong Kong) to the British.

Efforts at Reform

By the late 1870s, the old dynasty was well on the road to internal disintegration. In fending off the Taiping Rebellion, the Manchus had been compelled to rely for support on armed forces under regional command. After quelling the revolt, many of these regional commanders refused to disband their units and, with the support of the local gentry, continued to collect local taxes for their own use. The dreaded pattern of imperial breakdown, so familiar in Chinese history, was beginning to appear once again.

In their weakened state, the Qing rulers finally began to listen to the appeals of reform-minded officials, who called for a new policy of "self-strengthening," under which Western technology would be adopted while Confucian principles and institutions were maintained intact. This policy, popularly known by its slogan "East for essence, West for practical use," remained the guiding standard for Chinese foreign and domestic policy for decades. Some people even called for reforms in education and in China's hallowed political institutions. Pointing to the power and prosperity of Great Britain, the journalist Wang Tao (Wang T'ao, 1828–1897) remarked, "The real strength of England . . . lies in the fact that there is a sympathetic understanding between the governing and the governed, a close relationship between the ruler and the people. . . . My observation is that the daily domestic political life of England actually embodies the traditional ideals of our ancient Golden Age."[1] Such democratic ideas were too radical for most reformers, however. One of the leading court officials of the day, Zhang Zhidong (Chang Chih-tung), countered:

> The doctrine of people's rights will bring us not a single benefit but a hundred evils. Are we going to establish a parliament? . . . Even supposing the confused and clamorous people are assembled in one house, for every one of them who is clear-sighted, there will be a hundred others whose vision is beclouded; they will converse at random and talk as if in a dream—what use will it be?[2]

For the time being, Zhang Zhidong's arguments won the day. During the last quarter of the century, the Manchus attempted to modernize their military establishment and build up an industrial base without disturbing the essential elements of traditional Chinese civilization. Railroads, weapons arsenals, and shipyards were built, but the value system remained essentially unchanged.

The Climax of Imperialism in China

In the end, the results spoke for themselves. During the last two decades of the nineteenth century, the European penetration of China, both political and military, intensified. At the outer edges of the Qing Empire, rapacious imperialists began to bite off territory. The Gobi Desert north of the Great Wall, Chinese Central Asia (known in Chinese as Xinjiang), and Tibet, all inhabited by non-Chinese peoples and never fully assimilated into the Chinese Empire, were now gradually removed totally from Beijing's control. In the north and northwest, the main beneficiary was Russia, which took advantage of the dynasty's weakness to force the cession of territories north of the Amur River in Siberia. In Tibet, competition between Russia and Great Britain prevented either power from seizing the territory

outright but at the same time enabled Tibetan authorities to revive local autonomy never recognized by the Chinese. On the southern borders of the empire, British and French advances in mainland Southeast Asia removed Burma and Vietnam from their traditional vassal relationship with the Manchu court.

Even more ominous developments were taking place in the Chinese heartland, where European economic penetration led to the creation of so-called spheres of influence dominated by diverse foreign powers. Although the imperial court retained theoretical sovereignty throughout the country, in practice its political, economic, and administrative influence beyond the region of the capital was increasingly circumscribed.

The breakup of the Manchu dynasty accelerated during the last five years of the nineteenth century. In 1894, the Qing went to war with Japan over Japanese incursions into the Korean peninsula, which threatened China's long-held suzerainty over the area (see "Joining the Imperialist Club" later in this chapter). To the surprise of many observers, the Chinese were roundly defeated, confirming to some critics the devastating failure of the policy of self-strengthening by halfway measures.

More humiliation came in 1897, when Germany, a new entrant in the race for spoils in East Asia, used the pretext of the murder of two German missionaries by Chinese rioters to demand the cession of territories in the Shandong peninsula. The approval of this demand by the imperial court set off a scramble for territory by other interested powers. Russia now demanded the Liaodong peninsula with its ice-free harbor at Port Arthur, and Great Britain weighed in with a request for a coaling station in northern China.

The latest scramble for territory had taken place at a time of internal crisis in China. In the spring of 1898, an outspoken advocate of reform, the progressive Confucian scholar Kang Youwei, won the support of the young emperor Guangxu for a comprehensive reform program patterned after recent changes initiated in Japan. Without change, Kang argued, China would perish. During the next several weeks, the emperor issued edicts calling for major political, administrative, and educational reforms. Not surprisingly, Kang's ideas for reform were opposed by many conservatives, who saw little advantage to copying the West. Most important, the new program was opposed by the emperor's aunt, the Empress Dowager Cixi, the real source of power at court. Cixi had begun her political career as a concubine to an earlier emperor. After his death, she became a dominant force at court and in 1878 placed her infant nephew, the future emperor Guangxu, on the throne. For two decades, she ruled in his name as regent. Cixi interpreted Guangxu's action as a British-supported effort to reduce her influence at court. With the aid of conservatives

Empress Dowager Cixi. Cixi was the most powerful figure in late-nineteenth-century China. Originally a concubine at the imperial court, she later placed a nephew on the throne and dominated the political scene for a quarter of a century until her death in 1908. Conservative in her views, she staunchly resisted her advisers' suggestions for changes to help China face the challenge posed by the West. Note the long fingernails, a symbol of the privileged class, in this photograph taken in her final years.

in the army, she arrested and executed several of the reformers and had the emperor incarcerated in the palace. Kang Youwei succeeded in fleeing abroad. With Cixi's palace coup, the so-called One Hundred Days of reform came to an end.

Opening the Door to China During the next two years, foreign pressure on the dynasty intensified (see Map 3.2 on p. 51). With encouragement from the British, who hoped to avert a total collapse of the Manchu Empire, U.S. Secretary of State John Hay presented the other imperialist powers with a proposal to ensure equal economic access to the China market for all nations. Hay also suggested that all powers join together to guarantee the territorial and administrative integrity of the Chinese Empire. When none of the other governments flatly opposed the idea, Hay issued a second note declaring that all major nations with economic interests in China had agreed to an "Open Door" policy in China.

Though probably motivated more by a U.S. desire for open markets than by a benevolent wish to protect China, the Open Door policy did have the practical effect of reducing the imperialist hysteria over access to the China market. That hysteria—a product of decades of mythologizing among Western commercial interests about the "400 million" Chinese customers—had accelerated at the end of the century as fear over China's imminent collapse increased. The "gentlemen's agreement" about the Open Door (it was not a treaty but merely a pious and nonbinding expression of intent) served to deflate fears in Britain, France, Germany, and Russia that other powers would take advantage of China's weakness to dominate the China market.

The Boxer Rebellion In the long run, then, the Open Door was a positive step that brought a measure of sanity to imperialist behavior in East Asia. Unfortunately, it came too late to stop the domestic explosion known as the Boxer Rebellion. The Boxers, so called because of the physical exercises they performed, were members of a secret society operating primarily in rural areas in North China. Provoked by a damaging drought and high levels of unemployment caused in part by foreign economic activity (the introduction of railroads and steamships, for example, undercut the livelihood of boatworkers who traditionally carried merchandise on the rivers and canals), the Boxers attacked foreign residents and besieged the foreign legation quarter in Beijing until the foreigners were rescued by an international expeditionary force in the late summer of 1900. As punishment, the foreign troops destroyed a number of temples in the capital suburbs, and the Chinese government was compelled to pay a heavy indemnity to the foreign governments involved in suppressing the uprising.

The Collapse of the Old Order

During the next few years, the old dynasty tried desperately to reform itself. The empress dowager, who had long resisted change, now embraced a number of reforms in education, administration, and the legal system. The venerable civil service examination system, based on knowledge of the Confucian classics, was replaced by a new educational system patterned after the Western model. In 1905, a commission was formed to study constitutional changes, and over the next few years, legislative assemblies were established at the provincial level. Elections for a national assembly were held in 1910.

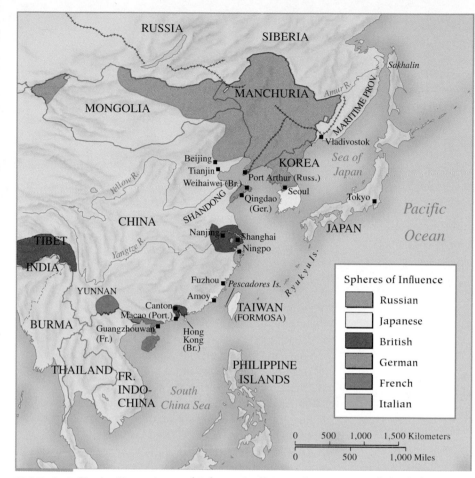

MAP 3.2 **Foreign Possessions and Spheres of Influence About 1900.** At the end of the nineteenth century, China was being carved up like a melon by foreign imperialist powers. **?** Which of the areas marked on the map were removed from Chinese control during the nineteenth century? **⊕** View an animated version of this map or related maps at the World History Resource Center, at worldrc.wadsworth.com/.

often centered on secret societies such as the Boxers, was an ominous sign of deep-seated resentment to which the dynasty would not, or could not, respond.

The Rise of Sun Yat-sen To China's reformist elite, such signs of social unrest were a threat to be avoided; to its tiny revolutionary movement, they were a harbinger of promise. The first physical manifestations of future revolution appeared during the last decade of the nineteenth century with the formation of the Revive China Society by the young radical Sun Yat-sen (1866–1925). Born to a peasant family in a village south of Canton, Sun was educated in Hawaii and returned to China to practice medicine. Soon he turned his full attention to the ills of Chinese society, leading bands of radicals in small-scale insurrections to attract attention.

At first, Sun's efforts yielded few positive results other than creating a symbol of resistance and the new century's first revolutionary martyrs. But at a convention in Tokyo in 1905, Sun managed to unite radical groups from across China in the so-called Revolutionary Alliance (Tongmenghui). The new organization's program was based on Sun's Three People's Principles: nationalism (meaning primarily the destruction of Manchu rule over China), democracy, and "people's livelihood" (a program to improve social and economic conditions; see the box on p. 52). Although the new organization was small and relatively inexperienced, it benefited from rising popular discontent with the failure of Manchu reforms to improve conditions in China.

Such moves helped shore up the dynasty temporarily, but history shows that the most dangerous period for an authoritarian system is when it begins to reform itself, because change breeds instability and performance rarely matches rising expectations. Such was the case in China. The emerging new provincial elite, composed of merchants, professionals, and reform-minded gentry, soon became impatient with the slow pace of political change and were disillusioned to find that the new assemblies were intended to be primarily advisory rather than legislative. The government also alienated influential elements by financing railway development projects through lucrative contracts to foreign firms rather than by turning to local investors. The reforms also had little meaning for peasants, artisans, miners, and transportation workers, whose living conditions were being eroded by rising taxes and official venality. Rising rural unrest, as yet poorly organized and

The 1911 Revolution In October 1911, followers of Sun Yat-sen launched an uprising in the industrial center of Wuhan, in central China. With Sun traveling in the United States, the insurrection lacked leadership, but the decrepit government's inability to react quickly encouraged political forces at the provincial level to take measures into their own hands. The dynasty was now in a state of virtual collapse: the dowager empress had died in 1908, one day after her nephew Guangxu; the throne was now occupied by the

PROGRAM FOR A NEW CHINA

*n 1905, Sun Yat-sen united a number of anti-Manchu groups into a single patriotic organization called the Revolutionary Alliance (Tongmenghui). The new organization was eventually renamed the *Guomindang,* or Nationalist Party. This excerpt is from the organization's manifesto, published in 1905 in Tokyo. Note that Sun believed that the Chinese people were not ready for democracy and required a period of tutelage to prepare them for constitutional political government. This was a formula that would be adopted by many other political leaders in Asia and Africa after World War II.

What are Sun Yat-sen's key proposals for the modernization of Chinese society? Why can he be described as a revolutionary rather than a reformer?

Sun Yat-sen, Manifesto for the Tongmenghui

By order of the Military Government, . . . the Commander-in-Chief of the Chinese National Army proclaims the purposes and platform of the Military Government to the people of the nation:

Therefore we proclaim to the world in utmost sincerity the outline of the present revolution and the fundamental plan for the future administration of the nation.

1. *Drive out the Tartars:* The Manchus of today were originally the eastern barbarians beyond the Great Wall. They frequently caused border troubles during the Ming dynasty; then when China was in a disturbed state they came inside Shanhaikuan, conquered China, and enslaved our Chinese people. . . . The extreme cruelties and tyrannies of the Manchu government have now reached their limit. With the righteous army poised against them, we will overthrow that government, and restore our sovereign rights.

2. *Restore China:* China is the China of the Chinese. The government of China should be in the hands of the Chinese. After driving out the Tartars we must restore our national state. . . .

3. *Establish the Republic:* Now our revolution is based on equality, in order to establish a republican government. All our people are equal and all enjoy political rights. . . .

4. *Equalize land ownership:* The good fortune of civilization is to be shared equally by all the people of the nation. We should improve our social and economic organization, and assess the value of all the land in the country. Its present price shall be received by the owner, but all increases in value resulting from reform and social improvements after the revolution shall belong to the state, to be shared by all the people, in order to create a socialist state, where each family within the empire can be well supported, each person satisfied, and no one fail to secure employment. . . .

The above four points will be carried out in three steps in due order. The first period is government by military law. When the righteous army has arisen, various places will join the cause. . . . Evils like the oppression of the government, the greed and graft of officials, . . . the cruelty of tortures and penalties, the tyranny of tax collections, shall all be exterminated together with the Manchu rule. Evils in social customs, such as the keeping of slaves, the cruelty of foot binding, the spread of the poison of opium, should also all be prohibited. . . .

The second period is that of government by a provisional constitution. When military law is lifted in each *hsien,* the Military Government shall return the right of the self-government to the local people. . . .

The third period will be government under the constitution. Six years after the provisional constitution has been enforced, a constitution shall be made. The military and administrative powers of the Military Government shall be annulled; the people shall elect the president, and elect the members of parliament to organize the parliament.

SOURCE: *Sources of Chinese Tradition* by William Theodore de Bary. Copyright © 1960 by Columbia University Press, New York. Reprinted with permission of the publisher.

---

infant Puyi, the son of Guangxu's younger brother. Sun's party, however, had neither the military strength nor the political base necessary to seize the initiative and was forced to turn to a representative of the old order, General Yuan Shikai. A prominent figure in military circles since the beginning of the century, Yuan had been placed in charge of the imperial forces sent to suppress the rebellion, but now he abandoned the Manchus and acted on his own behalf. In negotiations with representatives of Sun Yat-sen's party (Sun himself had arrived in China in January 1912), he agreed to serve as president of a new Chinese republic. The old dynasty and the age-old system it had attempted to preserve were no more.

Propagandists for Sun Yat-sen's party have often portrayed the events of 1911 as a glorious revolution that brought two thousand years of imperial tradition to an end. But a true revolution does not just destroy an old order; it also brings new political and social forces into power and creates new institutions and values that provide a new framework for a changing society. In this sense, the 1911 revolution did not live up to its name. Sun and his followers were unable to consolidate their gains. The Revolutionary Alliance found the bulk of its support in an emerging urban middle class and set forth a program based generally on Western liberal democratic principles. That class and that program had provided the foundation for the capitalist democratic revolutions in western Europe and North America in the late eighteenth and nineteenth centuries, but the bourgeois class in China was too small to form the basis for a new post-Confucian political order. The vast majority of the Chinese people still lived on the land. Sun had hoped to win their support with a land reform program that relied on fiscal incentives to persuade landlords to sell excess lands to their tenants, but few peasants had participated in the 1911 revolution. In effect, then, the events of 1911 were less a revolution than a collapse of the old order. Undermined by imperialism and its own internal weaknesses, the old dynasty had come to an abrupt end before new political and social forces were ready to fill the vacuum.

What China had experienced was part of a historical process that was bringing down traditional empires across the globe, both in regions threatened by Western imperialism and in Europe itself, where tsarist Russia, the Austro-Hungarian Empire, and the Ottoman Empire all came to an end within a few years of the collapse of the Qing (see Chapter 4). The circumstances of their demise were not all the same, but all four regimes shared the responsibility for their common fate because they had failed to meet the challenges posed by the times. All had responded to the forces of industrialization and popular participation in the political process with hesitation and reluctance, and their attempts at reform were too little and too late. All paid the supreme price for their folly.

Chinese Society in Transition

The growing Western presence in China during the late nineteenth and early twentieth centuries provided the imperial government with an opportunity to benefit from the situation. The results, however, were meager. Although foreign concession areas in the coastal cities provided a conduit for the importation of Western technology and modern manufacturing methods, the Chinese borrowed less than they might have. Foreign manufacturing enterprises could not legally operate in China until the last decade of the nineteenth century, and their methods had little influence beyond the concession areas. Chinese efforts to imitate Western methods, notably in shipbuilding and weapons manufacture,

were dominated by the government and often suffered from mismanagement.

Equally serious problems persisted in the countryside. The rapid increase in population had led to smaller plots and growing numbers of tenant farmers. Whether per capita consumption of food was on the decline is not clear from the available evidence, but apparently, rice as a staple of the diet was increasingly being replaced by less nutritious foods. Some farmers benefited from switching to commercial agriculture to supply the markets of the growing coastal cities. The shift entailed a sizable investment, however, and many farmers went so deeply into debt that they eventually lost their land. At the same time, the traditional patron-client relationship was frayed as landlords moved to the cities to take advantage of the glittering urban lifestyle.

The Impact of Western Imperialism

The advent of the imperialist era in the second half of the nineteenth century thus came in a society already facing serious problems. Whether the Western intrusion was beneficial or harmful is debated to this day. The Western presence undoubtedly accelerated the development of the Chinese economy in some ways: the introduction of modern means of production, transport, and communications; the appearance of an export market; and the steady integration of the Chinese market into the nineteenth-century global economy. To many Westerners at the time, it was self-evident that such changes would ultimately benefit the Chinese people. Critics retorted that Western imperialism actually hindered the process of structural change in preindustrial societies because it thwarted the rise of a local industrial and commercial sector so as to maintain colonies and semicolonies as a market for Western manufactured goods and a source of cheap labor and materials. If the West had not intervened, some argued, China would have found its own road to becoming an advanced industrial society.

Many historians today would say that the encounters with the West did both harm and good. By shaking China out of its traditional mind-set, Western imperialism accelerated the process of change that had begun in the late Ming and early Qing periods and forced the Chinese to adopt new ways of thinking and acting. At the same time, China paid a heavy price in the destruction of its local industry, while many of the profits flowed abroad. Although industrial revolution is a painful process whenever and wherever it occurs, the Chinese found the experience doubly painful because it was foisted on China from the outside. Whatever benefits it may have offered, imperialism created serious distortions in the local economy that resulted in massive changes in Chinese society during the twentieth century.

Daily Life

At the beginning of the nineteenth century, daily life for most Chinese was not substantially different from what it had been for centuries. Most were farmers, living in millions of villages in rice fields and on hillsides throughout the countryside. Their lives were governed by the harvest cycle, village custom, and family ritual. Their roles in society were firmly fixed by the time-honored principles of Confucian social ethics. Male children, at least the more fortunate ones, were educated in the Confucian classics, while females remained in the home or in the fields. All children were expected to obey their parents, wives to submit to their husbands.

A visitor to China a hundred years later would have seen a very different society, although still recognizably Chinese. Change was most striking in the coastal cities, where the educated and affluent had been visibly affected by the growing Western cultural presence. Confucian social institutions and behavioral norms were declining rapidly in influence, while those of Europe and North America were on the ascendant. Change was much less noticeable in the countryside, but even there, the customary bonds had been dangerously frayed by the rapidly changing times.

Some of the change can be traced to the educational system. During the nineteenth century, the importance of a Confucian education steadily declined as up to half of the degree holders had purchased their degrees. After 1906, when the government abolished the civil service examinations, a Confucian education ceased to be the key to a successful career, and Western-style education became more desirable. The old dynasty attempted to modernize by establishing an educational system on the Western model with universal education at the elementary level. Such plans had some effect in the cities, where public schools, missionary schools, and other private institutions educated a new generation of Chinese with little knowledge of or respect for the past.

The Status of Women

The status of women was also in transition. During the mid-Qing era, women were still expected to remain in the home. Their status as useless sex objects was painfully symbolized by the practice of foot binding, a custom that had probably originated among court entertainers in the eighth century and later spread to the common people. By the mid-nineteenth century, more than half of all adult women probably had bound feet.

During the second half of the nineteenth century, signs of change began to appear. Women began to seek employment in factories—notably in cotton mills and in the silk industry, established in Shanghai in the 1890s. Some women were active in dissident activities, such as the Taiping Rebellion and the Boxer movement, and a few fought beside men in the 1911 revolution. Qiu Jin, a well-known female revolutionary, wrote a manifesto calling for women's liberation and then organized a revolt against the Manchu government, only to be captured and executed at the age of thirty-two in 1907.

By the end of the century, educational opportunities for women began to appear for the first time. Christian missionaries began to open girls' schools, mainly in the foreign concession areas. Although only a relatively small number of women were educated in these schools, they had a significant impact on Chinese society as progressive intellectuals began to argue that ignorant women produced

Women with Bound Feet. To provide the best possible marriage for their daughters, upper-class families began to perform foot binding during the Song dynasty (960–1279). Eventually, the practice spread to all social classes in China. Although small feet were supposed to denote a woman of leisure, most Chinese women with bound feet contributed to the labor force, working mainly in textiles and handicrafts to supplement the family income. Here we see five women with bound feet sorting tea leaves in Shanghai.

ignorant children. In 1905, the court announced its intention to open public schools for girls, but few such schools ever materialized. The government also began to take steps to discourage the practice of foot binding, initially with only minimal success.

Traditional Japan and the End of Isolation

While Chinese rulers were coping with the dual problems of external threat and internal instability, similar developments were taking place in Japan. An agricultural society like its powerful neighbor, Japan had borrowed extensively from Chinese civilization for more than a millennium; its political institutions, religious beliefs, and cultural achievements all bore the clear imprint of the Chinese model. Nevertheless, throughout the centuries, the Japanese were able to retain not only their political independence but also their cultural uniqueness and had created a distinct civilization.

One reason for the historical differences between China and Japan is that China is a large continental country and Japan a small island nation. Proud of their own considerable cultural achievements and their dominant position throughout the region, the Chinese have traditionally been reluctant to dilute the purity of their culture with foreign innovations. Often subject to invasion by nomadic peoples from the north, the Chinese viewed culture rather than race as a symbol of their sense of identity. By contrast, the island character of Japan probably had the effect of strengthening the Japanese sense of ethnic and cultural distinctiveness. Although the Japanese self-image of ethnic homogeneity may not be entirely justified, it enabled them to import ideas from abroad without the risk of destroying the uniqueness of their own culture.

As a result, although the Japanese borrowed liberally from China over the centuries, they turned Chinese ideas and institutions to their own uses. In contrast to China, where a centralized political system was viewed as crucial to protect the vast country from foreign conquest or internal fractionalization, a decentralized political system reminiscent of the feudal system in medieval Europe held sway in Japan under the hegemony of a powerful military leader, or *shogun*, who ruled with varying degrees of effectiveness in the name of the hereditary emperor. This system lasted until the early seventeenth century, when a strong shogunate called the Tokugawa rose to power after a protracted civil war. The Tokugawa managed to revitalize the traditional system in a somewhat more centralized form that enabled it to survive for another 250 years.

A "Closed Country"

One of the many factors involved in the rise of the Tokugawa was the impending collapse of the old system. Another was contact with the West, which had begun with the arrival of Portuguese ships in Japanese ports in the middle of the sixteenth century. Japan initially opened its doors eagerly to European trade and missionary activity, but later Japanese elites became concerned at the corrosive effects of Western ideas and practices and attempted to evict the foreigners. For the next two centuries, the Tokugawa adopted a policy of "closed country" (to use the contemporary Japanese phrase) to keep out foreign ideas and protect native values and institutions. In spite of such efforts, however, Japanese society was changing from within and by the early nineteenth century was quite different from what it had been two centuries earlier. Traditional institutions and the feudal aristocratic system were under increasing strain, not only from the emergence of a new merchant class but also from the centralizing tendencies of the powerful shogunate.

Some historians have noted strong parallels between Tokugawa Japan and early modern Europe, which gave birth to centralized empires and a strong merchant class during the same period. Certainly, there were signs that the shogunate system was becoming less effective. Factionalism and corruption plagued the central bureaucracy. Feudal lords in the countryside (known as *daimyo,* or "great names") reacted to increasing economic pressures by intensifying their exactions from the peasants who farmed their manor holdings and by engaging in manufacturing and commercial pursuits, such as the sale of textiles, forestry products, and *sake* (Japanese rice wine). As peasants were whipsawed by rising manorial exactions and a series of poor harvests caused by bad weather, rural unrest swept the countryside.

Japan, then, was ripe for change. Some historians maintain that the country was poised to experience an industrial revolution under the stimulus of internal conditions. As in China, the resumption of contacts with the West in the middle of the nineteenth century rendered the question somewhat academic. To the Western powers, the continued isolation of Japanese society was an affront and a challenge. Driven by growing rivalry among themselves and convinced by their own propaganda and the ideology of world capitalism that the expansion of trade on a global basis would benefit all nations, Western nations began to approach Japan in the hope of opening up the hermit kingdom to foreign economic interests.

The Opening of Japan

The first to succeed was the United States. American whalers and clipper ships following the northern route across the Pacific needed a fueling station before completing their long journey to China and other ports in the area. The first efforts to pry the Japanese out of their cloistered existence in the 1830s and 1840s failed, but the Americans persisted. In the summer of 1853, an American fleet of four warships under Commodore Matthew C. Perry arrived in Edo Bay (now Tokyo Bay) with a letter from President Millard Fillmore addressed to the shogun. A few months later, Japan agreed to the Treaty of Kanagawa, providing for the opening of two ports and the establishment of a U.S. consulate on Japanese soil. In 1858, U.S. Consul Townsend Harris signed a more elaborate commercial treaty calling for the opening of several ports to U.S. trade and residence, an exchange of ministers, and extraterritorial privileges for U.S. residents in Japan. The Japanese soon signed similar treaties with several European nations.

The decision to open relations with the Western barbarians was highly unpopular in some quarters, particularly in regions distant from the shogunate headquarters in Edo. Resistance was especially strong in two of the key outside daimyo territories in the south, Satsuma and Choshu, both of which had strong military traditions. In 1863, the "Sat-Cho" alliance forced the hapless shogun to promise to bring relations with the West to an end, but the rebellious groups soon disclosed their own weakness. When Choshu troops fired on Western ships in the Strait of Shimonoseki, the Westerners fired back and destroyed the Choshu fortifications. The incident convinced the rebellious samurai ("retainers," the traditional warrior class) of the need to strengthen their own military and intensified their unwillingness to give in to the West. Having strengthened their influence at the imperial court in Kyoto, they demanded the resignation of the shogun and the restoration of the power of the emperor. In January 1868, rebel armies attacked the shogun's palace in Kyoto and proclaimed the restored authority of the emperor. After a few weeks, resistance collapsed, and the venerable shogunate system was brought to an end.

Rich Country, Strong Army

Although the victory of the Sat-Cho faction over the shogunate appeared on the surface to be a struggle between advocates of tradition and proponents of conciliation toward the West, in fact the new leadership soon realized that Japan must change to survive and embarked on a policy of comprehensive reform that would lay the foundations of a modern industrial nation within a generation. The symbol of the new era was the young emperor himself, who had taken the reign name Meiji ("enlightened rule") on ascending the throne after the death of his father in 1867. Although the post-Tokugawa period was termed a "restoration," the Meiji ruler was controlled by the new

leadership just as the shogun had controlled his predecessors. In tacit recognition of the real source of political power, the new capital was located at Edo, which was renamed Tokyo ("Eastern Capital"), and the imperial court was moved to the shogun's palace in the center of the city.

The Transformation of Japanese Politics

Once in power, the new leaders launched a comprehensive reform of Japanese political, social, economic, and cultural institutions and values. They moved first to abolish the remnants of the old order and strengthen executive power in their hands. To undercut the power of the daimyo, hereditary privileges were abolished in 1871, and the great lords lost title to their lands. As compensation, they were named governors of the territories formerly under their control. The samurai received a lump-sum payment to replace their traditional stipends but were forbidden to wear the sword, the symbol of their hereditary status.

The abolition of the legal underpinnings of the Tokugawa system permitted the Meiji modernizers to embark on the creation of a modern political system based on the Western model. In the Charter Oath of 1868, the new leaders promised to create a new deliberative assembly within the framework of continued imperial rule (see the box on p. 57). Although senior positions in the new government were given to the daimyo, the key posts were dominated by modernizing samurai, known as the *genro*, from the Sat-Cho clique.

During the next two decades, the Meiji government undertook a systematic study of Western political systems. A constitutional commission under Prince Ito Hirobumi traveled to several Western countries, including Great Britain, Germany, Russia, and the United States, to study their political institutions. As the process evolved, a number of factions appeared, each representing different ideas. The most prominent were the Liberals, who favored political reform on the Western liberal democratic model, and the Progressives, who called for a division of power between the legislative and executive branches, with a slight nod to the latter. There was also an imperial party that advocated the retention of supreme authority in the hands of the emperor.

The Meiji Constitution During the 1870s and 1880s, these factions competed for preeminence. In the end, the Progressives emerged victorious. The Meiji constitution, adopted in 1890, vested authority in the executive branch, although the imperialist faction was pacified by the statement that the constitution was the gift of the emperor. Members of the cabinet were to be handpicked by the Meiji oligarchs. The upper house of parliament was to be appointed and have equal legislative powers with the lower house,

A PROGRAM FOR REFORM IN JAPAN

In the spring of 1868, the reformers drew up a program for transforming Japanese society along Western lines in the post-Tokugawa era. Though vague in its essentials, the Charter Oath is a good indication of the plans that were carried out during the Meiji Restoration.

Do these basic principles all conform to the basic concepts of liberal democracy as practiced in Western societies? To what degree did the Meiji political system put them into effect? How did the Meiji constitution differ from those in the West?

The Charter Oath of Emperor Meiji

By this oath we set up as our aim the establishment of the national weal on a broad basis and the framing of a constitution and laws.

1. Deliberative assemblies shall be widely established and all matters decided by public discussion.
2. All classes, high and low, shall unite in vigorously carrying out the administration of affairs of state.
3. The common people, no less than the civil and military officials, shall each be allowed to pursue his own calling so that there may be no discontent.
4. Evil customs of the past shall be broken off and everything based upon the just laws of Nature.
5. Knowledge shall be sought throughout the world so as to strengthen the foundations of imperial rule.

SOURCE: From *Sources of Japanese Tradition* by William Theodore de Bary. Copyright © 1958 by Columbia University Press. Reprinted with permission of the publisher.

---

called the Diet, whose members would be elected. The core ideology of the state was called the *kokutai* (national polity), which embodied (although in very imprecise form) the concept of the uniqueness of the Japanese system based on the supreme authority of the emperor.

The result was a system that was democratic in form but despotic in practice, modern in external appearance but still recognizably traditional in that power remained in the hands of a ruling oligarchy. The system permitted the traditional ruling class to retain its influence and economic power while acquiescing in the emergence of a new set of institutions and values.

Meiji Economics

With the end of the daimyo domains, the government needed to establish a new system of land ownership that would transform the mass of the rural population from indentured serfs into citizens. To do so, it enacted a land reform program that redefined the domain lands as the private property of the tillers while compensating the previous owner with government bonds. One reason for the new policy was that the government needed operating revenues. At the time, public funds came mainly from customs duties, which were limited by agreement with the foreign powers to 5 percent of the value of the product. To remedy the problem, the Meiji leaders added a new agriculture tax, which was set at an annual rate of 3 percent of the estimated value of the land. The new tax proved to be a lucrative and dependable source of income for the government, but it was quite onerous for the farmers, who had previously paid a fixed percentage of their harvest to the landowner. As a result, in bad years, many taxpaying peasants were unable to pay their taxes and were forced to sell their lands to wealthy neighbors. Eventually, the government reduced the tax to 2.5 percent of the land value. Still, by the end of the century, about 40 percent of all farmers were tenants.

Launching the Industrial Revolution With its budget needs secured, the government turned to the promotion of industry. A small but growing industrial economy had already existed under the Tokugawa. In its early stages, manufacturing in Japan had been the exclusive responsibility of an artisan caste, who often worked for the local daimyo. Eventually, these artisans began to expand their activities, hiring workers and borrowing capital from merchants. By the end of the seventeenth century, manufacturing centers had developed in Japan's growing cities, such as Edo, Kyoto, and Osaka. According to one historian, by 1700, Japan already had four cities with a population over 100,000 and was one of the most urbanized societies in the world.

Japan's industrial sector received a massive stimulus from the Meiji Restoration. The government provided financial subsidies to needy industries, imported foreign advisers, improved transport and communications, and established a universal system of education emphasizing applied science. In contrast to China, Japan was able to achieve results with minimum reliance on foreign capital. Although the first railroad—built in 1872—was underwritten by a loan from Great Britain, future projects were all financed locally. Foreign-currency holdings came largely from tea and silk, which were exported in significant quantities during the latter half of the nineteenth century.

During the late Meiji era, Japan's industrial sector began to grow. Besides tea and silk, other key industries were weaponry, shipbuilding, and *sake*. From the start, the distinctive feature of the Meiji model was the intimate relationship between government and private business in terms of operations and regulations. Once an individual enterprise or industry was on its feet (or sometimes, when it had ceased to make a profit), it was turned over entirely to private ownership, although the government often continued to play some role even after its direct involvement in management was terminated.

Also noteworthy is the effect that the Meiji reforms had on rural areas. As we have seen, the new land tax provided the government with funds to subsidize the industrial sector, but it imposed severe hardship on the rural population, many of whom abandoned their farms and fled to the cities in search of jobs. This influx of people in turn benefited Japanese industry by providing an abundant source of cheap labor. As in early modern Europe, the Industrial Revolution was built on the strong backs of the long-suffering peasantry.

Building a Modern Social Structure

The Meiji Restoration also transformed several other feudal institutions. A key focus of their attention was the army. The Sat-Cho reformers had been struck by the weakness of the Japanese armed forces in clashes with the Western powers and embarked on a major program to create a modern military force that could compete in a Darwinist world governed by the survival of the fittest. The old feudal army based on the traditional warrior class was abolished, and an imperial army based on universal conscription was formed in 1871. The army also played an important role in Japanese society, becoming a route of upward mobility for many rural males.

Education   Education also underwent major changes. The Meiji leaders recognized the need for universal education, including instruction in modern technology. After a few years of experimenting, they adopted the American model of a three-tiered system culminating in a series of universities and specialized institutes. In the meantime, they sent bright students to study abroad and brought foreign specialists to Japan to teach in their new schools. Much of the content of the new system was Western in inspiration. Yet its ethical foundations had a distinctly Confucian orientation, emphasizing such values as filial piety and loyalty to the emperor.

The Role of Women   The Meiji reforms also had an impact on the role of women in Japan. In the traditional era, women were constrained by the "three obediences" imposed on their gender: child to father, wife to husband, and widow to son. Husbands could easily obtain a divorce, but wives could not (one regulation allegedly decreed that a husband could divorce his spouse if she drank too much tea or talked too much). Marriages were arranged, and the average age of marriage for females was sixteen years. Females did not share inheritance rights with males, and few received any education outside the family.

By the end of the nineteenth century, women were beginning to play a crucial role in their nation's effort to modernize. Urged by their parents to augment the family income, as well as by the government to fulfill their patriotic duty, young girls were sent en masse to work in textile mills. From 1894 to 1912, women represented 60 percent of the Japanese labor force. Thanks to them, by 1914, Japan was the world's leading exporter of silk and dominated cotton manufacturing. If it had not been for the export revenues earned from textile exports, Japan might not have been able to develop its heavy industry and military prowess without an infusion of foreign capital.

Japanese women received few rewards, however, for their contribution to the nation. In 1900, new regulations prohibited women from joining political organizations or attending public meetings. Beginning in 1905, a group of independent-minded women petitioned the Japanese parliament to rescind this restriction, but it was not repealed until 1922.

Joining the Imperialist Club

Japan's rapid advance was viewed with proprietary pride and admiration by sympathetic observers around the world. Unfortunately, the Japanese did not just imitate the domestic policies of their Western mentors; they also emulated the latter's aggressive approach to foreign affairs. That they adopted this course is perhaps not surprising. In their own minds, the Japanese were particularly vulnerable in the world economic arena. Their territory was small, lacking in resources, and densely populated, and they had no natural outlet for expansion. To observant Japanese, the lessons of history were clear. Western nations had amassed wealth and power not only because of their democratic systems and high level of education but also because of their colonies, which provided them with sources of raw materials, cheap labor, and markets for their manufactured products.

Traditionally, Japan had not been an expansionist country. The Japanese had generally been satisfied to remain on their home islands and had even deliberately isolated themselves from their neighbors during the Tokugawa era. Perhaps the most notable exception was a short-lived attempt at the end of the sixteenth century to extend Japanese control over the Korean peninsula.

The Japanese began their program of territorial expansion (see Map 3.3) close to home. In 1874, they claimed compensation from China for fifty-four sailors from the Ryukyu Islands who had been killed by aborigines on the island of Taiwan and sent a Japanese fleet to Taiwan to punish the perpetrators. When the Qing dynasty evaded responsibility for the incident while agreeing to pay an indemnity to Japan to cover the cost of the expedition, it weakened its claim to ownership of the island of Taiwan. Japan was then able to claim suzerainty over the Ryukyu Islands, long tributary to the Chinese Empire. Two years later, Japanese naval pressure forced the opening of Korean ports to Japanese commerce.

During the 1880s, as Meiji leaders began to modernize their military forces along Western lines, Sino-Japanese rivalry over Korea intensified. In 1894, China and Japan intervened on opposite sides of an internal rebellion in Korea. When hostilities broke out between the two powers, Japanese ships destroyed the Chinese fleet and seized the Manchurian city of Port Arthur. In the Treaty of Shimonoseki, the Manchus were forced to recognize the independence of Korea and to cede Taiwan and the Liaodong peninsula, with its strategic naval base at Port Arthur, to Japan.

Shortly thereafter, under pressure from the European powers, the Japanese returned the Liaodong peninsula to China, but in the early twentieth century, they returned to the offensive. Rivalry with Russia over influence in Korea led to increasingly strained relations between the two countries. In 1904, Japan launched a surprise attack on the Russian naval base at Port Arthur, which Russia had taken from China in 1898. The Japanese armed forces were weaker, but Russia faced difficult logistical problems along its new Trans-Siberian Railway and severe political instability at home. In 1905, after Japanese warships sank almost the entire Russian

Seitoku Kinen Kaigakan hekigashu, 1932, Special Collections, D. H. Ramsey Library, University of North Carolina at Asheville, NC 28804

The Emperor Reviews His Fleet In 1868, reformist elements overthrew the Tokugawa shogunate and launched an era of rapid modernization in Japanese society. Emperor Meiji, who had mounted the throne the previous year, became the symbol of his nation's effort to transform itself along Western lines. Although according to tradition the emperor played no military role in Japanese society, Emperor Meiji is shown here surveying a parade of warships in 1905 following the Japanese victory over Imperial Russia. On the right is Admiral Togo, who had commanded the fleet in its stunning victory over Russian naval forces in the Sea of Japan.

MAP 3.3 **Japanese Overseas Expansion During the Meiji Era.** Beginning in the late nineteenth century, Japan ventured beyond its home islands and became an imperialist power. The extent of Japanese colonial expansion through World War I is shown here. [?] Which parts of Imperial China were now under Japanese influence? View an animated version of this map or related maps at worldrc.wadsworth.com/.

fleet off the coast of Korea, the Russians agreed to a humiliating peace, ceding the strategically located Liaodong peninsula back to Japan, along with southern Sakhalin and the Kurile Islands. Russia also agreed to abandon its political and economic influence in Korea and southern Manchuria, which now came increasingly under Japanese control. The Japanese victory stunned the world, including the colonial peoples of Southeast Asia, who now began to realize that Europeans were not necessarily invincible.

During the next few years, the Japanese consolidated their position in northeastern Asia, annexing Korea in 1908 as an integral part of Japan. When the Koreans protested the seizure, Japanese reprisals resulted in thousands of deaths. The United States was the first nation to recognize the annexation in return for Tokyo's declaration of respect for U.S. authority in the Philippines. In 1908, the two countries reached an agreement in which the United States recognized Japanese interests in the region in return for Japanese acceptance of the principles of the Open Door. But mutual suspicion between the two countries was growing, sparked in part by U.S. efforts to restrict immigration from all Asian countries. President Theodore Roosevelt, who mediated the Russo-Japanese War, had aroused the anger of many Japanese by turning down a Japanese demand for reparations from Russia. In turn, some Americans began to fear the rise of a "yellow peril" manifested by Japanese expansion in East Asia.

CONCLUSION

*T*HE MEIJI RESTORATION was one of the great success stories of modern times. Not only did the Meiji leaders put Japan firmly on the path to economic and political development, but they also managed to remove the unequal treaty provisions that had been imposed at mid-century. Japanese achievements are especially impressive when compared with the difficulties experienced by China, which was not only unable to effect significant changes in its traditional society but had not even reached a consensus on the need for doing so. Japan's achievements more closely resemble those of Europe, but whereas the West needed a century and a half to achieve a significant level of industrial development, the Japanese achieved it in forty years.

The differences between the Japanese and Chinese responses to the West have sparked considerable debate among students of comparative history. Some have argued that Japan's success was partly due to good fortune; lacking abundant natural resources, it was exposed to less pressure from the West than many of its neighbors. That argument, however, is not very persuasive, since it does not explain why nations under considerably less pressure, such as Laos and Nepal, did not advance even more quickly.

One possible explanation has already been suggested: Japan's unique geographic position in Asia.

China, a continental nation with a heterogeneous ethnic composition, was distinguished from its neighbors by its Confucian culture. By contrast, Japan was an island nation, ethnically and linguistically homogeneous, which had never been conquered. Unlike the Chinese, the Japanese had little to fear from cultural change in terms of its effect on their national identity. If Confucian culture, with all its accouterments, was what defined the Chinese gentleman, his Japanese counterpart, in the familiar image, could discard his sword and kimono and don a modern military uniform or a Western business suit and still feel comfortable in both worlds.

Whatever the case, the Meiji Restoration was possible because aristocratic and capitalist elements managed to work together in a common effort to achieve national wealth and power. The nature of the Japanese value system, with its emphasis on practicality and military achievement, may also have contributed. Finally, the Meiji benefited from the fact that the pace of urbanization and commercial and industrial development had already begun to quicken under the Tokugawa. Japan, it has been said, was ripe for change, and nothing could have been more suitable as an antidote for the collapsing old system than the Western emphasis on wealth and power. It was a classic example of challenge and response.

TIMELINE

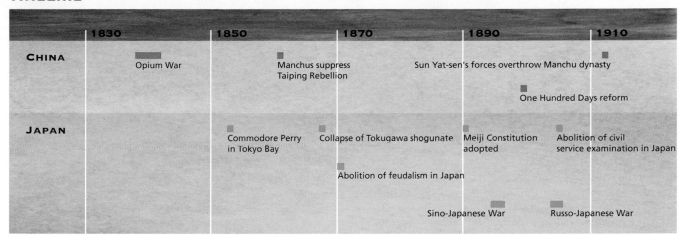

	1830	1850	1870	1890	1910
CHINA	■ Opium War	■ Manchus suppress Taiping Rebellion	■ Sun Yat-sen's forces overthrow Manchu dynasty ■ One Hundred Days reform		
JAPAN		■ Commodore Perry in Tokyo Bay	■ Collapse of Tokugawa shogunate ■ Abolition of feudalism in Japan	■ Meiji Constitution adopted ■ Sino-Japanese War	■ Abolition of civil service examination in Japan ■ Russo-Japanese War

---

CHAPTER NOTES

1. Quoted in Ssu-yu Teng and John K. Fairbank, eds., *China's Response to the West: A Documentary Survey, 1839–1923* (New York, 1970), p. 140.
2. Ibid., p. 167.

WORLD HISTORY
RESOURCE CENTER

Visit the *Twentieth-Century World History* Book Companion website for resources specific to this textbook:

academic.cengage.com/history/duiker

The Wadsworth World History Resource Center at worldrc.wadsworth.com/ offers a variety of tools to help you succeed in this course, including access to quizzes; images; documents; interactive simulations, maps, and timelines; movie explorations; and a wealth of other sources.

THE LATE NINETEENTH CENTURY witnessed two major developments: the Industrial Revolution and European domination of the world. Of these two factors, the first was clearly the more important, for it created the conditions for the latter. It was, of course, the major industrial powers—Great Britain, France, and later Germany, Japan, and the United States—that took the lead in building large colonial empires. European nations that did not achieve a high level of industrial advancement, such as Spain and Portugal, declined in importance as colonial powers.

Why some societies were able to master the challenge of industrialization and others were not has been a matter of considerable scholarly debate. Some observers have found the answer in the cultural characteristics of individual societies, such as the Protestant work ethic in parts of Europe or the tradition of social discipline and class hierarchy in Japan. According to the historian David Landes, cultural differences are the key reason the Industrial Revolution first took place in Europe rather than elsewhere in the world. While admitting that other factors, such as climate and the presence of natural resources, played a role in the process, what is most important, he maintains in his provocative book *The Wealth and Poverty of Nations,* are "work, thrift, honesty, patience, and tenacity," all characteristics that are present to a greater or lesser degree in European civilization. Other societies were entangled in a "web of tradition" comprised of political authoritarianism, religious prejudice, and a suspicion of material wealth. Thus, they failed to overcome obstacles to rapid economic development. Only Japan, with its own tradition of emphasis on hard work, self-sacrifice, and high achievement, succeeded in emulating the European experience.

Other scholars criticize Landes's approach as Eurocentric and marked by lamentable ignorance of the dynamic forces at work in the non-Western world. In their view, other more practical considerations may have played an equally important role in determining society's winners and losers, such as the lack of an urban market for agricultural goods in China (which reduced the landowners' incentives to introduce mechanized farming) or the relative absence of a foreign threat in Japan (which provided increased opportunities for local investment). In the view of some theorists of the "world systems" school, it was in fact as a result of the successes achieved during the early stages of European expansion during the sixteenth and seventeenth centuries that major European powers amassed the capital, developed the experience, and built the trade networks that would later fuel the Industrial Revolution. In that interpretation, vigorously argued by the sociologist Andre Gunder Frank, the latter event is less important as the driving force of the modern age than the period—marked by Western military conquest and the degradation of many non-Western peoples—that immediately preceded it.

It is clear that neither side possesses a monopoly of truth in this debate. Although culture clearly matters, other factors, such as climate, geography, the quality of political leadership, and what has been called "social capital" (such as the strength of the civil society), are also important. On the other hand, the argument that imperialism is the main culprit cannot explain why some previously colonial societies have succeeded in mounting the ladder of economic success so much more successfully than others. What is increasingly clear is that there is no single answer, or solution, to the question.

Whatever the ultimate causes, the advent of the Industrial Age had a number of lasting consequences for the world at large. On the one hand, the material wealth of those nations that successfully passed through the process increased significantly. In many cases, the creation of advanced industrial societies strengthened democratic institutions and led to a higher standard of living for the majority of the population. The spread of technology and trade outside of Europe created the basis for a new international economic order based on the global exchange of goods.

On the other hand, as we have seen, not all the consequences of the Industrial Revolution were beneficial. In the industrializing societies themselves, rapid economic change often led to resentment over the vast disparities in the distribution of wealth and a sense of rootlessness and alienation among much of the population. Some societies were able to manage these problems with some degree of success, but others experienced a breakdown of social values and the rise of widespread political instability. Industrialization also had destabilizing consequences on the global scene. Rising economic competition among the industrial powers was a major contributor to heightened international competition in the world.

Elsewhere in Europe, old empires found it increasingly difficult to respond to new problems. The Ottoman Empire appeared helpless to curb unrest in the Balkans. In Imperial

Russia, internal tensions became too much for the traditional landholding elites to handle, leading to significant political and social unrest in the first decade of the twentieth century. In Austria-Hungary, deep-seated ethnic and class antagonisms remained under the surface but reached a point where they might eventually threaten the survival of that multinational state.

In the meantime, the Industrial Revolution was creating the technological means by which the West would achieve domination of much of the rest of the world by the end of the nineteenth century. Europeans had begun to explore the world in the fifteenth century, but even as late as 1870, they had not yet completely penetrated North America, South America, and Australia. In Asia and Africa, with a few notable exceptions, the Western presence was limited to trading posts. Between 1870 and 1914, Western civilization expanded into the rest of the Americas and Australia, while most of Africa and Asia was divided into European colonies or spheres of influence. Two major factors explain this remarkable expansion: the migration of many Europeans to other parts of the world as a result of population growth and the revival of imperialism made possible by the West's technological advances.

The European population increased dramatically between 1850 and 1910, rising from 270 million to 460 million. Although agricultural and industrial prosperity supported an increase in the European population, it could not do so indefinitely, especially in areas that had little industry and severe rural overpopulation. Some of the excess labor from underdeveloped areas migrated to the industrial regions of Europe. By 1913, for example, more than 400,000 Poles were working in the heavily industrialized Ruhr region of western Germany. But the industrialized regions of Europe could not absorb the entire surplus population of the agricultural regions. A booming American economy after 1898 and cheap shipping fares after 1900 led to mass emigration from southern and eastern Europe to North America at the beginning of the twentieth century. In 1880, on average, around half a million people departed annually from Europe, but between 1906 and 1910, their numbers increased to 1.3 million, many of them from southern and eastern Europe. Altogether, between 1846 and 1932, probably 60 million Europeans left Europe, half of them bound for the United States and most of the rest for Canada or Latin America.

Beginning in the 1880s, European states began an intense scramble for overseas territory. This "new imperialism," as some have called it, led Europeans to carve up Asia and Africa. Imperialism was not really a new phenomenon. Since the Crusades of the Middle Ages and the overseas expansion of the sixteenth and seventeenth centuries, when Europeans established colonies in North and South America and trading posts around Africa and the Indian Ocean, Europeans had shown a marked proclivity for the domination of less technologically oriented, non-European peoples. Nevertheless, the imperialism of the late nineteenth century was different from that of earlier periods. First, it occurred after a period in which Europeans had reacted against imperial expansion. Between 1775 and 1875, European states actually lost more colonial territory than they acquired as many Europeans had come to regard colonies as expensive and useless. Second, the new imperialism was more rapid and resulted in greater and deeper penetrations into non-European societies. Finally, most of the new imperialism was directed toward Africa and Asia, two regions that had been largely ignored until then.

The new imperialism had a dramatic effect on Africa and Asia as European powers competed for control of these two continents. In contrast, Latin America was able to achieve political independence from its colonial rulers in the course of the nineteenth century and embark on the process of building new nations. Like the Ottoman Empire, however, Latin America remained subject to commercial penetration by Western merchants.

Another part of the world that escaped total domination by the West was East Asia, where China and Japan were able to maintain at least the substance of national independence during the height of the Western onslaught at the end of the nineteenth century. For China, once the most advanced country in the world, survival was very much in doubt for many decades as the waves of Western political, military, and economic influence lapped at the edges of the Chinese Empire and appeared on the verge of dividing up the Chinese heartland into separate spheres of influence. Only Japan responded with vigor and effectiveness, launching a comprehensive reform program that by the end of the century had transformed the island nation into an emerging member of the imperialist club. ◆

II

CULTURES IN COLLISION

Japanese troops enter the Chinese city of Nanjing

4

WAR AND REVOLUTION:
WORLD WAR I AND ITS AFTERMATH

As THE TWENTIETH-CENTURY DAWNED, the magnificent promise offered by recent scientific advances and the flowering of the Industrial Revolution appeared about to be fulfilled. Few expressed this mood of optimism better than the renowned British historian Arnold Toynbee. In a retrospective look at the opening of a tumultuous century written many years later, Toynbee remarked:

> [We had expected] that life throughout the world would become more rational, more humane, and more democratic and that, slowly, but surely, political democracy would produce greater social justice. We had also expected that the progress of science and technology would make mankind richer, and that this increasing wealth would gradually spread from a minority to a majority. We had expected that all this would happen peacefully. In fact we thought that mankind's course was set for an earthly paradise.[1]

Such bright hopes about the future of humankind were sadly misplaced. In the summer of 1914, simmering rivalries between the major imperialist powers erupted into full-scale war, causing extensive physical destruction and the deaths of millions. The Great War, as it was then labeled, was to be an eerie prelude to a tumultuous century marked by widespread violence and dramatic change. ◇

International Rivalry and the Coming of War

Between 1871 and 1914, Europeans experienced a long period of peace as the great powers managed to achieve a fragile balance of power in an effort to avert a re-creation of the destructive forces unleashed during the Napoleonic era. But rivalries among the major world powers continued, and even intensified, leading to a series of crises that might have erupted into a general war. Some of these crises, as we have seen in Chapters 2 and 3, took place outside Europe, as the imperialist nations scuffled for advantage in the race for new colonial territories. But the main focus of European statesmen remained on Europe itself, where the emergence of Germany as the most powerful state on the Continent threatened to upset the fragile balance of power that had been established at the Congress of Vienna in 1815. Fearful of a possible anti-German alliance between France and Russia, German Chancellor Otto von Bismarck signed a defensive treaty with Austria in 1879. Three years later, the alliance was enlarged to include Italy, increasingly angry with the French over conflicting colonial ambitions in North Africa. The so-called Triple Alliance of 1882 committed the three powers to support the existing political and social order while maintaining a defensive alliance against France.

While Bismarck was chancellor, German policy had been essentially cautious, as he sought to prevent rival powers from conspiring against Berlin. But in 1890 Emperor William II dismissed the "iron chancellor" from office and embarked on a more aggressive foreign policy dedicated to providing Germany with its rightful "place in the sun." As Bismarck had feared, France and Russia responded by concluding a military alliance in 1894. By 1907, a loose confederation of Great Britain, France, and Russia—known as the Triple Entente—stood opposed to the Triple Alliance of Germany, Austria-Hungary, and Italy. Europe was divided into two opposing camps that became more and more inflexible and unwilling to compromise. The stage was set for war.

Crises in the Balkans, 1908–1913

In such an environment, where potentially hostile countries are locked in an awkward balance of power, it often takes only a spark to set off a firestorm. Such was the case in 1908, when a major European crisis began to emerge in the Balkans, where the decline of Ottoman power had turned the region into a tinderbox of ethnic and religious tensions.

The Bosnian crisis of 1908–1909 began a chain of events that eventually spun out of control. Since the Russian victory over the Turks in 1878, Bosnia and Herzegovina had been under the protection of Austria, but in 1908, Austria took the drastic step of annexing the two Slavic-speaking territories. Serbia was outraged at this action because it dashed the Serbs' hopes of creating a large kingdom that would include most of the southern Slavs. But this possibility was precisely why the Austrians had annexed Bosnia and Herzegovina. The creation of a large Serbia would be a threat to the unity of their empire, with its large Slavic population. The Russians, desiring to increase their own authority in the Balkans, supported the Serbs, who then prepared for war against Austria. At this point, William II demanded that the Russians accept Austria's annexation of Bosnia and Herzegovina or face war with Germany. Weakened from their defeat in the Russo-Japanese War in 1904–1905, the Russians backed down but privately vowed revenge.

The crisis intensified in 1912 when Serbia, Bulgaria, Montenegro, and Greece organized the Balkan League and defeated the Turks in the First Balkan War. When the victorious allies were unable to agree on how to divide the conquered Turkish provinces in the area, a second conflict erupted in 1913. Greece, Serbia, Romania, and the Ottoman Empire attacked and defeated Bulgaria, which was left with only a small part of Macedonia. Most of the rest was divided

MAP 4.1 **Europe in 1914.** By 1914, two alliances dominated Europe: the Triple Entente of Britain, France, and Russia and the Triple Alliance of Germany, Austria-Hungary, and Italy. Russia sought to bolster fellow Slavs in Serbia, whereas Austria-Hungary was intent on increasing its power in the Balkans and thwarting Serbia's ambitions. Thus, the Balkans became the flash point for World War I. ❓ Which nonaligned nations were positioned between the two alliances? 🌐 **View an animated version of this map or related maps at the World History Resource Center, at** worldrc.wadsworth.com/.

between Serbia and Greece. Yet Serbia's aspirations remained unfulfilled. The two Balkan wars left the inhabitants embittered and created more tensions among the great powers.

By now Austria-Hungary was convinced that Serbia was a mortal threat to its empire and must at some point be crushed. Meanwhile, the French and Russian governments renewed their alliance as Britain drew closer to France. By the beginning of 1914, two armed camps viewed each other with suspicion. The European "age of progress" was about to come to an inglorious and bloody end (see Map 4.1).

The Road to World War I

On June 28, 1914, the heir to the Austrian throne, Archduke Francis Ferdinand, and his wife, Sophia, were assassinated in the Bosnian city of Sarajevo. The assassination was carried out by a Bosnian activist who worked for the Black Hand, a Serbian terrorist organization dedicated to the creation of a pan-Slavic kingdom. Although the Austrian government had no proof the Serbian government had been directly involved in the archduke's assassination, it saw an opportunity to "render Serbia innocuous once and for all by a display of force," as the Austrian foreign minister put it. Austrian leaders sought the backing of their German allies, who gave their assurance that Austria-Hungary could rely on Germany's "full support," even if "matters went to the length of a war between Austria-Hungary and Russia."

On July 23, Austrian leaders issued an ultimatum to Serbia in which they made such extreme demands that Serbia felt it had little choice but to reject some of them to preserve its sovereignty. Austria then declared war on Serbia on July 28. Still smarting from its humiliation in the Bosnian crisis of 1908, Russia was determined to support Serbia's cause. On July 28, Tsar Nicholas II ordered a partial mobilization of the Russian army against Austria (see the box on p. 69). The Russian general staff informed the tsar that their mobilization plans were based on a war against both Germany and Austria simultaneously. They could not execute a partial mobilization without creating chaos in the army. Consequently, the Russian government ordered a full mobilization on July 29, knowing that the Germans would consider this an act of war against them. Germany responded by demanding that the Russians halt their mobilization within twelve hours. When the Russians ignored the ultimatum, Germany declared war on Russia on August 1.

The Schlieffen Plan Under the guidance of General Alfred von Schlieffen, chief of staff from 1891 to 1905, the German general staff had devised a military plan based on the assumption of a two-front war with France and Russia, which had formed a military alliance in 1894. The Schlieffen Plan called for only a minimal troop deployment against Russia. Most of the German army would execute a rapid invasion of France before Russia could become effective in the east or the British could cross the English Channel to help France. To achieve this rapid invasion, the Germans would advance through neutral Belgium, with its level coastal plain, where the army could move faster than on the rougher terrain to the southeast. After the planned quick defeat of the French, the German army would then redeploy to the east against Russia. Under the Schlieffen Plan, Germany could not mobilize its troops solely against Russia; therefore, on August 2, Germany issued an ultimatum to Belgium demanding the right of German troops to pass through Belgian territory and, on August 3, declared war on France. On August 4, Great Britain declared war on Germany, officially in response to this violation of Belgian neutrality but in fact because of Britain's desire to maintain its world power. As one British diplomat argued, if Germany and Austria were to win the war, "What would be the position of a friendless England?" Thus, by August 4, all the great powers of Europe were at war.

The War

Before 1914, many political leaders had become convinced that war involved so many political and economic risks that it was not worth fighting. Others believed that "rational" diplomats could control any situation and prevent the outbreak of war. At the beginning of August 1914, both of these prewar illusions were shattered, but the new illusions that replaced them soon proved to be equally foolish.

Illusions and Stalemate, 1914–1915

Europeans went to war in 1914 with remarkable enthusiasm. Government propaganda had been successful in stirring up national antagonisms before the war. Now, in August 1914, the urgent pleas of governments for defense against aggressors fell on receptive ears in every belligerent nation. Most people seemed genuinely convinced that their nation's cause was just. A new set of illusions also fed the enthusiasm for war. In August 1914, almost everyone believed that because of the risk of damage to the regional economy, the war would be over in a few weeks. People were reminded that all European wars since 1815 had in fact ended in a matter of weeks. Both the soldiers who exuberantly boarded the trains for the war front in August 1914 and the jubilant citizens who bombarded them with flowers as they departed believed that the warriors would be home by Christmas.

German hopes for a quick end to the war rested on a military gamble. The Schlieffen Plan had called for the German army to make a vast encircling movement through Belgium into northern France that would sweep around Paris and encircle most of the French army. But the high command had not heeded Schlieffen's advice to place sufficient numbers of troops on the western salient near the English Channel to guarantee success, and the German advance was halted only 20 miles from Paris at the First Battle of the Marne (September 6–10). The war quickly turned into a stalemate as neither the Germans nor the French could dislodge the other from the trenches they had begun to dig for shelter. Two lines of trenches soon extended from the English Channel to the frontiers of Switzerland (see Map 4.2 on p. 70). The Western Front had become bogged down in a trench warfare that kept both sides immobilized in virtually the same positions for four years.

"YOU HAVE TO BEAR THE RESPONSIBILITY FOR WAR OR PEACE"

*A*fter Austria declared war on Serbia on July 28, 1914, Russian support of Serbia and German support of Austria threatened to escalate the conflict in the Balkans into a wider war. As we can see in these last-minute telegrams between the Russians and Germans (known as the "Willy-Nicky letters"), the rigidity of the military war plans on both sides made it difficult to avoid a confrontation once the process got under way.

Based on these letters, what was the chief issue that led to the outbreak of war? Was Emperor William II correct when he told Tsar Nicholas II that the latter would "have to bear the responsibility for war or peace"?

Communications Between Berlin and Saint Petersburg on the Eve of World War I

Emperor William II to Tsar Nicholas II, July 28, 10:45 P.M.

I have heard with the greatest anxiety of the impression which is caused by the action of Austria-Hungary against Servia [Serbia]. The inscrupulous agitation which has been going on for years in Servia has led to the revolting crime of which Archduke Franz Ferdinand has become a victim. . . . Doubtless You will agree with me that both of us, You as well as I, and all other sovereigns, have a common interest to insist that all those who are responsible for this horrible murder shall suffer their deserved punishment. . . .

Your most sincere and devoted friend and cousin

(*Signed*)   WILHELM

Tsar Nicholas II to Emperor William II, July 29, 1 P.M.

I am glad that you are back in Germany. In this serious moment I ask You earnestly to help me. An ignominious war has been declared against a weak country and in Russia the indignation which I fully share is tremendous. I fear that very soon I shall be unable to resist the pressure exercised upon me and that I shall be forced to take measures which will lead to war. To prevent a calamity as a European war would be, I urge You in the name of our old friendship to do all in Your power to restrain Your ally from going too far.

(*Signed*)   NICOLAS

Emperor William II to Tsar Nicholas II, July 29, 6:30 P.M.

I have received Your telegram and I share Your desire for the conservation of peace. However: I cannot—as I told You in my first telegram—consider the action of Austria-Hungary as an "ignominious war." Austria-Hungary knows from experience that the promises of Servia as long as they are merely on paper are entirely unreliable. . . . I believe that a direct understanding Is possible and desirable between Your Government and Vienna, an understanding which—as I have already telegraphed You—my Government endeavors to aid with all possible effort. Naturally military measures by Russia, which might be construed as a menace by Austria-Hungary, would accelerate a calamity which both of us desire to avoid and would undermine my position as mediator which—upon Your appeal to my friendship and aid—I willingly accepted.

(*Signed*)   WILHELM

Emperor William II to Tsar Nicholas II, July 30, 1 A.M.

My Ambassador has instructions to direct the attention of Your Government to the dangers and serious consequences of a mobilization. I have told You the same in my last telegram. Austria-Hungary has mobilized only against Servia, and only a part of her army. If Russia, as seems to be the case, according to Your advice and that of Your Government, mobilizes against Austria-Hungary, the part of the mediator with which You have entrusted me in such friendly manner and which I have accepted upon Your express desire, is threatened if not made impossible. The entire weight of decision now rests upon Your shoulders; You have to bear the responsibility for war or peace.

(*Signed*)   WILHELM

German Chancellor to German Ambassador at Saint Petersburg, July 31, URGENT

In spite of negotiations still pending and although we have up to this hour made no preparations for mobilization, Russia has mobilized her entire army and navy, hence also against us. On account of these Russian measures, we have been forced, for the safety of the country, to proclaim the threatening state of war, which does not yet imply mobilization. Mobilization, however, is bound to follow if Russia does not stop every measure of war against us and against Austria-Hungary within 12 hours, and notifies us definitely to this effect. Please to communicate this at once to M. Sazonoff and wire hour of communication.

SOURCE: *The Western World: From 1700*, Vol. II, by W. E. Adams, R. B. Barlow, G. R. Kleinfeld, and R. D. Smith (Dodd, Mead, and Co., 1968), pp. 421–442.

Eastern Front:

⟆ Battle site, 1914

–·–· Russian advances, 1914–1916

····· Deepest German penetration

—— Brest-Litovsk boundary, 1918

Western Front:

—— Farthest German advance, September 1914

—— German offensive, March–July 1918

– – – Winter, 1914–1915

—— Armistice line

⟵ German advances

⟵ Allied advances

(CRIMEA) Regions of national states

MAP 4.2 World War I, 1914–1918. This map shows how greatly the Western and Eastern Fronts of World War I differed. After initial German gains in the west, the war became bogged down in trench warfare, with little change in the battle lines throughout the war. The Eastern Front was marked by considerable mobility, with battle lines shifting by hundreds of miles. ❓ How do you explain the difference in the two fronts? 🌐 **View an animated version of this map or related maps at the World History Resource Center, at** worldrc.wadsworth.com/.

The War in the East In contrast to the west, the war in the east was marked by much more mobility, although the cost in lives was equally enormous. At the beginning of the war, the Russian army moved into eastern Germany but was decisively defeated at the battles of Tannenberg on August 30 and the Masurian Lakes on September 15. The Russians were no longer a threat to German territory.

The Austrians, Germany's allies, fared less well initially. After they were defeated by the Russians in Galicia

and thrown out of Serbia as well, the Germans came to their aid. A German-Austrian army defeated and routed the Russian army in Galicia and pushed the Russians back 300 miles into their own territory. Russian casualties stood at 2.5 million killed, captured, or wounded; the Russians had almost been knocked out of the war. Buoyed by their success, the Germans and Austrians, joined by the Bulgarians in September 1915, attacked and eliminated Serbia from the war.

© Hulton Archive/Stringer/Getty Images

The Horrors of War. The slaughter of millions of men in the trenches of World War I created unimaginable horrors for the participants. For the sake of survival, many soldiers learned to harden themselves against the stench of decomposing bodies and the sight of bodies horribly dismembered by artillery barrages.

The Great Slaughter, 1916–1917

The successes in the east enabled the Germans to move back to the offensive in the west. The early trenches dug in 1914 had by now become elaborate systems of defense.

Both lines of trenches were protected by barbed-wire entanglements 3 to 5 feet high and 30 yards wide, concrete machine-gun nests, and mortar batteries, supported farther back by heavy artillery. Troops lived in holes in the ground, separated from the enemy by a no-man's land.

The unexpected development of trench warfare baffled military leaders who had been trained to fight wars of movement and maneuver. Taking advantage of the recent American invention of the Caterpillar tractor, the British introduced tanks on the Western Front in 1915, but their effectiveness in breaking through enemy defenses was not demonstrated. The only plan generals could devise was to attempt a breakthrough by throwing

German Possessions in Africa, 1914

masses of men against enemy lines that had first been battered by artillery barrages. Periodically, the high command on either side would order an offensive that would begin with an artillery barrage to flatten the enemy's barbed wire and leave the enemy in a state of shock. After "softening up" the enemy in this fashion, a mass of soldiers would climb out of their trenches with fixed bayonets and hope to work their way toward the opposing trenches. The attacks rarely worked, as the machine gun put hordes of men advancing unprotected across open fields at a severe disadvantage. In 1916 and 1917, millions of young men were sacrificed in the search for the elusive breakthrough. In ten months at Verdun, 700,000 men lost their lives over a few miles of terrain.

Warfare in the trenches of the Western Front produced unimaginable horrors. Battlefields were hellish landscapes of barbed wire, shell holes, mud, and injured and dying men (see the box on p. 72). The introduction of poison gas in 1915 produced new forms of injuries, but the first aerial battles were a rare sideshow and gave no hint of the horrors to come with air warfare in the future.

Soldiers in the trenches also lived with the persistent presence of death. Since combat went on for months, soldiers had to carry on in the midst of countless bodies of dead men or the remains of men dismembered by artillery barrages. Many soldiers remembered the stench of decomposing bodies and the swarms of rats that grew fat in the trenches.

The Widening of the War

As another response to the stalemate on the Western Front, both sides looked for new allies who might provide a winning advantage. The Ottoman Empire, hoping to drive the British from Egypt, had already come into the war on Germany's side in August 1914. Russia, Great Britain, and France declared war on the Ottoman Empire in November. Although the Allies attempted to open a Balkan front by landing forces at Gallipoli, southwest of Constantinople, in April 1915, the campaign was a disaster. The Italians also entered the war on the Allied side after France and Britain promised to further their acquisition of Austrian territory.

By 1917, the war that had originated in Europe had truly become a world conflict. In the Middle East, the dashing but eccentric British adventurer T. E. Lawrence, popularly known as Lawrence of Arabia (1888–1935), incited Arab princes to revolt against their Ottoman overlords in 1917. In 1918, British forces from Egypt destroyed the rest of the Ottoman Empire in the Middle East. For these campaigns, the British mobilized

THE EXCITEMENT AND THE REALITY OF WAR

The incredible outpouring of patriotic enthusiasm that greeted the declaration of war at the beginning of August 1914 in many European countries demonstrated the power that nationalistic feeling had attained at the beginning of the twentieth century. Many Europeans seemingly believed that the war had given them a higher purpose, a renewed dedication to the greatness of their nation. That sense of enthusiasm was captured by the Austrian writer Stefan Zweig in his book *The World of Yesterday*.

The reality of war was entirely different. Soldiers who had left for the front in August 1914 in the belief that they would be home by Christmas found themselves shivering and dying in the vast networks along the battlefront. Few expressed the horror of trench warfare as well as the German writer Erich Maria Remarque in his famous novel *All Quiet on the Western Front*, written in 1929.

Why, according to author Stefan Zweig, did so many Europeans welcome the outbreak of war in 1914? Why had they so badly underestimated the cost?

Stefan Zweig, *The World of Yesterday*

The next morning I was in Austria. In every station placards had been put up announcing general mobilization. The trains were filled with fresh recruits, banners were flying, music sounded, and in Vienna I found the entire city in a tumult.... There were parades in the street, flags, ribbons, and music burst forth everywhere, young recruits were marching triumphantly, their faces lighting up at the cheering....

And to be truthful, I must acknowledge that there was a majestic, rapturous, and even seductive something in this first outbreak of the people from which one could escape only with difficulty. And in spite of all my hatred and aversion for war, I should not like to have missed the memory of those days. As never before, thousands and hundreds of thousands felt what they should have felt in peace time, that they belonged together.

What did the great mass know of war in 1914, after nearly half a century of peace? They did not know war, they had hardly given it a thought. It had become legendary, and distance had made it seem romantic and heroic. They still saw it in the perspective of their school readers and of paintings in museums; brilliant cavalry attacks in glittering uniforms, the fatal shot always straight through the heart, the entire campaign a resounding march of victory—"We'll be home at Christmas," the recruits shouted laughingly to their mothers in August of 1914.... A rapid excursion into the romantic, a wild, manly adventure—that is how the war of 1914 was painted in the imagination of the simple man, and the younger people were honestly afraid that they might miss this most wonderful and exciting experience of their lives; that is why they hurried and thronged to the colors, and that is why they shouted and sang in the trains that carried them to the slaughter; wildly and feverishly the red wave of blood coursed through the veins of the entire nation.

Erich Maria Remarque, *All Quiet on the Western Front*

We wake up in the middle of the night. The earth booms. Heavy fire is falling on us. We crouch into corners.... Every man is aware of the heavy shells tearing down the parapet, rooting up the embankment and demolishing the upper layers of concrete.... Already by morning a few of the recruits are green and vomiting....

No one would believe that in this howling waste there could still be men, but steel helmets now appear on all sides out of the trench, and fifty yards from us a machine-gun is already in position and barking.

[Finally the attack begins.]

The wire-entanglements are torn to pieces. Yet they offer some obstacle. We see the storm-troops coming.... We recognize the distorted faces, the smooth helmets: they are French. They have already suffered heavily when they reach the remnants of the barbed wire entanglements.

I see one of them, his face upturned, fall into a wire cradle. His body collapses, his hands remain suspended as thought he were praying. Then his body drops clear away and only his hands with the stumps of his arms, shot off, now hang in the wire.

SOURCES: From *The World of Yesterday* by Stefan Zweig translated by Helmut Ripperger. Translation copyright 1943 by the Viking Press, Inc.; All Quiet on the Western Front by Erich Maria Remarque. "Im Westen Nichts Neues," copyright 1928 by Ullstein A. G.; copyright renewed © 1956 by Erich Maria Remarque. All Quiet on the Western Front, copyright 1929, 1930 by Little. Brown and Company: Copyright renewed © 1957, 1958 by Erich Maria Remarque. All Rights Reserved.

forces from India, Australia, and New Zealand. The Allies also took advantage of Germany's preoccupations in Europe and lack of naval strength to seize German colonies elsewhere in the world. Japan seized a number of German-held islands in the Pacific, and Australia took over German New Guinea (see Chapter 5).

The Yanks Are Comin' Most important to the Allied cause was the entry of the United States into the war. At first, the United States tried to remain neutral, but that became more difficult as the war dragged on. The immediate cause of U.S. involvement grew out of the naval conflict between Germany and Great Britain. Britain used its superior naval power to maximum effect by imposing a naval blockade on Germany. Germany retaliated with a counterblockade enforced by the use of unrestricted submarine warfare. Strong U.S. protests over the German sinking of passenger liners—especially the British ship *Lusitania* on May 7, 1915, in which more than one hundred Americans lost their lives—forced the German government to suspend unrestricted submarine warfare in September 1915 to avoid further antagonizing the Americans.

In January 1917, however, eager to break the deadlock in the war, German naval officers convinced Emperor William II that the renewed use of unrestricted submarine warfare could starve the British into submission within five months, certainly before the Americans could act. To distract the Wilson administration in case it should decide to enter the war on the side of the Allied powers, German Foreign Minister Alfred von Zimmerman secretly encouraged the Mexican government to launch a military attack to recover territories lost to the United States in the American Southwest.

Berlin's decision to return to unrestricted submarine warfare, combined with outrage in Washington over the Zimmerman telegram (which had been decoded by the British and provided to U.S. diplomats in London), finally brought the United States into the war on April 6, 1917. Although American troops did not arrive in Europe in large numbers until 1918, U.S. entry into the war gave the Allied Powers a badly needed psychological boost. The year 1917 was not a good year for them. Allied offensives on the Western Front were disastrously defeated. The Italian armies were smashed in October, and in November 1917, the Bolshevik Revolution in Russia (discussed later in this chapter) led to Russia's withdrawal from the war, leaving Germany free to concentrate entirely on the Western Front.

The Home Front: The Impact of Total War

As the war dragged on, conditions on the home front became a matter of concern for all the participants. The prolongation of the war had transformed it into a total conflict that affected the lives of all citizens, however remote they might be from the battlefields. The need to organize masses of men and matériel for years of combat (Germany alone had 5.5 million men in active units in 1916) led to increased centralization of government powers, economic regimentation, and manipulation of public opinion to keep the war effort going.

Because the war was expected to be short, little thought had been given to economic problems and long-term wartime needs. Governments had to respond quickly, however, when the war machines failed to achieve their knockout blows and made ever-greater demands for men and matériel. The extension of government power was a logical outgrowth of these needs. Most European countries had already devised some system of mass conscription or military draft. It was now carried to unprecedented heights as countries mobilized tens of millions of young men for that elusive breakthrough to victory. Even countries that continued to rely on volunteers (Great Britain had the largest volunteer army in modern history—one million men—in 1914 and 1915) were forced to resort to conscription, especially to ensure that skilled laborers did not enlist but remained in factories that were important to the production of munitions. In the meantime, thousands of laborers were shipped in from the colonies to work on farms and in factories as replacements for Europeans mobilized to serve on the battlefield.

Throughout Europe, wartime governments expanded their powers over their economies. Free market capitalistic systems were temporarily shelved as governments experimented with price, wage, and rent controls; the rationing of food supplies and materials; the regulation of imports and exports; and the nationalization of transportation systems and industries. Some governments even moved toward compulsory employment. In effect, to mobilize the entire resources of the nation for the war effort, European countries had moved toward planned economies directed by government agencies. Under total war mobilization, the distinction between soldiers at war and civilians at home was narrowed. As U.S. President Woodrow Wilson expressed it, the men and women "who remain to till the soil and man the factories are no less a part of the army than the men beneath the battle flags."

Morale Problems As the Great War dragged on and both casualties and privations worsened, internal dissatisfaction replaced the patriotic enthusiasm that had marked the early stages of the conflict. By 1916, there were numerous signs that civilian morale was beginning to crack under the pressure of total war. War governments, however, fought back against the growing opposition to the war, as even parliamentary regimes resorted to an expansion of police powers to stifle internal dissent. At the very beginning of the war, the British Parliament passed the Defence of the Realm Act (DORA), which allowed the public authorities to arrest dissenters as traitors. The act was later extended to authorize public officials to censor newspapers by deleting objectionable material and even to suspend newspaper publication. In France, government authorities had initially been lenient about public opposition to the war, but by 1917, they began to fear that open opposition to the war might weaken the French will to fight. When Georges Clemenceau (1841–1929) became premier near the end of 1917, the lenient French policies came to an end, and basic civil liberties were suppressed for the duration of the war. When a former premier publicly advocated a negotiated peace, Clemenceau's government had him sentenced to prison for two years for treason.

Wartime governments made active use of propaganda to arouse enthusiasm for the war. The British and French, for example, exaggerated German atrocities in Belgium and found that their citizens were only too willing to believe these accounts. But as the war dragged on and morale sagged, governments were forced to devise new techniques for stimulating declining enthusiasm. In one British recruiting poster, for example, a small daughter asked her father, "Daddy, what did YOU do in the Great War?" while her younger brother played with toy soldiers and a cannon.

Total war made a significant impact on European society, most visibly by bringing an end to unemployment. The withdrawal of millions of men from the labor market to fight, combined with the heightened demand for wartime products, led to jobs for everyone able to work.

Women in World War I The war also created new roles for women. Because so many men went off to fight at the front, women were called on to take over jobs and responsibilities that had not been available to them before. Overall, the number of women employed in Britain who held new jobs or replaced men rose by 1,345,000. Women were also now employed in jobs that had been considered "beyond the capacity of women." These included such occupations as chimney sweeps, truck drivers, farm laborers, and factory workers in heavy industry. By 1918, some 38 percent of the workers in the Krupp armaments factories in Germany were women.

While male workers expressed concern that the employment of females at lower wages would depress their own wages, women began to demand equal pay legislation. A law passed by the French government in July 1915 established a minimum wage for women homeworkers in textiles, an industry that had grown dramatically thanks to the demand for military uniforms. Later in 1917, the government decreed that men and women should receive equal rates for piecework. Despite the noticeable increase in women's wages that resulted from government regulations, women's industrial wages still were not equal to men's wages by the end of the war.

Even worse, women's place in the workforce was far from secure. At the end of the war, governments moved quickly to remove women from the jobs they had encouraged them to take earlier. By 1919, there were 650,000 unemployed women in Britain, and wages for women who were still employed were lowered. The work benefits for women from World War I seemed to be short-lived as demobilized men returned to the job market.

Nevertheless, in some countries, the role played by women in the wartime economy did have a positive impact on the women's movement for social and political emancipation. The most obvious gain was the right to vote, granted to women in Britain in January 1918 and in Germany and

Austria immediately after the war. Contemporary media, however, tended to focus on the more noticeable, yet in some ways more superficial, social emancipation of upper- and middle-class women. In ever-larger numbers, these young women took jobs, had their own apartments, and showed their new independence by smoking in public and wearing shorter dresses, cosmetics, and new hairstyles.

War and Revolution

In the summer of 1914, Tsar Nicholas II of Russia had almost appeared to welcome the prospect of a European war. It seemed to him that such a conflict would unite his subjects at a time when his empire was passing through a period of rapid social change and political unrest. The imperial government had survived the popular demonstrations that erupted during the Russo-Japanese War of 1904–1905, but the tsar had been forced to grant a series of reforms in a desperate effort to restore political stability and forestall the collapse of the traditional system (see Chapter 1).

As it turned out, the onset of war served not to revive the Russian monarchy, but rather—as is so often the case with decrepit empires undergoing dramatic change—to undermine its already fragile foundations. World War I broke the trajectory of Russia's economic growth and set the stage for the final collapse of the old order. After stirring victories in the early stages of the war, news from the battlefield turned increasingly grim as poorly armed Russian soldiers were slaughtered by the modern armies of the German emperor. Between 1914 and 1916, two million Russian soldiers were killed, and another four to six million were wounded or captured. The conscription of peasants from the countryside caused food prices to rise and led to periodic bread shortages in the major cities. Workers grew increasingly restive at the wartime schedule of long hours with low pay and joined army deserters in angry marches through the capital of Saint Petersburg (now renamed Petrograd).

It was a classic scenario for revolution—discontent in the big cities fueled by mutinous troops streaming home from the battlefield and a rising level of lawlessness in rural areas as angry peasants seized land and burned the manor houses of the wealthy. Even the urban middle class, always a bellwether on the political scene, grew impatient with the economic crisis and the bad news from the front and began to question the competence of the tsar and his advisers. In March 1917 (late February according to the old style Julian calendar still in use in Russia), government troops fired at demonstrators in the streets of the capital and killed several. An angry mob marched to the Duma, where restive delegates demanded the resignation of the tsar's cabinet.

The March Revolution in Russia

Nicholas II had never wanted to share the supreme power he had inherited with the throne. After a brief period of hesitation, he abdicated, leaving a vacuum that was quickly seized by leading elements in the Duma, who formed a provisional government to steer Russia through the crisis. On the left, reformist and radical political parties—including the Social Revolutionaries (the legal successors of the outlawed terrorist organization Narodnaya Volya) and the Russian Social Democratic Labor Party (RSDLP), the only orthodox Marxist party active in Russia—cooperated in creating a shadow government called the Saint Petersburg Soviet. This shadow government supported the provisional government in pursuing the war but attempted to compel it to grant economic and social reforms that would benefit the masses.

The uprising of March 1917 had forced the collapse of the monarchy but showed little promise of solving the deeper problems that had led Russia to the brink of civil war. As the crisis continued, radical members of the RSDLP began to hope that a real social revolution was at hand.

Marxism had made its first appearance in the Russian environment in the 1880s. Early Marxists, aware of the primitive conditions in their country, asked Karl Marx himself for advice. The Russian proletariat was oppressed—indeed, brutalized—but small in numbers and unsophisticated. Could agrarian Russia make the transition to socialism without an intervening stage of capitalism? Marx, who always showed more flexibility than the rigid determinism of his system suggested, replied that it was possible that Russia could avoid the capitalist stage by building on the communal traditions of the Russian village, known as the *mir*.

But as Russian Marxism evolved, its leaders turned more toward Marxist orthodoxy. Founding member George Plekhanov saw signs in the early stages of the Industrial Revolution that Russia would follow the classic pattern. In 1898, Plekhanov's Russian Social Democratic Labor Party held its first congress.

Lenin and the Bolsheviks During the last decade of the nineteenth century, a new force entered the Russian Marxist movement in the figure of Vladimir Ulyanov, later to be known as Lenin (1870–1924). Initially radicalized by the execution of his older brother for terrorism in 1886, he became a revolutionary and a member of Plekhanov's RSDLP. Like Plekhanov, Lenin believed in the revolution, but he was a man in a hurry. Whereas Plekhanov wanted to prepare patiently for revolution by education and mass work, Lenin wanted to build up the party rapidly as a vanguard instrument to galvanize the masses and spur the workers to revolt. In a pamphlet titled "What Is to Be Done?" he proposed the transformation of the RSDLP into a compact and highly disciplined group of professional revolutionaries that would not merely ride the crest of the revolutionary wave but would unleash the storm clouds of revolt.

At the Second National Congress of the RSDLP, held in 1903 in Brussels and London, Lenin's ideas were supported by a majority of the delegates (thus the historical term *Bolsheviks,* or "majorityites," for his followers). His victory was short-lived, however, and for the next decade, Lenin, living in exile, was a brooding figure on the fringe of the Russian revolutionary movement, which was now dominated by the Mensheviks ("minorityites"), who opposed Lenin's single-minded pursuit of violent revolution.

From his residence in exile in Switzerland, Lenin heard the news of the collapse of the tsarist monarchy and decided to return to Russia. The German government thoughtfully provided him and his followers with a sealed railroad car to travel through Germany, undoubtedly in the hope that his presence would promote instability in Russia. On his arrival in Petrograd in April 1917, Lenin laid out a program for his followers: all power to the soviets (locally elected government councils), an end to the war, and the distribution of land to poor peasants. But Lenin's April Theses were too radical even for his fellow Bolsheviks, and his demands were ignored by other leaders, who continued to cooperate with the provisional government while attempting to push it to the left (see the box on p. 76).

The Bolshevik Revolution

During the summer, the crisis worsened, and in July, riots by workers and soldiers in the capital led the provisional government to outlaw the Bolsheviks and call for Lenin's arrest. The "July Days," raising the threat of disorder and class war, aroused the fears of conservatives and split the fragile political consensus within the provisional government. In September, General Lavr Kornilov, commander in chief of Russian imperial forces, launched a coup d'état to seize power from Alexander Kerensky, now the dominant figure in the provisional government. The revolt was put down with the help of so-called Red Guard units, formed by the Bolsheviks within army regiments in the capital area (these troops would later be regarded as the first units of the Red Army), but Lenin now sensed the weakness of the provisional government and persuaded his colleagues to prepare for revolt. On the night of November 7 (October 25 old style), forces under the command of Lenin's lieutenant, Leon Trotsky (1879–1940), seized key installations in the capital area. Kerensky fled from Russia in disguise. The following morning, at a national congress of delegates from soviet organizations throughout the country, the Bolsheviks declared a new socialist order. Moderate elements from the Menshevik faction and the Social Revolutionary Party protested the illegality of the Bolshevik action and left the conference hall in

ALL POWER TO THE SOVIETS!

*O*n his return to Petrograd in April 1917, the revolutionary Marxist Vladimir Lenin issued a series of proposals designed to overthrow the provisional government and bring his Bolshevik Party to power in Russia. At the time his April Theses were delivered, his ideas appeared to be too radical, even for his closest followers. By the end of the year, however, Lenin's compelling vision had been realized, and the world would never be the same again.

What were the key provisions of Lenin's April Theses? To what degree were they carried out?

Lenin's April Theses, 1917

2. The specific feature of the present situation in Russia is that the country is *passing* from the first stage of the revolution—which, owing to the insufficient class-consciousness and organisation of the proletariat, placed power in the hands of the bourgeoisie—to its *second* stage, which must place power in the hands of the proletariat and the poorest sections of the peasants. . . .

    This peculiar situation demands of us an ability to adapt ourselves to the *special* conditions of Party work among unprecedentedly large masses of proletarians who have just awakened to political life. . . .

3. No support for the Provisional Government: the utter falsity of all the promises should be made clear, particularly of those relating to the renunciation of annexations. Exposure in place of the impermissible, illusion-breeding

"demand" that *this* government of capitalists should *cease* to be an imperialist government.

The masses must be made to see that the Soviets of Workers' Deputies are the *only possible* form of revolutionary government, and that therefore our task is, as long as *this* government yields to the influence of the bourgeoisie, to present a patient, systematic and persistent explanation of the errors of their tactics, an explanation especially adapted to the practical needs of the masses.

As long as we are in the minority we carry on the work of criticising and exposing errors and at the same time we preach the necessity of transferring the entire state power to the Soviets of Workers' Deputies, so that the people may overcome their mistakes by experience.

Nationalisation of *all* lands in the country, the land to be disposed of by the local Soviets of Agricultural Labourers' and Peasants' Deputies. The organisation of separate Soviets of Deputies of Poor Peasants. The setting up of a model farm on each of the large estates (ranging in size from 100 to 300 dessiatines [about 270 to 810 acres], according to local and other conditions, and to the decisions of the local bodies) under the control of the Soviets of Agricultural Labourers' Deputies and for the public account.

SOURCE: V. I. Lenin, *Collected Works*, 4th ed. (Moscow: Progress, 1964), Vol. XXIV, pp. 21–24.

---

anger. They were derided by Trotsky, who proclaimed that they were relegated "to the dustbin of history."

With the Bolshevik Revolution of November 1917, Lenin was now in command. His power was tenuous and extended only from the capital to a few of the larger cities, such as Moscow and Kiev, that had waged their own insurrections. There were, in fact, few Bolsheviks in rural areas, where most peasants supported the moderate leftist Social Revolutionaries. On the fringes of the Russian Empire, restive minorities prepared to take advantage of the anarchy to seize their own independence, while "White Russian" supporters of the monarchy began raising armies to destroy the "Red menace" in Petrograd. Lenin was in power, but for how long?

The Bolshevik Revolution in Retrospect The Russian Revolution of 1917 has been the subject of vigorous debate by scholars and students of world affairs. Could it have been avoided if the provisional government had provided more effective leadership, or was it inevitable? Did Lenin stifle

Russia's halting progress toward a Western-style capitalist democracy, or was the Bolshevik victory preordained by the autocratic conditions and lack of democratic traditions in Imperial Russia? Such questions have no simple answers, but some hypotheses are possible. The weakness of the moderate government created by the March Revolution was probably predictable, given the political inexperience of the urban middle class and the deep divisions within the ruling coalition over issues of peace and war. On the other hand, it seems highly unlikely that the Bolsheviks would have possessed the self-confidence to act without the presence of their leader, Vladimir Lenin, who employed his strength of will to urge his colleagues almost single-handedly to make their bid for power. Without Lenin, it would probably have been left to the army to intervene in an effort to maintain law and order, as would happen so often elsewhere during the turbulent twentieth century.

In any event, the Bolshevik Revolution was a momentous development for Russia and for the entire world.

Lenin Addresses a Crowd. Vladimir Lenin was the driving force behind the success of the Bolsheviks in seizing power in Russia and creating the Union of Soviet Socialist Republics. Here Lenin is seen addressing a rally in Moscow in 1917.

Not only did it present Western capitalist societies with a brazen new challenge to their global supremacy, but it also demonstrated that Lenin's concept of revolution, carried through at the will of a determined minority of revolutionary activists "in the interests of the masses," could succeed in a society going through the difficult early stages of the Industrial Revolution. It was a repudiation of orthodox "late Marxism" and a return to Marx's pre-1848 vision of a multiclass revolt leading rapidly from a capitalist to a proletarian takeover (see Chapter 1). It was, in short, a lesson that would not be ignored by radical intellectuals throughout the world.

The Civil War

The Bolshevik seizure of power in Petrograd (soon to be renamed Leningrad after Lenin's death in 1924) was only the first, and not necessarily the most difficult, stage in the Russian Revolution. Although the Bolshevik slogan of "Peace, Land, and Bread" had earned considerable appeal among workers, petty merchants, and soldiers in the vicinity of the capital and other major cities, the party—only fifty thousand strong in November—had little representation in the rural areas, where the moderate leftist Social Revolutionary Party received majority support from the peasants. On the fringes of the Russian Empire, ethnic minority groups took advantage of the confusion in Petrograd to launch movements to restore their own independence or achieve a position of autonomy within the Russian state. In the meantime, supporters of the deposed Romanov dynasty and other political opponents of the Bolsheviks attempted to mobilize support to drive the Bolsheviks out of the capital and reverse the verdict of "Red October." And beyond all that, the war with Germany continued.

Lenin was aware of these problems and hoped that a wave of socialist revolutions in the economically advanced countries of central and western Europe would bring the world war to an end and usher in a new age of peace, socialism, and growing economic prosperity. In the meantime, his first priority was to consolidate the rule of the working class and its party vanguard (now to be renamed the Communist Party) in Russia. The first step was to set up a new order in Petrograd to replace the provisional government that itself had been created after the March Revolution. For lack of a better alternative, outlying areas were simply informed of the change in government—a "revolution by telegraph," as Leon Trotsky termed it. Then Lenin moved to create new organs of proletarian power, setting up the Council of People's Commissars to serve as a provisional government. Lenin was unwilling to share power with moderate leftists who had resisted the Bolshevik coup in November, and he created security forces (popularly called the Cheka, or "extraordinary commission"), which imprisoned and sometimes executed opponents of the new regime. In January 1918, the Constituent Assembly, which had been elected on the basis of plans established by the previous government, convened in Petrograd. Composed primarily of delegates from the Social Revolutionary Party and other parties opposed to the Bolsheviks, it showed itself critical of the new regime and was immediately abolished.

In foreign affairs, Lenin's first major decision was to seek peace with Germany in order to permit the new government to focus its efforts on the growing threat posed by White Russian forces within the country. In March 1918, a peace settlement with Germany was reached at Brest-Litovsk, although at enormous cost. Soviet Russia lost nearly one-fourth of the territory and one-third of the population of the prewar Russian Empire. In retrospect, however, Lenin's controversial decision to accept a punitive peace may have been a stroke of genius, for it gained time for the regime to build up its internal strength and defeat its many adversaries in the Russian Civil War (1918–1920). The White Russian forces were larger than those of the Red Army; they were supported by armed contingents sent by Great Britain, France, and the United States to assist in the extinction of the "Red menace"; but they were also rent by factionalism and hindered by the tendency of White

Russian leaders to return conquered land to the original landowners, thus driving many peasants to support the Soviet regime. By 1920, the civil war was over, and Soviet power was secure.

The Last Year of the War

For Germany, the withdrawal of the Russians from the war in March 1918 offered renewed hope for a favorable end to the war. The victory over Russia persuaded Erich von Ludendorff (1865–1937), who guided German military operations, and most German leaders to make one final military gamble—a grand offensive in the west to break the military stalemate. The German attack was launched in March and lasted into July, but an Allied counterattack, supported by the arrival of 140,000 fresh American troops, defeated the Germans at the Second Battle of the Marne on July 18. Ludendorff's gamble had failed. With the arrival of two million more American troops on the Continent, Allied forces began to advance steadily toward Germany.

On September 29, 1918, General Ludendorff informed German leaders that the war was lost and demanded that the government sue for peace at once. When German officials discovered that the Allies were unwilling to make peace with the autocratic imperial government, reforms were instituted to create a liberal government. But these constitutional reforms came too late for the exhausted and angry German people. On November 3, naval units in Kiel mutinied, and within days, councils of workers and soldiers were forming throughout northern Germany and taking over civilian and military administrations. William II, capitulating to public pressure, abdicated on November 9, and the Socialists under Friedrich Ebert (1871–1925) announced the establishment of a republic. Two days later, on November 11, 1918, the new German government agreed to an armistice. The war was over.

The final tally of casualties from the war was appalling. Nearly 10 million soldiers were dead, including 5 million on the Allied side and 3.5 million from the Central Powers (as Germany and its allies were known). Civilian deaths were nearly as high. France, which had borne much of the burden of the war, suffered nearly 2 million deaths, almost one-tenth of the entire male population of the country.

The Versailles Peace Conference

In January 1919, the delegations of twenty-seven victorious Allied nations gathered at the Palace of Versailles near Paris to conclude a final settlement of the Great War. Some delegates believed that this conference would avoid the mistakes made at Vienna in 1815 by aristocrats who rearranged the map of Europe to meet the selfish desires of the great powers. Harold Nicolson, one of the British delegates,

expressed what he believed this conference would achieve instead: "We were journeying to Paris not merely to liquidate the war, but to found a New Order in Europe. We were preparing not Peace only, but Eternal Peace. There was about us the halo of some divine mission. . . . For we were bent on doing great, permanent and noble things."[2]

The Vision of Woodrow Wilson National expectations, however, made Nicolson's quest for "eternal peace" a difficult one. Over the years, the reasons for fighting World War I had been transformed from selfish national interests to idealistic principles. No one expressed the latter better than Woodrow Wilson. The American president outlined to the U.S. Congress "Fourteen Points" that he believed justified the enormous military struggle then being waged. Later, Wilson spelled out additional steps for a truly just and lasting peace. Wilson's proposals included "open covenants of peace, openly arrived at" instead of secret diplomacy; the reduction of national armaments to a "point consistent with domestic safety"; and the self-determination of people so that "all well-defined national aspirations shall be accorded the utmost satisfaction." Wilson characterized World War I as a people's war waged against "absolutism and militarism," two scourges of liberty that could only be eliminated by creating democratic governments and a "general association of nations" that would guarantee "political independence and territorial integrity to great and small states alike." As the spokesman for a new world order based on democracy and international cooperation, Wilson was enthusiastically cheered by many Europeans when he arrived in Europe for the peace conference.

Wilson soon found, however, that other states at the conference were guided by considerably more pragmatic motives. The secret treaties and agreements that had been made before and during the war could not be totally ignored, even if they did conflict with Wilson's principle of self-determination (see Chapter 5). National interests also complicated the deliberations of the conference. David Lloyd George (1863–1945), prime minister of Great Britain, had won a decisive electoral victory in December 1918 on a platform of making the Germans pay for this dreadful war.

France's approach to peace was determined primarily by considerations of national security. To Georges Clemenceau, the feisty French premier who had led his country to victory, the French people had borne the brunt of German aggression and deserved security against any possible future attack. Clemenceau wanted a demilitarized Germany, vast reparations to pay for the costs of the war, and a separate Rhineland as a buffer state between France and Germany—demands that Wilson viewed as vindictive and contrary to the principle of national self-determination.

Although twenty-seven nations were represented at the Paris Peace Conference, the most important decisions were made by Wilson, Clemenceau, and Lloyd George. Italy was considered one of the so-called Big Four powers but played a much less important role than the other three countries. Germany was not invited to attend, and Russia could not because it was embroiled in civil war.

Forming the League of Nations In view of the many conflicting demands at Versailles, it was inevitable that the Big Three would quarrel. Wilson was determined to create a League of Nations to prevent future wars. Clemenceau and Lloyd George were equally determined to punish Germany. In the end, only compromise made it possible to achieve a peace settlement. On January 25, 1919, the conference adopted the principle of the League of Nations (the details of its structure were left for later sessions); Wilson willingly agreed to make compromises on territorial arrangements to guarantee the League's establishment, believing that a functioning League could later rectify bad arrangements. Clemenceau also compromised to obtain some guarantees for French security. He renounced France's desire for a separate Rhineland and instead accepted a defensive alliance with Great Britain and the United States, both of which pledged to help France if it were attacked by Germany.

The Peace Settlement The final peace settlement at Paris consisted of five separate treaties with the defeated nations—Germany, Austria, Hungary, Bulgaria, and Turkey. The Treaty of Versailles with Germany, signed on June 28, 1919, was by far the most important one. The Germans considered it a harsh peace and were particularly unhappy with Article 231, the so-called war guilt clause, which declared Germany (and Austria) responsible for starting the war and ordered Germany to pay reparations for all the damage to which the Allied governments and their people had been subjected as a result of the war "imposed upon them by the aggression of Germany and her allies."

The military and territorial provisions of the treaty also rankled the Germans, although they were by no means as harsh as the Germans claimed. Germany had to lower its army to 100,000 men, reduce its navy, and eliminate its air force. German territorial losses included the return of Alsace and Lorraine to France and sections of Prussia to the new Polish state. German land west and as far as 30 miles east of the Rhine was established as a demilitarized zone and stripped of all armaments or fortifications to serve as a barrier to any future German military moves westward against France. Outraged by the "dictated peace," the new German government complained but accepted the treaty.

The separate peace treaties made with the other Central Powers extensively redrew the map of eastern Europe (see Map 4.3). Many of these changes merely ratified what the war had already accomplished. Both Germany and Russia lost considerable territory in eastern Europe;

the Austro-Hungarian Empire disappeared altogether. New nation-states emerged from the lands of these three empires: Finland, Latvia, Estonia, Lithuania, Poland, Czechoslovakia, Austria, and Hungary. Territorial rearrangements were also made in the Balkans. Romania acquired additional lands from Russia, Hungary, and Bulgaria. Serbia formed the nucleus of a new South Slav state, called Yugoslavia, which combined Serbs, Croats, and Slovenes. Although the Paris Peace Conference was supposedly guided by the principle of self-determination, the mixtures of peoples in eastern Europe made it impossible to draw boundaries along neat ethnic lines. Compromises had to be made, sometimes to satisfy the national interest of the victors. France, for example, had lost Russia as its major ally on Germany's eastern border and wanted to strengthen and expand Poland, Czechoslovakia, Yugoslavia, and Romania as much as possible so that those states could serve as barriers against Germany and Communist Russia. As a result of compromises, virtually every eastern European state was left with a minorities problem that could lead to future conflicts. Germans in Poland; Hungarians, Poles, and Germans in Czechoslovakia; and the combination of Serbs, Croats, Slovenes, Macedonians, and Albanians in Yugoslavia all became sources of later conflict. Moreover, the new map of eastern Europe was based on the temporary collapse of power in both Germany and Russia. As neither country accepted the new eastern frontiers, it seemed only a matter of time before a resurgent Germany or Russia would seek to make changes.

A Punitive Peace? Within twenty years after the signing of the peace treaties, Europe was again engaged in deadly conflict. Some historians have suggested that the cause was the punitive nature of the peace terms imposed on the defeated powers, provoking anger that would lead to the rise of revanchist sentiment in Germany and Austria. Others maintain that the cause was less in the structure of the Versailles Treaty than in its lack of enforcement. Successful enforcement of the peace necessitated the active involvement of its principal architects, especially in helping the new German state develop a peaceful and democratic republic. By the end of 1919, however, the United States was already retreating into isolationism. The failure of the U.S. Senate to ratify the Treaty of Versailles meant that the United States never joined the League of Nations. The Senate also rejected Wilson's defensive alliance with Great Britain and France.

American withdrawal from the defensive alliance with Britain and France led Britain to withdraw as well. By removing itself from European affairs, the United States forced France to face its old enemy alone, leading the embittered nation to take strong actions against Germany that only intensified German resentment. By the end of 1919, it appeared that the peace was already beginning to unravel.

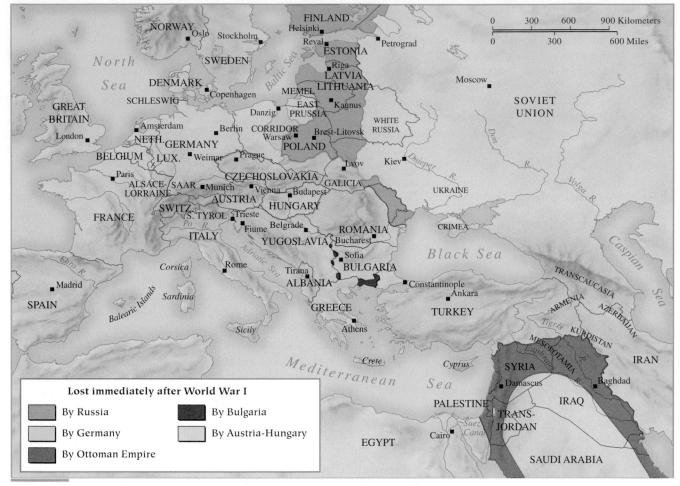

MAP 4.3 **Territorial Changes in Europe and the Middle East After World War I.** The victorious Allies met in Paris to determine the shape and nature of postwar Europe. At the urging of U.S. President Woodrow Wilson, many nationalist aspirations of former imperial subjects were realized with the creation of several new countries from the prewar territory of Austria-Hungary, Germany, Russia, and the Ottoman Empire. ❓ What new countries emerged in Europe and the Middle East?

🌀 View an animated version of this map or related maps at the World History Resource Center, at worldrc.wadsworth.com/.

The Failure of the Peace

In the years following the end of the war, many people hoped that Europe and the world were about to enter a new era of international peace, economic growth, and political democracy. In all of these areas, the optimistic hopes of the 1920s failed to be realized.

The Search for Security

The peace settlement at the end of World War I had tried to fulfill the nineteenth-century dream of nationalism by creating new boundaries and new states. From the outset, however, the settlement had left nations unhappy. Conflicts over disputed border regions between Germany and Poland, Poland and Lithuania, Poland and Czechoslovakia, Austria and Hungary, and Italy and Yugoslavia poisoned mutual relations in eastern Europe for years. Many Germans viewed the peace of Versailles as a dictated peace and vowed to seek its revision.

To its supporters, the League of Nations was the place to resolve such problems. The League, however, proved ineffectual in maintaining the peace. The failure of the United States to join the League (partially a consequence of public disillusionment with disputes at the Versailles conference) undermined the effectiveness of the League right from the start. Moreover, the League could use only economic sanctions to halt aggression. The French attempt to strengthen the League's effectiveness as an instrument of collective security by creating a peacekeeping force was rejected by nations that feared giving up any of their sovereignty to a larger international body.

The weakness of the League of Nations and the failure of both the United States and Great Britain to honor their defensive military alliances with France led the latter to insist on a strict enforcement of the Treaty of Versailles. This tough policy toward Germany began with the issue of reparations—the payments that the Germans were supposed to make to compensate for the "damage done to the civilian population of the Allied and Associated Powers and to their property," as the treaty asserted. In April 1921, the Allied Reparations Commission settled on a sum of 132 billion marks ($33 billion) for German reparations, payable in annual installments of 2.5 billion (gold) marks. Allied threats to occupy the Ruhr valley, Germany's chief industrial and mining center, induced the new German republic to accept the reparations settlement and to make its first payment in 1921. By the following year, however, facing rising inflation, domestic turmoil, and lack of revenues because of low tax rates, the German government announced that it was unable to pay more. Outraged by what they considered to be Germany's violation of one aspect of the peace settlement, the French government sent troops to occupy the Ruhr valley. If the Germans would not pay reparations, the French would collect reparations in kind by operating and using the Ruhr mines and factories.

French occupation of the Ruhr seriously undermined the fragile German economy. The German government adopted a policy of passive resistance to French occupation that was largely financed by printing more paper money, thus intensifying the inflationary pressures that had already begun at the end of the war. The German mark became worthless. Economic disaster fueled political upheavals as Communists staged uprisings in October and Adolf Hitler's band of Nazis attempted to seize power in Munich in 1923. The following year, a new conference of experts was convened to reassess the reparations problem.

The formation of liberal-socialist governments in both Great Britain and France opened the door to conciliatory approaches to Germany and the reparations problem. At the same time, a new German government led by Gustav Stresemann (1878–1929) ended the policy of passive resistance and committed Germany to carry out the provisions of the Versailles Treaty while seeking a new settlement of the reparations question.

In August 1924, an international commission produced a new plan for reparations. Named the Dawes Plan after the American banker who chaired the commission, it reduced reparations and stabilized Germany's payments on the basis of its ability to pay. The Dawes Plan also granted an initial $200 million loan for German recovery, which opened the door to heavy American investments in Europe that helped create a new era of European prosperity between 1924 and 1929.

The Spirit of Locarno A new approach to European diplomacy accompanied the new economic stability. A spirit of international cooperation was fostered by the foreign ministers of Germany and France, Gustav Stresemann and Aristide Briand (1862–1932), who concluded the Treaty of Locarno in 1925. This treaty guaranteed Germany's new western borders with France and Belgium. Although Germany's new eastern borders with Poland were conspicuously absent from the agreement, the Locarno pact was viewed by many as the beginning of a new era of European peace. On the day after the pact was concluded, the headline in the *New York Times* read "France and Germany Ban War Forever," and the London *Times* declared "Peace at Last."[3]

Germany's entry into the League of Nations in March 1926 soon reinforced the atmosphere of conciliation engendered at Locarno. Two years later, similar optimistic attitudes prevailed in the Kellogg-Briand Pact, drafted by U.S. Secretary of State Frank B. Kellogg and French Foreign Minister Briand. Sixty-three nations signed this accord, in which they pledged "to renounce war as an instrument of national policy." Nothing was said, however, about what would be done if anyone violated the treaty.

The spirit of Locarno was based on little real substance. Germany lacked the military power to alter its western borders even if it wanted to. Pious promises to renounce war without mechanisms to enforce them were virtually worthless. And the issue of disarmament soon proved that paper promises could not bring nations to cut back on their weapons. The League of Nations Covenant had recommended the "reduction of national armaments to the lowest point consistent with national safety." Numerous disarmament conferences, however, failed to achieve anything substantial as states proved unwilling to trust their security to anyone but their own military forces. By the time the World Disarmament Conference finally met in Geneva in 1932, the issue was already dead.

No Return to Normalcy

According to Woodrow Wilson, World War I had been fought "to make the world safe for democracy." In 1919, there seemed to be some justification for his claim. Four major European states and a host of minor ones had functioning political democracies. In a number of states, universal male suffrage had even been replaced by universal suffrage as male politicians rewarded women for their contributions to World

War I by granting them the right to vote (except in Italy, Switzerland, France, and Spain, where women had to wait until the end of World War II). In the 1920s, Europe seemed to be returning to the political trends of the prewar era—the broadening of parliamentary regimes and the fostering of individual liberties. But it was not an easy process; four years of total war and four years of postwar turmoil made "return to normalcy," in the words of Warren G. Harding, Wilson's successor as president, both difficult and troublesome.

After World War I, Great Britain went through a period of painful readjustment and serious economic difficulties. During the war, Britain had lost many of the markets for its industrial products, especially to the United States and Japan. The postwar decline of such staple industries as coal, steel, and textiles led to a rise in unemployment, which reached the two million mark in 1921. Britain experienced renewed prosperity between 1925 and 1929, but it proved relatively superficial. British exports in the 1920s never compensated for the overseas investments lost during the war, and even in these purportedly prosperous years, unemployment remained at a startling 10 percent. Coal miners were especially affected by the decline of the antiquated and inefficient British coal mines, which also suffered from a world glut of coal.

After the defeat of Germany and the demobilization of the German army, France became the strongest power on the European continent. Its biggest problem involved the reconstruction of the devastated areas of northern and eastern France. But neither the conservative National Bloc government nor a government coalition of leftist parties (the Cartel of the Left) seemed capable of solving France's financial problems between 1921 and 1926. The failure of the Cartel of the Left led to the return of the conservative Raymond Poincaré (1860–1934), whose government from 1926 to 1929 stabilized the French economy by means of a substantial increase in taxes during a period of relative prosperity.

When the German Empire came to an end with Germany's defeat in World War I, a democratic state known as the Weimar Republic was established. From its beginnings, the new republic was plagued by a series of problems. It had no truly outstanding political leaders, and those who were relatively able—including Friedrich Ebert, who served as president, and Gustav Stresemann, the foreign minister and chancellor—died in the 1920s. When Ebert died in 1925, Paul von Hindenburg (1847–1934), a World War I military hero, was elected president. Hindenburg was a traditional military officer, a monarchist in sentiment, who at heart was not in favor of the republic. The young republic also suffered politically from attempted uprisings and attacks from both the left and the right.

The Weimar Republic also faced serious economic difficulties. Germany experienced runaway inflation in 1922 and 1923, with grave social effects. Widows, orphans, the elderly, army officers, teachers, civil servants, and others who lived on fixed incomes all watched their monthly stipends become worthless or their lifetime savings disappear. Their economic losses increasingly pushed the middle class to the young German Communist Party or to rightist parties that were equally hostile to the republic.

The Great Depression

After World War I, most European states hoped to return to the liberal ideal of a market economy largely free of state intervention. But the war had vastly strengthened business cartels and labor unions, making some government regulation of these powerful organizations necessary. At the same time, reparations and war debts had severely distorted the postwar international economy, making the prosperity that did occur between 1924 and 1929 at best a fragile one and the dream of returning to a self-regulating market economy merely an illusion. What destroyed the concept altogether was the Great Depression.

Two factors played a major role in the coming of the Great Depression: a downturn in European economies and an international financial crisis created by the collapse of the American stock market in 1929. Already in the mid-1920s, prices for agricultural goods were beginning to decline rapidly as a result of the overproduction of basic commodities, such as wheat. In 1925, states in central and eastern Europe began to impose tariffs to close their markets to other countries' goods. And an increase in the use of oil and hydroelectricity led to a slump in the coal industry.

Much of the European prosperity in the mid-1920s was built on American bank loans to Germany, but in 1928 and 1929, American investors began to pull money out of Germany to invest in the booming New York stock market. When that market crashed in October 1929, panicky American investors withdrew even more of their funds from Germany and other European markets. The withdrawal of funds seriously weakened the banks of Germany and other central European states. The Credit-Anstalt, Vienna's most prestigious bank, collapsed on May 31, 1931. By that time, trade was slowing down, industrialists were cutting back production, and unemployment was increasing as the ripple effects of international bank failures had a devastating impact on domestic economies.

Repercussions in Europe Economic downturns were by no means a new phenomenon in European history, but the Great Depression was exceptionally severe and had immediate political repercussions. In Great Britain, the Labour Party, now the largest in the country, failed to resolve the crisis (at one point in the early 1930s, one British worker in four was unemployed) and fell from power in 1931. A new

The Great Depression: Bread Lines in Paris.
The Great Depression devastated the world economy and had serious political repercussions in many countries. Because of its more balanced economy, France did not feel the effects of the depression as quickly as other European countries. By 1931, however, even France was experiencing lines of unemployed people at free-food centers. Such scenes became familiar in industrialized countries around the world.

government dominated by the Conservatives took office and soon claimed credit for lifting the country out of the worst stages of the depression, primarily by using the traditional policies of balanced budgets and protective tariffs. British politicians largely ignored the new ideas of a Cambridge economist, John Maynard Keynes (1883–1946), whose 1936 *General Theory of Employment, Interest, and Money* took issue with the traditional view that depressions should be left to work themselves out through the self-regulatory mechanisms of a free economy. Keynes argued that unemployment stemmed not from overproduction but from a decline in consumer demand, which could be increased by public works, financed if necessary through deficit spending to stimulate production. Such policies, however, could be accomplished only by government intervention in the economy, a measure that British political leaders were unwilling to undertake.

France did not suffer from the effects of the Great Depression as soon as other countries because its economy was almost evenly divided between urban and agricultural pursuits, and a slight majority of French industrial plants were small enterprises. Consequently, France did not begin to face the crisis until 1931, but then it quickly led to political repercussions. During a nineteen-month period from 1932 to 1933, six different cabinets were formed as France faced political chaos.

The European nation that suffered the most damage from the depression was probably Germany. Unemployment increased to over four million by the end of 1930. For many Germans, who had already suffered through difficult times in the early 1920s, the democratic experiment represented by the Weimar Republic had become a nightmare. Some reacted by turning to Marxism because Karl Marx had long predicted that capitalism would destroy itself through overpopulation. As in several other European countries, communism took on a new popularity, especially with workers and intellectuals. But in Germany, the real beneficiary of the Great Depression was Adolf Hitler, whose Nazi Party came to power in 1933.

Franklin Roosevelt and the New Deal After Germany, no Western nation was more affected by the Great Depression than the United States. The full force of the depression had struck the United States by 1932. In that year, industrial production fell to 50 percent of what it had been in 1929. By 1933, there were 15 million unemployed. Under these circumstances, Democrat Franklin Delano Roosevelt (1882–1945) was able to win a landslide victory in the presidential election of 1932. Following the example of the American experience during World War I, his administration pursued a Keynesian policy of active government intervention in the economy that came to be known as the New Deal.

Initially, the New Deal attempted to restore prosperity by creating the National Recovery Administration (NRA), which required government, labor, and industrial leaders to work out regulations for each industry. Declared unconstitutional by the Supreme Court in 1935, the NRA was soon superseded by other efforts collectively known as the Second New Deal. Its programs included the Works Progress Administration (WPA), established in 1935, which employed between two and three million people building bridges, roads, post offices, airports, and other public works. The Roosevelt administration was also responsible for new social legislation that launched the American welfare state. In 1935, the Social Security Act created a system of old-age pensions and unemployment insurance. At the same time, the National Labor Relations Act of 1935 encouraged the rapid growth of labor unions.

The New Deal undoubtedly provided some social reform measures and may even have averted social revolution in the United States; it did not, however, solve the unemployment problems of the Great Depression. In May 1937, during what was considered a period of full recovery, American unemployment still stood at 7 million; a recession the following year increased that number to 11 million. Only World War II and the subsequent growth of armaments industries brought American workers back to full employment.

Socialism in One Country

With their victory over the White Russians in 1920, Soviet leaders now could turn for the first time to the challenging task of building the first socialist society in a world dominated by their capitalist enemies. In his writings, Karl Marx had said little about the nature of the final communist utopia or how to get there. He had spoken briefly of a transitional phase, variously known as "raw communism" or "socialism," that would precede the final stage of communism. During this phase, the Communist Party would establish a "dictatorship of the proletariat" to rid society of the capitalist oppressors, set up the institutions of the new order, and indoctrinate the population in the communist ethic. In recognition of the fact that traces of "bourgeois thinking" would remain among the population, profit incentives would be used to encourage productivity (in the slogan of Marxism, payment would be on the basis of "work" rather than solely on "need"), but major industries would be nationalized and private landholdings eliminated. After seizing power in 1917, however, the Bolsheviks were too preoccupied with survival to give much attention to the future nature of Soviet society. "War communism"—involving the government seizure of major industries, utilities, and sources of raw materials and the requisition of grain from private farmers—was, by Lenin's own admission, just a makeshift policy to permit the regime to mobilize resources for the civil war.

The New Economic Policy In 1920, it was time to adopt a more coherent approach. The realities were sobering. Soviet Russia was not an advanced capitalist society in the Marxist image, blessed with modern technology and an impoverished and politically aware underclass imbued with the desire to advance to socialism. It was poor and primarily agrarian, and its small but growing industrial sector had been ravaged by years of war. Under the circumstances, Lenin called for caution. He won his party's approval for a moderate program of social and economic development known as the New Economic Policy, or NEP. The program was based on a combination of capitalist and socialist techniques designed to

increase production through the use of profit incentives while at the same time promoting the concept of socialist ownership and maintaining firm party control over the political system and the overall direction of the economy. The "commanding heights" of the Soviet economy (heavy industry, banking, utilities, and foreign trade) remained in the hands of the state, while private industry and commerce were allowed to operate at the lower levels. The forced requisition of grain, which had caused serious unrest among the peasantry, was replaced by a tax, and land remained firmly in private hands. The theoretical justification for the program was that Soviet Russia now needed to go through its own "capitalist stage" (albeit under the control of the party) before beginning the difficult transition to socialism.

As an economic strategy, the NEP succeeded brilliantly. During the early and mid-1920s, the Soviet economy recovered rapidly from the doldrums of war and civil war. A more lax hand over the affairs of state allowed a modest degree of free expression of opinion within the ranks of the party and in Soviet society at large. Under the surface, however, trouble loomed. Lenin had been increasingly disabled by a bullet lodged in his neck from an attempted assassination, and he began to lose his grip over a fractious party. Even before his death in 1924, potential successors had begun to scuffle for precedence in the struggle to assume his position as party leader, the most influential position in the state. The main candidates were Leon Trotsky and a rising young figure from the state of Georgia, Joseph Djugashvili, better known by his revolutionary name, Stalin (1879–1953). Lenin had misgivings about all the candidates hoping to succeed him and suggested that a collective leadership best represented the interests of the party and the revolution. After his death in 1924, factional struggle among the leading figures in the party intensified. Although in some respects it was a pure power struggle, it did have policy ramifications as party factions debated about the NEP and its impact on the future of the Russian Revolution.

At first, the various factions were relatively evenly balanced, but Stalin proved adept at using his position as general secretary of the party to outmaneuver his rivals. By portraying himself as a centrist opposed to the extreme positions of his "leftist" (too radical in pursuit of revolutionary goals) or "rightist" (too prone to adopt moderate positions contrary to Marxist principles) rivals, he gradually concentrated power in his own hands.

In the meantime, the relatively moderate policies of the NEP continued to operate as the party and the state vocally encouraged the Soviet people, in a very un-Marxist manner, to enrich themselves. Capital investment and technological assistance from Western capitalist countries were actively welcomed. An observer at the time might reasonably have concluded that the Marxist vision of a world characterized by class struggle had become a dead letter.

The Advance to Socialism

Stalin had previously joined with the moderate members of the party to defend the NEP against Trotsky, whose "left opposition" wanted a more rapid advance toward socialism. Trotsky, who had become one of Stalin's chief critics, was expelled from the party in 1927. Then, in 1928, Stalin reversed course: he now claimed that the NEP had achieved its purpose and called for a rapid advance to socialist forms of ownership. Beginning in 1929, a series of new programs changed the face of Soviet society. Private capitalism in manufacturing and trade was virtually abolished, and state control over the economy was extended. The first of a series of five-year plans was launched to promote rapid "socialist industrialization," and in a massive effort to strengthen the state's hold over the agricultural economy, all private farmers were herded onto collective farms.

The bitter campaign to collectivize the countryside aroused the antagonism of many peasants and led to a decline in food production and in some areas to mass starvation. It also further divided the Communist Party and led to a massive purge of party members at all levels who opposed Stalin's effort to achieve rapid economic growth and the socialization of Russian society. A series of brutal purge trials eliminated thousands of "Old Bolsheviks" (people who had joined the party before the 1917 Revolution) and resulted in the conviction and death of many of Stalin's chief rivals. Trotsky, driven into exile, was dispatched by Stalin's assassin in 1940. Of the delegates who attended the National Congress of the CPSU (Communist Party of the Soviet Union) in 1934, fully 70 percent had been executed by the time of the National Congress in 1939.

The Legacy of Stalinism By the late 1930s, as the last of the great purge trials came to an end, the Russian Revolution had been in existence for more than two decades. It had achieved some successes. Stalin's policy of forced industrialization had led to rapid growth in the industrial sector, surpassing in many respects what had been achieved in the capitalist years prior to World War I. Between 1918 and 1937, steel production increased from 4 to 18 million tons per year, and hard coal output went from 36 to 128 million tons. New industrial cities sprang up overnight in the Urals and Siberia. The Russian people in general were probably better clothed, better fed, and better educated than they had ever been before. The cost had been enormous, however. Millions had died by bullet or starvation. Thousands, perhaps millions, languished in Stalin's concentration camps. The remainder of the population lived in a society now officially described as socialist, under the watchful eye of a man who had risen almost to the rank of a deity, the great leader of the Soviet Union, Joseph Stalin.

The impact of Joseph Stalin on Soviet society in one decade had been enormous. If Lenin had brought the party to power and nursed it through the difficult years of the civil war, it was Stalin, above all, who had mapped out the path to economic modernization and socialist transformation. To many foreign critics of the regime, the Stalinist terror and autocracy were an inevitable consequence of the concept of the vanguard party and the centralized state built by Lenin. Others traced Stalinism back to Marx. It was he, after all, who had formulated the idea of the dictatorship of the proletariat, which now provided ideological justification for the Stalinist autocracy. Still others found the ultimate cause in the Russian political culture, which had been characterized by autocracy since the emergence of Russian society from Mongol control in the fifteenth century.

Was Stalinism an inevitable outcome of Marxist-Leninist doctrine and practice? Or as Mikhail Gorbachev later claimed, were Stalin's crimes "alien to the nature of socialism" and a departure from the course charted by Lenin before his death? Certainly, Lenin had not envisaged a party dominated by a figure who became even larger than the organization itself and who, in the 1930s, almost destroyed the party. On the other hand, recent evidence shows that Lenin was capable of brutally suppressing perceived enemies of the revolution in a way that is reminiscent in manner, if not in scope, of Stalin's actions. It is also true that the state created by Lenin provided the conditions for a single-minded leader like Stalin to rise to absolute power. The great danger that neither Marx nor Lenin had foreseen had come to pass: the party itself, the vanguard organization leading the way into the utopian future, had become corrupted.

The Search for a New Reality in the Arts

The mass destruction brought on by World War I precipitated a general disillusionment with Western civilization on the part of artists and writers throughout Europe. Avant-garde art, which had sought to discover alternative techniques to portray reality, now gained broader acceptance as Europeans began to abandon classical traditions in an attempt to come to grips with the anxieties of the new age.

New Schools of Artistic Expression

A number of the artistic styles that gained popularity during the 1920s originated during the war in neutral Switzerland, where alienated intellectuals congregated at cafés to decry the insanity of the age and to exchange ideas on how to create a new and better world. One such group was the Dadaists, who sought to destroy the past with a vengeance, proclaiming their right to complete freedom of expression in art.

A flagrant example of Dada's revolutionary approach to art was the decision by French artist Marcel Duchamp (1887–1968) to enter a porcelain urinal in a 1917 art exhibit held in New York City. By signing it and giving it a title, Duchamp proclaimed that he had transformed the urinal into a work of art. Duchamp's Ready-Mades (as such art would henceforth be labeled) declared that whatever the artist proclaimed to be art was art. Duchamp's liberating concept served to open the floodgates of the art world, obliging the entire twentieth century to swim in this free-flowing, exuberant, exploratory, and often frightening torrent.

Probing the Subconscious While Dadaism flourished in Germany during the Weimar era, a school of Surrealism was established in Paris to liberate the total human experience from the restraints of the rational world. By using the subconscious, Surrealists hoped to resurrect the whole personality and reveal a submerged and illusive reality. Normally unrelated objects and people were juxtaposed in dreamlike and frequently violent paintings that were intended to shock the viewer into approaching reality from a totally fresh perspective. Most famous of the Surrealists was the Spaniard Salvador Dalí (1904–1989), who subverted the sense of reality in his painting by using near photographic detail in presenting a fantastic and irrational world.

Yet another modernist movement born on the eve of World War I was Abstract, or Nonobjective, painting. As one of its founders, Swiss artist Paul Klee (1879–1940), observed, "the more fearful this world becomes, . . . the more art becomes abstract."[4] Two of the movement's principal founders, Wassily Kandinsky (1866–1944) and Piet Mondrian (1872–1944), were followers of Theosophy, a religion that promised the triumph of the spirit in a new millennium. Since they viewed matter as an obstacle to salvation, the art of the new age would totally abandon all reference to the material world. Only abstraction, in the form of colorful forms and geometric shapes floating in space, could express the bliss and spiritual beauty of this terrestrial paradise.

A Musical Revolution Just as artists began to experiment with revolutionary ways to represent reality in painting, musicians searched for new revolutionary sounds. Austrian composer Arnold Schoenberg (1874–1951) rejected the traditional tonal system based on the harmonic triad that had dominated Western music since the Renaissance. To free the Western ear from traditional harmonic progression, Schoenberg substituted a radically new "atonal" system in which each piece established its own individual set of relationships and structure. In 1923, he devised a twelve-tone system in which he placed the twelve

Nonobjective Art. One artist who sought to break completely with the tradition of representative art was the Russian Kazimir Malevich (1878–1935), who painted geometric shapes that he felt expressed the dynamic rhythms of human experience. For Malevich, the square was the ideal geometric pattern because it is never found in nature, only in the mind, thus symbolizing his belief in the supremacy of pure thought. In this 1915 painting, *Red Square,* the color red seems to be thrusting outward as if seething with the political turmoil of Russia on the eve of the 1917 revolution. The square subsequently became a common motif in twentieth-century art.

pitches of the chromatic scale found on the piano in a set sequence for a musical composition. The ordering of these twelve tones was to be repeated throughout the piece, for all instrumental parts, constituting its melody and harmony. Even today, such atonal music seems inaccessible and incomprehensible to the uninitiated. Yet Schoenberg, perhaps more than any other modern composer, influenced the development of twentieth-century music.

Modernism in Architecture Other fields of artistic creativity, including sculpture, ballet, and architecture, also reflected these new directions. In Germany, a group of imaginative architects called the Bauhaus School created what is widely known as the international school, which soon became the dominant school of modern architecture. Led by the famous German architect Ludwig Mies van der Rohe (1881–1969), the internationalists promoted a new functional and unadorned style (Mies was widely known for observing that "less is more") characterized by high-rise towers of steel and glass that were reproduced endlessly throughout the second half of the century all around the world.

For many postwar architects, the past was the enemy of the future. In 1925, the famous French architect Le Corbusier (1877–1965) advocated razing much of the old city of Paris, to be replaced by modern towers of glass. In his plan, which called for neat apartment complexes separated by immaculate areas of grass, there was no room for people, pets, or nature. Fortunately, it was rejected by municipal authorities.

Culture for the Masses

During the postwar era, writers followed artists and architects in rejecting traditional forms in order to explore the subconscious. In his novel *Ulysses*, published in 1922, Irish author James Joyce (1882–1941) invented the "stream of consciousness" technique to portray the lives of ordinary people through the use of inner monologue. Joyce's technique exerted a powerful influence on literature for the remainder of the century. Some American writers, such as Ernest Hemingway (1899–1961), Theodore Dreiser (1871–1945), and Sinclair Lewis (1885–1951), reflected the rising influence of mass journalism in a new style designed to "tell it like it is." Such writers sought to report the "whole truth" in an effort to attain the authenticity of modern photography.

For much of the Western world, however, the best way to find (or escape) reality was in the field of mass entertainment. The 1930s represented the heyday of the Hollywood studio system, which in the single year of 1937 turned out nearly six hundred feature films. Supplementing the movies were cheap paperbacks and radio, which brought sports, soap operas, and popular music to the mass of the population. The radio was a great social leveler, speaking to all classes with the same voice. Such new technological wonders offered diversion even to the poor while helping to define the twentieth century as the era of the common people.

CONCLUSION

*W*ORLD WAR I SHATTERED the image of a liberal, rational society in early-twentieth-century Europe. The incredible destruction and the deaths of millions of people undermined the whole idea of progress. New propaganda techniques had manipulated entire populations into sustaining their involvement in a meaningless slaughter.

Who was responsible for the carnage? To the victorious Allied leaders, it was their defeated former adversaries, on whom they imposed harsh terms at the Versailles Peace Conference at the end of the war. In later years, however, some historians placed the blame on Russia for its decision to order full military mobilization in response to events taking place in the Balkans.

Perhaps, however, the real culprit was the system itself. In the first half of the nineteenth century, liberals had maintained that the organization of European states along national lines would lead to a peaceful Europe based on a sense of international fraternity. They had

been very wrong. The system of nation-states that emerged in Europe in the second half of the nineteenth century led not to cooperation but to competition. Governments that exercised restraint to avoid war wound up being publicly humiliated; those that went to the brink of war to maintain their national interests were often praised for having preserved national honor. As the British historian John Keegan has noted, for European statesmen in the early twentieth century, "the fear of not meeting a challenge was greater than the fear of war." In either case, by 1914, the major European states had come to believe that their allies were important and that their security depended on supporting those allies, even when they took foolish risks.

The growth of nationalism in the nineteenth century had yet another serious consequence. Not all ethnic groups had achieved the goal of nationhood. Slavic minorities in the Balkans and the polyglot Austro-Hungarian Empire, for example, still dreamed of creating their own national states. So did the Irish in the British Empire and the Poles in the Russian Empire, not to speak of the subject peoples living in colonial areas elsewhere around the globe. To a close observer of the global scene, the future must have looked ominous.

To make matters worse, the very industrial and technological innovations that brought the prospect of increased material prosperity for millions also led to the manufacture of new weapons of mass destruction such as long-range artillery, the tank, poison gas, and the airplane that would make war a more terrible prospect for those involved, whether military or civilian. If war did come, it would be highly destructive.

Victorious world leaders gathering at Versailles hoped to forge a peace settlement that would say good-bye to all that. But as it turned out, the turmoil wrought by World War I seemed to open the door to even greater insecurity. Revolutions in Russia and the Middle East dismembered old empires and created new states that gave rise to unexpected problems. Expectations that Europe and the world would return to normalcy were soon dashed by the failure to achieve a lasting peace, economic collapse, and the rise of authoritarian governments that not only restricted individual freedoms but sought even greater control over the lives of their subjects, manipulating and guiding their people to achieve the goals of their totalitarian regimes.

Finally, World War I brought an end to the age of European hegemony over world affairs. By virtually demolishing their own civilization on the battlegrounds of Europe in World War I, Europeans inadvertently encouraged the subject peoples of their vast colonial empires to initiate movements for national independence. In the next chapter, we examine some of those movements.

TIMELINE

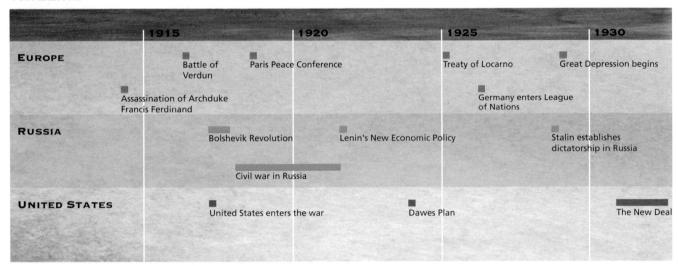

CHAPTER NOTES

1. A. Toynbee, *Surviving the Future* (New York, 1971), pp. 106–107.
2. Harold Nicolson, *Peacemaking, 1919* (Boston and New York, 1933), pp. 31–32.
3. Quoted in Robert Paxton, *Europe in the Twentieth Century*, 2d ed. (San Diego, 1985), p. 237.
4. Quoted in Nikos Stangos, *Concepts of Modern Art: From Fauvism to Postmodernism*, 3d ed. (London, 1994), p. 44.

WORLD HISTORY
RESOURCE CENTER

Visit the *Twentieth-Century World History* Book Companion Website for resources specific to this textbook:
academic.cengage.com/history/duiker
The Wadsworth World History Resource Center at worldrc.wadsworth.com/ offers a variety of tools to help you succeed in this course, including access to quizzes; images; documents; interactive simulations, maps, and timelines; movie explorations; and a wealth of other sources.

CHAPTER

5

NATIONALISM, REVOLUTION, AND DICTATORSHIP: AFRICA, ASIA, AND LATIN AMERICA FROM 1919 TO 1939

IN 1930, MOHANDAS GANDHI, the sixty-one-year-old leader of the nonviolent movement for Indian independence from British rule, began a march to the sea with seventy-eight followers. Their destination was Dandi, a little coastal town some 240 miles away. The group covered about 12 miles a day. As they went, Gandhi preached his doctrine of nonviolent resistance to British rule in every village he passed through: "Civil disobedience is the inherent right of a citizen. He dare not give it up without ceasing to be a man." By the time he reached Dandi, twenty-four days later, his small group had become a nonviolent army of thousands. When they arrived at Dandi, Gandhi picked up a pinch of salt from the sand. All along the coast, thousands did likewise, openly breaking British laws that prohibited Indians from making their own salt. The British had long profited from their monopoly on the making and sale of salt, an item much in demand in a tropical country. By their simple acts of disobedience, Gandhi and the Indian people had taken a bold step on their long march to independence.

The salt march was but one of many nonviolent activities that Mohandas Gandhi undertook between World War I and World War II to win India's goal of national independence from British rule. World War I had not only deeply affected the lives of Europeans, but also undermined the prestige of Western civilization in the minds of many observers in the rest of the world. When Europeans devastated their own civilization on the battlefields of Europe, the subject peoples of their vast colonial empires were quick to understand what it meant. In Africa and Asia, movements for national independence began to take shape. Some were inspired by the nationalist and liberal movements of the West, while others began to look toward the new Marxist model provided by the victory of the Communists in the Soviet Union, who soon worked to spread their revolutionary vision to African and Asian societies. In the Middle East, World War I ended the rule of the Ottoman Empire and led to the creation of new states, some of which adopted Western features. For some Latin American countries, the fascist dictatorships of Italy and Germany provided models for change. ◇

The Rise of Nationalism in Asia and Africa

Although the West had emerged from World War I relatively intact, its political and social foundations and its self-confidence had been severely undermined by the experience. Within Europe, doubts about the future viability of Western civilization were widespread, especially among the intellectual elite. These doubts were quick to reach the attention of perceptive observers in Asia and Africa and contributed to a rising tide of unrest against Western political domination throughout the colonial and semicolonial world. That unrest took a variety of forms but was most notably displayed in increasing worker activism, rural protest, and a rising sense of national fervor among anticolonialist intellectuals. Where independent states had successfully resisted the Western onslaught, the discontent fostered by the war and later by the Great Depression led to a loss of confidence in democratic institutions and the rise of political dictatorships.

As we have seen (see Chapter 1), nationalism refers to a state of mind rising out of an awareness of being part of a community that possesses common institutions, traditions, language, and customs. Unfortunately, even today few nations in the world meet such criteria. Most modern states contain a variety of ethnic, religious, and linguistic communities, each with its own sense of cultural and national identity. How does nationalism differ from tribal, religious, linguistic, or other forms of affiliation? Should every group that resists assimilation into a larger cultural unity be called nationalist?

Such questions complicate the study of nationalism and make agreement on a definition elusive. They create a particular dilemma in discussing Asia and Africa, where most societies are deeply divided by ethnic, linguistic, and religious differences and the very concept of nationalism is a foreign phenomenon imported from the West. Prior to the colonial era, most traditional societies in Africa and Asia were unified on the basis of religious beliefs, community loyalties, or devotion to hereditary monarchies. Individuals in some countries identified themselves as members of a particular national group, while others viewed themselves as subjects of a king, members of a caste, or adherents of a particular religion.

The advent of European colonialism brought the consciousness of modern nationhood to many societies in Asia and Africa. The creation of colonies with defined borders and a powerful central government weakened local ties and reoriented individuals' sense of political identity. The introduction of Western ideas of citizenship and representative government engendered a new sense of participation in the affairs of government. At the same time, the appearance of a new elite class based not on hereditary privilege or religious sanction but on alleged racial or cultural superiority aroused a shared sense of resentment among the subject peoples who felt a common commitment to the creation of an independent society. By the first quarter of the twentieth century, political movements dedicated to the overthrow of colonial rule had arisen throughout much of the non-Western world.

Nationalist movements in Asia and Africa, then, were a product of colonialism and, in a sense, a reaction to it. But a sense of nationhood does not emerge full-blown in a society. It begins among a few members of the educated elite (most commonly among articulate professionals such as lawyers, teachers, journalists, and doctors) and spreads gradually to the mass of the population. Only then has a true sense of nationhood been created.

Traditional Resistance: A Precursor to Nationalism

If we view the concept of nationalism as a process by which people in a given society gradually become aware of themselves as members of a particular nation, with its own culture and aspirations, then it is reasonable to seek the beginnings of modern nationalism in Asia and Africa in the initial resistance by the indigenous peoples to the colonial conquest itself. Although essentially motivated by the desire to defend traditional institutions, such movements reflected an early awareness of nationhood in that they sought to protect the homeland from the invader. Thus, traditional resistance to colonial conquest may logically be viewed as the first stage in the development of modern nationalism.

Such resistance took various forms. For the most part, it was led by the existing ruling class. In the Ashanti kingdom in West Africa and in Burma and Vietnam in Southeast Asia, the resistance to Western domination was initially directed by the imperial courts. In some cases, however, traditionalist elements continued to oppose foreign conquest even after resistance had collapsed at the center. In Japan, conservative elements opposed the decision of the Tokugawa shogunate in Tokyo to accommodate the Western presence and launched an abortive movement to defeat the foreigners and restore Japan to its previous policy of isolation (see Chapter 3). In India, Tipu Sultan resisted the British in the Deccan plateau region of central India after the collapse of the Mughal dynasty. Similarly, after the decrepit monarchy in Vietnam had bowed to French pressure and agreed to the concession of territory in the south and the establishment of a protectorate over the remainder of the country, a number of civilian and military officials set up an organization called Can Vuong (literally,

"Save the King") and continued their resistance without imperial sanction.

The Sepoy Rebellion Sometimes traditional resistance had a religious basis, as in the Sudan, where a revolt against the growing British presence had strong Islamic overtones, although it was initially provoked by Turkish misrule in Egypt. More significant was the famous Sepoy Rebellion of 1857 in India. The sepoys (derived from the Turkish word for "horseman" or "soldier") were native troops hired by the East India Company to protect British interests in the region. Unrest within Indian units of the colonial army had been common since early in the century, when it had been sparked by economic issues, religious sensitivities, or nascent anticolonial sentiment. Such attitudes intensified in the mid-1850s when the British instituted a new policy of shipping Indian troops abroad—a practice that exposed Hindus to pollution by foreign cultures. In 1857, tension erupted when the British adopted the new Enfield rifle for use by sepoy infantrymen. The new weapon was a muzzle-loader that used paper cartridges covered with animal fat and lard; the cartridge had to be bitten off, but doing so violated strictures against high-caste Hindus' eating animal products and Muslim prohibitions against eating pork. Protests among sepoy units in northern India turned into a full-scale rebellion, supported by uprisings in rural districts in various parts of the country. But the revolt lacked clear goals, and rivalries between Hindus and Muslims and discord among leaders within each community prevented coordination of operations. Although Indian troops often fought bravely and outnumbered the British by 240,000 to 40,000, they were poorly organized, and the British forces (supplemented in many cases by sepoy troops) suppressed the rebellion.

Still, the revolt frightened the British and led to a number of major reforms. The proportion of native troops relative to those from Great Britain was reduced, and precedence was given to ethnic groups likely to be loyal to the British, such as the Sikhs of Punjab and the Gurkhas, an upland people from Nepal in the Himalaya Mountains. To avoid religious conflicts, ethnic groups were spread throughout the service rather than assigned to special units. The British also decided to suppress the final remnants of the hapless Mughal dynasty, which had supported the rebellion, and place the governance of India directly under the British Crown.

As noted earlier, such forms of resistance cannot properly be called nationalist because they were essentially attempts to protect or restore traditional society and its institutions and were not motivated by the desire to create a nation in the modern sense of the word. In any event, such movements rarely met with success. Peasants armed with pikes and spears were no match for Western armies possessing the most terrifying weapons then known to human society, including the Gatling gun, the first rapid-fire weapon and the precursor of the modern machine gun.

Modern Nationalism

The first stage of resistance to the West in Asia and Africa must have confirmed many Westerners' conviction that colonial peoples lacked both the strength and the know-how to create modern states and govern their own destinies.

In fact, however, the process was just beginning. The next phase began to take shape at the beginning of the twentieth century and was the product of the convergence of several factors. The primary sources of anticolonialist sentiment were found in a new class of Westernized intellectuals in the urban centers created by colonial rule. In many cases, this new urban middle class, composed of merchants, petty functionaries, clerks, students, and professionals, had been educated in Western-style schools. A few had spent time in the West. In either case, they were the first generation of Asians and Africans to possess more than a rudimentary understanding of the institutions and values of the modern West.

The Paradox of Nationalism The results were paradoxical. On the one hand, this new class admired Western culture and sometimes harbored a deep sense of contempt for traditional ways. On the other hand, many strongly resented the gap between ideal and reality, theory and practice, in colonial policy. Although Western political thought exalted democracy, equality, and individual freedom, these values were generally not applied in the colonies. Democratic institutions were primitive or nonexistent, and colonial subjects usually had access to only the most menial positions in the colonial bureaucracy.

Equally important, the economic prosperity of the West was only imperfectly reflected in the colonies. Normally, middle-class Asians did not suffer in the same manner as impoverished peasants or menial workers on sugar or rubber plantations, but they, too, had complaints. They usually qualified only for menial jobs in the government or business. Even when employed, their salaries were normally lower than those of Europeans in similar occupations. The superiority of the Europeans over the natives was expressed in a variety of ways, including "whites only" clubs and the forms of language used to address colonial subjects. For example, Europeans would characteristically use the familiar form of direct address (normally used by adults to children) when talking to members of the local population in their own language.

Out of this mixture of hopes and resentments emerged the first stirrings of modern nationalism in Asia and Africa. During the first quarter of the twentieth century, in colonial and semicolonial societies across the entire arc of Asia from the Suez Canal to the shores of the Pacific Ocean, educated native peoples began to organize political parties and movements seeking reforms or the end of foreign rule and the restoration of independence.

At first, many of the leaders of these movements did not focus clearly on the idea of nationhood but tried to defend the economic interests or religious beliefs of the native population. In Burma, for example, the first expression of modern nationalism came from students at the University of Rangoon, who formed an organization to protest against official persecution of the Buddhist religion and British lack of respect for local religious traditions. Calling themselves Thakin (a polite term in the Burmese language meaning "lord" or "master," thus emphasizing their demand for the right to rule themselves), they protested against British arrogance and failure to observe local customs in Buddhist temples (visitors are expected to remove their footwear in a temple, a custom that was widely ignored by Europeans in colonial Burma). Eventually, however, they began to focus specifically on the issue of national independence.

A similar movement arose in the Dutch East Indies, where the first quasi-political organization dedicated to the creation of a modern Indonesia, the Sarekat Islam (Islamic Association), began as a self-help society among Muslim merchants to fight against domination of the local economy by Chinese interests. Eventually, activist elements began to realize that the source of the problem was not the Chinese merchants but the colonial presence, and in the 1920s, Sarekat Islam was transformed into a new organization—the Nationalist Party of Indonesia (PNI)—that focused on the issue of national independence. Like the Thakins in Burma, this party would eventually lead the country to independence after World War II.

Independence or Modernization? The Nationalist Quandary
Building a new nation, however, requires more than a shared sense of grievances against the foreign invader. By what means was independence to be achieved? Should independence or modernization be the first priority? What kind of political and economic system should be adopted once colonial rule had been overthrown? What national or cultural concept should be adopted as the symbol of the new nation, and which institutions and values should be preserved from the past?

Questions such as these triggered lively and sometimes acrimonious debates among patriotic elements throughout the colonial world. If national independence was the desired end, how could it be achieved? Could the

Westerners be persuaded to leave by nonviolent measures, or would force be required? If the Western presence could be beneficial in terms of introducing much-needed reforms in traditional societies, then a gradualist approach made sense. On the other hand, if the colonial regime was viewed as an impediment to social and political change, then the first priority was to bring it to an end.

Another problem was how to adopt modern Western ideas and institutions while preserving the essential values that defined the indigenous culture. One of the reasons for using traditional values was to provide ideological symbols that the common people could understand. If the desired end was national independence, then the new political parties needed to enlist the mass of the population in the common struggle. But how could peasants, plantation workers, fishermen, and shepherds be made to understand complicated and unfamiliar concepts like democracy, industrialization, and nationhood? The problem was often one of communication, for most urban intellectuals had little in common with the teeming population in the countryside. As the Indonesian intellectual Sutan Sjahrir lamented, many Westernized intellectuals had more in common with their colonial rulers than with the native population in the rural villages (see the box on p. 93).

Gandhi and the Indian National Congress

Nowhere in the colonial world were these issues debated more vigorously than in India. Before the Sepoy Rebellion, Indian consciousness had focused primarily on the question of religious identity. But in the latter half of the nineteenth century, a stronger sense of national consciousness began to arise, provoked by the conservative policies and racial arrogance of the British colonial authorities.

The first Indian nationalists were almost invariably upper class and educated. Many of them were from urban areas such as Bombay, Madras, and Calcutta. Some were trained in law and were members of the civil service. At first, many tended to prefer reform to revolution and accepted the idea that India needed modernization before it could handle the problems of independence. An exponent of this view was Gopal Gokhale (1866–1915), a moderate nationalist who hoped that he could convince the British to bring about needed reforms in Indian society. Gokhale and other like-minded reformists did have some effect. In the 1880s, the government launched a series of reforms introducing a measure of self-government for the first time. All too often, however, such efforts were sabotaged by local British officials.

The Indian National Congress The slow pace of reform convinced many Indian nationalists that relying on British benevolence was futile. In 1885, a small group of Indians met in Bombay to form the Indian National Congress (INC).

THE DILEMMA OF THE INTELLECTUAL

Sutan Sjahrir (1909–1966) was a prominent leader of the Indonesian nationalist movement who briefly served as prime minister of the Republic of Indonesia in the 1950s. Like many Western-educated Asian intellectuals, he was tortured by the realization that by education and outlook he was closer to his colonial masters—in his case, the Dutch— than to his own people. He wrote the following passage in a letter to his wife in 1935 and later included it in his book Out of Exile.

Why does the author feel estranged from his native culture? What is his answer to the challenges faced by his country in coming to terms with the modern world?

Sutan Sjahrir, *Out of Exile*

Am I perhaps estranged from my people? . . . Why are the things that contain beauty for them and arouse their gentler emotions only senseless and displeasing for me? In reality, the spiritual gap between my people and me is certainly no greater than that between an intellectual in Holland . . . and the undeveloped people of Holland. . . . The difference is rather . . . that the intellectual in Holland does not feel this gap because there is a portion—even a fairly large portion—of his own people on approximately the same intellectual level as himself. . . .

This is what we lack here. Not only is the number of intellectuals in this country smaller in proportion to the total population—in fact, very much smaller—but in addition, the few who are here do not constitute any single entity in spiritual outlook, or in any spiritual life or single culture

whatsoever. . . . It is for them so much more difficult than for the intellectuals in Holland. In Holland they build—both consciously and unconsciously—on what is already there. . . . Even if they oppose it, they do so as a method of application or as a starting point.

In our country this is not the case. Here there has been no spiritual or cultural life, and no intellectual progress for centuries. There are the much-praised Eastern art forms but what are these except bare rudiments from a feudal culture that cannot possibly provide a dynamic fulcrum for people of the twentieth century? . . . Our spiritual needs are needs of the twentieth century; our problems and our views are of the twentieth century. Our inclination is no longer toward the mystical, but toward reality, clarity, and objectivity. . . .

We intellectuals here are much closer to Europe or America than we are to the Borobudur or Mahabharata or to the primitive Islamic culture of Java and Sumatra. . . .

So, it seems, the problem stands in principle. It is seldom put forth by us in this light, and instead most of us search unconsciously for a synthesis that will leave us internally tranquil. We want to have both Western science and Eastern philosophy, the Eastern "spirit," in the culture. But what is this Eastern spirit? It is, they say, the sense of the higher, of spirituality, of the eternal and religious, as opposed to the materialism of the West. I have heard this countless times, but it has never convinced me.

SOURCE: From *The World of Southeast Asia: Selected Historical Readings,* Harry J. Benda and John A. Larkin, eds. Copyright © 1967 by Harper & Row, Publishers.

They hoped to speak for all India, but most were high-caste English-trained Hindus. Like their reformist predecessors, members of the INC did not demand immediate independence and accepted the need for reforms to end traditional abuses like child marriage and *sati* (see Chapter 2). At the same time, they called for an Indian share in the governing process and more spending on economic development and less on military campaigns along the frontier.

The British responded with a few concessions, such as accepting the principle of elective Indian participation on government councils, but in general, change was glacially slow. As impatient members of the INC became disillusioned, radical leaders such as Balwantrao Tilak (1856–1920) openly criticized the British while defending traditional customs like child marriage to solicit support from conservative elements within the local population. Tilak's activities split the INC between moderates and radicals, and he and

his followers formed the New Party, which called for the use of terrorism and violence to achieve national independence. Tilak was eventually convicted of sedition.

The INC also had difficulty reconciling religious differences within its ranks. The stated goal of the INC was to seek self-determination for all Indians regardless of class or religious affiliation, but many of its leaders were Hindu and inevitably reflected Hindu concerns. By the first decade of the twentieth century, Muslims began to call for the creation of a separate Muslim League to represent the interests of the millions of Muslims in Indian society.

India's "Great Soul," Mohandas Gandhi In 1915, the return of a young Hindu lawyer from South Africa transformed the movement and galvanized India's struggle for independence and identity. Mohandas Gandhi was born in 1869 in Gujarat, in western India, the son of a government minister. In the late nineteenth century, he studied in London and became a lawyer. In 1893, he went to South Africa to work in a law firm serving Indian émigrés working as laborers there. He soon became aware of the racial prejudice and exploitation experienced by Indians living in the territory and tried to organize them to protest their living conditions.

Nonviolent Resistance On his return to India, Gandhi immediately became active in the independence movement. Using his experience in South Africa, he set up a movement based on nonviolent resistance (the Indian term was *satyagraha,* "hold fast to the truth") to try to force the British to improve the lot of the poor and grant independence to India. Gandhi was particularly concerned about the plight of the millions of "untouchables" (the lowest social class in traditional India), whom he called *harijans,* or "children of God." When the British attempted to suppress dissent, he called on his followers to refuse to obey British regulations. He began to manufacture his own clothes (dressing in a simple *dhoti* made of coarse homespun cotton) and adopted the spinning wheel as a symbol of Indian resistance to imports of British textiles.

Gandhi, now increasingly known as India's "Great Soul" (*Mahatma*), organized mass protests to achieve his aims, but in 1919, they got out of hand and led to British reprisals. British troops killed hundreds of unarmed protesters in the enclosed square in the city of Amritsar in northwestern India. When the protests spread, Gandhi was horrified at the violence and briefly retreated from active politics. Nevertheless, he was arrested for his role in the protests and spent several years in prison.

Gandhi combined his anticolonial activities with an appeal to the spiritual instincts of all Indians. Though born and raised a Hindu, he possessed a universalist approach to the idea of God that transcended individual religion, although it was shaped by the historical themes of Hindu religious belief. At a speech given in London in September 1931, he expressed his view of the nature of God as "an indefinable mysterious power that pervades everything . . . , an unseen power which makes itself felt and yet defies all proof."

In 1921, the British passed the Government of India Act to expand the role of Indians in the governing process and transform the heretofore advisory Legislative Council into a bicameral parliament, two-thirds of whose members would be elected. Similar bodies were created at the provincial level. In a stroke, five million Indians were enfranchised. But such reforms were no longer enough for many members of the INC, which under its new leader, Motilal Nehru, wanted to

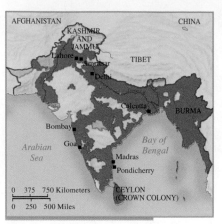

British India Between the Wars

push aggressively for full independence. The British exacerbated the situation by increasing the salt tax and prohibiting the Indian people from manufacturing or harvesting their own salt. On release from prison, Gandhi resumed his policy of civil disobedience by openly joining several dozen supporters in a 240-mile walk to the sea, where he picked up a lump of salt and urged Indians to ignore the law. Gandhi and many other members of the INC were arrested.

New Leaders, New Problems In the 1930s, a new figure entered the movement in the person of Jawaharlal Nehru (1889–1964), son of the INC leader Motilal Nehru. Educated in the law in Great Britain and a *brahmin* (member of the highest social class) by birth, Nehru personified the new Anglo-Indian politician: secular, rational, upper class, and intellectual. In fact, he appeared to be everything that Gandhi was not. With his emergence, the independence movement embarked on dual paths: religious and secular, native and Western, traditional and modern. The dichotomous

Nehru and Gandhi. Mahatma Gandhi (on the right), India's "Great Soul," became the emotional leader of India's struggle for independence from British colonial rule. Unlike many other nationalist leaders, Gandhi rejected the materialistic culture of the West and urged his followers to return to the native traditions of the Indian village. To illustrate his point, Gandhi dressed in the simple Indian *dhoti* rather than in the Western fashion favored by many of his colleagues. Along with Gandhi, Jawaharlal Nehru was a leading figure in the Indian struggle for independence. Unlike Gandhi, however, his goal was to transform India into a modern industrial society. After independence, he became the nation's prime minister until his death in 1964.

character of the INC leadership may well have strengthened the movement by bringing together the two primary impulses behind the desire for independence: elite nationalism and the primal force of Indian traditionalism. But it portended trouble for the nation's new leadership in defining India's future path in the contemporary world. In the meantime, Muslim discontent with Hindu dominance over the INC was increasing. In 1940, the Muslim League called for the creation of a separate Muslim state, to be known as Pakistan ("Land of the Pure"), in the northwest. As communal strife between Hindus and Muslims increased, many Indians came to realize with sorrow (and some British colonialists with satisfaction) that British rule was all that stood between peace and civil war.

The Nationalist Revolt in the Middle East

In the Middle East, as in Europe, World War I hastened the collapse of old empires. The Ottoman Empire, which had been growing steadily weaker since the end of the eighteenth century, would not long survive the end of the war.

The Ottoman Empire in Transition Reformist elements in Istanbul (as Constantinople was officially renamed in 1930), to be sure, had tried to resist the decline. The first efforts had taken place in the eighteenth century, when Westernizing forces, concerned at the shrinkage of the empire, had tried to modernize the army. One energetic sultan, Selim III (r. 1789–1807), tried to establish a "new order" that would streamline both the civilian and military bureaucracies, but conservative elements in the emperor's private guard, alarmed at the potential loss of their power, revolted and brought the experiment to an end. Further efforts during the first half of the nineteenth century were somewhat more successful and resulted in a series of bureaucratic, military, and educational reforms. New roads were built, the power of local landlords was reduced, and an Imperial Rescript issued in 1856 granted equal rights to all subjects of the empire, whatever their religious preference. In the 1870s, a new generation of reformers seized power in Istanbul and pushed through a constitution aimed at forming a legislative assembly that would represent all the peoples in the state. But the sultan they placed on the throne, Abdulhamid (r. 1876–1909), suspended the new charter and attempted to rule by traditional authoritarian means.

The "Young Turks" By the end of the nineteenth century, the defunct 1876 constitution had become a symbol of change for reformist elements,

now grouped together under the common name Young Turks. In 1908, Young Turk elements forced the sultan to restore the constitution, and he was removed from power the following year.

But the Young Turks had appeared at a moment of extreme fragility for the empire. Internal rebellions, combined with Austrian annexations of Ottoman territories in the Balkans, undermined support for the new government and provoked the army to step in. With most minorities from the old empire now removed from Turkish authority, many ethnic Turks began to embrace a new concept of a Turkish state based on all residents of Turkish nationality.

The final blow to the old empire came in World War I, when the Ottoman government chose the wrong side during the war and lost much of its territory in the peace settlement. To gain Arab support against the Turks, the Western allies had promised to recognize the independence of Arab areas then under Ottoman occupation. But imperialist habits died hard. Although Saudi Arabia eventually received full independence, much of the remainder of the region was assigned to Great Britain (Iraq and Jordan) and France (Syria and Lebanon) as mandates under the new League of Nations. The peace settlement had established the mandate system at the insistence of Woodrow Wilson, who opposed outright annexation of colonial territories by the allies.

Mustafa Kemal and the Modernization of Turkey As the Ottoman Empire began to fall apart at the end of the war, the Greeks won Allied approval to seize the western parts of the Anatolian peninsula for their dream of re-creating the substance of the old Byzantine Empire. The impending collapse energized key elements in Turkey under the leadership of war hero Colonel Mustafa Kemal (1881–1938), who had commanded Turkish forces in their heroic defense of the Dardanelles against a British invasion during World War I. Now he resigned from the army and convoked a national congress that called for the creation of an elected government and the preservation of the remaining territories of the old empire in a new republic of Turkey. Establishing the new capital at Ankara, Kemal's forces drove the Greeks from the Anatolian peninsula and persuaded the British to agree to a new treaty. In 1923, the last of the Ottoman sultans fled the country, which was now declared a Turkish republic. The Ottoman Empire had finally come to an end.

During the next few years, President Mustafa Kemal (now popularly known as Atatürk, or "Father Turk") attempted to transform Turkey

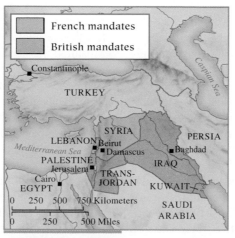

French mandates

British mandates

Constantinople

TURKEY

Caspian Sea

SYRIA

LEBANON Beirut

PERSIA

Mediterranean Sea Damascus Baghdad

PALESTINE IRAQ

Jerusalem

Cairo TRANS-

EGYPT JORDAN KUWAIT

0 250 500 750 Kilometers

SAUDI

0 250 500 Miles ARABIA

The Middle East in 1919

MUSTAFA KEMAL'S CASE AGAINST THE CALIPHATE

*A*s part of his plan to transform Turkey into a modern society, Mustafa Kemal Atatürk proposed bringing an end to the caliphate, which had been in the hands of Ottoman sultans since the formation of the empire. In the following passage from a speech to the National Assembly, he gives his reasons.

When and why was the caliphate system first established? Why does Mustafa Kemal believe that it no longer meets the needs of the Turkish people?

Atatürk's Speech to the Assembly, October 1924

The monarch designated under the title of Caliph was to guide the affairs of [all] Muslim peoples and to secure the execution of the religious prescriptions which would best correspond to their worldly interests. He was to defend the rights of all Muslims and concentrate all the affairs of the Muslim world in his hands with effective authority.

The sovereign entitled Caliph was to maintain justice among the three hundred million Muslims on the terrestrial globe, to safeguard the rights of these peoples, to prevent any event that could encroach upon order and security, and confront every attack which the Muslims would be called upon to encounter from the side of other nations. It was to be part of his attributes to preserve by all means the welfare and spiritual development of Islam. . . .

If the Caliph and Caliphate, as they maintained, were to be invested with a dignity embracing the whole of Islam, ought they not to have realized in all justice that a crushing burden would be imposed on Turkey, on her existence; her entire resources and all her forces would be placed at the disposal of the Caliph? . . .

For centuries our nation was guided under the influence of these erroneous ideas. But what has been the result of it? Everywhere they have lost millions of men. "Do you know," I asked, "how many sons of Anatolia have perished in the scorching deserts of the Yemen? Do you know the losses we have suffered in holding Syria and Egypt and in maintaining our position in Africa? And do you see what has come out of it? Do you know?

"Those who favor the idea of placing the means at the disposal of the Caliph to brave the whole world and the power to administer the affairs of the whole of Islam must not appeal to the population of Anatolia alone but to the great Muslim agglomerations which are eight or ten times as rich in men.

"New Turkey, the people of New Turkey, have no reason to think of anything else but their own existence and their own welfare. She has nothing more to give away to others."

SOURCE: From *Atatürk's Speech to the Assembly*, pp. 432–433. A speech delivered by Ghazi Mustafa Kemal, President of the Turkish Republic, October 1927.

into a modern secular republic. The trappings of a democratic system were put in place, centered on the elected Grand National Assembly, but the president was relatively intolerant of opposition and harshly suppressed critics of his rule. Turkish nationalism was emphasized, and the Turkish language, now written in the Roman alphabet, was shorn of many of its Arabic elements. Popular education was emphasized, old aristocratic titles like *pasha* and *bey* were abolished, and all Turkish citizens were given family names in the European style.

Atatürk also took steps to modernize the economy, overseeing the establishment of a light industrial sector producing textiles, glass, paper, and cement and instituting a five-year plan on the Soviet model to provide for state direction over the economy. Atatürk was no admirer of Soviet communism, however, and the Turkish economy can be better described as a form of state capitalism. He also encouraged the modernization of the agricultural sector through the establishment of training institutions and model farms, but such reforms had relatively little effect on the nation's predominantly conservative rural population.

Perhaps the most significant aspect of Atatürk's reform program was his attempt to limit the power of the Islamic religion and transform Turkey into a secular state. The caliphate (according to which the Ottoman sultan was recognized as the temporal leader of the global Islamic community) was formally abolished in 1924, and the *Shari'a* (Islamic law) was replaced by a revised version of the Swiss law code (see the box above). The fez (the brimless cap worn by Turkish Muslims) was abolished as a form of headdress, and women were discouraged from wearing the veil in the traditional Islamic custom. Women received the right to vote in 1934 and were legally guaranteed equal rights with men in all aspects of marriage and inheritance. Education and the professions were now open to citizens of both genders, and some women even began to take part in politics. All citizens were given the right to convert to another religion at will.

The legacy of Mustafa Kemal Atatürk was enormous. Although not all of his reforms were widely accepted in practice, especially by devout Muslims, most of the changes that he introduced were retained after his death in 1938. In virtually every respect, the Turkish republic was the product of his determined efforts to create a modern nation, a Turkish version of the "revolution from above" in Meiji Japan.

Modernization in Iran In the meantime, a similar process was under way in Persia. Under the Qajar dynasty (1794–1925), the country had not been very successful in resisting Russian advances in the Caucasus or a growing European presence farther south. To secure themselves from foreign influence, the shahs moved the capital from Tabriz to Tehran, in a mountainous area just south of the Caspian Sea. During the mid-nineteenth century, one modernizing shah attempted to introduce political and economic reforms but was impeded by resistance from tribal and religious forces. The majority of Persians were Shi'ites, one of the two main branches of Islam (as opposed to Sunni Muslims, who predominated in most of the Muslim world). Many Shi'ites adopted a strict interpretation of the Muslim faith.

Eventually, the growing foreign presence led to the rise of an indigenous nationalist movement. Its efforts were largely directed against Russian advances in the northwest and growing European influence in the small modern industrial sector, the profits from which left the country or disappeared into the hands of the dynasty's ruling elite. Supported actively by Shi'ite religious leaders, opposition to the regime rose steadily among both peasants and merchants in the cities, and in 1906, popular pressures forced the reigning shah to grant a constitution on the Western model.

As in the Ottoman Empire and Qing China, however, the modernizers had moved before their power base was secure. With the support of the Russians and the British, the shah was able to retain control, and the two foreign powers began to divide the country into separate spheres of influence. One reason for the growing foreign presence in Persia was the discovery of oil reserves in the southern part of the country in 1908. Within a few years, oil exports increased rapidly, with the bulk of the profits going into the pockets of British investors.

In 1921, a Persian army officer by the name of Reza Khan (1878–1944) led a mutiny that seized power in Tehran. The new ruler's original intention had been to establish a republic, but resistance from traditional forces impeded his efforts, and in 1925, the new Pahlavi dynasty, with Reza Khan as shah, replaced the now defunct Qajar dynasty. During the next few years, Reza Khan attempted to follow the example of Mustafa Kemal Atatürk in Turkey, introducing a number of reforms to strengthen the central government, modernize the civilian and military bureaucracy, and establish a modern economic infrastructure.

Iran Under the Pahlavi Dynasty

Unlike Atatürk, Reza Khan did not attempt to destroy the power of Islamic beliefs, but he did encourage the establishment of a Western-style educational system and forbade women to wear the veil in public. To strengthen the sense of nationalism and reduce the power of Islam, he restored the country's ancient name, Iran, and attempted to popularize the symbols and beliefs of pre-Islamic times. Like his Qajar predecessors, however, Reza Khan was hindered by strong foreign influence. When the Soviet Union and Great Britain decided to send troops into the country during World War II, he resigned in protest and died three years later.

Nation Building in Iraq One consequence of the collapse of the Ottoman Empire was the emergence of a new political entity along the Tigris and Euphrates rivers, once the heartland of ancient empires. Lacking defensible borders and sharply divided along ethnic and religious lines—a Shi'ite majority in rural areas was balanced by a vocal Sunni minority in the cities and a largely Kurdish population in the northern mountains—the region had been under Ottoman rule since the seventeenth century. With the advent of World War I, the lowland area from Baghdad southward to the Persian Gulf was occupied by British forces, who hoped to protect oil-producing regions in neighboring Iran from a German takeover.

In 1920, the country was placed under British control as the mandate of Iraq under the League of Nations. Civil unrest and growing anti-Western sentiment rapidly dispelled any possible plans for the emergence of an independent government, and in 1921, after the suppression of resistance forces, the country became a monarchy under the titular authority of King Faisal of Syria, a descendant of the Prophet Muhammad. Faisal relied for support primarily on the politically more sophisticated urban Sunni population, although they represented less than a quarter of the population. The discovery of oil near Kirkuk in 1927 increased the value of the area to the British, who granted formal independence to the country in 1932, although British advisers retained a strong influence over the fragile government.

The Rise of Arab Nationalism and the Issue of Palestine As we have seen, the Arab uprising during World War I helped bring about the demise of the Ottoman Empire. Actually, unrest against Ottoman rule had existed in the Arabian peninsula since the eighteenth century, when the Wahhabi revolt attempted to purge the outside influences and cleanse Islam of corrupt practices that had developed in past centuries. The revolt was eventually suppressed, but the influence of the Wahhabi movement persisted, revitalized in part by resistance to the centralizing and modernizing efforts of reformist elements in the nineteenth century.

World War I offered an opportunity for the Arabs to throw off the shackles of Ottoman rule—but what would replace them? The Arabs were not a nation but an idea, a loose collection of peoples who often do not see eye to eye on what constitutes their community. Disagreement over what it means to be an Arab has plagued generations of political leaders who have sought unsuccessfully to knit together the disparate peoples of the region into a single Arab nation.

When the Arab leaders in Mecca declared their independence from Ottoman rule in 1916, they had hoped for British support, but they were sorely disappointed when much of the area was placed under British or French authority as mandates of the League of Nations. To add salt to the wound, the new state of Lebanon had been created to place the Christian peoples there under a Christian administration.

The land of Palestine—once the home of the Jews but now inhabited primarily by Muslim Arabs and a few thousand Christians—became a separate mandate. According to the Balfour Declaration, issued by the British foreign secretary Lord Balfour in November 1917, Palestine was to be a national home for the Jews. The declaration was ambiguous on the legal status of the territory and promised that the decision would not undermine the rights of the non-Jewish peoples currently living in the area. But Arab nationalists were incensed. How could a national home for the Jewish people be established in a territory where 90 percent of the population was Muslim?

In the early 1920s, a leader of the Wahhabi movement, Ibn Saud (1880–1953), united Arab tribes in the northern part of the Arabian peninsula and drove out the remnants of Ottoman rule. Ibn Saud was a descendant of the family that had led the Wahhabi revolt in the eighteenth century. Devout and gifted, he won broad support among Arab tribal peoples and established the kingdom of Saudi Arabia throughout much of the peninsula in 1932.

At first, his new kingdom, consisting essentially of the vast wastes of central Arabia, was desperately poor. Its financial resources were limited to the income from Muslim pilgrims visiting the holy sites in Mecca and Medina. But during the 1930s, American companies began to explore for oil, and in 1938, Standard Oil made a successful strike at Dahran, on the Persian Gulf. Soon an Arabian-American oil conglomerate, popularly called Aramco, was established, and the isolated kingdom was suddenly inundated by Western oilmen and untold wealth.

In the meantime, Jewish settlers began to arrive in Palestine in response to the promises made in the Balfour Declaration. As tensions between the new arrivals and existing Muslim residents began to escalate, the British tried to restrict Jewish immigration into the territory and rejected the concept of a separate state. They also created the separate emirate of Trans-Jordan out of the eastern portion of Palestine. After World War II, it would become the independent kingdom of Jordan. The stage was set for the conflicts that would take place in the region after World War II.

Nationalism and Communism in Asia and Africa

Before the Russian Revolution, to most observers in Asia and Africa, Westernization meant the capitalist democratic civilization of western Europe and the United States, not the doctrine of social revolution developed by Karl Marx. Until 1917, Marxism was regarded as a utopian idea rather than a concrete system of government. Moreover, Marxism appeared to have little relevance to conditions in Asia and Africa. Marxist doctrine, after all, declared that a communist society could arise only from the ashes of an advanced capitalism that had already passed through the stage of industrial revolution. From the perspective of Marxist historical analysis, most societies in Asia and Africa were still at the feudal stage of development; they lacked the economic conditions and political awareness to achieve a socialist revolution that would bring the working class to power. Finally, the Marxist view of nationalism and religion had little appeal to many patriotic intellectuals in the non-Western world. Marx believed that nationhood and religion were essentially false ideas that diverted the attention of the oppressed masses from the critical issues of class struggle and, in his phrase, the exploitation of one person by another. Instead, Marx stressed the importance of an "internationalist" outlook based on class consciousness and the eventual creation of a classless society with no artificial divisions based on culture, nation, or religion.

Lenin and the East The situation began to change after the Russian Revolution in 1917. The rise to power of Lenin's Bolsheviks demonstrated that a revolutionary party espousing Marxist principles could overturn a corrupt, outdated system and launch a new experiment dedicated to ending human inequality and achieving a paradise on earth. In 1920, Lenin proposed a new revolutionary strategy designed to relate Marxist doctrine and practice to non-Western societies. His reasons were not entirely altruistic. Soviet Russia, surrounded by capitalist powers, desperately needed allies in its struggle to survive in a hostile world. To Lenin, the anticolonial movements emerging in North Africa, Asia, and the Middle East after World War I were natural allies of the beleaguered new regime in Moscow. Lenin was convinced that only the ability of the imperialist powers to find markets, raw materials, and sources of capital investment in the non-Western world kept capitalism alive. If the tentacles of capitalist influence in Asia and Africa could be severed, imperialism itself would ultimately weaken and collapse.

Establishing such an alliance was not easy, however. Most nationalist leaders in colonial countries belonged to the urban middle class, and many abhorred the idea of a comprehensive revolution to create a totally egalitarian society. In addition, many still adhered to traditional religious beliefs and were opposed to the atheistic principles of classical Marxism.

Since it was unrealistic to expect bourgeois support for social revolution, Lenin sought a compromise by which Communist parties could be organized among the working classes in the preindustrial societies of Asia and Africa. These parties would then forge informal alliances with existing middle-class nationalist parties to struggle against the remnants of the traditional ruling class and Western imperialism. Such an alliance, of course, could not be permanent because many bourgeois nationalists in Asia and Africa would reject an egalitarian, classless society. Once the imperialists had been overthrown, therefore, the Communist parties would turn against their erstwhile nationalist partners to seize power on their own and carry out the socialist revolution. Lenin thus proposed a two-stage revolution: an initial "national democratic" stage followed by a "proletarian socialist" stage.

Lenin's strategy became a major element in Soviet foreign policy in the 1920s. Soviet agents fanned out across the world to carry Marxism beyond the boundaries of industrial Europe. The primary instrument of this effort was the Communist International, or Comintern for short. Formed in 1919 at Lenin's prodding, the Comintern was a worldwide organization of Communist parties dedicated to the advancement of world revolution. At its headquarters in Moscow, agents from around the world were trained in the precepts of world communism and then sent back to their own countries to form Marxist parties and promote the cause of social revolution. By the end of the 1920s, almost every colonial or semicolonial society in Asia had a party based on Marxist principles. The Soviets had less success in the Middle East, where Marxist ideology appealed mainly to minorities such as Jews and Armenians in the cities, or in sub-Saharan Africa, where Soviet strategists in any case did not feel conditions were sufficiently advanced for the creation of Communist organizations.

The Appeal of Communism According to Marxist doctrine, the rank and file of Communist parties should be urban workers alienated from capitalist society by inhumane working conditions. In practice, many of the leading elements even in European Communist parties tended to be intellectuals or members of the lower middle class (in Marxist parlance,

the "petty bourgeoisie"). That phenomenon was even more apparent in the non-Western world. Some were probably drawn into the movement for patriotic reasons and saw Marxist doctrine as a new and more effective means of modernizing their societies and removing the power of exploitative colonialism. Others were attracted by the utopian dream of a classless society. For those who had lost their faith in traditional religion, it often served as a new secular ideology, dealing not with the hereafter but with the here and now. All who joined found it a stirring message of release from oppression and a practical strategy for the liberation of their society from colonial rule. The young Ho Chi Minh, later to become the founder of the Vietnamese Communist Party, was quick to see the importance of Lenin's revolutionary strategy for his own country:

> There were political terms difficult to understand in this thesis. But by dint of reading it again and again, finally I could grasp the main part of it. What emotion, enthusiasm, clear-sightedness, and confidence it instilled in me! I was overjoyed to tears. Though sitting alone in my room, I shouted aloud as if addressing large crowds: "Dear martyrs, compatriots! This is what we need, this is the path to our liberation!"[1]

Of course, the new doctrine's appeal was not the same in all non-Western societies. In Confucian societies such as China and Vietnam, where traditional belief systems had been badly discredited by their failure to counter the Western challenge, communism had an immediate impact and rapidly became a major factor in the anticolonial movement. In Buddhist and Muslim societies, where traditional religion remained strong and actually became a cohesive factor within the resistance movement, communism had less success and was forced to adapt to local conditions to survive.

Sometimes, as in Malaya (where the sense of nationhood was weak) or Thailand (which, alone in Southeast Asia, had not fallen under colonial rule), support for the local Communist Party came from minority groups such as the overseas Chinese community. To maximize their appeal and minimize potential conflict with traditional ideas, Communist parties frequently attempted to adjust Marxist doctrine to indigenous values and institutions. In the Middle East, for example, the Ba'ath Party in Syria adopted a hybrid socialism combining Marxism with Arab nationalism. In Africa, radical intellectuals talked vaguely of a uniquely "African road to socialism."

The degree to which these parties were successful in establishing alliances with existing nationalist parties also varied from place to place. In some instances, the local Communists were briefly able to establish a cooperative relationship with bourgeois parties in the struggle against Western imperialism. In the Dutch East Indies, the Indonesian Communist Party (known as the PKI) allied with the middle-class nationalist group Sarekat Islam but later broke loose in an effort to organize its own mass movement among the poor peasants. Similar problems were encountered in French Indochina, where Vietnamese Communists organized by the Moscow-trained revolutionary Ho Chi Minh sought to cooperate with bourgeois nationalist parties against the colonial regime. In 1928, all such efforts were abandoned when the Comintern, reacting to Chiang Kai-shek's betrayal of the alliance with the Chinese Communist Party (see the next section), declared that Communist parties should restrict their recruiting efforts to the most revolutionary elements in society—notably, the urban intellectuals and the working class. Harassed by colonial authorities and saddled with strategic directions from Moscow that often had little relevance to local conditions, Communist parties in most colonial societies had little success in the 1930s and failed to build a secure base of support among the mass of the population.

Revolution in China

Overall, revolutionary Marxism had its greatest impact in China, where a group of young radicals, including several faculty and staff members from prestigious Beijing University, founded the Chinese Communist Party (CCP) in 1921. The rise of the CCP was a consequence of the failed revolution of 1911. When political forces are too weak or divided to consolidate their power during a period of instability, the military usually steps in to fill the vacuum. In China, Sun Yat-sen and his colleagues had accepted General Yuan Shikai as president of the new Chinese republic in 1911 because they lacked the military force to compete with his control over the army. Moreover, many feared, perhaps rightly, that if the revolt lapsed into chaos, the Western powers would intervene and the last shreds of Chinese sovereignty would be lost. But some had misgivings about Yuan's intentions. As one remarked in a letter to a friend, "We don't know whether he will be a George Washington or a Napoleon."

In fact, he was neither. Understanding little of the new ideas sweeping into China from the West, Yuan ruled in a traditional manner, reviving Confucian rituals and institutions and eventually trying to found a new imperial dynasty. Yuan's dictatorial inclinations led to clashes with Sun's party, now renamed the *Guomindang* (*Kuomintang*), or Nationalist Party. When Yuan dissolved the new parliament, the Nationalists launched a rebellion. When it failed, Sun Yat-sen fled to Japan.

Yuan was strong enough to brush off the challenge from the revolutionary forces but not to turn back the clock of history. He died in 1916 (apparently of natural causes) and was succeeded by one of his military subordinates. For the next several years, China slipped into anarchy as the power of the central government disintegrated and military warlords seized power in the provinces.

Mr. Science and Mr. Democracy: The New Culture Movement

Although the failure of the 1911 revolution was a clear sign that China was not yet ready for radical change, discontent with existing conditions continued to rise in various sectors of Chinese society. The most vocal protests came from radical elements who opposed Yuan Shikai's conservative agenda but were now convinced that political change could not take place until the Chinese people were more familiar with trends in the outside world. Braving the displeasure of Yuan Shikai and his successors, progressive intellectuals at Beijing University launched the New Culture Movement, aimed at abolishing the remnants of the old system and introducing Western values and institutions into China. Using the classrooms of China's most prestigious university as well as the pages of newly established progressive magazines and newspapers, they presented the Chinese people with a heady mix of new ideas, from the philosophy of Friedrich Nietzsche and Bertrand Russell to the educational views of the American John Dewey and the feminist plays of Henrik Ibsen. As such ideas flooded into China, they stirred up a new generation of educated Chinese youth, who chanted "Down with Confucius and sons" and talked of a new era dominated by "Mr. Sai" (Mr. Science) and "Mr. De" (Mr. Democracy). No one was a greater defender of free thought and speech than the chancellor of Beijing University, Cai Yuanpei:

> So far as theoretical ideas are concerned, I follow the principles of "freedom of thought" and an attitude of broad tolerance in accordance with the practice of universities the world over. . . . Regardless of what school of thought a person may adhere to, so long as that person's ideas are justified and conform to reason and have not been passed by through the process of natural selection, although there may be controversy, such ideas have a right to be presented.[2]

The problem was that appeals for American-style democracy and women's liberation had little relevance to Chinese peasants, most of whom were still illiterate and concerned above all with survival. Consequently, the New Culture Movement did not win widespread support outside the urban areas. It certainly earned the distrust of conservative military officers, one of whom threatened to lob artillery shells into Beijing University to destroy the poisonous new ideas and their advocates.

Discontent among intellectuals, however, was soon joined by the rising chorus of public protest against Japan's efforts to expand its influence on the mainland. During the first decade of the twentieth century, Japan had taken advantage of the Qing's decline to extend its domination over Manchuria and Korea (see Chapter 3). In 1915, the Japanese government insisted that Yuan Shikai accept a series of twenty-one demands that would have given Japan a virtual protectorate over the Chinese government and economy. Yuan was able to fend off the most far-reaching Japanese demands by arousing popular outrage in China, but at the Paris Peace Conference four years later, Japan received Germany's sphere of influence in Shandong Province as a reward for its support of the Allied cause in World War I. On hearing the news that the Chinese government had accepted the decision, on May 4, 1919, patriotic students, supported by other sectors of the urban population, demonstrated in Beijing and other major cities of the country. Although this May Fourth Movement did not result in a reversal of the decision to award Shandong to Japan, it did alert a substantial part of the politically literate population to the threat to national survival and the incompetence of the warlord government.

By 1920, central authority had almost ceased to exist in China. Two political forces now began to emerge as competitors for the right to bring order to the chaos of the early republican era. One was Sun Yat-sen's Nationalist Party. Driven from the political arena seven years earlier by Yuan Shikai, the party now reestablished itself on the mainland by making an alliance with the warlord ruler of Guangdong Province in South China. From Canton, Sun sought international assistance to carry out his national revolution. The other was the Chinese Communist Party. Following Lenin's strategy, the CCP sought to link up with the more experienced Nationalists. Sun Yat-sen needed the expertise and the diplomatic support that the Soviet Union could provide because his anti-imperialist rhetoric had alienated many Western powers. In 1923, the two parties formed an alliance to oppose the warlords and drive the imperialist powers out of China.

For three years, with the assistance of a Comintern mission in Canton, the two parties submerged their mutual suspicions and mobilized and trained a revolutionary army to march north and seize control over China. The so-called Northern Expedition began in the summer of 1926 (see Map 5.1). By the following spring, revolutionary forces were in control of all Chinese territory south of the Yangtze River, including the major river ports of Wuhan and Shanghai.

But tensions between the two parties now surfaced. Sun Yat-sen had died of cancer in 1925 and was succeeded as head of the Nationalist Party by his military subordinate, Chiang Kai-shek (1887–1975). Chiang feigned support for the alliance with the Communists but actually planned to destroy them. In April 1927, he struck against the Communists and their supporters in Shanghai, killing thousands. The CCP responded by encouraging revolts in central China and Canton, but the uprisings were defeated and their leaders were killed or forced into hiding.

The Nanjing Republic

In 1928, Chiang Kai-shek founded a new Republic of China at Nanjing, and over the next three years, he managed to reunify China by a combination of military operations and inducements (known as "silver bullets") to various northern warlords to join his movement. One of his key targets was warlord Zhang Zuolin, who controlled Manchuria under the tutelage of Japan. When Zhang allegedly agreed

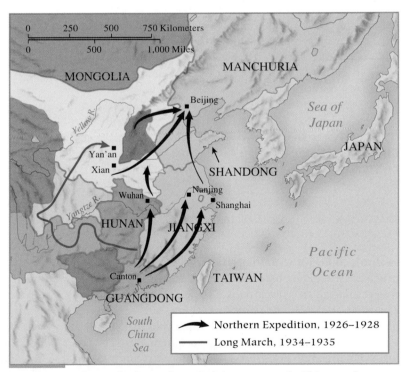

MAP 5.1 **The Northern Expedition and the Long March.** This map shows the routes taken by the combined Nationalist-Communist forces during the Northern Expedition of 1926–1928. The thinner arrow indicates the route taken by Communist units during the Long March led by Mao Zedong.
❔ Where did Mao establish his new headquarters? Why? 🌐 **View an animated version of this map or related maps at the World History Resource Center, at** worldrc.wadsworth.com/.

A CALL FOR REVOLT

In the fall of 1926, Nationalist and Communist forces moved north from Canton on their Northern Expedition in an effort to defeat the warlords. The young Communist Mao Zedong accompanied revolutionary troops into his home province of Hunan, where he submitted a report to the CCP Central Committee calling for a massive peasant revolt against the ruling order. The report shows his confidence that peasants could play an active role in the Chinese revolution despite the skepticism of many of his colleagues.

Why does Mao Zedong believe that rural peasants could help bring about a social revolution in China? How does his vision compare with the reality of the Bolshevik Revolution in Russia?

Mao Zedong, "The Peasant Movement in Hunan"

During my recent visit to Hunan I made a firsthand investigation of conditions. . . . In a very short time, . . . several hundred million peasants will rise like a mighty storm, . . . a force so swift and violent that no power, however great, will be able to hold it back. They will smash all the trammels that bind them and rush forward along the road to liberation. They will sweep all the imperialists, warlords, corrupt officials, local tyrants, and evil gentry into their graves. Every revolutionary party and every revolutionary comrade will be put to the test, to be accepted or rejected as they decide. There are three alternatives. To march at their head and lead them? To trail behind them, gesticulating and criticizing? Or to stand in their way and oppose them? Every Chinese is free to choose, but events will force you to make the choice quickly.

The main targets of attack by the peasants are the local tyrants, the evil gentry and the lawless landlords, but in passing they also hit out against patriarchal ideas and institutions, against the corrupt officials in the cities and against bad practices and customs in the rural areas. . . . As a result, the privileges which the feudal landlords enjoyed for thousands of years are being shattered to pieces. . . . With the collapse of the power of the landlords, the peasant associations have now become the sole organs of authority, and the popular slogan "All power to the peasant associations" has become a reality.

The peasants' revolt disturbed the gentry's sweet dreams. When the news from the countryside reached the cities, it caused immediate uproar among the gentry. . . . From the middle social strata upwards to the Kuomintang right-wingers, there was not a single person who did not sum up the whole business in the phrase, "It's terrible!" . . . Even quite progressive people said, "Though terrible, it is inevitable in a revolution." In short, nobody could altogether deny the word "terrible." But . . . the fact is that the great peasant masses have risen to fulfill their historic mission. . . . What the peasants are doing is absolutely right; what they are doing is fine! "It's fine!" is the theory of the peasants and of all other revolutionaries. Every revolutionary comrade should know that the national revolution requires a great change in the countryside. The Revolution of 1911 did not bring about this change, hence its failure. This change is now taking place, and it is an important factor for the completion of the revolution. Every revolutionary comrade must support it, or he will be taking the stand of counterrevolution.

SOURCE: From *Selected Works of Mao Tse-Tung* (London: Lawrence and Wishart, Ltd., 1954), vol. 1, pp. 21–23.

---

to throw in his lot with the Nationalists, the Japanese had him assassinated by placing a bomb under his train as he was returning to Manchuria. The Japanese hoped that Zhang Zuolin's son and successor, Zhang Xueliang, would be more cooperative, but they had miscalculated. Promised a major role in Chiang Kai-shek's government, Zhang began instead to integrate Manchuria politically and economically into the Nanjing republic.

Chiang Kai-shek saw the Japanese as a serious threat to Chinese national aspirations but considered them less dangerous than the Communists. (He once remarked to an American reporter that "the Japanese are a disease of the skin, but the Communists are a disease of the heart.") After the Shanghai massacre of April 1927, most of the Communist leaders went into hiding in the city, where they attempted to revive the movement in its traditional base among the urban working class. Shanghai was a rich recruiting ground for the party. A city of millionaires, paupers, prostitutes, gamblers, and adventurers, it had led one pious Christian missionary to comment, "If God lets Shanghai endure, He owes an apology to Sodom and Gomorrah."[3] Some party members, however, led by the young Communist organizer Mao Zedong (1893–1976), fled to the hilly areas south of the Yangtze River.

Unlike most other CCP leaders, Mao was convinced that the Chinese revolution must be based on the impoverished peasants in the countryside. The son of a prosperous peasant, Mao had helped organize a peasant movement in South China during the early 1920s and then served as an agitator in rural villages in his native province of Hunan during the Northern Expedition in the fall of 1926. At that time, he wrote a famous report to the party leadership suggesting that the CCP support peasant demands for a land revolution. But his superiors refused, fearing that adopting excessively radical policies would destroy the alliance with the Nationalists (see the box on p. 102).

After the spring of 1927, the CCP-Nationalist alliance ceased to exist. Chiang Kai-shek attempted to root the Communists out of their urban base in Shanghai. He succeeded in 1931, when most party leaders were forced to flee Shanghai for Mao's rural redoubt in the rugged hills of Jiangxi Province. Three years later, using their superior military strength, Chiang's troops surrounded the Communist base, inducing Mao's young People's Liberation Army (PLA) to abandon its guerrilla lair and embark on the famous Long March, an arduous journey of thousands of miles on foot through mountains, marshes, and deserts to the small provincial town of Yan'an 200 miles north of the modern-day city of Xian in the dusty hills of North China. Of the ninety thousand who embarked on the journey in October 1934, only ten thousand arrived in Yan'an a year later. Contemporary observers must have thought that the Communist threat to the Nanjing regime had been averted forever.

Meanwhile, Chiang Kai-shek was trying to build a new nation. When the Nanjing republic was established in 1928, Chiang publicly declared his commitment to Sun Yat-sen's Three People's Principles. In a program announced in 1918, Sun had written about the all-important second stage of "political tutelage":

> As a schoolboy must have good teachers and helpful friends, so the Chinese people, being for the first time under republican rule, must have a farsighted revolutionary government for their training. This calls for the period of political tutelage, which is a necessary transitional stage from monarchy to republicanism. Without this, disorder will be unavoidable.[4]

In keeping with Sun's program, Chiang announced a period of political indoctrination to prepare the Chinese people for a final stage of constitutional government. In the meantime, the Nationalists would use their dictatorial power to carry out a land reform program and modernize the urban industrial sector.

But it would take more than paper plans to create a new China. Years of neglect and civil war had severely frayed the political, economic, and social fabric of the nation. There were faint signs of an impending industrial revolution in the major urban centers, but most of the people in the countryside, drained by warlord exactions and civil strife, were still grindingly poor and overwhelmingly illiterate. A Westernized middle class had begun to emerge in the cities and formed much of the natural constituency of the Nanjing government. But this new Westernized elite, preoccupied with bourgeois values of individual advancement and material accumulation, had few links with the peasants in the countryside or the rickshaw drivers "running in this world of suffering," in the poignant words of a Chinese poet. In an expressive phrase, some critics dismissed Chiang Kai-shek and his chief followers as "banana Chinese"—yellow on the outside, white on the inside.

© Keystone/Getty Images/Hulton Archive

Mao Zedong on the Long March. In 1934, Mao Zedong led his bedraggled forces on the famous Long March from southern China to a new location at Yan'an, in the hills just south of the Gobi Desert. In the photo above, Mao Zedong poses with Zhou Enlai, one of his chief supporters. By this time, Mao had become the leader of the Communist movement, although his party did not take complete control of China until 1949.

Blending East and West Chiang was aware of the difficulty of introducing exotic foreign ideas into a society still culturally conservative. While building a modern industrial sector and rejecting what he considered the excessive individualism and material greed of Western capitalism, Chiang sought to propagate traditional Confucian values of hard work, obedience, and moral integrity through the officially promoted New Life Movement, sponsored by his Wellesley-educated wife, Mei-ling Soong.

Unfortunately for Chiang, Confucian ideas—at least in their institutional form—had been widely discredited by the failure of the traditional system to solve China's growing problems. Critics noted, as well, that Chiang's government did not practice what it preached. Much of the national wealth was in the hands of the so-called four families, composed of senior officials and close subordinates of the ruling elite. Lacking the political sensitivity of Sun Yat-sen and fearing Communist influence, Chiang repressed all opposition and censored free expression, thereby alienating many intellectuals and political moderates.

Promoting Economic Development With only a tenuous hold over the vast countryside (the Nanjing republic had total control over a handful of provinces in the Yangtze valley), Chiang Kai-shek's government had little more success in promoting economic development. Although mechanization was gradually beginning to replace manual labor in a number of traditional industries (notably in the manufacture of textile goods), about 75 percent of all industrial production was still craft-produced in the mid-1930s. Then again, traditional Chinese exports, such as silk and tea, were hard-hit by the Great Depression. With military expenses consuming about half the national budget, distressingly little was devoted to economic development. During the decade of precarious peace following the Northern Expedition, industrial growth averaged only about 1 percent annually.

One of Sun Yat-sen's most prominent proposals was to redistribute land to poor peasants in the countryside. Whether overall per capita consumption declined during the early decades of the century is unclear, but there is no doubt that Chinese farmers were often victimized by high taxes imposed by local warlords and the endemic political and social conflict that marked the period. A land reform program was enacted in 1930, but it had little effect. Since the urban middle class and the landed gentry were Chiang Kai-shek's natural political constituency, he shunned programs that would lead to a radical redistribution of wealth.

Social Change in Republican China

The transformation of the old order that had commenced at the end of the Qing era continued into the period of the early Chinese republic. By 1915, the assault on the old system and values by educated youth was intense. The main focus of the attack was the Confucian concept of the family—in particular, filial piety and the subordination of women. Young people demanded the right to choose their own mates and their own careers. Women demanded rights and opportunities equal to those enjoyed by men.

More broadly, progressives called for an end to the concept of duty to the community and praised the Western individualist ethos. The prime spokesman for such views

was the popular writer Lu Xun, whose short stories criticized the Confucian concept of family as a "man-eating" system that degraded humanity. In a famous short story titled "Diary of a Madman," the protagonist remarks:

> I remember when I was four or five years old, sitting in the cool of the hall, my brother told me that if a man's parents were ill, he should cut off a piece of his flesh and boil it for them if he wanted to be considered a good son. I have only just realized that I have been living all these years in a place where for four thousand years they have been eating human flesh.[5]

Such criticisms did have some beneficial results. During the early republic, the tyranny of the old family system began to decline, at least in urban areas, under the impact of economic changes and the urgings of the New Culture intellectuals. Women, long consigned to an inferior place in the Confucian world order, began to escape their cloistered existence and seek education and employment alongside their male contemporaries. Free choice in marriage and a more relaxed attitude toward sex became commonplace among affluent families in the cities, where the teenage children of Westernized elites aped the clothing, social habits, and musical tastes of their contemporaries in Europe and the United States.

But as a rule, the new consciousness of individualism and women's rights that marked the early republican era in the major cities did not penetrate to the villages, where traditional attitudes and customs held sway. Arranged marriages continued to be the rule rather than the exception, and concubinage remained common. According to a survey taken in the 1930s, well over two-thirds of the marriages, even among urban couples, had been arranged by their parents; in one rural area, only 3 of 170 villagers interviewed had heard of the idea of "modern marriage." Even the tradition of binding the feet of female children continued despite efforts by the Nationalist government to eradicate the practice.

Down with Confucius and Sons Nowhere was the struggle between traditional and modern more visible than in the field of culture. Beginning with the New Culture era during the early years of the first Chinese republic, radical reformists criticized traditional culture as the symbol and instrument of feudal oppression that must be entirely eradicated to create a new China that could stand on its feet with dignity in the modern world.

For many reformers, that new culture must be based on that of the modern West. During the 1920s and 1930s, Western literature and art became popular in China, especially among the urban middle class. Traditional culture continued to prevail among more conservative elements of the population, and some intellectuals argued for the creation of a new art that would synthesize the best of Chinese and foreign culture. But the most creative artists were interested in imitating foreign trends, whereas traditionalists were more concerned with preservation.

Literature in particular was influenced by foreign ideas as Western genres like the novel and the short story attracted a growing audience. Although most Chinese novels written after World War I dealt with Chinese subjects, they reflected the Western tendency toward social realism and often dealt with the new Westernized middle class (Mao Dun's *Midnight,* for example, describes the changing mores of Shanghai's urban elites) or the disintegration of the traditional Confucian family. Most of China's modern authors displayed a clear contempt for the past.

Japan Between the Wars

By the beginning of the twentieth century, Japan had made steady progress toward the creation of an advanced society on the Western model. Economic and social reforms launched during the Meiji era led to increasing prosperity and the development of a modern industrial and commercial sector. Although the political system still retained many authoritarian characteristics, optimists had reason to hope that Japan was on the road to becoming a full-fledged democracy.

Experiment in Democracy

During the first quarter of the twentieth century, the Japanese political system appeared to evolve significantly toward the Western democratic model. Political parties expanded their popular following and became increasingly competitive, while individual pressure groups such as labor unions began to appear in Japanese society, along with an independent press and a bill of rights. The influence of the old ruling oligarchy, the *genro,* had not yet been significantly challenged, however, nor had that of its ideological foundation, which focused on national wealth and power.

The fragile flower of democratic institutions was able to survive throughout the 1920s. During that period, the military budget was reduced, and a suffrage bill enacted in 1925 granted the vote to all Japanese adult males. Women remained disenfranchised, but women's associations gained increased visibility during the 1920s, and women became active in the labor movement and in campaigns for various social reforms.

But the era was also marked by growing social turmoil, and two opposing forces within the system were gearing up to challenge the prevailing wisdom. On the left, a Marxist labor movement, which reflected the tensions within the working class and the increasing radicalism among the rural poor, began to take shape in the early 1920s in response to growing economic difficulties. Attempts to suppress labor disturbances led to further radicalization. On the right, ultranationalist groups called for a rejection of Western models of development and a more militant approach to realizing national objectives. In 1919, radical nationalist Kita Ikki called for a military takeover and the establishment of a new system bearing a strong resemblance to what would later be called fascism in Europe (see Chapter 6).

This cultural conflict between old and new, native and foreign, was reflected in the world of literature. Japanese self-confidence had been somewhat restored after victories over China and Russia, and this resurgence sparked a great age of creativity in the early twentieth century. Japanese writers blended Western psychology with Japanese sensibility in exquisite novels reeking with nostalgia for the old Japan. A well-known example is Junichiro Tanizaki's *Some Prefer Nettles,* published in 1928, which delicately juxtaposes the positive aspects of both traditional and modern Japan. By the 1930s, however, military censorship increasingly inhibited free literary expression. Many authors continued to write privately, producing works that reflected the gloom of the era. This attitude is perhaps best exemplified by Shiga Naoya's novel *A Dark Night's Journey,* written during the early 1930s and capturing a sense of the approaching global catastrophe. It is regarded as the masterpiece of modern Japanese literature.

A Zaibatsu Economy

Japan also continued to make impressive progress in economic development. Spurred by rising domestic demand as well as a continued high rate of government investment in the economy, the production of raw materials tripled between 1900 and 1930, and industrial production increased more than twelvefold. Much of the increase went into the export market, and Western manufacturers began to complain about the rising competition for markets from the Japanese.

As often happens, rapid industrialization was accompanied by some hardship and rising social tensions. A characteristic of the Meiji model was the concentration of various manufacturing processes within a single enterprise, the so-called *zaibatsu,* or financial clique. Some of these firms were existing merchant companies that had the capital and the foresight to move into new areas of opportunity. Others were formed by enterprising samurai, who used their status and experience in management to good account in a new environment. Whatever their origins, these firms gradually developed, often with official encouragement, into large conglomerates that controlled a major segment of the Japanese industrial sector. According to one source, by 1937, the four largest *zaibatsu* (Mitsui, Mitsubishi, Sumitomo, and Yasuda) controlled 21 percent of the banking industry, 26 percent of mining, 35 percent of shipbuilding, 38 percent of commercial shipping, and more than 60 percent of paper manufacturing and insurance.

© Fortune Magazine, 1933

Swinging to the Latest Tunes. Whereas women of the old regime were swathed in colorful floor-length kimonos, elaborate coiffures, and traditional Japanese sandals, in the early 1930s many young Japanese adopted Western dress and leisure pursuits. Here we see young women with bobbed hair, short skirts, and high heels, performing the latest dances with young men in Western suits to the syncopation of a swinging brass band.

This concentration of power and wealth in the hands of a few major industrial combines resulted in the emergence of a form of dual economy: on the one hand, a modern industry characterized by up-to-date methods and massive government subsidies and, on the other, a traditional manufacturing sector characterized by conservative methods and small-scale production techniques.

Concentration of wealth also led to growing economic inequalities. As we have seen, economic growth had been achieved at the expense of the peasants, many of whom fled to the cities to escape rural poverty. That labor surplus benefited the industrial sector, but the urban proletariat was still poorly paid and ill-housed. Rampant inflation in the price of rice led to food riots shortly after World War I. A rapid increase in population (the total population of the Japanese islands increased from an estimated 43 million in 1900 to 73 million in 1940) led to food shortages and the threat of rising unemployment. Intense competition and the global recession in the early 1920s led to a greater concentration of industry and a perceptible rise in urban radicalism, marked by the appearance of a Marxist labor movement. In the meantime, those left on the farm continued to suffer. As late as the beginning of World War II, an estimated half of all Japanese farmers were tenants.

Shidehara Diplomacy

A final problem for Japanese leaders in the post-Meiji era was the familiar capitalist dilemma of finding sources of raw materials and foreign markets for the nation's manufactured goods. Until World War I, Japan had dealt with the problem by seizing territories such as Taiwan, Korea, and southern Manchuria and transforming them into colonies or protectorates of the growing Japanese Empire. That policy had succeeded brilliantly, but it had also begun to arouse the concern and, in some cases, the hostility of the Western nations. China was also becoming apprehensive; as we have seen, Japanese demands for Shandong Province at the Paris Peace Conference in 1919 aroused massive protests in major Chinese cities.

The United States was especially concerned about Japanese aggressiveness. Although the United States had been less active than some European states in pursuing colonies in the Pacific, it had a strong interest in keeping the area open for U.S. commercial activities. American anxiety about Tokyo's twenty-one demands on China in 1915 led to a new agreement in 1917, which essentially repeated the compromise provisions of the agreement reached nine years earlier.

In 1922, in Washington, D.C., the United States convened a major conference of nations with interests in the Pacific to discuss problems of regional security. The Washington Conference led to agreements on several issues, but the major accomplishment was the conclusion of a nine-power treaty recognizing the territorial integrity of China and the Open Door. The other participants induced Japan to accept these provisions by accepting its special position in Manchuria.

During the remainder of the 1920s, Japanese governments attempted to play by the rules laid down at the Washington Conference. Known as Shidehara diplomacy, after the foreign minister (and later prime minister) who attempted to carry it out, this policy sought to use diplomatic and economic means to realize Japanese interests in Asia. But this approach came under severe pressure as Japanese industrialists began to move into new areas of opportunity, such as heavy industry, chemicals, mining, and the manufacturing of appliances and automobiles. Because such industries desperately needed resources not found in abundance locally, the Japanese government came under increasing pressure to find new sources abroad.

The Rise of Militant Nationalism Throughout the 1920s, Japan sought to operate within a cooperative framework with other nations. In the early 1930s, however, with the onset of the Great Depression and growing tensions in the international arena, nationalist forces rose to dominance in the government. These elements, a mixture of military officers and ultranationalist politicians, were convinced that the diplomacy of the 1920s had failed and advocated a more aggressive approach to protecting national interests in a brutal and competitive world. We shall discuss the factors involved and the impact of these developments on the international scene in the next chapter.

Nationalism and Dictatorship in Latin America

Although the nations of Latin America played little role in World War I, that conflict nevertheless exerted an impact on the region, especially on its economy. By the end of the following decade, the region was also strongly influenced by another event of global proportions—the Great Depression.

A Changing Economy

At the beginning of the twentieth century, the economy of Latin America was based largely on the export of foodstuffs and raw materials. Some countries were compelled to rely on the export earnings of only one or two products. Argentina, for example, relied on the sale of beef and wheat; Chile exported nitrates and copper; Brazil and the Caribbean nations sold sugar; and the Central American states relied on the export of bananas. Such exports brought large profits to a few, but for the majority of the population, the returns were meager.

During World War I, the export of some products, such as Chilean nitrates (used to produce explosives), increased dramatically. In general, however, the war led to a decline in European investment in Latin America and a rise in the U.S. role in the local economies. That process was accelerated in the early years of the twentieth century when the United States intervened in Latin American politics to undertake construction of the Panama Canal, which dramatically reduced the time and distance needed for ships to pass between the Atlantic and Pacific Oceans.

The Role of the Yankee Dollar By the late 1920s, the United States had replaced Great Britain as the foremost source of foreign investment in Latin America. Unlike the British, however, U.S. investors placed funds directly into production enterprises, causing large segments of the area's export industry to fall into American hands. A number of Central American states, for example, were popularly labeled "banana republics" because of the power and influence of the U.S.-owned United Fruit Company. American firms also dominated the copper mining industry in Chile and Peru and the oil industry in Mexico, Peru, and Bolivia.

Increasing economic power served to reinforce the traditionally high level of U.S. political influence in Latin America, especially in Central America, a region that many Americans considered vital to U.S. national security. American troops occupied parts of both Nicaragua and Honduras to pacify unrest or protect U.S. interests there. The growing U.S. presence in the region provoked hostility among Latin Americans, who resented their dependent relationship on the United States, which they viewed as an aggressive imperialist power. Some charged that Washington worked, sometimes through U.S. military intervention, to keep ruthless dictators, such as Juan Vicente Gómez of Venezuela and Fulgencio Batista of Cuba, in power to preserve U.S. economic influence. In a bid to improve relations with Latin American countries, President Franklin D. Roosevelt in 1936 promulgated the Good Neighbor Policy, which rejected the use of U.S. military force in the region. To underscore his sincerity, Roosevelt ordered the withdrawal of U.S. marines from the island nation of Haiti in 1936. For the first time in thirty years, there were no U.S. occupation troops in Latin America.

Because so many Latin American nations depended for their livelihood on the export of raw materials and food products, the Great Depression of the 1930s was a disaster for the region. The total value of Latin American exports in 1930 was almost 50 percent below the figure for the previous five years. Spurred by the decline in foreign revenues, Latin American governments began to encourage the development of new industries to reduce dependence on imports. In some cases—the steel industry in Chile and Brazil, the oil industry in Argentina and Mexico—government investment made up for the absence of local sources of capital.

The Effects of Dependency

During the late nineteenth century, most governments in Latin America had been dominated by landed or military elites, who governed by the blatant use of military force. This trend continued during the 1930s as domestic instability caused by the effects of the Great Depression led to the creation of military dictatorships throughout the region, especially in Argentina and Brazil and, to a lesser degree, in Mexico—three countries that together possessed more than half of the land and wealth of Latin America (see Map 5.2).

MAP 5.2 **Latin America in the First Half of the Twentieth Century.** Shown here are the boundaries dividing the countries of Latin America after the independence movements of the nineteenth century. **?** Which areas remained under European rule? 🐢 **View an animated version of this map or related maps at the World History Resource Center, at** worldrc.wadsworth.com/.

Argentina Autocratic rule by an elite minority often had disastrous effects. The government of Argentina, controlled by landowners who had benefited from the export of beef and wheat, was slow to recognize the need to establish a local industrial base. In 1916, Hipólito Irigoyen (1852–1933), head of the Radical Party, was elected president on a program to improve conditions for the middle and lower classes. Little was achieved, however, as the party became increasingly corrupt and drew closer to the large landowners. In 1930, the army overthrew Irigoyen's government and reestablished the power of the landed class. But their effort to return to the past and suppress the growing influence of labor unions failed, and in 1946, General Juan Perón—claiming the support of the *descamisados* ("shirtless ones")—seized sole power (see Chapter 9).

Brazil Brazil followed a similar path. In 1889, the army overthrew the Brazilian monarchy, installed by Portugal decades before, and established a republic. But it was dominated by landed elites, many of whom had grown wealthy through their ownership of coffee plantations. By 1900, three-quarters of the world's coffee was grown in Brazil. As in Argentina, the ruling oligarchy ignored the importance of establishing an urban industrial base. When the Great Depression ravaged profits from coffee exports, a wealthy rancher, Getúlio Vargas (1883–1954), seized power and served as president from 1930 to 1945. At first, Vargas sought to appease workers by declaring an eight-hour day and a minimum wage, but influenced by the apparent success of fascist regimes in Europe, he ruled by increasingly autocratic means and relied on a police force that used torture to silence his opponents. His industrial policy was successful, however, and by the end of World War II, Brazil had become Latin America's major industrial power. In 1945, the army, concerned that Vargas was turning increasingly to leftist elements for support, forced him to resign.

Mexico Mexico, in the early years of the twentieth century, was in a state of turbulence. Under the rule of dictator

Porfirio Díaz (see Chapter 1), the real wages of the working class had declined. Moreover, 95 percent of the rural population owned no land, and about a thousand families ruled almost all of Mexico. When a liberal landowner, Francisco Madero, forced Díaz from power in 1910, he opened the door to a wider revolution. Madero's ineffectiveness triggered a demand for agrarian reform led by Emiliano Zapata (1879–1919), who aroused the masses of landless peasants in southern Mexico and began to seize the haciendas of wealthy landholders.

For the next several years, Zapata and rebel leader Pancho Villa (1878–1923), who operated in the northern state of Chihuahua, became an important political force in the country by publicly advocating efforts to redress the economic grievances of the poor. But neither had a broad grasp of the challenges facing the country, and power eventually gravitated to a more moderate group of reformists around the Constitutionalist Party. The latter were intent on breaking the power of the great landed families and U.S. corporations, but without engaging in radical land reform or the nationalization of property. After a bloody conflict that cost the lives of thousands, the moderates consolidated power, and in 1917, they promulgated a new constitution that established a strong presidency, initiated land reform policies, established limits on foreign investment, and set an agenda for social welfare programs.

In 1920, Constitutionalist leader Alvaro Obregón assumed the presidency and began to carry out his reform program. But real change did not take place until the presidency of General Lazaro Cárdenas (1895–1970) in 1934. Cárdenas won wide popularity with the peasants by ordering the redistribution of 44 million acres of land controlled by landed elites. He also seized control of the oil industry, which had hitherto been dominated by major U.S. oil companies. Alluding to the Good Neighbor Policy, President Roosevelt refused to intervene, and eventually Mexico agreed to compensate U.S. oil companies for their lost property. It then set up PEMEX, a governmental organization, to run the oil industry. By now, the revolution was democratic in name only, as the official political party, known as the Institutional Revolutionary Party (PRI), controlled the levers of power throughout society. Every six years, for more than half

Struggle for the Banner. Like Diego Rivera, David Alfaro Siqueiros (1896–1974) painted on public buildings large murals that celebrated the Mexican Revolution and the workers' and peasants' struggle for freedom. Beginning in the 1930s, Siqueiros expressed sympathy for the exploited and downtrodden peoples of Mexico in dramatic frescoes such as this one. He painted similar murals in Uruguay, Argentina, and Brazil and was once expelled from the United States, where his political art and views were considered too radical.

a century, PRI presidential candidates automatically succeeded each other in office.

Latin American Culture

The first half of the twentieth century witnessed a dramatic increase in literary activity in Latin America, a result in part of its ambivalent relationship with Europe and the United States. Many authors, while experimenting with imported modernist styles, felt compelled to proclaim Latin America's unique identity through the adoption of native themes and social issues. In *The Underdogs* (1915), for example, Mariano Azuela (1873–1952) presented a sympathetic but not uncritical portrait of the Mexican Revolution as his country entered an era of unsettling change.

In their determination to commend Latin America's distinctive characteristics, some writers extolled the promise of the region's vast virgin lands and the diversity of its peoples. In *Don Segundo Sombra*, published in 1926, Ricardo Guiraldes (1886–1927) celebrated the life of the ideal *gaucho* (cowboy), defining Argentina's hope and strength through the enlightened management of its fertile earth. Likewise, in *Dona Barbara*, Rómulo Gallegos (1884–1969) wrote in a similar vein about his native Venezuela. Other authors pursued the theme of solitude and detachment, a product of the region's physical separation from the rest of the world.

Latin American artists followed their literary counterparts in joining the Modernist movement in Europe, yet they too were eager to promote the emergence of a new regional and national essence. In Mexico, where the government provided financial support for painting murals on public buildings, the artist Diego Rivera (1886–1957) began to produce a monumental style of mural art that served two purposes: to illustrate the national past by portraying Aztec legends and folk customs and to popularize a political message in favor of realizing the social goals of the Mexican Revolution. His wife, Frida Kahlo (1907–1954), incorporated Surrealist whimsy in her own paintings, many of which were portraits of herself and her family.

CONCLUSION

*T*HE TURMOIL BROUGHT ABOUT by World War I not only resulted in the destruction of several of the major Western empires and a redrawing of the map of Europe but also opened the door to political and social upheavals elsewhere in the world. In the Middle East, the decline and fall of the Ottoman Empire led to the creation of the secular republic of Turkey and several other new states carved out of the carcass of the old empire.

Other parts of Asia and Africa also witnessed the rise of movements for national independence. In India, Gandhi and his campaign of civil disobedience played a crucial role in his country's bid to be free of British rule. China waged its own dramatic struggle to establish a modern nation as two dynamic political organizations—the Nationalists and the Communists—competed for legitimacy as the rightful heirs of the old order. Japan continued to follow its own path to modernization, which, although successful from an economic point of view, took a menacing turn during the 1930s.

The nations of Latin America faced their own economic problems because of their dependence on exports. Increasing U.S. investments in Latin America contributed to growing hostility against the powerful neighbor to the north. The Great Depression forced the region to begin developing new industries, but it also led to the rise of authoritarian governments, some of them modeled after the fascist regimes of Italy and Germany.

By demolishing the remnants of their old civilization on the battlefields of World War I, Europeans had inadvertently encouraged the subject peoples of their vast colonial empires to begin their own movements for national independence. The process was by no means completed in the two decades following the Treaty of Versailles, but the bonds of imperial rule had been severely strained. Once Europeans began to weaken themselves in the even more destructive conflict of World War II, the hopes of African and Asian peoples for national independence and freedom could at last be realized. It is to that devastating world conflict that we now turn.

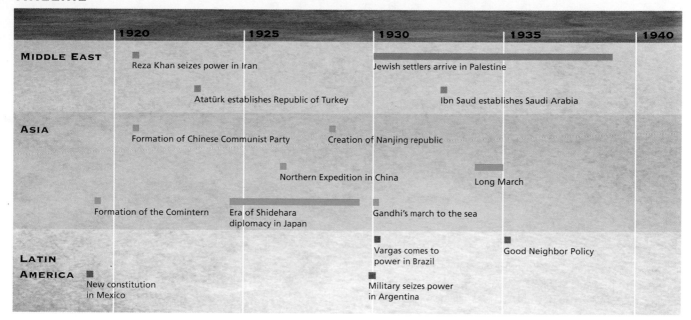

	1920	**1925**	**1930**	**1935**	**1940**
MIDDLE EAST	Reza Khan seizes power in Iran		Jewish settlers arrive in Palestine		
		Atatürk establishes Republic of Turkey	Ibn Saud establishes Saudi Arabia		
ASIA	Formation of Chinese Communist Party		Creation of Nanjing republic		
		Northern Expedition in China		Long March	
	Formation of the Comintern	Era of Shidehara diplomacy in Japan	Gandhi's march to the sea		
LATIN AMERICA	New constitution in Mexico		Vargas comes to power in Brazil	Good Neighbor Policy	
			Military seizes power in Argentina		

CHAPTER NOTES

1. Quoted in M. Gettleman, ed., *History, Documents, and Opinion on a Major World Crisis* (New York, 1965.), p. 32.
2. Ts'ai Yuan-p'ei, "Ta Lin Ch'in-nan Han," in *Ts'ai Yuan-p'ei Hsien-sheng Ch'uan-chi* [Collected Works of Mr. Ts'ai Yuan-p'ei] (Taipei, 1968), pp. 1057–1058.
3. Quoted in Nicholas Rowland Clifford, *Spoilt Children of Empire: Westerners in Shanghai and the Chinese Revolution of the 1920s* (Hanover, N.H., 1991), p. 16.
4. Quoted in William Theodore de Bary et al., eds., *Sources of Chinese Tradition* (New York, 1963), p. 783.
5. Lu Xun, "Diary of a Madman," in *Selected Works of Lu Hsun* (Beijing, 1957), vol. 1, p. 20.

THE CRISIS DEEPENS: THE OUTBREAK OF WORLD WAR II

IN SEPTEMBER 1931, acting on the pretext that Chinese troops had attacked a Japanese railway near the northern Chinese city of Mukden, Japanese military units stationed in the area seized control throughout Manchuria. Although Japanese military authorities in Manchuria announced that China had provoked the action, the "Mukden incident," as it was called, had actually been carried out by Japanese saboteurs. Eventually, worldwide protests against the Japanese action led the League of Nations to send an investigative commission to Manchuria. When the commission issued a report condemning the seizure, Japan angrily withdrew from the League. Over the next several years, the Japanese consolidated their hold on Manchuria, renaming it Manchukuo and placing it under the titular authority of former Chinese emperor and now Japanese puppet, Pu Yi.

Although no one knew it at the time, the Mukden incident would later be singled out by some observers as the opening shot of World War II. The failure of the League of Nations to take decisive action sent a strong signal to Japan and other potentially aggressive states that they might seek their objectives without the risk of united opposition by the major world powers. Despite its agonizing efforts to build a system of peace and stability that would prevent future wars, the League had failed dismally, and the world was once again about to slide inexorably into a new global conflict. ◇

The Rise of Dictatorial Regimes

In Europe, the first clear step to war took place two years later. On February 3, 1933, only four days after he had been appointed chancellor of Germany, Adolf Hitler met secretly with Germany's leading generals. He revealed to them his desire to remove the "cancer of democracy," create a new authoritarian leadership, and forge a new domestic unity. His foreign policy objectives were equally striking. Since Germany's living space was too small for its people, Hitler said, Germany must rearm and prepare for "the conquest of new living space in the east and its ruthless Germanization." From the outset, Adolf Hitler had a clear vision of his goals, and their implementation meant another war.

There was thus a close relationship between the rise of dictatorial regimes in the 1930s and the coming of World War II. The apparent triumph of liberal democracy in 1919 proved extremely short-lived. By 1939, only two major states in Europe, France and Great Britain, remained democratic. Italy and Germany had installed fascist regimes, and the Soviet Union under Joseph Stalin was a repressive dictatorial state. A host of other European states, and Latin American countries as well, adopted authoritarian systems, while a militarist regime in Japan moved that country down the path to war.

Dictatorships, of course, were hardly a new phenomenon as a means of governing human societies, but the type of political system that emerged after World War I did exhibit some ominous new characteristics. The modern "totalitarian" state, as it is sometimes labeled, transcended the ideal of passive obedience expected in a traditional dictatorship or authoritarian monarchy. It required the active loyalty and commitment of all its citizens to the regime and its goals and used modern mass propaganda techniques and high-speed communications to conquer citizens' minds and hearts. That control had a purpose: the active involvement of the masses in the achievement of the regime's goals, whether they be war, a classless utopia, or a thousand-year Reich.

The modern totalitarian state—whether of the right (as in Germany) or of the left (as in the Soviet Union—was to be led by a single leader and a single party. It ruthlessly rejected the liberal ideal of limited government power and constitutional guarantees of individual freedoms. Indeed, individual freedom was to be subordinated to the collective will of the masses, organized and determined for them by a leader or leaders. Modern technology also gave totalitarian states the ability to use unprecedented police powers to impose their wishes on their subjects.

What explains the emergence of this frightening new form of government at a time when the Enlightenment and the Industrial Revolution had offered such a bright perspective on the improvement of the human condition? According to the philosopher Hannah Arendt, in her renowned study, *The Origins of Totalitarianism* (1951), the totalitarian state was a direct product of the modern age. At a time when traditional sources of identity, such as religion and the local community, were in a state of decline, alienated intellectuals found fertile ground for their radical ideas among rootless peoples deprived of their communal instincts and their traditional faiths by the corrosive effects of the Industrial Age.

The Birth of Fascism

In the early 1920s, in the wake of economic turmoil, political disorder, and the general insecurity and fear stemming from World War I, Benito Mussolini (1883–1945) burst upon the Italian scene with the first Fascist movement in Europe. Mussolini began his political career as a socialist but was expelled from the Socialist Party after supporting Italy's entry into World War I, a position contrary to the socialist principle of ardent neutrality in imperialist wars. In 1919, Mussolini established a new political group, the *Fascio di Combattimento,* or League of Combat. It received little attention in the parliamentary elections of 1919, but Italy's three major political parties were unable to form an effective governmental coalition. When socialists began to speak of the need for revolution, provoking worker strikes and a general climate of class violence, alarmed conservatives turned to the Fascists, who formed armed squads to attack socialist offices and newspapers. By 1922, Mussolini's nationalist rhetoric and ability to play to middle-class fears of radicalism, revolution, and disorder were attracting ever more adherents. On October 29, 1922, after Mussolini and the Fascists threatened to march on Rome

if they were not given power, King Victor Emmanuel III (r. 1900–1946) capitulated and made Mussolini prime minister of Italy.

By 1926, Mussolini had established the institutional framework for his Fascist dictatorship. Press laws gave the government the right to suspend any publication that fostered disrespect for the Catholic church, the monarchy, or the state. The prime minister was made "head of government" with the power to legislate by decree. A police law empowered the police to arrest and confine anybody for both nonpolitical and political crimes without due process of law. In 1926, all anti-Fascist parties were outlawed. By the end of 1926, Mussolini ruled Italy as *Il Duce,* the leader.

Mussolini left no doubt of his intentions. Fascism, he said, "is totalitarian, and the Fascist State, the synthesis and unity of all values, interprets, develops and gives strength to the whole life of the people."[1] His regime attempted to mold Italians into a single-minded community by developing Fascist organizations. By 1939, about two-thirds of the population between eight and eighteen had been enrolled in some kind of Fascist youth group. Activities for these groups included Saturday afternoon marching drills and calisthenics, seaside and mountain summer camps, and youth contests. Beginning in the 1930s, all young men were given some kind of premilitary exercises to develop discipline and provide training for war.

Mussolini hoped to create a new Italian: hardworking, physically fit, disciplined, intellectually sharp, and martially inclined. In practice, the Fascists largely reinforced traditional social attitudes, as is evident in their policies toward women. The Fascists portrayed the family as the pillar of the state and women as the foundation of the family. "Woman into the home" became the Fascist slogan. Women were to be homemakers and baby producers, "their natural and fundamental mission in life," according to Mussolini, who viewed population growth as an indicator of national strength. A practical consideration also underlay the Fascist attitude toward women: working women would compete with males for jobs in the depression economy of the 1930s. Eliminating women from the market reduced male unemployment.

Hitler and Nazi Germany

As Mussolini began to lay the foundations of his Fascist state in Italy, a young admirer was harboring similar dreams in Germany. Born on April 20, 1889, Adolf Hitler was the son of an Austrian customs official. He had done poorly in secondary school and eventually made his way to Vienna to become an artist. Through careful observation of the political scene, Hitler became an avid German nationalist who learned from his experience in mass politics in Austria how political parties could use propaganda and terror effectively. But it was only after World War I, during which he had served as a soldier on the Western Front, that Hitler became actively involved in politics. By then, he had become convinced that the cause of German defeat had been the Jews, for whom he now developed a fervent hatred.

The Roots of Anti-Semitism Anti-Semitism, of course, was not new to European civilization. Since the Middle Ages, Jews had been portrayed as the murderers of Christ and were often subjected to mob violence and official persecution. Their rights were restricted, and they were physically separated from Christians in residential quarters known as ghettos. By the nineteenth century, as a result of the ideals of the Enlightenment and the French Revolution, Jews were increasingly granted legal equality in many European countries. Nevertheless, Jews were not completely accepted, and this ambivalence was apparent throughout Europe.

Nowhere in Europe were Jews more visible than in Germany and the German-speaking areas of Austria-Hungary. During the nineteenth century, many Jews in both countries had left the ghetto and become assimilated into the surrounding Christian population. Some entered what had previously been the closed world of politics and the professions. Many Jews became successful as bankers, lawyers, scientists, scholars, journalists, and stage performers. In 1880, for example, Jews made up 10 percent of the population of Vienna but accounted for 39 percent of its medical students and 23 percent of its law students.

All too often, such achievements provoked envy and distrust. During the last two decades of the century, conservatives in Germany and Austria founded right-wing parties that used dislike of Jews to win the votes of traditional lower-middle-class groups who felt threatened by changing times. Such parties also played on the rising sentiment of racism in German society. Spurred by social Darwinian ideas that nations, like the human species, were engaged in a brutal struggle for survival, rabid German nationalists promoted the concept of the *Volk* (nation, people, or race) as an underlying idea in German history since the medieval era. Portraying the German people as the successors of the pure "Aryan" race, the true and original creators of Western culture, nationalist groups called for Germany to take the lead in a desperate struggle to fight for European civilization and save it from the destructive assaults of such allegedly lower races as Jews, blacks, and Asians.

Hitler's Rise to Power, 1919–1933 At the end of World War I, Hitler joined the obscure German Workers' Party, one of a number of right-wing nationalist parties in Munich. By the summer of 1921, he had assumed total control over

the party, which he renamed the National Socialist German Workers' Party (NSDAP), or Nazi for short. Hitler worked assiduously to develop the party into a mass political movement with flags, party badges, uniforms, its own newspaper, and its own police force or party militia known as the SA—the *Sturmabteilung,* or Storm Troops. The SA added an element of force and terror to the growing Nazi movement. Hitler's own oratorical skills were largely responsible for attracting an increasing number of followers.

In November 1923, Hitler staged an armed uprising against the government in Munich, but the so-called Beer Hall Putsch was quickly crushed, and Hitler was sentenced to prison. During his brief stay in jail, he wrote *Mein Kampf* (My Struggle), an autobiographical account of his movement and its underlying ideology. Virulent German nationalism, anti-Semitism, and anticommunism were linked together by a social Darwinian theory of struggle that stressed the right of superior nations to *Lebensraum* ("living space") through expansion and the right of superior individuals to secure authoritarian leadership over the masses.

After his release from prison, Hitler worked assiduously to reorganize the Nazi Party on a regional basis and expand it to all parts of Germany, increasing its size from 27,000 members in 1925 to 178,000 by the end of 1929. Especially noticeable was the youthfulness of the regional, district, and branch leaders of the Nazi organization. Many young Germans were fiercely committed to Hitler because he gave them the promise of a new life.

By 1932, the Nazi Party had 800,000 members and had become the largest party in the Reichstag, the German parliament. No doubt, Germany's economic difficulties were a crucial factor in the Nazis' rise to power. Unemployment rose dramatically, from 4.35 million in 1931 to 6 million by the winter of 1932. The economic and psychological impact of the Great Depression made extremist parties more attractive. But Hitler claimed to stand above politics and promised to create a new Germany free of class differences and party infighting. His appeal to national pride, national honor, and traditional militarism struck chords of emotion in his listeners.

Increasingly, the conservative elites of Germany—the industrial magnates, landed aristocrats, military establishment, and higher bureaucrats—came to see Hitler as the man who had the mass support to establish a right-wing, authoritarian regime that would save Germany from a Communist takeover. Under pressure, President Paul von Hindenburg agreed to allow Hitler to become chancellor on January 30, 1933, and form a new government.

Within two months, Hitler had laid the foundations for the Nazis' complete control over Germany. On February 27, he convinced Hindenburg to issue a decree suspending all basic rights for the full duration of the emergency, thus enabling the Nazis to arrest and imprison anyone without redress. The crowning step in Hitler's "legal" seizure of power came on March 23, when the Reichstag passed the Enabling Act by a two-thirds vote. This legislation, which empowered the government to dispense with constitutional forms for four years while it issued laws that dealt with the country's problems, provided the legal basis for Hitler's subsequent acts. In effect, Hitler became a dictator appointed by the parliamentary body itself.

With their new source of power, the Nazis acted quickly to consolidate their control. The civil service was purged of Jews and democratic elements, concentration camps were established for opponents of the new regime, trade unions were dissolved, and all political parties except the Nazis were abolished. When Hindenburg died on August 2, 1934, the office of Reich president was abolished, and Hitler became sole ruler of Germany. Public officials and soldiers were all required to take a personal oath of loyalty to Hitler as the "Führer (leader) of the German Reich and people."

The Nazi State, 1933–1939 Having smashed the Weimar Republic, Hitler now turned to his larger objective, the creation of an Aryan racial state that would dominate Europe and possibly the world for generations to come. The Nazis pursued the vision of this totalitarian state in a variety of ways. Most dramatic were the mass demonstrations and spectacles employed to integrate the German nation into a collective fellowship and to mobilize it as an instrument for Hitler's policies. In the economic sphere, the Nazis pursued the use of public works projects and "pump-priming" grants to private construction firms to foster employment and end the depression. But there is little doubt that rearmament contributed far more to solving the unemployment problem. Unemployment, which had stood at 6 million in 1932, dropped to 2.6 million in 1934 and less than 500,000 in 1937. The regime claimed full credit for solving Germany's economic woes, although much of the success must be ascribed to decisions made at the initiative of local officials. Hitler himself had little interest in either economics or administration, and his prestige undoubtedly benefited enormously from spontaneous efforts undertaken throughout the country by his followers.

For its enemies, the Nazi totalitarian state had its instruments of terror and repression. Especially important was the SS (*Schutzstaffel*, or "protection echelon"). Originally created as Hitler's personal bodyguard, the SS, under the direction of Heinrich Himmler (1900–1945), came to control all of the regular and secret police forces. Himmler and the SS functioned on the basis of two principles, ideology and terror, and would eventually play a major role in the execution squads and death camps for the extermination of the Jews.

Other institutions, including the Catholic and Protestant churches, primary and secondary schools, and universities, were also brought under the control of the state. Nazi professional organizations and leagues were formed for civil servants, teachers, women, farmers, doctors, and lawyers, and youth organizations—the *Hitler Jugend* (Hitler Youth) and

© Hugo Jaeger, Life Magazine/Time Life Pictures/Getty Images

The Nazi Mass Spectacle. Hitler and the Nazis made clever use of mass spectacles to rally the German people behind the Nazi regime. These mass demonstrations evoked intense enthusiasm, as is evident in this photograph of Hitler arriving at the Bückeberg near Hamelin for the Harvest Festival in 1937. Almost one million people were present for the celebration.

its female counterpart, the *Bund Deutscher Mädel* (League of German Maidens)—were given special attention.

The Nazi attitude toward women was largely determined by ideological considerations. Women played a crucial role in the Aryan racial state as bearers of the children who would ensure the triumph of the Aryan race. To the Nazis, the differences between men and women were quite natural. Men were warriors and political leaders, while women were destined to be wives and mothers. Certain professions, including university teaching, medicine, and law, were considered inappropriate for women, especially married women. Instead, the Nazis encouraged women to pursue professional occupations that had direct practical application, such as social work and nursing. In addition to restrictive legislation against females, the Nazi regime pushed its campaign against working women with such poster slogans as "Get hold of pots and pans and broom and you'll sooner find a groom!"

From the beginning, the Nazi Party reflected the strong anti-Semitic beliefs of Adolf Hitler. Many of the early attacks on Jews, however, were essentially spontaneous in character. The regime quickly took note, and in September 1935, the Nazis announced new racial laws at the annual party rally in Nuremberg. These Nuremberg laws excluded German Jews from German citizenship and forbade marriages and extramarital relations between Jews and German citizens. But a more violent phase of anti-Jewish activity was initiated on November 9–10, 1938, the infamous *Kristallnacht,* or night of shattered glass. The assassination of a German diplomat in Paris became the excuse for a Nazi-led destructive rampage against the Jews, in which synagogues were burned, seven thousand Jewish businesses were destroyed, and at least one hundred Jews were killed. Moreover, twenty thousand Jewish males were rounded up and sent to concentration camps. Jews were now barred from all public buildings and prohibited from owning, managing, or working in any retail store. Finally, under the direction of the SS, Jews were encouraged to "emigrate from Germany." After the outbreak of World War II, the policy of emigration was replaced by a more gruesome one.

The Spread of Authoritarianism in Europe

Nowhere had the map of Europe been more drastically altered by World War I than in eastern Europe. The new states of Austria, Poland, Czechoslovakia, and Yugoslavia adopted parliamentary systems, and the preexisting kingdoms of Romania and Bulgaria gained new parliamentary constitutions in 1920. Greece became a republic in 1924. Hungary's government was parliamentary in form but controlled by its landed aristocrats. Thus, at the beginning of the 1920s, political democracy seemed well established.

Yet almost everywhere in eastern Europe, parliamentary governments soon gave way to authoritarian regimes.

Several problems helped create this situation. Eastern European states had little tradition of liberalism or parliamentary politics and no substantial middle class to support them. Then, too, these states were largely rural and agrarian. Many of the peasants were largely illiterate, and much of the land was still dominated by large landowners who feared the growth of agrarian peasant parties with their schemes for land redistribution. Ethnic conflicts also threatened to tear these countries apart. Fearful of land reform, Communist agrarian upheaval, and ethnic conflict, powerful landowners, the churches, and even some members of the small middle class looked to authoritarian governments to maintain the old system. Only Czechoslovakia, with its substantial middle class, liberal tradition, and strong industrial base, maintained its political democracy.

In Spain, democracy also failed to survive. Fearful of the rising influence of left-wing elements in the government, in July 1936 Spanish military forces led by General Francisco Franco (1892–1975) launched a brutal and bloody civil war that lasted three years. Foreign intervention complicated the situation. Franco's forces were aided by arms, money, and men from Italy and Germany, while the government was assisted by forty thousand foreign volunteers and trucks, planes, tanks, and military advisers from the Soviet Union. After Franco's forces captured Madrid on March 28, 1939, the Spanish Civil War finally came to an end. General Franco soon established a dictatorship that favored large landowners, businessmen, and the Catholic clergy.

The Rise of Militarism in Japan

The rise of militant forces in Japan resulted not from a seizure of power by a new political party but from the growing influence of such elements at the top of the political hierarchy. During the 1920s, a multiparty system based on democratic practices appeared to be emerging. Two relatively moderate political parties, the Minseito and the Seiyukai, dominated the Diet and took turns providing executive leadership in the cabinet. Radical elements existed at each end of the political spectrum, but neither militant nationalists nor violent revolutionaries appeared to present a threat to the stability of the system.

In fact, the political system was probably weaker than it seemed at the time. Both of the major parties were deeply dependent on campaign contributions from powerful corporations (the *zaibatsu*), and conservative forces connected to the military or the old landed aristocracy were still highly influential behind the scenes. As in the Weimar Republic in Germany during the same period, the actual power base of moderate political forces was weak, and politicians unwittingly undermined the fragility of the system by engaging in bitter attacks on each other.

Political tensions in Japan increased in 1928 when Zhang Xueliang, son and successor of the Japanese puppet Marshall Zhang Zuolin (see Chapter 5), decided to integrate Manchuria into the Nanjing republic. Appeals from Tokyo to Washington for a U.S. effort to restrain Chiang Kai-shek were rebuffed.

Already suffering from the decline of its business interests on the mainland, after 1929 Japan began to feel the impact of the Great Depression when the United States and major European nations raised their tariff rates against Japanese imports in a desperate effort to protect local businesses and jobs. The value of Japanese exports dropped by 50 percent from 1929 to 1931, and wages dropped nearly as much. Hardest hit were the farmers as the price of rice and other staple food crops plummeted. At the same time, militant nationalists, outraged at Japan's loss of influence in Manchuria, began to argue that the Shidehara policy of peaceful cooperation with other nations in maintaining the existing international economic order had been a failure. It was undoubtedly that vision that had motivated the military coup d'état launched in Mukden in the early fall of 1931.

During the early 1930s, civilian cabinets sought to cope with the economic challenges presented by the Great Depression. By abandoning the gold standard, Prime Minister Inukai Tsuyoshi was able to lower the price of Japanese goods on the world market, and exports climbed back to earlier levels. But the political parties were no longer able to stem the growing influence of militant nationalist elements. Despite its doubts about the wisdom of the Mukden incident, the cabinet was too divided to disavow it, and military officers in Manchuria increasingly acted on their own initiative.

In May 1932, Inukai Tsuyoshi was assassinated by right-wing extremists. He was succeeded by a moderate, Admiral Saito Makoto, but ultranationalist patriotic societies began to terrorize opponents, assassinating businessmen and public figures identified with the policy of conciliation toward the outside world. Some, like the publicist Kita Ikki, were convinced that the parliamentary system had been corrupted by materialism and Western values and should be replaced by a system that would return to traditional Japanese values and imperial authority. His message, "Asia for the Asians," had not won widespread support during the relatively prosperous 1920s but increased in popularity after the Great Depression, which convinced many Japanese that capitalism was unsuitable for Japan.

During the mid-1930s, the influence of the military and extreme nationalists over the government steadily increased.

Minorities and left-wing elements were persecuted, and moderates were intimidated into silence. Terrorists tried for their part in assassination attempts portrayed themselves as selfless patriots and received light sentences. Japan continued to hold national elections, and moderate candidates continued to receive substantial popular support, but the cabinets were dominated by the military or advocates of Japanese expansionism. In February 1936, junior officers in the army led a coup in the capital city of Tokyo, briefly occupying the Diet building and other key government installations and assassinating several members of the cabinet. The ringleaders were quickly tried and convicted of treason, but widespread sympathy for the defendants strengthened the influence of the military in the halls of power even further.

The Path to War in Europe

When Hitler became chancellor on January 30, 1933, Germany's situation in Europe seemed weak. The Versailles Treaty had created a demilitarized zone on Germany's western border that would allow the French to move into the heavily industrialized parts of Germany in the event of war. To Germany's east, the smaller states, such as Poland and Czechoslovakia, had defensive treaties with France. The Versailles Treaty had also limited Germany's army to 100,000 troops with no air force and only a small navy.

Posing as a man of peace in his public speeches, Hitler emphasized that Germany wished only to revise the unfair provisions of Versailles by peaceful means and occupy Germany's rightful place among the European states. On March 9, 1935, he announced the creation of a new air force and, one week later, the introduction of a military draft that would expand Germany's army (the *Wehrmacht*) from 100,000 to 550,000 troops. France, Great Britain, and Italy condemned Germany's unilateral repudiation of the Versailles Treaty but took no concrete action.

On March 7, 1936, buoyed by his conviction that the Western democracies had no intention of using force to maintain the Treaty of Versailles, Hitler sent German troops into the demilitarized Rhineland. According to the Versailles Treaty, the French had the right to use force against any violation of the demilitarized Rhineland. But France would not act without British support, and the British viewed the occupation of German territory by German troops as reasonable action by a dissatisfied power. The London *Times,* reflecting the war-weariness that had gripped much of the European public since the end of the Great War, noted that the Germans were only "going into their own back garden."

Meanwhile, Hitler gained new allies. In October 1935, Mussolini committed Fascist Italy to imperial expansion by invading Ethiopia. Angered by French and British opposition to his invasion, Mussolini welcomed Hitler's support and began to draw closer to the German dictator he had once called a buffoon. The joint intervention of Germany and Italy on behalf of General Franco in the Spanish Civil War in 1936 also drew the two nations closer together. In October 1936, Mussolini and Hitler concluded an agreement that recognized their common political and economic interests. One month later, Germany and Japan concluded the Anti-Comintern Pact and agreed to maintain a common front against communism.

Stalin Seeks a United Front

From behind the walls of the Kremlin in Moscow, Joseph Stalin undoubtedly observed the effects of the Great Depression with a measure of satisfaction. During the early 1920s, once it became clear that the capitalist states in Europe had managed to survive without socialist revolutions, Stalin decided to improve relations with the outside world as a means of obtaining capital and technological assistance in promoting economic growth in the Soviet Union. But Lenin had predicted that after a brief period of stability in Europe, a new crisis brought on by overproduction and intense competition was likely to occur in the capitalist world. That, he added, would mark the beginning of the next wave of revolution. In the meantime, he declared, "We will give the capitalists the shovels with which to bury themselves."

To Stalin, the onset of the Great Depression was a signal that the next era of turbulence in the capitalist world was at hand, and during the early 1930s, Soviet foreign policy returned to the themes of class struggle and social revolution. When the influence of the Nazi Party reached significant proportions in the early 1930s, Stalin viewed it as a pathological form of capitalism and ordered the Communist Party in Germany not to support the fragile Weimar Republic. Hitler would quickly fall, he reasoned, leading to a Communist takeover.

By 1935, Stalin became uneasily aware that Hitler was not only securely in power in Berlin but also represented a serious threat to the Soviet Union. That summer, at a major meeting of the Communist International held in Moscow, Soviet officials announced a shift in policy. The Soviet Union would now seek to form a united front with capitalist democratic nations throughout the world against the common danger of Nazism and fascism. Communist parties in capitalist countries and in colonial areas were instructed to cooperate with "peace-loving democratic forces" in forming coalition governments called Popular Fronts.

In most capitalist countries, Stalin's move was greeted with suspicion, but in France, a coalition of leftist parties—Communists, Socialists, and Radicals—fearful that rightists intended to seize power, formed a Popular Front government in June 1936. The new government succeeded in launching a program for workers that some called the French New Deal. It included the right of collective bargaining, a forty-hour workweek, two-week paid vacations, and minimum wages. But such policies failed to solve the problems of the depression, and although it survived until 1938, the Front was for all intents and purposes dead before then. Moscow signed a defensive treaty with France and reached an agreement with three non-Communist states in eastern Europe (Czechoslovakia, Romania, and Yugoslavia), but talks with Great Britain achieved little result. The Soviet Union, rebuffed by London and disappointed by Paris, feared that it might be forced to face Hitler alone.

Decision at Munich

By the end of 1936, the Treaty of Versailles had been virtually scrapped, and Germany had erased much of the stigma of defeat. Hitler, whose foreign policy successes had earned him much public acclaim, was convinced that neither the French nor the British would provide much opposition to his plans and decided in 1938 to move on Austria. By threatening Austria with invasion, Hitler coerced the Austrian chancellor into putting Austrian Nazis in charge of the government. The new government promptly invited German troops to enter Austria and assist in maintaining law and order. One day later, on March 13, 1938, Hitler formally annexed Austria to Germany.

The annexation of Austria, which had not raised objections in other European capitals, put Germany in position for Hitler's next objective—the destruction of Czechoslovakia. Although the latter was quite prepared to defend itself and was well supported by pacts with France and the Soviet Union, Hitler believed that its allies would not use force to defend it against a German attack.

He was right again. On September 15, 1938, Hitler demanded the cession to Germany of the Sudetenland (an area in western Czechoslovakia that was inhabited largely by ethnic Germans) and expressed his willingness to risk "world war" to achieve his objective. Instead of objecting, the British, French, Germans, and Italians—at a hastily arranged conference at Munich—reached an agreement that essentially met all of Hitler's demands. German troops were allowed to occupy the Sudetenland as the Czechs, abandoned by their Western allies, as well as by the Soviet Union, stood by helplessly. The Munich Conference was the high point of Western appeasement of Hitler. British Prime Minister Neville Chamberlain returned to England from Munich boasting that the agreement meant "peace in our time." Hitler had promised Chamberlain that he had made his last demand (see the box on p. 119).

THE MUNICH CONFERENCE

At the Munich Conference, the leaders of France and Great Britain capitulated to Hitler's demands on Czechoslovakia. When British Prime Minister Neville Chamberlain defended his actions at Munich as necessary for peace, another British statesman, Winston Churchill, characterized the settlement at Munich as "a disaster of the first magnitude." After World War II, political figures in western Europe and the United States would cite the example of appeasement at Munich to encourage vigorous resistance to expansionism by the Soviet Union.

What were the opposing views of Churchill and Chamberlain on how to respond to Hitler's demands at Munich? Do these arguments have any wider relevance for other world crises?

Winston Churchill, Speech to the House of Commons (October 5, 1938)

I will begin by saying what everybody would like to ignore or forget but which must nevertheless be stated, namely, that we have sustained a total and unmitigated defeat, and that France has suffered even more than we have. . . . The utmost my right honorable Friend the Prime Minister . . . has been able to gain for Czechoslovakia and in the matters which were in dispute has been that the German dictator, instead of snatching his victuals from the table, has been content to have them served to him course by course. . . . And I will say this, that I believe the Czechs, left to themselves and told they were going to get no help from the Western Powers, would have been able to make better terms than they have got. . . .

We are in the presence of a disaster of the first magnitude which has befallen Great Britain and France. Do not let us blind ourselves to that. . . .

And do not suppose that this is the end. This is only the beginning of the reckoning. This is only the first sip, the first foretaste of a bitter cup which will be proffered to us year by year unless by a supreme recovery of moral health and martial vigor, we arise again and take our stand for freedom as in the olden time.

Neville Chamberlain, Speech to the House of Commons (October 6, 1938)

That is my answer to those who say that we should have told Germany weeks ago that, if her army crossed the border of Czechoslovakia, we should be at war with her. We had no treaty obligations and no legal obligations to Czechoslovakia. . . . When we were convinced, as we became convinced, that nothing any longer would keep the Sudetenland within the Czechoslovakian State, we urged the Czech Government as strongly as we could to agree to the cession of territory, and to agree promptly. . . . It was a hard decision for anyone who loved his country to take, but to accuse us of having by that advice betrayed the Czechoslovakian State is simply preposterous. What we did was save her from annihilation and give her a chance of new life as a new State, which involves the loss of territory and fortifications, but may perhaps enable her to enjoy in the future and develop a national existence under a neutrality and security comparable to that which we see in Switzerland today. Therefore, I think the Government deserves the approval of this House for their conduct of affairs in this recent crisis, which has saved Czechoslovakia from destruction and Europe from Armageddon.

SOURCES: *Parliamentary Debates, House of Commons* (London: His Majesty's Stationery Office, 1938), vol. 339, pp. 361–369; Neville Chamberlain, *In Search of Peace* (New York: Putnam, 1939), pp. 215, 217.

In fact, Munich confirmed Hitler's perception that the Western democracies were weak and would not fight. Increasingly, he was convinced of his own infallibility and had by no means been satisfied at Munich. In March 1939, Hitler occupied the Czech lands (Bohemia and Moravia), and the Slovaks, with his encouragement, declared their independence of the Czechs and set up the German puppet state of Slovakia. On the evening of March 15, 1939, Hitler triumphantly declared in Prague that he would be known as the greatest German of them all.

At last, the Western states reacted vigorously to the Nazi threat. Hitler's naked aggression had made it clear that his promises were utterly worthless. When he began to demand the return to Germany of Danzig (which had been made a free city by the Treaty of Versailles to serve as a seaport for Poland), Britain recognized the danger and offered to protect Poland in the event of war. Both France and Britain realized that they needed Soviet help to contain Nazi aggression and began political and military negotiations with Stalin. Their distrust of Soviet communism, however, made an alliance unlikely.

Meanwhile, Hitler pressed on in the belief that Britain and France would not go to war over Poland. To preclude an alliance between the western European states and the Soviet Union, which would create the danger of a two-front war, Hitler, ever the opportunist, approached Stalin, who had given up hope of any alliance with Britain and France. The announcement on August 23, 1939, of the Nazi-Soviet Nonaggression Pact shocked the world. The treaty with the Soviet Union gave Hitler the freedom he sought, and on September 1, German forces invaded Poland. Two days later, Britain and France declared war on Germany. Europe was again at war.

The Path to War in Asia

In the years immediately following the Japanese seizure of Manchuria in the fall of 1931, Japanese military forces began to expand gradually into North China. Using the tactics of military intimidation and diplomatic bullying rather than all-out attack, Japanese military authorities began to carve out a new "sphere of influence" south of the Great Wall.

Not all politicians in Tokyo agreed with this aggressive policy—the young Emperor Hirohito, who had succeeded to the throne in 1926, was initially nervous about possible international repercussions—but right-wing terrorists assassinated some of its key critics and intimidated others into silence. The United States refused to recognize the Japanese takeover of Manchuria, which Secretary of State Henry L. Stimson declared an act of "international outlawry," but was unwilling to threaten the use of force. Instead, the Americans attempted to appease Japan in the hope of encouraging moderate forces in Japanese society. As one senior U.S. diplomat with long experience in Asia warned in a memorandum to the president:

> Utter defeat of Japan would be no blessing to the Far East or to the world. It would merely create a new set of stresses, and substitute for Japan the USSR—as the successor to Imperial Russia—as a contestant (and at least an equally unscrupulous and dangerous one) for the mastery of the East. Nobody except perhaps Russia would gain from our victory in such a war.[2]

For the moment, the prime victim of Japanese aggression was China. Nevertheless, Chiang Kai-shek attempted to avoid a confrontation with Japan so that he could deal with what he considered the greater threat from the Communists. When clashes between Chinese and Japanese troops broke out, he sought to appease the Japanese by granting them the authority to administer areas in North China. But, as the Japanese moved steadily southward, popular protests in Chinese cities against Japanese aggression intensified. In December 1936,

Chiang was briefly kidnapped by military forces commanded by General Zhang Xueliang, who compelled him to end his military efforts against the Communists in Yan'an and form a new united front against the Japanese. After Chinese and Japanese forces clashed at Marco Polo Bridge, south of Beijing, in July 1937, China refused to apologize, and hostilities spread.

A Monroe Doctrine for Asia

Japan had not planned to declare war on China, but neither side would compromise, and the 1937 incident eventually turned into a major conflict. The Japanese advanced up the Yangtze valley and seized the Chinese capital of Nanjing, raping and killing thousands of innocent civilians in the process. But Chiang Kai-shek refused to capitulate and moved his government upriver to Hankou. When the Japanese seized that city, he moved on to Chungking, in remote Sichuan Province. Japanese strategists had hoped to force Chiang to join a Japanese-dominated New Order in East Asia, comprising Japan, Manchuria, and China. Now they established a puppet regime in Nanjing that would cooperate with Japan in driving Western influence out of East Asia. Tokyo hoped eventually to seize Soviet Siberia, rich in resources, and to create a new "Monroe Doctrine for Asia" under which Japan would guide its Asian neighbors on the path to development and prosperity (see the box on p. 122). After all, who better to instruct Asian societies on modernization than the one Asian country that had already achieved it?

Tokyo's "Southern Strategy"

During the late 1930s, Japan began to cooperate with Nazi Germany on a plan to launch a joint attack on the Soviet Union and divide up its resources between them. But when Germany surprised Tokyo by signing a nonaggression pact with the Soviets in August 1939, Japanese strategists were compelled to reevaluate their long-term objectives. Japan was not strong enough to defeat the Soviet Union alone, as a small but bitter border war along the Siberian frontier near Manchukuo had amply demonstrated. So the Japanese began to shift their gaze southward to the vast resources of Southeast Asia—the oil of the Dutch East Indies, the rubber and tin of Malaya, and the rice of Burma and Indochina.

A move southward, of course, would risk war with the European colonial powers and the United States.

Japanese Advances into China, 1931–1938

A Japanese Victory in China. After consolidating its authority over Manchuria, Japan began to expand into northern China. Direct hostilities between Japanese and Chinese forces began in 1937. A year later Japanese troops seized Chiang Kai-shek's capital at Nanjing, where they proceeded to massacre much of the local population. This photograph shows Japanese units entering the city through one of the main city gates.

© Topham/The Image Works

Japan's attack on China in the summer of 1937 had already aroused strong criticism abroad, particularly from the United States, where President Franklin D. Roosevelt threatened to "quarantine" the aggressors after Japanese military units bombed an American naval ship operating in China. Public fear of involvement forced the president to draw back, but when Japan suddenly demanded the right to occupy airfields and exploit economic resources in French Indochina in the summer of 1940, the United States warned the Japanese that it would impose economic sanctions unless Japan withdrew from the area and returned to its borders of 1931.

Tokyo viewed the U.S. threat of retaliation as an obstacle to its long-term objectives. Japan badly needed liquid fuel and scrap iron from the United States. Should they be cut off, Japan would have to find them elsewhere. The Japanese were thus caught in a vise. To obtain guaranteed access to the natural resources that were necessary to fuel the Japanese military machine, Japan must risk being cut off from its current source of the raw materials that would be needed in case of a conflict. After much debate, the Japanese decided to launch a surprise attack on U.S. and European colonies in Southeast Asia in the hope of a quick victory that would evict the United States from the region.

The World at War

Using *Blitzkrieg*, or "lightning war," Hitler stunned Europe with the speed and efficiency of the German attack on Poland. Panzer divisions (a panzer division was a strike force of about three hundred tanks and accompanying forces and supplies), supported by airplanes, broke quickly through Polish lines and encircled the bewildered Polish troops, whose courageous cavalry units were no match for the mechanized forces of their adversary. Conventional infantry units then moved in to hold the newly conquered territory. Within four weeks, Poland had surrendered. On September 28, 1939, Germany and the Soviet Union officially divided Poland between them.

The War in Europe

Although Hitler was apparently surprised when France and Britain declared war on September 3, he was confident of ultimate victory. After a winter of waiting (called the "phony war"), on April 9, 1940, Germany launched a *Blitzkrieg* against Denmark and Norway. One month later, the Germans attacked the Netherlands, Belgium, and France. German panzer divisions broke through the weak French defensive positions in the Ardennes forest and raced across northern France, splitting the Allied armies and trapping French troops and the entire British army on the beaches of Dunkirk. Only by heroic efforts did the British succeed in a gigantic evacuation of 330,000 Allied (mostly British) troops. The French capitulated on June 22. German armies occupied about three-fifths of France while the French hero of World War I, Marshal Philippe Pétain (1856–1951), established a puppet regime (known as Vichy France) over the remainder. Germany was now in control of western and

JAPAN'S JUSTIFICATION FOR EXPANSION

Advocates of Japanese expansion in the 1920s and 1930s justified their proposals by claiming both economic necessity and moral imperatives. Note the familiar combination of motives, so often cited by advocates of colonial expansion, in this passage written by an extremist military leader in the late 1930s.

How do Japanese reasons for expansion in Asia compare with the concept of social Darwinism that served to justify the actions of Western imperialist powers?

Hashimoto Kingoro, "The Need for Emigration and Expansion"

We have already said that there are only three ways left to Japan to escape from pressure of surplus population. We are like a great crowd of people packed into a small and narrow room, and there are only three doors through which we might escape, namely emigration, advance into world markets, and expansion of territory. The first door, emigration, has been barred to us by the anti-Japanese immigration policies of other countries. The second door, advance into world markets, is being pushed shut by tariff barriers and the abrogation of commercial treaties. What should Japan do when two of the three doors have been closed against her?

It is quite natural that Japan should rush upon the last remaining door.

It may sound dangerous when we speak of territorial expansion, but the territorial expansion of which we speak does not in any sense of the word involve the occupation of the possessions of other countries, the planting of the Japanese flag thereon, and the declaration of the annexation to Japan. It is just that since the Powers have suppressed the circulation of Japanese materials and merchandise abroad, we are looking for some place overseas where Japanese capital, Japanese skills and Japanese labor can have free play, free from the oppression of the white race.

We would be satisfied with just this much. What moral right do the world powers who have themselves closed to us the two doors of emigration and advance into world markets have to criticize Japan's attempt to rush out of the third and last door?

If they do not approve of this, they should open the door which they have closed against us and permit the free movement overseas of Japanese emigrants and merchandise. . . .

At the time of the Manchurian incident, the entire world joined in criticism of Japan. They said that Japan was an untrustworthy nation. They said that she had recklessly brought cannon and machine guns into Manchuria, which was the territory of another country, flown airplanes over it, and finally occupied it. But the military action taken by Japan was not in the least a selfish one. Moreover, we do not recall ever having taken so much as an inch of territory belonging to another nation. The result of this incident was the establishment of the splendid new nation of Manchuria. The Powers are still discussing whether or not to recognize this new nation, but regardless of whether or not other nations recognize her, the Manchurian empire has already been established, and now, seven years after its creation, the empire is further consolidating its foundations with the aid of its friend, Japan.

And if it is still protested that our actions in Manchuria were excessively violent, we may wish to ask the white race just which country it was that sent warships and troops to India, South Africa, and Australia and slaughtered innocent natives, bound their hands and feet with iron chains, lashed their backs with iron whips, proclaimed these territories as their own, and still continues to hold them to this very day.

SOURCE: From *Sources of Japanese Tradition* by William Theodore de Bary. Copyright © 1958 by Columbia University Press, New York. Reprinted with permission of the publisher.

central Europe (see Map 6.1). Britain had still not been defeated, but it was reeling, and the wartime cabinet under Prime Minister Winston Churchill debated whether to seek a negotiated peace settlement.

The Battle of Britain As Hitler realized, an amphibious invasion of Britain could succeed only if Germany gained control of the air. In early August 1940, the *Luftwaffe* (German air force) launched a major offensive against British air and naval bases, harbors, communication centers, and war industries. The British fought back doggedly, supported by an effective radar system that gave them early warning of German attacks. Nevertheless, the British air force suffered critical losses and was probably saved by Hitler's change in strategy. In September, in retaliation for a British attack on Berlin, Hitler ordered a shift from military targets to massive bombing of cities to break British morale. The British rebuilt their air strength quickly and were soon inflicting major losses on *Luftwaffe* bombers. By the end of September, Germany had lost the

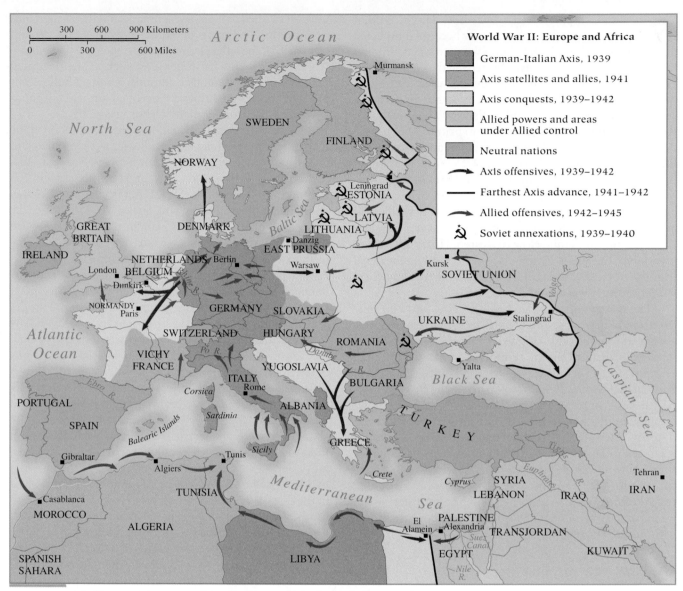

MAP 6.1 **World War II in Europe and North Africa.** With its fast and effective military, Germany quickly overwhelmed much of western Europe. However, Hitler overestimated his country's capabilities and underestimated those of his foes. By late 1942, his invasion of the Soviet Union was failing, and the United States had become a major factor in the war. The Allies successfully invaded Italy in 1943 and France in 1944. [?] Which countries were neutral, and how did geography help make their neutrality an option? 🌐 **View an animated version of this map or related maps at the World History Resource Center, at** worldrc.wadsworth.com/.

Battle of Britain, and the invasion of the British Isles had to be abandoned.

At this point, Hitler pursued a new strategy, which would involve the use of Italian troops to capture Egypt and the Suez Canal, thus closing the Mediterranean to British ships and thereby shutting off Britain's supply of oil. This strategy failed when the British routed the Italian army.

Although Hitler then sent German troops to the North African theater of war, his primary concern lay elsewhere; he had already reached the decision to fulfill his long-time obsession with the acquisition of territory in the east. In *Mein Kampf*, Hitler had declared that future German expansion must lie in the east, in the vast plains of southern Russia.

The Russian Campaign Hitler was now convinced that Britain was remaining in the war only because it expected Soviet support. If the Soviet Union were smashed, Britain's last hope would be eliminated. Moreover, the German general staff was convinced that the Soviet Union, whose military leadership had been decimated by Stalin's purge trials, could be defeated quickly and decisively. The invasion of the Soviet Union was scheduled for spring 1941 but was delayed because of problems in the Balkans. Mussolini's disastrous invasion of Greece in October 1940 exposed Italian forces to attack from British air bases in that country. To secure their Balkan flank, German troops seized both Yugoslavia and Greece in April 1941. Hitler had already obtained the political cooperation of Hungary, Bulgaria, and Romania. Now reassured, Hitler ordered an invasion of the Soviet Union on June 22, 1941, in the belief that the Soviets could still be decisively defeated before winter set in. It was a fateful miscalculation.

The massive attack stretched out along an 1,800-mile front. German troops, supported by powerful panzer units, advanced rapidly, capturing two million Russian soldiers. By November, one German army group had swept through Ukraine and a second was besieging Leningrad; a third approached within 25 miles of Moscow, the Russian capital. An early winter and unexpected Soviet resistance, however, brought a halt to the German advance. For the first time in the war, German armies had been stopped. A counterattack in December 1941 by Soviet army units newly supplied with U.S. weapons came as an ominous ending to the year for the Germans. "We knew we were in trouble," remarked one German war veteran many years later, "when we became aware that many Russian soldiers were armed with American rifles."

The New Order in Europe

After the German victories in Europe, Nazi propagandists created glowing images of a new European order based on the equality of all nations in an integrated economic community. The reality was rather different. Hitler saw the Europe he had conquered simply as subject to German domination. Only the Germans, he once said, "can really organize Europe."

The Nazi empire, which at its greatest extent stretched across continental Europe from the English Channel in the west to the outskirts of Moscow in the east, was organized in two different ways. Some areas, such as western Poland, were annexed and transformed into German provinces. Most of occupied Europe, however, was administered indirectly by German officials with the assistance of collaborationist regimes.

Racial considerations played an important role in how conquered peoples were treated. German civil administrations were established in Norway, Denmark, and the Netherlands because the Nazis considered their peoples to be Aryan, or racially akin to the Germans, and hence worthy of more lenient treatment. Latin peoples, such as the occupied French, were given military administrations. All the occupied territories were ruthlessly exploited for material goods and manpower for Germany's labor needs.

Because the conquered lands in the east contained the living space for German expansion and were populated in Nazi eyes by racially inferior Slavic peoples, Nazi administration there was considerably more ruthless. Heinrich Himmler, the leader of the SS, was put in charge of German resettlement plans in the region. His task was to replace the indigenous population with Germans, a policy first applied to the new German provinces created in western Poland. One million Poles were uprooted and dumped in southern Poland. Hundreds of thousands of ethnic Germans (descendants of Germans who had migrated years earlier from Germany to different parts of southern and eastern Europe) were encouraged to colonize designated areas in Poland. By 1942, two million ethnic Germans had been settled in Poland.

The invasion of the Soviet Union inflated Nazi visions of German colonization in the east. Hitler spoke to his intimate circle of a colossal project of social engineering after the war, in which Poles, Ukrainians, and Russians would become slave labor while German peasants settled on the abandoned lands and Germanized them. Nazis involved in this kind of planning were well aware of the human costs. Himmler told a gathering of SS officers that the destruction of 30 million Slavs was a prerequisite for German plans in the east. "Whether nations live in prosperity or starve to death interests me only insofar as we need them as slaves for our culture. Otherwise it is of no interest."[3]

Labor shortages in Germany led to a policy of ruthless mobilization of foreign labor. After the invasion of the Soviet Union, the four million Russian prisoners of war captured by the Germans, along with more than two million workers conscripted in France, became a major source of heavy labor. In 1942, a special office was created to recruit labor for German farms and industries. By the summer of 1944, seven million foreign workers were laboring in Germany, constituting 20 percent of Germany's labor force. At the same time, another seven million workers were supplying forced labor in their own countries on farms, in industries, and even in military camps. The brutal character of Germany's recruitment policies often led more and more people to resist the Nazi occupation forces.

The Holocaust No aspect of the Nazi new order was more tragic than the deliberate attempt to exterminate the Jewish people of Europe. By the beginning of 1939, Nazi policy focused on promoting the "emigration" of German Jews from Germany. Once the war began in September 1939, the so-called Jewish problem took on new dimensions. For a while, there was discussion of the Madagascar Plan—a mass shipment of Jews to the African island of Madagascar. When war contingencies made this plan impracticable, an even more drastic policy was conceived.

The SS was given responsibility for what the Nazis called the Final Solution to the Jewish problem—the annihilation of the Jewish people. Reinhard Heydrich (1904–1942), head of the SS's Security Service, was given administrative responsibility for the Final Solution. After the defeat of Poland, Heydrich ordered his special strike forces (*Einsatzgruppen*) to round up all Polish Jews and concentrate them in ghettos established in a number of Polish cities.

In June 1941, the *Einsatzgruppen* were given new responsibilities as mobile killing units. These death squads followed the regular army's advance into the Soviet Union. Their job was to round up Jews in the villages and execute and bury them in mass graves, often giant pits dug by the victims themselves before they were shot. Such constant killing produced morale problems among the SS executioners. During a visit to Minsk in the Soviet Union, Himmler tried to build morale by pointing out that

> he would not like it if Germans did such a thing gladly. But their conscience was in no way impaired, for they were soldiers who had to carry out every order unconditionally. He alone had responsibility before God and Hitler for everything that was happening, . . . and he was acting from a deep understanding of the necessity for this operation.[4]

Although it has been estimated that as many as one million Jews were killed by the *Einsatzgruppen,* this approach to solving the Jewish problem was soon perceived as inadequate. Instead, the Nazis opted for the systematic annihilation of the European Jewish population in specially built death camps. Jews from occupied countries would be rounded up, packed like cattle into freight trains, and shipped to Poland, where six extermination centers were built for this purpose. The largest and most famous was Auschwitz-Birkenau. Zyklon B (the commercial name for hydrogen cyanide) was selected as the most effective gas for quickly killing large numbers of people in gas chambers designed to look like shower rooms to facilitate the cooperation of the victims.

By the spring of 1942, the death camps were in operation. Although initial priority was given to the elimination of the ghettos in Poland, Jews were soon also being shipped from France, Belgium, and the Netherlands and eventually from Greece and Hungary. Despite desperate military needs, the Final Solution had priority in using railroad cars to transport Jews to the death camps.

About 30 percent of the arrivals at Auschwitz were sent to a labor camp, and the remainder went to the gas chambers.

After they had been gassed, the bodies were burned in crematoria. The victims' goods and even their bodies were used for economic gain. Women's hair was cut off, collected, and turned into mattresses or cloth. Some inmates were also subjected to cruel and painful "medical" experiments. The Germans killed between five and six million Jews, more than three million of them in the death camps. Virtually 90 percent of the Jewish populations of Poland, the Baltic countries, and Germany were exterminated. Overall, the Holocaust was responsible for the death of nearly two of every three European Jews.

The Nazis were also responsible for the death by shooting, starvation, or overwork of at least another nine to ten million people. Because the Nazis considered the Gypsies (like the Jews) an alien race, they were systematically rounded up for extermination. About 40 percent of Europe's one million Gypsies were killed in the death camps. The leading elements of the Slavic peoples—the clergy, intelligentsia, civil leaders, judges, and lawyers—were also arrested and executed. Probably an additional four million Poles, Ukrainians, and Belorussians lost their lives in the concentration camps or as slave laborers for Nazi Germany, and at least three to four million Soviet prisoners of war were killed in captivity. The Nazis also singled out homosexuals for persecution, and thousands lost their lives in concentration camps.

War Spreads in Asia

On December 7, 1941, Japanese carrier-based aircraft attacked the U.S. naval base at Pearl Harbor in the Hawaiian Islands. The same day, other units launched assaults on the Philippines and began advancing toward the British colony of Malaya. Shortly thereafter, Japanese forces seized the British island of Singapore, invaded the Dutch East Indies, and occupied a number of islands in the Pacific Ocean. In some cases, as on the Bataan peninsula and the island of Corregidor in the Philippines, resistance was fierce, but by the spring of 1942, almost all of Southeast Asia and much of the western Pacific had fallen into Japanese hands. Placing the entire region under Japanese tutelage, Japan declared the creation of a so-called Great East Asia Co-Prosperity Sphere, and announced its intention to liberate Southeast Asia from Western rule. For the moment, however, Japan needed the resources of the region for its war machine and placed its conquests under its rule on a wartime footing.

Japanese leaders had hoped that their strike at American bases would destroy the U.S. Pacific Fleet and persuade the Roosevelt administration to accept Japanese domination of the Pacific. The American people, in the eyes of Japanese leaders, had been made soft by material indulgence. But the Japanese had miscalculated. The attack on Pearl Harbor galvanized American opinion and won broad support for Roosevelt's war policy. The United States now joined with European nations and the embattled peoples of Nationalist China in a combined effort to defeat Japan's plan to achieve hegemony in the Pacific.

U.S. Strategy in the Pacific On December 11, 1941, four days after the Japanese attack on Pearl Harbor, Germany declared war on the United States. Confronted with the reality of a two-front war, President Roosevelt decided that because of the overwhelming superiority of the *Wehrmacht* in Europe, the war effort in that theater should receive priority over the conflict with Japan in the Pacific. Accordingly, U.S. war strategists drafted plans to make maximum use of their new ally in China. An experienced U.S. military commander, Lieutenant General Joseph Stilwell, was appointed as Roosevelt's special adviser to Chiang Kai-shek. His objective was to train Chinese Nationalist forces in preparation for an Allied advance through mainland China toward the Japanese islands. By the fall of 1942, Allied forces were beginning to gather for offensive operations into South China from Burma, while U.S. cargo planes continued to fly "over the hump" through the Himalaya Mountains to supply the Chinese government in Chungking with desperately needed war supplies.

In the meantime, the tide of battle began to turn in the Pacific. In the Battle of the Coral Sea in early May 1942, U.S. naval forces stopped the Japanese advance and temporarily relieved Australia of the threat of invasion. On June 4, American carrier planes destroyed all four of the attacking Japanese aircraft carriers near Midway Island and established U.S. naval superiority in the Pacific, even though almost all of the American planes were shot down in the encounter. Farther to the south, U.S. troops under the command of General Douglas MacArthur launched their own campaign (dubbed "island hopping") by invading the Japanese-held island of New Guinea, at the eastern end of the Dutch East Indies. After a series of bitter engagements in the Solomon Islands from August to November 1942, Japanese fortunes in the area began to fade (see Map 6.2).

The New Order in Asia

Once their military takeover was completed, Japanese policy in the occupied areas of Asia became essentially defensive, as Japan hoped to use its new possessions to meet its burgeoning needs for raw materials, such as tin, oil, and rubber, as well as an outlet for Japanese manufactured goods. To provide an organizational structure for the new Great East Asia Co-Prosperity Sphere, a Ministry for Great East Asia, staffed by civilians, was established in Tokyo in

October 1942 to handle relations between Japan and the conquered territories (see the box on p. 128).

Asia for the Asians? The Japanese conquest of Southeast Asia had been accomplished under the slogan "Asia for the Asians," and many Japanese sincerely believed that their government was bringing about the liberation of the Southeast Asian peoples from European colonial rule. Japanese officials in the occupied territories made contact with nationalist elements and promised that independent governments would be established under Japanese tutelage. Such governments were eventually set up in Burma, the Dutch East Indies, Vietnam, and the Philippines.

In fact, however, real power rested with the Japanese military authorities in each territory, and the local Japanese military command was directly subordinated to the Army General Staff in Tokyo. The economic resources of the colonies were exploited for the benefit of the Japanese war machine, while natives were recruited to serve in local military units or conscripted to work on public works projects. In some cases, the people living in the occupied areas were subjected to severe hardships. In Indochina, for example, forced requisitions of rice by the local Japanese authorities for shipment abroad created a food shortage that caused the starvation of more than a million Vietnamese in 1944 and 1945.

The Japanese planned to implant a new moral and social order as well as a new political and economic order in the occupied areas. Occupation policy stressed traditional values such as obedience, community spirit, filial piety, and discipline that reflected the prevailing political and cultural bias in Japan, while supposedly Western values such as materialism, liberalism, and individualism were strongly discouraged. To promote the creation of this new order, occupation authorities gave particular support to local religious organizations but discouraged the formation of formal political parties.

At first, many Southeast Asian nationalists took Japanese promises at face value and agreed to cooperate with their new masters. In Burma, an independent government was established in 1943 and subsequently declared war on the Allies. But as the exploitative nature of Japanese occupation policies became increasingly clear, sentiment turned against the new order. Japanese officials sometimes unwittingly provoked resentment by their arrogance and contempt for local customs. In the Dutch East Indies, for example, Indonesians were required to bow in the direction of Tokyo and recognize the divinity of the Japanese emperor, practices that were repugnant to Muslims. In Burma, Buddhist pagodas were sometimes used as military latrines.

Like German soldiers in occupied Europe, Japanese military forces often had little respect for the lives of their subject peoples and viewed the Geneva Convention governing

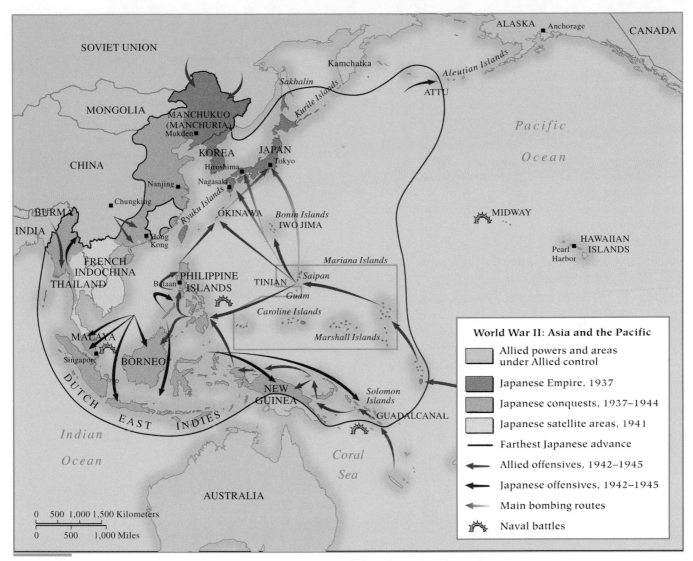

MAP 6.2 **World War II in Asia and the Pacific.** In 1937, Japan invaded northern China, beginning its effort to create the "Great East Asia Co-Prosperity Sphere." Further expansion induced America to end iron and oil sales to Japan. Deciding that war with the United States was inevitable, Japan engineered a surprise attack on Pearl Harbor. [?] Why was control of the islands in the western Pacific of great importance both to the Japanese and to the Allies? [icon] **View an animated version of this map or related maps at the World History Resource Center, at** worldrc.wadsworth.com/.

the treatment of prisoners of war as little more than a fabrication of the Western countries to tie the hands of their adversaries. In their conquest of northern and central China, the Japanese freely used poison gas and biological weapons, leading to the deaths of millions of Chinese citizens. The Japanese occupation of the onetime Chinese capital of Nanjing was especially brutal. In what has become notorious as the "Nanjing incident," they spent several days killing, raping, and looting the local population.

Japanese soldiers were also savage in their treatment of Koreans. Almost 800,000 Koreans were sent overseas, most of them as forced laborers, to Japan. Tens of thousands of Korean women were forced to be "comfort women" (prostitutes) for Japanese troops. In construction projects to help their war effort, the Japanese also made extensive use of labor forces composed of both prisoners of war and local peoples. In building the Burma-Thailand railway in 1943, for example,

JAPAN'S PLAN FOR ASIA

The Japanese objective in World War II was to create a vast Great East Asia Co-Prosperity Sphere to provide Japan with needed raw materials and a market for its exports. The following passage is from a secret document produced by a high-level government committee in January 1942.

What were Japan's proposals for a Japanese-led Asia? How did the government committee that produced this document distinguish between "Occidental individualism and materialism" and "the Imperial Way"? From the evidence of this document, were individualism and materialism a part of the Imperial Way?

Draft Plan for the Establishment of the Great East Asia Co-Prosperity Sphere

The Plan. The Japanese empire is a manifestation of morality and its special characteristic is the propagation of the Imperial Way. It is necessary to foster the increased power of the empire, to cause East Asia to return to its original form of independence and co-prosperity by shaking off the yoke of Europe and America, and to let its countries and peoples develop their respective abilities in peaceful cooperation and secure livelihood.

The Form of East Asiatic Independence and Co-Prosperity. The states, their citizens, and resources, comprised in those areas pertaining to the Pacific, Central Asia, and the Indian Oceans formed into one general union are to be established as an autonomous zone of peaceful living and common prosperity on behalf of the peoples of the nations of East Asia. The area including Japan, Manchuria, North China, lower Yangtze River, and the Russian Maritime Province, forms the nucleus of the East Asiatic Union. The Japanese empire possesses a duty as the leader of the East Asiatic Union.

The above purpose presupposes the inevitable emancipation or independence of Eastern Siberia, China, Indo-China, the South Seas, Australia, and India. . . .

Outline of East Asiatic Administration. It is intended that the unification of Japan, Manchoukuo, and China in neighborly friendship be realized by the settlement of the Sino-Japanese problems through the crushing of hostile influences in the Chinese interior, and through the construction of a new China. . . . Aggressive American and British influences in East Asia shall be driven out of the area of Indo-China and the South Seas, and this area should be brought into our defense sphere. The war with Britain and America shall be prosecuted for that purpose. . . .

Chapter 3: Political Construction

Basic Plan. The realization of the great ideal of constructing Greater East Asia Co-Prosperity requires not only the complete prosecution of the current Greater East Asia War but also presupposes another great war in the future. . . .

The following are the basic principles for the political construction of East Asia. . . .

The desires of the peoples in the sphere for their independence shall be respected, and endeavors shall be made for their fulfillment, but proper and suitable forms of government shall be decided for them in consideration of military and economic requirements and of the historical, political, and cultural elements peculiar to each area.

It must also be noted that the independence of various peoples of East Asia should be based on the idea of constructing East Asia as "independent countries existing within the New Order of East Asia" and that this conception differs from an independence based on the idea of liberalism and national self-determination. . . .

Western individualism and materialism shall be rejected, and a moral worldview, the basic principle of whose morality shall be the Imperial Way, shall be established. The ultimate object to be achieved is not exploitation but co-prosperity and mutual help, not competitive conflict but mutual assistance and mild peace, not a formal view of equality but a view of order based on righteous classification, not an idea of rights but an idea of service, and not several worldviews but one unified worldview.

SOURCE: From *Sources of Japanese Tradition* by William Theodore de Bary. Copyright © 1958 by Columbia University Press, New York. Reprinted with permission of the publisher.

---

the Japanese used 61,000 Australian, British, and Dutch prisoners of war and almost 300,000 workers from Burma, Malaya, Thailand, and the Dutch East Indies. An inadequate diet and appalling work conditions in an unhealthy climate led to the deaths of 12,000 Allied prisoners of war and 90,000 native workers by the time the railway was completed.

Such Japanese behavior created a dilemma for many nationalists, who had no desire to see the return of the colonial powers. Some turned against the Japanese, and others lapsed into inactivity. Indonesian patriots tried to have it both ways, feigning support for Japan while attempting to sabotage the Japanese administration. In Indochina, Ho Chi Minh's Indochinese Communist

Party established contacts with American military units in South China and agreed to provide information on Japanese troop movements and rescue downed American fliers in the area. In Malaya, where Japanese treatment of ethnic Chinese residents was especially harsh, many joined a guerrilla movement against the occupying forces. By the end of the war, little support remained in the region for the erstwhile "liberators."

The Turning Point of the War, 1942–1943

The entry of the United States into the war created a coalition, called the Grand Alliance, that ultimately defeated the Axis Powers (Germany, Italy, and Japan). Nevertheless, the three major Allies—Britain, the United States, and the Soviet Union—had to overcome mutual suspicions before they could operate as an effective alliance. In a bid to allay Stalin's suspicion of U.S. intentions, President Roosevelt declared that the defeat of Germany should be the first priority of the alliance. The United States, under its Lend-Lease program, also sent large amounts of military aid, including $50 billion worth of trucks, planes, and other arms, to the Soviet Union. In 1943, the Allies agreed to fight until the Axis Powers surrendered unconditionally. This had the effect of making it nearly impossible for Hitler to divide his foes. On the other hand, it likely discouraged dissident Germans and Japanese from overthrowing their governments to arrange a negotiated peace.

Victory, however, was only a vision for the distant future in the minds of Allied leaders at the beginning of 1942. As Japanese forces advanced into Southeast Asia and the Pacific after crippling the American naval fleet at Pearl Harbor, Axis forces continued the war in Europe against Britain and the Soviet Union. Reinforcements in North Africa enabled the Afrika Korps under General Erwin Rommel to break through the British defenses in Egypt and advance toward Alexandria. In the spring of 1942, a renewed German offensive in the Soviet Union led to the capture of the entire Crimean peninsula, causing Hitler to boast that in two years, German divisions would be on the Indian border.

The Battle of Stalingrad By that fall, however, the war had begun to turn against the Germans. In North Africa, British forces stopped Rommel's troops at El Alamein in the summer of 1942 and then forced them back across the desert. In November, U.S. forces landed in French North Africa and forced the German and Italian troops to surrender in May 1943. Allied war strategists drew up plans for an invasion of Italy, on the "soft underbelly" of Europe.

But the true turning point of the war undoubtedly occurred on the Eastern Front, at Stalingrad. After capturing the Crimea, Hitler's generals wanted him to concentrate on the Caucasus and its oil fields, but Hitler decided that Stalingrad, a major industrial center on the Volga, should be taken as well. Accordingly, German forces advancing in the southern Soviet Union were divided. After three months of bitter fighting, German troops occupied the city of Stalingrad, but Soviet troops in the area counterattacked. Besieged from all sides, the Germans were forced to surrender on February 2, 1943. The entire German Sixth Army of 300,000 men was lost, with the survivors sent off to prison camps. Soviet casualties were estimated at nearly one million, more than the United States lost in the entire war. By spring, long before Allied troops landed on the European continent, even Hitler knew that the Germans would not defeat the Soviet Union. The *Wehrmacht* was now in full retreat all across the Eastern Front.

The Last Years of the War

By the beginning of 1943, the tide of battle had begun to turn against the Axis. On July 10, the Allies crossed the Mediterranean and carried the war to Italy. After taking Sicily, Allied troops began the invasion of mainland Italy in September. Following the ouster and arrest of Mussolini, a new Italian government offered to surrender to Allied forces. But the Germans, in a daring raid, liberated Mussolini and set him up as the head of a puppet German state in northern Italy while German troops occupied much of Italy. The new defensive lines established by the Germans in the hills south of Rome were so effective that the Allied advance up the Italian peninsula was slow and marked by heavy casualties. Rome finally fell on June 4, 1944. By that time, the Italian war had assumed a secondary role as the Allies opened their long-awaited second front in western Europe.

Operation Overlord Since the autumn of 1943, under considerable pressure from Stalin, the Allies had been planning a cross-channel invasion of France (known as Operation Overlord) from Great Britain. Under the direction of U.S. General Dwight D. Eisenhower (1890–1969), five assault divisions landed on the Normandy beaches on June 6, 1944, in history's greatest naval invasion. An initially indecisive German response enabled the Allied forces to establish a beachhead. Within three months, they had landed two million men and a half-million vehicles that pushed inland and broke through the German defensive lines.

After the breakout, Allied troops moved south and east, liberating Paris by the end of August. By March 1945, they had crossed the Rhine and advanced into

Refugees Flee Yokohama. American bombing attacks on Japanese cities, which began in earnest in November 1944, were designed to undermine the morale of the civilian population as well as to destroy Japan's industrial base. Built of flimsy materials, Japan's crowded cities were soon devastated by these air raids. This photograph shows a homeless family fleeing Yokohama, a shelter for refugees until American bombers devastated the city on May 29, 1945.

Germany. The Allied advance northward through Belgium encountered greater resistance, as German troops launched a desperate counterattack known as the Battle of the Bulge. The Allies weathered the German attack, however, and in late April, they finally linked up with Soviet units at the Elbe River.

Advance in the East The Soviets had come a long way since the Battle of Stalingrad in 1943. In the summer of 1943, Hitler gambled on taking the offensive by making use of newly developed "Tiger" tanks. At the Battle of Kursk (July 5–12), the greatest tank battle of World War II, the Soviets soundly defeated the German forces. Soviet forces, now supplied with their own "T-34" heavy tanks, began a relentless advance westward. The Soviets reoccupied the Ukraine by the end of 1943, lifted the siege of Leningrad, and moved into the Baltic states by the beginning of 1944. Advancing along a northern front, Soviet troops occupied Warsaw in January 1945 and entered Berlin in April. Meanwhile,

Soviet troops along a southern front swept through Hungary, Romania, and Bulgaria.

In January 1945, Hitler moved into a bunker 55 feet under Berlin to direct the final stages of the war. He committed suicide on April 30, two days after Mussolini was shot by partisan Italian forces. On May 7, German commanders surrendered. The war in Europe was over.

The War in the Pacific Ends The war in Asia continued, although with a significant change in approach. Allied war planners had initially hoped to focus their main effort on an advance through China with the aid of Chinese Nationalist forces trained and equipped by the United States. But Roosevelt became disappointed with Chiang Kai-shek's failure to take the offensive against Japanese forces in China and eventually approved a new strategy to strike toward the Japanese home islands directly across the Pacific. This "island-hopping" approach took an increasing toll on enemy resources, especially at sea and in the air. Meanwhile, new U.S. long-range B-29 bombers unleashed a wave of destruction on all major cities in the Japanese homeland.

As Allied forces drew inexorably closer to the main Japanese islands in the summer of 1945, President Harry Truman, who had succeeded to the presidency on the death of Franklin Roosevelt in April, had an excruciatingly difficult decision to make. Should he use atomic weapons (at the time, only two bombs were available, and their effectiveness had not been demonstrated) to bring the war to an end without the necessity of an Allied invasion of the Japanese homeland? The invasion of the island of Okinawa in April had resulted in thousands of casualties on both sides, with many Japanese troops committing suicide rather than surrendering to enemy forces.

After an intensive debate, Truman approved the use of America's new superweapon. The first bomb was dropped on the city of Hiroshima on August 6. Truman then called on Japan to surrender or expect a "rain of ruin from the air." When the Japanese did not respond, a second bomb was dropped on Nagasaki. The destruction in Hiroshima was incredible. Of 76,000 buildings near the center of the explosion, 70,000 were flattened, and 140,000 of the city's 400,000 inhabitants died by the end of 1945. By the end of 1950, another 50,000 had perished from the effects of radiation. The dropping of the first atomic bomb introduced the world to the nuclear age.

The nuclear attack on Japan did have its intended effect, however. Japan surrendered unconditionally on August 14. World War II, in which 17 million combatants died in battle and almost 20 million civilians perished as well, was finally over.

In the years following the end of the war, Truman's decision to approve the use of nuclear weapons to compel Japan to surrender was harshly criticized, not only for causing thousands of civilian casualties but also for introducing a frightening new weapon that could threaten the survival of the human race. Some have even charged that Truman's real purpose in ordering the nuclear strikes was to intimidate the Soviet Union. Defenders of the decision argue that the human costs of invading the Japanese home islands would have been infinitely higher had the bombs not been dropped and that the Soviet Union would have had ample time to consolidate its control over Manchuria and command a larger role in the postwar occupation of Japan.

The Home Front: Three Examples

World War II was even more of a global war than World War I. Fighting was much more widespread, economic mobilization was more extensive, and so was the mobilization of women. And the number of civilians killed was far higher: almost 20 million were killed by bombing raids, mass extermination policies, and attacks by invading armies.

The Soviet Union

The home fronts of the major belligerents varied with the local circumstances. World War II had an enormous impact on the Soviet Union. Two of every five persons killed in World War II were Soviet citizens. Leningrad experienced nine hundred days of siege, during which its inhabitants became so desperate for food that they ate dogs, cats, and mice. As the German army made its rapid advance into Soviet territory, the factories in the western part of the Soviet Union were dismantled and shipped to the interior—to the Urals, western Siberia, and the Volga region.

Soviet women played a major role in the war effort. Women and girls worked in industries, mines, and railroads. Overall, the number of women working in industry increased by almost 60 percent. Soviet women were also expected to dig antitank ditches and work as air-raid wardens. Finally, the Soviet Union was the only country to use women as combatants in World War II. Soviet women functioned as snipers and also as air crews in bomber squadrons. The female pilots who helped defeat the Germans at Stalingrad were known as the "Night Witches."

The United States

The home front in the United States was quite different from those of its chief wartime allies, largely because the United States faced no threat of war on its own territory. Although the economy and labor force were slow to mobilize, the United States eventually became the arsenal of the Allied Powers, producing the military equipment they needed. At the height of war production in 1943, the nation was constructing six ships a day and $6 billion worth of war-related goods a month. Much of this industrial labor was done by American women, who, despite some public opposition, willingly took jobs in factories to replace husbands and brothers who had gone off to war.

The mobilization of the U.S. economy caused social problems. The construction of new factories created boomtowns where thousands came to work but then faced shortages of housing, health facilities, and schools. More than one million African Americans migrated from the rural South to the industrial cities of the North and West, looking for jobs in industry. The presence of African Americans in areas where they had not been present before led to racial tensions and sometimes even race riots.

Japanese Americans were treated especially shabbily. On the West Coast, 110,000 Japanese Americans, 65 percent of them born in the United States, were removed to camps encircled by barbed wire and made to take loyalty oaths. Although public officials claimed that this policy was necessary for security reasons, no similar treatment of German Americans or Italian Americans ever took place. Eventually, President Roosevelt agreed to alleviate the situation for Japanese Americans, and by 1943, one-third of those interned had been released from the camps to work in factories or enter military service.

Japan

In Japan, society had been put on a wartime footing even before the attack on Pearl Harbor. A conscription law was passed in 1938, and economic resources were placed under strict government control. Two years later, all political parties were merged into the so-called Imperial Rule Assistance Association. Labor unions were dissolved, and education and culture were purged of all "corrupt" Western ideas in favor of traditional values emphasizing the divinity of the emperor and the higher spirituality of Japanese civilization. During the war, individual rights were severely curtailed as the entire population was harnessed to the needs of the war effort.

Japan was reluctant, however, to mobilize women on behalf of the war effort. General Hideki Tojo, prime minister from 1941 to 1944, opposed female employment, arguing that "the weakening of the family system would be the weakening of the nation. . . . We are able to do our duties only because we have wives and mothers at home."[5] Female employment increased during the war, but only in areas, such as the textile industry and farming, where women traditionally worked. Instead of using women to meet labor shortages, the Japanese government brought in Korean and Chinese laborers.

The Peace Settlement

In November 1943, Stalin, Roosevelt, and Churchill, the leaders of the Grand Alliance, met at Tehran (the capital of Iran) to decide the future course of the war. Their major strategic decision involved approval for an American-British invasion of the Continent through France, which they scheduled for the spring of 1944. The acceptance of this plan had important consequences. It meant that Soviet and British-American forces would meet in defeated Germany along a north-south dividing line and that eastern Europe would most likely be liberated by Soviet forces. The Allies also agreed to a partition of postwar Germany until denazification could take place. Roosevelt privately assured Stalin that Soviet borders in Europe would be moved westward to compensate for the loss of territories belonging to the old Russian Empire after World War I. Poland would receive lands in eastern Germany to make up for territory lost in the east to the Soviet Union.

In February 1945, the three Allied leaders met once more at Yalta, on the Crimean peninsula of the Soviet Union. Since the defeat of Germany was a foregone conclusion, much of the attention focused on the war in the Pacific. Roosevelt sought Soviet military help against Japan. Development of the atomic bomb was not yet assured, and U.S. military planners feared the possibility of heavy casualties in amphibious assaults on the Japanese home islands. Roosevelt therefore agreed to Stalin's price for military assistance against Japan: possession of Sakhalin and the Kurile Islands, as well as two warm-water ports and railroad rights in Manchuria.

The creation of a new United Nations to replace the now discredited League of Nations was a major U.S. concern at Yalta. Roosevelt hoped to ensure the participation of the Big Three Powers in a postwar international organization before difficult issues divided them into hostile camps. After a number of compromises, both Churchill and Stalin accepted Roosevelt's plans for the United Nations organization and set the first meeting for San Francisco in April 1945.

The issues of Germany and eastern Europe were treated less decisively. The Big Three reaffirmed that Germany must surrender unconditionally and created four occupation zones. German reparations were set at $20 billion. A compromise was also worked out in regard to Poland. Stalin agreed to free elections in the future to determine a new government. But the issue of free elections in eastern Europe would ultimately cause a serious rift between the Soviets and the Americans. The Allied leaders agreed on an ambiguous statement that eastern European governments would be freely elected but were also supposed to be friendly to the Soviet Union. This attempt to reconcile the irreconcilable was doomed to failure.

Even before the next conference at Potsdam, Germany, took place in July 1945, Western relations with the Soviets had begun to deteriorate rapidly. The Grand Alliance had been one of necessity in which ideological incompatibility had been subordinated to the pragmatic concerns of the war. The Allied Powers' only common aim was the defeat of Nazism. Once this aim had been all but accomplished, the many differences that antagonized East-West relations came to the surface.

The Victorious Allied Leaders at Yalta.
Even before World War II ended, the leaders of the Big Three of the Grand Alliance—Churchill, Roosevelt, and Stalin (shown seated from left to right)—met in wartime conferences to plan the final assault on Germany and negotiate the outlines of the postwar settlement. At the Yalta meeting (February 5–11, 1945), the three leaders concentrated on postwar issues. The American president, visibly weary at Yalta, died two months later.

The Potsdam Conference of July 1945, the last Allied conference of World War II, consequently began under a cloud of mistrust. Roosevelt had died on April 12 and had been succeeded as president by Harry Truman. During the conference, Truman received word that the atomic bomb had been successfully tested. Some historians have argued that this knowledge stiffened Truman's resolve against the Soviets. Whatever the reasons, there was a new coldness in the relations between the Soviets and the Americans. At Potsdam, Truman demanded free elections throughout eastern Europe. After a bitterly fought and devastating war, however, Stalin sought absolute military security, which in his view could be ensured only by the presence of Communist states in eastern Europe. Free elections might result in governments hostile to the Soviet Union. By the middle of 1945, only an invasion by Western forces could undo developments in eastern Europe, and in the immediate aftermath of the world's most destructive conflict, few people favored such a policy. But the stage was set for a new confrontation, this time between the two major victors of World War II.

CONCLUSION

ORLD WAR II WAS THE MOST DEVASTATING total war in human history. Germany, Italy, and Japan had been utterly defeated. Perhaps as many as 40 million people—soldiers and civilians—had been killed in only six years. In Asia and Europe, cities had been reduced to rubble, and millions of people faced starvation as once fertile lands stood neglected or wasted. Untold millions of people had become refugees.

What were the underlying causes of the war? One direct cause was the effort by two rising capitalist powers, Germany and Japan, to make up for their relatively late arrival on the scene by carving out their own global empires. Key elements in both countries had resented the agreements reached after the end of World War I that divided the world in a manner favorable to their rivals and hoped to overturn them at the earliest opportunity. Neither Germany nor Japan possessed a strong tradition of political pluralism; to the contrary, in both countries, the legacy of a feudal past marked by a strong military tradition still wielded strong influence over the political system and the mind-set of the entire population. It is no surprise that under the impact of the Great Depression, the effects of which were severe in both countries, fragile democratic institutions were soon overwhelmed by militant forces determined to enhance national wealth and power.

Unlike World War I, which has often been blamed on the entire system of balance-of-power politics, the consensus among most Western observers is that responsibility for World War II falls squarely on the shoulders of leaders in Berlin and Tokyo who were willfully determined to reverse the verdict of Versailles and divide the world between them. That view is not accepted in Japan, where many feel that they were punished for doing the same things that had previously been done by the Western imperialist powers.

Whatever the causes of World War II and its controversial conclusion, the consequences were soon to be evident. European hegemony over the world was at an end, and two new superpowers on the fringes of Western civilization had emerged to take its place. Even before the last battles had been fought, the United States and the Soviet Union had arrived at different visions of the postwar world. No sooner had the war ended than their differences gave rise to a new and potentially even more devastating conflict: the Cold War. Though Europeans seemed merely pawns in the struggle between the two superpowers, they managed to stage a remarkable recovery of their own civilization. In Asia, defeated Japan made a miraculous economic recovery, and the era of European domination finally came to an end.

TIMELINE

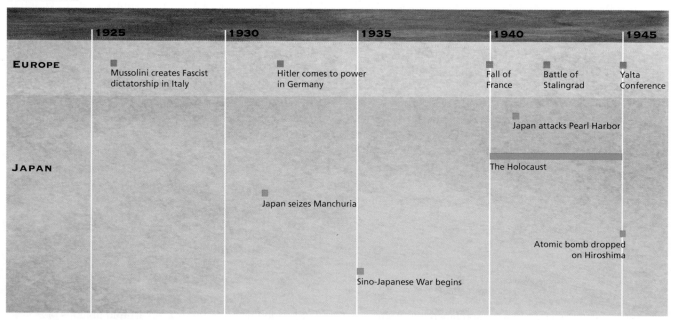

	1925	1930	1935	1940	1945
EUROPE	Mussolini creates Fascist dictatorship in Italy	Hitler comes to power in Germany		Fall of France / Battle of Stalingrad	Yalta Conference
				Japan attacks Pearl Harbor	
JAPAN				The Holocaust	
		Japan seizes Manchuria			Atomic bomb dropped on Hiroshima
			Sino-Japanese War begins		

CHAPTER NOTES

1. Benito Mussolini, "The Doctrine of Fascism," in *Italian Fascisms from Pareto to Gentile,* ed. Adrian Lyttleton (London, 1973), p. 42.
2. John Van Antwerp MacMurray, quoted in Arthur Waldron, *How the Peace Was Lost: The 1935 Memorandum* (Stanford, Calif., 1992), p. 5.
3. International Military Tribunal, *Trial of the Major War Criminals* (Nuremberg, 1947–1949), vol. 22, p. 480.
4. Quoted in Raul Hilberg, *The Destruction of the European Jews,* rev. ed. (New York, 1985), vol. 1, pp. 332–333.
5. Quoted in John Campbell, *The Experience of World War II* (New York, 1989), p. 143.

By 1945, THE ERA OF EUROPEAN HEGEMONY over world affairs was over. As World War I was followed by revolutions, the Great Depression, the mass murder machines of totalitarian regimes, and the destructiveness of World War II, it appeared that Western civilization had become a nightmare. Europeans, accustomed to dominating the world at the beginning of the twentieth century, now watched helplessly at mid-century as two new superpowers from outside the margins of heartland Europe—the United States and the Soviet Union—took control of their destinies. Moreover, the imperialist European states no longer had the energy or the wealth to maintain their colonial empires after the war. With the decline of the Old World, a new era of global relationships was about to begin.

What were the underlying causes of the astounding spectacle of self-destruction that engaged the European powers in two bloody internecine conflicts within a period of less than a quarter of a century? One factor was the rise of the spirit of nationalism. In the first half of the nineteenth century, nationalism in Europe was closely identified with liberals, who maintained that unified, independent nation-states could best preserve individual rights.

After the unification of Italy and Germany in 1871, however, nationalism became loud and chauvinistic. As one exponent expressed it, "A true nationalist places his country above everything"; he believes in the "exclusive pursuit of national policies" and "the steady increase in national power—for a nation declines when it loses military might." It was sentiments such as these that resulted in bitter disputes and civil strife in a number of countries and contributed to the competition among nations that eventually erupted into world war.

Nationalism was also inherently divisive in its political ramifications. Most European countries consisted of a patchwork of different ethnic, linguistic, and religious communities, a product of centuries of migration, war, and dynastic alliances. How could a system of stable nation-states, each based on a single national community, ever emerge from such a bewildering amalgam of cultures and peoples? The peace treaties signed after the Great War replaced one set of territorial boundaries with another, but hardly resolved the underlying problem.

Another factor that contributed to the violence of the early twentieth century was the Industrial Revolution. Technology transformed the nature of war itself. New weapons of mass destruction created the potential for a new kind of warfare that reached beyond the battlefield into the very heartland of the enemy's territory, while the concept of nationalism transformed war from the sport of kings to a matter of national honor and commitment. Since the French Revolution, when the government in Paris had mobilized the entire country to fight against the forces that opposed the revolution, governments had relied on mass conscription to defend the national cause while their engines of destruction reached far into enemy territory to destroy the industrial base and undermine the will to fight. This trend was amply demonstrated in the two world wars of the twentieth century. Each was a product of antagonisms that had been unleashed by economic competition and growing national consciousness. Each resulted in a level of destruction that severely damaged the material foundations and eroded the popular spirit of the participants, the victors as well as the vanquished.

In the end, then, industrial power and the driving force of nationalism, the very factors that had created the conditions for European global dominance, contained the seeds for the decline of that dominance. These seeds germinated during the 1930s, when the Great Depression sharpened international competition and mutual antagonisms, and then sprouted in the ensuing conflict, which embraced the entire globe. By the time World War II came to an end, the once-powerful countries of Europe were exhausted, leaving the door ajar not only for the emergence of the United States and the Soviet Union to global dominance but also for the collapse of the European colonial empires.

If in Europe the dominant challenge of the era had been to come to terms with the impact of the Industrial Revolution, in the rest of the world it was undoubtedly the sheer fact of Western imperialism. By the end of the nineteenth century, European powers, or their rivals in Japan and the United States, had achieved political mastery over virtually the entire remainder of the world. While the overall effect of imperialism on the subject peoples is still open to debate, it seems clear that for much of the population in colonial areas, Western domination was rarely beneficial and was often destructive. Although a limited number of merchants, large landowners, and traditional hereditary elites undoubtedly prospered under the umbrella of the expanding imperialist economic order, the majority of people, urban and rural alike, suffered considerable hardship as a result of the policies adopted by their foreign rulers. The effects of the Industrial Revolution on the poor had been felt in Europe, too, but there the pain was eased somewhat by the fact that the industrial era had laid the foundations for future technological advances and material abundance. In the colonial territories, the importation of modern technology was limited, while most of the profits from manufacturing and commerce fled abroad. For too many, the "white man's burden" was shifted to the shoulders of the colonial peoples.

In response, the latter turned to another European import, the spirit of nationalism. Some European historians of the phenomenon have argued that the spirit of nationalism was an artificial flower in much of the non-Western world, where allegiance was more often directed to the local community, the kinship group, or a religious faith. Even if that contention is justified—and the examples of Japan, Vietnam, and Thailand appear to suggest the opposite—the concept of nationalism served a useful role in many countries in Asia and Africa, where it provided colonial peoples with a sense of common purpose that later proved vital in knitting together diverse elements in their societies to oppose colonial regimes and create the conditions for future independent states. At first, such movements achieved relatively little success, but they began to gather momentum in the second quarter of the twentieth century, when full-fledged nationalist movements began to appear throughout the colonial world to lead their people in the struggle for independence.

Another idea that gained currency in colonial areas was that of democracy. As a rule, colonial regimes did not make a serious attempt to introduce democratic institutions to their subject populations out of concern that such institutions would inevitably undermine colonial authority. Nevertheless, Western notions of representative government and individual freedom had their advocates in colonial areas well before the end of the nineteenth century. Later, countless Asians and Africans were exposed to such ideas in schools set up by the colonial regime or in the course of travel to Europe or the United States. Most of the nationalist parties founded in colonial territories espoused democratic principles and attempted to apply them when they took power after the restoration of independence.

As we shall see later, in most instances, such programs were premature. For the most part, the experiment with democracy in postwar African and Asian societies was brief. But the popularity of democratic ideals among educated elites in colonial societies was a clear indication of democracy's universal appeal and a sign that it would become a meaningful part of the political culture after the dismantling of the colonial regimes. The idea of the nation, composed of free, educated, and politically active citizens, was now widely accepted throughout much of the non-Western world.

Chapter 2 attempted to draw up a balance sheet on the era of Western imperialism, and the arguments presented in the conclusion of that chapter do not need to be repeated here. What is clear is that if there were any lasting benefits for the colonial peoples related to the era of imperialism, they have to be seen in terms of their potential rather than their immediate effects. The spread of European power throughout the world took place at a time of spectacular achievements in the realm of science and technology as well as economics. Advances in health and sanitation, engineering, transportation, communications, and the food sciences began to enrich the human experience in ways that never before seemed possible. And although most of the immediate benefits from these developments accrued to the imperialist countries themselves, they carried the promise of an ultimate transformation of traditional societies throughout the globe in ways that are even today as yet unforeseen. For countless millions of peoples who suffered through the colonial era, of course, that may be poor consolation indeed.

The final judgment on the age of European dominance, then, is mixed. It was a time of unfulfilled expectations, of altruism and greed, of bright promise and tragic failure. The fact is that human beings had learned how to master some of the forces of nature before they had learned how to order relations among themselves or temper their own natures for the common good. The consequences were painful, for European and non-European peoples alike. ◆

III

ACROSS THE IDEOLOGICAL DIVIDE

*Nixon lectures Soviet Communist Party chief Nikita Khrushchev
on the technology of the U.S. kitchen*

AP Images

EAST AND WEST IN THE GRIP OF THE COLD WAR

$\mathcal{O}$UR MEETING HERE IN THE CRIMEA has reaffirmed our common determination to maintain and strengthen in the peace to come that unity of purpose and of action which has made victory possible and certain for the United Nations in this war. We believe that this is a sacred obligation which our Governments owe to our peoples and to all the peoples of the world.[1]

With these ringing words, drafted at the Yalta Conference in February 1945, President Franklin D. Roosevelt, Marshal Joseph Stalin, and Prime Minister Winston Churchill affirmed their common hope that the Grand Alliance, which had brought their countries to victory in World War II, could be sustained in the postwar era. Only through the continuing and growing cooperation and understanding among the three victorious allies, the statement asserted, could a secure and lasting peace be realized that, in the words of the Atlantic Charter, would "afford assurance that all the men in all the lands may live out their lives in freedom from fear and want."

Roosevelt hoped that the decisions reached at Yalta would provide the basis for a stable peace in the postwar era. Allied occupation forces—American, British, and French in the west and Soviet in the east—were to bring about the end of Axis administration and the holding of free elections to form democratic governments throughout Europe. To foster an attitude of mutual trust and an end to the suspicions that had marked relations between the capitalist world and the Soviet Union prior to World War II, Roosevelt tried to reassure Stalin that Moscow's legitimate territorial aspirations and genuine security needs would be adequately met in a durable peace settlement.

It was not to be. Within months after the German surrender, the attitude of mutual trust among the victorious allies—if it had ever existed—rapidly disintegrated, and the dream of a stable peace was replaced by the specter of a nuclear holocaust. As the Cold War conflict between Moscow and Washington intensified, Europe was divided into two armed camps, and the two superpowers, glaring at each other across a deep ideological divide, held the survival of the entire world in their hands. ◇

The Collapse of the Grand Alliance

The problem started in Europe. At the end of the war, Soviet military forces occupied all of Eastern Europe and the Balkans (except for Greece, Albania, and Yugoslavia), while U.S. and other Allied forces completed their occupation of the western part of the Continent. Roosevelt had assumed that free elections administered by "democratic and peace-loving forces" would lead to the creation of democratic governments responsive to the aspirations of the local population. But it soon became clear that Moscow and Washington differed in their interpretations of the Yalta agreement. When Soviet occupation authorities turned their attention to forming a new Polish government in Warsaw, Stalin refused to accept the legitimacy of the Polish government in exile—headquartered in London during the war, it was composed primarily of representatives of the landed aristocracy who harbored a deep distrust of the Soviets—and instead installed a government composed of Communists who had spent the war in Moscow. Roosevelt complained to Stalin but, preoccupied with other problems, he eventually agreed to a compromise solution whereby two members of the exile government in London were included in a new regime dominated by the Communists. A week later, Roosevelt was dead of a cerebral hemorrhage.

The Iron Curtain Descends

Similar developments took place elsewhere in Eastern Europe as all of the states occupied by Soviet troops became part of Moscow's sphere of influence. Coalitions of all political parties (except Fascist or right-wing parties) were formed to run the government, but within a year or two, the Communist parties in these coalitions had assumed the lion's share of power. The next step was the creation of one-party Communist governments. The timetables for these takeovers varied from country to country, but between 1945 and 1947, Communist governments became firmly entrenched in East Germany, Bulgaria, Romania, Poland, and Hungary. In Czechoslovakia, with its strong tradition of democratic institutions, the Communists did not achieve their goals until 1948. In the elections of 1946, the Communist Party became the largest party but was forced to share control of the government with non-Communist rivals. When it appeared that the latter might win new elections early in 1948, the Communists seized control of the government on February 25. All other parties were dissolved, and Communist

Eastern Europe in 1948

leader Klement Gottwald became the new president of Czechoslovakia.

Yugoslavia was a notable exception to the pattern of growing Soviet dominance in Eastern Europe. The Communist Party there had led resistance to the Nazis during the war and easily took over power when the war ended. Josip Broz, known as Tito (1892–1980), the leader of the Communist resistance movement, appeared to be a loyal Stalinist. After the war, however, he moved toward the establishment of an independent Communist state in Yugoslavia. Stalin hoped to take control of Yugoslavia, just as he had done in other Eastern European countries. But Tito refused to capitulate to Stalin's demands and gained the support of the people (and some sympathy in the West) by portraying the struggle as one of Yugoslav national freedom. In 1958, the Yugoslav party congress asserted that Yugoslav Communists did not see themselves as deviating from communism, only from Stalinism. They considered their more decentralized economic and political system, in which workers could manage themselves and local communes could exercise some political power, closer to the Marxist-Leninist ideal.

To Stalin (who had once boasted, "I will shake my little finger, and there will be no more Tito"), the creation of pliant pro-Soviet regimes throughout Eastern Europe may simply have represented his interpretation of the Yalta peace agreement and a reward for sacrifices suffered during the war while satisfying Moscow's aspirations for a buffer zone against the capitalist West. Recent evidence suggests that Stalin did not decide to tighten Communist control over the new Eastern European governments until U.S. actions—notably the promulgation of the Marshall Plan (see below)—threatened to undermine Soviet authority in the region. If the Soviet leader had any intention of promoting future Communist revolutions in Western Europe—and there is some indication that he did—in his mind such developments would have to await the appearance of a new capitalist crisis a decade or more into the future. As Stalin undoubtedly recalled, Lenin had always maintained that revolutions come in waves.

The Truman Doctrine and the Beginnings of Containment

In the United States, the Soviet takeover of Eastern Europe represented an ominous development that threatened Roosevelt's vision of a durable peace. Public suspicion of Soviet intentions grew rapidly, especially among the millions of Americans who still had relatives

A Call to Arms. In March 1946, former British prime minister Winston Churchill gave a speech before a college audience in Fulton, Missouri, that electrified the world. Soviet occupation of the countries of Eastern Europe, he declared, had divided the Continent into two conflicting halves, separated by an "Iron Curtain." Churchill's speech has often been described as the opening salvo in the Cold War, and Moscow responded by labeling the speech "reactionary" and "unconvincing." In the photo, Churchill, with President Harry Truman behind him, prepares to give his address.

living in Eastern Europe. Winston Churchill was quick to put such fears into words. In a highly publicized speech given to an American audience at Westminster College in Fulton, Missouri, in March 1946, the former British prime minister declared that an "Iron Curtain" had "descended across the continent," dividing Germany and Europe itself into two hostile camps. Stalin responded by branding Churchill's speech a "call to war with the Soviet Union." But he need not have worried. Although public opinion in the United States placed increasing pressure on Washington to devise an effective strategy to counter Soviet advances abroad, the American people were in no mood for another war.

A civil war in Greece created another potential arena for confrontation between the superpowers and an opportunity for the Truman administration to take a stand. Communist guerrilla forces supported by Tito's Yugoslavia had taken up arms against the pro-Western government in Athens. Great Britain had initially assumed primary responsibility for promoting postwar reconstruction in the eastern Mediterranean, but in 1947, continued postwar economic problems caused the British to withdraw from the active role they had been playing in both Greece and Turkey. U.S. President Harry S Truman (1884–1972), alarmed by British weakness and the possibility of Soviet expansion into the eastern Mediterranean, responded with the Truman Doctrine, which said in essence that the United States would provide money to

countries that claimed they were threatened by Communist expansion. If the Soviets were not stopped in Greece, the Truman argument ran, then the United States would have to face the spread of communism throughout the free world. As Dean Acheson, the American secretary of state, explained, "Like apples in a barrel infected by disease, the corruption of Greece would infect Iran and all the East . . . likewise Africa . . . Italy . . . France. . . . Not since Rome and Carthage has there been such a polarization of power on this earth." [2]

The Marshall Plan The U.S. suspicion that Moscow was actively supporting the insurgent movement in Greece was inaccurate. Stalin was apparently unhappy with Tito's promoting of the conflict, not only because it suggested that the latter was attempting to create his own sphere of influence in the Balkans but also because it risked provoking a direct confrontation between the Soviet Union and the United States. The proclamation of the Truman Doctrine was soon followed in June 1947 by the European Recovery Program, better known as the Marshall Plan. Intended to rebuild prosperity and stability, this program included $13 billion for the economic recovery of war-torn Europe. Underlying the program was the belief that Communist aggression fed off economic turmoil. General George C. Marshall noted in a speech at Harvard, "Our policy is not directed against any country or doctrine but against hunger, poverty, desperation and chaos." [3]

From the Soviet perspective, the Marshall Plan was nothing less than capitalist imperialism, a thinly veiled attempt to buy the support of the smaller European countries, which in return would be expected to submit to economic exploitation by the United States. The White House indicated that the Marshall Plan was open to the Soviet Union and its Eastern European satellite states, but they refused to participate. The Soviets, however, were in no position to compete financially with the United States and could do little to counter the Marshall Plan except to tighten their control in Eastern Europe.

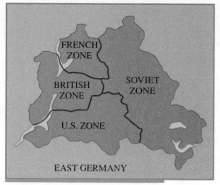

Berlin at the Start of the Cold War

Europe Divided

By 1947, the split in Europe between East and West had become a fact of life. At the end of World War II, the United States had favored a quick end to its commitments in Europe. But U.S. fears of Soviet aims caused the United States to play an increasingly important role in European affairs. In an article in *Foreign Affairs* in July 1947, George Kennan, a well-known U.S. diplomat with much knowledge of Soviet affairs, advocated a policy of containment against further aggressive Soviet moves. Kennan favored the "adroit and vigilant application of counter-force at a series of constantly shifting geographical and political points, corresponding to the shifts and maneuvers of Soviet policy." After the Soviet blockade of Berlin in 1948, containment of the Soviet Union became formal U.S. policy.

The fate of Germany had become a source of heated contention between East and West. Besides denazification and the partitioning of Germany (and Berlin) into four occupied zones, the Allied Powers had agreed on little with regard to the conquered nation. Even denazification proceeded differently in the various zones of occupation. The Americans and British proceeded methodically—the British had tried two million cases by 1948—while the Soviets went after major criminals and allowed lesser officials to go free. The Soviet Union, hardest hit by the war, took reparations from Germany in the form of booty. The technology-starved Soviets dismantled and removed to Russia 380 factories from the western zones of Berlin before transferring their control to the Western powers. By the summer of 1946, two hundred chemical, paper, and textile factories in the East German zone had likewise been shipped to the Soviet Union. At the same time, the German Communist Party was reestablished under the

control of Walter Ulbricht (1893–1973) and was soon in charge of the political reconstruction of the Soviet zone in eastern Germany.

The Berlin Blockade Although the foreign ministers of the four occupying powers (the United States, the Soviet Union, Great Britain, and France) kept meeting in an attempt to arrive at a final peace treaty with Germany, they grew further and further apart. At the same time, the British, French, and Americans gradually began to merge their zones economically and by February 1948 were making plans for unification of these sectors and the formation of a national government. The Soviet Union responded with a blockade of West Berlin that prevented all traffic from entering the city's three western zones through Soviet-controlled territory in East Germany. The Soviets hoped to force the Western powers to stop the creation of a separate West German state, which threatened Stalin's plan to create a reunified Germany that could eventually be placed under Soviet domination.

The Western powers faced a dilemma. Direct military confrontation seemed dangerous, and no one wished to risk World War III. Therefore, an attempt to break through the blockade with tanks and trucks was ruled out. The solution was the Berlin Airlift: supplies for the city's inhabitants were brought in by plane. At its peak, the airlift flew 13,000 tons of supplies daily into Berlin. The Soviets, also not wanting war, did not interfere and finally lifted the blockade in May 1949. The blockade of Berlin had severely increased tensions between the United States and the Soviet Union and confirmed the separation of Germany into two states. The Federal Republic of Germany (FRG) was formally created from the three Western zones in September 1949, and a month later, the separate German Democratic Republic (GDR) was established in East Germany. Berlin remained a divided city and the source of much contention between East and West.

NATO and the Warsaw Pact The search for security in the new world of the Cold War also led to the formation of military alliances. The North Atlantic Treaty Organization (NATO) was formed in April 1949 when Belgium, Luxembourg, the Netherlands, France, Britain, Italy, Denmark, Norway, Portugal, and Iceland signed a treaty with the United States and Canada (see Map 7.1). All the powers agreed to provide mutual assistance if any one of them was attacked. A few years later, West Germany, Greece, and Turkey joined NATO.

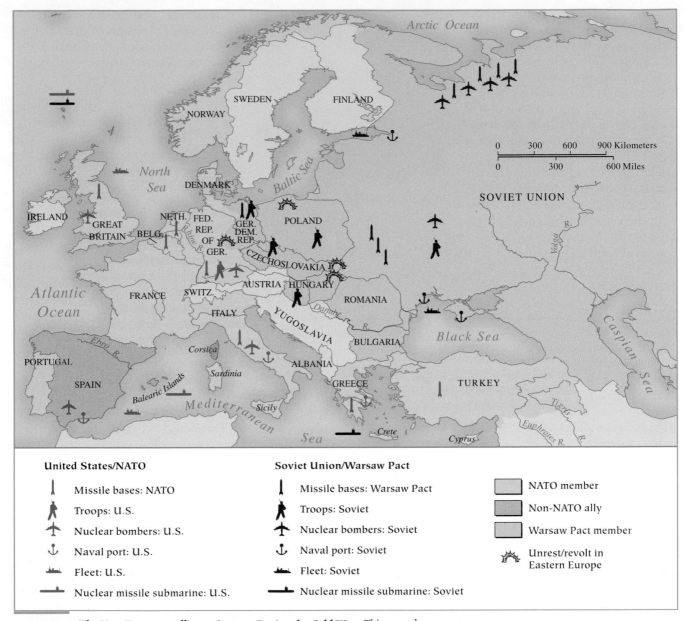

MAP 7.1 **The New European Alliance Systems During the Cold War.** This map shows postwar Europe as it was divided during the Cold War into two contending power blocs, the NATO alliance and the Warsaw Pact. Major military and naval bases are indicated by symbols on the map. ❓ Where on the map was the so-called Iron Curtain? 🌐 View an animated version of this map or related maps at the **World History Resource Center,** at worldrc.wadsworth.com/.

The Eastern European states soon followed suit. In 1949, they formed the Council for Mutual Economic Assistance (COMECON) for economic cooperation. Then, in 1955, Albania, Bulgaria, Czechoslovakia, East Germany, Hungary, Poland, Romania, and the Soviet Union organized a formal military alliance, the Warsaw Pact. Once again, Europe was tragically divided into hostile alliance systems.

Who Started the Cold War? By the end of the 1950s, then, the dream of a stable peace in Europe had been obliterated. There has been considerable historical debate over who bears the most responsibility for starting what would henceforth be called the Cold War. In the 1950s, most scholars in the West assumed that the bulk of the blame must fall on the shoulders of Joseph Stalin, whose determination to impose Soviet rule on the countries of Eastern Europe snuffed out hopes for freedom and self-determination there and aroused justifiable fears of Communist expansion in the Western democracies. During the next decade, however, a new school of revisionist historians—influenced in part by aggressive U.S. policies to prevent a Communist victory in Southeast Asia—began to argue that the fault lay primarily in Washington, where President Truman and his anti-Communist advisers abandoned the precepts of Yalta and sought to encircle the Soviet Union with a tier of pliant U.S. client states.

Both the United States and the Soviet Union took steps at the end of World War II that were unwise or might have been avoided. Both nations, however, were working within a framework conditioned by the past. Ultimately, the rivalry between the two superpowers stemmed from their different historical perspectives and their irreconcilable political ambitions. Intense competition for political and military supremacy had long been a regular feature of Western civilization. The United States and the Soviet Union were the heirs of that European tradition of power politics, and it should not come as a surprise that two such different systems would seek to extend their way of life to the rest of the world. Because of its need to feel secure on its western border, the Soviet Union was not prepared to give up the advantages it had gained in Eastern Europe from Germany's defeat. But neither were Western leaders prepared to accept without protest the establishment of a system of Soviet satellites that not only threatened the security of Western Europe but also deeply offended Western sensibilities because of its blatant disregard of the Western concept of human rights.

This does not necessarily mean that both sides bear equal responsibility for starting the Cold War. Some revisionist historians have claimed that the U.S. doctrine of containment was a provocative action that aroused Stalin's suspicions and drove Moscow into a position of hostility to the West. This charge lacks credibility. As information from the Soviet archives and other sources has become available, it is increasingly clear that Stalin's suspicions of the West were rooted in his Marxist-Leninist worldview and long predated Washington's enunciation of the doctrine of containment. As his foreign minister, Vyacheslav Molotov, once remarked, Soviet policy was inherently aggressive and would be triggered whenever the opportunity offered. Although Stalin apparently had no master plan to advance Soviet power into Western Europe, he was probably prepared to make every effort to do so once the next revolutionary wave appeared on the horizon. Western leaders were fully justified in reacting to this possibility by strengthening their own lines of defense. On the other hand, it has been argued—by no less than George Kennan himself—that in deciding to respond to the Soviet challenge in a primarily military manner, Western leaders overreacted to the situation and virtually guaranteed that the Cold War would be transformed into an arms race that could quite conceivably result in a new and uniquely destructive war.

Cold War in Asia

The Cold War was somewhat slower to make its appearance in Asia. At Yalta, Stalin formally agreed to enter the Pacific war against Japan three months after the close of the conflict with Germany. As a reward for Soviet participation in the struggle against Japan, Roosevelt promised that Moscow would be granted "preeminent interests" in Manchuria (interests reminiscent of those possessed by Imperial Russia prior to its defeat by Japan in 1904–1905) and the establishment of a Soviet naval base at Port Arthur. In return, Stalin promised to sign a treaty of alliance with the Republic of China, thus implicitly committing the Soviet Union not to provide the Chinese Communists with support in a possible future civil war. Although many observers would later question Stalin's sincerity in making such a commitment to the vocally anti-Communist Chiang Kai-shek, in Moscow the decision probably had a logic of its own. Stalin had no particular liking for the independent-minded Mao Zedong and did not anticipate a victory by the Chinese Communist Party (CCP) in the eventuality of a civil war in China. Only an agreement with Chiang Kai-shek could provide the Soviet Union with a strategically vital economic and political presence in North China.

Despite these commitments, Allied agreements soon broke down, and the region was sucked into the vortex of the Cold War by the end of the decade. The root of the problem lay in the underlying weakness of Chiang Kai-shek's regime, which threatened to create a political vacuum in East Asia that both Moscow and Washington would be tempted to fill.

The Chinese Civil War

As World War II came to an end in the Pacific, relations between the government of Chiang Kai-shek in China and its powerful U.S. ally had become frayed. Although Roosevelt had hoped that China would be the keystone of his plan for peace and stability in Asia after the war, he eventually became disillusioned with the corruption of Chiang's government and his unwillingness to risk his forces against the Japanese (he hoped to save them for use against the Communists after the war in the Pacific ended), and China became a backwater as the war came to a close. Nevertheless, U.S. military and economic aid to China had been substantial, and at war's end, the Truman administration still hoped that it could rely on Chiang to support U.S. postwar goals in the region.

While Chiang Kai-shek wrestled with Japanese aggression and problems of postwar reconstruction, the Communists were building up their liberated base in North China. An alliance with Chiang in December 1936 had relieved them from the threat of immediate attack from the south, although Chiang was chronically suspicious of the Communists and stationed troops near Xian to prevent them from infiltrating areas under his control.

He had good reason to fear for the future. During the war, the Communists patiently penetrated Japanese lines and built up their strength in North China. To enlarge their political base, they carried out a "mass line" policy designed to win broad popular support by reducing land rents and confiscating the lands of wealthy landlords. By the end of World War II, according to Communist estimates, 20 to 30 million Chinese were living under their administration, and their People's Liberation Army (PLA) included nearly one million troops.

As the war came to an end, world attention began to focus on the prospects for renewed civil strife in China. Members of a U.S. liaison team stationed in Yan'an during the last months of the war were impressed by the performance of the Communists, and some recommended that the United States should support them or at least remain neutral in a possible conflict between Communists and Nationalists for control of China. The Truman administration, though skeptical of Chiang's ability to forge a strong and prosperous country, was increasingly concerned over the spread of communism in Europe and tried to find a peaceful solution through the formation of a coalition government of all parties in China.

The effort failed. By 1946, full-scale war between the Nationalist government, now reinstalled in Nanjing, and the Communists resumed. The Communists, having taken advantage of the Soviet occupation of Manchuria in the last days of the war, occupied rural areas in the region and laid siege to Nationalist garrisons hastily established there. Now Chiang Kai-shek's errors came home to roost. In the countryside, millions of peasants, attracted to the Communists by promises of land and social justice, flocked to serve in the PLA. In the cities, middle-class Chinese, who were normally hostile to communism, were alienated by Chiang's brutal suppression of all dissent and

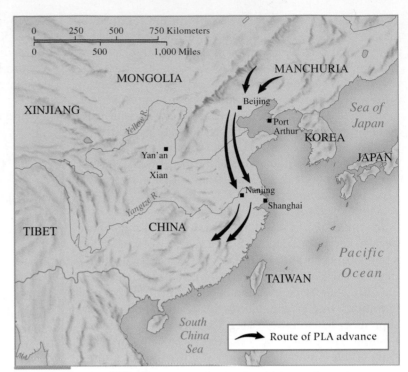

MAP 7.2 **The Chinese Civil War.** After the close of the Pacific war in 1945, the Nationalist government and the Chinese Communists fought a bitter civil war that ended with a victory by the latter in 1949. The path of Communist advance is displayed on the map. **?** Where did Chiang Kai-shek's government retreat to after its defeat? **🌐** View an animated version of this map or related maps at worldrc.wadsworth.com/.

his government's inability to slow the ruinous rate of inflation or solve the economic problems it caused. With morale dropping, Chiang's troops began to defect to the Communists. Sometimes whole divisions, officers as well as ordinary soldiers, changed sides. By 1948, the PLA was advancing south out of Manchuria and had encircled Beijing (see Map 7.2). Communist troops took the old imperial capital, crossed the Yangtze the following spring, and occupied the commercial hub of Shanghai. During the next few months, Chiang's government and two million of his followers fled to Taiwan, which the Japanese had returned to Chinese control after World War II.

The Truman administration reacted to the spread of Communist power in China with acute discomfort. Washington had no desire to see a Communist government on the mainland, but it had little confidence in Chiang Kai-shek's ability to realize Roosevelt's dream of a strong, united, and prosperous China. In December 1946, President Truman's emissary, General George C. Marshall, sought and received permission from the White House to abandon his mission, arguing that neither side was cooperating in the effort. During the next two years,

WHO LOST CHINA?

*I*n 1949, with China about to fall under the control of the Communists, President Harry S Truman instructed the State Department to prepare a White Paper explaining why the U.S. policy of seeking to avoid a Communist victory in China had failed. The authors of the White Paper concluded that responsibility lay at the door of Nationalist Chinese leader Chiang Kai-shek and that there was nothing the United States could have reasonably done to alter the result. Most China observers today would accept that assessment, but it did little at the time to deflect criticism of the administration for selling out the interests of the U.S. ally in China.

How do the authors of the White Paper explain the Communist victory in China? What actions do they think might have prevented it?

U.S. State Department White Paper on China, 1949

When peace came the United States was confronted with three possible alternatives in China: (1) it could have pulled out lock, stock, and barrel; (2) it could have intervened militarily on a major scale to assist the Nationalists to destroy the Communists; (3) it could, while assisting the Nationalists to assert their authority over as much of China as possible, endeavor to avoid a civil war by working for a compromise between the two sides.

The first alternative would, and I believe American public opinion at the time so felt, have represented an abandonment of our international responsibilities and of our traditional policy of friendship for China before we had made a determined effort to be of assistance. The second alternative policy, while it may look attractive theoretically, in retrospect, was wholly impracticable. The Nationalists had been unable to destroy the Communists during the ten years before the war. Now after the war the Nationalists were . . . weakened, demoralized, and unpopular. They had quickly dissipated

their popular support and prestige in the areas liberated from the Japanese by the conduct of their civil and military officials. The Communists on the other hand were much stronger than they had ever been and were in control of most of North China. Because of the ineffectiveness of the Nationalist forces, which was later to be tragically demonstrated, the Communists probably could have been dislodged only by American arms. It is obvious that the American people would not have sanctioned such a colossal commitment of our armies in 1945 or later. We therefore came to the third alternative policy whereunder we faced the facts of the situation and attempted to assist in working out a *modus vivendi* which would avert civil war but nevertheless preserve and even increase the influence of the National Government. . . .

The distrust of the leaders of both the Nationalist and Communist Parties for each other proved too deep-seated to permit final agreement, notwithstanding temporary truces and apparently promising negotiations. The Nationalists, furthermore, embarked in 1946 on an overambitious military campaign in the face of warnings by General Marshall that it not only would fail but would plunge China into economic chaos and eventually destroy the National Government. . . .

The unfortunate but inescapable fact is that the ominous result of the civil war in China was beyond the control of the government of the United States. Nothing that this country did or could have done within the reasonable limits of its capabilities could have changed that result; nothing that was left undone by this country has contributed to it. It was the product of internal Chinese forces, forces which this country tried to influence but could not. A decision was arrived at within China, if only a decision by default.

SOURCE: *United States Relations with China* (Washington, D.C.: U.S. Department of State, 1949), pp. xv–xvi.

---

the United States gave limited military support to the Nanjing regime but refused to commit U.S. power to guarantee its survival. The administration's hands-off policy deeply angered many in Congress, who charged that the White House was "soft on communism" and declared further that Roosevelt had betrayed Chiang at Yalta by granting privileges in Manchuria to the Soviets. In their view, Soviet troops had hindered the dispatch of Chiang's forces to the area and provided the PLA with weapons to use against their rivals.

In later years, evidence accumulated that the Soviet Union had given little assistance to the CCP in its struggle against the Nanjing regime. In fact, Stalin periodically

advised Mao against undertaking the effort. Although Communist forces undoubtedly received some assistance from Soviet occupation troops in Manchuria, the underlying reasons for their victory stemmed from conditions inside China, not from the intervention of outside powers. So indeed argued the Truman administration, when in 1949 it issued a white paper that placed most of the blame for the debacle at the feet of the Chiang Kai-shek regime (see the box above).

Many Americans, however, did not agree. The Communist victory on the mainland of China injected Asia directly into American politics as an integral element of the Cold War. During the spring of 1950, under pressure from

Congress and public opinion to define U.S. interests in Asia, the Truman administration adopted a new national security policy (known as NSC-68) that implied that the United States would take whatever steps were necessary to stem the further expansion of communism in the region.

The Korean War

Communist leaders in China, from their new capital at Beijing, hoped that their accession to power in 1949 would bring about an era of peace in the region and permit their new government to concentrate on domestic goals. But the desire for peace was tempered by their determination to erase a century of humiliation at the hands of imperialist powers and to restore the traditional outer frontiers of the empire. In addition to recovering territories that had been part of the Manchu Empire, such as Manchuria, Taiwan, and Tibet, the Chinese leaders also hoped to restore Chinese influence in former tributary areas such as Korea and Vietnam.

It soon became clear that these two goals were not always compatible. Negotiations with Moscow led to the signing of a mutual security treaty and Soviet recognition of Chinese sovereignty over Manchuria and Xinjiang (the desolate lands north of Tibet that were known as Chinese Turkestan because many of the peoples in the area were of Turkish origin), although the Soviets retained a measure of economic influence in both areas. Chinese troops occupied Tibet in 1950 and brought it under Chinese administration for the first time in more than a century. But in Korea and Taiwan, China's efforts to re-create the imperial buffer zone threatened to provoke new conflicts with foreign powers.

The problem of Taiwan was a consequence of the Cold War. As the civil war in China came to an end, the Truman administration appeared determined to avoid entanglement in China's internal affairs and indicated that it would not seek to prevent a Communist takeover of the island, now occupied by Chiang Kai-shek's Republic of China. But as tensions between the United States and the new Chinese government escalated during the winter of 1949–1950, influential figures in the United States began to argue that Taiwan was crucial to U.S. defense strategy in the Pacific.

The outbreak of war in Korea also helped bring the Cold War to East Asia.

A Meeting of Communist Leaders. Soviet leader Nikita Khrushchev and North Vietnamese President Ho Chi Minh are hosted by CCP Chairman Mao Zedong at a banquet in Beijing in October 1959.

As we have seen in Chapter 3, Korea, long a Chinese tributary, was annexed into the Japanese Empire in 1908 and remained there until 1945. The removal of Korea from Japanese control had been one of the stated objectives of the Allies in World War II, and on the eve of Japanese surrender in August 1945, the Soviet Union and the United States agreed to divide the country into two separate occupation zones at the 38th parallel. They originally planned to hold national elections after the restoration of peace to reunify Korea under an independent government. But as U.S.-Soviet relations deteriorated, two separate governments emerged in Korea, Communist in the north and anti-Communist in the south.

Tensions between the two governments ran high along the dividing line, and on June 25, 1950, with Stalin's apparently reluctant approval, North Korean troops invaded the south. The Truman administration immediately ordered U.S. naval and air forces to support South Korea, and the United Nations Security Council (with the Soviet delegate absent to protest the failure of the UN to assign China's seat to the new government in Beijing) passed a resolution calling on member nations to jointly resist the invasion. By September, UN forces under the command of U.S. General Douglas MacArthur marched northward across the 38th parallel with the aim of unifying Korea under a single non-Communist government.

President Truman worried that by approaching the Chinese border at the Yalu River, the UN troops could trigger

The Korean Peninsula

Chinese intervention but was assured by MacArthur that China would not respond. In November, however, Chinese "volunteer" forces intervened on the side of North Korea and drove the UN troops southward in disarray. A static defense line was eventually established near the original dividing line at the 38th parallel, although the war continued.

To many Americans, the Chinese intervention in Korea was clear evidence that China intended to promote communism throughout Asia, and recent evidence does suggest that Mao Zedong, convinced that a revolutionary wave was on the rise in Asia, argued to his colleagues that they should not fear a confrontation with the United States on the Korean peninsula. China's decision to enter the war was probably also motivated by the fear that hostile U.S. forces might be stationed on the Chinese frontier and perhaps even launch an attack across the border. MacArthur intensified such fears by calling publicly for air attacks, possibly including nuclear weapons, on Manchurian cities in preparation for an attack on Communist China. In any case, the outbreak of the Korean War was particularly unfortunate for China. Immediately after the invasion, President Truman dispatched the U.S. Seventh Fleet to the Taiwan Strait to prevent a possible Chinese invasion of Taiwan. Even more unfortunate, the invasion hardened Western attitudes against the new Chinese government and led to China's isolation from the major capitalist powers for two decades. As a result, China was cut off from all forms of economic and technological assistance and was forced to rely almost entirely on the Soviet Union.

Conflict in Indochina

A cease-fire agreement brought the Korean War to an end in July 1953, and China signaled its desire to live in peaceful coexistence with other independent countries in the region. But a relatively minor conflict now began to intensify on Beijing's southern flank, in French Indochina. The struggle had begun after World War II, when Ho Chi Minh's Indochinese Communist Party, at the head of a multiparty nationalist alliance called the Vietminh Front, seized power in northern and central Vietnam after the surrender of Imperial Japan. After abortive negotiations between Ho's

Indochina After 1954

government and the French over a proposed "free state" of Vietnam under French tutelage, war broke out in December 1946. French forces occupied the cities and the densely populated lowlands, while the Vietminh took refuge in the mountains.

For three years, the Vietminh waged a "people's war" of national liberation from colonial rule, gradually increasing in size and effectiveness. At the time, however, the conflict in Indochina attracted relatively little attention from world leaders, who viewed events there as only one aspect of the transition to independence of colonialized territories in postwar Asia. The Truman administration was uneasy about Ho's long-time credentials as a Soviet agent, but was equally reluctant to anger anticolonialist elements in the area by intervening on behalf of the French. Moscow had even less interest in the region. Stalin—still hoping to see the Communist Party come to power in Paris—ignored Ho's request for recognition of his movement as the legitimate representative of the national interests of the Vietnamese people.

But what had begun as an anticolonial struggle by the Vietminh Front against the French became entangled in the Cold War after the CCP came to power in China. In early 1950, Beijing began to provide military assistance to the Vietminh to burnish its revolutionary credentials and protect its own borders from hostile forces. The Truman administration, increasingly concerned that a revolutionary "red tide" was sweeping through the region, decided to support the French, while pressuring them to prepare for an eventual transition to independent non-Communist governments in Vietnam, Laos, and Cambodia.

With casualties mounting and the French public tired of fighting the "dirty war" in Indochina, the French agreed to a peace settlement with the Vietminh at the Geneva Conference in 1954. Vietnam was temporarily divided into a northern Communist half (known as the Democratic Republic of Vietnam or DRV) and a non-Communist southern half based in Saigon (eventually to be known as the Republic of Vietnam). Elections were to be held in two years to create a unified government. Cambodia and Laos were both declared independent under neutral governments. French forces, which had suffered a major defeat at the hands of Vietminh troops at the battle of Dien Bien Phu in the spring of 1954, were withdrawn from all three countries.

Ho Chi Minh Plans an Attack on the French. Unlike many peoples in Southeast Asia, the Vietnamese had to fight for their independence after World War II. That fight was led by the talented Communist leader Ho Chi Minh. In this photograph, Ho (in the center), assisted by his chief strategist, Vo Nguyen Giap (at the far right), plans an attack on French positions in Vietnam.

China had played an active role in bringing about the agreement and clearly hoped that a settlement would lead to a reduction of tensions in the area, but subsequent efforts to bring about improved relations between China and the United States foundered on the issue of Taiwan. In the fall of 1954, the United States signed a mutual security treaty with the Republic of China guaranteeing U.S. military support in case of an invasion of Taiwan. When Beijing demanded U.S. withdrawal from Taiwan as the price for improved relations, diplomatic talks between the two countries collapsed.

From Confrontation to Coexistence

The 1950s opened with the world teetering on the edge of a nuclear holocaust. The Soviet Union had detonated its first nuclear device in 1949, and the two blocs—capitalist and socialist—viewed each other across an ideological divide that grew increasingly bitter with each passing year. Yet as the decade drew to a close, a measure of sanity crept into the Cold War, and the leaders of the major world powers began to seek ways to coexist in an increasingly unstable world (see Map 7.3).

Khrushchev and the Era of Peaceful Coexistence

The first clear sign occurred after Stalin's death in early 1953. His successor, Georgy Malenkov (1902–1988), hoped to improve relations with the Western powers to reduce defense expenditures and shift government spending to growing consumer needs. During his campaign to replace Malenkov two years later, Nikita Khrushchev (1894–1971) appealed to powerful pressure groups in the party Politburo (the governing body of the Communist Party of the Soviet Union) by calling for higher defense expenditures, but once in power, he resumed his predecessor's efforts to reduce tensions with the West and improve the living standards of the Soviet people.

In an adroit public relations touch, Khrushchev publicized Moscow's appeal for a new policy of "peaceful coexistence" with the West. In 1955, he surprisingly agreed to negotiate an end to the postwar occupation of Austria by the victorious allies and allow the creation of a neutral country with strong cultural and economic ties with the West. He also called for a reduction in defense expenditures and reduced the size of the Soviet armed forces.

At first, Washington was suspicious of Khrushchev's motives, especially after the Soviet crackdown in Hungary in the fall of 1956 (see Chapter 10), an event that sharply increased Cold War tensions on both sides of the Iron Curtain.

The Berlin Crisis A new crisis over Berlin added to the tension. The Soviets had launched their first intercontinental ballistic missile (ICBM) in August 1957, arousing U.S. fears—fueled by a partisan political debate—of a "missile gap" between the United States and the Soviet Union. Khrushchev attempted to take advantage of the U.S. frenzy over missiles to solve the problem of West Berlin, which had remained a

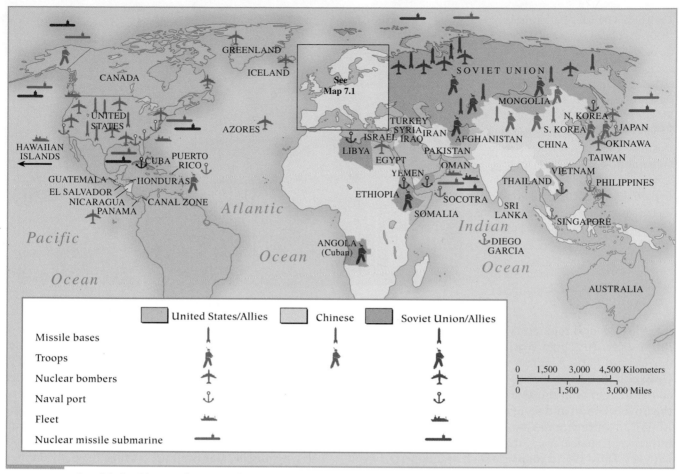

MAP 7.3 The Global Cold War. This map indicates the location of major military bases and missile sites possessed by the contending power blocs throughout the world at the height of the Cold War. ❓ Which continents are the most heavily armed? 🖱 **View an animated version of this map or related maps at the World History Resource Center, at** worldrc.wadsworth.com/.

"Western island" of prosperity inside the relatively poverty-stricken state of East Germany. Many East Germans sought to escape to West Germany by fleeing through West Berlin—a serious blot on the credibility of the GDR and a potential source of instability in East-West relations. In November 1958, Khrushchev announced that unless the West removed its forces from West Berlin within six months, he would turn over control of the access routes to the East Germans. Unwilling to accept an ultimatum that would have abandoned West Berlin to the Communists, President Eisenhower and the West stood firm, and Khrushchev eventually backed down.

The Spirit of Camp David Despite such periodic crises in East-West relations, there were tantalizing signs that an era of true peaceful coexistence between the two power blocs could be achieved. In the late 1950s, the United States and the Soviet Union initiated a cultural exchange program, helping the peoples of one bloc to become acquainted with

the nature of life in the other. While the Leningrad Ballet appeared at theaters in the United States, Benny Goodman and the film of Leonard Bernstein's *West Side Story* played in Moscow. In 1958, Nikita Khrushchev visited the United States and had a brief but friendly encounter with President Eisenhower at Camp David, his presidential retreat in northern Maryland. Predictions of improved future relations led reporters to laud "the spirit of Camp David."

Yet Khrushchev could rarely avoid the temptation to gain an advantage over the United States in the competition for influence throughout the world, and this resulted in an unstable relationship that prevented a lasting accommodation between the two superpowers. West Berlin was an area of persistent tension (a boil on the foot of the United States, Khrushchev derisively termed it), and in January 1961, just as newly elected president John F. Kennedy (1917–1963) came into office, Moscow threatened once again to turn over responsibility for access to the East German government.

The Kitchen Debate. During the late 1950s, the United States and the Soviet Union sought to defuse Cold War tensions by encouraging cultural exchanges between the two countries. On one occasion, U.S. Vice President Richard M. Nixon visited Moscow in conjunction with the arrival of an exhibit to introduce U.S. culture and society to the Soviet people. Here Nixon lectures Soviet party chief Nikita Khrushchev on the technology of the U.S. kitchen. On the other side of Nixon is future Soviet president Leonid Brezhnev (at the far right).

AP Images

Moscow also took every opportunity to promote its interests in the Third World, as the countries of Asia, Africa, and Latin America were now popularly called. Unlike Stalin, Khrushchev viewed the dismantling of colonial regimes in the area as a potential advantage for the Soviet Union and sought especially to exploit anti-American sentiment in Latin America. To improve Soviet influence in such areas, Khrushchev established alliances with key Third World countries such as Indonesia, Egypt, India, and Cuba. In January 1961, just as Kennedy assumed the presidency, Khrushchev unnerved the new president at an informal summit meeting in Vienna by declaring that Moscow would provide active support to national liberation movements throughout the world. There were rising fears in Washington of Soviet meddling in such sensitive trouble spots as Southeast Asia, Central Africa, and the Caribbean.

The Cuban Missile Crisis and the Move Toward Détente

The Cold War confrontation between the United States and the Soviet Union reached frightening levels during the Cuban Missile Crisis. In 1959, a left-wing revolutionary named Fidel Castro (b. 1927) overthrew the Cuban dictator Fulgencio Batista and established a Soviet-supported totalitarian regime. As tensions increased between the new government in Havana and the United States, the Eisenhower administration broke relations with Cuba and drafted plans to overthrow Castro, who reacted by drawing closer to Moscow.

Soon after taking office, in early 1961 Kennedy approved a plan to support an invasion of Cuba by anti-Castro exiles. But the attempt to land in the "Bay of Pigs"

in southern Cuba was an utter failure. At Castro's request, the Soviet Union then decided to place nuclear missiles in Cuba. The Kennedy administration was not prepared to allow nuclear weapons within such close striking distance of the American mainland, although the United States had placed nuclear weapons in Turkey within easy range of the Soviet Union, a fact that Khrushchev was quick to point out. When U.S. intelligence discovered that a Soviet fleet carrying missiles was heading to Cuba, Kennedy decided to dispatch U.S. warships into the Atlantic to prevent the fleet from reaching its destination.

This approach to the problem was risky but had the benefit of delaying confrontation and giving the two sides time to find a peaceful solution. After a tense standoff during which the two countries came frighteningly close to a direct nuclear confrontation (the Soviet missiles already in Cuba, it turned out, were operational), Khrushchev finally sent a conciliatory letter to Kennedy agreeing to turn back the fleet if Kennedy pledged not to invade Cuba. In a secret concession not revealed until many years later, the latter also promised to dismantle U.S. missiles in Turkey. To the world, however (and to an angry Castro), it appeared that Kennedy had bested Khrushchev. "We were eyeball to eyeball," noted U.S. Secretary of State Dean Rusk, "and they blinked."

The intense feeling that the world might have been annihilated in a few days had a profound influence on both sides. A communication hotline between Moscow and Washington was installed in 1963 to expedite rapid communication between the two superpowers in time of crisis. In the same year, the two powers agreed to ban nuclear tests in the atmosphere, a step that served to lessen the tensions between the two nations.

A PLEA FOR PEACEFUL COEXISTENCE

The Soviet leader Vladimir Lenin had contended that war between the socialist and imperialist camps was inevitable because the imperialists would never give up without a fight. That assumption had probably guided the thoughts of Joseph Stalin, who told colleagues shortly after World War II that a new war would break out in fifteen to twenty years. But Stalin's successor, Nikita Khrushchev, feared that a new world conflict could result in a nuclear holocaust and contended that the two sides must learn to coexist, although peaceful competition would continue. In this speech given in Beijing in 1959, Khrushchev attempted to persuade the Chinese to accept his views. But Chinese leaders argued that the "imperialist nature" of the United States would never change and warned that they would not accept any peace agreement in which they had no part.

Why does Nikita Khrushchev feel that a conflict between the socialist and the capitalist camps is no longer inevitable, as Lenin had predicted?

Khrushchev's Speech to the Chinese, 1959

Comrades! Socialism brings to the people peace—that greatest blessing. The greater the strength of the camp of socialism grows, the greater will be its possibilities for successfully defending the cause of peace on this earth. The forces of socialism are already so great that real possibilities are being created for excluding war as a means of solving international disputes. . . .

When I spoke with President Eisenhower—and I have just returned from the United States of America—I got the impression that the President of the U.S.A.—and not a few people support him—understands the need to relax international tension. . . .

There is only one way of preserving peace—that is the road of peaceful coexistence of states with different social systems. The question stands thus: either peaceful coexistence or war with its catastrophic consequences. Now, with the present relation of forces between socialism and capitalism being in favor of socialism, he who would continue the "cold war" is moving towards his own destruction. . . .

Already in the first years of the Soviet power the great Lenin defined the general line of our foreign policy as being directed towards the peaceful coexistence of states with different social systems. For a long time, the ruling circles of the Western Powers rejected these truly humane principles. Nevertheless the principles of peaceful coexistence made their way into the hearts of the vast majority of mankind. . . .

It is not at all because capitalism is still strong that the socialist countries speak out against war, and for peaceful coexistence. No, we have no need of war at all. If the people do not want it, even such a noble and progressive system as socialism cannot be imposed by force of arms. The socialist countries therefore, while carrying through a consistently peace-loving policy, concentrate their efforts on peaceful construction; they fire the hearts of men by the force of their example in building socialism, and thus lead them to follow in their footsteps. The question of when this or that country will take the path to socialism is decided by its own people. This, for us, is the holy of holies.

SOURCE: From G. F. Hudson et al., eds., *The Sino-Soviet Dispute* (New York: Frederick Praeger, 1961), pp. 61–63, cited in *Peking Review*, no. 40, 1959.

The Sino-Soviet Dispute

Nikita Khrushchev had launched his slogan of peaceful coexistence as a means of improving relations with the capitalist powers; ironically, one result of the campaign was to undermine Moscow's ties with its close ally China. During Stalin's lifetime Beijing had accepted the Soviet Union as the official leader of the socialist camp. After Stalin's death, however, relations began to deteriorate. Part of the reason may have been Mao Zedong's contention that he, as the most experienced Marxist leader, should now be acknowledged as the most authoritative voice within the socialist community. But another determining factor was that just as Soviet policies were moving toward moderation, China's were becoming more radical.

Several other issues were involved, including territorial disputes and China's unhappiness with limited Soviet economic assistance. But the key sources of disagreement involved ideology and the Cold War. Chinese leaders were convinced that the successes of the Soviet space program confirmed that the socialists were now technologically superior to the capitalists (the East wind, trumpeted the Chinese official press, had now triumphed over the West wind), and they urged Soviet leader Nikita Khrushchev to go on the offensive to promote world revolution. Specifically, China wanted Soviet assistance in retaking Taiwan from Chiang Kai-shek. But Khrushchev was trying to improve relations with the West and rejected Chinese demands for support against Taiwan (see the box above).

By the end of the 1950s, the Soviet Union had begun to remove its advisers from China, and in 1961, the dispute broke into the open. Increasingly isolated, China voiced its hostility to what Mao described as the "urban industrialized

COMBATING THE AMERICANS

In December 1960, the National Liberation Front of South Vietnam, or NLF, was born. Composed of political and social leaders opposed to the anti-Communist government of Ngo Dinh Diem in South Vietnam, it operated under the direction of the Vietnam Workers' Party in North Vietnam and served as the formal representative of revolutionary forces in the south throughout the remainder of the Vietnam War. When, in the spring of 1965, President Lyndon Johnson began to dispatch U.S. combat troops to Vietnam to prevent a Communist victory there, the NLF issued the following declaration.

How does the NLF justify its claim to represent the legitimate aspirations of the people of South Vietnam? Do you agree with its argument?

Statement of the National Liberation Front of South Vietnam

American imperialist aggression against South Vietnam and interference in its internal affairs have now continued for more than ten years. More American troops and supplies, including missile units, Marines, B-57 strategic bombers, and mercenaries from South Korea, Taiwan, the Philippines, Australia, Malaysia, etc., have been brought to South Vietnam. . . .

The Saigon puppet regime, paid servant of the United States, is guilty of the most heinous crimes. These despicable traitors, these boot-lickers of American imperialism, have brought the enemy into our country. They have brought to South Vietnam armed forces of the United States and its satellites to kill our compatriots, occupy and ravage our sacred soil and enslave our people.

The Vietnamese, the peoples of all Indo-China and Southeast Asia, supporters of peace and justice in every part of the world, have raised their voice in angry protest against this criminal unprovoked aggression of the United States imperialists.

In the present extremely grave situation, the South Vietnam National Liberation Front considers it necessary to proclaim anew its firm and unswerving determination to resist the U.S. imperialists and fight for the salvation of our country. . . . [It] will continue to rely chiefly on its own forces and potentialities, but it is prepared to accept any assistance, moral and material, including arms and other military equipment, from all the socialist countries, from nationalist countries, from international organizations, and from the peace-loving peoples of the world.

SOURCE: "Statement of the National Liberation Front of South Vietnam," *New Times* (March 27, 1965), pp. 36–40.

countries" (which included the Soviet Union) and portrayed itself as the leader of the "rural underdeveloped countries" of Asia, Africa, and Latin America in a global struggle against imperialist oppression. In effect, China had applied Mao's famous concept of people's war in an international framework.

The Second Indochina War

The Eisenhower administration had opposed the peace settlement at Geneva in 1954, which divided Vietnam temporarily into two separate regroupment zones, specifically because the provision for future national elections opened up the possibility of placing the entire country under Communist rule. But President Eisenhower had been unwilling to introduce U.S. military forces to continue the conflict without the full support of the British and the French, who preferred to seek a negotiated settlement. In the end, Washington promised not to break the provisions of the agreement but refused to commit itself to the results.

During the next several months, the United States began to provide aid to a new government in South Vietnam. Under the leadership of the anti-Communist politician Ngo Dinh Diem, the Saigon regime began to root out dissidents while refusing to hold the national elections called for by the Geneva Accords. It was widely anticipated, even in Washington, that the Communists would win such elections. In 1959, Ho Chi Minh, despairing of the peaceful unification of the country under Communist rule, returned to a policy of revolutionary war in the south. Late the following year, a broad political organization that was designed to win the support of a wide spectrum of the population was founded in an isolated part of South Vietnam. Known as the National Liberation Front, or NLF, it was under firm leadership from Communist leaders in North Vietnam (see the box above).

By 1963, South Vietnam was on the verge of collapse. Diem's autocratic methods and inattention to severe economic inequality had alienated much of the population, and revolutionary forces, popularly known as the Viet Cong (Vietnamese Communists), expanded their influence throughout much of the country. In the fall of 1963, with the approval of the Kennedy administration, senior military officers overthrew the Diem regime. But factionalism kept the new military leadership from reinvigorating the struggle against the insurgent forces, and by early 1965, the Viet Cong, their ranks now swelled by military units infiltrating from North Vietnam, were on the verge of seizing control of the entire country. In desperation, President Lyndon Johnson (1908–1973) decided to launch bombing raids on the north and send U.S. combat troops to South Vietnam to prevent a total defeat for the anti-Communist government in Saigon.

The Role of China Chinese leaders observed the gradual escalation of the conflict in South Vietnam with mixed feelings. They were undoubtedly pleased to have a firm Communist ally—and indeed one that had in so many ways followed the path of Mao Zedong—just beyond their southern frontier. Yet they could not relish the possibility that renewed bloodshed in South Vietnam might enmesh China in a new conflict with the United States. Nor could they have welcomed the specter of a powerful and ambitious united Vietnam that might wish to extend its influence throughout mainland Southeast Asia, which Beijing considered its own backyard.

Chinese leaders therefore tiptoed delicately through the minefield of the Indochina conflict, seeking to maintain good relations with their ally in Hanoi while avoiding a confrontation with the United States. As the war escalated in 1964 and 1965, Beijing publicly announced that the Chinese people would give their full support to their fraternal comrades seeking national liberation in South Vietnam but privately assured Washington that China would not directly enter the conflict unless U.S. forces threatened its southern border. Beijing also refused to cooperate fully with Moscow in shipping Soviet goods to North Vietnam through Chinese territory.

Despite its dismay at the lack of full support from China, the Communist government in North Vietnam responded to U.S. escalation by infiltrating more of its own regular force troops into the south, and by 1968, the war was a virtual stalemate. The Communists were not strong enough to overthrow the Saigon regime, whose weakness was shielded by the presence of half a million U.S. troops, but President Johnson was reluctant to engage in all-out war on North Vietnam for fear of provoking a global nuclear conflict. In the fall, after the Communist-led Tet offensive aroused heightened antiwar protests in the United States, peace negotiations began in Paris.

The Road to Peace Richard Nixon (1913–1994) came into the White House in 1969 on a pledge to bring an honorable

end to the Vietnam War. With U.S. public opinion sharply divided on the issue, he began to withdraw U.S. troops while continuing to hold peace talks in Paris. But the centerpiece of his strategy was to improve relations with China and thus undercut Chinese support for the North Vietnamese war effort. During the 1960s, relations between Moscow and Beijing had reached a point of extreme tension, and thousands of troops were stationed on both sides of their long common frontier. To intimidate their Communist rivals, Soviet sources dropped the hint that they might decide to launch a preemptive strike to destroy Chinese nuclear facilities in Xinjiang. Sensing an opportunity to split the onetime allies, Nixon sent his emissary Henry Kissinger on a secret trip to China. Responding to the latter's assurances that the United States was determined to withdraw from Indochina and hoped to improve relations with the mainland regime, Chinese leaders invited President Nixon to visit China in early 1972.

Incensed at the apparent betrayal by their close allies, in January 1973 North Vietnamese leaders signed a peace treaty in Paris calling for the removal of all U.S. forces from South Vietnam. In return, the Communists agreed to seek a political settlement of their differences with the Saigon regime. But negotiations between north and south over the political settlement soon broke down, and in early 1975, convinced that Washington would not intervene, the Communists resumed the offensive. At the end of April, under a massive assault by North Vietnamese military forces, the South Vietnamese government surrendered. A year later, the country was unified under Communist rule.

Why had the United States lost the Vietnam War? Many Americans argued that by not taking the war directly to North Vietnam, the White House had forced the U.S. armed forces to fight "with one hand tied behind their backs." Others retorted that the United States should not have gotten involved in a struggle for national liberation in the first place. Dean Rusk, secretary of state during the Kennedy and Johnson administrations, declared many years later that U.S. political leaders had underestimated the determination of the enemy and overestimated the patience of the American people. Perhaps, too, they had overestimated the ability of the Saigon government to take charge of its own destiny.

The Communist victory in Vietnam was a humiliation for the United States, but its strategic impact was limited because of the new relationship with China. During the next decade, Sino-American relations continued to improve. In 1979, diplomatic ties were established between the two countries under an arrangement whereby the United States renounced its mutual security treaty with the Republic of China in return for a pledge from China to seek reunification with Taiwan by peaceful means. By the end of the 1970s, China and the United States had forged a "strategic relationship" in which each would cooperate with the other against the common threat of Soviet "hegemonism" (as China described Soviet policy) in Asia.

An Era of Equivalence

The Johnson administration sent U.S. combat troops to South Vietnam in 1965 in an effort to prevent the expansion of communism in Southeast Asia. Washington's primary concern, however, was not Moscow but Beijing. By the mid-1960s, U.S. officials viewed the Soviet Union as an essentially conservative power, more concerned with protecting its vast empire than with expanding its borders. In fact, U.S. policy makers periodically sought Soviet assistance in achieving a peaceful settlement of the Vietnam War. As long as Khrushchev was in power, they found a receptive ear in Moscow. Khrushchev had sternly advised the North Vietnamese against a resumption of revolutionary war in South Vietnam.

After October 1964, when Khrushchev was replaced by a new leadership headed by party chief Leonid Brezhnev (1906–1982) and Prime Minister Alexei Kosygin (1904–1980), Soviet attitudes about Vietnam became more ambivalent. On the one hand, the new Soviet leadership had no desire to see the Vietnam conflict poison relations between the great powers. On the other hand, Moscow was anxious to demonstrate its support for the North Vietnamese to deflect Chinese charges that the Soviet Union had betrayed the interests of the oppressed peoples of the world. As a result, Soviet officials voiced sympathy for the U.S. predicament in Vietnam but put no pressure on their allies to bring an end to the war. Indeed, the Soviets became Hanoi's main supplier of advanced military equipment in the final years of the war.

Still, Brezhnev and Kosygin continued to pursue the Khrushchev line of peaceful coexistence with the West and adopted a generally cautious posture in foreign affairs. By the early 1970s, a new age in Soviet-American relations had emerged, often referred to by the French term *détente*, meaning a reduction of tensions between the two sides. One symbol of the new relationship was the Antiballistic Missile (ABM) Treaty, often called SALT I (for Strategic Arms Limitation Talks), signed in 1972, in which the two nations agreed to limit their missile systems.

Washington's objective in pursuing such a treaty was to make it unprofitable for either superpower to believe that it could win a nuclear exchange by launching a preemptive strike against the other. U.S. officials believed that a policy of "equivalence," in which there was a roughly equal power balance on each side, was the best way to avoid a nuclear confrontation. Détente was pursued in other ways as well. When President Nixon took office in 1969, he sought to increase trade and cultural contacts with the Soviet Union. His purpose was to set up a series of "linkages" in U.S.-Soviet relations that would persuade Moscow of the economic and social benefits of maintaining good relations with the West.

A symbol of that new relationship was the Helsinki Agreement of 1975. Signed by the United States, Canada, and all European nations on both sides of the Iron Curtain, these accords recognized all borders in Central and Eastern Europe established since the end of World War II, thereby formally acknowledging for the first time the Soviet sphere of influence. The Helsinki Agreement also committed the signatory powers to recognize and protect the human rights of their citizens, a clear effort by the Western states to improve the performance of the Soviet Union and its allies in that area.

An End to Détente?

Protection of human rights became one of the major foreign policy goals of the next U.S. president, Jimmy Carter (b. 1924). Ironically, just at the point when U.S. involvement in Vietnam came to an end and relations with China began to improve, the mood in U.S.-Soviet relations began to sour, for several reasons.

Renewed Tensions in the "Third World" Some Americans had become increasingly concerned about aggressive new tendencies in Soviet foreign policy. The first indication came in Africa. Soviet influence was on the rise in Somalia, across the Red Sea in South Yemen, and later in Ethiopia. Soviet involvement was also on the increase in southern Africa, where an insurgent movement supported by Cuban troops came to power in Angola, once a colony of Portugal. Then, in 1979, Soviet troops were sent to neighboring Afghanistan to protect a newly installed Marxist regime facing rising internal resistance from fundamentalist Muslims. Some observers suspected that the Soviet advance into hitherto neutral Afghanistan was to extend Soviet power into the oil fields of the Persian Gulf. To deter such a possibility, the White House promulgated the Carter Doctrine, which stated that the United States would use its military power, if necessary, to safeguard Western access to the oil reserves in the Middle East. In fact, sources in Moscow later disclosed that the Soviet advance into Afghanistan had little to do with a strategic drive toward the Persian Gulf but represented an effort to take advantage of the recent disarray in U.S. foreign policy in the aftermath of defeat in Vietnam to increase Soviet influence in a sensitive region increasingly beset with Islamic fervor. Soviet officials feared that the wave of Islamic activism could spread to the Muslim populations in the Soviet republics in central Asia and were confident that the United States was too distracted by the "Vietnam syndrome" (the public fear of U.S. involvement in another Vietnam-type conflict) to respond.

Other factors contributed to the growing suspicion of the Soviet Union in the United States. During the era of détente, Washington officials had assumed that Moscow accepted the U.S. doctrine of equivalence—the idea that both sides possessed sufficient strength to destroy the other in the event of a surprise attack. By the end of the decade, however, some U.S. defense analysts began to charge that the Soviets were seeking strategic superiority in nuclear weapons and argued for a substantial increase in U.S. defense spending. Such charges, combined with evidence of Soviet efforts in Africa and the Middle East and reports of the persecution of Jews and dissidents in the Soviet Union, helped undermine public support for détente in the United States. These changing attitudes were reflected in the failure of the Carter administration to obtain congressional approval of a new arms limitation agreement (SALT II) signed with the Soviet Union in 1979.

Northern Central America

Countering the Evil Empire

The early years of the administration of President Ronald Reagan (1911–2004) witnessed a return to the harsh rhetoric, if not all of the harsh practices, of the Cold War. President Reagan's anti-Communist credentials were well known. In a speech given shortly after his election in 1980, he referred to the Soviet Union as an "evil empire" and frequently voiced his suspicion of its motives in foreign affairs. In an effort to eliminate perceived Soviet advantages in strategic weaponry, the White House began a military buildup that stimulated a renewed arms race. In 1982, the Reagan administration introduced the nuclear-tipped cruise missile, whose ability to fly at low altitudes made it difficult to detect by enemy radar. Reagan also became an ardent exponent of the Strategic Defense Initiative (SDI), nicknamed "Star Wars." Its purposes were to create a space shield that could destroy incoming missiles and to force Moscow into an arms race that it could not hope to win.

The Reagan administration also adopted a more activist, if not confrontational, stance in the Third World. That attitude was most directly demonstrated in Central America, where the revolutionary Sandinista regime had come to power in Nicaragua with the overthrow of the Somoza dictatorship in 1979. Charging that the Sandinista regime was supporting a guerrilla insurgency movement in nearby El Salvador, the Reagan administration began to provide material aid to the government in El Salvador while simultaneously applying pressure on the Sandinistas by giving support to an anti-Communist guerrilla movement (called the Contras) in Nicaragua. The administration's Central

American policy caused considerable controversy in Congress, and critics charged that growing U.S. involvement there could lead to a repeat of the nation's bitter experience in Vietnam.

By providing military support to the anti-Soviet insurgents in Afghanistan, the White House helped maintain a Vietnam-like war in Afghanistan that would embed the Soviet Union in its own quagmire. Like the Vietnam War, the conflict in Afghanistan resulted in heavy casualties and demonstrated that the influence of a superpower was limited in the face of strong nationalist, guerrilla-type opposition.

Toward a New World Order

In 1985, Mikhail Gorbachev was elected secretary of the Communist Party of the Soviet Union in Moscow. During Brezhnev's last years and the brief tenures of his two successors (see Chapter 10), the Soviet Union had entered an era of serious economic decline, and the dynamic new party chief was well aware that drastic changes would be needed to rekindle the dreams that had inspired the Bolshevik Revolution. During the next few years, he launched a program of restructuring (*perestroika*) to revitalize the Soviet system. As part of that program, he set out to improve relations with the United States and the rest of the capitalist world. When he met with President Reagan in Reykjavik, the capital of Iceland, the two leaders agreed to set aside their ideological differences.

Gorbachev's desperate effort to rescue the Soviet Union from collapse was too little and too late. In 1991, the Soviet Union, so long an apparently permanent fixture on the global scene, suddenly disintegrated. In its place arose several new nations from the ashes of the Soviet empire. Meanwhile, the string of Soviet satellites in Eastern Europe broke loose from Moscow's grip and declared their independence from Communist rule. The era of the Cold War was over.

The end of the Cold War lulled many observers into the seductive vision of a new world order that would be characterized by peaceful cooperation and increasing prosperity. Sadly, such hopes have not been realized. A bitter civil war in the Balkans in the mid-1990s graphically demonstrated that old fault lines of national and ethnic hostility still divided the post–Cold War world. Elsewhere, bloody ethnic and religious disputes broke out in Africa and the Middle East. Then, on September 11, 2001, the world entered a dangerous new era when terrorists attacked the nerve centers of U.S. power in New York City and Washington, D.C., inaugurating a new round of tension between the West and the forces of militant Islam. These events will be discussed in greater detail in the chapters that follow.

Beyond these immediate problems, other issues clamor for attention. Environmental pollution and the threat of global warming, the widening gap between rich and poor nations, and growing tensions caused by the migration of peoples all present a threat to political stability and the pursuit of happiness. Today, the task of guaranteeing the survival of the human race appears to be equally as challenging as it was during the era of the Cold War—and even more complex. We will return to these issues in the final chapter.

CONCLUSION

A T THE END OF WORLD WAR II, a new conflict appeared in Europe as the two superpowers, the United States and the Soviet Union, began to compete for political domination. This ideological division soon spread to the rest of the world as the United States fought in Korea and Vietnam to prevent the spread of communism, promoted by the new Maoist government in China, while the Soviet Union used its influence to prop up pro-Soviet regimes in Asia, Africa, and Latin America.

What had begun, then, as a confrontation across the great divide of the Iron Curtain in Europe eventually took on global significance, much as the major European powers had jostled for position and advantage in Africa and eastern Asia prior to World War I. As a result, both Moscow and Washington became entangled in areas that in themselves had little importance in terms of real national security interests.

As the twentieth century entered its last two decades, however, there were tantalizing signs of a thaw in the Cold War. In 1979, China and the United States decided to establish mutual diplomatic relations, a consequence of Beijing's decision to focus on domestic reform and stop supporting wars of national liberation in Asia. Six years later, the ascent of Mikhail Gorbachev to leadership, culminating in the collapse of the Soviet Union in 1991, brought a final end to almost half a century of bitter rivalry between the world's two superpowers.

The Cold War had thus ended without the horrifying vision of a mushroom cloud. Unlike earlier rivalries that had culminated in the century's two world wars, the antagonists had gradually come to realize that the struggle for supremacy could best be carried out in the political and economic arena rather than on the battlefield. And in the final analysis, it was not military superiority, but political, economic, and cultural factors that had brought about the triumph of Western civilization over the Marxist vision of a classless utopia. The world's statesmen could now shift their focus to other problems of mutual concern.

TIMELINE

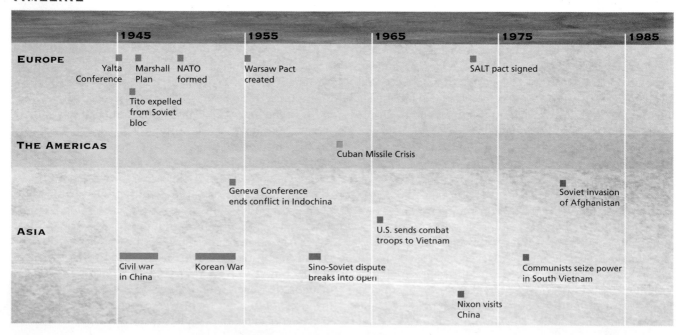

CHAPTER NOTES

1. *Department of State Bulletin,* February 11, 1945, p. 213.
2. Quoted in Joseph M. Jones, *The Fifteen Weeks (February 21–June 5, 1947),* 2d ed. (New York, 1964), pp. 140–141.
3. Quoted in Walter Laqueur, *Europe in Our Time* (New York, 1992), p. 111.

CHAPTER

8

THE UNITED STATES, CANADA, AND LATIN AMERICA

$\mathcal{O}$N MAY 22, 1964, President Lyndon B. Johnson gave a policy speech before an assembled audience of students at the University of Michigan in Ann Arbor. He used the occasion to propose a new domestic strategy—to be known as the "Great Society"—to bring about major economic and social reforms in the United States. The aim of these reforms, he said, would be to use the national wealth "to enrich and elevate our national life and to advance the quality of our American civilization."[1]

In his State of the Union address the following January, President Johnson unveiled some of the details of his plan. They included increased funding for education, urban renewal, the fight on crime and disease, a new Medicare program, and a war on poverty. Finally, he called for an extension of voting rights to guarantee the franchise to all citizens.

During the next few years, the U.S. Congress enacted many of the programs drafted by the Johnson administration, and the Great Society became a familiar part of the American landscape. A few years, later, however, it came under attack, as a more conservative electorate turned away from expensive welfare programs and endorsed a more cautious approach to meeting the social needs of the American people. An era of active government intervention to bring about changes in the fabric of American society had came to an end. ◇

The United States Since 1945

Between 1945 and 1970, the legacy of Franklin Roosevelt's New Deal largely determined the parameters of American domestic politics. The New Deal gave rise to a distinct pattern that signified a basic transformation in American society. This pattern included a dramatic increase in the role and power of the federal government, the rise of organized labor as a significant force in the economy and politics, a commitment to the welfare state, albeit a restricted one (Americans did not have access to universal health care as most other industrialized societies did), a grudging acceptance of the need to resolve minority problems, and a willingness to experiment with deficit spending as a means of spurring the economy.

An Era of Prosperity

The influence of New Deal politics was bolstered by the election of Democratic presidents—Harry Truman in 1948, John F. Kennedy in 1960, and Lyndon B. Johnson in 1964. Even the election of a Republican president, Dwight D. Eisenhower, in 1952 and 1956, did not significantly alter the fundamental direction of the New Deal. As Eisenhower conceded in 1954, "Should any political party attempt to abolish Social Security and eliminate labor laws and farm programs, you would not hear of that party again in our political history."

No doubt, the economic boom that took place after World War II fueled public confidence in the new American way of life. A shortage of consumer goods during the war left Americans with both surplus income and the desire to purchase these goods after the war. Then, too, the growing power of organized labor enabled more and more workers to obtain the wage increases that fueled the growth of the domestic market. Increased government expenditures (justified by the theory of English economist John Maynard Keynes that government spending could stimulate a lagging economy to reach higher levels of productivity) also indirectly subsidized the American private enterprise system. Especially after the Korean War began in 1950, outlays on defense provided money for scientific research in the universities and markets for weapons industries. After 1955, tax dollars built a massive system of interstate highways, and tax deductions for mortgages subsidized homeowners. Between 1945 and 1973, real wages grew at an average rate of 3 percent a year, the most prolonged advance in American history.

America on the Move The prosperity of the 1950s and 1960s also translated into significant social changes. More workers left the factories and fields and moved into white-collar occupations, finding jobs as professional and technical employees, managers, proprietors, and clerical and sales workers. In 1940, blue-collar workers made up 52 percent of the labor force; farmers and farmworkers, 17 percent; and white-collar workers, 31 percent. By 1970, blue-collar workers constituted 50 percent; farmers and farmworkers, 3 percent; and white-collar workers, 47 percent.

One consequence of this change was a movement from rural areas and central cities into the suburbs. In 1940, just 19 percent of the American population lived in suburbs, with 49 percent in rural areas and 32 percent in central cities. By 1970, those figures had changed to 38, 31, and 31 percent, respectively. The move to the suburbs also produced an imposing number of shopping malls and reinforced the American passion for the automobile, which provided the means of transport from suburban home to suburban mall and workplace. Finally, the search for prosperity led to new migration patterns. As the West and South experienced rapid economic growth through the development of new industries, especially in the defense field, massive numbers of people made the exodus from the cities of the Northeast and Midwest to the Sunbelt of the South and West. Between 1940 and 1980, cities like Chicago, Philadelphia, Detroit, and Cleveland lost between 13 and 36 percent of their populations, while Los Angeles, Dallas, and San Diego grew between 100 and 300 percent.

Although the country was becoming more affluent, it was also feeling more vulnerable as Cold War confrontations abroad had repercussions at home. The Communist victory in China aroused fears that Communists had infiltrated the United States. A demagogic senator from Wisconsin, Joseph McCarthy, helped intensify a massive "Red scare" with unsubstantiated allegations that there were hundreds of Communists in high government positions. But McCarthy went too far when he attacked alleged "Communist conspirators" in the U.S. Army, and he was censured by Congress in 1954. Shortly after, his anti-Communist crusade came to an end. The pervasive fear of communism and the possibility of a nuclear war, however, remained strong.

Toward the Great Society While the 1950s have been characterized (erroneously) as a tranquil age, the period between 1960 and 1973 was clearly a time of upheaval that brought to the fore some of the problems that had been glossed over in the 1950s. The era began on an optimistic note. At age forty-three, John F. Kennedy (1917–1963) became the youngest elected president in the history of the United States and the first born in the twentieth century. His own administration, cut short by an assassin's bullet on November 22, 1963, focused primarily on foreign affairs, although it inaugurated an extended period of increased economic growth. Kennedy's successor, Lyndon B. Johnson (1908–1973), who won a new term as president in a landslide in 1964, used his stunning mandate to pursue the growth of the welfare state, first begun in the New Deal. Johnson's Great Society programs included health care for the elderly, a "war on poverty" to be fought with food stamps and a "job corps," the new Department of Housing and Urban Development to deal with the problems of the cities, and federal assistance for education.

Focus on Civil Rights Johnson's other domestic passion was the achievement of equal rights for African Americans. The civil rights movement began in earnest in 1954 when the U.S. Supreme Court took the dramatic step of striking down the practice of maintaining racially segregated public schools. According to Chief Justice Earl Warren, "Separate educational facilities are inherently unequal." A year later, during a boycott of segregated buses in Montgomery, Alabama, the eloquent Martin Luther King Jr. (1929–1968) surfaced as the leader of a growing movement for racial equality.

By the early 1960s, a number of groups, including King's Southern Christian Leadership Conference (SCLC), were organizing demonstrations and sit-ins across the South to end racial segregation. In August 1963, King led the March on Washington for Jobs and Freedom. This march and King's impassioned plea for racial equality had an electrifying effect on the American people (see the box on p. 162). By the end of 1963, a majority of Americans (52 percent) called civil rights the most significant national issue; only 4 percent had done so eight months earlier.

President Johnson took up the cause of civil rights. As a result of his initiative, Congress in 1964 enacted the Civil Rights Act, which ended segregation and discrimination in the workplace and in all public accommodations. The Voting Rights Act, passed the following year, eliminated racial obstacles to voting in southern states. But laws alone

"I Have a Dream"

In the spring of 1963, a bomb attack on a church that killed four African American children and the brutal fashion in which police handled black demonstrators brought the nation's attention to the policies of racial segregation in Birmingham, Alabama. A few months later, on August 28, 1963, Martin Luther King Jr. led a march on Washington, D.C., and gave an inspired speech at the Lincoln Memorial that catalyzed the civil rights movement.

Martin Luther King Jr. was known as a highly skilled and moving orator. What are some of the rhetorically effective elements in this speech?

Martin Luther King Jr., "I Have a Dream"

I am happy to join with you today in what will go down in history as the greatest demonstration for freedom in the history of our nation.

Five score years ago, a great American, in whose symbolic shadow we stand today, signed the Emancipation Proclamation. This momentous decree came as a great beacon light of hope to millions of Negro slaves, who had been seared in the flames of withering injustice. It came as a joyous daybreak to end the long night of their captivity.

But one hundred years later, the Negro still is not free; one hundred years later, the life of the Negro is still sadly crippled by the manacles of segregation and the chains of discrimination; one hundred years later, the Negro lives on a lonely island of poverty in the midst of a vast ocean of material prosperity; one hundred years later, the Negro is still languished in the corners of American society and finds himself in exile in his own land. . . .

So we've come here today to dramatize a shameful condition. In a sense we've come to our nation's capital to cash a check. When the architects of our republic wrote the magnificent words of the Constitution and the Declaration of Independence, they were signing a promissory note to which every American was to fall heir. This note was the promise that all men, yes, black men as well as white men, would be guaranteed the unalienable rights of life, liberty, and the pursuit of happiness.

It is obvious today that America has defaulted on this promissory note in so far as her citizens of color are concerned. Instead of honoring this sacred obligation, America has given the Negro people a bad check, a check which has come back marked "insufficient funds." But we refuse to believe that the bank of justice is bankrupt. . . .

We have also come to this hallowed spot to remind America of the fierce urgency of now. This is no time to engage in the luxury of cooling off or to take the tranquilizing drug of gradualism. Now is the time to make real the promises of democracy; now is the time to rise from the dark and desolate valley of segregation to the sunlit path of racial justice; now is the time to lift our nation from the quicksands of racial injustice to the solid rock of brotherhood; now is the time to make justice a reality for all of God's children. It would be fatal for the nation to overlook the urgency of the moment. . . .

I say to you today, my friends, so even though we face the difficulties of today and tomorrow, I still have a dream. It is a dream deeply rooted in the American dream. I have a dream that one day this nation will rise up and live out the true meaning of its creed, "We hold these truths to be self-evident, that all men are created equal." I have a dream that one day on the red hills of Georgia, sons of former slaves and the sons of former slave owners will be able to sit down together at the table of brotherhood. . . . I have a dream that my four little children will one day live in a nation where they will not be judged by the color of their skin, but by the content of their character. . . .

This is our hope. This is the faith that I go back to the South with. With this faith we will be able to hew out of the mountain of despair a stone of hope. With this faith we will be able to transform the jangling discords of our nation into a beautiful symphony of brotherhood. With this faith we will be able to work together, to pray together, to struggle together, to go to jail together, to stand up for freedom together, knowing that we will be free one day. And this will be the day. This will be the day when all of God's children will be able to sing with new meaning, "My country 'tis of thee, sweet land of liberty, of thee I sing. Land where my father died, land of the pilgrims' pride, from every mountainside, let freedom ring." And if America is to be a great nation, this must become true. . . .

And when this happens, and when we allow freedom to ring, when we let it ring from every village and every hamlet, from every state and every city, we will be able to speed up that day when all of God's children, black men and white men, Jews and Gentiles, Protestants and Catholics, will be able to join hands and sing in the words of the old Negro spiritual: "Free at last. Free at last. Thank God Almighty, we are free at last."

SOURCE: From Martin Luther King, Jr., 1963. Copyright © 1963 by Martin Luther King, Jr. Copyright renewed 1991 by Coretta Scott King. Reprinted by arrangement with the Estate of Martin Luther King, Jr., c/o Writers House, Inc. as agent for the proprietor, New York, NY.

could not guarantee a "great society," and Johnson soon faced bitter social unrest, both from African Americans and from the burgeoning antiwar movement.

In the North and West, African Americans had had voting rights for many years, but local patterns of segregation resulted in considerably higher unemployment rates for blacks (and Hispanics) than for whites and left blacks segregated in huge urban ghettos. In these ghettos, calls for militant action by radical black nationalist leaders, such as Malcolm X of the Black Muslims, attracted more attention than the nonviolent appeals of Martin Luther King. In the summer of 1965, race riots erupted in the Watts district of Los Angeles that led to thirty-four deaths and the destruction of more than one thousand buildings. Cleveland, San Francisco, Chicago, Newark, and Detroit likewise exploded in the summers of 1966 and 1967. After the assassination of Martin Luther King in 1968, more than one hundred cities experienced rioting, including Washington, D.C., the nation's capital. The combination of riots and extremist comments by radical black leaders led to a "white backlash" and a severe division of American society. In 1964, only 34 percent of white Americans agreed with the statement that blacks were asking for "too much"; by late 1966, that number had risen to 85 percent.

A Nation Divided Antiwar protests also divided the American people after President Johnson committed American troops to the costly war in Vietnam (see Chapter 7). The antiwar movement arose out of the free speech movement that began in 1964 at the University of California at Berkeley as a protest against the impersonality and authoritarianism of the large university. As the war progressed and U.S. casualties mounted, protests escalated. Teach-ins, sit-ins, and the occupation of university buildings alternated with more radical demonstrations that increasingly led to violence. The killing of four students at Kent State University in 1970 by the Ohio National Guard caused a reaction, and the antiwar movement began to subside. By that time, however, antiwar demonstrations had helped weaken the willingness of many Americans to continue the war. But the combination of antiwar demonstrations and ghetto riots in the cities also prepared many people to embrace "law and order," an appeal used by Richard M. Nixon (1913–1994), the Republican presidential candidate in 1968. With Nixon's election in 1968, a shift to the right in American politics had begun.

Move to the Right

Nixon eventually ended U.S. involvement in Vietnam by gradually withdrawing American troops and appealing to the "silent majority" of Americans for patience in bringing the conflict to an end. A slowdown in racial desegregation appealed to southern whites, who had previously tended

The Anti-War Movement. As U.S. military casualties in South Vietnam began to mount in the mid-1960s, public protests against the war began to intensify on the home front. Many of the protesters were young Americans subject to the draft, but opposition to U.S. policies in Vietnam gradually spread throughout the country and eventually forced President Lyndon Johnson and his successor Richard M. Nixon to withdraw American troops from the country. Shown here is a vast protest demonstration against the backdrop of the U.S. Capitol Building in Washington, D.C.

to vote Democratic. The Republican strategy also gained support among white Democrats in northern cities, where court-mandated busing to achieve racial integration had produced a white backlash. Nixon was less conservative on other issues, notably when, breaking with his strong anti-Communist past, he visited China in 1972 and opened the door toward the eventual diplomatic recognition of that Communist state.

Nixon was paranoid about conspiracies, however, and began to use illegal methods of gaining political intelligence about his political opponents. One of the president's advisers explained that their intention was to "use the available federal machinery to screw our political enemies." Nixon's zeal led to the infamous Watergate scandal—the attempted bugging of Democratic National Headquarters. Although Nixon repeatedly lied to the American public about his involvement in the affair, secret tapes of his own conversations in the White House revealed the truth. On August 9, 1974, Nixon resigned from office, an act that saved him from almost certain impeachment and conviction.

After Watergate, American domestic politics focused on economic issues. Gerald B. Ford (b. 1913) became president when Nixon resigned, only to lose in the 1976 election to the Democratic former governor of Georgia, Jimmy Carter (b. 1924), who campaigned as an outsider against the Washington establishment. Both Ford and Carter faced severe economic problems. The period from 1973 to the mid-1980s was one of economic stagnation, which came to be known as stagflation—a combination of high inflation and high unemployment. In 1984, median family income was 6 percent below that of 1973.

The First Oil Crisis The economic downturn stemmed at least in part from a dramatic rise in oil prices. Oil had been a cheap and abundant source of energy in the 1950s, but by the late 1970s, half of the oil used in the United States came from the Middle East. An oil embargo imposed by the Organization of Petroleum Exporting Countries (OPEC) cartel as a reaction to the Arab-Israeli War in 1973 and OPEC's subsequent raising of prices led to a quadrupling of the cost of oil. By the end of the 1970s, oil prices had increased twentyfold, encouraging inflationary tendencies throughout the entire economy. Although the Carter administration produced a plan for reducing oil consumption at home while spurring domestic production, neither Congress nor the American people could be persuaded to follow what they regarded as drastic measures.

By 1980, the Carter administration was facing two devastating problems. High inflation and a noticeable decline in average weekly earnings were causing a perceptible drop in American living standards. At the same time, a crisis abroad had erupted when fifty-three Americans were taken and held hostage by the Iranian government of Ayatollah Khomeini. Although Carter had little control over the situation, his inability to gain the release of the American hostages led to the perception at home that he was a weak president. His overwhelming loss to Ronald Reagan (1911–2004) in the election of 1980 brought forward the chief exponent of conservative Republican policies and a new political order.

Dismantling the Welfare State The conservative trend continued in the 1980s. The election of Ronald Reagan changed the direction of American policy on several fronts. Reversing decades of the expanding welfare state, Reagan cut spending on food stamps, school lunch programs, and job programs. At the same time, his administration fostered

the largest peacetime military buildup in American history. Total federal spending rose from $631 billion in 1981 to more than $1 trillion by 1986. But instead of raising taxes to pay for the new expenditures, which far outweighed the budget cuts in social areas, Reagan convinced Congress to support supply-side economics. Massive tax cuts were designed to stimulate rapid economic growth and produce new revenues.

Reagan's policies seemed to work in the short run, and the United States experienced an economic upturn that lasted until the end of the 1980s, although most of the benefits accrued to the most affluent members of American society. But the spending policies of the Reagan administration also produced record government deficits, which loomed as an obstacle to long-term growth. In the 1970s, the total deficit was $420 billion; between 1981 and 1987, Reagan budget deficits were three times that amount. The inability of George H. W. Bush (b. 1924), Reagan's successor, to deal with the deficit problem or with the continuing economic downslide led to the election of a Democrat, Bill Clinton (b. 1946), in November 1992.

Seizing the Political Center

The new president was a southerner who claimed to be a new Democrat—one who favored fiscal responsibility and a more conservative social agenda—a clear indication that the rightward drift in American politics had not been reversed by his victory. During his first term in office, Clinton reduced the budget deficit and signed a bill turning the welfare program back to the states while pushing measures to strengthen the educational system and provide job opportunities for those Americans removed from the welfare rolls. By seizing the center of the American political agenda, Clinton was able to win reelection in 1996, although the Republican Party now held a majority in both houses of Congress.

President Clinton's political fortunes were helped considerably by a lengthy economic revival. Thanks to downsizing, major U.S. corporations began to recover the competitive edge they had lost to Japanese and European firms in previous years. At the same time, a steady reduction in the annual government budget deficit strengthened confidence in the performance of the national economy. Although wage increases were modest, inflation was securely in check, and public confidence in the future was on the rise.

Many of the country's social problems, however, remained unresolved. Although crime rates were down, drug use, smoking, and alcoholism among young people remained high, and the specter of rising medical costs loomed as a generation of baby boomers (those born in the two decades after World War II) neared retirement age. Americans remained bitterly divided over such issues as abortion and affirmative action programs to rectify past discrimination on the basis of gender, race, or sexual orientation.

President Clinton contributed to the national sense of unease by becoming the focus of a series of financial and sexual scandals that aroused concerns among many Americans that the moral fiber of the country had been severely undermined. Accused of lying under oath in a judicial hearing, he was impeached by the Republican-led majority in Congress. Although the effort to remove Clinton from office failed, his administration was tarnished, and in 2000, Republican candidate George W. Bush (b. 1946), the son of Clinton's predecessor, narrowly defeated Clinton's vice president, Albert Gore, in the race for the presidency. Bush too sought to occupy the center of the political spectrum while heeding the concerns of his conservative base.

The Politics of Terrorism On September 11, 2001, terrorists hijacked four commercial jet planes shortly after taking off from Boston, Newark, and Washington, D.C. Two of the planes were flown directly into the twin towers of the World Trade Center in New York City, causing both buildings to collapse; a third slammed into the Pentagon, near Washington, D.C.; and the fourth crashed in a field in central Pennsylvania. About three thousand people were killed, including everyone aboard the four airliners.

The hijackings were carried out by a terrorist organization known as al-Qaeda, which had been suspected of bombing two U.S. embassies in Africa in 1998 and attacking a U.S. naval ship, the U.S.S. *Cole,* two years later. Its leader, Osama bin Laden, was a native of Saudi Arabia who was allegedly angry at the growing U.S. presence in the Middle East. U.S. President George W. Bush vowed to wage an offensive war on terrorism, and in October, with broad international support, including from the United Nations, U.S. forces attacked al-Qaeda bases in Afghanistan (see Chapter 15).

The Bush administration had less success in gaining UN approval for an attack on the brutal regime of Saddam Hussein in Iraq, which the White House accused of amassing weapons of mass destruction and providing support to terrorist groups in the region. Nevertheless, in March 2003, U.S. forces invaded Iraq and quickly overthrew the regime of Saddam Hussein. Initially, the invasion had broad popular support in the United States, but as insurgent activities continued to inflict casualties on U.S. and Allied occupation forces—not to speak of the deaths of thousands of Iraqi civilians—the war became more controversial. Some Americans called for an immediate pullout of U.S. troops.

The Bush administration was also dogged by an economic downturn and a number of other domestic problems, including the outsourcing of American jobs to Asian countries and the failure to control illegal immigration from Mexico. But it benefited from the public perception that the Republican Party was more effective in protecting the American people from the threat of terrorism than its Democratic rival. Evangelical Christians—one of the nation's most vocal communities—were also drawn to the Republican Party for its emphasis on traditional moral values and the sanctity of the family and its opposition to abortion. Riding the wave of such concerns, President Bush defeated the Democratic candidate John F. Kerry in the presidential election of 2004.

After the election, the Bush administration sought to rein in the rising cost of domestic spending by presenting new proposals to reform Social Security and the Medicare program. But the war in Iraq continued to distract the White House from other pressing issues, including a dramatic rise in the price of oil and an exploding national budget deficit, that demanded the urgent attention of the nation and its political leaders.

The Changing Face of American Society

Major changes took place in American society in the decades following World War II. New technologies such as television, jet planes, medical advances, and the computer revolution all dramatically altered the pace and nature of American life. Increased prosperity led to the growth of the middle class, the expansion of higher education, and a rapid increase in consumer demand for the products of a mass society. The building of a nationwide system of superhighways, combined with low fuel prices and steady improvements in the quality and operability of automobiles, produced a highly mobile society in which the average American family moved at least once every five years, sometimes from one end of the continent to the other.

A Consumer Society, a Permissive Society

These changes in the physical surroundings of the country were matched by equally important shifts in the social fabric. Boosted by rising incomes, a new generation of baby boomers grew up with higher expectations about their future material prospects than their parents had had. The members of this new "consumer society" focused much of their attention on achieving the "good life"—a middle-class lifestyle, complete with a home in the suburbs, two automobiles, and ample time for leisure activities. The growing predilection for buying on the installment plan was an important factor in protecting the national economy from the cycle of "boom and bust" that had characterized the prewar period, while also increasing the level of personal debt.

American social mores were also changing. Casual attitudes toward premarital sex (a product in part of the introduction of the birth control pill) and the use of drugs (a practice that increased dramatically during the Vietnam War) marked the emergence of a youth movement in the 1960s that questioned all authority and fostered rebellion against older generations.

The new standards were evident in the breakdown of the traditional nuclear family. Divorce rates increased exponentially to the point that at the end of the century, one of every two marriages was likely to end in divorce. Attitudes toward extramarital sex and homosexuality were also changing, and the stigma attached to children born out of wedlock eroded dramatically, although such evolving values were more evident in large cities than in the American heartland.

The Melting Pot in Action

One of the primary visual factors that helped shape American society in the postwar era was the increasing pace of new arrivals from abroad. As restrictions on immigration were loosened after World War II, millions of immigrants began to arrive from all over the world. Although the majority came from Latin America, substantial numbers came from China, Vietnam, and the countries of southern Asia. By 2003, people of Hispanic origin surpassed African Americans as the largest minority group in the country.

In recent years, illegal immigration—primarily from Mexico but also to a lesser extent from other countries in Central America—has become a controversial issue in American politics. Since many illegal immigrants gravitate to low-paying jobs not attractive to most Americans, they have usually been tacitly accepted by the public as a necessary evil. Now, however, their numbers have increased dramatically (an estimated 500,000 have crossed the border illegally each year since 2000), and critics point to the financial burden the new arrivals place on the nation's educational and medical systems. The number of Hispanics living in the southwestern states has increased to the extent that some argue the melting pot has become a "salad bowl" of unassimilated minorities living inside the borders of the United States. Yet recent immigrants, many of them undocumented, have became an increasingly indispensable element in the U.S. economy, comprising one-quarter of all farmworkers and 14 percent of all those employed in construction jobs.

Women and Society

Many of the changes taking place in American life reflected the fact that the role of women was in a state of rapid transition. In the years immediately following World War II, many women gave up their jobs in factories and returned to their traditional role as homemakers, sparking the "baby boom" of the late 1940s and 1950s. Eventually, however, many women became restive with their restrictive role as wives and mothers and began to enter the workforce at an increasing rate. Unlike the situation before the war, many of them were married. In 1900, for example, married women made up about 15 percent of the female labor force. By 1970, their number had increased to 62 percent.

American women were still not receiving equal treatment in the workplace, however, and by the late 1960s, some began to assert their rights and speak as feminists. Leading advocates of women's rights in the United States included Betty Friedan and Gloria Steinem. A journalist and the mother of three children, Friedan (1921–2006) grew increasingly uneasy with her attempt to fulfill the traditional role of housewife and mother. In 1963, she published *The Feminine Mystique,* in which she analyzed the problems of middle-class women in the 1950s and argued that women were systematically being denied equality with men. *The Feminine Mystique* became a best-seller and transformed Friedan into a prominent spokeswoman for women's rights in the United States.

As women became more actively involved in public issues, their role in education increased as well. Beginning in the 1980s, women's studies programs began to proliferate on college campuses throughout the United States. Women also became active in promoting women's rights in countries around the world, and they helped organize international conferences on the subject in Mexico City, Copenhagen, Nairobi, and Beijing.

Although women have steadily made gains in terms of achieving true equality in legal rights and economic opportunity in American society, much remains to be done. In recent years, much of the energy in the women's movement has focused on maintaining the right to legalized abortion. In 1973, the U.S. Supreme Court's decision in *Roe v. Wade* established the legal right to abortion. That ruling, however, has been under attack from those Americans who believe that an abortion is an act of murder against an unborn child.

The Environment

Concern over environmental problems first began to engage public opinion in the United States during the 1950s, when high pollution levels in major cities such as Los Angeles, Chicago, and Pittsburgh, combined with the popularity of Rachel Carson's book, *Silent Spring,* aroused concerns over the impact that unfettered industrialization was having on the quality of life and the health of the American people. During the next several decades, federal, state, and local governments began to issue regulations directed at reducing smog in urban areas and improving the quality of rivers and streams throughout the country.

In general, most Americans reacted favorably to such regulations, but by the 1980s, the environmental movement had engendered a backlash as some people complained that excessively radical measures could threaten the pace of economic growth and a loss of jobs in the workforce. By the end of the century, environmental issues had become deeply entangled with worries about the state of the national economy. Still, growing concerns about the potential impact of global warming kept the state of the environment alive as a serious problem in the world community (see Chapter 16).

Cultural Trends

The changing character of American society was vividly reflected in the world of culture.

The World of Painting

After World War II, the capital of the Western art world shifted from Paris to New York. Continuing the avant-garde quest to express reality in new ways, a group of New York artists known as Abstract Expressionists began to paint large nonrepresentational canvases in an effort to express a spiritual essence beyond the material world. Among the first was Jackson Pollock (1912–1956), who developed the technique of dripping and flinging paint onto a canvas spread out on the floor. Pollock's large paintings of swirling colors expressed the energy of primal forces as well as the vast landscapes of his native Wyoming.

During the 1960s, many American artists began to reject the emotional style of the previous decade and chose to deal with familiar objects from everyday experience. Some feared that art was being drowned out by popular culture, which bombarded Americans with the images of mass culture in newspapers, in the movies, or on television. In the hope of making art more relevant and accessible to the public, artists sought to pattern their work on aspects of everyday life to reach and manipulate the masses. Works such as those by Andy Warhol (1930–1987), which repeated images such as soup cans, dollar bills, and the faces of the *Mona Lisa* and Marilyn Monroe, often left the viewer with a detached numbness and a sense of being trapped in an impersonal, mechanized world. Repetitious and boring, most such paintings did little to close the gap between popular culture and serious art.

Perhaps the most influential American artist of the postwar era was Robert Rauschenberg (b. 1925), whose works broke through the distinctions between painting and other art forms such as sculpture, photography, dance, and theater. In his "collages" or "combines," he juxtaposed disparate images and everyday objects—photographs, clothing, letters, even dirt and cigarette butts—to reflect the energy and disorder of the world around us. He sought to reproduce the stream of images projected by flicking the channels on a TV set. His works represented an encapsulated documentary of American life in the 1960s, filled with news events, celebrities, war, sports, and advertisements.

Beginning in the late 1960s, a new school of conceptual art began to reject the commercial marketability of an art object and seek the meaning of art in ideas. Art as idea could be philosophy, linguistics, mathematics, or social criticism, existing solely in the mind of the artist and the audience. In a related attempt to free art from the shackles of tradition, a school of performance art used the body as a means of living sculpture. Often discomfiting or shocking in its intimate revelations, performance art expanded the horizons of modern creativity but also widened the gap between modern art and the public, many of whom now considered art as socially dysfunctional and totally lacking in relevance to their daily lives.

From Modernism to Postmodernism By the early 1970s, Postmodernism became the new art of revolt. Although some artists persevered in the Modernist tradition of formal experimentation, many believed that art should serve society; thus, their work expressed political concerns, seeking to redress social inequities by addressing issues of gender, race, sexual orientation, ecology, and globalization. This new style was called conceptual art, because it was primarily preoccupied with ideas. Using innovative techniques such as photography, video, and even representational painting, such artists produced shocking works with the intent of motivating the viewer to political action.

One of the most popular genres in the 1990s was the installation. The artist "installs" machine- or human-made objects, sometimes filling a large room, with the aim of transporting the viewer to another environment so as to experience new ideas and self-awareness. A powerful example is found in the untitled installation of 1997 by Robert Gober (b. 1955): in its center, a stereotypical statue of the Virgin Mary stands over an open drain while a wide steel pipe pierces her body. Such a violent violation of the Madonna can be viewed by Christians as depicting the victory and resilience of faith despite the century's philosophical discourse denying the existence of God.

New Concepts in Music and Architecture

Musical composers also experimented with radically new concepts. One such innovator was John Cage (1912–1992), who defined music as the "organization of sound" and included all types of noise in his music. Any unconventional sound was welcomed: electronic buzzers and whines, tape recordings played at altered speeds, or percussion from any household item. In wanting to make music "purposeless,"

Robert Gober's Madonna Installation.
Here the Virgin Mary is welcoming the faithful with outstretched arms, inviting them to unburden their suffering and tears by putting them down the drain at her feet. By combining such dramatically opposed visual objects, Gober succeeds in making the Madonna's pain palpably real, bringing her down to our level and overwhelming us with sadness and awe. For the unbeliever, Gober's installation is equally moving, representing as it does humankind's indomitable spirit. For despite the absurdity of one's existence, like this statue with its insides pierced, we are somehow still standing, still persevering in our quest for joy and meaning in life.

Cage removed the composer's control over the sounds. Rather, he sought to let the sounds, unconnected to one another, exist on their own. His most discussed work, called "4′ 33″," was four minutes and thirty-three seconds of silence—the "music" being the sounds the audience heard in the hall during the "performance," such as coughing, the rustling of programs, the hum of air conditioning, and the shuffling of feet.

In the 1960s, minimalism took hold in the United States. Largely influenced by Indian music, minimalist composers such as Philip Glass (b. 1937) focus on the subtle nuances in the continuous repetitions of a melodic or rhythmic pattern. Yet another musical development was microtonality, which expands the traditional twelve-tone chromatic scale to include quarter tones and even smaller intervals. Since the 1960s, there has also been much experimental electronic and computer music. Despite the excitement of such musical exploration, however, much of it is considered too cerebral and alien, even by the educated public.

One of the most accomplished and accessible contemporary American composers, John Adams (b. 1947), has labeled much of twentieth-century experimental composition as the "fussy, difficult music of transition." His music blends Modernist elements with classical traditions using much minimalist repetition interspersed with dynamic rhythms. Critics applaud his operas *Nixon in China* (1987) and *Doctor Atomic* (2005), which dramatizes the anxious countdown to the detonation of the first atomic bomb in New Mexico in 1945.

Architecture best reflects the extraordinary global economic expansion of the second half of the twentieth century, from the rapid postwar reconstruction of Japan and Europe to the phenomenal prosperity of the West and the newfound affluence of emerging Third World nations. No matter where one travels today, from Kuala Lumpur to Johannesburg, from Buenos Aires to Shanghai, the world's cities boast the identical monolithic rectangular skyscraper, which is the international symbol of modernization, money, and power.

Postmodern American architects, however, grew tired of the repetition and impersonality of the international style. Inspired by a new enthusiasm for historical preservation and urban renewal, they began to reincorporate traditional materials, shapes, and decorative elements into their buildings. Anyone sighting an American city today cannot fail to observe its Postmodern skyline, with pyramidal and cupolaed skyscrapers of blue-green glass and brick. Even Modernist rectangular malls have tacked on Greek columns and entryways shaped like Egyptian pyramids.

The arts are affected by the technological discoveries of their age, and today's marvel is undoubtedly the computer. In recent years, all the arts have been grappling with computerizing their medium. In architecture, for example, the computer is used as an engineering tool to solve construction problems for buildings imagined on the drawing board. What is more, architects today bypass the drawing board completely and let the computer conceive the building all by itself. In the visual arts, many artists compose abstract designs or representational paintings directly on the computer, forsaking canvas and brush entirely.

New Trends in Literature

Fictional writing in the 1960s reflected growing concerns about the materialism and superficiality of American culture and often took the form of exuberant and comic verbal fantasies. As the pain of the Vietnam War and the ensuing social and political turmoil intensified, authors turned to satire, using "black humor" and cruelty in the hope of shocking the American public into a recognition of its social ills. Many of these novels—such as Thomas Pynchon's *V.* (1963), Joseph Heller's *Catch-22* (1961), and John Barth's *Sot-Weed Factor* (1960)—were wildly imaginative, highly entertaining, and very different from the writing of the first half of the century, which had detailed the "real" daily lives of small-town or big-city America.

In the 1970s and 1980s, American fiction relinquished the extravagant verbal displays of the 1960s, returning to a more sober exposition of social problems, this time related to race, gender, and sexual orientation. Much of the best fiction explored the moral dimensions of contemporary life from Jewish, African American, feminist, or gay perspectives. Bernard Malamud (1914–1986), Saul Bellow (1915–2005), and Philip Roth (b. 1933) presented the Jewish American experience, while Ralph Ellison (1914–1994), James Baldwin (1924–1987), and Toni Morrison (b. 1931) dramatized the African American struggle.

Some outstanding women's fiction was written by foreign-born writers from Asia and Latin America, who examined the problems of immigrants, such as cultural identity and assimilation into the American mainstream.

Popular Culture

Popular culture has always played an important role in helping the American people define themselves. It also reflects the economic system that supports it, for it is this system that manufactures, distributes, and sells the images that people consume as popular culture. As popular culture and its economic support system have become increasingly intertwined, leisure industries have emerged. Modern popular culture is thus inextricably tied to the mass consumer society in which it has emerged. This consumer-oriented aspect of popular culture delineates it clearly from the folk culture of preceding centuries; folk culture is something people make, whereas popular culture is something people buy.

The United States has been the most influential force in shaping popular culture in the West and, to a lesser degree, throughout the world. Through movies, music, advertising, and television, the United States has spread its particular form of consumerism and the American dream to millions around the world. As we shall see in later chapters, however, American culture is also resented in many parts of the world for its role in eroding traditional values and the ability of individual nations to define their own social mores.

Motion pictures were the primary vehicle for the diffusion of American popular culture in the years immediately following World War II and continued to dominate both European and American markets in the next decades. Although developed in the 1930s, television did not become readily available until the late 1940s. By 1954, there were 32 million sets in the United States as television became the centerpiece of middle-class life. In the 1960s, as television spread around the world, American networks unloaded their products on Europe and developing countries at extraordinarily low prices. Only the establishment of quota systems prevented American television from completely inundating these countries.

The United States has also dominated popular music since the end of World War II. Jazz, blues, rhythm and blues, rock, rap, and hip-hop have been the most popular music forms in the Western world—and much of the non-Western world—during this time. All of them originated in the United States, and all are rooted in African American musical innovations. These forms later spread to the rest of the world, inspiring local artists, who then transformed the music in their own way.

In the postwar years, sports became a major product of both popular culture and the leisure industry. The emergence of professional football and basketball leagues, as well as the increasing popularity of their college equivalents, helped to transform sports into something akin to a national obsession. Sports became a cheap form of entertainment for consumers, as fans did not have to leave their homes to enjoy athletic competitions. In fact, some sports organizations initially resisted television, fearing that it would hurt ticket sales. The tremendous revenues possible from television contracts overcame this hesitation, however. As sports television revenue escalated, many sports came to receive the bulk of their yearly revenue from broadcasting contracts.

Sports became intertwined with international politics as well as big business. Politicization was one of the most significant trends in sports during the second half of the twentieth century. Football (soccer) remains the dominant world sport and more than ever has become a vehicle for nationalist sentiment and expression. It has yet to establish a mass viewing base in the United States, however. On the other hand, the Olympic Games are one of the most watched events on television.

Science and Technology

Since the Scientific Revolution of the seventeenth century and the Industrial Revolution of the nineteenth, science and technology have played increasingly important roles in the growth of Western civilization. Before World War II, theoretical science and technology were largely separated. Pure science was the domain of university professors, far removed from the practical technological matters of technicians and engineers. But during World War II, university scientists were recruited to work for their governments to develop new weapons and practical instruments of war. British physicists played a crucial role in developing an improved radar system in 1940 that helped defeat the German air force in the Battle of Britain. The computer, too, was a wartime creation. British mathematician Alan Turing designed a primitive computer to assist British intelligence in breaking the secret codes of German ciphering machines. The most famous product of wartime scientific research was the atomic bomb, created by a team of American and European scientists under the guidance of the physicist J. Robert Oppenheimer. Obviously, most wartime devices were created for destructive purposes, but computers and breakthrough technologies such as nuclear energy were soon adapted for peacetime uses.

The sponsorship of research by governments and the military during World War II led to a new scientific model. Science had become very complex, and only large organizations with teams of scientists, huge laboratories, and complicated equipment could undertake such large-scale projects. Such facilities were so expensive, however, that only governments and large corporations could support them. Because of its postwar prosperity, the United States was able to lead in the development of the new science. Almost 75 percent of all scientific research funds in the United States came from the government in 1965. In fact, the U.S. defense establishment generated much of the scientific research of the postwar era. One of every four scientists and engineers trained after 1945 was engaged in the creation of new weapons systems. Universities found their research agendas increasingly determined by government funding for military-related projects.

There was no more stunning example of how the new scientific establishment operated than the space race of the 1960s. In 1957, the Soviet Union announced that it had sent the first space satellite, *Sputnik I,* into orbit around the earth. In response, the United States launched a gigantic project to land a manned spacecraft on the moon within a decade. Massive government funding financed the scientific research and technological advances that attained this goal in 1969.

The postwar alliance of science and technology led to an accelerated rate of change that became a fact of life throughout Western society. The emergence of the computer has revolutionized American business practices and transformed the way individuals go about their lives and communicate with each other. Although early computers, which required thousands of vacuum tubes to function, were quite large, the development of the transistor and the silicon chip enabled manufacturers to reduce the size of their products dramatically. By the 1990s, the personal computer had become a fixture in businesses, schools, and homes around the country. The Internet—the world's largest computer network—provides millions of people around the world with quick access to immense quantities of information, as well as rapid communication and commercial transactions. By 2000, an estimated 500 million people were using the Internet. The United States has been at the forefront of this process, and the Clinton administration established the goal of providing instruction in computers in every school in the country.

Science is also being harnessed to serve other social purposes, including the development of biologically engineered food products, the formulation of new medicines to fight age-old diseases, and the development of alternative fuels to replace oil and the internal combustion engine. Recent interest has focused on the invention of new automobile engines that—like the hybrid varieties now entering the market—rely on some combination of electrical power and liquid energy.

Canada: In the Shadow of Goliath

Canada experienced many of the same developments as the United States in the postwar years. For twenty-five years after World War II, Canada realized extraordinary economic prosperity as it set out on a new path of industrial development. Canada had always had a strong export economy based on its abundant natural resources. Now it also developed electronic, aircraft, nuclear, and chemical engineering industries on a large scale. Much of the Canadian growth, however, was financed by capital from the United States, which resulted in U.S. ownership of Canadian businesses. While many Canadians welcomed the economic growth, others feared U.S. economic domination of Canada and its resources.

Canada's close relationship with the United States has been a notable feature of its postwar history. In addition to fears of economic domination, Canadians have also worried about playing a subordinate role politically and militarily to their neighboring superpower. Canada agreed to join the North Atlantic Treaty Organization in 1949 and even sent military contingents to fight in Korea the following year.

But to avoid subordination to the United States or any other great power, Canada has consistently and actively supported the United Nations. Nevertheless, concerns about the United States have not kept Canada from maintaining a special relationship with its southern neighbor. The North American Air Defense Command (NORAD), formed in 1957, was based on close cooperation between the air forces of the two countries for the defense of North America against aerial attack. As another example of their close cooperation, in 1972, Canada and the United States signed the Great Lakes Water Quality Agreement to regulate water quality of the lakes that border both countries.

Quebec

After 1945, the Liberal Party continued to dominate Canadian politics until 1957, when John Diefenbaker (1895–1979) achieved a Conservative victory. But a major recession returned the Liberals to power, and under Lester Pearson (1897–1972), they created Canada's welfare state by enacting a national social security system (the Canada Pension Plan) and a national health insurance program.

The most prominent Liberal government, however, was that of Pierre Trudeau (1919–2000), who came to power in 1968. Although French Canadian in background, Trudeau was dedicated to Canada's federal union. In 1968, his government passed the Official Languages Act, creating a bilingual federal civil service and encouraging the growth of French culture and language in Canada. Although Trudeau's government vigorously pushed an industrialization program, high inflation and Trudeau's efforts to impose the will of the federal government on the powerful provincial governments alienated voters and weakened his government.

For Canada, the vigor of the U.S. economy in the 1980s and 1990s was a mixed blessing, for the American behemoth was all too often inclined to make use of its power to have its way with its neighbors. Economic recession had brought Brian Mulroney (b. 1939), leader of the Progressive Conservative Party, to power in Canada in 1984. Mulroney's government sought to privatize many of Canada's state-run corporations and negotiated a free trade agreement with the United States. Bitterly resented by many Canadians as a sellout, the agreement cost Mulroney's government much of its popularity. In 1993, the ruling Conservatives were drastically defeated in national elections, winning only two seats in the House of Commons. The Liberal leader, Jean Chrétien (b. 1934), took over as prime minister with the charge of stimulating the nation's sluggish economy.

The new Liberal government also faced an ongoing crisis over the French-speaking province of Quebec. In the late 1960s, the Parti Québécois, headed by René Lévesque, campaigned on a platform of Quebec's secession from the Canadian confederation. In 1970, the party won 24 percent of the popular vote in Quebec's provincial elections. To pursue their dream of separation, some underground separatist groups even used terrorist bombings and kidnapped two prominent government officials. In 1976, the Parti Québécois won Quebec's provincial elections and in 1980 called for a referendum that would enable the provincial government to negotiate Quebec's independence from the rest of Canada. But voters in Quebec rejected the plan in 1995, and debate over Quebec's status continued to divide Canada as the decade came to a close. Provincial elections held in April 2003 delivered a stunning defeat to the Parti Québécois and a decisive victory to federalist elements. By then, however, the ruling Liberal Party was plagued by scandals, and in 2006, national elections brought the Conservatives, under new prime minister Stephen Harper (b. 1959), to power in Ottawa. Observers speculated that the new government would seek to repair strained relations with the United States.

Democracy, Dictatorship, and Development in Latin America Since 1945

The Great Depression of the 1930s caused political instability in many Latin American countries that led to military coups and militaristic regimes (see Chapter 5). But it also helped transform Latin America from a traditional to a modern economy. Since the nineteenth century, Latin Americans had exported raw materials, especially minerals and foodstuffs, while buying the manufactured goods of the industrialized countries, particularly Europe and the United States. Despite a limited degree of industrialization, Latin America was still dependent on an export-import economy. As a result of the Great Depression, however, exports were cut in half, and the revenues available to buy manufactured goods declined. In response, many Latin American countries encouraged the development of new industries to produce goods that were formerly imported. Due to a shortage of capital in the private sector, governments often invested in the new industries, thereby leading, for example, to government-run steel industries in Chile and Brazil and petroleum industries in Argentina and Mexico.

An Era of Dependency

In the 1960s, however, most Latin American countries were still dependent on the United States, Europe, and now Japan for the advanced technology needed for modern industries. To make matters worse, poverty conditions in some countries limited the size of domestic markets, and many countries were unable to find markets abroad for their products.

These failures resulted in takeovers by military regimes that sought to curb the demands of the new industrial middle class and a working class that had increased in size and power as a result of industrialization. In the 1960s, repressive military regimes in Chile, Brazil, and Argentina abolished political parties and turned to export-import economies financed by foreigners while encouraging multinational corporations to come into their countries. Because these companies were primarily interested in taking advantage of Latin America's raw materials and abundant supply of cheap labor, their presence often offered little benefit to the local economy and contributed to the region's dependence on the industrially developed nations.

In the 1970s, Latin American regimes grew even more reliant on borrowing from abroad, especially from banks in Europe and the United States. Between 1970 and 1982, debt to foreigners increased from $27 billion to $315.3 billion. By 1982, a number of governments announced that they could no longer pay interest on their debts to foreign banks, and their economies began to crumble. Wages fell, and unemployment skyrocketed. Governments were forced to undertake fundamental reforms to qualify for additional loans, reducing the size of the state sector and improving agricultural production in order to stem the flow of people from the countryside to the cities and strengthen the domestic market for Latin American products. In many cases, these reforms were launched by democratic governments that began to replace the discredited military regimes in power during the 1980s.

In the 1990s, the opening of markets to free trade and other consequences of the globalization process began to exert a growing impact on Latin American economies. As some countries faced the danger of bankruptcy, belt-tightening measures undertaken to reassure foreign investors provoked social protests and threatened to undermine the

South America

precarious political stability in the region.

Not all political parties in Latin America opted to adopt the capitalist model. In some countries, resentment at economic and social inequities led to the emergence of strong leftist movements or even to social revolution. The most prominent example was Cuba, where in the late 1950s Fidel Castro established a regime based loosely on the Soviet model. Eventually, other revolutionary movements flourished or even came to power in Chile, Uruguay, and parts of Central America as well (see "The Marxist Variant" below).

The Role of the Catholic Church The Catholic church has sometimes played a significant role in the process of social and political change. A powerful force in Latin America for centuries, the church often applied its prestige on the side of the landed elites, helping them maintain their grip on power. Eventually, however, the church adopted a middle stance in Latin American society, advocating a moderate capitalist system that would respect workers' rights, institute land reform, and provide for the poor. Some Catholics, however, took a more radical path to change by advocating a theology of liberation. Influenced by Marxist ideas, advocates of liberation theology believed that Christians must fight to free the oppressed, using violence if necessary. Some Catholic clergy recommended armed rebellions and even teamed up with Marxist guerrillas in rural areas. Other radical priests worked in factories alongside workers or carried on social work among the poor in the slums. Liberation theology was by no means the ideology of the majority of Latin American Catholics and was rejected by the church hierarchy. Nevertheless, the Catholic church continued to play an important role in Latin America by becoming the advocate of human rights against authoritarian regimes.

The Behemoth to the North Throughout the postwar era, the United States has cast a large shadow over Latin America. In 1948, the nations of the region formed the Organization of American States (OAS), which was intended to eliminate unilateral action by one state in the internal or external affairs of another state, while encouraging regional cooperation to maintain peace. It did not end U.S. interference in Latin American affairs, however.

The United States returned to a policy of unilateral action when it believed that Soviet agents were attempting to use local Communists or radical reformers to establish governments hostile to U.S. interests. In the 1960s, President Kennedy's Alliance for Progress encouraged social reform and economic development by providing private and public funds to elected governments whose reform programs were acceptable to the United States. But when Marxist-led insurrections began to spread throughout the region, the United States responded by providing massive military aid to anti-Communist regimes to forestall the possibility of a Soviet bastion in the Western Hemisphere.

Since the 1990s, the United States has played an active role in persuading Latin American governments to open their economies to the international marketplace. Though globalization has had some success in promoting prosperity in the region, it has also led to economic dislocation and hardship in some countries, provoking familiar cries of "Yanqui imperialismo" from protest groups in the region.

Nationalism and the Military: The Examples of Argentina and Brazil

The military became the power brokers of twentieth-century Latin America. Especially in the 1960s and 1970s, military leaders portrayed themselves as the guardians of national honor and orderly progress. In the mid-1970s, only Colombia, Venezuela, and Costa Rica maintained democratic governments.

A decade later, pluralistic systems had been installed virtually everywhere except in Cuba, Paraguay, and some of the Central American states. The establishment of democratic institutions, however, has not managed to solve all the chronic problems that have plagued the states of Latin America. Official corruption continues in many countries, and the gap between rich and poor is growing, most notably in Brazil and in Venezuela, where a leftist regime led by President Hugo Chávez adopted policies designed to redistribute the wealth in this oil-rich country.

Argentina Fearful of the forces unleashed by the development of industry, the military intervened in Argentinian politics in 1930 and propped up the cattle and wheat oligarchy that had controlled the government since the beginning of the twentieth century. In 1943, restless military officers staged a coup and seized power. But the new regime was not sure how to deal with the working classes. One of its members, Juan Perón (1895–1974), thought that he could manage the workers and used his position as labor secretary in the military government to curry favor with them. He encouraged workers to join labor unions and increased job benefits as well as the number of paid holidays

and vacations. But as Perón grew more popular, other army officers began to fear his power and arrested him. An uprising by workers forced the officers to back down, and in 1946, Perón was elected president.

Perón pursued a policy of increased industrialization to please his chief supporters—labor and the urban middle class (known rhetorically as the *descamisados*, or "shirtless ones"). At the same time, he sought to free Argentina from foreign investors. The government bought the railways; took over the banking, insurance, shipping, and communications industries; and assumed regulation of imports and exports. But Perón's regime was also authoritarian. His wife, Eva Perón, organized women's groups to support the government while Perón created fascist gangs, modeled after Hitler's Storm Troops, that used violence to overawe his opponents. But growing corruption in the Perón government and the alienation of more and more people by the regime's excesses encouraged the military to overthrow him in September 1955. Perón went into exile in Spain.

It had been easy for the military to seize power, but it was harder to rule, especially now that Argentina had a party of *Peronistas* clamoring for the return of the exiled leader. In the 1960s and 1970s, military and civilian governments (the latter closely watched by the military) alternated in power. When both failed to provide economic stability, military leaders decided to allow Juan Perón to return. Reelected president in September 1973, Perón died one year later. In 1976, the military installed a new regime, using the occasion to kill more than six thousand leftists in what was called the "Dirty War." With economic problems still unsolved, the regime tried to divert popular attention by invading the Falkland Islands in April 1982. Great Britain, which had controlled the islands since the nineteenth century, decisively defeated the Argentine forces. The loss discredited the military and opened the door once again to civilian rule. In 1983, Raúl Alfonsín (b. 1927) was elected president and sought to reestablish democratic processes.

In 1989, however, Alfonsín was defeated in the presidential elections by the Peronist candidate, Carlos Saúl Menem (b. 1930). During his first term, the charismatic Menem won broad popularity for his ability to control the army, long an active force in politics, and he was reelected in 1995. But when he sought to control rampant inflation by curbing government spending, rising unemployment and an economic recession cut into his public acclaim. Plagued with low growth, rising emigration (a growing number of descendants of European settlers were returning to live in Europe), and shrinking markets abroad, the government defaulted on its debt to the International Monetary Fund (IMF) in 2001, initiating an era of political chaos. In May 2003, Nestor Kirchner (b. 1950) assumed the presidency and sought to revive public confidence in an economy in paralysis.

The new president took decisive steps to end the crisis, adopting measures to stimulate economic growth and promote exports. By 2005, the debt to the IMF had been fully paid off. Kirchner has also encouraged measures designed to bring the military officers who carried out the "Dirty War" of the 1970s to justice. Critics charge, however, that his efforts to centralize power in his hands are reminiscent of Perónism and threaten to undermine the country's fragile democratic institutions.

Brazil   After Getúlio Vargas was forced to resign from the presidency in 1945 (see Chapter 5), a second Brazilian republic came into being. In 1949, Vargas was elected to the presidency. But he was unable to solve Brazil's economic problems, especially its soaring inflation, and in 1954, after the armed forces called on him to resign, Vargas committed suicide. Subsequent democratically elected presidents had no better success in controlling inflation while trying to push rapid industrialization. In the spring of 1964, the military decided to intervene and took over the government.

The armed forces remained in direct control of the country for twenty years, setting a new economic course, cutting back somewhat on state control of the economy and emphasizing market forces. The new policies seemed to work, and during the late 1960s, Brazil experienced an "economic miracle" as it moved into self-sustaining economic growth, generally the hallmark of a modern economy. Promoters also pointed to the country's success in turning a racially diverse population into a relatively color-blind society.

Rapid economic growth carried with it some potential drawbacks. The economic exploitation of the Amazon River basin opened the region to farming but in the view of some critics threatened the ecological balance not only of Brazil but of the earth itself. Ordinary Brazilians hardly benefited as the gulf between rich and poor, always wide, grew even wider. In 1960, the wealthiest 10 percent of Brazil's population, most of whom were of European descent, received 40 percent of the nation's income; in 1980, they received 51 percent. At the same time, rapid development led to an inflation rate of 100 percent a year, and an enormous foreign debt added to the problems. Overwhelmed, the generals resigned from power and opened the door for a return to democracy in 1985.

In 1990, national elections brought a new president into office—Fernando Collor de Mello (b. 1949). The new administration promised to reduce inflation with a drastic

Copacabana, Tourist Mecca for the Americas.   Copacabana Beach in Rio de Janeiro is one of the glamour locations of the global tourist industry. The "beautiful people" of Brazil have gathered here to see and be seen for decades, and the resort is one of the most popular tourist destinations in Latin America. Behind the glittering facade, however, the poor residents of the city gather in neighborhoods (*favellas*) without sanitation facilities and running water. High poverty rates represent one of the major challenges for Brazil, the most dynamic of South American countries.

reform program based on squeezing money out of the economy by stringent controls on wages and prices, drastic reductions in public spending, and cuts in the number of government employees. But Collor de Mello's efforts—reminiscent of Menem's in Argentina—were undermined by reports of official corruption, and he resigned at the end of 1992 after having been impeached. In new elections two years later, Fernando Cardoso (b. 1931) was elected president by an overwhelming majority of the popular vote.

Cardoso, a member of the Brazilian Social Democratic Party, introduced measures to privatize state-run industries and to reform social security and the pension system. He rode a wave of economic prosperity to reelection in 1998. But economic problems, combined with allegations of official corruption and rising factionalism within the ruling party, undermined his popularity, leading to the victory of the Workers' Party in elections held in 2003. The new president, ex-lathe operator Luiz Inacio "Lula" da Silva (b. 1945), however, immediately cautioned his supporters that the party's ambitious plans could not be realized until urgent financial reforms had been enacted. That remark effectively sums up the challenge that the new administration has faced in its first years in power: how to satisfy the pent-up demands of its traditional constituency—the millions of Brazilians still living in poverty conditions—while dealing effectively with the realities of exercising power. So far, the government has sought to straddle the issue, with only limited success.

The Mexican Way

During the presidency of Lázaro Cárdenas in the 1930s, the Mexican government returned to some of the original revolutionary goals by distributing 44 million acres of land to landless Mexican peasants, thereby appealing to the rural poor.

In the 1950s and 1960s, Mexico's ruling party, the Institutional Revolutionary Party (PRI), focused on a balanced industrial program. Fifteen years of steady economic growth combined with low inflation and real gains in wages for more and more people made those years appear to be a golden age in Mexico's economic development. But at the end of the 1960s, one implication of Mexico's domination by one party became apparent with the rise of the student protest movement. On October 2, 1968, a demonstration by university students in Tlaltelolco Square in Mexico City was met by police, who opened fire and killed hundreds of students. Leaders of the PRI became concerned about the need to change the system.

The next two presidents, Luis Echeverría (b. 1922) and José López Portillo (1920–2004), introduced political reforms. The government eased rules for the registration of political parties and allowed greater freedom of debate in the press and universities. But economic problems continued to trouble Mexico.

In the late 1970s, vast new reserves of oil were discovered in Mexico. As the sale of oil abroad rose dramatically, the government became increasingly dependent on oil revenues. When world oil prices dropped in the mid-1980s, Mexico was no longer able to make payments on its foreign debt, which had reached $80 billion in 1982. The government was forced to adopt new economic policies, including the sale of publicly owned companies to private parties.

The debt crisis and rising unemployment increased dissatisfaction with the government. In the 1988 elections, the PRI's choice for president, Carlos Salina (b. 1948), who had been expected to win in a landslide, won by only a 50.3 percent majority. The new president continued the economic liberalization of his predecessors and went even further by negotiating the North American Free Trade Agreement (NAFTA) with the United States and Canada. Although NAFTA was highly controversial in the United States because of the fear that U.S. firms would move factories to Mexico, where labor costs are cheaper and environmental standards less stringent, some observers assert that the impact of NAFTA has been more beneficial to the U.S. economy than to its southern neighbor. Reflecting Mexico's continuing economic problems was rising popular unrest in southern parts of the country, where unhappy farmers, many of whom are native Amerindians, have grown increasingly vocal in protesting endemic poverty and widespread neglect of the needs of the indigenous peoples, who comprise about 10 percent of the total population of 100 million people.

In the summer of 2000, a national election suddenly swept the ruling PRI from power. The new president, Vicente Fox (b. 1942), promised to address the many problems affecting the country, including political corruption, widespread poverty, environmental concerns, and a growing population. But he faced vocal challenges from the PRI, which still controlled many state legislatures and a plurality in Congress, as well as from the protest movement in rural areas in the south. Calling themselves Zapatistas in honor of the revolutionary leader Emiliano Zapata (see Chapter 5), the rebels demanded passage of legislation to protect the rights of the indigenous Indian population and increasing autonomy for regions such as the southern state of Chiapas, where Amerindians make up a substantial percentage of the population. Although the movement has since faded, it aroused such a groundswell of support from around the country that President Fox and his successor have been under considerable pressure to deal with generations of neglect in solving the problems of Mexico. The problems are enormous. Forty percent of Mexicans live in poverty, and one in ten earns less than the equivalent of one U.S. dollar a day.

Mexico Possible: The New Politics. With its long tradition of male pride, the continent of Latin America has been slow to advance the cause of women in their struggle for gender equality. But efforts are now under way in several countries to redress the balance, as this billboard erected in the Mexican resort city of Acapulco indicates. The English translation reads: "In Mexico there are few vocations where women earn more than men. Is a better society possible?" The photograph on the left side of the billboard seems self-explanatory.

The Marxist Variant

Until the 1960s, Marxism played little role in the politics of Latin America. The success of Fidel Castro in Cuba, however, opened the door for other revolutionary movements that aimed to gain the support of peasants and industrial workers and bring radical change to Latin America.

The Cuban Revolution An authoritarian regime, headed by Fulgencio Batista (1901–1973) and closely tied economically to U.S. investors, had ruled Cuba since 1934. A strong opposition movement to Batista's government developed, led by Fidel Castro (b. 1926) and assisted by Ernesto "Ché" Guevara (1928–1967), an Argentinian who believed that revolutionary upheaval was necessary for change to occur. Castro maintained that only armed force could overthrow Batista, but when their initial assaults on Batista's regime brought little success, Castro's forces, based in the Sierra Maestra mountains, turned to guerrilla warfare (see the box on p. 177). As the rebels gained more support, Batista responded with such brutality that he alienated his own supporters. The dictator fled in December 1958, and Castro's revolutionaries seized Havana on January 1, 1959.

Relations between Cuba and the United States quickly deteriorated. An agrarian reform law in May 1959 nationalized all landholdings over 1,000 acres. A new level of antagonism arose early in 1960 when the Soviet Union agreed to buy Cuban sugar and provide $100 million in credits. On March 17, 1960, President Eisenhower directed the Central Intelligence Agency (CIA) to "organize the training of Cuban exiles, mainly in Guatemala, against a possible future day when they might return to their homeland."[2] Arms from Eastern Europe began to arrive in Cuba, the United States cut its purchases of Cuban sugar, and the Cuban government nationalized U.S. companies and banks. In October 1960, the United States declared a trade embargo of Cuba, driving Castro closer to the Soviet Union.

On January 3, 1961, the United States broke diplomatic relations with Cuba. The new U.S. president, John F. Kennedy, approved a plan originally drafted by the previous administration to launch an invasion to overthrow Castro's government, but the landing of fourteen hundred CIA-assisted Cubans in Cuba on April 17, 1961, known as the Bay of Pigs, turned into a total military disaster. This fiasco encouraged the Soviets to make an even greater commitment to Cuban independence by attempting to place nuclear missiles in the country, an act that led to a showdown with the United States (see Chapter 7). As its part of the bargain to defuse the missile crisis, the United States agreed not to invade Cuba.

Courtesy of William J. Duiker

CASTRO'S REVOLUTIONARY IDEALS

*O*n July 26, 1953, Fidel Castro and a small group of supporters launched an ill-fated attack on the Moncada Barracks in Santiago de Cuba. Castro was arrested and put on trial. This excerpt is taken from his defense speech, in which he discussed the goals of the revolutionaries.

What did Fidel Castro intend to accomplish by his revolution in Cuba? On whose behalf did he fight this revolution?

Fidel Castro, "History Will Absolve Me"

I stated that the second consideration on which we based our chances for success was one of social order because we were assured of the people's support. When we speak of the people we do not mean the comfortable ones, the conservative elements of the nation, who welcome any regime of oppression, any dictatorship, and despotism, prostrating themselves before the master of the moment until they grind their foreheads into the ground. When we speak of struggle, the people means the vast unredeemed masses, to whom all make promises and whom all deceive; we mean the people who yearn for a better, more dignified, and more just nation; who are moved by ancestral aspirations of justice, for they have suffered injustice and mockery, generation after generation; who long for great and wise changes in all aspects of their life; people, who, to attain these changes, are ready to give even the very last breath of their lives—when they believe in something or in someone, especially when they believe in themselves.

In the brief of this cause there must be recorded the five revolutionary laws that would have been proclaimed immediately after the capture of the Moncada barracks and would have been broadcast to the nation by radio. . . .

The First Revolutionary Law would have returned power to the people and proclaimed the Constitution of 1940 the supreme Law of the land, until such time as the people should decide to modify or change it. . . .

The Second Revolutionary Law would have granted property, not mortgageable and not transferable, to all planters, subplanters, lessees, partners, and squatters who hold parcels of five or less *caballerias* [tract of land, about 33 acres] of land, and the state would indemnify the former owners on the basis of the rental which they would have received for these parcels over a period of ten years.

The Third Revolutionary Law would have granted workers and employees the right to share 30 percent of the profits of all the large industrial, mercantile, and mining enterprises, including the sugar mills. . . .

The Fourth Revolutionary Law would have granted all planters the right to share 55 percent of the sugar production and a minimum quota of forty thousand *arrobas* [25 pounds] for all small planters who have been established for three or more years.

The Fifth Revolutionay Law would have ordered the confiscation of all holdings and ill-gotten gains of those who had committed frauds during previous regimes, as well as the holdings and ill-gotten gains of all their legatees and heirs. . . .

Furthermore, it was to be declared that the Cuban policy in the Americas would be one of close solidarity with the democratic people of this continent, and that those politically persecuted by bloody tyrants oppressing our sister nations would find generous asylum, brotherhood, and bread in [Cuba]. Not the persecution, hunger, and treason that they find today. Cuba should be the bulwark of liberty and not a shameful link in the chain of despotism.

SOURCE: Excerpt from *Latin American Civilization* by Benjamin Keen, ed. (Boston: Houghton Mifflin, 1974), pp. 369–373.

But the missile crisis affected Cuba in another way as well. Castro, who had urged Soviet leader Nikita Khrushchev to stand firm even at the risk of nuclear war with the United States, now realized that the Soviet Union was unreliable. If revolutionary Cuba was to be secure and no longer encircled by hostile states tied to U.S. interests, the Cubans would have to instigate social revolution in the rest of Latin America. He believed that once guerrilla wars were launched, peasants would flock to the movement and overthrow the old regimes. Guevara attempted to launch a guerrilla war in Bolivia but was caught and killed by the Bolivian army in the fall of 1967. The Cuban strategy had failed.

In Cuba, however, Castro's socialist revolution proceeded, with mixed results. The Cuban Revolution did secure some social gains for its people, especially in health care and education. The regime provided free medical services for all citizens, and a new law code expanded the rights of women. Illiteracy was wiped out by creating new schools and establishing teacher-training institutes that tripled the number of teachers within ten years. Eschewing the path of rapid industrialization, Castro encouraged agricultural diversification. But the Cuban economy continued to rely on the production and sale of sugar. Economic problems forced the Castro regime to depend on Soviet subsidies and the purchase of Cuban sugar by Soviet bloc countries.

The disintegration of the Soviet Union was a major blow to Cuba, as the new government in Moscow no longer had a reason to continue to subsidize the onetime Soviet ally.

During the 1990s, Castro began to introduce limited market reforms and to allow the circulation of U.S. dollars. But although most Cubans remain locked in poverty, the regime has refused to liberalize the political system, and although limited Cuban contacts with the United States were permitted by the Clinton administration, the U.S. embargo is still in place today.

Chile Another challenge to U.S. influence in Latin America appeared in 1970 when a Marxist, Salvador Allende (1908–1973), was elected president of Chile and attempted to create a socialist society by constitutional means. Chile suffered from a number of economic problems. Wealth was concentrated in the hands of large landowners and a few large corporations. Inflation, foreign debts, and a decline in the mining industry (copper exports accounted for 80 percent of Chile's export income) caused untold difficulties. Right-wing control of the government had failed to achieve any solutions, especially since foreign investments were allowed to expand. There was growing resentment of U.S. corporations, especially Anaconda and Kennecott, which controlled the copper industry.

In the 1970 elections, a split in the moderate forces enabled Allende to become president of Chile as head of a coalition of Socialists, Communists, and Catholic radicals. A number of labor leaders, who represented the interests of the working classes, were given the ministries of labor, finance, public works, and interior in the new government. Allende increased the wages of industrial workers and began to move toward socialism by nationalizing the largest domestic and foreign-owned corporations. Nationalization of the copper industry—essentially without compensation for the owners—caused the Nixon administration to cut off all aid to Chile, creating serious problems for the Chilean economy. At the same time, the government offered only halfhearted resistance to radical workers who were beginning to take control of the landed estates.

These actions brought growing opposition from the upper and middle classes, who began, with covert support from the CIA, to organize strikes against the government. Allende attempted to stop the disorder by bringing three military officers into his cabinet. They succeeded in ending the strikes, but when Allende's coalition increased its vote in the congressional elections of March 1973, the Chilean army, under the direction of General Augusto Pinochet (b. 1915), decided on a coup d'état. In September 1973, Allende and thousands of his supporters were killed. Contrary to the expectations of many right-wing politicians, the military remained in power and set up a dictatorship. The regime moved quickly to outlaw all political parties, disband the congress, and restore many nationalized industries and landed estates to their original owners. The copper industry, however, remained in government

hands. Although Pinochet's regime liberalized the economy, its flagrant abuse of human rights led to growing unrest against the government in the mid-1980s. In 1989, free elections produced a Christian Democratic president who advocated free market economics.

The shadow of the Pinochet era continued to hover over Chilean politics, however, as many citizens demanded that the general, now living in exile, be brought to justice for his crimes against humanity. In 2000, he was returned to the country from Europe and placed on trial for crimes that had allegedly taken place under his rule. In the meantime, the Socialist Party returned to power through national elections under a program to bring about moderate reforms while simultaneously opening the country to the global trade network. In 2006, Socialist Michelle Bachelet (b. 1951) was elected president, the first woman chief executive in Latin America.

Nicaragua The United States intervened in Nicaraguan domestic affairs in the early twentieth century, and U.S. Marines actually remained there for long periods of time. The leader of the U.S.-supported National Guard, Anastasio Somoza (1896–1956), seized control of the government in 1937, and his family remained in power for the next forty-three years. U.S. support for the Somoza military regime enabled the family to overcome any opponents while enriching themselves at the expense of the state.

Opposition to the regime finally arose from Marxist guerrilla forces known as the Sandinista National Liberation Front. By mid-1979, military victories by the Sandinistas left them in virtual control of the country. Inheriting a poverty-stricken nation, the Sandinistas organized a provisional government and aligned themselves with the Soviet Union. The Reagan and Bush administrations, believing that Central America faced the danger of another Communist state, financed the counterrevolutionary Contra rebels in a guerrilla war against the Sandinista government. The Contra war and a U.S. economic embargo undermined support for the Sandinistas, and in 1990, they agreed to hold free elections. Although they lost to a coalition headed by Violetta Barrios de Chamorro (b. 1929), the Sandinistas remained a significant political force in Nicaragua.

Venezuela: The New Cuba? With the discovery of oil in the small town of Cabímas in the early 1920s, Venezuela took its first step toward becoming a major exporter of oil and one of the wealthiest countries in Latin America. At first, profits from "black rain" accrued mainly to the nation's elite families, but in 1976 the oil industry was nationalized, and Venezuela entered an era of national prosperity. But when the price of oil on world markets dropped sharply in the 1980s, the country's economic honeymoon came to an end, and in 1989 President Carlos

Andrés Pérez launched an austerity program that cut deeply into the living standards of much of the population.

After popular demonstrations led to an army crackdown in 1992, restive military forces launched an abortive coup to seize power. Five years later, one of the leading members of the plot—a paratroop commander named Hugo Chávez (b. 1954)—was elected president in national elections. Taking advantage of rising oil prices, Chávez launched an ambitious spending program to improve living conditions for the poor. Although such measures have earned his regime broad national support, critics charge that Chávez' efforts to strengthen presidential powers—including a program to organize his supporters into "Bolívarian circles" (in honor of the nineteenth-century Venezuelan liberator Simón Bolívar) at the local level—display his all-too-evident dictatorial tendencies.

A longtime admirer of Fidel Castro, Chávez has strengthened relations with Cuba and encourages leftist movements throughout Latin America. As an outspoken opponent of "Yanqui imperialismo," he has also proposed resistance to U.S. proposals for a hemispheric free trade zone, charging that such an organization would operate only for the benefit of the United States. Today, Chávez has replaced Fidel Castro as Washington's most dangerous adversary in Latin America.

Trends in Latin American Culture

Postwar literature in Latin America has been vibrant. Writers such as Mario Vargas Llosa, Nobel Prize winner Gabriel García Márquez, Jorge Luis Borges, and Carlos Fuentes are among the most respected literary names of the last half century. These authors often use dazzling language and daring narrative experimentation to make their point. Master of this new style is Gabriel García Márquez (b. 1938), from Colombia. In *One Hundred Years of Solitude* (1967), he explores the transformation of a small town under the impact of political violence, industrialization, and the arrival of a U.S. banana company. Especially noteworthy is his use of magical realism, relating the outrageous events that assail the town in a matter-of-fact voice, thus transforming the fantastic into the commonplace.

Unlike novelists in the United States and Western Europe, who tend to focus their attention on the interior landscape within the modern personality in an industrial society, fiction writers in Latin America, like their counterparts in Africa and much of Asia, have sought to project an underlying political message. Many have been inspired by a sense of social and political injustice, a consequence of the economic inequality and authoritarian politics that marked the local scene throughout much of the twentieth century. Some, like the Peruvian José Maria Arguedas (1911–1969), have championed the cause of the Amerindian and lauded the diversity that marks the ethnic mix throughout the continent. Others have run for high political office as a means of remedying social problems. Some have been women, reflecting the rising demand for sexual equality in a society traditionally marked by male domination. The memorable phrase of the Chilean poet Gabriela Mistral (1889–1957)—"I have chewed stones with woman's gums"—encapsulates the plight of Latin American women.

A powerful example of Postmodern art in Latin America is found in the haunting work of the Colombian artist Doris Salcedo (b. 1958). Her art evokes disturbing images of her country's endless civil war and violent drug trade. Salcedo often presents everyday wooden furniture, over which she has applied a thin layer of cement and fragments of personal mementos from the owner's past life: a remnant of lace curtain, a lock of hair, or a handkerchief. Frozen in time, these everyday souvenirs evoke the pain of those who were dragged from their homes in the middle of the night and senselessly murdered. Salcedo's work can be experienced as an impassioned plea to stop the killing of innocent civilians or as the fossilized artifact from some future archaeologist's dig, showing traces of our brief and absurd sojourn on earth.

CONCLUSION

*D*URING THE SECOND HALF of the twentieth century, the United States emerged as the preeminent power in the world, dominant in its economic and technological achievements as well as in terms of military hardware. Although the Soviet Union was a serious competitor in the arms race engendered by the Cold War, its economic achievements paled in comparison with those of the U.S. behemoth. Beginning in the 1970s, Japan began to rival the United States in the realm of industrial production, but the challenge faded in the 1990s, when structural weaknesses began to tarnish the Japanese miracle.

The worldwide dominance of the United States was a product of a combination of political, economic, and cultural factors and showed no signs of abating as the new century began. But there were some warning signs that bore watching: a growing gap in the distribution of wealth that could ultimately threaten the steady growth in consumer spending; an educational system that all too often fails to produce graduates with the skills needed to master the challenges of a technology-driven economy; and a racial divide that threatens to undermine America's historical role as a melting pot of peoples.

As the new century dawned, America's global hegemony was also threatened from abroad in the form of a militant terrorist movement originating in the Middle East. So far, the U.S. response, led by the administration of President George W. Bush, has been primarily military, but whether the political and social forces driving the movement can be defeated by such means alone has been a matter of vigorous debate.

The United States also faces a growing challenge in the economic realm from a resurgent Asia and a united Europe. As Americans become increasingly concerned

about the threat to national security, their primacy in other areas no longer seems assured, and the future remains in serious doubt.

For most of the nations elsewhere in the Americas, U.S. dominance has mixed consequences. As a vast consumer market and a source of capital, the dynamism of the U.S. economy helped stimulate growth throughout the region. But recent studies suggest that for many countries in Latin America, the benefits of globalization have been slower to appear than originally predicted and have often flowed primarily to large transnational corporations at the expense of smaller domestic firms. At the same time, the U.S. penchant for interfering in the affairs of its neighbors has aroused anger and frequently undermined efforts by local governments to deal with problems within their own borders. As the world enters a new millennium, the United States is still finding it difficult to be a good neighbor.

TIMELINE

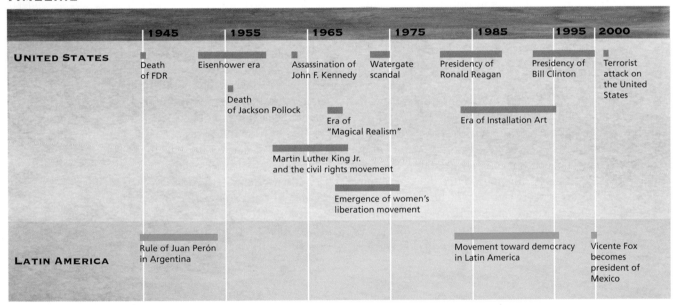

CHAPTER NOTES

1. *Public Papers of the Presidents of the United States: Lyndon B. Johnson*, Bk. 1, 1963–64 (Washington, D.C., 1965), p. 704.
2. Dwight D. Eisenhower, *The White House Years: Waging Peace, 1956–1961* (Garden City, 1965), p. 533.

WORLD HISTORY
RESOURCE CENTER

Visit the *Twentieth-Century World History* Book Companion Website for resources specific to this textbook:

academic.cengage.com/history/duiker

The Wadsworth World History Resource Center at worldrc.wadsworth.com/ offers a variety of tools to help you succeed in this course, including access to quizzes; images; documents; interactive simulations, maps, and timelines; movie explorations; and a wealth of other sources.

Brave New World: The Rise and Fall of Communism in the Soviet Union and Eastern Europe

According to Karl Marx, capitalism is a system that involves the exploitation of man by man; under socialism, it is the other way around. That wry joke, an ironic twist on the familiar Marxist remark a century previously, was typical of popular humor in post–World War II Moscow, where the dreams of a future Communist utopia had faded in the grim reality of life in the Soviet Union.

Nevertheless, the Communist monopoly on power seemed secure, as did Moscow's hold over its client states in Eastern Europe. In fact, for three decades after the end of World War II, the Soviet Empire appeared to be a permanent feature of the international landscape. But by the early 1980s, it became clear that there were cracks in the facade of the Kremlin wall. The Soviet economy was stagnant, the minority nationalities were restive, and Eastern European leaders were increasingly emboldened to test the waters of the global capitalist marketplace. In the United States, newly elected President Ronald Reagan boldly predicted the imminent collapse of the "evil empire." ◇

The Postwar Soviet Union

World War II had left the Soviet Union as one of the world's two superpowers and its leader, Joseph Stalin, at the height of his power. As a result of the war, Stalin and his Soviet colleagues were now in control of a vast empire that included Eastern Europe, much of the Balkans, and territory gained from Japan in East Asia.

From Stalin to Khrushchev

World War II devastated the Soviet Union. Twenty million citizens lost their lives, and cities such as Kiev, Kharkov, and Leningrad suffered enormous physical destruction. As the lands that had been occupied by the German forces were liberated, the Soviet government turned its attention to restoring their economic structures. Nevertheless, in 1945, agricultural production was only 60 percent and steel output only 50 percent of prewar levels. The Soviet people faced incredibly difficult conditions: they worked longer hours; they ate less; they were ill-housed and poorly clothed.

In the immediate postwar years, the Soviet Union removed goods and materials from occupied Germany and extorted valuable raw materials from its satellite states in Eastern Europe. More important, however, to create a new industrial base, Stalin returned to the method he had used in the 1930s—the extraction of development capital from Soviet labor. Working hard for little pay and for precious few consumer goods, Soviet laborers were expected to produce goods for export with little in return for themselves. The incoming capital from abroad could then be used to purchase machinery and Western technology. The loss of

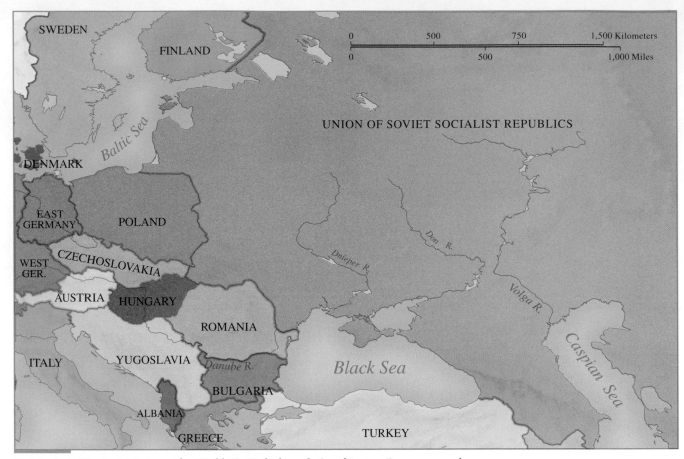

MAP 9.1 **The Soviet Union.** After World War II, the boundaries of Eastern Europe were redrawn as a result of Allied agreements reached at the Tehran and Yalta conferences. This map shows the new boundaries that were established throughout the region, placing Soviet power in the center of Europe.
❓ How had the boundaries changed from the prewar era? 🌐 **View an animated version of this map or related maps at the World History Resource Center, at** worldrc.wadsworth.com/.

millions of men in the war meant that much of this tremendous workload fell to Soviet women, who performed almost 40 percent of the heavy manual labor.

An Industrial Powerhouse The pace of economic recovery in the Soviet Union was impressive. By 1947, Russian industrial production had attained 1939 levels; three years later, it had surpassed those levels by 40 percent. New power plants, canals, and giant factories were built, and new industrial enterprises and oil fields were established in Siberia and Soviet Central Asia. A new five-year plan, announced in 1946, reached its goals in less than five years. Returning to his prewar forced-draft system, Stalin had created an industrial powerhouse (see Map 9.1).

Although Stalin's economic recovery policy was successful in promoting growth in heavy industry, primarily for the benefit of the military, consumer goods remained scarce. The development of thermonuclear weapons,

MIG fighters, and the first space satellite (*Sputnik*) in the 1950s may have elevated the Soviet state's reputation as a world power abroad, but domestically, the Soviet people were shortchanged. Heavy industry grew at a rate three times that of personal consumption. Moreover, the housing shortage was acute, with living conditions especially difficult in the overcrowded cities.

When World War II ended, Stalin had been in power for more than fifteen years. During that time, he had removed all opposition to his rule and remained the undisputed master of the Soviet Union. Increasingly distrustful of competitors, Stalin exercised sole authority and pitted his subordinates against one another. One of these subordinates, Lavrenti Beria, head of the secret police, controlled a force of several hundred thousand agents, leaving Stalin's colleagues completely cowed. As Stalin remarked mockingly on one occasion, "When I die, the imperialists will strangle all of you like a litter of kittens."[1]

Courtesy of William J. Duiker

The Portals of Doom. Perhaps the most feared location in the Soviet Union was Lyubyanka Prison, an ornate prerevolutionary building in the heart of Moscow. Taken over by the Bolsheviks after the 1917 revolution, it became the headquarters of the Soviet secret police, the Cheka, later to be known as the KGB. It was here that many Soviet citizens accused of "counterrevolutionary acts" were imprisoned and executed. The figure on the pedestal is that of Felix Dzerzhinsky, first director of the Cheka. After the dissolution of the Soviet Union, the statue was removed.

Stalin's morbid suspicions added to the constantly increasing repression of the regime. In 1946, government decrees subordinated all forms of literary and scientific expression to the political needs of the state. Along with the anti-intellectual campaign came political terror. By the late 1940s, an estimated nine million people were in Siberian concentration camps. Stalin's distrust of potential threats to his power even extended to some of his closest colleagues. In 1948, Andrei Zhdanov, his presumed successor and head of the Leningrad party organization, died under mysterious circumstances, presumably at Stalin's order. Within weeks, the Leningrad party organization was purged of several top leaders, many of whom were charged with traitorous connections with Western intelligence agencies. In succeeding years, Stalin directed his suspicion at other members of the inner circle, including Foreign Minister Vyacheslav Molotov. Known as "Old Stone Butt" in the West for his stubborn defense of Soviet security interests, Molotov had been a loyal lieutenant since the early years of Stalin's rise to power. Now Stalin distrusted Molotov and had his Jewish wife placed in a Siberian concentration camp.

The Rise and Fall of Nikita Khrushchev Stalin died in 1953 and, after some bitter infighting within the party leadership, was succeeded by Georgy Malenkov, a veteran administrator and ambitious member of the Politburo. Malenkov came to power with a clear agenda. In foreign affairs, he hoped to promote an easing of Cold War tensions and improve relations with the Western powers. For Moscow's Eastern European allies, he advocated a "new course" in their mutual relations and a decline in Stalinist methods of rule. Inside the Soviet Union, he hoped to reduce defense expenditures and assign a higher priority to improving the standard of living. Such goals were laudable and probably had the support of the majority of the Russian people, but they were not necessarily appealing to key pressure groups within the Soviet Union—the army, the Communist Party, the managerial elite, and the security services (now known as the Committee on Government Security, or KGB). Malenkov was soon removed from his position as prime minister, and power shifted to his rival, the new party general secretary, Nikita Khrushchev.

During his struggle for power with Malenkov, Khrushchev had outmaneuvered him by calling for heightened defense expenditures and a continuing emphasis on heavy industry. Once in power, however, Khrushchev showed the political dexterity displayed by many an American politician and reversed his priorities. He now resumed the efforts of his predecessor to reduce tensions with the West and improve the standard of living of the Russian people. He moved vigorously to improve the performance of the Soviet economy and revitalize Soviet society. By nature, Khrushchev was a man of enormous energy

CHAPTER 9 BRAVE NEW WORLD: THE RISE AND FALL OF COMMUNISM IN THE SOVIET UNION **183** as well as an innovator. In an attempt to release the stranglehold of the central bureaucracy over the national economy, he abolished dozens of government ministries and split up the party and government apparatus. Khrushchev also attempted to rejuvenate the stagnant agricultural sector, long the Achilles heel of the Soviet economy. He attempted to spur production by increasing profit incentives and opened "virgin lands" in Soviet Kazakhstan to bring thousands of acres of new land under cultivation.

Like any innovator, Khrushchev had to overcome the inherently conservative instincts of the Soviet bureaucracy, as well as of the mass of the Soviet population. His plan to remove the "dead hand" of the state, however laudable in intent, alienated much of the Soviet official class, and his effort to split the party angered those who saw it as the central force in the Soviet system. Khrushchev's agricultural schemes inspired similar opposition. Although the Kazakhstan wheat lands would eventually demonstrate their importance in the overall agricultural picture, progress was slow, and his effort to persuade the Russian people to eat more corn (an idea he had apparently picked up during a visit to the United States) led to the mocking nickname of "Cornman." Disappointing agricultural production, combined with high military spending, hurt the Soviet economy. The industrial growth rate, which had soared in the early 1950s, now declined dramatically from 13 percent in 1953 to 7.5 percent in 1964.

Khrushchev was probably best known for his policy of destalinization. Khrushchev had risen in the party hierarchy as a Stalin protégé, but he had been deeply disturbed by his mentor's excesses and, once in a position of authority, moved to excise the Stalinist legacy from Soviet society. The campaign began at the Twentieth National Congress of the Communist Party in February 1956, when Khrushchev gave a long speech criticizing some of Stalin's major shortcomings. The speech had apparently not been intended for public distribution, but it was quickly leaked to the Western press and created a sensation throughout the world (see the box on p. 185). During the next few years, Khrushchev encouraged more freedom of expression for writers, artists, and composers, arguing that "readers should be given the chance to make their own judgments" regarding the acceptability of controversial literature and that "police measures shouldn't be used."[2] At Khrushchev's order, thousands of prisoners were released from concentration camps.

Khrushchev's personality, however, did not endear him to higher Soviet officials, who frowned at his tendency to crack jokes and play the clown. Nor were the higher members of the party bureaucracy pleased when Khrushchev tried to curb their privileges. Foreign policy failures further damaged Khrushchev's reputation among his colleagues. Relations with China deteriorated badly under his leadership.

His plan to install missiles in Cuba was the final straw (see Chapter 7). While he was away on vacation in 1964, a special meeting of the Soviet Politburo voted him out of office (because of "deteriorating health") and forced him into retirement. Although a group of leaders succeeded him, real power came into the hands of Leonid Brezhnev (1906–1982), the "trusted" supporter of Khrushchev who had engineered his downfall.

The Brezhnev Years, 1964–1982

The ouster of Nikita Khrushchev in October 1964 vividly demonstrated the challenges that would be encountered by any Soviet leader sufficiently bold to try to reform the Soviet system. In democratic countries, pressure on the government comes from various sources within society at large—the business community and labor unions, interest groups, and the general public. In the Soviet Union, pressure on government and party leaders originated from sources essentially operating inside the system—from the government bureaucracy, the party apparatus, the KGB, and the armed forces.

Leonid Brezhnev, the new party chief, was undoubtedly aware of these realities of Soviet politics, and his long tenure in power was marked, above all, by the desire to avoid changes that might provoke instability, either at home or abroad. Brezhnev was himself a product of the Soviet system. He had entered the ranks of the party leadership under Joseph Stalin, and although he was not a particularly avid believer in party ideology—indeed, his years in power gave rise to innumerable stories about his addiction to "bourgeois pleasures," including expensive country houses in the elite Moscow suburb of Zhukovka and fast cars (many of them gifts from foreign leaders)—he was no partisan of reform.

Still, Brezhnev sought stability in the domestic arena. He and his prime minister, Alexei Kosygin, undertook what might be described as a program of "de-Khrushchevization," returning the responsibility for long-term planning to the central ministries and reuniting the Communist Party apparatus. Despite some cautious attempts to stimulate the stagnant farm sector, increasing capital investment in agriculture and raising food prices to increase rural income and provide additional incentives to collective farmers, there was no effort to revise the basic structure of the collective system. In the industrial sector, the regime launched a series of reforms designed to give factory managers (themselves employees of the state) more responsibility for setting prices, wages, and production quotas. These "Kosygin reforms" had little effect, however, because they were stubbornly resisted by the bureaucracy and were eventually adopted by relatively few enterprises within the vast state-owned industrial sector.

KHRUSHCHEV DENOUNCES STALIN

Three years after Stalin's death, the new Soviet premier, Nikita Khrushchev, addressed the Twentieth Congress of the Communist Party and denounced the former Soviet dictator for his crimes. This denunciation, which caused consternation in Communist parties around the world, was the beginning of a policy of destalinization in the Soviet Union.

What were Stalin's major crimes, according to Khrushchev? To what degree were these problems resolved under later Soviet leaders?

Khrushchev Addresses the Twentieth Party Congress, February 1956

Comrades, . . . quite a lot has been said about the cult of the individual and about its harmful consequences. . . . The cult of the person of Stalin . . . became at a certain specific stage the source of a whole series of exceedingly serious and grave perversions of Party principles, of Party democracy, of revolutionary legality.

Stalin absolutely did not tolerate collegiality in leadership and in work and . . . practiced brutal violence, not only toward everything which opposed him, but also toward that which seemed to his capricious and despotic character, contrary to his concepts.

Stalin abandoned the method of ideological struggle for that of administrative violence, mass repressions and terror. . . . Arbitrary behavior by one person encouraged and permitted arbitrariness in others. Mass arrests and deportations of many thousands of people, execution without trial and without normal investigation created conditions of insecurity, fear, and even desperation.

Stalin showed in a whole series of cases his intolerance, his brutality, and his abuse of power. . . . He often chose the path of repression and annihilation, not only against actual enemies, but also against individuals who had not committed any crimes against the Party and the Soviet government. . . .

Many Party, Soviet, and economic activists who were branded in 1937–38 as "enemies" were actually never enemies, spies, wreckers, and so on, but were always honest communists; they were only so stigmatized, and often, no longer able to bear barbaric tortures, they charged themselves (at the order of the investigative judges-falsifiers) with all kinds of grave and unlikely crimes.

This was the result of the abuse of power by Stalin, who began to use mass terror against the Party cadres. . . . Stalin put the Party and the NKVD up to the use of mass terror when the exploiting classes had been liquidated in our country and when there were no serious reasons for the use of extraordinary mass terror. The terror was directed . . . against the honest workers of the Party and the Soviet state. . . .

Stalin was a very distrustful man, sickly, suspicious. . . . Everywhere and in everything he saw "enemies," "two-facers," and "spies." Possessing unlimited power, he indulged in great willfulness and choked a person morally and physically. A situation was created where one could not express one's own will. When Stalin said that one or another would be arrested, it was necessary to accept on faith that he was an "enemy of the people." What proofs were offered? The confession of the arrested. . . . How is it possible that a person confesses to crimes that he had not committed? Only in one way—because of application of physical methods of pressuring him, tortures, bringing him to a state of unconsciousness, deprivation of his judgment, taking away of his human dignity.

SOURCE: *Congressional Record*, 84th Congress, 2d session, vol. 102, pt. 7 (June 4, 1956), pp. 9389–9402.

A Controlled Society Brezhnev also initiated a significant retreat from the policy of destalinization adopted by Nikita Khrushchev. Criticism of the "Great Leader" had angered conservatives both within the party hierarchy and among the public at large, many of whom still revered Stalin as a hero of the Soviet system and a defender of the Russian people against Nazi Germany. Many influential figures in the Kremlin feared that destalinization could lead to internal instability and a decline in public trust in the legitimacy of party leadership—the hallowed "dictatorship of the proletariat." Early in Brezhnev's reign, Stalin's reputation began to revive. Although his alleged "shortcomings" were not totally ignored, he was now described in the official press as "an outstanding party leader" who had been primarily responsible for the successes achieved by the Soviet Union.

The regime also adopted a more restrictive policy toward free expression and dissidence in Soviet society. Critics of the Soviet system, such as the physicist Andrei Sakharov, were harassed and arrested or, like the famous writer Alexander Solzhenitsyn (who had written about the horrors of Soviet concentration camps), forced to leave the country. There was also a qualified return to the anti-Semitic policies and attitudes that had marked the Stalin era. Such indications of renewed repression aroused concern in the West and were instrumental in the inclusion of a statement on human rights in the 1975 Helsinki Agreement, which guaranteed the sanctity of international frontiers throughout the continent of Europe (see Chapter 7).

The political stamp of the Brezhnev era was formally enshrined in a new state constitution, promulgated in 1977. Although the preamble declared that the Soviet Union was no longer a proletarian dictatorship but rather a "state of all the people," comprising workers, farmers, and "socialist intellectuals," it confirmed the role of the Communist Party as "the predominant force" in Soviet society. Article 49 stated that "persecution for criticism shall be prohibited," but Article 62 qualified the rights of the individual by declaring that citizens "shall be obligated to safeguard the interests of the Soviet state and to contribute to the strength of its might and prestige."

There were, of course, no rival voices to compete with the party and the government in defining national interests. The media were controlled by the state and presented only what the state wanted people to hear. The two major newspapers, *Pravda* (Truth) and *Izvestiya* (News), were the agents of the party and the government, respectively. Cynics joked that there was no news in *Pravda* and no truth in *Izvestiya*. Reports of airplane accidents in the Soviet Union were rarely publicized on the grounds that doing so would raise questions about the quality of the Soviet airline industry. The government made strenuous efforts to prevent the Soviet people from being exposed to harmful foreign ideas, especially modern art, literature, and contemporary Western rock music. When the Summer Olympic Games were held in Moscow in 1980, Soviet newspapers advised citizens to keep their children indoors to protect them from being polluted with "bourgeois" ideas passed on by foreign visitors.

For citizens of Western democracies, such a political atmosphere would seem highly oppressive, but for the people in the Soviet republics, an emphasis on law and order was an accepted aspect of everyday life inherited from the tsarist period. Conformism was the rule in virtually every corner of Soviet society, from the educational system (characterized at all levels by rote memorization and political indoctrination) to child rearing (it was forbidden, for example, to be left-handed) and even to yearly vacations (most workers took their vacations at resorts run by their employer, where the daily schedule of activities was highly regimented). Young Americans studying in the Soviet Union reported that friends there were often shocked to hear U.S. citizens criticizing their own president and to learn that they did not routinely carry identity cards.

A Stagnant Economy Soviet leaders also failed to achieve their objective of revitalizing the national economy. Whereas growth rates during the early Khrushchev era had been impressive (prompting Khrushchev during a reception at the Kremlin in 1956 to chortle, "We will bury you,"

referring to the Western countries), under Brezhnev, industrial growth declined to an annual rate of less than 4 percent in the early 1970s and less than 3 percent in the period 1975–1980. Successes in the agricultural sector were equally meager. Grain production rose from less than 90 million tons in the early 1950s to nearly 200 million tons in the 1970s but then stagnated at that level (though it should be noted that Soviet statistics were notoriously unreliable).

One of the primary problems with the Soviet economy was the absence of incentives. Salary structures offered little reward for hard labor and extraordinary achievement. Pay differentials operated within a much narrower range than in most Western societies, and there was little danger of being dismissed. According to the Soviet constitution, every Soviet citizen was guaranteed an opportunity to work.

There were, of course, some exceptions to this general rule. Athletic achievement was highly prized, and a gymnast of Olympic stature would receive great rewards in the form of prestige and lifestyle. Senior officials did not receive high salaries but were provided with countless "perquisites," such as access to foreign goods, official automobiles with a chauffeur, and entry into prestigious institutions of higher learning for their children. For the elite, it was *blat* (influence) that most often differentiated them from the rest of the population. The average citizen, however, had little material incentive to produce beyond the minimum acceptable level of effort. It is hardly surprising that overall per capita productivity was only about half that realized in most capitalist countries. At the same time, the rudeness of clerks and waiters toward their customers in Soviet society became legendary.

The problem of incentives existed at the managerial level as well, where the practice of centralized planning discouraged initiative and innovation. Factory managers, for example, were assigned monthly and annual quotas by the Gosplan (the "state plan," drawn up by the central planning commission). Because state-owned factories faced little or no competition, factory managers did not care whether their products were competitive in terms of price and quality, so long as the quota was attained. One of the key complaints of Soviet citizens was the low quality of most locally made consumer goods. Knowledgeable consumers quickly discovered that products manufactured at the end of the month were often of lower quality (because factory workers had to rush to meet their quotas at the end of their production cycle) and attempted to avoid purchasing them.

Often consumer goods were simply unavailable. Soviet citizens automatically got in line when they saw a queue forming in front of a store because they never knew when something might be available again. When they reached the head of the line, most would purchase several of the same item to swap with their friends and neighbors. Giving in to

How to Shop in Moscow. Because of the policy of state control over the Soviet economy, the availability of goods was a consequence not of market factors but of decisions made by government bureaucrats. As a result, needed goods were often in short supply. When Soviet citizens heard that a shipment of a particular product had arrived at a state store, they queued up to buy it. Here shoppers line up in front of a store selling dinnerware in Moscow.

this "queue psychology," of course, was a time-consuming process and inevitably served to reduce the per capita rate of productivity.

Soviet citizens often tried to overcome the shortcomings of the system by operating "on the left" (the black market). Private economic activities, of course, were illegal in the socialized Soviet system, but many workers took to "moonlighting" to augment their meager salaries. An employee in a state-run appliance store, for example, would promise to repair a customer's television set on his own time in return for a payment "under the table." Otherwise, servicing of the set might require several weeks. Knowledgeable observers estimated that as much as one-third of the entire Soviet economy operated outside the legal system.

Another major obstacle to economic growth was inadequate technology. Except in the area of national defense, the overall level of Soviet technology was not comparable to that of the West or the advanced industrial societies of East Asia. Part of the problem, of course, stemmed from the issues already described. With no competition, factory managers had little incentive to improve the quality of their products. But another reason was the high priority assigned to defense. The military sector of the economy regularly received the most resources from the government and attracted the cream of the country's scientific talent.

An Aging Leadership Such problems would be intimidating for any government; they were particularly so for the elderly generation of party leaders surrounding Leonid Brezhnev, many of whom were cautious to a fault.

Although some undoubtedly recognized the need for reform and innovation, they were paralyzed by the fear of instability and change. The problem worsened during the late 1970s, when Brezhnev's health began to deteriorate.

Brezhnev died in November 1982 and was succeeded by Yuri Andropov (1914–1984), a party veteran and head of the Soviet secret services. During his brief tenure as party chief, Andropov was a vocal advocate of reform, but most of his initiatives were limited to the familiar nostrums of punishment for wrongdoers and moral exhortations to Soviet citizens to work harder. At the same time, material incentives were still officially discouraged and generally ineffective. Andropov had been ailing when he was selected to succeed Brezhnev as party chief, and when he died after only a few months in office, little had been done to change the system. He was succeeded, in turn, by a mediocre party stalwart, the elderly Konstantin Chernenko (1911–1985). With the Soviet system in crisis, Moscow seemed stuck in a time warp. As one concerned observer told an American journalist, "I had a sense of foreboding, like before a storm. That there was something brewing in people and there would be a time when they would say, 'That's it. We can't go on living like this. We can't. We need to redo everything.'"[3]

Ferment in Eastern Europe

The key to Moscow's security along the western frontier of the Soviet Union was the string of satellite states that had been created in Eastern Europe after World War II.

Once Communist power had been assured in Warsaw, Prague, Sofia, Budapest, Bucharest, and East Berlin, a series of "little Stalins" put into power by Moscow instituted Soviet-type five-year plans that emphasized heavy industry rather than consumer goods, the collectivization of agriculture, and the nationalization of industry. They also appropriated the political tactics that Stalin had perfected in the Soviet Union, eliminating all non-Communist parties and establishing the standard institutions of repression—the secret police and military forces. Dissidents were tracked down and thrown into prison, while "national Communists" who resisted total subservience to the nation were charged with treason in mass show trials and executed.

Eastern Europe Under Communist Rule

to warn his Polish colleague against adopting policies that could undermine the "dictatorship of the proletariat" (the Marxist phrase for the political dominance of the party) and even weaken security links with the Soviet Union. After a brief confrontation, during which both sides threatened to use military force to punctuate their demands, Gomulka and Khrushchev reached a compromise according to which Poland would adopt a policy labeled "internal reform, external loyalty." Poland agreed to remain in the Warsaw Pact and to maintain the sanctity of party rule. In return, Warsaw was authorized to adopt domestic reforms, such as easing restrictions on religious practice and ending the policy of forced collectivization in rural areas.

Despite such repressive efforts, however, Soviet-style policies aroused growing discontent in several Eastern European societies. Hungary, Poland, and Romania harbored bitter memories of past Russian domination and suspected that Stalin, under the guise of proletarian internationalism, was seeking to revive the empire of the Romanovs. For the vast majority of peoples in Eastern Europe, the imposition of the "people's democracies" (a euphemism invented by Moscow to refer to a society in the early stage of socialist transition) resulted in economic hardship and severe threats to the most basic political liberties.

Unrest in Poland

The first indications of unrest appeared in 1953, when popular riots broke out against Communist rule in East Berlin. The riots eventually subsided, but the virus had begun to spread to neighboring countries. In Poland, public demonstrations against an increase in food prices in 1956 escalated into widespread protests against the regime's economic policies, restrictions on the freedom of Catholics to practice their religion, and the continued presence of Soviet troops (as called for by the Warsaw Pact) on Polish soil. In a desperate effort to defuse the unrest, in October the Polish party leader stepped down and was replaced by Wladyslaw Gomulka (1905–1982), a popular figure who had previously been demoted for his "nationalist" tendencies. When Gomulka took steps to ease the crisis, the new Soviet party chief, Nikita Khrushchev, flew to Warsaw

The Hungarian Uprising

The developments in Poland sent shock waves throughout the region. The impact was strongest in neighboring Hungary, where the methods of the local "little Stalin," Matyas Rakosi, were so brutal that he had been summoned to Moscow for a lecture. In late October, student-led popular riots broke out in the capital of Budapest and soon spread to other towns and villages throughout the country. Rakosi was forced to resign and was replaced by Imre Nagy (1896–1958), a "national Communist" who attempted to satisfy popular demands without arousing the anger of Moscow. Unlike Gomulka, however, Nagy was unable to contain the zeal of leading members of the protest movement, who sought major political reforms and the withdrawal of Hungary from the Warsaw Pact. On November 1, Nagy promised free elections, which, given the mood of the country, would probably have brought an end to Communist rule. Moscow decided on firm action. Soviet troops, recently withdrawn at Nagy's request, returned to Budapest and installed a new government under the more pliant party leader János Kádár (1912–1989). While Kádár rescinded many of Nagy's measures, Nagy sought refuge in the Yugoslav Embassy. A few weeks later, he left the embassy under the promise of safety but was quickly arrested, convicted of treason, and executed.

The dramatic events in Poland and Hungary graphically demonstrated the vulnerability of the Soviet satellite system in Eastern Europe, and many observers throughout the world anticipated an attempt by the United States to intervene on behalf of the freedom fighters in Hungary. After all, the Eisenhower administration had promised that it would "roll back" communism, and radio broadcasts by the U.S.-sponsored Radio Liberty and Radio Free Europe had encouraged the peoples of Eastern Europe to rise up against Soviet domination. In reality, Washington was well aware that U.S. intervention could lead to nuclear war and limited itself to protests against Soviet brutality in crushing the uprising.

The year of discontent was not without its consequences, however. Soviet leaders now recognized that Moscow could maintain control over its satellites in Eastern Europe only by granting them the leeway to adopt domestic policies appropriate to local conditions. Khrushchev had already embarked on this path when, during a visit to Belgrade in 1955, he assured Josip Tito that there were "different roads to socialism." Eastern European Communist leaders now took Khrushchev at his word and adopted reform programs to make socialism more palatable to their subject populations. Even János Kádár, derisively labeled the "butcher of Budapest," managed to preserve many of Imre Nagy's reforms and allow a measure of capitalist incentive and freedom of expression in Hungary.

The Prague Spring

Czechoslovakia did not share in the thaw of the mid-1950s and remained under the rule of Antonín Novotný (1904–1975), who had been placed in power by Stalin himself. By the late 1960s, however, Novotný's policies had led to widespread popular alienation, and in 1968, with the support of intellectuals and reformist party members, Alexander Dubček (1921–1992) was elected first secretary of the Communist Party. He immediately attempted to create what was popularly called "socialism with a human face," relaxing restrictions on freedom of speech and the press and the right to travel abroad. Reforms were announced for the economic sector, and party control over all aspects of society was reduced. A period of euphoria erupted that came to be known as the "Prague Spring."

It proved to be short-lived. Encouraged by Dubček's actions, some Czechs called for more far-reaching reforms, including neutrality and withdrawal from the Soviet bloc. To forestall the spread of this "spring fever," the Soviet Red Army, supported by troops from other Warsaw Pact states, invaded Czechoslovakia in August 1968 and crushed the reform movement. Gustav Husák (1913–1991), a committed Stalinist, replaced Dubček and restored the old order (see the box on p. 190).

Elsewhere in Eastern Europe, Stalinist policies continued to hold sway. The ruling Communist government in East Germany, led by Walter Ulbricht (1893–1973),

consolidated its position in the early 1950s and became a faithful Soviet satellite. Industry was nationalized and agriculture collectivized. After the 1953 workers' revolt was crushed by Soviet tanks, a steady flight of East Germans to West Germany ensued, primarily through the city of Berlin. This exodus of mostly skilled laborers (soon only party chief Ulbricht would be left, remarked one Soviet observer sardonically) created economic problems and in 1961 led the East German government to erect the infamous Berlin Wall separating West from East Berlin, as well as even more fearsome barriers along the entire border with West Germany.

After walling off the West, East Germany succeeded in developing the strongest economy among the Soviet Union's Eastern European satellites. In 1971, Walter Ulbricht was succeeded by Erich Honecker (1912–1994), a party hardliner who was deeply committed to the ideological battle against détente. Propaganda increased, and the use of the Stasi, the secret police, became a hallmark of Honecker's virtual dictatorship. Honecker ruled unchallenged for the next eighteen years.

Culture and Society in the Soviet Bloc

In his occasional musings about the future Communist utopia, Karl Marx had predicted the emergence of a classless society to replace the exploitative and hierarchical systems of feudalism and capitalism. Workers would take part in productive activities but would share equally in the fruits of their labor. In their free time, they would help produce a new, advanced culture, proletarian in character and egalitarian in content.

Cultural Expression

The reality in the post–World War II Soviet Union and in Eastern Europe was somewhat different. Beginning in 1946, a series of government decrees made all forms of literary and scientific expression dependent on the state. All Soviet culture was expected to follow the party line. Historians, philosophers, and social scientists all grew accustomed to quoting Marx, Lenin, and, above all, Stalin as their chief authorities. Novels and plays, too, were supposed to portray Communist heroes and their efforts to create a better society. No criticism of existing social conditions was permitted. Even distinguished composers such as Dmitri Shostakovich (1906–1975) were compelled to heed Stalin's criticisms, including his view that contemporary Western music was nothing but a "mishmash." Some areas of intellectual activity were virtually abolished; the science of

THE BREZHNEV DOCTRINE

In the summer of 1968, when the new Communist Party leaders in Czechoslovakia were seriously considering proposals for reforming the totalitarian system there, the Warsaw Pact nations met under the leadership of Soviet party chief Leonid Brezhnev to assess the threat to the socialist camp. Shortly after, military forces of several Soviet bloc nations entered Czechoslovakia and imposed a new government subservient to Moscow. The move was justified by the spirit of "proletarian internationalism" and was widely viewed as a warning to China and other socialist states not to stray too far from Marxist-Leninist orthodoxy, as interpreted by the Soviet Union. The principle came to be known as the Brezhnev Doctrine.

How does Leonid Brezhnev justify the Soviet invasion of Czechoslovakia in 1968? Do you find his argument persuasive?

A Letter to Czechoslovakia

To the Central Committee of the Communist Party of Czechoslovakia   Warsaw, July 15, 1968

Dear comrades!

On behalf of the Central Committees of the Communist and Workers' Parties of Bulgaria, Hungary, the German Democratic Republic, Poland, and the Soviet Union, we address ourselves to you with this letter, prompted by a feeling of sincere friendship based on the principles of Marxism-Leninism and proletarian internationalism and by the concern of our common affairs for strengthening the positions of socialism and the security of the socialist community of nations.

The development of events in your country evokes in us deep anxiety. It is our firm conviction that the offensive of the reactionary forces, backed by imperialists, against your Party and the foundations of the social system in the Czechoslovak Socialist Republic, threatens to push your country off the road of socialism and that consequently it jeopardizes the interests of the entire socialist system. . . .

We neither had nor have any intention of interfering in such affairs as are strictly the internal business of your Party and your state, nor of violating the principles of respect, independence, and equality in the relations among the Communist Parties and socialist countries. . . .

At the same time we cannot agree to have hostile forces push your country from the road of socialism and create a threat of severing Czechoslovakia from the socialist community. . . . This is the common cause of our countries, which have joined in the Warsaw Treaty to ensure independence, peace, and security in Europe, and to set up an insurmountable barrier against aggression and revenge. . . . We shall never agree to have imperialism, using peaceful or nonpeaceful methods, making a gap from the inside or from the outside in the socialist system, and changing in imperialism's favor the correlation of forces in Europe. . . .

That is why we believe that a decisive rebuff of the anti-communist forces, and decisive efforts for the preservation of the socialist system in Czechoslovakia are not only your task but ours as well. . . .

We express the conviction that the Communist Party of Czechoslovakia, conscious of its responsibility, will take the necessary steps to block the path of reaction. In this struggle you can count on the solidarity and all-round assistance of the fraternal socialist countries.

SOURCE: *Moscow News*, Supplement to No. 30 (917), 1968, pp. 3–6.

---

genetics disappeared, and few movies were made during Stalin's final years.

Stalin's death brought a modest respite from cultural repression. Writers and artists banned during Stalin's years were again allowed to publish. The writer Ilya Ehrenburg set the tone with his novel, significantly titled *The Thaw*. Still, Soviet authorities, including Khrushchev, were reluctant to allow cultural freedom to move far beyond official Soviet ideology.

These restrictions, however, did not prevent the emergence of some significant Soviet literature, although authors paid a heavy price if they alienated the Soviet authorities. Boris Pasternak (1890–1960), who began his literary career as a poet, won the Nobel Prize in 1958 for his celebrated novel *Doctor Zhivago*, published in Italy in 1957. But the Soviet government condemned Pasternak's anti-Soviet tendencies, banned the novel from the Soviet Union, and would not allow him to accept the prize. The author had alienated the authorities by describing a society scarred by the excesses of Bolshevik revolutionary zeal.

Alexander Solzhenitsyn (b. 1918) caused an even greater furor than Pasternak. Solzhenitsyn had spent eight years in forced-labor camps for criticizing Stalin, and his *One Day in the Life of Ivan Denisovich*, which won him the Nobel Prize in 1970, was an account of life in those camps. Later, Solzhenitsyn wrote *The Gulag Archipelago*, a detailed indictment of the whole system of Soviet oppression. Soviet authorities denounced Solzhenitsyn's efforts to inform the world of Soviet crimes against humanity and

Stalinist Heroic: An Example of Socialist Realism. Under Stalin and his successors, art was assigned the task of indoctrinating the Soviet population on the public virtues, such as hard work, loyalty to the state, and patriotism. Grandiose statuary erected to commemorate the heroic efforts of the Red Army during World War II appeared in every Soviet city. Here is an example in Minsk, today the capital of Belarus.

Courtesy of William J. Duiker

arrested and expelled him from the Soviet Union after he published *The Gulag Archipelago* abroad in 1973.

Although restrictive policies continued into the late 1980s, some Soviet authors learned how to minimize battles with the censors by writing under the guise of humor or fantasy. Two of the most accomplished and popular Soviet novelists of the period, Yury Trifonov (1925–1981) and Fazil Iskander (b. 1929), focused on the daily struggle of Soviet citizens to live with dignity. Trifonov depicted with grim realism the everyday life of ordinary Russians, while Iskander used humor to poke fun at the incompetence of the Soviet regime.

Cultural Change in Eastern Europe In the Eastern European satellites, cultural freedom varied considerably from country to country. In Poland, intellectuals had access to Western publications as well as greater freedom to travel to the West. Hungarian and Yugoslav Communists, too, tolerated a certain level of intellectual activity that was not liked but not prohibited. Elsewhere, intellectuals were forced to conform to the regime's demands. After the Soviet invasion of Czechoslovakia in 1968, Czech Communists pursued a policy of strict cultural control.

The socialist camp also experienced the many facets of modern popular culture. By the early 1970s, there were 28 million television sets in the Soviet Union, although state authorities controlled the content of the programs that the Soviet people watched. Tourism, too, made inroads into the Communist world as state-run industries provided vacation time and governments facilitated the establishment of resorts for workers on the coasts of the Black Sea and

the Adriatic. In Poland, the number of vacationers who used holiday retreats increased from 700,000 in 1960 to 2.8 million in 1972.

Spectator sports became a large industry and were also highly politicized as the result of Cold War divisions. Victory in international athletic events was viewed as proof of the superiority of the socialist system over its capitalist rival. Accordingly, the state provided money for the construction of gymnasiums and training camps and portrayed athletes as superheroes.

Social Changes in the Soviet Union and Eastern Europe

The imposition of Marxist systems in Eastern Europe had far-reaching social consequences. Most Eastern European countries made the change from peasant societies to modern industrialized economies. In Bulgaria, for example, 80 percent of the labor force was engaged in agriculture in 1950, but only 20 percent was still there in 1980. Although the Soviet Union and its Eastern European satellites never achieved the high standards of living of the West, they did experience some improvement. In 1960, the average real income of Polish peasants was four times higher than before World War II. Consumer goods also became more widespread. In East Germany, only 17 percent of families had television sets in 1960, but 75 percent had acquired them by 1972.

According to Marxist doctrine, government control of industry and the elimination of private property were supposed to lead to a classless society. Although the classless society was never achieved, that ideal did have important social consequences. For one thing, traditional ruling classes were stripped of their special status after 1945. The Potocki family in Poland, for example, which had owned 9 million acres of land before the war, lost all of its possessions, and family members were reduced to the ranks of common laborers.

The desire to create a classless society led to noticeable changes in education. In some countries, the desire to provide equal educational opportunities led to laws that mandated quota systems based on class. In East Germany, for example, 50 percent of the students in secondary schools had to be children of workers and peasants. The sons of manual workers constituted 53 percent of university students in Yugoslavia in 1964 and 40 percent in East Germany, compared to only 15 percent in Italy and 5.3 percent in West Germany. Social mobility also increased. In Poland in 1961, half of the white-collar workers came from blue-collar families. A significant number of judges, professors, and industrial managers stemmed from working-class backgrounds.

Education became crucial in preparing for new jobs in the Communist system and led to higher enrollments in both secondary schools and universities. In Czechoslovakia, for example, the number of students in secondary schools tripled between 1945 and 1970, and the number of university students quadrupled between the 1930s and the 1960s. The type of education that students received also changed. In Hungary before World War II, 40 percent of students studied law, 9 percent engineering and technology, and 5 percent agriculture. In 1970, the figures were 35 percent in engineering and technology, 9 percent in agriculture, and only 4 percent in law.

By the 1970s, the new managers of society, regardless of class background, realized the importance of higher education and used their power to gain special privileges for their children. By 1971, fully 60 percent of the children of white-collar workers attended a university, and even though blue-collar families constituted 60 percent of the population, only 36 percent of their children attended institutions of higher learning. Even East Germany dropped its requirement that 50 percent of secondary students had to be the offspring of workers and peasants.

This shift in educational preferences demonstrates yet another aspect of the social structure in the Communist world: the emergence of a new privileged class, made up of members of the Communist Party, state officials, high-ranking officers in the military and secret police, and a few special professional groups. The new elite not only possessed political power but also received special privileges, including the right to purchase high-quality goods in special stores (in Czechoslovakia, the elite could obtain organically grown produce not available to anyone else), paid vacations at special resorts, access to good housing and superior medical services, and advantages in education and jobs for their children.

Ideals of equality did not include women. Men dominated the leadership positions of the Communist parties in the Soviet Union and Eastern Europe. Women did have greater opportunities in the workforce and even in the professions, however. In the Soviet Union, women comprised 51 percent of the labor force in 1980; by the mid-1980s, they constituted 50 percent of the engineers, 80 percent of the doctors, and 75 percent of the teachers and teachers' aides. But many of these were low-paying jobs; most female doctors, for example, worked in primary care and were paid less than skilled machinists. The chief administrators in hospitals and schools were still men.

Moreover, although women were part of the workforce, they were never freed of their traditional roles in the home. Most women confronted what came to be known as the "double shift." After working eight hours in their jobs, they came home to face the housework and care of the children. They might spend two hours a day in long lines at a number of stores waiting to buy food and clothes. Because of the housing situation, they were forced to use kitchens that were shared by a number of families.

Nearly three-quarters of a century after the Bolshevik Revolution, then, the Marxist dream of an advanced, egalitarian society was as far away as ever. Although in some respects conditions in the socialist camp were an improvement over those before World War II, many problems and inequities were as intransigent as ever.

The Disintegration of the Soviet Empire

On the death of Konstantin Chernenko in 1985, party leaders selected the talented and vigorous Soviet official Mikhail Gorbachev to succeed him. The new Soviet leader had shown early signs of promise. Born into a peasant family in 1931, Gorbachev combined farmwork with school and received the Order of the Red Banner for his agricultural efforts. This award and his good school record enabled him to study law at the University of Moscow. After receiving his law degree in 1955, he returned to his native southern Russia, where he eventually became first secretary of the Communist Party in the city of Stavropol and then first secretary of the regional party committee. In 1978, Gorbachev was made a member of the party's Central Committee in Moscow. Two years later, he became a full member of the ruling Politburo and secretary of the Central Committee.

During the early 1980s, Gorbachev began to realize the extent of Soviet problems and the crucial importance of massive reform to transform the system. During a visit to Canada in 1983, he discovered to his astonishment that Canadian farmers worked hard on their own initiative. "We'll never have this for fifty years," he reportedly remarked.[4] wOn his return to Moscow, he established a series of committees to evaluate the situation and recommend measures to improve the system.

The Gorbachev Era

With his election as party general secretary in 1985, Gorbachev seemed intent on taking earlier reforms to their logical conclusions. The cornerstone of his reform program was *perestroika,* or "restructuring." At first, it meant only a reordering of economic policy, as Gorbachev called for the beginning of a market economy with limited free enterprise and some private property. Initial economic reforms were difficult to implement, however. Radicals demanded decisive measures; conservatives feared that rapid changes would be too painful. In his attempt to achieve compromise, Gorbachev often pursued partial liberalization, which satisfied neither faction and also failed to work, producing only more discontent.

Gorbachev soon perceived that in the Soviet system, the economic sphere was intimately tied to the social and political spheres. Any efforts to reform the economy without political or social reform would be doomed to failure. One of the most important instruments of *perestroika* was *glasnost,* or "openness." Soviet citizens and officials were encouraged to openly discuss the strengths and weaknesses of the Soviet Union. This policy could be seen in *Pravda,* the official newspaper of the Communist Party, where disasters such as the nuclear accident at Chernobyl in 1986 and collisions of ships in the Black Sea received increasing coverage. Soon this type of reporting was extended to include reports of official corruption, sloppy factory work, and protests against government policy. The arts also benefited from the new policy as previously banned works were now allowed to circulate and motion pictures began to depict negative aspects of Soviet life. Music based on Western styles, such as jazz and rock, began to be performed openly. Religious activities, previously banned by Soviet authorities, were once again tolerated.

Political reforms were equally revolutionary. In June 1987, the principle of two-candidate elections was introduced; previously, voters had been presented with only

Courtesy of William J. Duiker

Behind the Mask. After the Bolshevik Revolution, Soviet writers and artists were compelled to follow the dictates of socialist realism. All creative work was expected to glorify the state and the superiority of the socialist system. As official restrictions began to loosen under Gorbachev's policy of *glasnost,* however, books and paintings began to offer a more critical view of the Soviet system. In the paintings shown here, displayed at an exhibit in Moscow in 1989, an artist seeks to expose the harsh inner nature of hallowed Soviet leaders.

one candidate. Most dissidents, including Andrei Sakharov, who had spent years in internal exile, were released. At the Communist Party conference in 1988, Gorbachev called for the creation of a new Soviet parliament, the Congress of People's Deputies, whose members were to be chosen in competitive elections. It convened in 1989, the first such meeting since 1918. Now as an elected member of the Congress, Sakharov called for an end to the Communist monopoly of power and on December 11, 1989, the day he died, urged the creation of a new, non-Communist party. Early in 1990, Gorbachev legalized the formation of other political parties and struck out Article 6 of the Soviet constitution, which guaranteed the "leading role" of the Communist Party. Hitherto, the position of first secretary of the party was the most important post in the Soviet Union, but as the Communist Party became less closely associated with the state, the powers of this office diminished. Gorbachev attempted to consolidate his power by creating a new state presidency, and in March 1990, he became the Soviet Union's first president.

Eastern Europe: From Soviet Satellites to Sovereign Nations

The progressive decline of the Soviet Union had an impact on its neighbors to the west. First to respond, as in 1956, was Poland, where popular protests of high food prices had erupted in the early 1980s, leading to the rise of an independent labor movement called Solidarity. Led by Lech Walesa (b. 1943), Solidarity rapidly became an influential force for change and a threat to the government's monopoly of power. The union was outlawed in 1981, but martial law did not solve Poland's serious economic problems, and in 1988, the Communist government bowed to the inevitable and permitted free national elections to take place, resulting in the election of Walesa as president of Poland in December 1990. Unlike the situation in 1956, when Khrushchev had intervened to prevent the collapse of the Soviet satellite system in Eastern Europe, in the late 1980s, Moscow—inspired by Gorbachev's policy of encouraging "new thinking" to improve relations with the Western powers—took no action to reverse the verdict in Warsaw.

In Hungary, as in Poland, the process of transition had begun many years previously. After crushing the Hungarian revolution of 1956, the Communist government of János Kádár had tried to assuage popular opinion by enacting a series of far-reaching economic reforms (labeled "communism with a capitalist face-lift"), but as the 1980s progressed, the economy sagged, and in 1989, the regime permitted the formation of opposition political parties, leading eventually to the formation of a

non-Communist coalition government in elections held in March 1990.

The transition in Czechoslovakia was more abrupt. After Soviet troops crushed the Prague Spring in 1968, hard-line Communists under Gustav Husák followed a policy of massive repression to maintain their power. In 1977, dissident intellectuals formed an organization called Charter 77 as a vehicle for protest against violations of human rights. Regardless of the repressive atmosphere, dissident activities continued to grow during the 1980s, and when massive demonstrations broke out in several major cities in 1989, President Husák's government, lacking any real popular support, collapsed. At the end of December, he was replaced by Václav Havel (b. 1936), a dissident playwright who had been a leading figure in Charter 77.

But the most dramatic events took place in East Germany, where a persistent economic slump and the ongoing oppressiveness of the regime of Erich Honecker led to a flight of refugees and mass demonstrations against the regime in the summer and fall of 1989. Capitulating to popular pressure, the Communist government opened its entire border with the West. The Berlin Wall, the most tangible symbol of the Cold War, became the site of a massive celebration, and most of it was dismantled by joyful Germans from both sides of the border. In March 1990, free elections led to the formation of a non-Communist government that began to negotiate political and economic reunification with West Germany.

End of Empire

The events in Eastern Europe were being watched closely in Moscow. One of Gorbachev's most serious problems stemmed from the nature of the Soviet Union. The Union of Soviet Socialist Republics was a truly multiethnic country, containing 92 nationalities and 112 recognized languages. Previously, the iron hand of the Communist Party, centered in Moscow, had kept a lid on the centuries-old ethnic tensions that had periodically erupted throughout the history of this region. As Gorbachev released this iron grip, tensions resurfaced, a by-product of *glasnost* that Gorbachev had not anticipated. Ethnic groups took advantage of the new openness to protest what they perceived to be ethnically motivated slights. As violence erupted, the Soviet army, in disarray since the Soviet intervention in Afghanistan in 1979, had difficulty controlling the situation. In some cases, independence movements and ethnic causes became linked, as in Azerbaijan, where the National Front became the spokesgroup for the Muslim Azerbaijanis in the conflict with Christian Armenians.

The period from 1988 to 1990 witnessed the emergence of nationalist movements in all fifteen republics of the Soviet Union. Often motivated by ethnic concerns,

MAP 9.2 **Eastern Europe and the Former Soviet Union.** After the disintegration of the Soviet Union in 1991, several onetime Soviet republics declared their independence. This map shows the new configuration of the states that emerged in the 1990s from the former Soviet Union. The breakaway region of Chechnya is indicated on the map. **?** What new nations have appeared in the territory of the old Soviet Union since the end of the Cold War? 🌐 **View an animated version of this map or related maps at** worldrc.wadsworth.com/.

many of them called for sovereignty of the republics and independence from Russian-based rule centered in Moscow. Such movements sprang up first in Georgia in late 1988 and then in Moldavia, Uzbekistan, Azerbaijan, and the three Baltic republics.

In December 1989, the Communist Party of Lithuania declared itself independent of the Communist Party of the Soviet Union. Gorbachev made it clear that he supported self-determination but not secession, which he believed would be detrimental to the Soviet Union. Nevertheless, on March 11, 1990, the Lithuanian Supreme Council unilaterally declared Lithuania independent. Its formal name was now the Lithuanian Republic; the adjectives *Soviet* and *Socialist* had been dropped. On March 15, the Soviet Congress of People's Deputies, though recognizing a general right to secede from the Union of Soviet Socialist Republics, declared the Lithuanian declaration null and void; the Congress stated that proper procedures must be established and followed before secession would be acceptable.

During 1990 and 1991, Gorbachev struggled to deal with the problems unleashed by his reforms. On the one hand, he tried to appease the conservative forces who complained about the growing disorder within the Soviet Union. On the other hand, he tried to accommodate the liberal forces who increasingly favored a new kind of decentralized

Soviet federation. Gorbachev especially labored to cooperate more closely with Boris Yeltsin (b. 1931), elected president of the Russian Republic in June 1991. Conservative elements from the army, the party, and the KGB, however, had grown increasingly worried about the potential dissolution of the Soviet Union. On August 19, 1991, a group of these discontented rightists arrested Gorbachev and attempted to seize power. Gorbachev's unwillingness to work with the conspirators and the brave resistance in Moscow of Yeltsin and thousands of Russians who had grown accustomed to their new liberties caused the coup to disintegrate rapidly. The actions of these right-wing plotters served to accelerate the very process they had hoped to stop—the disintegration of the Soviet Union.

Despite desperate pleas from Gorbachev, all fifteen republics soon opted for complete independence (see Map 9.2). Ukraine voted for independence on December 1, 1991. A week later, the leaders of Russia, Ukraine, and Belarus announced that the Soviet Union had "ceased to exist" and would be replaced by a much looser federation, the Commonwealth of Independent States. Gorbachev resigned on December 25, 1991, and turned over his responsibilities as commander in chief to Boris Yeltsin, the president of Russia. By the end of 1991, one of the largest empires in world history had come to an end, and a new era had begun in its lands.

The New Russia: From Empire to Nation

In Russia, by far the largest of the former Soviet republics, a new power struggle soon ensued. Yeltsin, a onetime engineer who had been dismissed from the Politburo in 1987 for his radicalism, was committed to introducing a free market economy as quickly as possible. In December 1991, the Congress of People's Deputies granted Yeltsin temporary power to rule by decree. But former Communist Party members and their allies in the Congress were opposed to many of Yeltsin's economic reforms and tried to place new limits on his powers. Yeltsin fought back. After winning a vote of confidence on April 25, 1993, Yeltsin pushed ahead with plans for a new Russian constitution that would abolish the Congress of People's Deputies, create a two-chamber parliament, and establish a strong presidency. A hard-line parliamentary minority resisted and in early October took the offensive, urging supporters to take over government offices and the central television station. Yeltsin responded by ordering military forces to storm the parliament building and arrest hard-line opponents. Yeltsin used his victory to consolidate his power in parliamentary elections held in December.

During the mid-1990s, Yeltsin was able to maintain a precarious grip on power while seeking to implement reforms that would place Russia on a firm course toward a pluralistic political system and a market economy. But the new post-Communist Russia remained as fragile as ever. Burgeoning economic inequality and rampant corruption aroused widespread criticism and shook the confidence of the Russian people in the superiority of the capitalist system over the one that existed under Communist rule. A nagging war in the Caucasus—where the Muslim people of Chechnya sought national independence from Russia—drained the government's budget and exposed the decrepit state of the once vaunted Red Army. In presidential elections held in 1996, Yeltsin was reelected, but the rising popularity of a revived Communist Party and the growing strength of nationalist elements, combined with Yeltsin's precarious health, raised serious questions about the future of the country.

What had happened to derail Yeltsin's plan to transform Soviet society? To some critics, Yeltsin and his advisers tried to achieve too much too fast. Between 1991 and 1995, state firms that had previously provided about 80 percent of all industrial production and employment had been privatized, and the prices of goods (previously subject to government regulation) were allowed to respond to market forces. Only agriculture—where the decision to privatize collective farms had little impact in rural areas—was left substantially untouched. The immediate results were disastrous: industrial output dropped by more than one-third, and unemployment levels and prices rose dramatically. Many Russian workers and soldiers were not paid their salaries for months on end, and many social services came to an abrupt halt.

With the harsh official and ideological constraints of the Soviet system suddenly removed, corruption—labeled by one observer "criminal gang capitalism"—became rampant, and the government often appeared inept in coping with complexities of a market economy. Few Russians appeared to grasp the realities of modern capitalism and understandably reacted to the inevitable transition pains from the old system by heaping all the blame on the new one. The fact is that Yeltsin had attempted to change the structure of the Soviet system without due regard to the necessity of changing the mentality of the people as well. The result was a high level of disenchantment. A new joke circulated among the Russian people: "We know now that everything they told us about communism was false. And everything they told us about capitalism was true."

The Putin Era At the end of 1999, Yeltsin suddenly resigned his office and was replaced by Vladimir Putin (b. 1952), a former member of the KGB. Putin vowed to bring an end to the rampant corruption and inexperience that permeated Russian political culture and to strengthen the role of the central government in managing the affairs of state. During the succeeding months, the parliament approved his proposal to centralize power in the hands of the federal government in Moscow; in early 2001, he presented a new plan to regulate political parties, which had risen in number to more than fifty. Parties at both extremes of the political spectrum, the Yabloko (apple) faction representing Western-style liberal policies and Gennadi Zyuganov's revived Communist Party, opposed the legislation, without success.

Putin also vowed to bring the breakaway state of Chechnya back under Russian authority and to adopt a more assertive role in international affairs. The new president took advantage of growing public anger at Western plans to expand the NATO (North Atlantic Treaty Organization) alliance into Eastern Europe, as well as aggressive actions by NATO countries against Serbia in the Balkans (see Chapter 10), to restore Russia's position as an influential force in the world. To undercut U.S. dominance on the political scene, Moscow has improved relations with neighboring China and simultaneously sought to cooperate with European nations on issues of common concern. To assuage national pride, Putin has entered negotiations with such former republics of the old Soviet Union as Belarus and Ukraine to tighten forms of mutual political and economic cooperation.

Pride in the recent achievements of the Russian nation, however, is hard to come by these days. Not only have the boundaries of the old Soviet Empire shrunk by one-third, but the living standards of the Russian people have declined as well. According to recent statistics, mortality rates have risen by an estimated 40 percent in the last three decades, and the national population is predicted to decline by almost 50 million in the next half-century. Since the early 1980s, marriage rates have declined by over 30 percent, and the rate of divorce has increased by a similar measure. For the Russian people, there is very little good news these days.

Among the most acute observers of the current mood in Russia are the country's writers. Some have reacted to the lifting of decades of political restraint by experimenting with irreverent or pornographic fiction. But others urge Russians to firmly face their past. One of the most popular Russian novelists today is Viktor Pelevin (b. 1962), who combines acid social commentary with dramatic narrative. In *The Yellow Arrow* (1993), he critically depicts the Russian people trapped on a never-ending train ride, too lethargic to leave the train to embark on a new life.

Echoing this sentiment is Alexander Solzhenitsyn, one of Russia's greatest living writers, who recently returned from exile in the United States. At first, his warnings to fellow authors against the danger of "pessimistic relativism" were ignored, but in 2006, *The First Circle*, his gripping account of the Soviet labor camps, received popular acclaim when it was shown as a ten-part miniseries on a state-owned television network.

President Putin has attempted to deal with the chronic problems in Russian society by centralizing his control over the system, and by silencing critics—notably in the Russian media. Such moves have aroused unease among many observers in the West and provoked the United States to warn him against derailing the trend toward democratic institutions and practices in the old Soviet bloc. But there is a widespread sense of unease in Russia today about the decline of social order—marked by a rising incidence of alcoholism, sexual promiscuity, criminal activities, and the disintegration of the traditional family system in post-Soviet Russia— and many of Putin's compatriots express sympathy with his attempt to restore a sense of pride and discipline in Russian society. He was not alone in expressing the view in the spring of 2005 that the breakup of the Soviet Union was a national tragedy.

CONCLUSION

*T*HE SOVIET UNION HAD EMERGED FROM WORLD WAR II as one of the world's two superpowers. Its armies had played an instrumental role in the final defeat of the powerful German war machine and had installed pliant Communist regimes throughout Eastern Europe. No force of comparable strength had occupied the plains of western Russia since the Mongols in the thirteenth and fourteenth centuries.

During the next four decades, the Soviet Union appeared to be secure in its power. Its military and economic performance during the first postwar decade was sufficiently impressive to create an atmosphere of incipient panic in Washington. By the mid-1980s, however, fears that the Soviet Union would surpass the United States as an economic power had long since dissipated, and the Soviet system appeared to be mired in a state of near paralysis. Economic growth had slowed to a snail's pace, corruption had reached epidemic levels, and leadership had passed to a generation of elderly party bureaucrats who appeared incapable of addressing the burgeoning problems that affected Soviet society.

What had happened to tarnish the dream that had inspired Lenin and his fellow Bolsheviks to believe they could create a Marxist paradise? Some analysts argue that the ambitious defense policies adopted by the Reagan administration forced Moscow into an arms race it could not afford and thus ultimately led to a collapse of the Soviet economy. Others suggest that Soviet problems were more deeply rooted and would have led to the disintegration of the Soviet Union even without outside stimulation. The latter argument is surely closer to the mark. For years, if not decades, leaders in the Kremlin had disguised or ignored the massive inefficiencies of the Soviet system. It seems clear in retrospect that the Soviet command economy proved better at managing the early stages of the Industrial Revolution than at moving on to the next stage of an advanced technological society and that the Leninist concept of democratic centralism failed to provide the quality of leadership and political courage needed to cope with the challenges of nation building. By the 1980s, behind the powerful shield of the Red Army, the system had become an empty shell.

In the years immediately preceding his ascent to power in the Politburo, the perceptive Mikhail Gorbachev had recognized the crucial importance of instituting radical reforms. At the time, he hoped that by doing so, he could save the socialist system. By then, however, it was too late. Restive minorities that had long resented the suppression of their national or cultural identities under Moscow's heavy hand now saw their opportunity to break away from the Soviet system. Even the Russian people no longer were confident that the bright vision of a Marxist utopia could be transformed into reality.

The dissolution of the Soviet Union and its satellite system in Eastern Europe brought a dramatic end to the Cold War. At the dawn of the 1990s, a generation of global rivalry between two ideological systems had come to a close, and world leaders turned their attention to the construction of what U.S. President George Herbert Walker Bush called the New World Order. But what sort of new order would it be?

TIMELINE

	1945	1955	1965	1975	1985	1995	2000

SOVIET UNION AND RUSSIA

- Death of Stalin and emergence of Khrushchev
- Brezhnev era
- Dissolution of the Soviet Union
- Gorbachev years
- Yeltsin era
- Vladimir Putin to power in Moscow

EASTERN EUROPE

- "Prague Spring"
- Hungarian uprising
- Communist governments in Eastern Europe
- Revolutions in Eastern Europe

CHAPTER NOTES

1. Vladislav Zubok and Constantin Pleshakov, *Inside the Kremlin's Cold War: From Stalin to Khrushchev* (Cambridge, England, 1996), p. 166.
2. Nikita Khrushchev, *Khrushchev Remembers*, trans. Strobe Talbott (Boston, 1970), p. 77.
3. Quoted in Hedrick Smith, *The New Russians* (New York, 1990), p. 30.
4. Smith, *The New Russians*, p. 74.

WORLD HISTORY
RESOURCE CENTER

Visit the *Twentieth-Century World History* Book Companion Website for resources specific to this textbook:

academic.cengage.com/history/duiker

The Wadsworth World History Resource Center at worldrc.wadsworth.com/ offers a variety of tools to help you succeed in this course, including access to quizzes; images; documents; interactive simulations, maps, and timelines; movie explorations; and a wealth of other sources.

10

POSTWAR EUROPE: ON THE PATH TO UNITY?

*A*T THE END OF WORLD WAR II, European civilization was in ruins. Almost 40 million people had been killed in six years. Massive air raids and artillery bombardments had reduced many of the great cities of Europe to rubble. An American general described the German capital of Berlin: "Wherever we looked, we saw desolation. It was like a city of the dead. Suffering and shock were visible in every face. Dead bodies still remained in canals and lakes and were being dug out from under bomb debris." Berlin was not alone in its devastation. Dozens of other cities around Europe had been equally damaged by Allied bombing raids during the war, as air attacks were used for the first time as a deliberate means of intimidating the enemy. Millions of Europeans now faced starvation as grain harvests were only half of what they had been in 1939. Countless others had been uprooted by the war; now they became "displaced persons," trying to find food and then their way home. The fruits of the Industrial Revolution, when mixed with the heady brew of virulent nationalism and the struggle for empire, were bitter indeed.

Between 1945 and 1970, Europe not only recovered from the devastating effects of World War II but also experienced an economic resurgence that seemed nothing less than miraculous. Economic growth and virtually full employment continued so long that the first postwar recession, in 1973, came as a shock to Western Europe. It was short-lived, however, and economic growth returned.

In the meantime, the historical animosities that had fueled two catastrophic world wars were replaced by a determination to bring about a new united Europe, based on mutual cooperation and equal opportunity for all. Although the process is by no means complete, Europe has made great strides in seeking to guarantee that the horrors of the recent past will never be repeated. ◆

Western Europe: Recovery and Renewal

In the immediate postwar era, the challenge was clear and intimidating. The peoples of Europe needed to rebuild their national economies and reestablish and strengthen their democratic institutions. They needed to find the means to cooperate in the face of a potential new threat from the east in the form of the Soviet Union. Above all, they needed to restore their confidence in the continuing vitality and future promise of European civilization—a civilization whose image had been badly tarnished by two bitter internal conflicts in the space of a quarter century.

In confronting the challenge, the Europeans possessed one significant trump card: the support and assistance of the United States. The United States had entered World War II as a major industrial power, but its global influence had been limited by the effects of the Great Depression and a self-imposed policy of isolation that had removed it from active involvement in world affairs. But after the United States helped bring the conflict to a close, the nation bestrode the world like a colossus. Its military power was enormous, its political influence was unparalleled, and its economic potential, fueled by the demands of building a war machine to defeat the Axis, seemed unlimited. When on June 5, 1947, Secretary of State George C. Marshall told the graduating class at Harvard University that the United States was prepared to assist the nations of Europe in the task of recovery from "hunger, poverty, desperation, and chaos," he offered a beacon of hope to a region badly in need of reasons for optimism.

Armageddon, 1945. In the last months of World War II, the German capital of Berlin was exposed to a relentless bombing campaign by the Allied forces. As the war came to an end in May 1945, the once-stylish city was in ruins. Shown here is a view of Berlin's most fashionable street, Unter den Linden. In the foreground is the Brandenburg Gate, soon to become the point of division between East and West Berlin.

© William Vandivert/Time Life Pictures/Getty Images

The Triumph of Democracy in Postwar Europe

With the economic aid of the Marshall Plan, the countries of Western Europe (see Map 10.1) recovered relatively rapidly from the devastation of World War II. Between 1947 and 1950, European countries received $9.4 billion to be used for new equipment and raw materials. By the late 1970s, industrial production had surpassed all previous records, and Western Europe experienced virtually full employment. Social welfare programs included affordable health care; housing; family allowances to provide a minimum level of material care for children; increases in sickness, accident, unemployment, and old-age benefits; and educational opportunities. Despite economic recessions in the mid-1970s and early 1980s, caused in part by dramatic increases in the price of oil, the economies of Western Europe had never been so prosperous, leading some observers to label the period a "golden age" of political and economic achievement. Western Europeans were full participants in the technological advances of the age and seemed quite capable of standing up to competition from the other global economic powerhouses, Japan and the United States.

A major challenge for Europe in the postwar era was to restore confidence in the democratic institutions that had become the hallmark of advanced Western civilization during the nineteenth century. The Western democracies had been unable to confront the threat of fascism when the armies of the Wehrmacht began their march across Europe at the end of the 1930s, and most succumbed rapidly to the Nazi juggernaut. As the war came to a close, many Europeans, their confidence shaken by bleak prospects for the future, turned their eyes to the Soviet model. In France and Italy, local Communist parties received wide support in national elections, raising fears in the United States that they might eventually be voted into power in Paris and Rome.

By the late 1940s, however, confidence in democratic institutions began to revive as economic conditions started to improve. Even Spain and Portugal, which retained their prewar dictatorial regimes until the mid-1970s, established democratic systems in the late 1970s. Moderate political

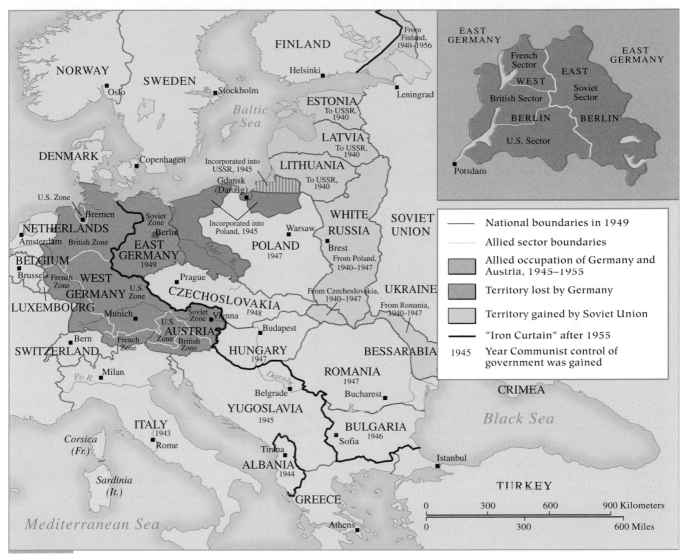

MAP 10.1 Territorial Changes in Europe After World War II. In the last months of World War II, the Red Army occupied much of Eastern Europe. Stalin sought pro-Soviet satellite states in the region as a buffer against future invasions from Western Europe, whereas Britain and the United States wanted democratically elected governments. Soviet military control of the territory settled the question. **?** Which country gained the greatest territory at the expense of Germany? 👁 **View an animated version of this map or related maps at the World History Resource Center, at** worldrc.wadsworth.com/.

parties, especially the Christian Democrats in Italy and Germany, played a particularly important role in Europe's economic restoration. Overall, the influence of Communist parties declined, although reformist mass parties only slightly left of center, such as the Labour Party in Britain and the Social Democrats in West Germany, continued to share power. During the mid-1970s, a new variety of communism, called Eurocommunism, emerged briefly when Communist parties tried to work within the democratic system as mass movements committed to better government. But by the 1980s, internal political developments in Western Europe

and events within the Communist world had combined to undermine the Eurocommunist experiment.

The Modern Welfare State: Three European Models

The European welfare state that began to take shape in the years following World War II represented a distinct effort to combine the social benefits provided by the reformist brand of social democracy (see Chapter 1) with the dynamic qualities of modern capitalism. The results varied from country to country, and not all political parties approved of the social democratic model. Eventually, though, virtually all the nations in Western Europe adopted some elements of the system, which differed sharply from the mostly laissez-faire capitalist model practiced in the United States.

France

The history of France for nearly a quarter century after the war was dominated by one man, Charles de Gaulle (1890–1970), who possessed an unshakable faith in his own historic mission to reestablish the greatness of the French nation. During the war, de Gaulle, then a colonel in the French army, had assumed leadership of resistance groups known as the "Free French," and he played an important role in ensuring the establishment of a French provisional government after the war. But immediately following the war, the creation of the Fourth Republic, with a return to a multiparty parliamentary system that de Gaulle considered inefficient, led him to withdraw temporarily from politics. Eventually, he formed the French Popular Movement, a political organization based on conservative principles that blamed the multiparty system for France's political mess and called for a stronger presidency, a goal—and role—that de Gaulle finally achieved in 1958.

Expectations of Grandeur At the time of his election as president, the fragile political stability of the Fourth Republic was shaken by a crisis in Algeria, France's large North African colony. The French army, having suffered a humiliating defeat in Indochina in 1954, was determined to resist demands for independence by Algeria's Muslim majority. Independence was also opposed by the large French community living in Algeria. But a strong antiwar movement among French intellectuals and church leaders led to bitter divisions in France that opened the door to the possibility of civil war. The panic-stricken leaders of the Fourth Republic offered to let de Gaulle take over the government and revise the constitution.

In 1958, de Gaulle drafted a new constitution for a Fifth Republic that greatly enhanced the power of the French president, who now had the right to choose the prime minister, dissolve parliament, and supervise both defense and foreign policy. As the new president, de Gaulle sought to return France to a position of power and influence. In the belief that an independent role in the Cold War might enhance France's stature, he pulled France out of the NATO (North Atlantic Treaty Organization) high command. He sought to increase French prestige in the Third World by consenting to Algerian independence despite strenuous opposition from the army and offered French colonies in Africa membership in a new French community of nations under French tutelage. France invested heavily in the nuclear arms race and exploded its first nuclear bomb in 1960. Despite his successes, however, de Gaulle did not really achieve his ambitious goals of world power.

Although the cost of the nuclear program increased the defense budget, de Gaulle did not neglect the French economy. Economic decision making was centralized, a reflection of the overall centralization undertaken by the Gaullist government. Between 1958 and 1968, the French gross national product (GNP) grew by 5.5 percent annually, faster than U.S. GNP. By the end of the Gaullist era, France was a major industrial producer and exporter, particularly in such areas as automobiles and armaments. Nevertheless, problems remained. The expansion of traditional industries, such as coal, and railroads, which had been nationalized, led to large government deficits. The cost of living increased faster than in the rest of Europe.

Shift to the Left Public dissatisfaction with the government's inability to deal with these problems soon led to more violent action. In May 1968, a series of student protests, provoked by conditions in the country's anachronistic educational system as well as the ongoing war in Vietnam, was followed by a general strike by the labor unions. Although de Gaulle managed to restore order, the events of May 1968 seriously undermined popular respect for the aloof and imperious president. Tired and discouraged, de Gaulle resigned from office in April 1969 and died within a year.

During the 1970s, the French economic situation worsened, bringing about a political shift to the left. By 1981, the Socialists had become the dominant party in the National Assembly, and the veteran Socialist leader, François Mitterrand (1916–1996), was elected president. Mitterrand's first concern was to resolve France's economic difficulties. In 1982, he froze prices and wages in the hope of reducing the huge budget deficit and high inflation. Mitterrand also passed a number of measures to aid workers: an increased minimum wage, expanded social benefits, a mandatory fifth week of paid vacation for salaried workers, a thirty-nine-hour workweek, and higher taxes for the rich. Mitterrand's administrative reforms included both centralization (nationalization of banks and industry) and decentralization (granting local governments greater powers). Their victory also convinced the Socialists that they could enact some of their more radical reforms. Consequently, the government nationalized the steel industry, major banks, the space and electronics industries, and important insurance firms.

A Season of Discontent The policies adopted during the early 1980s by the Socialist majority under President Mitterrand failed to work, however, and within three years the Mitterrand government returned some of the economy to private enterprise. Mitterrand was able to win a second seven-year term in the 1988 presidential election, but France's economic decline continued. In 1993, French unemployment stood at 10.6 percent, and in the elections in March of that year, the Socialists won only 28 percent of the vote while a coalition of conservative parties won 80 percent of the seats in the National Assembly. The move to the right was strengthened when the conservative mayor of Paris, Jacques Chirac, was elected president in May 1995. The center-right government remained in power as the new century opened.

By now, resentment against foreign-born residents had become a growing political reality. Spurred by rising rates of unemployment and large numbers of immigrants from North Africa (often identified in the public mind with terrorist actions committed by militant groups based in the Middle East), many French voters gave their support to Jean-Marie Le Pen's National Front, which openly advocated restrictions on all new immigration and limited assimilation of immigrants already living in France.

In the fall of 2005, however, antiforeign sentiment provoked a backlash of its own, as young Muslims in the crowded suburbs of Paris rioted against dismal living conditions and the lack of employment opportunities for foreign residents in France. After the riots subsided, government officials promised to adopt measures to respond to the complaints, but tensions between the Muslim community and the remainder of the French population have become a chronic source of social unrest throughout the country.

West Germany

The unification of the three Western zones into the Federal Republic of Germany (West Germany) became a reality in 1949. Konrad Adenauer (1876–1967), the leader of the Christian Democratic Union (CDU), served as chancellor from 1949 to 1963 and became the "founding hero" of the FRG. Adenauer, who had opposed Hitler's regime, sought respect for Germany by cooperating with the United States and the other Western European nations. He was especially desirous of reconciliation with France—Germany's longtime rival. The beginning of the Korean War in June 1950 had unexpected repercussions for West Germany. The fear that South Korea might fall to the Communists led many in the West to worry about the security of West Germany and inspired calls for German rearmament. Although some people, concerned about a revival of German militarism, condemned this proposal, Cold War tensions were decisive. West Germany rearmed in 1955 and became a member of NATO.

The Economic Miracle The Adenauer era witnessed a resurrection of the West German economy that was so remarkable it earned a reputation as the "economic miracle."

Clash of Civilizations? In the late fall of 2005, violent youth riots suddenly erupted in the primarily Muslim suburbs of more than 300 cities and towns across France, leaving a trail of shattered shopwindows and burned automobiles in their wake. The outbreak served to highlight the growing difficulties of assimilating the country's five million Muslims—many of whom are faced with limited employment opportunities and institutionalized racism—into French society.

Although West Germany had only 75 percent of the population and 52 percent of the territory of prewar Germany, by 1955 the West German GNP exceeded that of prewar Germany. Real wages doubled between 1950 and 1965, even though working hours were cut by 20 percent. Unemployment fell from 8 percent in 1950 to 0.4 percent in 1965. To maintain its economic expansion, West Germany imported hundreds of thousands of "guest" workers, primarily from Italy, Spain, Greece, Turkey, and Yugoslavia.

The Federal Republic had established its capital at Bonn, a sleepy market town on the Rhine River, to erase memories of the Nazi era, when the capital was at Berlin. Still, the country was troubled by its past. The surviving major Nazi leaders had been tried and condemned as war criminals at the Nuremberg war crimes trials in 1945 and 1946. As part of the denazification of Germany, the victorious Allies continued to try lesser officials for war crimes, but these trials diminished in number as the Cold War produced a shift in attitudes. By 1950, German courts had begun to take over the war crimes trials, and the German legal machine persisted in prosecuting cases. Beginning in 1953, the West German government also began to make payments to Israel and to Holocaust survivors and their relatives to make some restitution for, in the words of German president Richard von Weizsäcker, "the unspeakable sorrow that occurred in the name of Germany."

Willy Brandt and *Ostpolitik* After the Adenauer era ended in the mid-1960s, the Social Democrats became the leading party. By forming a ruling coalition with the small Free Democratic Party, the Social Democrats remained in power until 1982. The first Social Democratic chancellor was Willy Brandt (1913–1992). Brandt was especially successful with his "opening toward the east" (known as *Ostpolitik*), for which he received the Nobel Peace Prize in 1972. On March 19, 1971, Brandt met with Walter Ulbricht, the leader of East Germany, and worked out the details of a treaty that was signed in 1972. This agreement did not establish full diplomatic relations with East Germany but did call for "good neighborly" relations. As a result, it led to greater cultural, personal, and economic contacts between West and East Germany. Despite this success, the discovery of an East German spy among Brandt's advisers caused his resignation in 1974.

His successor, Helmut Schmidt (b. 1918), was more of a technocrat than a reform-minded socialist and concentrated on the economic problems brought about largely by high oil prices between 1973 and 1975. Schmidt was successful in eliminating a deficit of 10 billion marks in three years. In 1982, when the coalition of Schmidt's Social Democrats with the Free Democrats fell apart over the reduction of social welfare expenditures, the Free Democrats joined with the Christian Democratic Union of Helmut Kohl (b. 1930) to form a new government.

Germany United: The Party's Over With the end of the Cold War, West Germany faced a new challenge. Chancellor Helmut Kohl had benefited greatly from an economic boom in the mid-1980s. Gradually, however, discontent with the Christian Democrats increased, and by 1988, their political prospects seemed diminished. But unexpectedly, the 1989 revolution in East Germany led to the reunification of the two Germanies (see Chapter 9), leaving the new Germany, with its 79 million people, the leading power in Europe. Reunification, accomplished during Kohl's administration, brought rich political dividends to the Christian Democrats. In the first all-German federal election, Kohl's Christian Democrats won 44 percent of the vote, and their coalition partners, the Free Democrats, received 11 percent.

But the euphoria over reunification soon dissipated as the realization set in that the revitalization of eastern Germany would take far more money than was originally thought, and Kohl's government was soon forced to face the politically undesirable task of raising taxes substantially. Moreover, the virtual collapse of the economy in eastern Germany led to extremely high levels of unemployment and severe discontent. One reason for the problem was the government's decision to establish a 1:1 ratio between the East and West German marks. This policy raised salaries for East German workers, but it increased labor costs and provoked many companies into hiring workers abroad.

Increasing unemployment in turn led to growing resentment against foreigners. For years, foreigners seeking asylum or employment found haven in Germany because of its extremely liberal immigration laws. In 1992, more than 440,000 immigrants came to Germany seeking asylum, 123,000 of them from former Yugoslavia alone. Attacks against foreigners by right-wing extremists—many of them espousing neo-Nazi beliefs—killed seventeen people in 1992 and became an all too frequent occurrence in German life.

East Germans were also haunted by another memory from their recent past. The opening of the files of the secret police (the *Stasi*) showed that millions of East Germans had spied on their neighbors and colleagues, and even their spouses and parents, during the Communist era. A few senior *Stasi* officials were put on trial for their past actions, but many Germans preferred simply to close the door on an unhappy period in their lives.

As the century neared its close, then, Germans struggled to cope with the challenge of building a new, united

© BPA Bernd Kühler/dpa/CORBIS

Berlin Reunited. Few cities in Europe have been so transformed since the end of World War II as Berlin, once the nerve center of Hitler's Third Reich. Long divided from its hinterland by the Cold War, since 1991 it has once again become the capital of a united Germany and is returning to its traditional role as one of the great cities of modern Europe.

nation. To reduce the debt incurred because of economic reconstruction in the east, the government threatened to cut back on many of the social benefits West Germans had long been accustomed to receiving. This in turn sharpened resentments that were already beginning to emerge between the two zones. Although the Berlin Wall had been removed, the gap between East and West remained (see box on p. 000). In 1998, voters took out their frustations at the ballot box. Helmut Kohl's conservative coalition was defeated in national elections, and a new prime minister, Social Democrat Gerhard Schröder, came into office. Schröder had no better luck than his predecessor at reviving the economy, however. In 2003, with nearly five million workers unemployed, the government announced plans to scale back welfare benefits that had long been a familiar part of life for the German people. In 2005, national elections brought the Christian Democrats back into power under the leadership of Germany's first woman chancellor, Angela Merkel (b. 1954).

Great Britain

The end of World War II left Britain with massive economic problems. In elections held immediately after the war, the Labour Party overwhelmingly defeated Churchill's Conservative Party. The Labour Party had promised far-reaching reforms, particularly in the area of social welfare—an appealing platform in a country with a tremendous shortage of consumer goods and housing. Clement Atlee (1883–1967), the new prime minister, was a pragmatic reformer rather than the leftist revolutionary that Churchill had warned against during the election campaign.

THE GREAT WALL OF GERMANY

*C*he unification of the two Germanys after the fall of
the Berlin Wall was widely hailed as a symbol of the
end of the Cold War in Europe. It even inspired fear among
many Europeans living in neighboring countries as the harbinger of the rise of a new and more powerful Germany. In fact,
unification has given birth to a number of major political,
economic, and social problems. Although the new Germany
is administratively united, it remains divided in culture and
outlook, as the following article suggests.

*What possible reasons might explain the difficulties experi-
enced by the former East Germany in overcoming the challenge of reunification?*

Remembrance of Things Past

There's a widespread feeling among East Germans that
something new should have emerged out of unification,
combining the best of both worlds.

"We suddenly saw that there is a different mentality,
even a different language in some areas," says Western
psychologist Uwe Wetter, "a different tradition, and cultural
differences all around. But we tried to address these differences by giving our knowledge—what we thought was the
best—to the Easterners. We thought that would be the way
to handle the situation."

Many Easterners have not been able to reestablish the
sense of identity. They pine for what they regard to be the
sunny side of the former East German state: a sense of
belonging, and a cozy feeling that they were being taken
care of by the system. Some former East Germans continue
to gather at frequently held nostalgia parties.

Stefan Winkler, from the eastern part of Berlin, is one of
them: "I have mixed emotions about these nostalgia parties.
I still have a GDR flag. I don't think it's for nostalgia reasons;
it's more of a political statement. I think people tend to forget
about the bad things after a while and only remember the
good. There were a couple of really good things in East
Germany. A lot of [East Germans] feel quite unsafe at the
moment. Not only because they lost their jobs. It's also
because many lost their identity—and that's where their
nostalgia comes in."

(Hardy Graupner, *Deutsche Welle* [independent world
radio], Cologne, November 1999.)

SOURCE: *World Press Review,* January 2000, p. 9.

His Labour government proceeded to enact reforms that
created a modern welfare state.

The establishment of the British welfare state began
with the nationalization of the Bank of England, the coal
and steel industries, public transportation, and public utilities such as electricity and gas. In the area of social welfare,
the new government enacted the National Insurance Act
and the National Health Service Act, both in 1946. The
insurance act established a comprehensive social security
program and nationalized medical insurance, thereby
enabling the state to subsidize the unemployed, the sick, and
the aged. The health act created a system of socialized medicine that forced doctors and dentists to work with state
hospitals, although private practices could be maintained.
This measure was especially costly for the state, but within
a few years, 90 percent of the medical profession was par-
ticipating. The British welfare state became the model for
most European countries after the war.

Sunset for the Empire The cost of building a welfare state
at home forced the British to reduce expenses abroad. This
meant dismantling the British Empire and reducing military
aid to such countries as Greece and Turkey, a decision that
inspired the enunciation in Washington of the Truman
Doctrine (see Chapter 7). Economic necessity, and not just
a belief in the morality of self-determination, brought an
end to the British Empire.

Continuing economic problems brought the Conservatives back into power from 1951 to 1964. Although they
favored private enterprise, the Conservatives accepted the
welfare state and even extended it, undertaking an ambitious
construction program to improve British housing. Although
the British economy had recovered from the war, it had done
so at a slower rate than other European countries. This slow
recovery masked a long-term economic decline caused by
a variety of factors, including trade union demands for wages
that rose faster than productivity and the unwillingness of
factory owners to invest in modern industrial machinery and
to adopt new methods. Underlying the immediate problems,
however, was a deeper issue. As a result of World War II,
Britain had lost much of its prewar revenue from abroad but
was left with a burden of debt from its many international
commitments. At the same time, with the rise of the United
States and the Soviet Union, Britain's ability to play the role
of a world power declined substantially.

Between 1964 and 1979, Conservatives and Labour
alternated in power. Both parties faced seemingly
intractable problems. Although separatist movements in
Scotland and Wales were overcome, a dispute between
Catholics and Protestants in Northern Ireland was marked

by violence as the rebel Irish Republican Army (IRA) staged a series of dramatic terrorist acts in response to the suspension of Northern Ireland's parliament in 1972 and the establishment of direct rule by London. The problem of Northern Ireland remained unresolved. Nor was either party able to deal with Britain's ailing economy. Failure to modernize made British industry less and less competitive. Britain was also hampered by frequent labor strikes, many of them caused by conflicts between rival labor unions.

"Thatcherism": The Conservatives in Ascendance

In 1979, after five years of Labour government and worsening economic problems, the Conservatives returned to power under Margaret Thatcher (b. 1925), the first woman prime minister in British history. Thatcher pledged to lower taxes, reduce government bureaucracy, limit social welfare, restrict union power, and end inflation. The "Iron Lady," as she was called, did break the power of the labor unions. Although she did not eliminate the basic components of the social welfare system, she did use austerity measures to control inflation. "Thatcherism," as her economic policy was termed, improved the British economic situation, but at a price. The south of England, for example, prospered, but the old industrial areas of the Midlands and north declined and were beset by high unemployment, poverty, and sporadic violence. Cutbacks in funding for education seriously undermined the quality of British schools, long regarded as among the world's finest.

In foreign policy, Thatcher took a hard-line approach against communism. She oversaw a large military buildup aimed at replacing older technology and reestablishing Britain as a world policeman. In 1982, when Argentina attempted to take control of the Falkland Islands (one of Britain's few remaining colonial outposts, known to Argentines as the Malvinas) 300 miles off its coast, the British successfully rebuffed the Argentines, although at considerable economic cost and the loss of 255 lives. The Falklands War, however, did generate popular support for Thatcher, as many in Britain reveled in memories of the nation's glorious imperial past.

The Era of Tony Blair

While Thatcher dominated politics in the 1980s, the Labour Party, beset by divisions between its moderate and radical wings, offered little effective opposition. Only in 1990 did Labour's fortunes seem to revive when Thatcher's government attempted to replace local property taxes with a flat-rate tax payable by every adult to his or her local authority. Although Thatcher argued that this would make local government more responsive to popular needs, many argued that this was nothing more than a poll tax that would enable the rich to pay the same rate as the poor. After antitax riots broke out, Thatcher's once legendary popularity plummeted to an all-time low. At the end of November, a revolt within her own party caused Thatcher to resign as prime minister. Her replacement was John Major, whose Conservative Party won a narrow victory in the general elections held in April 1992. But Major's lackluster leadership failed to capture the imagination of many Britons, and in new elections in May 1997, the Labour Party won a landslide victory. The new prime minister, Tony Blair, was a moderate whose youth and energy immediately instilled a new vigor into the political scene. Adopting centrist policies reminiscent of those followed by President Bill Clinton in the United States (see Chapter 8), his party dominated the political arena into the new century. Blair's decision to support the U.S.-led invasion of Iraq in 2003 was not popular with the British public, but the failure of the opposition Conservative Party to field a popular candidate kept him in power for nearly a decade.

Western Europe: The Search for Unity

As we have seen, the divisions created by the Cold War led the nations of Western Europe to form the North Atlantic Treaty Organization in 1949. But military cooperation was not the only kind of unity fostered in Europe after 1945. The destructiveness of two world wars caused many thoughtful Europeans to consider the need for additional forms of integration. National feeling was still too powerful, however, for European nations to give up their political sovereignty. Consequently, the quest for unity initially focused primarily on the economic arena rather than the political one.

The Curtain Rises: The Creation of the Common Market

In 1951, France, West Germany, the Benelux countries (Belgium, the Netherlands, and Luxembourg), and Italy formed the European Coal and Steel Community (ECSC). Its purpose was to create a common market for coal and steel products among the six nations by eliminating tariffs and other trade barriers. The success of the ECSC encouraged its members to proceed further, and in 1957, they created the European Atomic Energy Community (EURATOM) to further European research on the peaceful uses of nuclear energy.

In the same year, the same six nations signed the Rome Treaty, which created the European Economic Community (EEC), also known as the Common Market. The EEC eliminated customs barriers among the six member nations and created a large free-trade area protected from the rest of the world by a common external tariff. By promoting free trade, the EEC also encouraged cooperation and standardization in many aspects of the six nations' economies. All the member nations benefited economically.

Europeans moved toward further integration of their economies after 1970. The European Economic Community

Toward a United Europe

n December 1991, the nations of Europe took a significant step on the road to unity when they drafted the Treaty of Maastricht, which created the structure for a new European Union. The new organization, which represented a significant step beyond the forms of economic cooperation that had previously existed, envisaged integration in the fields of foreign and security policies and cooperation in the areas of justice and domestic affairs. In the years since the passing of the treaty, the European Union has successfully established a common currency—the euro—but resolving many of the other obstacles to unity has proved to be a severe challenge. Some of the key provisions of the treaty are presented here.

What are the key provisions of the Treaty of Maastricht? How do they appear to infringe on traditional standards of national sovereignty?

The Treaty of Maastricht

Article A

By this Treaty, the High Contracting Parties establish among themselves a European Union, hereinafter called "the Union."

This Treaty marks a new stage in the process of creating an ever closer union among the peoples of Europe, in which decisions are taken as closely as possible to the citizen.

The Union shall be founded on the European Communities, supplemented by the policies and forms of cooperation established by this Treaty. Its task shall be to organize, in a manner demonstrating consistency and solidarity, relations between the Member States and between their peoples.

Article B

The Union shall set itself the following objectives:
- to promote economic and social progress which is balanced and sustainable, in particular through

the creation of an area without internal frontiers, through the strengthening of economic and social cohesion and through the establishment of economic and monetary union, ultimately including a single currency in accordance with the provisions of this Treaty;
- to assert its identity on the international scene, in particular through the implementation of a common foreign and security policy including the eventual framing of a common defence policy, which might in time lead to a common defence;
- to strengthen the protection of the rights and interests of the nationals of its Member States through the introduction of a citizenship of the Union;
- to develop close cooperation on justice and home affairs. . . .

Article F

1. The Union shall respect the national identities of its Member States, whose systems of government are founded on the principles of democracy.
2. The Union shall respect fundamental rights, as guaranteed by the European Convention for the Protection of Human Rights and Fundamental Freedoms signed in Rome on 4 November 1950 and as they result from the constitutional traditions common to the Member States, as general principles of Community law.
3. The Union shall provide itself with the means necessary to attain its objectives and carry through its policies.

SOURCE: http://europa.eu.int/en/record/mt/title1.html.

expanded in 1973 when Great Britain, Ireland, and Denmark gained membership in what its members now began to call the European Community (EC). By 1986, three more members—Spain, Portugal, and Greece—had been added. The economic integration of the members of the EC led to cooperative efforts in international and political affairs as well. The foreign ministers of the twelve members consulted frequently and provided a common front in negotiations on important issues.

The European Union

By 1992, the EC included nearly 350 million people and constituted the world's largest single trading bloc, transacting

almost one-quarter of the world's commerce. In the early 1990s, EC members drafted the Treaty on European Union (known as the Maastricht Treaty, after the city in the Netherlands where the agreement was reached), seeking to create a true economic and monetary union of all members of the organization (see the box above). The treaty would not take effect, however, until all members agreed. On January 1, 1994, the European Community became the European Union (EU).

One of its first goals was to introduce a common currency, called the euro. But problems soon arose. Voters in many countries opposed the austerity measures that their governments would be compelled to take to reduce growing budget deficits. Germans in particular feared that replacing the rock-solid mark with a common European currency could lead to economic disaster. Yet the logic of the new union appeared inescapable if European nations were to improve their capacity to compete with the United States and the powerful industrializing nations of the Pacific Rim.

The Fall of the Iron Curtain

The fall of Communist governments in Eastern Europe during the revolutions of 1989 brought a wave of euphoria to Europe. The new structures meant an end to a postwar European order that had been imposed on unwilling peoples by the victorious forces of the Soviet Union. In 1989 and 1990, new governments throughout Eastern Europe worked diligently to scrap the remnants of the old system and introduce the democratic procedures and market systems they believed would revitalize their scarred lands (see Chapter 9). But this process proved to be neither simple nor easy.

Most Eastern European countries had little or no experience with democratic systems. Then, too, ethnic divisions, which had troubled these areas before World War II and had been forcibly submerged under Communist rule, reemerged with a vengeance. Finally, the rapid conversion to market economies also proved painful. The adoption of "shock therapy" austerity measures produced much suffering. Unemployment, for example, climbed to over 13 percent in Poland in 1992.

Nevertheless, by the beginning of the twenty-first century, many of these states were making a successful transition to both free markets and democracy. In Poland, Aleksander Kwasniewski, although a former Communist, was elected president in November 1995 and pushed Poland toward an increasingly prosperous free market economy. His success brought his reelection in October 2000. In Czechoslovakia, the shift to non-Communist rule was complicated by old problems, especially ethnic issues. Czechs and Slovaks disagreed over the makeup of the new state but were able to agree to a peaceful division of the country. On January 1, 1993, Czechoslovakia split into the Czech Republic and Slovakia (see Map 10.2 on p. 210). Václav Havel was elected the first president of the new Czech Republic.

The Disintegration of Yugoslavia The most difficult transition to the post–Cold War era in Eastern Europe was undoubtedly in Yugoslavia. From its beginning in 1919, Yugoslavia had been an artificial creation. After World War II, the dictatorial Marshal Tito had managed to hold its six republics and two autonomous provinces together. After his death in 1980, no strong leader emerged, and his responsibilities passed to a collective state presidency and the League of Communists of Yugoslavia. At the end of the 1980s, Yugoslavia was caught up in the reform movements

sweeping through Eastern Europe. The League of Communists collapsed, and new parties quickly emerged.

The Yugoslav political scene was complicated by the development of separatist movements. In 1990, the republics of Slovenia, Croatia, Bosnia-Herzegovina, and Macedonia began to lobby for a new federal structure of Yugoslavia that would fulfill their separatist desires. Slobodan Milošević (1941–2006), who had become the leader of the Serbian Communist Party in 1987 and had managed to stay in power by emphasizing his Serbian nationalism, rejected these efforts. He asserted that these republics could be independent only if new border arrangements were made to accommodate the Serb minorities in the republics who did not want to live outside the boundaries of Serbia. Serbs constituted about 12 percent of Croatia's population and 32 percent of Bosnia's.

After negotiations among the six republics failed, Slovenia and Croatia declared their independence in June 1991. Milošević's government sent the Yugoslavian army, which it controlled, into Slovenia, without much success. In September 1991, it began a full assault against Croatia. Increasingly, the Yugoslavian army was becoming the Serbian army, while Serbian irregular forces played a growing role in military operations. Before a cease-fire was arranged, the Serbian forces had captured one-third of Croatia's territory in brutal and destructive fighting.

The recognition of Slovenia, Croatia, and Bosnia-Herzegovina by many European states and the United States early in 1992 did not stop the Serbs from turning their guns on Bosnia. By mid-1993, Serbian forces had acquired 70 percent of Bosnian territory. The Serbian policy of "ethnic cleansing"—killing or forcibly removing Bosnian Muslims from their lands—revived memories of Nazi atrocities in World War II. Nevertheless, despite worldwide outrage, European governments failed to take a decisive and forceful stand against these Serbian activities, and by the spring of 1993, the Muslim population of Bosnia was in desperate straits. As the fighting spread, European nations and the United States began to intervene to stop the bloodshed, and in the fall of 1995, a fragile cease-fire agreement was reached at a conference held in Dayton, Ohio. An international peacekeeping force was stationed in the area to maintain tranquillity and monitor the accords.

Peace in Bosnia, however, did not bring peace to Yugoslavia. A new war erupted in 1999 over Kosovo, which had been made an autonomous province within Yugoslavia by Tito in 1974. Kosovo's inhabitants were mainly ethnic Albanians. But the province was also home to a Serbian minority that considered it sacred territory where Serbian forces in the fourteenth century had been defeated by the Ottoman Turks.

In 1989, Yugoslav President Milošević stripped Kosovo of its autonomous status and outlawed any official use

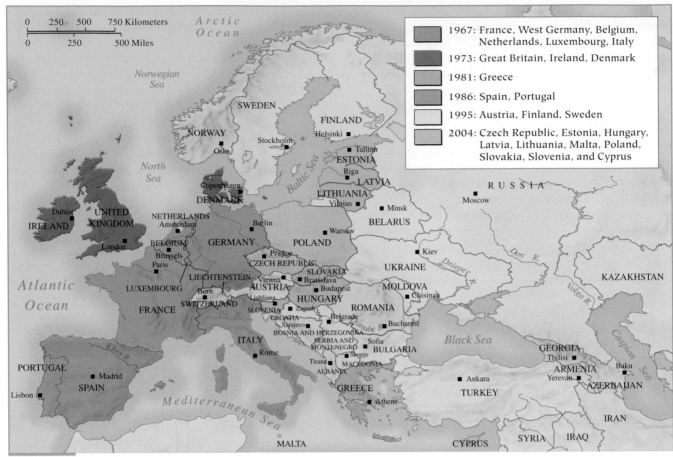

MAP 10.2 **European Union, 2004.** Beginning in 1957 as the European Economic Community, also known as the Common Market, the union of European states seeking to integrate their economies has gradually grown from six members to twenty-five in 2004. The European Union has achieved two major goals—the creation of a single internal market and a common currency—although it has been less successful at working toward common political and foreign policy goals. ❓ What additional nations do you think will join the European Union? Why? 🖰 **View an animated version of this map or related maps at the World History Resource Center, at** worldrc.wadsworth.com/.

of the Albanian language. In 1993, some groups of ethnic Albanians founded the Kosovo Liberation Army (KLA) and began a campaign against Serbian rule in Kosovo. When Serb forces began to massacre ethnic Albanians in an effort to crush the KLA, the United States and its NATO allies sought to arrange a settlement. When Milošević refused to sign the agreement, the United States and its NATO allies began a bombing campaign that forced the Yugoslavian government into compliance. In the fall elections of 2000, Milošević himself was ousted from power and was later put on trial by an international tribunal for war crimes against humanity for his ethnic cleansing policies throughout the disintegration of Yugoslavia, which has recently changed its name to Serbia and Montenegro.

Europe Reunited

On January 1, 2002, twelve members of the European Union (including all of the major European states except Great Britain) abandoned their national currencies in favor of the euro. The move hastened the transition of the EU into a single economic entity capable of competing in world markets with the United States and major Asian nations.

In the meantime, plans got under way to extend the EU into Eastern Europe, where several nations were just emerging from decades of domination by the Soviet Union. In December 2002, the EU voted to add ten new members, including Poland, the Baltic states, Hungary, Slovakia, and the Czech Republic, which joined the organization in 2004 (see Map 10.2). Yet not all are convinced that European integration is a good thing. Eastern Europeans fear that their countries will be dominated by investment from their prosperous neighbors, while their counterparts in Western Europe express concerns at a possible influx of low-wage workers from the new member countries. All in all, a true sense of a unified Europe is still lacking among the population throughout the region, and the rising wave of antiforeign sentiment and anger at government belt tightening are issues that will not go away in the near future.

The growing antiforeign sentiment in Europe has had an additional impact in the reaction to Turkey's application to join the EU. Although the Turkish government has sought to assuage European criticisms of its record in the area of human rights (notably in the treatment of its Kurdish minority), many Europeans remain uneasy about the prospect of admitting an Islamic nation of more than 70 million people into an organization of predominantly Christian nations already facing serious concerns over their growing Muslim minorities. The proposal is currently under consideration, but Turkey's admission is by no means assured. In the meantime, popular anger over Turkey's application and a variety of other issues has undermined the transition to a more unified Europe. In 2005, voters in several EU countries rejected the draft of a new constitution that would have strengthened the political and economic integration of the nations within the EU.

Meanwhile, the NATO alliance continues to serve as a powerful force for European unity. Yet it too faces new challenges as Moscow's former satellites in Eastern Europe clamor for membership in the hope that it will spur economic growth and reduce the threat from a revival of Russian expansionism. In 1999, the Czech Republic, Hungary, and Poland joined the alliance, and the Baltic states have expressed an interest in doing so in the future. Some observers express concern, however, that an expanded NATO will not only reduce the cohesiveness of the organization but also provoke Russia into a new posture of hostility to the outside world. There is also some disagreement between the United States and some European members over the use of NATO forces in other parts of the world, such as the Middle East.

Aspects of Society in Postwar Europe

Socially, intellectually, and culturally, Western Europe changed significantly during the second half of the twentieth century. Although many trends represented a continuation of prewar developments, in other cases the changes were quite dramatic, leading some observers in the 1980s to begin speaking of the gradual emergence of a postmodern age.

An Age of Affluence

In the decades following the end of World War II, Western Europe witnessed remarkably rapid change. Such products of new technologies as computers, television, jet planes, contraceptive devices, and new surgical techniques all dramatically and quickly altered the pace and nature of human life. Called variously a technocratic society, an affluent society, or the consumer society, postwar Europe was characterized by changing social values and new attitudes toward the meaning of the human experience.

The structure of European society was also altered in major respects after 1945. Especially noticeable were changes in the nature of the middle class. Traditional occupations such as merchants and the professions (law, medicine, and the universities) were greatly augmented by a new group of managers and technicians, as large companies and government agencies employed increasing numbers of white-collar supervisory and administrative personnel. In most cases, success depended on specialized knowledge acquired from some form of higher education. Since their jobs usually depended on their skills, these individuals took steps to ensure that their children would be similarly educated.

Changes occurred in other areas as well. Especially noticeable was the dramatic shift from the countryside to the cities. The number of people in agriculture declined by 50 percent. Yet the industrial working class did not expand. In West Germany, industrial workers made up 48 percent of the labor force throughout the 1950s and 1960s. Thereafter, the number of industrial workers began to dwindle as the number of white-collar service employees increased. At the same time, a substantial increase in their real wages enabled the working classes to aspire to the consumption patterns of the middle class. Buying on the installment plan, introduced in the 1930s, became widespread in the 1950s and gave workers a chance to imitate the middle class by buying such products as televisions, washing machines, refrigerators, vacuum cleaners, and stereos. But the most visible symbol of mass consumerism was the automobile. Before World War II, cars were reserved mostly for the upper classes. In 1948, there were 5 million cars in all of Europe, but by 1957, the number had tripled. By the mid-1960s, there were almost 45 million cars.

Rising incomes, combined with shorter working hours, created an even greater market for mass leisure activities. Between 1900 and 1980, the workweek was reduced from sixty hours to about forty hours (or even less in some countries), and the number of paid holidays increased. All aspects of popular culture—music, sports, media—became commercialized and offered opportunities for leisure activities, including concerts, sporting events, and television viewing.

Another very visible symbol of mass leisure was the growth of tourism. Before World War II, most persons who traveled for pleasure were from the upper and middle classes. After the war, the combination of more vacation time, increased prosperity, and the flexibility provided by package tours with their lower rates and low-budget rooms enabled millions to expand their travel possibilities. By the mid-1960s, some 100 million tourists were crossing European borders each year.

The Youth Revolution Social change was also evident in new educational patterns. Before World War II, higher education was largely the preserve of Europe's wealthier classes. Even in 1950, only 3 or 4 percent of Western European young people were enrolled in a university. European higher education remained largely centered on the liberal arts, pure science, and preparation for the professions of law and medicine.

Much of this changed in the 1950s and 1960s. European states began to foster greater equality of opportunity in higher education by eliminating fees, and universities experienced an influx of students from the middle and lower classes. Enrollments grew dramatically. In France, 4.5 percent of young people went to a university in 1950; by 1965, the figure had increased to 14.5 percent. Enrollments in European universities more than tripled between 1940 and 1960.

With growth came problems. Overcrowded classrooms, unapproachable professors, and authoritarian administrators aroused student resentment. In addition, despite changes in the curriculum, students often felt that the universities were not providing an education relevant to the modern age. This discontent led to an outburst of student revolts in the late 1960s. In part, these protests were an extension of the disruptions in American universities in the mid-1960s, which were often sparked by student opposition to the Vietnam War. Protesters also criticized other aspects of Western society, such as its materialism, and expressed concern about becoming cogs in the large and impersonal bureaucratic jungles of the modern world.

The most famous student revolt occurred in France in 1968. It erupted at the University of Nanterre outside Paris but soon spread to the Sorbonne, the main campus of the University of Paris. French students demanded a greater voice in the administration of the university, took over buildings, and then expanded the scale of their protests by inviting workers to support them. Half of France's workforce went on strike in May 1968. After the Gaullist government instituted a hefty wage hike, the workers returned to work, and the police repressed the remaining student protesters.

One source of anger among the student revolutionaries of the late 1960s was the lingering influence of traditional institutions and values. World War I had seen the first significant crack in the rigid code of manners and morals of the nineteenth century. The 1920s had witnessed experimentation with drugs, the appearance of hard-core pornography, and a new sexual freedom. But these changes appeared mostly in major cities and touched only small numbers of people. After World War II, they were more extensive and far more noticeable.

Sweden took the lead in the so-called sexual revolution of the 1960s, but the rest of Europe soon followed. Sex education in the schools and the decriminalization of homosexuality were but two aspects of Sweden's liberal legislation. Introduction of the birth control pill, which became widely available by the mid-1960s, gave people more freedom in sexual behavior. Meanwhile, sexually explicit movies, plays, and books broke new ground in the treatment of once-hidden subjects.

The new standards were evident in the breakdown of the traditional family. Divorce rates increased dramatically, especially in the 1960s, while premarital and extramarital sexual experiences also rose substantially. The 1960s also saw the emergence of a drug culture. Marijuana use was widespread among college and university students, and Timothy Leary, a professor who had done research at Harvard on the effects of LSD (lysergic acid diethylamide), promulgated the purported "mind-expanding" effects of hallucinogenics.

Rethinking the Welfare State The slowdown in the European economy at the end of the twentieth century, combined with the changing social fabric, has begun to erode the region's long-standing commitment to the concept of the welfare state. Aging populations, high unemployment rates, and heavy outlays for social programs have compelled some European governments—notably, France and Germany—to consider reducing some of the vaunted social benefits that their citizens view as a birthright. Measures designed to raise taxes, increase the number of working hours, and reduce pension and health benefits have run into strong popular resistance, however, and have led, in some cases, to a change in governments.

Expanding Roles for Women

Another area that saw significant change in postwar European society was the role of women. Although women were found in professional careers and a number of other vocations in the 1920s and 1930s, the place for most women was still in the home. Half a century later, there were almost as many women as men in the workplace, many of them employed in professions hitherto reserved for men.

One consequence of the trend toward greater employment outside the home for women was a drop in the birthrate. The percentage of married women in the female labor force in Sweden, for example, increased from 47 to 66 percent between 1963 and 1975. In many European countries, zero population growth was reached in the 1960s, and increases since then have been due solely to immigration. In Italy and Spain, the flood of women into the workplace resulted in a dramatic reduction in the number of children born annually, leading to fears of an absolute decline in total population. In newly united Germany, it has been estimated that nearly half a million immigrants will be required annually to maintain the current level of economic growth.

But the increased number of women in the workforce has not changed some old patterns. Working-class women in particular still earn salaries lower than those paid to men for equal work. Women still tend to enter traditionally female jobs. A 1980 study of twenty-five European nations revealed that women still made up more than 80 percent of typists, nurses, tailors, and dressmakers in those countries. Many European women also still face the double burden of earning income on the one hand and raising a family and maintaining the household on the other. Such inequalities have led increasing numbers of women to rebel against their conditions.

The participation of women in World Wars I and II helped them achieve one of the major aims of the nineteenth-century feminist movement—the right to vote. After World War I, governments in many countries—Sweden, Great Britain, Germany, Poland, Hungary, Austria, and Czechoslovakia—acknowledged the contributions of women to the war effort by granting them the vote. Women in France and Italy finally gained the right to vote in 1945.

After World War II, European women tended to fall back into the traditional roles expected of them, and little was heard of feminist concerns. But with the student upheavals of the late 1960s came a renewed interest in feminism, or the women's liberation movement, as it was now called. Increasingly, women protested that the acquisition of political and legal equality had not brought true equality with men.

A leading role in the movement was played by French writer Simone de Beauvoir (1908–1986). Born into a middle-class Catholic family and educated at the Sorbonne in Paris, she joined the existentialist movement, which was the leading intellectual movement of its time in Western Europe, and became active in political causes. In 1949, she published *The Second Sex,* in which she argued that living in male-dominated societies, women had been defined by their differences from men and consequently received second-class status. "What particularly signalizes the situation of woman is that she—a free autonomous being like all human creatures—nevertheless finds herself in a world where men compel her to assume the status of the Other." De Beauvoir played an active role in the women's movement during the 1970s, and her book was a major influence on women in both Western Europe and the United States.

Feminists in Europe came to believe that women must transform the fundamental conditions of their lives. They did so in a variety of ways, forming numerous "consciousness-raising" groups to further awareness of women's issues and working to legalize both contraception and abortion. A French law passed in 1968 legalized the sale of contraceptive devices. In 1979, abortion became legal in France. Even in countries where the Catholic church remained strongly opposed to contraception and legalized abortion, legislation allowing them passed in the 1970s and 1980s.

The Environment and the Green Movements

Beginning in the 1970s, environmentalism became a serious item on the political agenda throughout the Western world. By that time, serious ecological problems had become all too apparent in the crowded countries of Western Europe. Air pollution, produced by nitrogen oxide and sulfur dioxide emissions from road vehicles, power plants, and industrial factories, was causing respiratory illnesses and having corrosive effects on buildings as well as on historical monuments such as the Parthenon in Athens. Many rivers, lakes, and seas had become so polluted that they posed serious health risks. Dying forests (such as the famous Black Forest in southern Germany) and disappearing wildlife alarmed more and more people.

Although the environmental movement first began to gain broad public attention in the United States, the problem was more serious in Europe, with its higher population density and high levels of industrial production in such countries as Great Britain and West Germany. The problem was compounded by the lack of antipollution controls in the industrial sectors of the Soviet satellite states to the east.

Growing ecological awareness gave rise to Green movements and Green parties throughout Europe in the 1970s. They came about in various ways. Some grew out of the antinuclear movement; others arose out of such causes as women's liberation and concern for foreign workers. Most started at the local level and then gradually extended their activities to the national level, where they became formally organized as political parties. Most visible was the Green Party in Germany, which was officially organized in 1979 and eventually elected forty-one delegates to the West German parliament, but Green parties also competed successfully in Sweden, Austria, and Switzerland.

As in the United States, however, the movement has been hindered by concerns that strict environmental regulations could sap economic growth and exacerbate unemployment. National rivalries and disagreements over how to deal with rising levels of pollution along international waterways such as the Rhine River have also impeded cooperation. Nevertheless, public alarm over potential effects of global warming has focused attention on the global character of environmental issues.

Aspects of Culture in Postwar Europe

During the German occupation of France, the French intellectual Jean-Paul Sartre (1905–1980) developed a philosophy of resistance and individual freedom called existentialism, whose fundamental premise was the absence of a god in the universe, thereby denying that humans had any preordained destiny. Humans were thus deprived of any absolute purpose or meaning, set adrift in an absurd world. Often reduced to despair and depression, the protagonists of Sartre's literary works were left with only one reason for hope—themselves, and their ability to voluntarily reach out and become involved in their community. In the early 1950s, Sartre became a devout Marxist, hitching his philosophy of freedom to one of political engagement to the Communist ideal.

One of Sartre's contemporaries, Albert Camus (1913–1960), greatly influenced generations of young people in the postwar era with writings that focused on the notion of the absurd. In his seminal novel, *The Stranger* (1942), the protagonist, having stumbled through a lethargic existence, realizes just before dying that regardless of the absurdity of life, humans still have the opportunity to embrace the joyful dimensions of experience—in his case, the warmth and splendor of the Algerian skies. Neither a political activist nor an ideologue, Camus broke with Sartre and other French leftists after the disclosure of the Stalinist atrocities in the Soviet gulags.

The existentialist worldview found expression in the Paris of the 1950s in the "theater of the absurd." One of its foremost proponents was the Irish dramatist Samuel Beckett (1906–1990), who lived in France. In his trailblazing play *Waiting for Godot* (1952), two nondescript men eagerly await the appearance of someone who never arrives. While they wait, they pass the time exchanging hopes and fears, with humor, courage, and touching friendship. This waiting represents the existential meaning of life, which is found in the daily activities and fellowship of the here and now, despite the absence of any absolute salvation for the human condition.

With the Soviet suppression of the Hungarian uprising in 1956, many Europeans became disenchanted with political systems of any kind and began to question the validity of reason, history, progress, and universal truths. In the late 1960s, the negation of prewar ideologies, now applied to all branches of learning, fused into a new doctrine of skepticism called deconstruction. Deconstruction cast doubt on all Western political and philosophical traditions, leaving a world in which human beings have lost their status as free agents dealing with universal verities and are reduced to empty vessels programmed by language and culture.

For deconstructionists, language was like quicksand, constantly moving, its intermittent layers hiding unlimited and opposing meanings. A word does not signify an objective meaning but rather is open to different associations by each speaker or listener. Consequently, a given text can never have one single meaning, since the intention of the author and the understanding of the reader will never be precisely the same. By denying any ultimate meaning to language, deconstruction thus negated the existence of any objective truth.

The philosophical skepticism reflected in this new approach quickly manifested itself in European literature as authors grappled with new ways to present reality in an uncertain and nonsensical world. Whereas the Modernists at the beginning of the century had celebrated the power of art to benefit humankind, placing their faith in the written word, much of the new "postmodern" literature reflected the lack of belief in anything, especially the written word.

Following in the footsteps of the Modernists, French authors in the 1960s experimented so radically with literary forms and language that they pushed fiction well beyond its traditional limits of rational understanding. In the "new novel," for example, authors like Alain Robbe-Grillet (b. 1922) and Nathalie Sarraute (1900–1999) delved deeply into stream-of-consciousness writing, literally abandoning the reader in the disorienting obsessions of the protagonist's unconscious mind.

Some authors, however, preferred to retrieve literary forms and values that Modernists had rejected, choosing to tell a "good" chronological story, to entertain as well as to deliver a moral message. Graham Greene (1904–1991) was one of Britain's more prolific, popular, and critically acclaimed authors of the century. He succeeded in combining psychological and moral depth with enthralling stories, often dealing with political conflicts set in exotic locales. A longtime critic of the United States, Greene forecast the American defeat in Vietnam in his 1955 novel *The Quiet American*. This and many of his other novels have been made into films.

Several other European authors have also combined a gripping tale and a fresh exciting narrative with seriousness

Glass Pyramid at the Louvre. The Louvre, residence of French kings since the sixteenth century and an art museum since the French Revolution, has traditionally represented classical symmetry and grandeur. In 1988, under the auspices of French President François Mitterrand, architect I. M. Pei added this imaginative and daring symmetrical pyramid of glass. It functions as an expedient entrance to the mammoth museum, while also allowing natural light to flood the lower floors. Its form incorporates the grandeur of Egypt with modernist simplicity.

of intent. In 1959, *The Tin Drum* by Gunter Grass (b. 1927) blasted German consciousness out of the complacency that had been induced by the country's postwar economic miracle. The novel reexamined Germany's infatuation with Hitler and warned German readers of the ever-present danger of repeating the evils of the past. Only recently, however, have German writers like Grass and W. C. Sebald (1944–2001), along with innumerable television documentaries, been examining the atrocities of the Nazi era. Germans are finally breaking their taboo of silence, which for long suppressed the memory of their own suffering during World War II, as well as the horrors inflicted on others.

In *The Cave* (2001), the Portuguese novelist José Saramago (b. 1922) focused on global issues, such as the erosion of individual cultures stemming from the tyranny of globalization, which, in his view, had not only led to the exploitation of poor countries but had also robbed the world's cultures of their uniqueness, thus reducing humankind to living in caves where communication is impossible and the only place of worship is the ubiquitous shopping mall. Like Grass, Saramago believed strongly in the Western humanist tradition and viewed authors as society's moral guardians and political mobilizers.

Addressing today's ethnic stew of intermarriage between Caribbean blacks, South Asians, and Caucasians, the British author Zadie Smith (b. 1975) explores the resulting amalgam of our globalized society in *White Teeth* (2000) and *On Beauty* (2005).

Since the end of World War II, serious music has witnessed a wide diversity of experimental movements, each searching for new tonal and rhythmic structures. Striving to go beyond Arnold Schoenberg's atonality, European composers in the 1950s set out to free their music from the traditional constraints of meter, form, and dynamics. Of special consideration are Frenchman Pierre Boulez (b. 1925) and German Karlheinz Stockhausen (b. 1928). They devised a new procedure called serialism, which is a mathematical ordering of musical components that, once set in motion, essentially writes itself automatically.

CONCLUSION

𝒟URING THE IMMEDIATE POSTWAR ERA, Western Europe emerged from the ashes of World War II and achieved a level of political stability and economic prosperity unprecedented in its long history. By the 1970s, European leaders were beginning to turn their attention to bringing about further political and economic unity among the nations in the region. With the signing of the Maastricht Treaty in 1994, a schedule had been established to put the dream into effect. But there have been some bumps along the way, as the pains of transition become more apparent and long-standing structural and cultural differences hinder the process of unification. A truly united Europe still remains a long way off.

TIMELINE

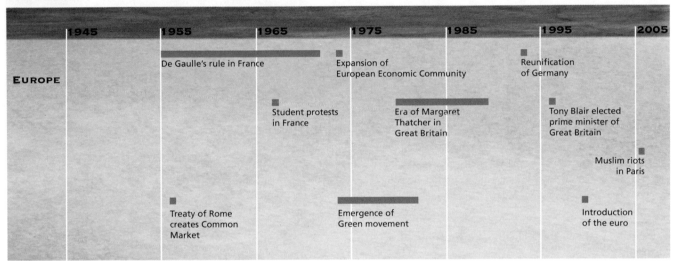

| | 1945 | 1955 | 1965 | 1975 | 1985 | 1995 | 2005 |

EUROPE

De Gaulle's rule in France

Expansion of European Economic Community

Reunification of Germany

Student protests in France

Era of Margaret Thatcher in Great Britain

Tony Blair elected prime minister of Great Britain

Muslim riots in Paris

Treaty of Rome creates Common Market

Emergence of Green movement

Introduction of the euro

11

THE EAST IS RED: CHINA UNDER COMMUNISM

"*A* REVOLUTION IS NOT A DINNER PARTY, or writing an essay, or painting a picture, or doing embroidery; it cannot be so refined, so leisurely and gentle, so temperate and kind, courteous, restrained, and magnanimous. A revolution is an insurrection, an act of violence by which one class overthrows another." [1] With these words—written in 1926, at a time when the Communists, in cooperation with Chiang Kai-shek's Nationalist Party, were embarked on their Northern Expedition to defeat the warlords and reunify China—the young revolutionary Mao Zedong warned his colleagues that the road to victory in the struggle to build a Communist society would be arduous and would inevitably involve acts of violence against the class enemy.

During the next twenty years, the mettle of the Communist Party was severely tested. It was harassed to near extinction by the Nationalist government and then attacked by the armed forces of imperial Japan. In the summer of 1949, it finally triumphed over Chiang in a bruising civil war that led to the latter's abandonment of the mainland and retreat to the island of Taiwan. By then, Mao had become the most powerful man in China, and people began to speculate about his future intentions. Did Mao's words two decades previously portend a new reign of terror that would—not for the first time—drown the Chinese Revolution in a sea of blood? Or were Mao and his colleagues—as some American observers had speculated in Mao's wartime capital of Yan'an—really "agrarian reformers," more patriots than revolutionaries, who would bind the wounds of war and initiate a period of peace and prosperity? As Mao and his colleagues mounted the rostrum of Beijing's Gate of Heavenly Peace in early October 1949 to declare their intentions, the fate of a nation lay in the balance. ◇

China Under Mao Zedong

The first signs were reassuring. In the fall of 1949, China was at peace for the first time in twelve years. The newly victorious Chinese Communist Party (CCP), under the leadership of its chairman, Mao Zedong, turned its attention to consolidating its power base and healing the wounds of war. Its long-term goal was to construct a socialist society, but its leaders realized that popular support for the revolution was based on the party's platform of honest government, land reform, social justice, and peace rather than on the utopian goal of a classless society. Accordingly, the new regime followed Soviet precedent in adopting a moderate program of political and economic recovery known as New Democracy.

New Democracy

Under New Democracy—patterned roughly after Lenin's New Economic Policy in Soviet Russia in the 1920s (see Chapter 4)—the capitalist system of ownership was retained in the industrial and commercial sectors. A program of land redistribution was adopted, but the collectivization of agriculture was postponed. Only after the party had consolidated its rule and brought a degree of prosperity to the national economy would the difficult transformation to a socialist society begin.

In following Soviet precedent, Chinese leaders tacitly recognized that time and extensive indoctrination would be needed to convince the Chinese people of the superiority of socialism. In the meantime, the party would rely on capitalist profit incentives to spur productivity. Manufacturing and commercial firms were permitted to remain in private hands, but they were placed under stringent government

LAND REFORM IN ACTION

One of the great achievements of the new Communist regime was the land reform program, which resulted in the redistribution of farmland to almost two-thirds of the rural population in China. The program consequently won the gratitude of millions of Chinese. But it also had a dark side as local land reform tribunals routinely convicted "wicked landlords" of crimes against the people and then put them to death. The following passage, written by a foreign observer, describes the process in one village.

What was the main purpose of the Communist Party in carrying out the land reform program in China? How did the tactics employed here support that strategy?

Revolution in a Chinese Village

T'ien-ming [a Party official] called all the active young cadres and the militiamen of Long Bow [village] together and announced to them the policy of the county government, which was to confront all enemy collaborators and their backers at public meetings, expose their crimes, and turn them over to the county authorities for punishment. He proposed that they start with Kuo Te-yu, the puppet village head. Having moved the group to anger with a description of Te-yu's crimes, T'ien-ming reviewed the painful life led by the poor peasants during the occupation and recalled how hard they had all worked and how as soon as they harvested all the grain the puppet officials, backed by army bayonets, took what they wanted, turned over huge quantities to the Japanese devils, forced the peasants to haul it away, and flogged those who refused.

As the silent crowd contracted toward the spot where the accused man stood, T'ien-ming stepped forward. . . . "This is our chance. Remember how we were oppressed. The traitors seized our property. They beat us and kicked us. . . ."

"Let us speak out the bitter memories. Let us see that the blood debt is repaid. . . ."

He paused for a moment. The peasants were listening to every word but gave no sign as to how they felt. . . .

"Come now, who has evidence against this man?"
Again there was silence.

Kuei-ts'ai, the new vice-chairman of the village, found it intolerable. He jumped up, struck Kuo Te-yu on the jaw with the back of his hand. "Tell the meeting how much you stole," he demanded.

The blow jarred the ragged crowd. It was as if an electric spark had tensed every muscle. Not in living memory had any peasant ever struck an official. . . .

The people in the square waited fascinated as if watching a play. They did not realize that in order for the plot to unfold they themselves had to mount the stage and speak out what was on their minds.

That evening T'ien-ming and Kuei-ts'ai called together the small groups of poor peasants from various parts of the village and sought to learn what it was that was really holding them back. They soon found the root of the trouble was fear of the old established political forces and their military backers. The old reluctance to move against the power of the gentry, the fear of ultimate defeat and terrible reprisal that had been seared into the consciousness of so many generations, lay like a cloud over the peasants' minds and hearts.

Emboldened by T'ien-ming's words, other peasants began to speak out. They recalled what Te-yu had done to them personally. Several vowed to speak up and accuse him the next morning. After the meeting broke up, the passage of time worked its own leaven. In many a hovel and tumble-down house talk continued well past midnight. Some people were so excited they did not sleep at all. . . .

On the following day the meeting was livelier by far. It began with a sharp argument as to who would make the first accusation, and T'ien-ming found it difficult to keep order. Before Te-yu had a chance to reply to any questions, a crowd of young men, among whom were several militiamen, surged forward ready to beat him.

SOURCE: Richard Solomon, _Mao's Revolution and the Chinese Political Culture_, pages 198–199. Copyright © 1971 Center for Chinese Studies, University of Michigan. Used with permission of the University of California Press.

regulations and were encouraged to form "joint enterprises" with the government. To win the support of the poorer peasants, who made up the majority of the population, the land reform program that had long been in operation in "liberated areas" was now expanded throughout the country. This strategy was designed not only to win the gratitude of the rural masses but also to undermine the political and economic influence of counterrevolutionary elements still loyal to Chiang Kai-shek.

In some ways, New Democracy was a success. About two-thirds of the peasant households in the country received property under the land reform program and thus had reason to be grateful to the new regime. Spurred by official tolerance for capitalist activities and the end of the civil war, the national economy began to rebound, although agricultural production still lagged behind both official targets and the growing population, which was increasing at an annual rate of more than 2 percent. But the picture had a number of blemishes. In the course of carrying out land redistribution, thousands, if not millions, of landlords and rich farmers lost their lands, their personal property, their freedom, and sometimes their lives. Many of those who died had been tried and convicted of "crimes against the people" in tribunals set up in towns and villages around the country. As Mao himself later conceded, many were innocent of any crime, but in the eyes of the party, their deaths were necessary to destroy the power of the landed gentry in the countryside (see the box on p. 218).

The Transition to Socialism

Originally, party leaders intended to follow the Leninist formula of delaying the building of a fully socialist society until China had a sufficient industrial base to permit the mechanization of agriculture. In 1953, they launched the nation's first five-year plan (patterned after earlier Soviet plans), which called for substantial increases in industrial output. Lenin had believed that the promise of mechanization would give Russian peasants an incentive to join collective farms, which, because of their greater size, could better afford to purchase expensive farm machinery. But the enormous challenge of providing tractors and reapers for millions of rural villages eventually convinced Mao Zedong and some of his colleagues that it would take years, if not decades, for China's infant industrial base to meet the burgeoning needs of a modernizing agricultural sector. He therefore decided to change the equation and urged that collectivization be undertaken immediately, in the hope that collective farms would increase food production and release land, labor, and capital for the industrial sector.

Accordingly, in 1955 the Chinese government launched a new program to build a socialist society. Beginning in that year, virtually all private farmland was collectivized, although peasant families were allowed to retain small plots for their private use (a Chinese version of the private plots adopted in the Soviet Union). In addition, most industry and commerce were nationalized.

Collectivization was achieved without provoking the massive peasant unrest that had taken place in the Soviet Union during the 1930s, perhaps because the Chinese government followed a policy of persuasion rather than compulsion (Mao remarked that Stalin had "drained the pond to catch the fish") and because the land reform program had already earned the support of millions of rural Chinese. But the hoped-for production increases did not materialize, and in 1958, at Mao's insistent urging, party leaders approved a more radical program known as the Great Leap Forward. Existing rural collectives, normally the size of a traditional village, were combined into vast "people's communes," each containing more than thirty thousand people. These communes were to be responsible for all administrative and economic tasks at the local level. The party's official slogan promised "Hard work for a few years, happiness for a thousand."[2]

Mao hoped this program would mobilize the population for a massive effort to accelerate economic growth and ascend to the final stage of communism before the end of the twentieth century. It is better, he said, to "strike while the iron is hot" and advance the revolution without interruption. Some party members were concerned that this ambitious program would threaten the government's rural base of support, but Mao argued that Chinese peasants were naturally revolutionary in spirit. The Chinese rural masses, he said, are

> first of all, poor, and secondly, blank. That may seem like a bad thing, but it is really a good thing. Poor people want change, want to do things, want revolution. A clean sheet of paper has no blotches, and so the newest and most beautiful words can be written on it, the newest and most beautiful pictures can be painted on it.[3]

Those words, of course, were *socialism* and *communism*.

The Great Leap Forward was a disaster. Administrative bottlenecks, bad weather, and peasant resistance to the new system (which, among other things, attempted to eliminate work incentives and destroy the traditional family as the basic unit of Chinese society) combined to drive food production downward, and over the next few years, as many as 15 million people may have died of starvation. Many peasants were reportedly reduced to eating the bark off trees and in some cases allowing infants to starve. In 1960, the commune experiment was essentially abandoned. Although the commune structure was retained, ownership and management were returned to the collective level. Mao was severely criticized by some of his more pragmatic colleagues (one remarked bitingly that "one cannot reach Heaven in a single step"), provoking him to complain that he had been relegated to the sidelines "like a Buddha on a shelf."

The Great Proletarian Cultural Revolution

But Mao, still an imposing figure within the party, was not yet ready to abandon either his power or his dream of an egalitarian society. In 1966, he returned to the attack, mobilizing discontented youth and disgruntled party members into revolutionary units known as Red Guards who were urged to take to the streets to cleanse Chinese society—from local schools and factories to government ministries in Beijing—of impure elements who in Mao's mind were guilty of "taking the capitalist road." Supported by his wife, Jiang Qing, and other radical party figures, Mao launched China on a new forced march toward communism.

The so-called Great Proletarian Cultural Revolution lasted for ten years, from 1966 to 1976. Some Western observers interpreted it as a simple power struggle between Mao and some of his key rivals such as head of state Liu Shaoqi (1898–1969) and Deng Xiaoping (1904–1997), the party's general secretary. Both were removed from their positions, and Liu later died, allegedly of torture, in a Chinese prison. But real policy disagreements were involved. One reason Mao had advocated the Great Leap Forward was to bypass the party and government bureaucracy, which in his view had lost their revolutionary zeal and were primarily concerned with protecting their power. Now he and his supporters feared that capitalist values and the remnants of "feudalist" Confucian ideas and practices would undermine ideological fervor and betray the revolutionary cause. Mao himself was convinced that only an atmosphere of constant revolutionary fervor (what he termed "uninterrupted revolution") could enable the Chinese to overcome the lethargy of the past and achieve the final stage of utopian communism. "I care not," he once wrote, "that the winds blow and the waves beat. It is better than standing idly in a courtyard."

His opponents, on the other hand, worried that Mao's "heaven-storming" approach could delay economic growth and antagonize the people. They argued for a more pragmatic strategy that gave priority to nation building over the ultimate Communist goal of spiritual transformation. But with Mao's supporters now in power, the party carried out vast economic and educational reforms that virtually eliminated any remaining profit incentives, established a new school system that emphasized "Mao Zedong Thought," and stressed practical education at the elementary level at the expense of specialized training in science and the humanities in the universities. School learning was discouraged as a legacy of capitalism, and Mao's famous *Little Red Book* (a slim volume of Maoist aphorisms to encourage good behavior and revolutionary zeal) was hailed as the most important source of knowledge in all areas.

Such efforts to destroy all vestiges of traditional society were reminiscent of the Reign of Terror in revolutionary France, when the Jacobins sought to destroy organized religion and even replaced the traditional Christian chronological system with a new revolutionary calendar. Red Guards rampaged through the country attempting to eradicate the "four olds" (old thought, old culture, old customs, and old habits). They destroyed temples and religious sculptures; they tore down street signs and replaced them with new ones carrying revolutionary names. At one point, the city of Shanghai even ordered that the significance of colors in stoplights be changed so that red (the revolutionary color) would indicate that traffic could move.

But a mood of revolutionary enthusiasm is difficult to sustain. Key groups, including party bureaucrats, urban professionals, and many military officers, did not share Mao's belief in the benefits of "uninterrupted revolution" and

constant turmoil. Many were alienated by the arbitrary actions of the Red Guards, who indiscriminately accused and brutalized their victims in a society where legal safeguards had almost entirely vanished. Whether the Cultural Revolution led to declining productivity is a matter of debate. Inevitably, however, the sense of anarchy and uncertainty caused popular support for the movement to erode, and when the end came with Mao's death in 1976, the vast majority of the population may well have welcomed its demise.

Personal accounts by young Chinese who took part in the Cultural Revolution show that their initial enthusiasm often turned to disillusionment. In *Son of the Revolution*, Liang Heng tells how at first he helped friends organize Red Guard groups: "I thought it was a great idea. We would be following Chairman Mao just like the grownups, and Father would be proud of me. I suppose I too resented the teachers who had controlled and criticized me for so long, and I looked forward to a little revenge."[4] Later, he had reason to repent. His sister ran off to join the local Red Guard group. Prior to her departure, she denounced her mother and the rest of her family as "rightists" and enemies of the revolution. Their home was regularly raided by Red Guards, and their father was severely beaten and tortured for having three neckties and "Western shirts." Books, paintings, and writings were piled in the center of the floor and burned before his eyes. On leaving, a few of the Red Guards helped themselves to his monthly salary and his transistor radio.

China After Mao

In September 1976, Mao Zedong died at the age of eighty-three. After a short but bitter succession struggle, the pragmatists led by Deng Xiaoping seized power from the radicals and brought the Cultural Revolution to an end. Mao's widow, Jiang Qing, and three other radicals (derisively called the "Gang of Four" by their opponents) were put on trial and sentenced to death or to long terms in prison. The egalitarian policies of the previous decade were reversed, and a new program emphasizing economic modernization was introduced.

The Four Modernizations

Under the leadership of Deng, who installed his supporters in key positions throughout the party and the government, attention focused on what were called the "Four Modernizations": industry, agriculture, technology, and national defense. Deng had been a leader of the faction that opposed Mao's program of rapid socialist transformation, and during the Cultural Revolution, he had been forced to perform menial labor to "sincerely correct his errors." But Deng continued to espouse the pragmatic approach and

AP Images

Punishing Chinese Enemies During the Cultural Revolution. The Cultural Revolution, which began in 1966, was a massive effort by Mao Zedong and his radical supporters to eliminate rival elements within the Chinese Communist Party and the government. Accused of being "capitalist roaders," such individuals were subjected to public criticism and removed from their positions. Some were imprisoned or executed. Here Red Guards parade a victim wearing a dunce cap through the streets of Beijing.

reportedly once remarked, "Black cat, white cat, what does it matter so long as it catches the mice?" Under the program of Four Modernizations, many of the restrictions against private activities and profit incentives were eliminated, and people were encouraged to work hard to benefit themselves and Chinese society. The government popularized the idea that all Chinese would prosper, although not necessarily at the same speed. Familiar slogans such as "Serve the people" and "Uphold the banner of Marxist-Leninist-Maoist thought" were replaced by new ones repugnant to the tenets of Mao Zedong Thought: "Create wealth for the people" and "Time is money." The party announced that China was still at the "primary stage of socialism" and might not reach the state of utopian communism for generations.

Crucial to the program's success was the government's ability to attract foreign technology and capital. For more than two decades, China had been isolated from technological advances taking place elsewhere in the world. Although China's leaders understandably prided themselves on their nation's capacity for "self-reliance," their isolationist policy

had been exceedingly costly for the national economy. China's post-Mao leaders blamed the country's backwardness on the "ten lost years" of the Cultural Revolution, but the "lost years," at least in technological terms, extended back to 1949 and in some respects even before. Now, to make up for lost time, the government encouraged foreign investment and sent thousands of students and specialists abroad to study capitalist techniques.

By adopting this pragmatic approach in the years after 1976, China made great strides in ending its chronic problems of poverty and underdevelopment. Per capita income roughly doubled during the 1980s; housing, education, and sanitation improved; and both agricultural and industrial output skyrocketed. Clearly, China had begun to enter the Industrial Age.

But critics, both Chinese and foreign, complained that Deng Xiaoping's program had failed to achieve a "fifth modernization": democracy. Official sources denied such charges and spoke proudly of restoring "socialist legality" by doing away with the arbitrary punishments applied during the Cultural Revolution. Deng himself encouraged the Chinese people to speak out against earlier excesses. In the late 1970s, ordinary citizens began to paste posters criticizing the abuses of the past on the so-called Democracy Wall near Tiananmen Square in downtown Beijing.

Yet it soon became clear that the new leaders would not tolerate any direct criticism of the Communist Party or of Marxist-Leninist ideology. Dissidents were suppressed, and some were sentenced to long prison terms. Among them was the well-known astrophysicist Fang Lizhi, who spoke out publicly against official corruption and the continuing influence of Marxist-Leninist concepts in post-Mao China, telling an audience in Hong Kong that "China will not be able to modernize if it does not break the shackles of Maoist and Stalinist-style socialism." Fang immediately felt the weight of official displeasure. He was refused permission to travel abroad, and articles that he submitted to official periodicals were rejected.

The problem began to intensify in the late 1980s, as more Chinese began to study abroad and more information about Western society reached educated individuals inside the country. Rising expectations aroused by the economic improvements of the early 1980s led to increasing pressure from students and other urban residents for better living conditions, relaxed restrictions on study abroad, and increased freedom to select employment after graduation.

Incident at Tiananmen Square

As long as economic conditions for the majority of Chinese were improving, other classes did not share the students' discontent, and the government was able to isolate them from other elements in society. But in the late 1980s, an overheated economy led to rising inflation and growing discontent among salaried workers, especially in the cities. At the same time, corruption, nepotism, and favored treatment for senior officials and party members were provoking increasing criticism. In May 1989, student protesters carried placards demanding Science and Democracy (reminiscent of the slogan of the May Fourth Movement, whose seventieth anniversary was celebrated in the spring of 1989), an end to official corruption, and the resignation of China's aging party leadership. These demands received widespread support from the urban population (although notably less in rural areas) and led to massive demonstrations in Tiananmen Square.

The demonstrations divided the Chinese leaders. Reformist elements around party general secretary Zhao Ziyang were sympathetic to the protesters, but veteran leaders such as Deng saw the students' demands for more democracy as a disguised call for an end to the CCP's rule. After some hesitation, the government sent tanks and troops into Tiananmen Square to crush the demonstrators. Dissidents were arrested, and the regime once again began to stress ideological purity and socialist values. Although the crackdown provoked widespread criticism abroad, Chinese leaders insisted that economic reforms could only take place in conditions of party leadership and political stability.

Deng and other aging party leaders turned to the army to protect their base of power and suppress what they described as "counterrevolutionary elements." Deng was undoubtedly counting on the fact that many Chinese, particularly in rural areas, feared a recurrence of the disorder

Give Me Liberty—Or Give Me Death!
The demonstrations that erupted in Tiananmen Square in the spring of 1989 spread rapidly to other parts of China, where students and other local citizens gave their vocal support to the popular movement in Beijing. Here students from a high school march to the city of Guilin to display their own determination to take part in the reform of Chinese society. Their call to "give me liberty or give me death" (in Patrick Henry's famous phrase) echoed the determination expressed by many of their counterparts in Beijing.

Courtesy of William J. Duiker

of the Cultural Revolution and craved economic prosperity more than political reform. In the months following the confrontation, the government issued new regulations requiring courses on Marxist-Leninist ideology in the schools, winnowed out dissidents in the intellectual community, and made it clear that while economic reforms would continue, the CCP's monopoly of power would not be allowed to decay. Harsh punishments were imposed on those accused of undermining the Communist system and supporting its enemies abroad.

From Marx to Confucius

In the 1990s, the government began to nurture urban support by reducing the rate of inflation and guaranteeing the availability of consumer goods in great demand among the rising middle class. Under Deng's successor, Jiang Zemin (b. 1926), who served as both party chief and president of China, the government promoted rapid economic growth while cracking down harshly on political dissent. That policy paid dividends in bringing about a perceptible decline in alienation among the population in the cities. Industrial production continued to surge, leading to predictions that China would become one of the economic superpowers of the twenty-first century. But problems in rural areas began to increase, as lagging farm income, high taxes, and official corruption sparked resentment among the rural populace.

Partly out of fear that such developments could undermine the socialist system and the rule of the CCP, conservative leaders attempted to curb Western influence and restore faith in Marxism-Leninism. Perhaps tacitly recognizing that Marxist exhortations were no longer an effective means of enforcing social discipline, the party turned to Confucianism as an antidote. Ceremonies celebrating the birth of Confucius now received official sanction, and the virtues he promoted, such as righteousness, propriety, and filial piety, were widely cited as the means to counter antisocial behavior.

Beijing's decision to emphasize traditional Confucian themes as a means of promoting broad popular support for its domestic policies was paralleled by a growing reliance on the spirit of nationalism to achieve its goals on the world stage. Today, China conducts an independent foreign policy and is playing an increasingly active role in the region. To some of its neighbors, including Japan, India, and Russia, China's new posture is cause for disquiet and has given rise to suspicions that it is once again preparing to assert its muscle as in the imperial era. A striking example of this new attitude took place as early as 1979, when Chinese forces briefly invaded Vietnam as punishment for the Vietnamese occupation of neighboring Cambodia. In the 1990s, China aroused concern in the region by claiming sole ownership over the Spratly Islands in the South China Sea and over Diaoyu Island (also claimed by Japan) near Taiwan (see Map 11.1).

To Chinese leaders, however, such actions simply represent legitimate efforts to resume China's rightful role in the affairs of the region. After a century of humiliation at the hands of the Western powers and neighboring Japan, the nation, in Mao's famous words of 1949, "has stood up" and no one will be permitted to humiliate it again. For the moment, at least, a fervent patriotism seems to be on the rise in China, actively promoted by the party as a means of holding the country together. Pride in the achievement of national sports teams is intense, and two young authors recently achieved wide acclaim with the publication of their book *The China That Can Say No,* a response to criticism of the country in the United States and Europe. The decision by the International Olympic Committee to award the 2008 Summer Games to Beijing led to widespread celebration throughout the country.

Pumping up the spirit of patriotism is not a solution for all of China's problems, however. Unrest is growing among China's national minorities: in Xinjiang, where restless Muslim peoples observe with curiosity the emergence of independent Islamic states in Central Asia, and in Tibet, where the official policy of quelling separatism has led to the violent suppression of Tibetan culture and an influx of thousands of ethnic Chinese immigrants. In the meantime, the Falun Gong religious movement, which the government has attempted to suppress as a potentially serious threat to its authority, is an additional indication that with the disintegration of the old Maoist utopia, the Chinese people will need more than a pallid version of Marxism-Leninism or a revived Confucianism to fill the gap.

Whether the current leadership will be able to prevent further erosion of the party's power and prestige is unclear. In the short term, efforts to slow the process of change may succeed because many Chinese are understandably fearful of punishment and concerned for their careers. And high economic growth rates can sometimes obscure a multitude of problems as many individuals will opt to chase the fruits of materialism rather than the less tangible benefits of personal freedom. But in the long run, the party leadership must resolve the contradiction between political authoritarianism and economic prosperity. One is reminded of Chiang Kai-shek's failed attempt during the 1930s to revive Confucian ethics as a standard of behavior for modern China: dead ideologies cannot be revived by decree.

New leaders installed in 2002 and 2003 appear to recognize the challenge. Hu Jintao (b. 1943), who replaced Jiang Zemin as CCP general secretary and head of state, appears to recognize the need for further reforms to open up Chinese society and bridge the yawning gap between rich

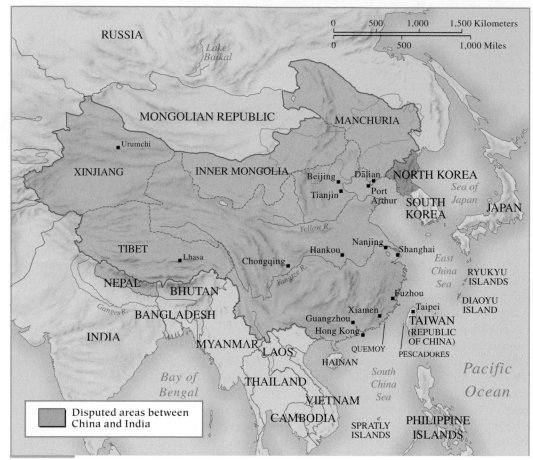

MAP 11.1 **The People's Republic of China.** This map shows China's current boundaries. Major regions are indicated in capital letters. ❓ In which regions are there movements against Chinese rule? 🌐 View an animated version of this map or related maps at the **World History Resource Center,** at worldrc.wadsworth.com/.

and poor. In recent years, the government has shown a growing tolerance for the public exchange of ideas, which has surfaced with the proliferation of bookstores, avant-garde theater, experimental art exhibits, and the Internet. In 2005, an estimated 27 percent of all Chinese citizens owned a cell phone. Today, despite the government's efforts to restrict access to certain websites, more people are "surfing" the Net in China than in any country except the United States.

Serve the People: Chinese Society Under Communism

Enormous changes took place in Chinese society after the Communist rise to power in 1949. Yet beneath the surface of rapid change were tantalizing hints of the survival of elements of the old China. Despite all the efforts of Mao Zedong and his colleagues, the ideas of Confucius and

Sons had still not been irrevocably discarded. China under communism remained a society that in many respects was enthralled by its past.

The Politics of the Mass Line

Nowhere was this uneasy balance between the old and the new more clearly demonstrated than in politics and government.

In its broad outlines, the new political system followed the Soviet pattern. Yet from the start, CCP leaders made it clear that the Chinese model would differ from the Soviet in important respects. Whereas the Bolsheviks had severely distrusted nonrevolutionary elements in Russia and established a minority government based on the radical left, Mao and his colleagues were more confident that they possessed the basic support of the majority of the Chinese people. Under New Democracy, the party attempted to reach out to all progressive classes in the population to maintain the alliance that had brought it to power in the first place.

The primary link between the regime and the population was the system of "mass organizations," representing peasants, workers, women, religious groups, writers, and artists. The party had established these associations during the 1920s to mobilize support for the revolution. Now they served as a conduit between party and people, enabling the leaders to assess the attitude of the masses while at the same time seeking their support for the party's programs. Behind this facade of representative institutions stood the awesome power of the CCP.

Initially, this "mass line" system worked fairly well. True, opposition to the regime was ruthlessly suppressed, but on the positive side, China finally had a government that appeared to be "for the people." Although there was no pretense at Western-style democracy, and official corruption and bureaucratic mismanagement and arrogance had by no means been entirely eliminated, the new ruling class came preponderantly from workers and peasants and was more willing than its predecessors to listen to the complaints and aspirations of its constituents.

A good example of the party's mass line policy was the land reform program, which redistributed farmland to the poor. The program was carried out at the village level by land reform cadres who urged local farmers to establish tribunals to confiscate the lands of the landlord class and assign them to poor or landless peasants, thus giving the impression that the policy was locally inspired rather than imposed, Soviet style, from the top down.

But the adoption of the Great Leap Forward betrayed a fundamental weakness in the policy of the mass line. While declaring his willingness to listen to the concerns of the population, Mao was also determined to build a utopian society based on Marxist-Leninist principles. Popular acceptance of nationalization and collectivization during the mid-1950s indicates that the Chinese people were not entirely hostile to socialism, but when those programs were carried to an extreme during the Great Leap Forward, many Chinese, even within the party, resisted and forced the government to abandon the program.

The failure of the Great Leap Forward split the CCP and led to the revolutionary disturbances of the following decade. Some of Mao's associates had opposed his radical approach and now sought to adopt a more cautious road to nation building. To Mao, such views were a betrayal of the party's revolutionary principles. The Cultural Revolution, which he launched in 1966, can be seen above all as his attempt to cleanse the system of its impurities and put Chinese society back on the straight road to egalitarian communism.

Many of his compatriots evidently shared his beliefs. Young people in particular, alienated by the lack of job opportunities, flocked to his cause and served with enthusiasm in the Red Guard organizations that became the shock troops of the revolution. But the enthusiasms aroused by the Cultural Revolution did not last. As in the French Revolution, the efforts to achieve revolutionary purity eventually alienated all except the most radical elements in the country, and a period of reaction inevitably set in. In China, revolutionary fervor gave way to a new era in which belief in socialist ideals was replaced by a more practical desire for material benefits.

Economics in Command

Deng Xiaoping recognized the need to restore a sense of "socialist legality" and credibility to a system that was on the verge of breakdown and hoped that rapid economic growth would satisfy the Chinese people and prevent them from demanding political reforms. The post-Mao leaders demonstrated a willingness to emphasize economic performance over ideological purity. To stimulate the stagnant industrial sector, which had been under state control since the end of the era of New Democracy, they reduced bureaucratic controls over state industries and allowed local managers to have more say over prices, salaries, and quality control. Productivity was encouraged by permitting bonuses to be paid for extra effort, a policy that had been discouraged during the Cultural Revolution. State firms were no longer guaranteed access to precious resources and were told to compete with each other for public favor and even to export goods on their own initiative. The regime also tolerated the emergence of a small private sector. Unemployed youth were encouraged to set up restaurants, bicycle or radio repair shops, and handicraft shops on their own initiative.

Finally, the regime opened up the country to foreign investment and technology. The Maoist policy of self-reliance was abandoned, and China openly sought the advice of foreign experts and the money of foreign capitalists. Special economic zones were established in urban centers near the coast (ironically, many were located in the old nineteenth-century treaty ports), where lucrative concessions were offered to encourage foreign firms to build factories. The tourist industry was encouraged, and students were sent abroad to study.

The new leaders especially stressed educational reform. The system adopted during the Cultural Revolution, emphasizing practical education and ideology at the expense of higher education and modern science, was rapidly abandoned (Mao's *Little Red Book* itself was withdrawn from circulation and could no longer be found on bookshelves), and a new system based generally on the Western model was instituted. Admission to higher education was based on success in merit examinations, and courses on science and mathematics received high priority.

Agricultural Reform No economic reform program could succeed unless it included the countryside. Three decades of socialism had done little to increase food production or to lay the basis for a modern agricultural sector. China, with a population numbering one billion in the mid-1970s, could still barely feed itself. Peasants had little incentive to work and few opportunities to increase production through mechanization, the use of fertilizer, or better irrigation.

Under Deng Xiaoping, agricultural policy made a rapid about-face. Under the new "rural responsibility system," adopted shortly after Deng had consolidated his authority, collectives leased land on contract to peasant families, who paid a quota as rent to the collective. Anything produced on the land above that payment could be sold on the private market or consumed. To soak up excess labor in the villages, the government encouraged the formation of so-called sideline industries, a modern equivalent of the traditional cottage industries in premodern China. Peasants raised fish or shrimp, made consumer goods, and even assembled living room furniture and appliances for sale to their newly affluent compatriots.

The reform program had a striking effect on rural production. Grain production increased rapidly, and farm income doubled during the 1980s. Yet it also created problems. In the first place, income at the village level became more unequal as some enterprising farmers (known locally as "ten thousand dollar" households) earned profits several times those realized by their less fortunate or less industrious neighbors. When some farmers discovered they could earn more by growing cash crops or other specialized commodities, they devoted less land to rice and other grain crops, thereby threatening to reduce the supply of China's most crucial staple. Finally, the agricultural policy threatened to undermine the government's population control program, which party leaders viewed as crucial to the success of the Four Modernizations.

Since a misguided period in the mid-1950s when Mao had argued that more labor would result in higher productivity, China had been attempting to limit its population growth. By 1970, the government had launched a stringent family planning program—including education, incentives, and penalties for noncompliance—to persuade the Chinese people to limit themselves to one child per family. The program did have some success, and the rate of population growth was reduced drastically in the early 1980s. The rural responsibility system, however, undermined the program because it encouraged farm families to pay the penalties for having additional children in the

China's "Little Emperors." Under China's massive family planning program to curtail population growth, urban families have been restricted to a single child. In conformity with tradition, sons are still especially prized, and some Chinese complain that many parents overindulge their only children, turning them into spoiled "little emperors." Despite such programs, China's population has continued to grow and now surpasses 1.3 billion.

belief that the labor of these offspring would increase family income and provide the parents with greater security in their old age.

Evaluating the Four Modernizations Still, the overall effects of the modernization program were impressive. The standard of living improved for the majority of the population. Whereas a decade earlier the average Chinese had struggled to earn enough to buy a bicycle, radio, watch, or washing machine, by the late 1980s many were beginning to purchase videocassette recorders, refrigerators, and color television sets.

Yet the rapid growth of the economy created its own problems: inflationary pressures, greed, envy, increased corruption, and—most dangerous of all for the regime—rising expectations. When the economy failed to live up to those expectations, as in the late 1980s, disillusionment ran high, especially in the cities, where high living by officials and rising prices for goods aroused widespread alienation and cynicism. Such attitudes undoubtedly contributed to the anger and frustration that burst out during the spring of 1989, when many workers, peasants, and functionaries joined the demonstrations in Tiananmen Square against official corruption and one-party rule.

During the 1990s, growth rates in the industrial sector remained high as domestic capital became increasingly available to compete with the growing presence of foreign enterprises. The government finally began to recognize the need to close down inefficient state enterprises, and by the end of the decade, the private sector, with official encouragement, accounted for over 10 percent of the gross domestic product. A stock market opened, and China's prowess in the international marketplace improved dramatically.

As a result of these developments, China now possesses a large and increasingly affluent middle class and a burgeoning domestic market for consumer goods. More than 80 percent of all urban Chinese now possess a color television set, a refrigerator, and a washing machine. One-third own their homes, and nearly as many have an air conditioner. For the more affluent, a private automobile is increasingly a possibility. Like their counterparts elsewhere in Asia, urban Chinese are increasingly brand-name conscious, a characteristic that provides a considerable challenge to local manufacturers.

But, as Chinese leaders have discovered, rapid economic change never comes without cost. The closing of state-run factories has led to the dismissal of millions of workers each year, and the private sector, although growing at more than 20 percent annually, is unable to absorb them all. Discontent has been increasing in the countryside as well, where farmers earn only about half the salary of their urban counterparts (the government tried to increase the official purchase price for grain but rescinded the order when it became too expensive). China's recent entry into the World Trade Organization (WTO) may help the nation as a whole, but is less likely to benefit farmers, who now face the challenge of cheap foreign imports. Taxes and local corruption add to their complaints as land seizures by the government or by local officials are a major source of anger in rural communities. In desperation, millions of rural Chinese have left for the big cities, where many of them are unable to find steady employment and are forced to live in squalid conditions in crowded tenements or in the sprawling suburbs. Millions of others remain on the farm but attempt to maximize their income by producing for the market or increasing the size of their families. Although China's population control program continues to limit rural couples to two children, such regulations are widely

© Xiaoyang Liu/CORBIS

Reach for the Sky. Shanghai, once Republican China's premier commercial and industrial center, languished during the early years of Communist rule, but is now reviving to become one of the modern cities in the world, a metropolis of superhighways and mushrooming skyscrapers. The eighty-story television tower in the background dominates a new urban sector teeming with hotels, office buildings, and entertainment centers.

VIEWS ON MARRIAGE

One of the major goals of the Communist government in China was to reform the tradition of marriage and place it on a new egalitarian basis. In the following excerpt, a writer with the magazine *China Youth Daily* describes the ideal marriage and explains how socialist marriage differs from its capitalist counterpart.

How, according to this document, will socialist marriage differ from its capitalist counterpart? In what ways will traditional Chinese practices be changed?

The Correct Viewpoint Toward Marriage

Now then, what is our viewpoint? Is it different from that of the exploiting bourgeois class?

For one, thing, our basic concept on marriage is and must be that we build our happiness upon the premise that happiness should be shared by all. We advocate equal rights for man and woman, equal rights for husband and wife. We oppose the idea that man is superior to woman or that the husband has special prerogatives over his wife. We also oppose any discrimination against or ill treatment of the wife.

We believe that marriage should be based solely upon mutual consent. We oppose the so-called arranged marriage, or the use of any deceitful or compulsory method by one of the parties in this matter. We uphold the system of monogamy. Husband and wife ought to have true and exclusive love toward each other, and concubinage is not permitted.

We believe that the very basic foundations for love between man and woman are common political understanding, comradeship in work, mutual help, and mutual respect. Money, position, or the so-called prettiness should not be taken into consideration for a right marriage, because they are not reliable foundations for love.

We also believe that solemnity and fidelity are important elements for a correct relationship between husband and wife, and for a happy family life. To abandon one's partner by any improper means is to be opposed. In our society, those who intend to pursue their happiness at the expense of others run contradictory to the moral principle of Communism and will never be happy.

For the exploiting class, the concept about marriage is just the opposite. The landlord class believes in pursuing happiness by making other people suffer. They subscribe to such biased viewpoints as "man is superior to woman," "man is more important than woman," "man should dominate woman," etc. Under this type of ideology, women are merely slaves and properties of men and marriage is nothing but a process of buying and selling with compulsion. In the bourgeois society the whole matrimonial relationship is built upon money, and becomes simply a "monetary relationship." In economic relationships women belong to men. Love is nothing but a merchandise; women trade their flesh for men's money. This concept about marriage is indeed reactionary and it shall meet with our firm opposition.

Among our young worker comrades there are still a few whose thinking is still under the influence of the exploiting class. They cannot do away with the thinking that man is superior to woman, they look down upon their own wives, especially those who have lower education and those who come from rural areas. When they look for lovers, what concerns the man most is whether the woman is pretty or not; what concerns the woman most is whether the man is earning high wages and has a high position. They disregard all the other elements for a good match.

Some of them even use deception to steal love or force the other party to marry them. Their attitude toward love and marriage is most revolting. They love the new ones and forsake the old, get themselves involved in multi-angle romance, or even seek excuses as grounds for divorce. All this sort of thinking and behavior are certainly contradictory to the moral quality of the working class and Communism, and contradictory to the socialist concept and system of marriage. Therefore those who have formed such a wrong concept about marriage ought to adopt a correct one in accordance with the moral principle of Communism. Only then will there be possibility for true love and happy family life.

SOURCE: From *Communist China*, Vol. 3 *of China Reader* by Franz Schurzmann and Orville Schell, copyright © 1966 by Franz Schurzmann. *Copyright © 1967 by Franz Schurzmann and Orville Schell.* Used by permission of Random House, Inc.

flouted despite stringent penalties. Chinese leaders must now face the reality that the pains of industrialization are not limited to capitalist countries.

Social Problems

At the root of Marxist-Leninist ideology is the idea of building a new citizen free from the prejudices, ignorance, and superstition of the "feudal" era and the capitalist desire for self-gratification. This new citizen would be characterized not only by a sense of racial and sexual equality but also by the selfless desire to contribute his or her utmost for the good of all. In the words of Mao Zedong's famous work "The Foolish Old Man Who Removed the Mountains," the people should "be resolute, fear no sacrifice, and surmount every difficulty to win victory."[5]

Women and the Family The new government wasted no time in keeping its promise. During the early 1950s, it took a number of steps to bring a definitive end to the old system in China. Women were permitted to vote and encouraged to become active in the political process. At the local level, an increasing number of women became active in the CCP and in collective organizations. In 1950, a new marriage law guaranteed women equal rights with men (see the box on p. 228). Most important, perhaps, it permitted women for the first time to initiate divorce proceedings against their husbands. Within a year, nearly one million divorces had been granted. The regime also undertook to destroy the influence of the traditional family system. To the Communists, loyalty to the family, a crucial element in the Confucian social order, undercut loyalty to the state and to the dictatorship of the proletariat.

At first, the new government moved carefully to avoid alienating its supporters in the countryside unnecessarily. When collective farms were established in the mid-1950s, each member of a collective accumulated "work points" based on the number of hours worked during a specified time period. Payment for work points was made not to the individual but to the family head. The payments, usually in the form of ration coupons, could then be spent at the collective community store. Because the payments went to the head of the family, the traditionally dominant position of the patriarch was maintained. When people's communes were established in the late 1950s, payments went to the individual.

During the political radicalism of the Great Leap Forward, children were encouraged to report to the authorities any comments by their parents that criticized the system. Such practices continued during the Cultural Revolution, when children were expected to report on their parents, students on their teachers, and employees on their superiors. Some have suggested that Mao deliberately encouraged such practices to bring an end to the traditional "politics of dependency." According to this theory, historically the famous "five relationships" forced individuals to swallow their anger and frustration (known in Chinese as "to eat bitterness") and accept the hierarchical norms established by Confucian ethics (the five relationships were the subordination of son to father, wife to husband, younger brother to older brother, and subject to ruler, and the proper relationship of friend to friend). By encouraging the oppressed elements in society—the young, the female, and the poor—to voice their bitterness, Mao was breaking down the tradition of dependency. Such denunciations had been issued against landlords and other "local tyrants" in the land reform tribunals of the late 1940s and early 1950s. Later, during the Cultural Revolution, they were applied to other authority figures in Chinese society.

Lifestyle Changes The post-Mao era brought a decisive shift away from revolutionary utopianism and a return to the pragmatic approach to nation building. For most people, it meant improved living conditions and a qualified return to family traditions. For the first time in more than a decade, enterprising Chinese began to concentrate on improving their standard of living. For the first time, millions of Chinese saw the prospect of a house or an urban flat with a washing machine, television set, and indoor plumbing. Young people whose parents had given them patriotic names such as Build the Country, Protect Mao Zedong, and Assist Korea began to choose more elegant and cosmopolitan names for their own children. Some names, such as Surplus Grain or Bring a Younger Brother, expressed hope for the future.

The new attitudes were also reflected in physical appearance. For a generation after the civil war, clothing had been restricted to the traditional baggy "Mao suit" in olive drab or dark blue, but by the 1980s, young people craved such fashionable Western items as designer jeans, trendy sneakers, and sweat suits (or reasonable facsimiles). Cosmetic surgery to create a more buxom figure or a more Western facial look became increasingly common among affluent young women in the cities. Many had the epicanthic fold over their eyelids removed or even enlarged their noses—a curious decision in view of the tradition of referring derogatorily to foreigners as "big noses."

Religious practices and beliefs also changed. As the government became more tolerant, some Chinese began returning to the traditional Buddhist faith or to folk religions, and Buddhist and Taoist temples were once again crowded with worshipers. Despite official efforts to suppress its more evangelical forms, Christianity became increasingly popular; like the "rice Christians" (persons who supposedly converted for economic reasons) of the past, many viewed it as a symbol of success and cosmopolitanism.

As with all social changes, China's reintegration into the outside world has had a price. Arranged marriages, nepotism, and mistreatment of females (for example, under the one-child program, many parents in rural areas reportedly killed female infants in the hope that the next one would be a son) have returned, although such behavior had likely continued under the cloak of revolutionary purity for a generation. Materialistic attitudes are highly prevalent among young people, along with a corresponding cynicism about politics and the CCP. Expensive weddings are now increasingly common, and bribery and favoritism are all too frequent. Crime of all types, including an apparently growing incidence of prostitution and sex crimes against women, appears to be on the rise. To discourage sexual abuse, the government now seeks to provide free legal services for women living in rural areas.

There is also a price to pay for the trend toward privatization. Under the Maoist system, the elderly and the sick received retirement benefits and health care from the state or the collective organizations. Today, with the collectives no longer playing such a social role and more workers operating in the private sector, the safety net has been removed. The government attempted to fill the gap by enacting a social security law, but because of a lack of funds, eligibility has been limited primarily to individuals in the urban sector of the economy. Those living in the countryside—who still represent 60 percent of the population—have essentially been left to their own devices, although in 2006 the government promised to provide improved education, medical care, and other social services to the rural population.

China's Changing Culture

Like their contemporaries all over Asia, Chinese artists were strongly influenced by the revolutionary changes that were taking place in the art world of the West in the early twentieth century. In the decades following the 1911 revolution, Chinese artists began to experiment with Western styles, although the more extreme schools, such as Surrealism and Abstract painting, had little impact.

The rise to power of the Communists in 1949 added a new dimension to the debate over the future of culture in China. Spurred by comments made by Mao Zedong at a cultural forum in Yan'an in 1942, leaders rejected the Western slogan of "Art for art's sake" and, like their Soviet counterparts, viewed culture as an important instrument of indoctrination. The standard would no longer be aesthetic quality or the personal preference of the artist but "Art for life's sake," whereby culture would serve the interests of socialism.

At first, the new emphasis on socialist realism did not entirely extinguish the influence of traditional culture. Mao and his colleagues saw the importance of traditional values and culture in building a strong new China and tolerated—and even encouraged—efforts by artists to synthesize traditional ideas with socialist concepts and Western techniques. During the Cultural Revolution, however, all forms of traditional culture came to be viewed as reactionary. Socialist realism became the only

Hail the Great Helmsman! During the Great Proletarian Cultural Revolution, Chinese art was restricted to topics that promoted revolution and the thoughts of Chairman Mao Zedong. All the knowledge that the true revolutionary required was to be found in Mao's *Little Red Book,* a collection of his sayings on proper revolutionary behavior. In this painting, Chairman Mao stands among his admirers, who wave copies of the book as a symbol of their total devotion to him and his vision of a future China.

acceptable standard in literature, art, and music. All forms of traditional expression were forbidden.

Characteristic of the changing cultural climate in China was the experience of author Ding Ling. Born in 1904 and educated in a school for women set up by leftist intellectuals during the hectic years after the May Fourth Movement, she began writing in her early twenties. At first, she was strongly influenced by prevailing Western styles, but after her husband, a struggling young poet and a member of the CCP, was executed by Chiang Kai-shek's government in 1931, she became active in party activities and sublimated her talent to the revolutionary cause.

In the late 1930s, Ding Ling settled in Yan'an, where she became a leader in the women's and literary associations of the CCP. Though she remained dedicated to revolution, years of service to the party did not stifle her individuality, and in 1942, she wrote critically of the incompetence, arrogance, and hypocrisy of many party officials, as well as the treatment of women in areas under Communist authority. Such conduct raised eyebrows, but she was able to survive criticism and in 1948 wrote her most famous novel, *The Sun Shines over the Sangan River,* which described the CCP's land reform program in favorable terms. It was awarded the Stalin Prize three years later.

During the early 1950s, Ding Ling was one of the most prominent literary lights of the new China, but in the more ideological climate at the end of the decade, she was attacked for her individualism and her previous criticism of the party. Although temporarily rehabilitated, during the Cultural Revolution she was sentenced to hard labor on a commune in the far north and was not released until the late 1970s after the death of Mao Zedong. Although crippled and in poor health, she began writing a biography of her mother that examined the role of women in twentieth-century China. She died in 1981. Ding Ling's story mirrored the fate of thousands of progressive Chinese intellectuals who, despite their efforts, were not able to satisfy the constantly changing demands of a repressive regime.

After Mao's death, Chinese culture was once again released from the shackles of socialist realism. In painting, the new policies led to a revival of interest in both traditional and Western forms. The revival of traditional art was in part a matter of practicality as talented young Chinese were trained to produce traditional paintings for export to earn precious foreign currency for the state. But the regime also showed a new tolerance for the imitation of Western styles as a necessary by-product of development, thus unleashing an impressive outpouring of artistic creativity later dubbed the "Beijing Spring." A new generation of Chinese painters, with the tacit permission of the government, has begun to experiment with a wide range of previously prohibited art styles, including Cubism and Abstract Expressionism.

An excellent illustration of Chinese artists' tireless battle for creative freedom is the painting *My Dream* (1988) by Xu Mangyao. It depicts an artist who has freed his hands from manacles and now seeks to escape from the confinement of a red brick wall. The painting represents the worldwide struggle by all the twentieth-century artists silenced by totalitarian regimes in the Soviet Union, Latin America, and Africa.

In music, too, the post-Mao era brought significant changes. Music academies closed during the Cultural Revolution for sowing the seeds of the bourgeois mentality were reopened. Students were permitted to study both Chinese and Western styles, but the vast majority selected the latter. To provide examples, leading musicians and composers, such as violinist Isaac Stern, were invited to China to lecture and perform before eager Chinese students.

The limits to freedom of expression were most apparent in literature. During the early 1980s, party leaders encouraged Chinese writers to express their views on the mistakes of the past, and a new "literature of the wounded" began to describe the brutal and arbitrary nature of the Cultural Revolution. One of the most prominent writers was Bai Hua, whose script for the film *Bitter Love* described the life of a young Chinese painter who joined the revolutionary movement during the 1940s but was destroyed during the Cultural Revolution when his work was condemned as counterrevolutionary. The film depicted the condemnation through a view of a street in Beijing "full of people waving the *Quotations of Chairman Mao,* all those devout and artless faces fired by a feverish fanaticism." Driven from his home for posting a portrait of a third-century B.C.E. defender of human freedom on a Beijing wall, the artist flees the city. At the end of the film, he dies in a snowy field, where his corpse and a semicircle made by his footprints form a giant question mark.

In criticizing the excesses of the Cultural Revolution, Bai Hua was only responding to Deng Xiaoping's appeal for intellectuals to speak out, but he was soon criticized for failing to point out the essentially beneficial role of the CCP in recent Chinese history, and his film was withdrawn from circulation in 1981. Bai Hua was compelled to recant his errors and to state that the great ideas of Mao Zedong on art and literature were "still of universal guiding significance today."[6]

As the attack on Bai Hua illustrates, many party leaders remain suspicious of the impact that "decadent" bourgeois culture could have on the socialist foundations of Chinese society, and the official press has periodically warned that China should adopt only the "positive" aspects of Western culture (notably, its technology and its work ethic) and not the "negative" elements such as drug use, pornography, and hedonism. One of the chief targets in China's recent "spiritual civilization" campaign was author Wang Shuo (b. 1958), whose writings have been banned for exhibiting a sense of "moral decay." In his novels *Playing for Thrills* (1989) and *Please Don't Call Me Human* (2000), Wang highlighted the seamier side of contemporary urban society, peopled with hustlers, ex-convicts, and other assorted hooligans. Spiritually depleted, hedonistic, and amoral in their approach to life, his characters represent the polar opposite of the socialist ideal.

Conservatives have been especially incensed by the tendency of many writers to dwell on the shortcomings of the socialist system and to come uncomfortably close to direct criticism of the role of the CCP. The works of Mo Yan (b. 1956), who is regarded as China's greatest writer, are a case in point. In his novels *The Garlic Ballads* (1988) and *The Republic of Wine* (2000), Mo exposes the rampant corruption of contemporary Chinese society, the roots of which he attributes to one-party rule.

CONCLUSION

O THE OUTSIDE OBSERVER, since the Communist takeover of power on the mainland, China has projected an image of almost constant turmoil and rapid change. That portrayal is not an inaccurate one, for Chinese society has undergone a number of major transformations since the establishment of the People's Republic of China in the fall of 1949. Even in the relatively stable 1980s, many a prudent China watcher undoubtedly wondered whether the prosperous and tolerant conditions of the era of Deng Xiaoping would long endure.

An extended period of political instability and domestic violence is hardly unusual in the years following a major revolutionary upsurge. Similar conditions existed in late-eighteenth-century France after the revolt that overthrew the ancient regime and in Russia after the Bolshevik seizure of power in 1917. In both cases, pragmatists in the pursuit of national wealth and power clashed with radicals who were determined to create a utopian society. In the end, the former were victorious, in a process sometimes known as the "routinization of the revolution." "The revolution," it has been astutely observed, "eats its own."

A similar course of events has been taking place in China since the Communist ascent to power. Radical elements grew restive at what they perceived as a relapse into feudal habits by "capitalist roaders" within the party and launched the Great Proletarian Cultural Revolution. What was distinctive about the Chinese case was that the movement was led by Mao Zedong himself, who risked the destruction of the very organization that had brought him to power in the first place—the Communist Party. Clearly, much about the Chinese Revolution cannot be explained without an understanding of the complex personality of its great leader.

With the death of Mao in 1976, the virulent phase of the revolution appeared to be at an end, and a more stable era of economic development is under way. Yet the Communist Party remains in power.

Why has communism survived in China, albeit in a substantially altered form, when it collapsed in Eastern Europe and the Soviet Union? One of the primary reasons is probably cultural. Although the doctrine of Marxism-Leninism originated in Europe, many of its main precepts, such as the primacy of the community over the individual and the denial of the concept of private property, run counter to the trends in Western civilization. This inherent conflict is especially evident in the societies of central and western Europe, which were strongly influenced by Enlightenment philosophy and the Industrial Revolution. These forces were weaker in the countries farther to the east, but both had begun to penetrate tsarist Russia by the end of the nineteenth century.

By contrast, Marxism-Leninism found a more receptive climate in China and other countries in the region influenced by Confucian tradition. In its political culture, the Communist system exhibits many of the same characteristics as traditional Confucianism—a single truth, an elite governing class, and an emphasis on obedience to the community and its governing representatives—while feudal attitudes regarding female inferiority, loyalty to the family, and bureaucratic arrogance are hard to break. On the surface, China today bears a number of uncanny similarities to the China of the past.

Yet these similarities should not blind us to the real changes that are taking place in the China of today, which is fundamentally different from that of the late Qing or even the early republic. Literacy rates and the standard of living, on balance, are far higher; the pressures of outside powers are less threatening; and China has entered the opening stages of its own industrial and technological revolution. For many Chinese, independent talk radio and the Internet are a greater source of news and views than the official media. Where Sun Yat-sen, Chiang Kai-shek, and even Mao Zedong broke their lances on the rocks of centuries of tradition, poverty, and ignorance, China's present leaders rule a country much more aware of the world and its place in it.

TIMELINE

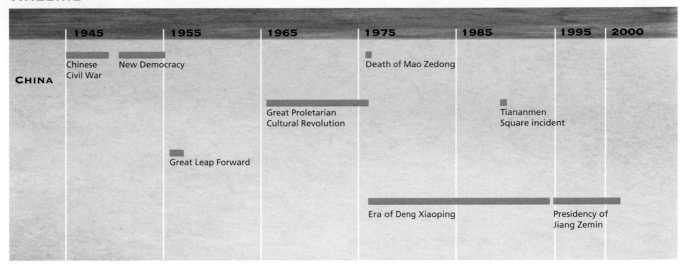

CHINA

| 1945 | 1955 | 1965 | 1975 | 1985 | 1995 | 2000 |

Chinese Civil War

New Democracy

Death of Mao Zedong

Great Proletarian Cultural Revolution

Tiananmen Square incident

Great Leap Forward

Era of Deng Xiaoping

Presidency of Jiang Zemin

CHAPTER NOTES

1. "Report on an Investigation of the Peasant Movement in Hunan (March 1927)," *Quotations from Chairman Mao Tse-tung* (Beijing, 1976), p. 12.
2. Quoted in Stanley Karnow, *Mao and China: Inside China's Cultural Revolution* (New York, 1972), p. 95.
3. Quoted from an article by Mao Zedong in the journal *Red Flag,* June 1, 1958. See Stuart R. Schram, *The Political Thought of Mao Tse-tung* (New York, 1963), p. 253. The quotation "strike while the iron is hot" is from Karnow, *Mao and China,* p. 93.
4. Liang Heng with Judith Shapiro, *Son of the Revolution* (New York, 1983).
5. "The Foolish Old Man Who Removed the Mountains," *Quotations from Chairman Mao,* p. 182.
6. Quoted in Jonathan Spence, *Chinese Roundabout: Essays in History and Culture* (New York, 1992), p. 285.

𝓐s WORLD WAR II CAME to an end, the survivors of that bloody struggle could afford to face the future with at least a measure of cautious optimism. With the death of Adolf Hitler in his bunker in Berlin, there were reasons to hope that the bitter rivalry that had marked relations among the Western powers would finally be put to an end and that the wartime alliance of the United States, Great Britain, and the Soviet Union could be maintained into the postwar era. In the meantime, the peoples of Asia and Africa could envision the possibility that the colonial system would soon end, ushering in a new era of political stability and economic development on a global scale.

With the perspective of more than half a century, we can see that these hopes have been only partly realized. In the decades following the war, the capitalist nations managed to recover from the extended economic depression that had contributed to the start of World War II and advanced to a level of economic prosperity never before seen in world history. The bloody conflicts that had erupted among European nations during the first half of the twentieth century came to an end, and Germany and Japan were fully integrated into the world community. At the same time, the colonial era gradually came to a close, enabling newly independent nations in Africa and Asia to seek to regain control over their own destinies.

On the other hand, the prospects for a stable, peaceful world and an end to balance-of-power politics were hampered by the emergence of the grueling and sometimes tense ideological struggle between the socialist and capitalist blocs, a competition headed by the only remaining great powers, the Soviet Union and the United States. Although the two superpowers were able to avoid a nuclear confrontation, the postwar world was divided into two heavily armed camps in a balance of terror that on one occasion—the Cuban Missile Crisis—brought the world briefly to the brink of nuclear holocaust.

Europe again became divided into hostile camps as the Cold War rivalry between the United States and the Soviet Union forced the European nations to ally with one or the other of the superpowers. The creation of two mutually antagonistic military alliances—NATO in 1949 and the Warsaw Pact in 1955—confirmed the new division of Europe, while a divided Germany, and within it, a divided Berlin, remained its most visible symbols. Repeated crises over the status of Berlin only intensified the fears on both sides of the ideological divide.

In the midst of this rivalry, the Western European nations, with the assistance of the United States, made a remarkable economic recovery and attained unprecedented levels of prosperity. In Eastern Europe, Soviet domination, both political and economic, seemed so complete that many doubted it could ever be undone. Although popular uprisings in Poland and Hungary in 1956, and in Czechoslovakia in 1968, were vivid reminders that the dream of a utopian society was far from a reality, communism appeared, at least for the time being, too powerful to be dislodged. The Helsinki Agreement, signed in 1975, appeared to be a tacit admission by the West that the Iron Curtain had taken on a near-permanent status.

Although the Cold War had begun in Europe at the end of World War II, it soon spread to Asia, with the rise of the Communist Party to power in China. By the mid-1950s, the bitter ideological rivalry between the two camps had taken on such a global character that events in such disparate areas as Southeast Asia, Central America, and the Middle East could send shock waves through world capitals.

In China, the utopian dream was kept alive by Mao Zedong and his radical disciples during the frenetic years between the Great Leap Forward and the Cultural Revolution. The ultimate failure of both programs was a striking testimonial to the difficulties of continually stoking the fires of social revolution.

In the West, economic affluence gave birth to its own set of problems. The voracious focus on material possessions, an intrinsic characteristic of the capitalist ethos, helped promote high levels of productivity in office and factory but at the same time produced a spiritual malaise in individual members of society, who increasingly began to question the meaning and purpose of life beyond the sheer accumulation of things. As the spread of scientific knowledge eroded religious belief, increasing social mobility undermined the traditional base-level structural units of human society—the family and the community. Modernity, as postwar society in the West was now commonly described, appeared to have no answer to the search for meaning in life beyond an unconfirmed and complacent belief in the Enlightenment doctrine of progress.

For the have-nots of capitalist society, the sources of discontent were more immediate, focusing on a lack of equal access to the cornucopia of goods produced by the capitalist machine. Political leaders in many countries sought ways to extend the benefits of an affluent society to their disadvantaged constituents, but success was limited, and experts searched without result for the ultimate solution.

As had been the case since the beginning of the nineteenth century, the driving force behind many of these changes in the postwar world was the Industrial Revolution, which relentlessly undermined the political, social, and economic foundations of traditional society, without disclosing the final destination. Human beings could only hope that as old ways were inexorably chucked aside in the new industrial world, the expanding power of scientific knowledge would provide them with clues on how to find a new purpose and a new meaning behind the mystery of life.

In the early 1990s, the Soviet Union and its system of satellites suddenly came tumbling down, leading to the emergence of truly independent nations in Eastern Europe. In China, the Communist Party managed to remain in power, but only by making an intense effort to abandon the key tenets of Mao Zedong Thought and adopt major components of the capitalist system.

The end of the Cold War spurred rising hopes for the emergence of a "new world order," marked by rising global prosperity and peaceful cooperation among nations. But it soon became clear that the end of the Cold War had also unleashed long-dormant ethnic and religious forces in various parts of the world, producing a new round of civil conflicts and a level of terrorist activity reminiscent of the early part of the twentieth century. In Part IV of this book, we will explore the impact of these events on the continents of Africa and Asia. Part V will focus on some of the key global challenges that face the peoples of the world in the new millennium.

IV

THIRD WORLD RISING

*In the city of Beijing, skyscrapers thrust up beyond the walls
of the fifteenth-century Imperial City*

12

TOWARD THE PACIFIC CENTURY?
JAPAN AND THE LITTLE TIGERS

*I*N AUGUST 1945, JAPAN WAS IN RUINS, its cities destroyed, its vast Asian empire in ashes, its land occupied by a foreign army. A decade earlier, Japanese leaders had proclaimed their national path to development as a model for other Asian nations to follow. But their Great East Asia Co-Prosperity Sphere, which had been designed to build a vast empire under Japanese tutelage, had led only to bloody war and ultimate defeat.

Half a century later, Japan had emerged as the second greatest industrial power in the world, democratic in form and content and a source of stability throughout the region. Praise of the so-called Japanese miracle became a growth industry in academic circles in the United States, and Japan's achievement spawned a number of Asian imitators. Known as the "Little Tigers," the four industrializing societies of Taiwan, Hong Kong, Singapore, and South Korea achieved considerable success by following the path originally charted by Japan. Along with Japan, they became economic powerhouses and ranked among the world's top seventeen trading nations. Other nations in Asia and elsewhere took note and began to adopt the Japanese formula. It is no wonder that observers relentlessly heralded the coming of the "Pacific Century."

The impressive success of some countries in East and Southeast Asia prompted several commentators in the region to declare that the global balance of power had shifted away from Europe and the United States toward the lands of the Pacific. When Western critics argued that eastern Asia's achievements had taken place at great cost, as authoritarian governments in the region trampled on human rights and denied their citizens the freedoms that they required to fulfill their own destiny, Asian observers retorted that freedom is not simply a matter of individuals' doing what they please but rather represents an opportunity and an obligation to serve their community and achieve the betterment of their fellow human beings. Such views reflected not only the growing self-confidence of many societies in East and Southeast Asia but also their growing inclination to defend Asian values and traditions against critics in the West. ◇

THE EMPEROR IS NOT DIVINE

t the close of World War II, the United States agreed that Japan could retain the emperor, but only on the condition that he renounce his divinity. When the governments of Great Britain and the Soviet Union advocated that Hirohito be tried as a war criminal, General Douglas MacArthur, the supreme commander of Allied occupation forces in Japan, argued that the emperor had a greater grasp of democratic principles than most other Japanese and that his presence was vital to the success of Allied occupation policy. That recommendation was upheld. On New Year's Day, 1946, the emperor issued a rescript denying his divinity. To many Japanese of the era, however, he remained a divine figure.

What promises is the Japanese emperor making to his subjects in this statement? Does he apologize for mistakes made in the past?

Hirohito, Rescript on Divinity

In greeting the New Year, we recall to mind that the Emperor Meiji proclaimed as the basis of our national policy the five clauses of the Charter at the beginning of the Meiji era. . . .

The proclamation is evident in its significance and high in its ideals. We wish to make this oath anew and restore the country to stand on its own feet again. We have to reaffirm the principles embodied in the Charter and proceed unflinchingly toward elimination of misguided practices of the past; and keeping in close touch with the desires of the people, we will construct a new Japan through thoroughly being pacific, the officials and the people alike obtaining rich culture and advancing the standard of living of the people.

The devastation of the war inflicted upon our cities, the miseries of the destitute, the stagnation of trade, shortage of food, and the great and growing number of unemployed are indeed heart-rending, but if the nation is firmly united in its resolve to face the present ordeal and to see civilization consistently in peace, a bright future will undoubtedly be ours, not only for our country but for the whole of humanity.

Love of the family and love of country are especially strong in this country. With more of this devotion should we now work toward love of mankind.

We feel deeply concerned to note that consequent upon the protracted war ending in our defeat our people are liable to grow restless and to fall into the slough of despond. Radical tendencies in excess are gradually spreading and the sense of morality tends to lose its hold on the people with the result that there are signs of confusion of thoughts.

We stand by the people and we wish always to share with them in their moment of joys and sorrows. The ties between us and our people have always stood upon mutual trust and affection. They do not depend upon mere legends and myths. They are not predicated on the false conception that the Emperor is divine and that the Japanese people are superior to other races and fated to rule the world.

Our Government should make every effort to alleviate their trials and tribulations. At the same time, we trust that the people will rise to the occasion and will strive courageously for the solution of their outstanding difficulties and for the development of industry and culture. Acting upon a consciousness of solidarity and of mutual aid and broad tolerance in their civil life, they will prove themselves worthy of their best tradition. By their supreme endeavors in that direction they will be able to render their substantial contribution to the welfare and advancement of mankind.

The resolution for the year should be made at the beginning of the year. We expect our people to join us in all exertions looking to accomplishment of this great undertaking with an indomitable spirit.

SOURCE: John David Lu, *Sources of Japanese Tradition* (New York: McGraw-Hill, 1974), vol. 2, pp. 190–191; from *New York Times*, January 1, 1946.

Japan: Asian Giant

For five years after the war in the Pacific, Japan was governed by an Allied administration under the command of U.S. General Douglas MacArthur. The occupation regime, which consisted of the Far Eastern Commission in Washington, D.C., and the four-power Allied Council in Tokyo, was dominated by the United States, although the country was technically administered by a new Japanese government. As commander of the occupation administration, MacArthur was responsible for demilitarizing Japanese society, destroying the Japanese war machine, trying Japanese civilian and military officials charged with war crimes, and laying the foundations of postwar Japanese society.

During the war, senior U.S. officials had discussed whether to insist on the abdication of the emperor as the symbol of Japanese imperial expansion. During the summer of 1945, the United States rejected a Japanese request to guarantee that the position of the emperor would be retained in any future peace settlement and reiterated its demand for unconditional surrender. After the war, however, the United States agreed to the retention of the emperor after he agreed publicly to renounce his divinity (see the box above). Although many historians have suggested that Emperor Hirohito opposed the war policy of his senior advisers, some recent studies have contended that he fully supported it.

Under MacArthur's firm tutelage, Japanese society was remodeled along Western lines. The centerpiece of occupation policy was the promulgation of a new constitution to replace the Meiji Constitution of 1889. The new charter, which was drafted by U.S. planners and imposed on the Japanese despite their objections to some of its provisions, was designed to transform Japan into a peaceful and pluralistic society that would no longer be capable of waging offensive war. The constitution specifically renounced war as a national policy, and Japan unilaterally agreed to maintain armed forces only sufficient for self-defense. Perhaps most important, the constitution established a parliamentary form of government based on a bicameral legislature, an independent judiciary, and a universal franchise; it also reduced the power of the emperor and guaranteed human rights.

But more than a written constitution was needed to demilitarize Japan and place it on a new course. Like the Meiji leaders in the late nineteenth century, occupation administrators wished to transform Japanese social institutions and hoped their policies would be accepted by the Japanese people as readily as those of the Meiji period had been. The Meiji reforms, however, had been crafted to reflect native traditions and had set Japan on a path quite different from that of the modern West. Some Japanese observers believed that a fundamental reversal of trends begun with the Meiji Restoration would be needed before Japan would be ready to adopt the Western capitalist, democratic model.

One of the sturdy pillars of Japanese militarism had been the giant business cartels, known as *zaibatsu*. Allied policy was designed to break up the *zaibatsu* into smaller units in the belief that corporate concentration, in Japan as in the United States, not only hindered competition but was inherently undemocratic and conducive to political authoritarianism. Occupation planners also intended to promote the formation of independent labor unions, to lessen the power of the state over the economy, and to provide a mouthpiece for downtrodden Japanese workers. Economic inequality in rural areas was to be reduced by a comprehensive land reform program that would turn the land over to the people who farmed it. Finally, the educational system was to be remodeled along American lines so that it would turn out independent individuals rather than automatons subject to manipulation by the state.

The Allied program was an ambitious and even audacious plan to remake Japanese society and has been justly praised for its clear-sighted vision and altruistic motives. Parts of the program, such as the constitution, the land

reform program, and the educational system, succeeded brilliantly. But as other concerns began to intervene, changes or compromises were made that were not always successful. In particular, with the rise of Cold War sentiment in the United States in the late 1940s, the goal of decentralizing the Japanese economy gave way to the desire to make Japan a key partner in the effort to defend East Asia against international communism. Convinced of the need to promote economic recovery in Japan, U.S. policymakers began to show more tolerance for the *zaibatsu*. Concerned at growing radicalism within the new labor movement, where left-wing elements were gaining strength, U.S. occupation authorities placed less emphasis on the independence of the labor unions.

Cold War concerns also affected U.S. foreign relations with Japan. On September 8, 1951, the United States and other former belligerent nations signed a peace treaty restoring Japanese independence. In turn, Japan renounced any claim to such former colonies or territories as Taiwan (which had been returned to the Republic of China), Korea (which, after a period of joint Soviet and U.S. occupation, had become two independent states), and southern Sakhalin and the Kurile Islands (which had been ceded to the Soviet Union). The Soviet Union refused to sign the treaty on the grounds that it had not been permitted to play an active role in the occupation. On the same day, the Japanese and Americans signed a defensive alliance and agreed that the United States could maintain military bases on the Japanese islands. Japan was now formally independent, but in a new dependency relationship with the United States.

The Transformation of Modern Japan: Politics and Government

Thus, by the early 1950s, Japan had regained at least partial control over its own destiny (see Map 12.1). Although it was linked closely to the United States through the new security treaty and the new U.S.-drafted constitution, Japan was now essentially free to move out on its own. As the world would soon discover, the Japanese adapted quickly to the new conditions. From a semifeudal society with autocratic leanings, Japan rapidly progressed into one of the most stable and advanced democracies in the world.

The Allied occupation administrators started with the conviction that Japanese expansionism was directly linked to the institutional and ideological foundations of the Meiji Constitution. Accordingly, they set out to change Japanese politics into something closer to the pluralistic approach used in most Western nations. The concepts of universal suffrage, governmental accountability, and a balance of

MAP 12.1 **Modern Japan.** Shown here are the four main islands that comprise the contemporary state of Japan. ❓ Which is the largest? 🌐 **View an animated version of this map or related maps at the World History Resource Center, at** worldrc.wadsworth.com/.

power among the executive, legislative, and judicial branches that were embodied in the constitution of 1947 have held firm, and Japan today is a stable and mature democratic society with a literate and politically active electorate and a government that usually seeks to meet the needs of its citizens.

Yet a number of characteristics of the current Japanese political system reflect the tenacity of the traditional political culture. Although postwar Japan had a multiparty system with two major parties, the Liberal Democrats and the Socialists, in practice there was a "government party" and a permanent opposition—the Liberal Democrats were not voted out of office for thirty years. The ruling Liberal Democratic Party included several factions, but disputes usually involved personalities rather than substantive issues. Many of the leading Liberal Democrats controlled factions on a patron-client basis, and decisions on key issues, such as who should assume the prime ministership, were decided by a modern equivalent of the *genro* oligarchs.

That tradition changed suddenly in 1993 when the ruling Liberal Democrats, shaken by persistent reports of corruption and cronyism between politicians and business

interests, failed to win a majority of seats in parliamentary elections. Mirohiro Hosokawa, the leader of one of several newly created parties in the Japanese political spectrum, was elected prime minister. He promised to launch a number of reforms to clean up the political system. The new coalition government quickly split into feuding factions, however, and in 1995, the Liberal Democratic Party returned to power. Successive prime ministers failed to carry out promised reforms, and in 2001, Junichiro Koizumi (b. 1942), a former minister of health and welfare, was elected prime minister on a promise that he would initiate far-reaching reforms to fix the political system and make it more responsive to the needs of the Japanese people. His charisma raised expectations that he might be able to bring about significant changes, but bureaucratic resistance to reform and chronic factionalism within the Liberal Democratic Party have largely thwarted his efforts.

Japan, Incorporated One of the problems plaguing the current system has been the centralizing tendencies that it inherited from the Meiji period. The government is organized on a unitary rather than a federal basis; the local administrative units, called prefectures, have few of the powers of states in the United States. Moreover, the central government plays an active and sometimes intrusive role in various aspects of the economy, mediating management-labor disputes, establishing price and wage policies, and subsidizing vital industries and enterprises producing goods for export. This government intervention in the economy has traditionally been widely accepted and is often cited as a key reason for the efficiency of Japanese industry and the emergence of the country as an industrial giant.

In recent years, though, the tradition of active government involvement in the economy has increasingly come under fire. Japanese business, which previously sought government protection from imports, now argues that deregulation is needed to enable Japanese firms to innovate in order to keep up with the competition. Such reforms, however, have been resisted by powerful government ministries in Tokyo, which are accustomed to playing an active role in national affairs.

A third problem is that the ruling Liberal Democratic Party has long been divided into factions that seek to protect their own interests and often resist changes that might benefit society as a whole. This tradition of factionalism has tended to insulate political figures from popular scrutiny and encouraged susceptibility to secret dealing and official corruption. A number of senior politicians, including two recent prime ministers, have been forced to resign because of serious questions about improper financial dealings with business associates. Concern over political corruption was undoubtedly a major factor in the defeat suffered by the

Liberal Democrats in the summer of 1993, and the issue continues to plague the political scene.

Last but certainly not least, minorities such as the *eta* (hereditary outcastes in traditional Japan, now known as the Burakumin) and Korean residents in Japan continue to be subjected to legal and social discrimination. For years, official sources were reluctant to divulge that thousands of Korean women were conscripted to serve as "comfort women" (prostitutes) for Japanese soldiers during the war, and many Koreans living in Japan contend that such condescending attitudes toward minorities continue to exist. Representatives of the "comfort women" have demanded both financial compensation and a formal letter of apology from the Japanese government for the treatment they received during the Pacific War. Negotiations over the issue are under way.

Atoning for the Past Japan's behavior during World War II has been an especially sensitive issue. During the early 1990s, critics at home and abroad charged that textbooks printed under the guidance of the Ministry of Education did not adequately discuss the atrocities committed by the Japanese government and armed forces during World War II. Other Asian governments were particularly incensed at Tokyo's failure to accept responsibility for such behavior and demanded a formal apology. The government expressed remorse, but only in the context of the aggressive actions of all colonial powers during the imperialist era. In the view of many Japanese, the actions of their government during the Pacific War were a form of self-defense. When new textbooks were published that openly discussed instances of Japanese wartime misconduct, including sex slavery, the use of slave labor, and the Nanjing Massacre (see Chapter 6), many Japanese were outraged and initiated a campaign to delete or tone down references to atrocities committed by imperial troops during the Pacific War. Prime Minister Koizumi has exacerbated the controversy by attending ceremonies at shrines dedicated to the spirits of Japan's war dead.

The issue is not simply an academic one, for fear of a revival of Japanese militarism is still strong in the region, where Japan's relations with other states have recently been strained by disputes with South Korea and China over ownership of small islands in the China Sea. The United States has not shared this concern, however, and applauded Japan's recent decision to enhance the ability of its self-defense forces to deal with potential disturbances within the region. The proper role of the military has provoked vigorous debate in Japan, where some observers have argued that their country should adopt a more assertive stance toward the United States and play a larger role in Asian affairs.

The Economy

Nowhere are the changes in postwar Japan so visible as in the economic sector, where the nation has developed into a major industrial and technological power in the space of a century, surpassing such advanced Western societies as Germany, France, and Great Britain. Here indeed is the Japanese miracle in its most concrete manifestation.

The process began a century ago in the single-minded determination of the Meiji modernizers to create a rich country and a strong state. Their initial motive was to ensure Japan's survival against Western imperialism, but this defensive urge evolved into a desire to excel and, during the years before World War II, to dominate. That desire led to the war in the Pacific and, in the eyes of some observers, still contributes to Japan's problems with its trading partners in the world today.

Occupation Reforms As we have seen, the officials of the Allied occupation identified the Meiji economic system with centralized power and the rise of Japanese militarism. Accordingly, MacArthur's planners set out to break up the *zaibatsu* and decentralize Japanese industry and commerce. But with the rise of Cold War tensions, the policy was scaled back in the late 1940s, and only the nineteen largest conglomerates were affected. In any event, the new antimonopoly law did not hinder the formation of looser ties between Japanese companies, and as a result, a new type of informal relationship, sometimes called the *keiretsu*, or "interlocking arrangement," began to take shape after World War II. Through such arrangements among suppliers, wholesalers, retailers, and financial institutions, the *zaibatsu* system was reconstituted under a new name.

The occupation administration had more success with its program to reform the agricultural system. Half of the population still lived on farms, and half of all farmers were still tenants. Under a stringent land reform program in the late 1940s, all lands owned by absentee landlords and all cultivated landholdings over an established maximum were sold on easy credit terms to the tenants. The maximum size of an individual farm was set at 7.5 acres, while an additional 2.5 acres could be leased to tenants. The reform program created a strong class of yeoman farmers, and tenants declined to about 10 percent of the rural population.

The Japanese Miracle During the next fifty years, Japan re-created the stunning results of the Meiji era. At the end of the Allied occupation in 1950, the Japanese gross domestic product was about one-third that of Great Britain or France. Today, it is larger than both put together and well over half that of the United States. For years, Japan was the greatest exporting nation in the world, and its per capita income equals or surpasses that of most advanced Western states. In terms of education, mortality rates, and health care, the quality of life in Japan is superior to that in the United States or the advanced nations of Western Europe.

By the mid-1980s, the economic challenge presented by Japan had begun to arouse increasing concern in both official and private circles in Europe and the United States. Explanations for the phenomenon tended to fall into two major categories. Some pointed to cultural factors: The Japanese are naturally group-oriented and find it easy to cooperate with one another. Traditionally hardworking and frugal, they are more inclined to save than to consume, a trait that boosts the savings rate and labor productivity. The Japanese are also family-oriented and therefore spend less on welfare for the elderly, who normally live with their children. Like all Confucian societies, the Japanese value education, and consequently, the labor force is highly skilled. Finally, Japan is a homogeneous society in which people share common values and respond in similar ways to the challenges of the modern world.

Others cited more practical reasons for Japanese success. Paradoxically, Japan benefited from the total destruction of its industrial base during World War II because it did not face the problem of antiquated plants that plagued many industries in the United States. Under the terms of its constitution and the security treaty with the United States, Japan spends less than 1 percent of its gross domestic product on national defense, whereas the United States spends about 5 percent. Labor productivity is high, not only because the Japanese are hard workers (according to statistics, Japanese workers spend more time on the job than workers in other advanced societies) but also because corporations reward innovation and have maintained good management-labor relations. Consequently, employee mobility and the number of days lost to labor stoppages are minimized (on an average day in the 1990s, according to one estimate, 603 Japanese workers were on strike compared to 11,956 Americans). Just as it did before World War II, the Japanese government promotes business interests rather than hindering them. Finally, some analysts have charged that Japan uses unfair trade practices, subsidizing exports through the Ministry of International Trade and Industry (MITI), dumping goods at prices below cost to break into a foreign market, maintaining an artificially low standard of living at home to encourage exports, and unduly restricting imports from other countries.

There is some truth on both sides of the argument. Undoubtedly, Japan benefited from its privileged position beneath the U.S. nuclear umbrella as well as from its ability to operate in a free trade environment that provided both export markets and access to Western technology. The Japanese also took a number of practical steps to improve their competitive position in the world and the effectiveness of their economic system at home.

Yet many of these steps were possible precisely because of the cultural factors described here. The tradition of loyalty to the firm, for example, derives from the communal tradition in Japanese society. The concept of sacrificing one's personal interests to those of the state, though not necessarily rooted in the traditional period, was certainly fostered by the *genro* oligarchy during the Meiji era.

The Miracle Tarnished By the 1990s, however, the Japanese economy had begun to run into serious difficulties, raising the question of whether the vaunted Japanese model is as appealing as many observers earlier declared. A rise in the value of the yen hurt exports and burst the bubble of investment by Japanese banks that had taken place under the umbrella of government protection. Lacking a domestic market equivalent in size to the United States, the Japanese economy slipped into a long-term recession that has only recently come to an end.

These economic difficulties have placed heavy pressure on some of the highly praised features of the Japanese economy. The tradition of lifetime employment created a bloated white-collar workforce and made downsizing difficult. Today, job security is on the decline as increasing numbers of workers are being laid off. Unfortunately, a disproportionate burden has fallen on women, who lack seniority and continue to suffer from various forms of discrimination in the workplace. A positive consequence is that job satisfaction is beginning to take precedence over security in the minds of many Japanese workers, and salary is beginning to reflect performance more than time on the job.

A final change is that slowly but inexorably, the Japanese market is beginning to open up to international competition. Foreign automakers are winning a growing share of the domestic market, while the government—concerned at the prospect of food shortages—has committed itself to facilitating the importation of rice from abroad. This last move was especially sensitive, given the almost sacred role that rice farming holds in the Japanese mind-set.

At the same time, greater exposure to foreign economic competition may improve the performance of Japanese manufacturers. In recent years, Japanese consumers have become increasingly concerned about the quality of some of their domestic products, provoking one cabinet minister to complain about "sloppiness and complacency" among Japanese firms (the scandal in the United States over defects in Firestone tires, produced by the Japanese tire manufacturer Bridgestone, was a case in point). One apparent reason for the country's quality problems is the cost-cutting measures adopted by Japanese companies to meet the challenges from abroad.

A Society in Transition

During the occupation, Allied planners set out to change social characteristics that they believed had contributed to Japanese aggressiveness before and during World War II. The new educational system removed all references to filial piety, patriotism, and loyalty to the emperor and emphasized the individualistic values of Western civilization. The new constitution and a revised civil code attempted to achieve true sexual equality by removing remaining legal restrictions on women's rights to obtain a divorce, hold a job, or change their domicile. Women were guaranteed the right to vote and were encouraged to enter politics.

Such efforts to remake Japanese behavior through legislation were only partly successful. Since the end of World War II, Japan has unquestionably become a more individualistic and egalitarian society. Freedom of choice in marriage and occupation is taken for granted, and social mobility, though not so extensive as in the United States, has increased considerably. Although Allied occupation policy established the legal framework for these developments, primary credit must be assigned to the evolution of the Japanese themselves into an urbanized and technologically advanced industrial society.

At the same time, many of the distinctive characteristics of traditional Japanese society have persisted, in somewhat altered form. The emphasis on loyalty to the group and community relationships, for example, known in Japanese as *amae,* is reflected in the strength of corporate loyalties in contemporary Japan. Even though competition among enterprises in a given industry is often quite vigorous, social cohesiveness among both management and labor personnel is exceptionally strong within each individual corporation, although, as we have seen, that attitude has eroded somewhat in recent years.

One possible product of this attitude may be the relatively egalitarian nature of Japanese society in terms of income. A chief executive officer in Japan receives, on average, about twenty times the salary of the average worker, compared with over two hundred times in the United States. The disparity between wealth and poverty is also generally less in Japan than in most European countries and certainly less than in the United States.

Japan's welfare system also differs profoundly from its Western counterparts. Applicants are required to seek assistance first from their own families, and the physically able are ineligible for government aid. As a result, less than 1 percent of the population receives welfare benefits, compared with more than 10 percent who receive some form of assistance in the United States. Outside observers interpret the difference as the product of several factors, including low levels of drug addiction and illegitimacy, as well as the importance in Japan of the work ethic and family responsibility.

Emphasis on the work ethic remains strong. The tradition of hard work is implanted at a young age by the educational system. The Japanese school year runs for 240 days, compared to 180 days in the United States, and work assignments outside class tend to be more extensive (according to one source, a Japanese student averages about five hours of homework per day). Competition for acceptance into universities is intense, and many young Japanese take cram courses to prepare for the "examination hell" that lies ahead. The results are impressive: the literacy rate in Japanese schools is almost 100 percent, and Japanese schoolchildren consistently earn higher scores on achievement tests than children in other advanced countries. At the same time, this devotion to success has often been accompanied by bullying by teachers and what Americans might consider an oppressive sense of conformity (see the box on p. 245).

Some young Japanese find suicide the only escape from the pressures emanating from society, school, and family. Parental pride often becomes a factor, with "education mothers" pressuring their children to work hard and succeed for the honor of the family. Ironically, once the student is accepted into college, the amount of work assigned tends to decrease because graduates of the best universities are virtually guaranteed lucrative employment offers. Nevertheless, the early training instills an attitude of deference to group interests that persists throughout life. Some outside observers, however, believe such attitudes can have a detrimental effect on individual initiative.

By all accounts, independent thinking is on the increase in Japan, and some schools are beginning to emphasize creativity over rote learning. In some cases, it leads to antisocial behavior, such as crime or membership in a teen gang. Usually, it is expressed in more indirect ways, such as the recent fashion among young people of dyeing their hair brown (known in Japanese as "tea hair"). Because the practice is banned in many schools and generally frowned on by the older generation (one police chief dumped a pitcher of beer on a student with brown hair that he noticed in a bar), many young Japanese dye their hair as a gesture of independence and a means of gaining acceptance among their peers. When seeking employment or getting married, however, they return their hair to its natural color.

Women in Japanese Society One of the more tenacious legacies of the past in Japanese society is sexual inequality. Although women are now legally protected against discrimination in employment, very few have reached senior levels in business, education, or politics, and in the words of one Western scholar, they remain "acutely disadvantaged"—though ironically, in a recent survey of business executives in Japan, a majority declared that women were smarter than men. Women now make up over 50 percent

GROWING UP IN JAPAN

*J*apanese schoolchildren are exposed to a much more regimented environment than U.S. children experience. Most Japanese schoolchildren, for example, wear black-and-white uniforms to school. These regulations are examples of rules adopted by middle school systems in various parts of Japan. The Ministry of Education in Tokyo concluded that these regulations were excessive, but they are probably typical.

What do you think is the purpose of establishing such regulations? How do they differ from standards of behavior in schools in the United States?

School Regulations: Japanese Style

1. Boys' hair should not touch the eyebrows, the ears, or the top of the collar.
2. No one should have a permanent wave, or dye his or her hair. Girls should not wear ribbons or accessories in their hair. Hair dryers should not be used.
3. School uniform skirts should be ____ centimeters above the ground, no more and no less (differs by school and region).
4. Keep your uniform clean and pressed at all times. Girls' middy blouses should have two buttons on the back collar. Boys' pant cuffs should be of the prescribed width. No more than 12 eyelets should be on the shoes. The number of buttons on a shirt and tucks in a shirt are also prescribed.
5. Wear your school badge at all times. It should be positioned exactly.
6. Going to school in the morning, wear your book bag strap on the right shoulder; in the afternoon on the way home, wear it on the left shoulder. Your book case thickness, filled and unfilled, is also prescribed.
7. Girls should wear only regulation white underpants of 100% cotton.
8. When you raise your hand to be called on, your arm should extend forward and up at the angle prescribed in your handbook.
9. Your own route to and from school is marked in your student rule handbook; carefully observe which side of each street you are to use on the way to and from school.
10. After school you are to go directly home, unless your parent has written a note permitting you to go to another location. Permission will not be granted by the school unless the other location is a suitable one. You must not go to coffee shops. You must be home by ____ o'clock.
11. It is not permitted to drive or ride a motorcycle, or to have a license to drive one.
12. Before and after school, no matter where you are, you represent our school, so you should behave in ways we can all be proud of.

SOURCE: Reprinted with permission of The Free Press, a division of Simon & Schuster Adult Publishing Group, from *The Material Child: Coming of Age in Japan and America* by Merry White. Copyright © 1993 by Merry White. All rights reserved.

---

of the workforce, but most are in retail or service occupations, and their average salary is only about half that of men.[1] There is a feminist movement in Japan, but it has none of the vigor and mass support of its counterpart in the United States.

Most women in Japan consider being a homemaker the ideal position. In the home, a Japanese woman has considerable responsibility. She is expected to be a "good wife and wise mother" and has the primary responsibility for managing the family finances and raising the children. Japanese husbands (known derisively in Japan as the "wet leaf tribe") perform little work around the house, spending an average of nine minutes a day on housework, compared to twenty-six minutes for American husbands. At the same time, Japanese divorce rates are well below those of the United States.

The Demographic Crisis Many of Japan's current dilemmas stem from its growing demographic problems. Today, Japan has the highest proportion of people older than sixty-five of any industrialized country—17 percent of the country's total population. By the year 2024, an estimated one-third of the Japanese population will be over the age of sixty-five, and the median age will be fifty, ten years older than the median in the United States. This demographic profile is due both to declining fertility and a low level of immigration. Immigrants make up only 1 percent of the total population of Japan. Together, the aging population and the absence of immigrants are creating the prospect of a dramatic labor shortage in coming years. Nevertheless, prejudice against foreigners persists in Japan, and the government has no plans to ease restrictions against immigrants from other countries in the region.

Japan's aging population has many implications for the future. Traditionally, it was the responsibility of the eldest child in a Japanese family to care for aging parents, but that system is beginning to break down because of limited housing space and the growing tendency of working-age

Cool *Otaku* Fashion Teens. Fashion-conscious teenagers have become Japan's most dedicated consumers. With the economy in the doldrums and real estate costs soaring, many young people live with their families well into their twenties and use the money they save to purchase the latest styles in clothing. Avid readers of fashion magazines, these *otaku* ("obsessed") teenagers—heirs of Japan's long affluence—pay exorbitant prices for hip-hop outfits, platform shoes, and layered dresses.

© Barry Cronin Newsmakers/Getty Images

women to seek jobs in the marketplace. The proportion of Japanese older than sixty-five years of age who live with their children has dropped from 80 percent in 1970 to about 50 percent today. At the same time, public and private pension plans are under increasing financial pressure, partly because of the low birthrate and the graying population.

Whether the unique character of modern Japan will endure is unclear. Confidence in the Japanese "economic miracle" has been shaken by the long recession, and there are indications of a growing tendency toward hedonism and individualism among Japanese youth. Older Japanese frequently complain that the younger generation lacks their sense of loyalty and willingness to sacrifice.[2] There are also signs that the concept of loyalty to one's employer may be beginning to erode among Japanese youth. Some observers have predicted that with increasing affluence, Japan will become more like the industrialized societies in the West. Nevertheless, Japan is unlikely to evolve into a photocopy of the United States. Not only is Japan a much more homogeneous society, but its small size and dearth of natural resources encourage a strong work ethic and a sense of togetherness that have dissipated in American society.

Religion and Culture

The sense of racial and cultural pride that characterizes contemporary Japan is rather different from Japanese attitudes at the beginning of the Meiji era. When Japan was opened to the West in the nineteenth century, many Japanese became convinced of the superiority of foreign ideas and institutions and were especially interested in Western religion and culture. Although Christian converts were few, numbering less than 1 percent of the population, the influence of Christianity was out of proportion to the size of the community. Many intellectuals during the Meiji era were impressed by the emotional commitment shown by missionaries in Japan and viewed Christianity as a contemporary version of Confucianism.

Today, Japan includes almost 1.5 million Christians along with 93 million Buddhists. Many Japanese also follow Shinto, no longer identified with reverence for the emperor and the state. As in the West, increasing urbanization has led to a decline in the practice of organized religion, although evangelical sects have proliferated in recent years. In all likelihood, their members, like those belonging to similar sects elsewhere, are seeking spiritual underpinnings in an increasingly secular and complex world. The largest and best-known sect is the Soka Gakkai, a lay Buddhist organization that has attracted millions of followers and formed its own political party, the Komeito.

Western literature, art, and music also had a major impact on Japanese society. Western influence led to the rapid decline of traditional forms of drama and poetry and the growth in popularity of the prose novel. After the Japanese defeat in World War II, many of the writers who had been active before the war resurfaced, but now their writing reflected their demoralization, echoing the spiritual vacuum of the times. Labeled *apure,* from the first part of the French *après-guerre* (postwar), these disillusioned authors were attracted to existentialism, and some turned to hedonism and nihilism. This "lost generation" described its anguish with piercing despair; several of its luminaries committed suicide. For them, defeat was compounded by fear of the Americanization of postwar Japan.

One of the best examples of this attitude was the novelist Yukio Mishima (1925–1970), who led a crusade to stem the tide of what he described as America's "universal and uniform 'Coca-Colonization'" of the world in general and Japan in particular.[3] In *Confessions of a Mask,* written in 1949, Mishima described the awakening of a young man to his own homosexuality. His later novels, *The Thirst for Love* and *The Temple of the Golden Pavilion,* are riveting narratives about disturbed characters. Mishima's ritual suicide in 1970 was the subject of widespread speculation and transformed him into a cult figure.

One of Japan's most serious-minded contemporary authors is Kenzaburo Oe (b. 1935). His work, which was rewarded with the Nobel Prize in Literature in 1994, presents Japan's ongoing quest for modern identity and purpose. His characters reflect the spiritual anguish precipitated by the collapse of the imperial Japanese tradition and the subsequent adoption of Western culture—a trend that, according to Oe, has culminated in unabashed materialism, cultural decline, and a moral void. Yet unlike Mishima, Oe does not wish to reinstill the imperial traditions of the past but rather seeks to regain spiritual meaning by retrieving the sense of communality and innocence found in rural Japan.

Haruki Murakami (b. 1949), one of Japan's most popular authors today, was one of the first to discard the introspective and somber style of the earlier postwar period. Characters in his novels typically take the form of a detached antihero, reflecting the emptiness of corporate life in contemporary Japan. In *The Wind-Up Bird Chronicle* (1997), Murakami highlights the capacity for irrational violence in Japanese society and the failure of the nation to accept its guilt for the behavior of Japanese troops during World War II.

Since the 1970s, increasing affluence and a high literacy rate have contributed to a massive quantity of publications, ranging from popular potboilers to first-rate fiction. Much of this new literature deals with the common concerns of all affluent industrialized nations, including the effects of urbanization, advanced technology, and mass consumption. A recent phenomenon is the so-called industrial novel, which seeks to lay bare the vicious infighting and pressure tactics that characterize Japanese business today. A wildly popular genre is the "art-manga," or literary cartoon. Manga has recently become popular in the United States, especially in the form of adventure stories appealing to young girls.

There were many women writers during early Japanese history, but they labored under many disabilities in a male-dominated society. Japanese literary critics, who were invariably men, accepted "female" literature as long as it dealt exclusively with what they viewed as appropriately "female" subjects, such as the "mysteries" of the female psyche and motherhood. Recently, however, a new generation of young women in their early twenties have emerged as serious writers who examine the alienation and irreverence of many Japanese youths today. Growing up after the "bubble" era of the boom economy, the wildly popular author Hitomi Kanehara (b. 1984) writes about the members of a dropout, downwardly mobile generation, who are repudiating traditional Japanese culture.

Other aspects of Japanese culture have also been influenced by Western ideas, although without the intense preoccupation with synthesis that is evident in literature. Western music is popular in Japan, and scores of Japanese classical musicians have succeeded in the West. Even rap music has gained a foothold among Japanese youth, although without the association with sex, drugs, and violence that it has in the United States. Although some of the lyrics betray an attitude of revolt against the uptight world of Japanese society, most lack any such connotations. An example is the rap song "Street Life":

> Now's the time to hip-hop,
> Everybody's crazy about rap,
> Hey, hey, you all, listen up,
> Listen to my rap and cheer up.

As one singer remarked, "We've been very fortunate, and we don't want to bother our moms and dads. So we don't sing songs that would disturb parents."[4]

No longer are Japanese authors and painters seeking to revive the old Japan of the tea ceremony and falling plum blossoms. Raised in the crowded cities of postwar Japan, soaking up movies and television, rock music and jeans, Coca-Cola and McDonald's, many contemporary Japanese speak the universal language of today's world. Yet even as the Japanese enter the global marketplace, they retain ties to their own traditions. Businesspeople sometimes use traditional Taoist forms of physical and mental training to reduce the stress inherent in their jobs, while others retreat to a Zen monastery to learn to focus their willpower as a means of besting a competitor.

There are some signs that under the surface, the tension between traditional and modern is exacting a price. As novelists such as Yukio Mishima and Kenzaburo Oe feared, the growing focus on material possessions and the decline of traditional religious beliefs have left a spiritual void that is undermining the sense of community and purpose that have motivated the country since the Meiji era. Some young people have reacted to the emptiness of their lives by joining religious cults such as Aum Shinri Kyo, which came to world attention in 1995 when members of the organization, inspired by their leader Asahara Shoko, carried out a poison gas attack on the Tokyo subway that killed several people. Such incidents serve as a warning that Japan is not immune to the social ills that plague many Western countries.

South Korea: A Peninsula Divided

While the world was focused on the economic miracle occurring on the Japanese islands, another miracle of sorts was taking place across the Sea of Japan on the Asian mainland. In 1953, the Korean peninsula was exhausted from three years of bitter fraternal war, a conflict that took the lives of an estimated four million Koreans on both sides of the 38th parallel and turned as much as one-quarter of the population into refugees. Although a cease-fire was signed at Panmunjom in July 1953, it was a fragile peace that left two heavily armed and mutually hostile countries facing each other suspiciously.

North of the truce line was the People's Republic of Korea (PRK), a police state under the dictatorial rule of Communist leader Kim Il Sung (1912–1994). To the south was the Republic of Korea, under the equally autocratic President Syngman Rhee (1875–1965), a fierce anti-Communist who had led the resistance to the northern invasion and now placed his country under U.S. military protection. But U.S. troops could not protect Rhee from his own people, many of whom resented his reliance on the political power of the wealthy landlord class. After several years of harsh rule, marked by government corruption, fraudulent elections, and police brutality, demonstrations broke out in the capital city of Seoul in the spring of 1960 and forced him into retirement.

The Korean Model

The Rhee era was followed by a brief period of multiparty democratic government, but in 1961, General Chung Hee Park (1917–1979) came to power through a coup d'état. The new regime promulgated a new constitution, and in 1963, Park was elected president of a civilian government. He set out to foster an economic recovery after decades of foreign occupation and civil war. Adopting the nineteenth-century Japanese slogan "Rich Country and Strong State," Park built up a strong military while relying on U.S. and later Japanese assistance to help build a strong manufacturing base in what had been a predominantly agricultural society. Because the private sector had been relatively weak under Japanese rule, the government played an active role in the process by instituting a series of five-year plans that targeted specific industries for development, promoted exports, and funded infrastructure development. Under a land reform program, large landowners were required to sell all their farmland above 7.4 acres to their tenants at low prices.

The program was a solid success. Benefiting from the Confucian principles of thrift, respect for education, and hard work (during the 1960s and 1970s, South Korean workers spent an average of sixty hours a week at their jobs), as well as from Japanese capital and technology, Korea gradually emerged as a major industrial power in East Asia. The economic growth rate rose from less than 5 percent annually in the 1950s to an average of 9 percent under Park.

Melding Past and Present in South Korea. South Korea has made a greater effort to preserve aspects of traditional culture than most of its neighbors in East Asia. Here an architect has tried to soften the impact of modernization by camouflaging a gas station in Seoul with a traditional Korean tile roof.

Courtesy of William J. Duiker

The largest corporations—including Samsung, Daewoo, and Hyundai—were transformed into massive conglomerates called *chaebol,* the Korean equivalent of the *zaibatsu* of prewar Japan. Taking advantage of relatively low wages and a stunningly high rate of saving, Korean businesses began to compete actively with the Japanese for export markets in Asia and throughout the world. The Japanese became concerned about their "hungry spirit" and began refusing to share technology with the South Koreans. Per capita income also increased dramatically, from less than $90 (in U.S. dollars) annually in 1960 to $1,560 (twice that of Communist North Korea) twenty years later.

But like many other countries in the region, South Korea was slow to develop democratic principles. Although his government functioned with the trappings of democracy, Park continued to rule by autocratic means and suppressed all forms of dissidence. In 1979, Park was assassinated, and after a brief interregnum of democratic rule, a new military government under General Chun Doo Hwan (b. 1931) seized power. The new regime was as authoritarian as its predecessors, but opposition to autocratic rule had now spread from the ranks of college and high school students, who had led the early resistance, to much of the urban population. Protests against government policies became increasingly frequent. In 1987, massive demonstrations drove government troops out of the southern city of Kwangju, but the troops returned in force and killed an estimated two thousand demonstrators.

The Transition to Democracy

With Chun under increasing pressure from the United States to moderate the oppressive character of his rule, national elections were finally held in 1989. The government nominee, Roh Tae Woo, won the election with less than 40 percent of the vote. New elections in 1992 brought Kim Young Sam to the presidency. Kim selected several women for his cabinet and promised to make South Korea "a freer and more mature democracy." He also attempted to crack down on the rising influence of the giant *chaebols,* accused of giving massive bribes in return for favors from government officials. In the meantime, representatives of South Korea had made tentative contacts with the

The Korean Peninsula Since 1953

Communist regime in North Korea on possible steps toward eventual reunification of the peninsula.

But the problems of South Korea were more serious than the endemic problem of corruption. A growing trade deficit, combined with a declining growth rate, led to a rising incidence of unemployment and bankruptcy. Ironically, a second problem resulted from the economic collapse of Seoul's bitter rival, the PRK. Under the rule of Kim Il Sung's son Kim Jong Il, the North Korean economy was in a free fall, raising the specter of an outflow of refugees that could swamp neighboring countries. To relieve the immediate effects of a food shortage, the Communist government in Pyongyang relaxed its restrictions on private farming, while Seoul agreed to provide food aid to alleviate the famine.

In the fall of 1997, a sudden drop in the value of the Korean currency, the *won,* led to bank failures and a decision to seek assistance from the International Monetary Fund (IMF). In December, an angry electorate voted Kim Young Sam (whose administration was tarnished by reports of corruption) out of office and elected his rival Kim Dae Jung to the presidency. But although the new chief executive promised drastic reforms, his regime too was charged with corruption and incompetence, while relations with North Korea, now on the verge of becoming a nuclear power, remained tense. On the economic front, South Korea has become a major player in the emerging field of information technology and a significant supplier of cell phones on a global basis.

Taiwan: The Other China

South Korea was not the only rising industrial power trying to imitate the success of the Japanese in East Asia. To the south on the island of Taiwan, the Republic of China began to do the same.

After retreating to Taiwan following their defeat by the Communists, Chiang Kai-shek and his followers established a new capital at Taipei and set out to build a strong and prosperous nation based on Chinese traditions and the principles of Sun Yat-sen. The government, which continued to refer to itself as the Republic of China (ROC),

Modern Taiwan

contended that it remained the legitimate representative of the Chinese people and that it would eventually return in triumph to the mainland.

The Nationalists had much more success on Taiwan than they had achieved on the mainland. In the relatively secure environment provided by a security treaty with the United States, signed in 1954, and the comforting presence of the U.S. Seventh Fleet in the Taiwan Strait, the ROC was able to concentrate on economic growth without worrying about a Communist invasion. The regime possessed a number of other advantages that it had not enjoyed in Nanjing. Fifty years of efficient Japanese rule had left behind a relatively modern economic infrastructure and an educated populace, although the island had absorbed considerable damage during World War II and much of its agricultural produce had been exported to Japan at low prices. With only a small population to deal with (about seven million in 1945), the ROC could make good use of foreign assistance and the efforts of its own energetic people to build a modern industrialized society.

The government moved rapidly to create a solid agricultural base. A land reform program, more effectively designed and implemented than the one introduced in the early 1930s on the mainland, led to the reduction of rents, while landholdings over 3 acres were purchased by the government and resold to the tenants at reasonable prices. As in Meiji Japan, the previous owners were compensated by government bonds. The results were gratifying: food production doubled over the next generation and began to make up a substantial proportion of exports.

In the meantime, the government strongly encouraged the development of local manufacturing and commerce. By the 1970s, Taiwan was one of the most dynamic industrial economies in East Asia. The agricultural proportion of the gross domestic product declined from 36 percent in 1952 to only 9 percent thirty years later. At first, the industrial and commercial sector was composed of relatively small firms engaged in exporting textiles and food products, but the 1960s saw a shift to heavy industry, including shipbuilding, steel, petrochemicals, and machinery, and a growing emphasis on exports. The government played a major role in the process, targeting strategic industries for support and investing in infrastructure. At the same time, as in Japan, the government stressed the importance of private enterprise and encouraged foreign investment and a high rate of internal savings. By the mid-1980s, more than three-quarters of the population lived in urban areas.

Taiwan Under Nationalist Rule

In contrast to the People's Republic of China (PRC) on the mainland, the ROC actively maintained Chinese tradition, promoting respect for Confucius and the ethical principles of

The Chiang Kai-shek Memorial in Taipei. While the Chinese government on the mainland attempted to destroy all vestiges of traditional culture, the Republic of China on Taiwan sought to preserve the cultural heritage as a link between past and present. This policy is graphically displayed in the mausoleum for Chiang Kai-shek in downtown Taipei, shown in this photograph. The mausoleum, with its massive entrance gate, not only glorifies the nation's leader, but recalls the grandeur of old China.

the past, such as hard work, frugality, and filial piety. Although there was some corruption in both the government and the private sector, income differentials between the wealthy and the poor were generally less than elsewhere in the region, and the overall standard of living increased substantially. Health and sanitation improved, literacy rates were quite high, and an active family planning program reduced the rate of population growth. Nevertheless, the total population on the island increased to about 20 million in the mid-1980s.

In one respect, however, Chiang Kai-shek had not changed: increasing prosperity did not lead to the democratization of the political process. The Nationalists continued to rule by emergency decree and refused to permit the formation of opposition political parties on the grounds that the danger of invasion from the mainland had not subsided. Propaganda material from the PRC was rigorously prohibited, and dissident activities (promoting either rapprochement with the mainland or the establishment of an independent Republic of Taiwan) were ruthlessly suppressed. Although representatives to the provincial government of the province of Taiwan were chosen in local elections, the central government (technically representing the entire population of China) was dominated by mainlanders who had fled to the island with Chiang in 1949.

Some friction developed between the mainlanders (as the new arrivals were called), who numbered about two million, and the native Taiwanese; except for a few aboriginal peoples in the mountains, most of the natives were ethnic Chinese whose ancestors had emigrated to the island during the Qing dynasty. While the mainlanders were dominant in government and the professions, the native Taiwanese were prominent in commerce. Mainlanders tended to view the local population with a measure of condescension, and at least in the early years, intermarriage between members of the two groups was rare. Many Taiwanese remembered with anger the events of March 1947, when Nationalist troops had killed hundreds of Taiwanese demonstrators in Taipei. More than one thousand leading members of the local Taiwanese community were arrested and killed in the subsequent repression. By the 1980s, however, these fissures in Taiwanese society had begun to diminish; by that time, an ever-higher proportion of the population had been born on the island and identified themselves as Taiwanese.

Crafting a Taiwanese Identity

During the 1980s, the ROC slowly began to evolve toward a more representative form of government—a process that was facilitated by the death of Chiang Kai-shek in 1975. Chiang Ching-kuo (1909–1988), his son and successor, was less concerned about the danger from the mainland and more tolerant of free expression. On his death, he was succeeded as president by Lee Teng-hui (b. 1923), a native

Taiwanese. By the end of the 1980s, democratization was under way, including elections and the formation of legal opposition parties. A national election in 1992 resulted in a bare majority for the Nationalists over strong opposition from the Democratic Progressive Party (DPP).

But political liberalization had its dangers; some leading Democratic Progressives began to agitate for an independent Republic of Taiwan, a possibility that aroused concern within the Nationalist government in Taipei and frenzied hostility in the PRC. In the spring of 2000, DPP candidate Chen Shuibian (b. 1950) was elected to the presidency, ending half a century of Nationalist Party rule on Taiwan. His elevation to the position angered Beijing, which noted that in the past he had called for an independent Taiwanese state. Chen backed away from that position and called for the resumption of talks with the PRC, but Chinese leaders remain suspicious of his intentions and reacted with hostility to U.S. plans to provide advanced military equipment to the island. In the meantime, charges of official corruption and economic problems have begun to erode support for the DPP on the island.

Whether Taiwan will remain an independent state or be united with the mainland is impossible to predict. Certainly, the outcome depends in good measure on developments in the PRC. During his visit to China in 1972, U.S. President Richard Nixon said that this was a question for the Chinese people to decide (see Chapter 7). In 1979, President Jimmy Carter abrogated the mutual security treaty between the United States and the ROC that had been in force since 1954 and switched U.S. diplomatic recognition from the Republic of China to the PRC. But the United States continues to provide defensive military assistance to the Taiwanese armed forces and has made it clear that it supports self-determination for the people of Taiwan and that it expects the final resolution of the Chinese civil war to be by peaceful means. In the meantime, economic and cultural contacts between Taiwan and the mainland are steadily increasing, making the costs of any future military confrontation increasingly expensive for both sides. Nevertheless, the Taiwanese have shown no inclination to accept the PRC's offer of "one country, two systems," under which the ROC would accept the PRC as the legitimate government of China in return for autonomous control over the affairs of Taiwan.

Singapore and Hong Kong: The Littlest Tigers

The smallest but by no means the least successful of the Little Tigers are Singapore and Hong Kong. Both are essentially city-states with large populations densely packed into small territories. Singapore, once a British crown colony and briefly a part of the state of Malaysia, is now an independent nation. Hong Kong was a British colony until it was returned to

You *Can* Take It with You. While wealthy Chinese in traditional China buried clay models of personal possessions to accompany the departed to the next world, ordinary people burned paper effigies, which were transported to the afterlife by means of the rising smoke. This custom survives in many Chinese communities today, as this photograph taken in modern-day Singapore demonstrates. Some merchants make their living by manufacturing paper replicas of elaborate houses as seen here, often featuring such embellishments as television sets, elegant furniture, and even Mercedes automobiles.

Courtesy of William J. Duiker

PRC control, but with autonomous status, in 1997. In recent years, both have emerged as industrial powerhouses with standards of living well above the level of their neighbors.

The success of Singapore must be ascribed in good measure to the will and energy of its political leaders. When it became independent in August 1965, Singapore was in a state of transition. Its longtime position as an entrepôt for trade between the Indian Ocean and the South China Sea was declining in importance. With only 618 square miles of territory, much of it marshland and tropical jungle, Singapore had little to offer but the frugality and industriousness of its predominantly overseas Chinese population. But a recent history of political radicalism, fostered by the rise of influential labor unions, had frightened away foreign investors.

Within a decade, Singapore's role and reputation had dramatically changed. Under the leadership of Prime Minister Lee Kuan-yew (b. 1923), once the firebrand leader of the radical People's Action Party, the government encouraged the growth of an attractive business climate while engaging in massive public works projects to feed, house, and educate the nation's two million citizens. The major components of success have been shipbuilding, oil refineries, tourism, electronics, and finance—the city-state has become the banking hub of the entire region.

Like the other Little Tigers, Singapore has relied on a combination of government planning, entrepreneurial spirit, export promotion, high productivity, and an exceptionally high rate of saving to achieve industrial growth rates of nearly

The Republic of Singapore

10 percent annually over the past quarter century. Unlike some other industrializing countries in the region, it has encouraged the presence of multinational corporations to provide much needed capital and technological input. Population growth has been controlled by a stringent family planning program, and literacy rates are among the highest in Asia.

As in the other Little Tigers, an authoritarian political system has guaranteed a stable environment for economic growth. Until his retirement in 1990, Lee Kuan-yew and his People's Action Party dominated Singaporean politics, and opposition elements were intimidated into silence or arrested. The prime minister openly declared that the Western model of pluralist democracy was not appropriate for Singapore and lauded the Meiji model of centralized development. Confucian values of thrift, hard work, and obedience to authority have been promoted as the ideology of the state. The government has had a passion for cleanliness and at one time even undertook a campaign to persuade its citizens to flush the public urinals. In 1989, the local *Straits Times,* a mouthpiece of the government, published a photograph of a man walking sheepishly from a row of urinals. The caption read "Caught without a flush: Mr. Amar Mohamed leaving the Lucky Plaza toilet without flushing the urinal."[5]

But economic success is beginning to undermine the authoritarian foundations of the system as a more sophisticated citizenry begins to demand more political freedoms and an end to government paternalism. Lee Kuan-yew's successor, Goh Chok Tong (b. 1941), promised a "kinder, gentler" Singapore, and political restrictions on individual behavior are gradually being relaxed. In the spring of 2000, the government announced the opening of a speaker's corner, where citizens would be permitted to express their views, provided they obtained a permit and did not break the law. While this was a small step, it provided a reason for optimism that a more pluralistic political system will gradually emerge under Goh's successor, Lee Hsien-luong, the son of Lee Kuan-yew.

The future of Hong Kong is not so clear-cut. As in Singapore, sensible government policies and the hard work of its people have enabled Hong Kong to thrive. At first, the prosperity of the colony depended on a plentiful supply of cheap labor. Inundated with refugees from the mainland during the 1950s and 1960s, the population of Hong Kong burgeoned

Hong Kong

to more than six million. Many of the newcomers were willing to work for starvation wages in sweatshops producing textiles, simple appliances, and toys for the export market. More recently, Hong Kong has benefited from increased tourism, manufacturing, and the growing economic prosperity of neighboring Guangdong Province, the most prosperous region of the PRC. In one respect, Hong Kong has differed from the other societies discussed in this chapter in that it has relied on an unbridled free market system rather than active state intervention in the economy. At the same time, by allocating substantial funds for transportation, sanitation, education, and public housing, the government has created favorable conditions for economic development.

Unlike the other Little Tigers, Hong Kong remained under colonial rule until very recently. British authorities

The Hong Kong Skyline. Hong Kong reverted to Chinese sovereignty in 1997 after a century of British rule. To commemorate the occasion, the imposing Conference Center, shown here in the foreground, was built on reclaimed shoreland in the Hong Kong harbor.

RETURN TO THE MOTHERLAND

*A*fter lengthy negotiations, in 1984 China and Great Britain agreed that on July 1, 1997, Hong Kong would return to Chinese sovereignty. Key sections of the agreement are included here. In succeeding years, authorities of the two countries held further negotiations. Some of the discussions raised questions in the minds of residents of Hong Kong as to whether their individual liberties would indeed be respected after the colony's return to China.

To what degree are the people of Hong Kong self-governing under these regulations? How do the regulations infringe on the freedom of the population?

The Joint Declaration on Hong Kong

The Hong Kong Special Administrative Region will be directly under the authority of the Central People's Government of the People's Republic of China. The Hong Kong Special Administrative Region will enjoy a high degree of autonomy, except in foreign and defense affairs, which are the responsibility of the Central People's Government.

The Hong Kong Special Administrative Region will be vested with executive, legislative, and independent judicial power, including that of final adjudication. The laws currently in force in Hong Kong will remain basically unchanged.

The Government of the Hong Kong Special Administrative Region will be composed of local inhabitants. The chief executive will be appointed by the Central People's Government on the basis of the results of elections or consultations by the chief executive of the Hong Kong Special Administrative Region for appointment by the Central People's Government. . . .

The current social and economic systems in Hong Kong will remain unchanged, and so will the lifestyle. Rights and freedoms, including those of the person, of speech, of the press, of assembly, of association, of travel, of movement, of correspondence, of strike, of choice of occupation, of academic research, and of religious belief will be ensured by law. . . . Private property, ownership of enterprises, legitimate right of inheritance, and foreign investment will be protected by law.

SOURCE: Kevin Rafferty, *City on the Rocks* (New York: Penguin, 1991).

---

did little to foster democratic institutions or practices, and most residents of the colony cared more about economic survival than political freedoms. In talks between representatives of Great Britain and the PRC, the Chinese leaders made it clear they were determined to have Hong Kong return to mainland authority in 1997, when the British ninety-nine-year lease over the New Territories, the foodbasket of the colony of Hong Kong, ran out. The British agreed, on condition that satisfactory arrangements could be made for the welfare of the population. The Chinese promised that for fifty years, the people of Hong Kong would live under a capitalist system and be essentially self-governing. Recent statements by Chinese leaders, however, have raised questions about the degree of autonomy Hong Kong will receive under Chinese rule, which began on July 1, 1997 (see the box above). In 2003, the local government's decision to expand security restrictions aroused widespread public protests, and pro-democratic candidates have done well in recent local elections.

On the Margins of Asia: Postwar Australia and New Zealand

Geographically, Australia and New Zealand are not part of Asia, and throughout their short history, both countries have identified culturally and politically with the West rather than with their Asian neighbors. Their political institutions and values are derived from Europe, and the form and content of their economies resemble those of the advanced countries of the world rather than the preindustrial societies of much of Southeast Asia. Both are currently members of the British Commonwealth and of the U.S.-led ANZUS alliance (Australia, New Zealand, and the United States), which serves to shield them from political turmoil elsewhere in the region.

Yet trends in recent years have been drawing both states, especially Australia, closer to Asia. In the first place, immigration from East and Southeast Asia has increased rapidly. More than one-half of current immigrants to Australia come from East Asia, and about 7 percent of the population of about 20 million people is now of Asian descent. In New Zealand, residents of Asian descent represent only about 3 percent of the population of four million, but about 12 percent of the population are Maoris, Polynesian peoples who settled on the islands about a thousand years ago. Second, trade relations with Asia are increasing rapidly. About 60 percent of Australia's export markets today are in East Asia, and the region is the source of about one-half of its imports. Asian trade with New Zealand is also on the increase.

At the same time, the links that bind both countries to Great Britain and the United States have been loosening.

Ties with London became increasingly distant after Great Britain decided to join the European Community in the early 1970s. There are moves under way in Australia and New Zealand to withdraw from the British Commonwealth, although the outcome is far from certain. Security ties with the United States remain important, but many Australians opposed their government's decision to cooperate with Washington during the Vietnam War, and the government today is seeking to establish closer political and military ties with the ASEAN alliance. Further removed from Asia both physically and psychologically, New Zealand assigns less importance to its security treaty with the United States and has been vocally critical of U.S. nuclear policies in the region.

Whether Australia and New Zealand will ever become an integral part of the Asia-Pacific region is uncertain. Cultural differences stemming from the European origins of the majority of the population in both countries hinder mutual understanding on both sides of the divide, and many ASEAN leaders (see Chapter 13) express reluctance to accept the two countries as full members of the alliance. Both countries continue to face problems in integrating indigenous peoples—the aborigines and the Maoris—into the general population. But economic and geographic realities act as a powerful force, and should the Pacific region continue on its current course toward economic prosperity and political stability, the role of Australia and New Zealand will assume greater significance.

CONCLUSION

WHAT EXPLAINS THE STRIKING ABILITY of Japan and the four Little Tigers to transform themselves into export-oriented societies capable of competing with the advanced nations of Europe and the Western Hemisphere? Some analysts point to the traditional character traits of Confucian societies, such as thrift, a work ethic, respect for education, and obedience to authority. In a recent poll of Asian executives, more than 80 percent expressed the belief that Asian values differ from those of the West, and most add that these values have contributed significantly to the region's recent success. Others place more emphasis on deliberate steps taken by government and economic leaders to meet the political, economic, and social challenges their societies face.

There seems no reason to doubt that cultural factors connected to East Asian social traditions have contributed to the economic success of these societies. Certainly, habits such as frugality, industriousness, and subordination of individual desires have all played a role in their governments' ability to concentrate on the collective interest. Political elites in these countries have been highly conscious of these factors and willing to use them for national purposes. Prime Minister Lee Kuan-yew of Singapore deliberately fostered the inculcation of such ideals among the citizens of his small nation and lamented the decline of Confucian values among the young.

As this and preceding chapters have shown, however, without active encouragement by political elites, such traditions cannot be effectively harnessed for the good of society as a whole. The creative talents of the

Chinese people, for example, were not efficiently utilized under Mao Zedong during the frenetic years of the Cultural Revolution. Only when Deng Xiaoping and other pragmatists took charge and began to place a high priority on economic development were the stunning advances of recent decades achieved. Rural poverty was reduced, if not eliminated, by stringent land reform and population control programs. Profit incentives and foreign investment were encouraged, and the development of export markets received high priority.

There was, of course, another common factor in the successes achieved by Japan and its emulators. All the Little Tigers received substantial inputs of capital and technology from the advanced nations of the West—Taiwan and South Korea from the United States, Hong Kong and Singapore from Britain. Japan relied to a greater degree on its own efforts but received a significant advantage by being placed under the U.S. security umbrella and guaranteed access to markets and sources of raw materials in a region dominated by U.S. naval power.

To some observers, economic growth in the region has sometimes been achieved at the cost of political freedom and individual human rights. Until recently, government repression of opposition has been common throughout East Asia except in Japan. In addition, the rights of national minorities and women are often still limited in comparison with the advanced countries of the West. Some commentators in the region take vigorous exception to such criticism and argue that pluralistic political systems could be very dangerous and destabilizing in the heterogeneous societies that currently exist in the region.

In any event, it should be kept in mind that progress in political pluralism and human rights has not always been easy to achieve in Europe and North America and even now frequently fails to match expectations. A rising standard of living, increased social mobility, and a changing regional environment brought about by the end of the Cold War should go far to enhance political freedoms and promote social justice in the countries bordering the western Pacific.

TIMELINE

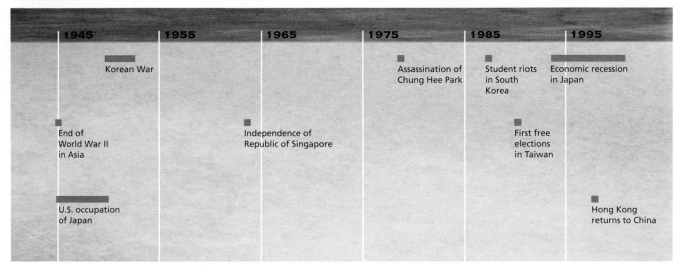

CHAPTER NOTES

1. In 2003, only about 8 percent of managers in Japanese firms were women, compared with 46 percent in the United States. *New York Times,* July 25, 2003.
2. Younger Japanese invest only about 6 percent of their annual income, whereas their parents save 25 percent. *Far Eastern Economic Review,* April 2005.
3. Yukio Mishima and Geoffrey Bownas, eds., *New Writing in Japan* (Harmondsworth, England, 1972), p. 16.
4. *New York Times,* January 29, 1996.
5. Stan Seser, "A Reporter at Large," *New Yorker,* January 13, 1992, p. 44.

CHAPTER

13

NATIONALISM TRIUMPHANT: THE EMERGENCE OF INDEPENDENT STATES IN SOUTH AND SOUTHEAST ASIA

*F*IRST-TIME VISITORS TO THE MALAYSIAN capital of Kuala Lumpur are astonished to observe a pair of twin towers thrusting up above the surrounding buildings into the clouds. The Petronas Towers rise 1,483 feet from ground level, leading to claims by Malaysian officials that they are the world's tallest buildings, at least for the time being.

More than an architectural achievement, the towers announced the emergence of Asia as a major player on the international scene. It is probably no accident that the foundations were laid on the site of the Selangor Cricket Club, symbol of colonial hegemony in Southeast Asia. "These towers," commented one local official, "will do wonders for Asia's self-esteem and confidence, which I think is very important, and which I think at this moment are at the point of takeoff."[1]

Slightly more than a year after that remark, Malaysia and several of its neighbors were mired in a financial crisis that threatened to derail their rapid advance to economic affluence and severely undermined the "self-esteem" that the Petronas Towers were meant to symbolize. For years after the buildings were completed, many of their offices were unoccupied. Today, however, the region is once again on the march. The nations of Southeast Asia have recovered from their brief economic malaise, while further to the West, India, the world's largest democracy, is beginning to shake off decades of economic lethargy and emerge as a vibrant force in the global marketplace.

The Petronas Towers, then, serve as a vivid demonstration in steel and glass of the dual face of modern Asia: a region seeking to compete with the advanced nations of the West while still struggling to overcome a legacy of economic underdevelopment and colonial rule. As Asian leaders have discovered, it is a path strewn with hidden obstacles but also opportunities. ◇

South Asia

In 1947, nearly two centuries of British colonial rule came to an end when two new independent nations, India and Pakistan, came into being. Under British authority, the subcontinent of South Asia had been linked ever more closely to the global capitalist economy. Yet as in other areas of Asia and Africa, the experience brought only limited benefits to the local peoples; little industrial development took place, and the bulk of the profits went into the pockets of Western entrepeneurs.

For half a century, nationalist forces had been seeking reforms in colonial policy and the eventual overthrow of colonial power. But the peoples of South Asia did not regain their independence until after World War II.

The End of the British Raj

During the 1930s, the nationalist movement in India was severely shaken by factional disagreements between Hindus and Muslims. The outbreak of World War II subdued these sectarian clashes, but they erupted again after the war ended in 1945. Battles between Hindus and Muslims broke out in several cities, and Mohammed Ali Jinnah (1876–1948), leader of the Muslim League, demanded the creation of a separate state for each. Meanwhile, the Labour Party, which had long been critical of the British colonial legacy on both moral and economic grounds, had come to power in Britain, and the new prime minister, Clement Attlee, announced that power would be transferred to "responsible Indian hands" by June 1948.

But the imminence of independence did not dampen communal strife. As riots escalated, the British reluctantly accepted the inevitability of partition and declared that on August 15, 1947, two independent nations—predominantly Hindu India and Muslim Pakistan—would be established. Pakistan would be divided between the main area of Muslim habitation in the Indus River valley in the west and a separate territory in east Bengal 2,000 miles to the east. Although Mahatma Gandhi warned that partition would provoke "an orgy of blood,"[2] he was increasingly regarded as a figure of the past, and his views were ignored.

The British instructed the rulers in the princely states to choose which state they would join by August 15, but problems arose in predominantly Hindu Hyderabad, where the nawab was a Muslim, and mountainous Kashmir, where a Hindu prince ruled over a Muslim population. After independence was declared, the flight of millions of Hindus and Muslims across the borders led to violence and the deaths of more than a million people. One of the casualties was Gandhi, who was assassinated on January 30, 1948, as he was going to morning prayer. The assassin, a Hindu militant, was apparently motivated by Gandhi's opposition to a Hindu India.

Independent India

With independence, the Indian National Congress, now renamed the Congress Party, moved from opposition to the responsibility of power under Jawaharlal Nehru (1889–1964), the new prime minister. The prospect must have been intimidating. The vast majority of India's 400 million people were poor and illiterate. The new nation encompassed a significant number of ethnic groups and fourteen major languages. Although Congress leaders spoke bravely of building a new nation, Indian society still bore the scars of past wars and divisions.

The government's first problem was to resolve disputes left over from the transition period. The rulers of Hyderabad and Kashmir had both followed their own preferences rather than the wishes of their subject populations. Nehru was determined to include both states within India. In 1948, Indian troops invaded Hyderabad and annexed the area. India also occupied most of Kashmir, but at the cost of creating an intractable problem that has poisoned relations with Pakistan to the present day.

An Experiment in Democratic Socialism Under Nehru's leadership, India adopted a political system on the British model, with a figurehead president and a parliamentary form of government. A number of political parties operated legally, but the Congress Party, with its enormous prestige and charismatic leadership, was dominant at both the central and the local levels. It was ably assisted by the Indian civil service, which had been created during the era of British colonial rule and provided solid expertise in the arcane art of bureaucracy.

Nehru had been influenced by British socialism and patterned his economic policy roughly after the program of the British Labour Party. The state took over ownership of the major industries and resources, transportation, and utilities, while private enterprise was permitted at the local and retail levels. Farmland remained in private hands, but rural cooperatives were officially encouraged. The government also sought to avoid excessive dependence on foreign investment and technological assistance. All businesses were required by law to have majority Indian ownership.

In other respects, Nehru was a devotee of Western materialism. He was convinced that to succeed, India must industrialize. In advocating industrialization, Nehru departed sharply from Gandhi, who believed that materialism was morally corrupting and that only simplicity and nonviolence (as represented by the traditional Indian village and the symbolic spinning wheel) could save India, and the world itself, from self-destruction (see the box on p. 259). Gandhi, Nehru complained, "just wants to spin and weave."

The primary themes of Nehru's foreign policy were anticolonialism and antiracism. Under his guidance, India took a neutral stance in the Cold War and sought to provide leadership to all newly independent nations in Asia, Africa, and Latin America. At the Bandung Conference, held in Indonesia in 1955, India promoted the concept of a bloc of "Third World" countries that would provide a balance between the capitalist world and the Communist bloc. It also sought good relations with the new People's Republic of China. India's neutrality put it at odds with the United States, which during the 1950s was trying to mobilize all nations against what it viewed as the menace of international communism.

Relations with Pakistan continued to be troubled. India refused to consider Pakistan's claim to Kashmir, even though the majority of the population there was Muslim. Tension between the two countries persisted, erupting into war in 1965. In 1971, when riots against the Pakistani government broke out in East Pakistan, India intervened on the side of East Pakistan, which declared its independence as the new nation of Bangladesh (see Map 13.1).

The Post-Nehru Era Nehru's death in 1964 aroused concern that Indian democracy was dependent on the Nehru mystique. When his successor, a Congress Party veteran, died in 1966, Congress leaders selected Nehru's daughter, Indira Gandhi (no relation to Mahatma Gandhi), as the new prime minister. Gandhi (1917–1984) was inexperienced in politics, but she quickly showed the steely determination of her father.

Like Nehru, Gandhi embraced democratic socialism and a policy of neutrality in foreign affairs, but she was more activist than her father. To combat rural poverty,

TWO VISIONS FOR INDIA

Although Jawaharlal Nehru and Mohandas Gandhi agreed on their desire for an independent India, their visions of the future of their homeland were dramatically different. Nehru favored industrialization to build material prosperity, whereas Gandhi praised the simple virtues of manual labor. The first excerpt is from a speech by Nehru; the second is from a letter written by Gandhi to Nehru.

What are the key differences between these two views of the future of India? Why do you think Nehru's vision triumphed over that of Mahatma Gandhi?

Nehru's Socialist Creed

I am convinced that the only key to the solution of the world's problems and of India's problems lies in socialism, and when I use this word I do so not in a vague humanitarian way but in the scientific economic sense. . . . I see no way of ending the poverty, the vast unemployment, the degradation and the subjection of the Indian people except through socialism. That involves vast and revolutionary changes in our political and social structure, the ending of vested interests in land and industry, as well as the feudal and autocratic Indian states system. That means the ending of private property, except in a restricted sense, and the replacement of the present profit system by a higher ideal of cooperative service. . . . In short, it means a new civilization, radically different from the present capitalist order. Some glimpse we can have of this new civilization in the territories of the U.S.S.R. Much has happened there which has pained me greatly and with which I disagree, but I look upon that great and fascinating unfolding of a new order and a new civilization as the most promising feature of our dismal age.

A Letter to Jawaharlal Nehru

I believe that if India, and through India the world, is to achieve real freedom, then sooner or later we shall have to go and live in the villages—in huts, not in palaces. Millions of people can never live in cities and palaces in comfort and peace. Nor can they do so by killing one another, that is, by resorting to violence and untruth. . . . We can have the vision of . . . truth and nonviolence only in the simplicity of the villages. That simplicity resides in the spinning wheel and what is implied by the spinning wheel. . . .

You will not be able to understand me if you think that I am talking about the villages of today. My ideal village still exists only in my imagination. . . . In this village of my dreams the villager will not be dull—he will be all awareness. He will not live like an animal in filth and darkness. Men and women will live in freedom, prepared to face the whole world. There will be no plague, no cholera, and no smallpox. Nobody will be allowed to be idle or to wallow in luxury. Everyone will have to do body labor. Granting all this, I can still envisage a number of things that will have to be organized on a large scale. Perhaps there will even be railways and also post and telegraph offices. I do not know what things there will be or will not be. Nor am I bothered about it. If I can make sure of the essential thing, other things will follow in due course. But if I give up the essential thing, I give up everything.

SOURCES: From *Sources of Indian Tradition* by William De Bary. Copyright © 1988 by Columbia University Press, New York, and excerpt from *Gandhi in India: In His Own Words*, Martin Green, ed. Copyright © 1987 by Navajian Trust, Lebanon, NH: University Press of New England.

---

she nationalized banks, provided loans to peasants on easy terms, built low-cost housing, distributed land to the landless, and introduced electoral reforms to enfranchise the poor.

Gandhi was especially worried by India's growing population and in an effort to curb the growth rate adopted a policy of enforced sterilization. This policy proved unpopular, however, and, along with growing official corruption and Gandhi's authoritarian tactics, led to her defeat in the general election of 1975, the first time the Congress Party had failed to win a majority at the national level.

A minority government of procapitalist parties was formed, but within two years, Gandhi was back in power. She now faced a new challenge, however, in the rise of religious strife. The most dangerous situation was in the Punjab, where militant Sikhs were demanding autonomy or even independence from India (the Sikh religion was created in the sixteenth century to combine the best elements of Islam and Hinduism). Gandhi did not shrink from a confrontation and attacked Sikh rebels hiding in their Golden Temple in the city of Amritsar. The incident aroused widespread anger among the Sikh community, and in 1984, Sikh members of Gandhi's personal bodyguard assassinated her.

By now, Congress politicians were convinced that the party could not remain in power without a member of the Nehru family at the helm. Gandhi's son Rajiv (1944–1991), a commercial airline pilot with little interest in politics, was persuaded to replace his mother as prime minister. Rajiv lacked the strong ideological and political convictions of his mother and grandfather and allowed a greater role for private enterprise. But his government was criticized for cronyism, inefficiency, and corruption, as well as insensitivity to the poor.

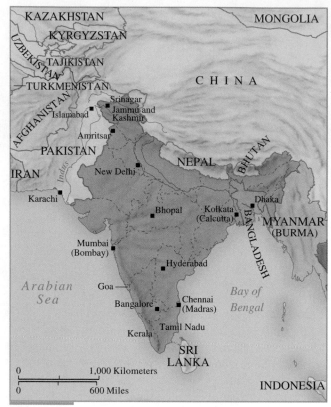

MAP 13.1 Modern South Asia. This map shows the boundaries of all the states in contemporary South Asia. India, the largest in area and population, is highlighted. [?] Which of the countries on this map have a Muslim majority? [icon] View an animated version of this map or related maps at the World History Resource Center, at worldrc.wadsworth.com/.

Rajiv Gandhi also sought to play a role in regional affairs, mediating a dispute between the government in Sri Lanka and Tamil rebels (known as the "Elam Tigers") who were ethnically related to the majority population in southern India. The decision cost him his life: while campaigning for reelection in 1991, he was assassinated by a member of the Tiger organization. India faced the future without a member of the Nehru family as prime minister.

During the early 1990s, Congress remained the leading party, but the powerful hold it had once had on the Indian electorate was gone. New parties, such as the militantly Hindu Bharata Janata Party (BJP), actively vied with Congress for control of the central and state governments. Growing political instability at the center was accompanied by rising tensions between Hindus and Muslims.

When a coalition government formed under Congress leadership collapsed, the BJP, under Prime Minister A. B. Vajpayee, ascended to power in 1998 and played on Hindu sensibilities to build its political base. The new government based its success on an aggressive program of privatization

in the industrial and commercial sectors and made a major effort to support the nation's small but growing technological base. But BJP leaders had underestimated the discontent of India's less affluent citizens (an estimated 350 million Indians earn less than one U.S. dollar a day), and in the spring of 2004, a stunning defeat in national elections forced the Vajpayee government to resign. The Congress Party returned to power at the head of a coalition government based on a commitment to maintain economic growth while carrying out reforms in rural areas, including public works projects and hot lunch programs for all primary school children.

The Land of the Pure: Pakistan Since Independence

When Pakistan achieved independence in August 1947, it was, unlike its neighbor India, in all respects a new nation, based on religious conviction rather than historical or ethnic tradition. The unique state united two separate territories 2,000 miles apart. West Pakistan, including the Indus River basin and the West Punjab, was perennially short of water and was populated by dry crop farmers and peoples of the steppe. East Pakistan was made up of the marshy deltas of the Ganges and Brahmaputra rivers. Densely populated with rice farmers, it was the home of the artistic and intellectual Bengalis.

Even though the new state was an essentially Muslim society, its first years were marked by intense internal conflicts over religious, linguistic, and regional issues. Mohammed Ali Jinnah's vision of a democratic state that would assure freedom of religion and equal treatment for all was opposed by those who advocated a state based on Islamic principles.

Even more dangerous was the division between east and west. Many in East Pakistan felt that the government, based in the west, ignored their needs. In 1952, riots erupted in East Pakistan over the government's decision to adopt Urdu, a language derived from Hindi and used by Muslims in northern India, as the national language of the entire country. Most East Pakistanis spoke Bengali, an unrelated language. Tensions persisted, and in March 1971, East Pakistan declared its independence as the new nation of Bangladesh. Pakistani troops attempted to restore central government authority in the capital of Dhaka, but rebel forces supported by India went on the offensive, and the government bowed to the inevitable and recognized independent Bangladesh.

The breakup of the union between East and West Pakistan undermined the fragile authority of the military regime that had ruled Pakistan since 1958 and led to its replacement by a civilian government under Zulfikar Ali Bhutto. But now religious tensions came to the fore, despite a new constitution that made a number of key concessions to conservative Muslims. In 1977, a new military government under General Zia Ul Ha'q came to power with a commitment to make Pakistan a truly Islamic state. Islamic law became the basis for social behavior as well as for the legal system. Laws governing the consumption of alcohol and the role of women were tightened in accordance with strict Muslim beliefs. But after Zia was killed in a plane crash, Pakistanis elected Benazir Bhutto (b. 1953), the daughter of Zulfikar Ali Bhutto and a supporter of secularism who had been educated in the United States. She too was removed from power by a military regime, in 1990, on charges of incompetence and corruption. Reelected in 1993, she attempted to crack down on opposition forces but was removed once again amid renewed charges of official corruption. Her successor soon came under fire for the same reason and in 1999 was ousted by a military coup led by General Pervaiz Musharraf (b. 1943), who promised to restore political stability and honest government.

In September 2001, Pakistan became the focus of international attention when a coalition of forces arrived in Afghanistan to overthrow the Taliban regime and destroy the al-Qaeda terrorist network. Despite considerable support for the Taliban among the local population, President Musharraf pledged his help in bringing terrorists to justice. He also promised to return his country to the secular principles espoused by Mohammed Ali Jinnah. His situation was complicated by intense popular anger at the U.S. invasion of Iraq (see Chapter 15) and by a series of violent clashes between Muslims and Hindus in India. In 2003, Pakistan's relations with India began to improve when both countries promised to seek a peaceful solution to the Kashmir dispute.

Poverty and Pluralism in South Asia

The leaders of the new states that emerged in South Asia after World War II faced a number of problems. The peoples of South Asia were still overwhelmingly poor and illiterate, and the sectarian, ethnic, and cultural divisions that had plagued Indian society for centuries had not dissipated.

The Politics of Communalism Perhaps the most sincere effort to create democratic instititutions was in India, where the new constitution called for social justice, liberty, equality of status and opportunity, and fraternity. All citizens were guaranteed protection from discrimination on the grounds of religious belief, race, caste, gender, or place of birth.

In theory, then, India became a full-fledged democracy on the British parliamentary model. In actuality, a number of distinctive characteristics made the system less than fully democratic in the Western sense but may also have enabled it to survive. As we have seen, India became in essence a one-party state. By leading the independence movement, the Congress Party had gained massive public support, which enabled it to retain its preeminent position in Indian politics for three decades. The party also avoided being identified as a party exclusively for the Hindu majority by including prominent non-Hindus among its leaders and favoring measures to protect minority groups such as Sikhs, untouchables, and Muslims from discrimination.

After Nehru's death in 1964, however, problems emerged that had been disguised by his adept maneuvering. Part of the problem was the familiar one of a party too long in power. Party officials became complacent and all too easily fell prey to the temptations of corruption and pork-barrel politics.

Another problem was communalism. Beneath the surface unity of the new republic lay age-old ethnic, linguistic, and religious divisions. Because of India's vast size and complex history, no national language had ever emerged. Hindi was the most prevalent, but it was the native language of less than one-third of the population. During the colonial period, English had served as the official language of government, and many non-Hindi speakers suggested making it the official language. But English was spoken only by the educated elite, and it represented an affront to national pride. Eventually, India recognized fourteen official tongues, making the parliament sometimes sound like the Tower of Babel.

Divisiveness increased after Nehru's death, and under his successors, official corruption grew. Only the lack of appeal of its rivals and the Nehru family charisma carried on by his daughter Indira Gandhi kept the party in power. But she was unable to prevent the progressive disintegration of the party's power base at the state level, where regional or ideological parties won the allegiance of voters by exploiting ethnic or social revolutionary themes.

During the 1980s, religious tensions began to intensify, not only among Sikhs in the northwest but also between Hindus and Muslims. As we have seen, Gandhi's uncompromising approach to Sikh separatism led to her assassination in 1984. Under her son, Rajiv Gandhi, Hindu militants demanded the destruction of a mosque built on a holy site at Ayodhya, in northern India, where a Hindu temple had previously existed. In 1992, Hindu demonstrators destroyed the mosque and erected a temporary temple at the site, provoking clashes between Hindus and Muslims throughout the country. In protest, rioters in neighboring Pakistan destroyed a number of Hindu shrines in that country.

In recent years, communal divisions have intensified as militant Hindu groups agitate for a state that caters to the Hindu majority, now numbering more than 700 million people. In the spring of 2002, violence between Hindus and Muslims flared up again over plans by Hindu activists to build a permanent temple at the site of the destroyed mosque at Ayodhya. In 2006, a terrorist attack on commuter trains killed scores of Indians in the city of Mumbai.

The Economy Nehru's answer to the social and economic inequality that had long afflicted the subcontinent was socialism. He instituted a series of five-year plans, which led to the creation of a relatively large and reasonably efficient industrial sector, centered on steel, vehicles, and textiles. Industrial production almost tripled between 1950 and 1965, and per capita income rose by 50 percent between 1950 and 1980, although it was still less than $300 (in U.S. dollars).

By the 1970s, however, industrial growth had slowed. The lack of modern infrastructure was a problem, as was the rising price of oil, most of which had to be imported. The relative weakness of the state-owned sector, which grew at an annual rate of only about 2 percent in the 1950s and 1960s, versus 5 percent for the private sector, also became a serious obstacle.

India's major economic weakness, however, was in agriculture. At independence, mechanization was almost unknown, fertilizer was rarely used, and most farms were small and uneconomical because of the Hindu tradition of dividing the land equally among all male children. As a result, the vast majority of the Indian people lived in conditions of abject poverty. Landless laborers outnumbered landowners by almost two to one. The government attempted to relieve the problem by redistributing land to the poor, limiting the size of landholdings, and encouraging farmers to form voluntary cooperatives. But all three programs ran into widespread opposition and apathy.

Another problem was overpopulation. Even before independence, the country had had difficulty supporting its people. In the 1950s and 1960s, the population grew by more than 2 percent annually, twice the nineteenth-century rate. Beginning in the 1960s, the Indian government sought to curb population growth. Indira Gandhi instituted a program combining monetary rewards and compulsory sterilization. Males who had fathered too many children were sometimes forced to undergo a vasectomy. Popular resistance undermined the program, however, and the goals were scaled back in the 1970s. As a result, India has made only limited progress in holding down its burgeoning population, now estimated at more than one billion. One factor in the continued growth has been a decline in the death rate, especially the rate of infant mortality. Nevertheless, as a result of media popularization and better government programs, the trend today, even in poor rural villages, is toward smaller families. The average number of children a woman bears has been reduced from six in 1950 to three today. As has occurred elsewhere, the decline in family size began among the educated and is gradually spreading throughout Indian society.

The "Green Revolution" that began in the 1960s helped reduce the severity of the population problem. The intro-duction of more productive, disease-resistant strains of rice and wheat doubled grain production between 1960 and 1980. But the Green Revolution also increased rural inequality. Only the wealthier farmers were able to purchase the necessary fertilizer, while poor peasants were often driven off the land. Millions fled to the cities, where they lived in vast slums, working at menial jobs or even begging for a living.

After the death of Indira Gandhi in 1984, her son Rajiv proved more receptive to foreign investment and a greater role for the private sector in the economy. India began to export more manufactured goods, including computer software. The pace of change has accelerated under Rajiv Gandhi's successors, who have continued to transfer state-run industries to private hands. These policies have stimulated the growth of a prosperous new middle class, now estimated at more than 100 million. Consumerism has soared, and sales of television sets, automobiles, DVD players, and cell phones have increased dramatically. Equally important, Western imports are being replaced by new products manufactured in India with Indian brand names.

One consequence of India's entrance into the industrial age is the emergence of a small but vibrant technological sector that provides many important services to the world's advanced nations. The city of Bangalore in South India has become an important technological center, benefiting from low wages and the presence of skilled labor with proficiency in the English language. It has also become a symbol of the "outsourcing" of jobs from the United States and Europe that has led to an increase in middle-class unemployment throughout the Western world.

Nevertheless, Nehru's dream of a socialist society remains strong. State-owned enterprises still produce about half of all domestic goods, and high tariffs continue to stifle imports. Nationalist parties have played on the widespread fear of foreign economic influence to force the cancellation of some contracts and the relocation of some foreign firms. A combination of religious and environmental groups attempted unsuccessfully to prevent Kentucky Fried Chicken from establishing outlets in major Indian cities (see the box on p. 263).

As in the industrialized countries of the West, economic growth has been accompanied by environmental damage. Water and air pollution has led to illness and death for many people, and an environmental movement has emerged. Some critics, reflecting the traditional anti-imperialist attitude of Indian intellectuals, blame Western capitalist corporations for the problem, as in the highly publicized case of leakage from a foreign-owned chemical plant at Bhopal. Much of the problem, however, comes from state-owned factories erected with Soviet aid. And not all the environmental damage can be ascribed to industrialization.

SAY NO TO McDONALD'S AND KFC!

*O*ne of the consequences of Rajiv Gandhi's decision to deregulate the Indian economy has been an increase in the presence of foreign corporations, including U.S. fast-food restaurant chains. Their arrival set off a storm of protest in India: from environmentalists concerned that raising grain for chickens is an inefficient use of land, from religious activists angry at the killing of animals for food, and from nationalists anxious to protect the domestic market from foreign competition. The author of this piece, which appeared in the *Hindustan Times*, was Maneka Gandhi, a daughter-in-law of Indira Gandhi and a onetime minister of the environment who has emerged as a prominent rival of Sonia Gandhi, the widow of Rajiv Gandhi and the Congress Party president.

Why does the author of this article oppose the introduction of Western-style fast-food restaurants in India? Do you think her comments apply in the United States as well?

Why India Doesn't Need Fast Food

India's decision to allow Pepsi Foods Ltd. to open 60 restaurants in India—30 each of Pizza Hut and Kentucky Fried Chicken—marks the first entry of multinational, meat-based junk-food chains into India. If this is allowed to happen, at least a dozen other similar chains will very quickly arrive, including the infamous McDonald's.

The implications of allowing junk-food chains into India are quite stark. As the name denotes, the foods served at Kentucky Fried Chicken (KFC) are chicken-based and fried. This is the worst combination possible for the body and can create a host of health problems, including obesity, high cholesterol, heart ailments, and many kinds of cancer. Pizza Hut products are a combination of white flour, cheese, and meat—again, a combination likely to cause disease. . . .

Then there is the issue of the environmental impact of junk-food chains. Modern meat production involves misuse of crops, water, energy, and grazing areas. In addition, animal agriculture produces surprisingly large amounts of air and water pollution.

KFC and Pizza Hut insist that their chickens be fed corn and soybeans. Consider the diversion of grain for this purpose. As the outlets of KFC and Pizza Hut increase in number, the poultry industry will buy up more and more corn to feed the chickens, which means that the corn will quickly disappear from the villages, and its increased price will place it out of reach for the common man. Turning corn into junk chicken is like turning gold into mud. . . .

It is already shameful that, in a country plagued by famine and flood, we divert 37 percent of our arable land to growing animal fodder. Were all of that grain to be consumed directly by humans, it would nourish five times as many people as it does after being converted into meat, milk, and eggs. . . .

Of course, it is not just the KFC and Pizza Hut chains of Pepsi Foods Ltd. that will cause all of this damage. Once we open India up by allowing these chains, dozens more will be eagerly waiting to come in. Each city in America has an average of 5,000 junk-food restaurants. Is that what we want for India?

SOURCE: From *World Press Review* (September 1995), p. 47.

The Ganges River is so polluted by human overuse that it is risky for Hindu believers to bathe in it.

Moreover, many Indians have not benefited from the new prosperity. Nearly one-third of the population lives below the national poverty line. Millions continue to live in urban slums, such as the famous "City of Joy" in Calcutta, and most farm families remain desperately poor. Despite the socialist rhetoric of India's leaders, the inequality of wealth in India is as pronounced as it is in capitalist nations in the West. Indeed, India has been described as two nations: an educated urban India of 100 million people surrounded by over 900 million impoverished peasants in the countryside. Such problems are even more serious in neighboring Pakistan and Bangladesh. The overwhelming majority of Pakistan's 150 million citizens are poor, and at least half are illiterate. Moreover, the nation lacks a modern technological sector to provide a magnet for the emergence of a modern middle class.

Caste, Class, and Gender Drawing generalizations about the life of the average Indian is difficult because of ethnic, religious, and caste differences, which are compounded by the vast gulf between town and country.

Although the constitution of 1950 guaranteed equal treatment and opportunity for all, regardless of caste, and prohibited discrimination based on untouchability, prejudice is hard to eliminate. Untouchability persists, particularly in the villages, where *harijans*, now called *dalits*, still perform menial tasks and are often denied fundamental human rights.

In general, urban Indians appear less conscious of caste distinctions. Material wealth rather than caste identity is increasingly defining status. Still, color consciousness based on the age-old distinctions between upper-class Aryans and lower-class Dravidians remains strong. Class-conscious Hindus still express a distinct preference for light-skinned marital partners.

Fetching Water at the Village Well. The scarcity of water will surely become one of the planet's most crucial problems. It will affect all nations, developed and developing, rich and poor. Although many Indians live with an inadequate water supply, these women are fortunate to have a well in their village. More typical is the image of the Indian woman, dressed in a colorful sari, children encircling her as she heads to her distant home on foot, carrying a heavy pail of water on her head.

Courtesy of William J. Duiker

In recent years, low-caste Indians (who represent more than 80 percent of the voting public) have begun to demand affirmative action to relieve their disabilities and give them a more equal share of the national wealth. Officials at U.S. consulates in India have noticed a rise in visa applications from members of the *brahmin* caste, who claim that they have "no future" in the new India. But opponents of such measures often are not reluctant to fight back. Phoolan Devi, known as the "bandit queen," spent several years in jail for taking part in the murder of twenty men from a landowning caste who had allegedly gang-raped her when she was an adolescent. Her campaign for office during the 1996 elections was the occasion of violent arguments between supporters and opponents, and she was assassinated by an unknown assailant in 2001.

In few societies was the life of women more restricted than in traditional India. Hindu favoritism toward men was compounded by the Muslim custom of *purdah* to create a society in which males were dominant in virtually all aspects of life. Females received no education and had no inheritance rights. They were restricted to the home and tied to their husbands for life. Widows were expected to shave their heads and engage in a life of religious meditation or even to immolate themselves on their husband's funeral pyre.

After independence, India's leaders sought to equalize treatment of the sexes. The constitution expressly forbade discrimination based on gender and called for equal pay for equal work. Laws prohibited child marriage and the payment of a dowry by the bride's family. Women were encouraged to attend school and enter the labor market.

Such laws, along with the dynamics of economic and social change, have had a major impact on the lives of many Indian women. Middle-class women in urban areas are much more likely to seek employment outside the home, and many hold managerial and professional positions. Some Indian women, however, choose to play a dual role—a modern one in their work and in the marketplace and a more submissive, traditional one at home.

Such attitudes are also reflected in the Indian movie industry, where aspiring actresses must often brave family disapproval to enter the entertainment world. Before World War II, female actors were routinely viewed as prostitutes or "loose women," and such views are still prevalent among conservative Indian families. Even Karisma Kapoor, one of India's current film stars and a member of the Kapoor clan, which has produced several generations of actors, had to defy her family's ban on its women entering show business.

Nothing more strikingly indicates the changing role of women in South Asia than the fact that in recent years, three of the major countries in the area—India, Pakistan, and Sri Lanka—have had women prime ministers. It is worthy of mention, however, that all three—Indira Gandhi, Benazir Bhutto, and Srimivao Bandaranaike—came from prominent political families and owed their initial success to a husband or a father who had served as prime minister before them.

Courtesy of William J. Duiker

Young Hindu Bride in Gold Bangles. Awaiting the marriage ceremony, a young bride sits with the female relatives of her family at the Meenakshi Hindu temple, one of the largest in southern India. Although child marriage is illegal, Indian girls are still married at a young age. With the marital union arranged by the parents, this young bride may never have met her future husband. Bedecked in gold jewelry and rich silks—part of her dowry—she nervously awaits the priest's blessing before she moves to her husband's home. There she will begin a life of servitude to her in-laws' family.

Like other aspects of life, the role of women has changed much less in rural areas. In the early 1960s, many villagers still practiced the institution of *purdah*. A woman who went about freely in society would get a bad reputation. Female children are still much less likely to receive an education. The overall literacy rate in India today is less than 40 percent, but it is undoubtedly much lower among women. Laws relating to dowry, child marriage, and inheritance are routinely ignored in the countryside. There have been a few highly publicized cases of *sati* (the immolation of widows on their deceased husband's funeral pyre) although undoubtedly more women die of mistreatment at the hands of their husband or of other members of his family.

Perhaps the most tragic aspect of continued sexual discrimination in India is the high mortality rate among girls. One-quarter of the female children born in India die before the age of fifteen as a result of neglect or even infanticide. Others are aborted before birth after gender-detection examinations. The results are striking. In most societies, the number of women equals or exceeds that of men; in India, according to one estimate, the ratio is only 933 females to 1,000 males.

South Asian Art and Literature Since Independence

Recent decades have witnessed a prodigious outpouring of literature in India. Most works have been written in one of the Indian languages and have not been translated into a foreign tongue. Many authors, however, choose to write in English for the Indian elite or for foreign audiences. For that reason, some critics charge that such literature lacks authenticity.

Because of the vast quantity of works published (India is currently the third-largest publisher of English-language books in the world), only a few of the most prominent fiction writers can be mentioned here. Anita Desai (b. 1937) was one of the first prominent female writers in contemporary India. Her writing focuses on the struggle of Indian women to achieve a degree of independence. In her first novel, *Cry, the Peacock,* the heroine finally seeks liberation by murdering her husband, preferring freedom at any cost to remaining a captive of traditional society.

The best-known female writer in South Asia today is Taslima Nasrin (b. 1962) of Bangladesh. She first became famous when she was sentenced to death for her novel *Shame* (1993), in which she criticized official persecution of the Hindu minority. An outspoken feminist, she is critical of Islam for obstructing human progress and women's equality. She now lives in exile in Europe.

The most controversial writer in India today is Salman Rushdie (b. 1947). In *Midnight's Children,* published in 1980, the author linked his protagonist, born on the night of independence, to the history of modern India, its achievements and its frustrations. Like his contemporaries Günter Grass and Gabriel García Márquez, Rushdie used the technique of magical realism to jolt his audience into a recognition of the inhumanity of modern society and the need to develop a sense of moral concern for the fate of the Indian people and for the world as a whole.

Rushdie's later novels have tackled such problems as religious intolerance, political tyranny, social injustice, and greed and corruption. His attack on Islamic fundamentalism in *The Satanic Verses* (1988) won plaudits from literary critics but provoked widespread criticism among Muslims, including a death sentence by Ayatollah Khomeini in Iran. *The Moor's Last Sigh* (1995) examined the alleged excesses of Hindu nationalism, and *Shalimar the Clown* (2005) addressed the quagmire in Kashmir.

Like Chinese and Japanese artists, Indian artists have agonized over how best to paint with a modern yet indigenous mode of expression. During the colonial period, Indian art went in several directions at once. One school of painters favored traditional themes; another experimented with a colorful primitivism founded on folk art. Many Indian artists painted representational social art extolling the suffering and silent dignity of India's impoverished millions. After 1960, however, most Indian artists adopted abstract art as their medium. Surrealism in particular, with its emphasis on spontaneity and the unconscious, appeared closer to the Hindu tradition of favoring intuition over reason. Yet Indian artists are still struggling to find the ideal way to be both modern and Indian.

Gandhi's Vision

Indian society looks increasingly Western in form, if not in content. As in a number of other Asian and African societies, the distinction between traditional and modern, or native and Westernized, sometimes seems to be a simple dichotomy between rural and urban. The major cities appear modern and Westernized, but the villages have changed little since precolonial days.

Yet traditional practices appear to be more resilient in India than in many other societies, and the result is often a synthesis rather than a clash between conflicting institutions and values. Unlike China, India has not rejected its past but merely adjusted it to meet the needs of the present. Clothing styles in the streets where the *sari* and *dhoti* continue to be popular, religious practices in the temples, and social relationships in the home all testify to the importance of tradition in India.

One disadvantage of the eclectic approach, which seeks to blend the old and the new rather than choosing one over the other, is that sometimes contrasting traditions cannot be reconciled. In *India: A Wounded Civilization,* V. S. Naipaul (b. 1932), a West Indian of Indian descent, charged that Mahatma Gandhi's glorification of poverty and the simple Indian village was an obstacle to efforts to overcome the poverty, ignorance, and degradation of India's past and build a prosperous modern society. Gandhi's vision of a spiritual India, Naipaul complained, was a balm for defeatism and an excuse for failure.

Certainly, India faces a difficult dilemma. Some problems are undoubtedly a consequence of the colonial era, but the British cannot be blamed for all of the country's economic and social ills. To build a democratic, prosperous society, the Indian people must discard many of their traditional convictions and customs. Belief in karma and inherent caste distinctions are incompatible with the democratic belief in equality before the law. These traditional beliefs also undercut the work ethic and the modern sentiment of nationalism.

So long as Indians accept their fate as predetermined, they will find it difficult to change their environment and create a new society. Yet their traditional beliefs provide a measure of identity and solace often lacking in other societies, where such traditional spiritual underpinnings have eroded. Destroying India's traditional means of coping with a disagreeable reality without changing that reality would be cruel indeed.

Southeast Asia

The Japanese wartime occupation had a great impact on attitudes among the peoples of Southeast Asia. It demonstrated the vulnerability of colonial rule in the region and showed that an Asian power could defeat Europeans. The Allied governments themselves also contributed—sometimes unwittingly—to rising aspirations for independence by promising self-determination for all peoples at the end of the war. Although Winston Churchill later said that the Atlantic Charter did not apply to the colonial peoples, it would be difficult to put the genie back in the bottle.

The End of the Colonial Era

Some did not try. In July 1946, the United States granted total independence to the Philippines. The Americans maintained a military presence on the islands, however, and U.S. citizens retained economic and commercial interests in the new country.

The British, too, under the Labour Party, were willing to bring an end to a century of imperialism in the region. In 1948, the Union of Burma received its independence. Malaya's turn came in 1957, after a Communist guerrilla movement had been suppressed.

The French and the Dutch, however, both regarded their colonies in the region as economic necessities as well as symbols of national grandeur and refused to turn them over to nationalist movements at the end of the war. The Dutch attempted to suppress a rebellion in the East Indies led by Sukarno (1901–1970), leader of the Indonesian Nationalist Party. But the United States, which feared a Communist victory there, pressured the Dutch to grant independence to Sukarno and his non-Communist forces, and in 1950, the Dutch finally agreed to recognize the new Republic of Indonesia.

The Franco-Vietminh War The situation was somewhat different in Vietnam, where the leading force in the anti-colonial movement was the local Indochinese Communist Party (ICP) led by the veteran Moscow-trained revolutionary Ho Chi Minh (1890–1969). In August 1945, virtually at the moment of Japanese surrender, the Vietminh Front, an alliance of patriotic forces under secret ICP leadership that had been founded to fight the Japanese in 1941, launched a general uprising and seized power throughout most of Vietnam.

In early September, Ho Chi Minh was declared president of a new provisional republic in Hanoi. In the meantime, French military units began arriving in Saigon, with the permission of the British occupation command there. The new government in Hanoi, formally known as the Democratic Republic of Vietnam (DRV), appealed to the victorious Allies for recognition but received no response, and by late fall, the southern part of the country was back under French rule. Ho signed a preliminary agreement with the French recognizing Vietnam as a "free state" within the French Union, but negotiations over the details broke down in the summer of 1946, and war between the two parties broke out in December. The French occupied the cities, while the Vietminh retreated into the countryside and began to carry out a guerrilla struggle. At the Geneva Conference in 1954, the French agreed to withdraw from all Indochina, and two new states emerged in Vietnam (see Chapter 7).

The Era of Independent States

Many of the leaders of the newly independent states in Southeast Asia (see Map 13.2) admired Western political institutions and hoped to adapt them to their own countries. New constitutions were patterned on Western democratic models, and multiparty political systems quickly sprang into operation.

The Search for a New Political Culture By the 1960s, most of these budding experiments in pluralist democracy had been abandoned or were under serious threat. Some had been replaced by military or one-party autocratic regimes. In Burma, a moderate government based on the British parliamentary system and dedicated to Buddhism and nonviolent Marxism had given way to a military government. In Thailand, too, the military now ruled. In the Philippines, President Ferdinand Marcos discarded democratic restraints and established his own centralized control. In South Vietnam (see Chapter 7), Ngo Dinh Diem and his

successors paid lip service to the Western democratic model but ruled by authoritarian means.

One problem faced by most of these states was that independence had not brought material prosperity or ended economic inequality and the domination of the local economies by foreign interests. Most economies in the region were still characterized by tiny industrial sectors; they lacked technology, educational resources, capital investment, and leaders trained in developmental skills.

The presence of widespread ethnic, linguistic, cultural, and economic differences also made the transition to Western-style democracy difficult. In Malaya, for example, the majority Malays—most of whom were farmers—feared economic and political domination by the local Chinese minority, who were much more experienced in industry and commerce. In 1961, the Federation of Malaya, whose ruling party was dominated by Malays, integrated former British possessions on the island of Borneo into the new Union of Malaysia in a move to increase the non-Chinese proportion of the country's population. Yet periodic conflicts persisted as the Malaysian government attempted to guarantee Malay control over politics and a larger role in the economy.

Sukarno and "Guided Democracy" The most publicized example of a failed experiment in democracy was in Indonesia. In 1950, the new leaders drew up a constitution creating a parliamentary system under a titular presidency. Sukarno was elected the first president. A spellbinding orator, Sukarno played a major role in creating a sense of national identity among the disparate peoples of the Indonesian archipelago (see the box on p. 269).

In the late 1950s, Sukarno, exasperated at the incessant maneuvering among devout Muslims, Communists, and the army, dissolved the constitution and attempted to rule on his own through what he called "guided democracy." As he described it, guided democracy was closer to Indonesian traditions and superior to the Western variety. The weakness of the latter was that it allowed the majority to dominate the minority, whereas guided democracy would reconcile different opinions and points of view in a government operated by consensus. Highly suspicious of the West, Sukarno nationalized foreign-owned enterprises and sought economic aid from China and the Soviet Union while relying for domestic support on the Indonesian Communist Party.

The army and conservative Muslims resented Sukarno's increasing reliance on the Communists, and the Muslims were further upset by his refusal to consider a state based on Islamic principles. In 1965, military officers launched a coup d'état that provoked a mass popular uprising, which resulted in the slaughter of several hundred

MAP 13.2 Modern Southeast Asia. Shown here are the countries of contemporary Southeast Asia. The major islands that make up the Republic of Indonesia are indicated in yellow. ❓ Which of the countries in Southeast Asia now have functioning democratic governments? Which appear to be the most prosperous? 🌐 **View an animated version of this map or related maps at the World History Resource Center, at** worldrc.wadsworth.com/.

thousand suspected Communists, many of whom were overseas Chinese, long distrusted by the Muslim majority. In 1967, a military government under General Suharto (b. 1921) was installed.

The new government made no pretensions of reverting to democratic rule, but it did restore good relations with the West and sought foreign investment to repair the country's ravaged economy. But it also found it difficult to placate Muslim demands for an Islamic state. In a few areas, including western Sumatra, militant Muslims took up arms against the state.

The one country in Southeast Asia that explicitly rejected the Western model was North Vietnam, which was occupied by Ho Chi Minh's DRV after the Geneva

Conference in 1954. Its leaders opted for the Stalinist pattern of national development, based on Communist Party rule and socialist forms of ownership. In 1958, stimulated by the success of collectivization in neighboring China, the government launched a three-year plan to lay the foundation for a socialist society. Collective farms were established, and all industry and commerce above the family level were nationalized.

Recent Trends

In recent years, some Southeast Asian societies have shown signs of evolving toward more democratic forms. In the Philippines, the dictatorial Marcos regime was overthrown

THE GOLDEN THROAT OF PRESIDENT SUKARNO

*P*resident Sukarno of Indonesia was a spellbinding speaker and a charismatic leader of his nation's struggle for independence. These two excerpts are from speeches in which Sukarno promoted two of his favorite projects: Indonesian nationalism and "guided democracy." The force that would guide Indonesia, of course, was to be Sukarno himself.

How does Sukarno justify his claim that Indonesia is as large as the United States?

Sukarno on Indonesian Greatness

What was Indonesia in 1945? What was our nation then? It was only two things, only two things. A flag and a song. That is all. (Pause, finger held up as afterthought.) But no, I have omitted the main ingredient. I have missed the most important thing of all. I have left out the burning fire of freedom and independence in the breast and heart of every Indonesian. That is the most important thing—this is the vital chord—the spirit of our people, the spirit and determination to be free. This was our nation in 1945—the spirit of our people!

And what are we today? We are a great nation. We are bigger than Poland. We are bigger than Turkey. We have more people than Australia, than Canada, we are bigger in area and have more people than Japan. In population now we are the fifth-largest country in the world. In area, we are even bigger than the United States of America. The American Ambassador, who is here with us, admits this. Of course, he points out that we have a lot of water in between our thousands of islands. But I say to him—America has a lot of mountains and deserts, too!

Sukarno on Guided Democracy

Indonesia's democracy is not liberal democracy. Indonesian democracy is not the democracy of the world of Montaigne or Voltaire. Indonesia's democracy is not à la America, Indonesia's democracy is not the Soviet—NO! Indonesia's democracy is the democracy which is implanted in the breasts of the Indonesian people, and it is that which I have tried to dig up again, and have put forward as an offering to you. . . . If you, especially the undergraduates, are still clinging to and being borne along the democracy made in England, or democracy made in France, or democracy made in America, or democracy made in Russia, you will become a nation of copyists!

SOURCE: From Howard Jones, *Indonesia: The Possible Dream* (New York: Harcourt Brace Jovanovich, Hoover Institute, 1971), pp. 223, 237.

---

by a massive public uprising in 1986 and replaced by a democratically elected government under President Corazon Aquino (b. 1933), the widow of a popular politician assassinated a few years earlier. Aquino was unable to resolve many of the country's chronic economic and social difficulties, however, and political stability remains elusive; one of her successors, ex-actor Joseph Estrada, was forced to resign on the charge of corruption. At the same time, Muslims in the southern island of Mindanao have mounted a terrorist campaign in their effort to obtain autonomy or independence.

In other nations, the results have also been mixed. Although Malaysia is a practicing democracy, tensions persist between Malays and Chinese as well as between secular and orthodox Muslims who seek to create an Islamic state. In neighboring Thailand, the military has found it expedient to hold national elections for civilian governments, but the danger of a military takeover is never far beneath the surface.

The Fall of the Suharto Regime In Indonesia, difficult economic conditions caused by the financial crisis of 1997 (see "Increasing Prosperity and Financial Crisis" later in the chapter), combined with popular anger against the Suharto government (several members of his family had reportedly used their positions to amass considerable wealth), led to violent street riots and demands for his resignation. Forced to step down in the spring of 1998, Suharto was replaced by his deputy B. J. Habibie, who called for the establishment of a national assembly to select a new government based on popular aspirations. The assembly selected a moderate Muslim leader as president, but he was charged with corruption and incompetence and was replaced in 2001 by his vice president, Sukarno's daughter Megawati Sukarnoputri (b. 1947).

The new government faced a severe challenge, not only from the economic crisis but also from dissident elements seeking autonomy or even separation from the republic. Under pressure from the international community, Indonesia agreed to grant independence to the onetime Portuguese colony of East Timor, where the majority of the people are Roman Catholics. But violence provoked by pro-Indonesian militia units forced many refugees to flee the country. Religious tensions have also erupted between Muslims and Christians elsewhere in the archipelago, and Muslim rebels in western Sumatra continue to agitate for a new state based on strict adherence to fundamentalist Islam. In the meantime, a terrorist attack directed at tourists on the island of Bali provoked fears that the Muslim nation had become a haven for terrorist elements throughout the region.

In direct elections held in 2004, General Susilo Yudhyono defeated Megawati Sukarnoputri and ascended to the presidency. The new chief executive promised a new era of political stability, honest government, and economic reform but faces a number of severe challenges. Concerned about high wages and the risk of terrorism, a number of foreign firms have relocated their factories elsewhere in Asia, forcing thousands of workers to return to the countryside. Pressure from traditional Muslims to abandon the nation's secular tradition and move toward the creation of an Islamic state continues to grow. That the country was able to hold democratic elections in the midst of such tensions holds some promise for the future.

The Vietnamese Model As always, Vietnam is a special case. After achieving victory over South Vietnam in the spring of 1975 (see Chapter 7), the Communist government pursued the rapid reunification of the two zones under Communist Party rule and laid plans to carry out a socialist transformation throughout the country, now renamed the Socialist Republic of Vietnam. The result was an economic disaster, and in 1986, party leaders followed the example of Mikhail Gorbachev in the Soviet Union and introduced their own version of *perestroika* in Vietnam (see Chapter 9). The trend in recent years has been toward a mixed capitalist-socialist economy and a greater popular role in the governing process. Elections for the unicameral parliament are more open than in the past. The government remains suspicious of Western-style democracy, however, and represses any opposition to the Communist Party's guiding role over the state.

The Burmese Exception Only in Burma (now renamed Myanmar), where the military has been in complete control since the early 1960s, have the forces of greater popular participation been virtually silenced. Even there, however, the power of the ruling regime of General Ne Win (1911–2003) and his successors, known as SLORC, has been vocally challenged by Aung San Huu Kyi (b. 1952), the admired daughter of one of the heroes of the country's struggle for national liberation after World War II.

Increasing Prosperity and Financial Crisis The trend toward more representative systems of government has been due in part to increasing prosperity and the growth of an affluent and educated middle class. Although Indonesia, Burma, and the three Indochinese states are still overwhelmingly agrarian, Malaysia and Thailand have been undergoing relatively rapid economic development.

In the late summer of 1997, however, these economic gains were threatened, and popular faith in the ultimate benefits of globalization was shaken as a financial crisis swept through the region. The crisis was triggered by a number of problems, including growing budget deficits caused by excessive government expenditures on ambitious development projects, irresponsible lending and investment practices by financial institutions, and an overvaluation of local currencies relative to the U.S. dollar. An underlying cause of these problems was the prevalence of backroom deals between politicians and business leaders that temporarily enriched both groups at the cost of eventual economic dislocation.

As local currencies plummeted in value, the International Monetary Fund agreed to provide assistance, but only on the condition that the governments concerned permit greater transparency in their economic systems and allow market forces to operate more freely, even at the price of bankruptcies and the loss of jobs. By the early 2000s, there were signs that the economies in the region were beginning to recover. The massive tsunami that struck in December 2004, however, was another setback to economic growth, as well as a human tragedy of enormous proportions.

Regional Conflict and Cooperation: The Rise of ASEAN

In addition to their continuing internal challenges, Southeast Asian states have been hampered by serious tensions among themselves. Some of these tensions were a consequence of historical rivalries and territorial disputes that had been submerged during the long era of colonial rule. In the 1960s, Indonesian president Sukarno briefly launched a policy of confrontation with the Federation of Malaya, contending that the Malayan peninsula had once been part of empires based on the Indonesian islands. The claim was dropped after Sukarno's fall from power in 1965.

Another chronic border dispute has long existed between Cambodia and its two neighbors, Thailand and Vietnam, both of which once exercised suzerainty over Cambodian territories. The frontiers established at the moment of Cambodian independence were originally drawn up by French colonial authorities for their own convenience.

After the reunification of Vietnam under Communist rule in 1975, the lingering border dispute between Cambodia and Vietnam erupted again. In April 1975, a brutal revolutionary regime under the leadership of the

Courtesy of William J. Duiker

Holocaust in Cambodia. When the Khmer Rouge seized power in Cambodia in April 1975, they immediately emptied the capital of Phnom Penh and systematically began to eliminate opposition elements throughout the country. Thousands were tortured in the infamous Tuol Sleng prison and then marched out to the countryside, where they were massacred. Their bodies were thrown into massive pits. The succeeding government disinterred the remains, which are now displayed at an outdoor museum on the site.

Khmer Rouge dictator Pol Pot came to power in Cambodia and proceeded to carry out the massacre of more than one million Cambodians. Then, claiming that vast territories in the Mekong delta had been seized from Cambodia by the Vietnamese in previous centuries, the Khmer Rouge regime launched attacks across the common border. In response, Vietnamese forces invaded Cambodia in December 1978 and installed a pro-Hanoi regime in Phnom Penh. Fearful of Vietnam's increasing power in the region, China launched a brief attack on Vietnam to demonstrate its displeasure.

The outbreak of war among the erstwhile Communist allies aroused the concern of other countries in the neighborhood. In 1967, several non-Communist countries had established the Association of Southeast Asian Nations (ASEAN). Composed of Indonesia, Malaysia, Thailand, Singapore, and the Philippines, ASEAN at first concentrated on cooperative social and economic endeavors, but after the end of the Vietnam War, it cooperated with other states in an effort to force the Vietnamese to withdraw. In 1991, the Vietnamese finally withdrew, and a new government was formed in Phnom Penh.

The growth of ASEAN from a weak collection of diverse states into a stronger organization whose members cooperate militarily and politically has helped provide the nations of Southeast Asia with a more cohesive voice to represent their interests on the world stage. They will need it,

for disagreements with Western countries over global economic issues and the rising power of China will present major challenges in coming years. That Vietnam was admitted into ASEAN in 1996 should provide both Hanoi and its neighbors with greater leverage in dealing with their powerful neighbor to the north. At present, China is pursuing a policy of conciliation toward the region and has surpassed the United States as Southeast Asia's major trading partner.

Daily Life: Town and Country in Contemporary Southeast Asia

The urban-rural dichotomy observed in India also is found in Southeast Asia, where the cities resemble those in the West while the countryside often appears little changed from precolonial days. In cities such as Bangkok, Manila, and Jakarta, broad boulevards lined with skyscrapers alternate with muddy lanes passing through neighborhoods packed with wooden shacks topped by thatch or rusty tin roofs. Nevertheless, in recent decades, millions of Southeast Asians have fled to these urban slums. Although most available jobs are menial, the pay is better than in the villages.

Traditional Customs, Modern Values The urban migrants change not only their physical surroundings but their attitudes

One World, One Fashion. One of the negative aspects of tourism is the eroding of distinctive ethnic cultures, even in previously less traveled areas. Nevertheless, fashions from other lands often seem exotic and enticing. This village chief from Flores, a remote island in the Indonesian archipelago, seems very proud of his designer sunglasses.

and values as well. Sometimes the move leads to a decline in traditional beliefs. Belief in the existence of nature and ancestral spirits, for example, has declined among the urban populations of Southeast Asia. In Thailand, Buddhism has come under pressure from the rising influence of materialism, although temple schools still educate thousands of rural youths whose families cannot afford the cost of public education.

Nevertheless, Buddhist, Muslim, and Confucian beliefs remain strong, even in cosmopolitan cities such as Bangkok, Jakarta, and Singapore. This preference for the traditional also shows up in lifestyle. Native dress—or an eclectic blend of Asian and Western attire—is still common. Traditional music, art, theater, and dance remain popular, although Western music has become fashionable among the young, and Indonesian filmmakers complain that Western films are beginning to dominate the market.

The increasing inroads made by Western culture have caused anxiety in some countries. In Malaysia, for example, fundamentalist Muslims criticize the prevalence of pornography, hedonism, drugs, and alcohol in Western culture and have tried to limit their presence in their own country. The Malaysian government has attempted to limit the number of U.S. entertainment programs shown on local television stations and has replaced them with shows on traditional themes.

Changing Roles for Women One of the most significant changes that has taken place in Southeast Asia in recent decades is in the role of women in society. In general, women in the region have historically faced fewer restrictions on their activities and enjoyed a higher status than women elsewhere in Asia. Nevertheless, they were not the equal of men in every respect. With independence, Southeast Asian women gained new rights. Virtually all of the constitutions adopted by the newly independent states granted women full legal and political rights, including the right to work. Today, women have increased opportunities for education and have entered careers previously reserved for men. Women have become more active in politics, and as we have seen, some have served as heads of state.

Yet women are not truly equal to men in any country in Southeast Asia. Sometimes the distinction is simply a matter of custom. In Vietnam, women are legally equal to men, yet until recently no women had served in the Communist Party's ruling Politburo. In Thailand, Malaysia, and Indonesia, women rarely hold senior positions in government service or in the boardrooms of major corporations. Similar restrictions apply in Burma, although Aung San Huu Kyi is the leading figure in the democratic opposition movement.

Sometimes, too, women's rights have been undermined by a social or religious backlash. The revival of Islamic fundamentalism has had an especially strong impact in Malaysia, where Malay women are expected to cover their bodies and wear the traditional Muslim headdress. Even in non-Muslim countries, women are still expected to behave demurely and exercise discretion in all contacts with the opposite sex.

Cultural Trends

In most countries in Southeast Asia, writers, artists, and composers are attempting to synthesize international styles and themes with local tradition and experience. The novel has become increasingly popular as writers seek to find the best medium to encapsulate the dramatic changes that have taken place in the region in recent decades.

The best-known writer in postwar Indonesia—at least to readers abroad—is Pramoedya Toer (1925–2006). Born in eastern Java, he joined the Indonesian nationalist movement in his early twenties. Arrested in 1965 on the charge of being a Communist, he spent the next fourteen years in prison. While incarcerated, he began writing his four-volume *Buru Quartet*, which recounts in fictional form the story of the struggle of the Indonesian people for freedom from colonial rule and the autocratic regimes of the independence period.

Among the most talented of contemporary Vietnamese novelists is Duong Thu Huong (b. 1947). A member of the Vietnamese Communist Party who served on the front lines during the Sino-Vietnamese war in 1979, she later became outspoken in her criticism of the party's failure to carry out democratic reforms and was briefly imprisoned in 1991. Undaunted by official pressure, she has written several novels that express the horrors experienced by guerrilla fighters during the Vietnam War and the cruel injustices perpetrated by the regime in the cause of building socialism.

Some popular musical styles have evolved out of Indonesia's growing familiarity with the West. Like young musicians in Africa, the rock group Slank, for example, uses music to attack corruption and social inequality. Shocked at the recent violent acts committed by Islamic fundamentalists, such as the 2002 bombing of a nightclub in Bali, the group promotes a nonviolent message of hope and tolerance for Indonesia's diverse ethnic and religious groups.

CONCLUSION: A REGION IN FLUX

T HE IMAGE OF SOUTHEAST ASIA mired in the Vietnam conflict and the tensions of the Cold War has become a distant memory. In ASEAN, the states in the region have created the framework for a regional organization that can serve their common political, economic, technological, and security interests. A few members of ASEAN are already on the road to advanced development. The remainder are showing signs of undergoing a similar process within the next generation. Although ethnic and religious tensions continue to exist in most ASEAN states, there are promising signs of increasing political stability and pluralism throughout the region.

To be sure, there are also continuing signs of trouble. The financial crisis of 1997 aroused serious political unrest in Indonesia, and although the region's economy has largely recovered, there are still lingering effects. Burma remains isolated and appears mired in a state of chronic underdevelopment and brutal military rule. The three states of Indochina remain potentially unstable and have not yet been fully integrated into the region as a whole. Finally, the increase in terrorist activity within the region, especially in Indonesia, is ominous. Although most Muslims in Southeast Asia have traditionally embraced moderate political, social, and religious views, radical agitators have made inroads through their presence in Muslim schools in the region.

All things considered, however, the situation is more promising today than would have seemed possible a generation ago. The nations of Southeast Asia appear capable of coordinating their efforts to erase the internal divisions and conflicts that have brought so much tragedy to the peoples of the region for centuries. If the original purpose of the U.S. intervention in the Indochina conflict was to buy time for the other nations of the region to develop, the gamble may have paid off. Although the war in Vietnam was lost at considerable cost and bloodshed to the participants, the dire predictions in Washington of a revolutionary reign of terror and falling dominoes were not fulfilled, and some countries in the region appear ready to join the steadily growing ranks of developing nations.

To some observers, economic success in the region has come at a high price, in the form of political authoritarianism and a lack of attention to human rights. Indeed, proponents of the view that Asian values are different from those of the West should not be too complacent in their conviction that there is no correlation between economic prosperity and democracy. Still, a look at the historical record suggests that political pluralism is often a by-product of economic advances and that political values and institutions evolve in response to changing societal conditions. In the end, the current growing pains in Southeast Asia may prove to be beneficial in their overall impact on societies in the region.

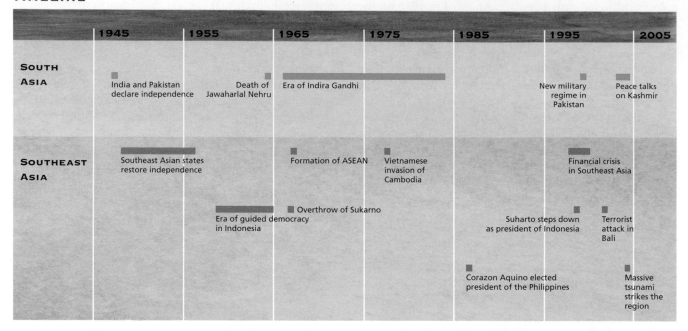

SOUTH ASIA

- India and Pakistan declare independence
- Death of Jawaharlal Nehru
- Era of Indira Gandhi
- New military regime in Pakistan
- Peace talks on Kashmir

SOUTHEAST ASIA

- Southeast Asian states restore independence
- Formation of ASEAN
- Vietnamese invasion of Cambodia
- Financial crisis in Southeast Asia
- Era of guided democracy in Indonesia
- Overthrow of Sukarno
- Suharto steps down as president of Indonesia
- Terrorist attack in Bali
- Corazon Aquino elected president of the Philippines
- Massive tsunami strikes the region

(Timeline axis: 1945, 1955, 1965, 1975, 1985, 1995, 2005)

CHAPTER NOTES

1. *New York Times,* May 2, 1996.
2. Quoted in Larry Collins and Dominique Lapierre, *Freedom at Midnight* (New York, 1975), p. 252.

WORLD HISTORY
RESOURCE CENTER

Visit the *Twentieth-Century World History* Book Companion website for resources specific to this textbook:

academic.cengage.com/history/duiker

The Wadsworth World History Resource Center at worldrc.wadsworth.com/ offers a variety of tools to help you succeed in this course, including access to quizzes; images; documents; interactive simulations, maps, and timelines; movie explorations; and a wealth of other sources.

CHAPTER

14

EMERGING AFRICA

*A*T THE END OF WORLD WAR II, Africa had already been exposed to over half a century of colonial rule. Although many Europeans complacently assumed that colonialism was a necessary evil in the process of introducing civilization to the backward peoples of Africa and Asia, to some African intellectuals, the Western drive for economic profit and political hegemony was a plague that threatened ultimately to destroy civilization. It was the obligation of Africans to use their own humanistic and spiritual qualities to help save the human race. The Ghanaian official Michael Francis Dei-Anang agreed. In *Whither Bound Africa,* written in 1946, he scathingly unmasked the pretensions of Western superiority:

> *Forward! To what?*
> *The Slums, where man is dumped upon man,*
> *Where penury*
> *And misery*
> *Have made their hapless homes,*
> *And all is dark and drear?*
> *Forward! To what?*
> *The factory*
> *To grind hard hours*
> *In an inhuman mill,*
> *In one long ceaseless spell?*
>
> *Forward! To what?*
> *To the reeking round*
> *Of medieval crimes,*
> *Where the greedy hawks*
> *of Aryan stock*
> *Prey with bombs and guns*
> *On men of lesser breed?*
> *Forward to CIVILIZATION.*[1]

To Africans like Dei-Anang, the new Africa that emerged from imperialist rule had a duty to seek new ways of resolving the problems of humanity.

In the three decades following the end of World War II, the peoples of Africa were gradually liberated from the formal trappings of European colonialism. The creation of independent states in Africa began in the late 1950s and proceeded gradually until the last colonial regimes were finally dismantled. But the transition to independence has not been an unalloyed success. The legacy of colonialism in the form of political inexperience and continued European economic domination has combined with overpopulation and climatic disasters to frustrate the new states' ability to achieve political stability and economic prosperity. At the same time, arbitrary boundaries imposed by the colonial powers and ethnic and religious divisions within the African countries have led to bitter conflicts, which have posed a severe obstacle to the dream of continental solidarity and cooperation in forging a common destiny. Today, the continent of Africa, although blessed with enormous potential, is one of the most volatile and conflict-ridden areas of the world. Michael Dei-Anang's dream of a unique African road has not yet been realized. ◇

Uhuru: The Struggle for Independence

After World War II, Europeans reluctantly recognized that the end result of colonial rule in Africa would be African self-government, if not full independence. Accordingly, the African population would have to be trained to handle the responsibilities of representative government. In many cases, however, relatively little had been done to prepare the local population for self-rule. Early in the colonial era, during the late nineteenth century, African administrators had held influential positions in several British colonies, and one even served as governor of the Gold Coast. Several colonies had legislative councils with limited African participation, although their functions were solely advisory. But with the formal institution of colonial rule, senior positions were reserved for the British, although local authority remained in the hands of native rulers.

Colonial Reforms

After World War II, most British colonies introduced reforms that increased the representation of the local population. Members of legislative and executive councils were increasingly chosen through elections, and Africans came to constitute a majority of these bodies. Elected councils at the local level were introduced in the 1950s to reduce the power of the tribal chiefs and clan heads, who had controlled local government under indirect rule. An exception was South Africa, where European domination continued. In the Union of South Africa, the franchise was restricted to whites except in the former territory of the Cape Colony, where persons of mixed ancestry had enjoyed the right to vote since the mid-nineteenth century. Black Africans did win some limited electoral rights in Northern and Southern Rhodesia (now Zambia and Zimbabwe), although whites generally dominated the political scene.

A similar process of political liberalization was taking place in the French colonies. In 1944, the Free French movement under General Charles de Gaulle issued the Brazzaville Declaration, which promised equal rights, though not self-government, in a projected French Union composed of France and its overseas possessions. After the war, a legislative assembly for the new organization was created, although its political powers were limited. At the same time, African representatives were elected to the French National Assembly in Paris. But even this new community of nations had separate categories of citizenship based on education and ethnic background, and decisions on major issues were still made in France or by French officials in French Africa.

The Legacy of Colonialism

As in Asia, colonial rule had a mixed impact on the societies and peoples of Africa. The Western presence brought a number of short-term and long-term benefits to Africa, such as improved transportation and communication facilities, and in a few areas laid the foundation for a modern industrial and commercial sector. Improved sanitation and medical care in all probability increased life expectancy. The introduction of selective elements of Western political systems laid the basis for the gradual creation of democratic societies.

Yet the benefits of Westernization were distributed unequally, and the vast majority of Africans found their lives little improved, if at all. Only South Africa and French-held Algeria, for example, developed modern industrial sectors, extensive railroad networks, and modern communications systems. In both countries, European settlers were numerous, most investment capital for industrial ventures was European, and whites comprised almost the entire professional and managerial class. Members of the native population were generally restricted to unskilled or semiskilled jobs at wages less than one-fifth of those enjoyed by Europeans. Those who worked in industry or on infrastructure projects often suffered from inhumane working conditions. Several thousand African conscripts reportedly died on press gangs building the new railroad system.

Many colonies concentrated on export crops—peanuts from Senegal and Gambia, cotton from Egypt and Uganda, coffee from Kenya, and palm oil and cocoa products from the Gold Coast. Here the benefits of development were somewhat more widespread. In some cases, the crops were grown on plantations, which were usually owned by Europeans. But plantation agriculture was not always suitable in Africa (sometimes the cultivation of cash crops eroded the fragile soil base and turned farmland into desert), and much farming was done by free or tenant farmers. In some areas, where land ownership was traditionally vested in the community, the land was owned and leased by the corporate village.

Even here, however, the vast majority of the profits from the export of tropical products accrued to Europeans or to merchants from other foreign countries, such as India and the Arab emirates. While a fortunate few benefited from the increase in exports, the vast majority of Africans continued to be subsistence farmers growing food for their own consumption. The gap was particularly wide in places like Kenya, where the best lands had been reserved for European settlers to make the colony self-sufficient. As in other parts of the world, the early stages of the Industrial Revolution were especially painful for the rural population, and ordinary subsistence farmers reaped few benefits from colonial rule.

The Rise of Nationalism

The African response to the loss of independence can be traced through several stages, beginning with resistance. In some cases, the opposition came from an organized state, such as Ashanti, which fought against the British takeover of the Gold Coast in the 1860s. Where formal states did not exist, the colonial takeover was often easier and more gradual; in a few instances, however, such as the Zulu tribesmen in South Africa in the 1880s and Abdel Qadir's rebellion against the French in Algeria, resistance to white rule was quite fierce.

Early Nationalist Movements But formal nationalist movements and parties generally arose later in Africa than in Asia. The first nationalist groups were formed in urban areas, primarily among people who had been exposed to Western civilization. The first Afro-Europeans, as such people are sometimes called, often benefited from the European presence, and some, as we have seen, held responsible positions in the colonial bureaucracy. But as the system became more formalized in the early twentieth century, more emphasis was placed on racial distinctions, and opportunities in government and other professional positions diminished, especially in the British colonies, where indirect rule was based on collaboration with the local tribal aristocracy. The result was a dissatisfied urban educated elite, who were all the angrier when they realized they would not benefit from the improved conditions.

Political organizations for African rights did not arise until after World War I, and then only in a few areas, such as British-ruled Kenya and the Gold Coast. At first, organizations such as the National Congress of British West Africa (formed in 1919 in the Gold Coast) and Jomo Kenyatta's Kikuyu Central Association in Kenya focused on improving African living conditions in the colonies rather than on national independence. After World War II, however, following the example of independence movements elsewhere, these groups became organized political parties with independence as their objective. In the Gold Coast, Kwame Nkrumah (1909–1972) led the Convention People's Party, the first formal political party in black Africa. In the late 1940s, Jomo Kenyatta (1894–1978) founded the Kenya African National Union (KANU), which focused on economic issues but had an implied political agenda as well.

For the most part, these political activities were basically nonviolent and were led by Western-educated African intellectuals. Their constituents were primarily urban professionals, merchants, and members of labor unions. But the demand for independence was not entirely restricted to the cities. In Kenya, for example, the widely publicized Mau Mau movement among the Kikuyu people used terrorism as an essential element of its program to achieve *uhuru* (Swahili for "freedom") from the British. Although most of the violence was directed against other Africans—only about a hundred Europeans were killed in the violence, compared with an estimated seventeen hundred Africans who lost their lives at the hands of the rebels—the specter of Mau Mau terrorism alarmed the European population and convinced the British government in 1959 to promise eventual independence.

The Transition to Independence A similar process was occurring in Egypt, which had been a protectorate of Great Britain (and under loose Turkish suzerainty until the breakup of the Ottoman Empire) since the 1880s. National consciousness had existed in Egypt since well before the colonial takeover, and members of the legislative council were calling for independence even before World War I. In 1918, a formal political party called the Wafd was formed to promote Egyptian independence. The intellectuals were opposed as much to the local palace government as to the British, however, and in 1952, an army coup overthrew King Farouk, the grandson of Khedive Ismail, and established an independent republic.

In areas such as South Africa and Algeria, where the political system was dominated by European settlers, the transition to independence was more complicated. In South Africa, political activity by local Africans began with the formation of the African National Congress (ANC) in 1912. Initially, the ANC was dominated by Western-oriented intellectuals and had little mass support. Its goal was to achieve economic and political reforms, including full equality for educated Africans, within the framework of the existing system. But the ANC's efforts met with little success, while conservative white parties managed to stiffen the segregation laws. In response, the ANC became increasingly radicalized, and by the 1950s, the prospects for a violent confrontation were growing.

In Algeria, resistance to French rule by Berbers and Arabs in rural areas had never ceased. After World War II, urban agitation intensified, leading to a widespread rebellion against colonial rule in the mid-1950s. At first, the French government tried to maintain its authority in Algeria, which was considered an integral part of metropolitan France. But when Charles de Gaulle became president in 1958, he reversed French policy, and Algeria became independent under President Ahmad Ben Bella (1918–2004) in 1962. The armed struggle in Algeria hastened the transition to statehood in its neighbors as well. Tunisia won its independence in 1956 after some urban agitation and rural unrest but retained close ties with Paris. The French attempted to suppress the nationalist movement in Morocco by sending Sultan Muhammad V into exile, but the effort failed, and in 1956, he returned as the ruler of the independent state of Morocco.

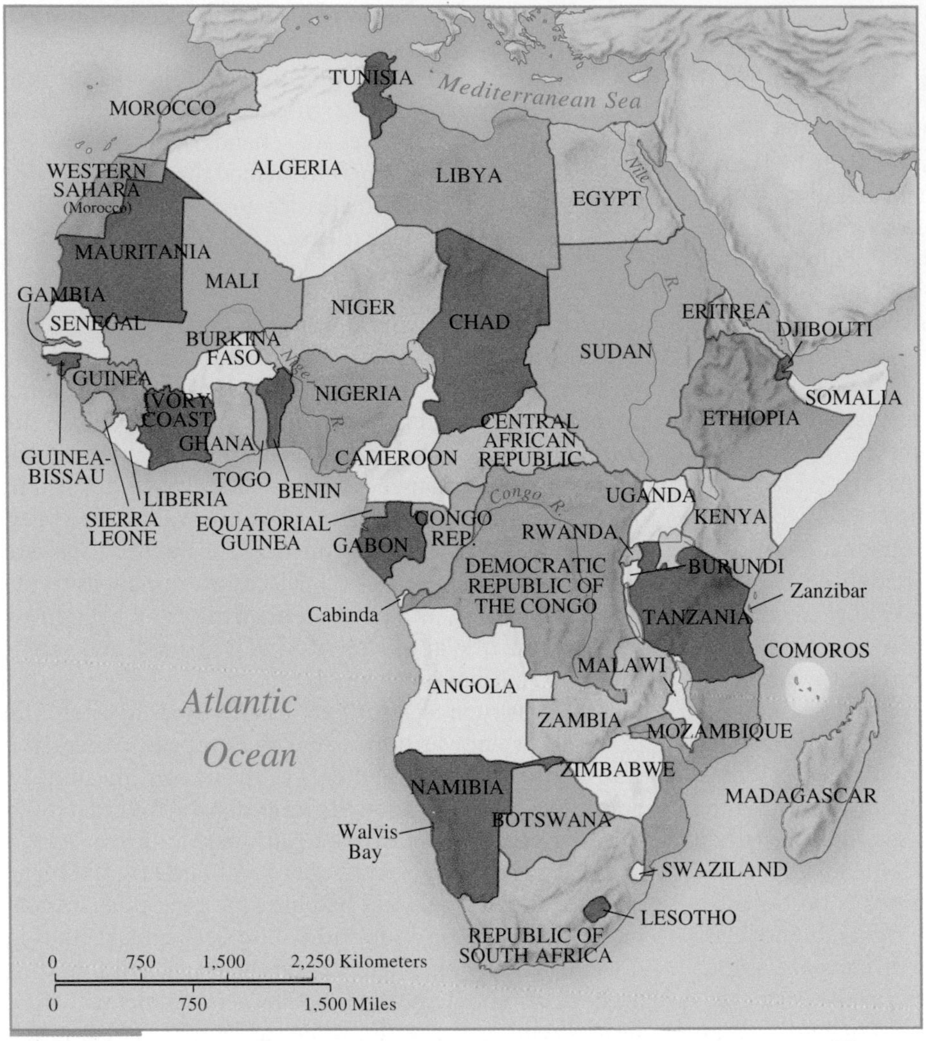

MAP 14.1 Modern Africa. This map shows the independent states in Africa today. Why was unity so difficult to achieve in African regions? **View an animated version of this map or related maps at the World History Resource Center, at** worldrc.wadsworth.com/.

Most black African nations achieved their independence in the late 1950s and 1960s, beginning with the Gold Coast, now renamed Ghana, in 1957 (see Map 14.1). Nigeria, the Belgian Congo (renamed Zaire and later the Democratic Republic of the Congo), Kenya, Tanganyika (renamed Tanzania after merging with Zanzibar), and several other countries soon followed. Most of the French colonies agreed to accept independence within the framework of de Gaulle's French Community. By the late 1960s, only parts of southern Africa and the Portuguese possessions of Mozambique and Angola remained under European rule.

Independence came later to Africa than to most of Asia. Several factors help explain the delay. For one thing, colonialism was established in Africa somewhat later than in most areas of Asia, and the inevitable reaction from the local population was consequently delayed. Furthermore, with the exception of a few areas in West Africa and along the Mediterranean, coherent states with a strong sense of cultural, ethnic, and linguistic unity did not exist in most of Africa. Most traditional states, such as Ashanti in West Africa, Songhai in the southern Sahara, and Bakongo in the Congo basin, were collections of heterogeneous peoples with little sense of national or cultural identity. Even after colonies were established, the European powers often practiced a policy of "divide and rule," while the British encouraged political decentralization by retaining the authority of the traditional native chieftains. It is hardly surprising that when opposition to colonial rule emerged, unity was difficult to achieve.

The Era of Independence

The newly independent African states faced intimidating challenges. Like the new states in South and Southeast Asia, they had been profoundly affected by colonial rule. Yet the experience had been highly unsatisfactory in most respects. Although Western political institutions, values, and technology had been introduced, at least into the cities, the exposure to European civilization had been superficial at best for most Africans and tragic for many. At the outset of independence, most African societies were still primarily agrarian and traditional, and their modern sectors depended mainly on imports from the West.

Pan-Africanism and Nationalism: The Destiny of Africa

Like the leaders of the new states in South and Southeast Asia, most African leaders came from the urban middle class. They had studied in Europe or the United States and spoke and read European languages. Although most were profoundly critical of colonial policies, they appeared to accept the relevance of the Western model to Africa and gave at least lip service to Western democratic values.

TOWARD AFRICAN UNITY

*I*n May 1963, the leaders of thirty-two African states met in Addis Ababa, the capital of Ethiopia, to discuss the creation of an organization that would represent the interests of all the newly independent countries of Africa. The result was the Organization of African Unity (OAU). An excerpt from its charter is presented here. Although the organization did not realize all of the aspirations of its founders, it provided a useful forum for the discussion and resolution of its members' common problems. In 2001, it was replaced by the African Union, which was designed to bring about increased cooperation among the states on the continent.

What were the key elements in the charter of the OAU? To what degree have these goals been realized?

Charter of the Organization of African Unity

We, the Heads of African States and Governments assembled in the City of Addis Ababa, Ethiopia;

CONVINCED that it is the inalienable right of all people to control their own destiny;

CONSCIOUS of the fact that freedom, equality, justice, and dignity are essential objectives for the achievement of the legitimate aspirations of the African peoples;

CONSCIOUS of our responsibility to harness the natural and human resources of our continent for the total advancement of our peoples in spheres of human endeavor;

INSPIRED by a common determination to promote understanding among our peoples and cooperation among our States in response to the aspirations of our peoples for brotherhood and solidarity, in a larger unity transcending ethnic and national differences;

CONVINCED that, in order to translate this determination into a dynamic force in the cause of human progress, conditions for peace and security must be established and maintained;

DETERMINED to safeguard and consolidate the hard-won independence as well as the sovereignty and territorial integrity of our States, and to fight against neocolonialism in all its forms;

DEDICATED to the general progress of Africa; . . .

DESIROUS that all African States should henceforth unite so that the welfare and well-being of their peoples can be assured;

RESOLVED to reinforce the links between our states by establishing and strengthening common institutions;

HAVE agreed to the present Charter.

SOURCE: *Organizing African Unity* by Jon Woronoff, pp. 642–649. Copyright © 1970 by Scarecrow Press, Inc. Used with permission of the publisher.

Their views on economics were somewhat more diverse. Some, like Jomo Kenyatta of Kenya and General Mobutu Sese Seko (1930–1998) of Zaire (previously the Belgian Congo), were advocates of Western-style capitalism. Others, like Julius Nyerere (1922–1999) of Tanzania, Kwame Nkrumah of Ghana, and Sékou Touré (1922–1984) of Guinea, preferred an "African form of socialism," which bore slight resemblance to the Marxist-Leninist socialism practiced in the Soviet Union and was more like the syndicalist movement in Western Europe. According to its advocates, it was descended from traditional communal practices in precolonial Africa.

Like the leaders of other developing countries, the new political leaders in Africa were strongly nationalistic and generally accepted the colonial boundaries. But as we have seen, these boundaries were artificial creations of the colonial powers. Virtually all of the new states included widely diverse ethnic, linguistic, and territorial groups. Zaire, for example, was composed of more than two hundred territorial groups speaking seventy-five different languages.

Some African leaders themselves harbored attitudes that undermined the fragile sense of common identity needed to knit these diverse groups together. A number of leaders—including Nkrumah of Ghana, Touré of Guinea, and Kenyatta of Kenya—were enticed by the dream of pan-Africanism, a concept of continental unity that transcended national boundaries and was to find its concrete manifestation in the Organization of African Unity (OAU), which was founded in Addis Ababa, Ethiopia, in 1963 (see the box above).

Pan-Africanism originated among African intellectuals during the first half of the twentieth century. A basic element was the conviction that there was a distinctive "African personality" that owed nothing to Western materialism and provided a common sense of destiny for all black African peoples. According to Aimé Césaire, a West Indian of African descent and a leading ideologist of the movement, whereas Western civilization prized rational thought and material achievement, African culture emphasized emotional expression and a common sense of humanity.

The concept of a unique African destiny (known to its originators by the French term *négritude*, or "blackness") was in part a natural defensive response to the social Darwinist concepts of Western racial superiority and

African inferiority that were popular in Europe and the United States during the early years of the twentieth century. At the same time, it was stimulated by growing self-doubt among many European intellectuals after World War I, who feared that Western civilization was on a path of self-destruction. Aimé Césaire compared the white world,

> *appalling weary from its immense effort*
> *the crack of its joints rebelling under the hardness*
>   *of the stars*

with that of the Africans,

> *Those who invented neither gunpowder nor compass*
> *those who tamed neither steam nor electricity*
> *those who explored neither sea nor sky*
> *but those who know the humblest corners of the*
>   *country suffering*
> *those whose only journeys were uprooting*
> *those who went to sleep on their knees*
> *those who were domesticated and christianized*
> *those who were inoculated with degeneration*[2]

The idea had more appeal to Africans from French colonies than to those from British possessions. Yet it also found adherents in the British colonies, as well as in the United States and elsewhere in the Americas. African American intellectuals such as W. E. B. Dubois and George Padmore and the West Indian politician Marcus Garvey attempted to promote a "black renaissance" by popularizing the idea of a distinct African personality. Their views were shared by several of the new African leaders, including Leopold Senghor (1906–2001) of Senegal, Kwame Nkrumah of Ghana, and Jomo Kenyatta of Kenya. Nkrumah in particular appeared to hope that a pan-African union could be established that would unite all of the new countries of the continent in a broader community.

Dream and Reality: Political and Economic Conditions in Independent Africa

The program of the OAU had forecast a future Africa based on freedom, equality, justice, and dignity and on the unity, solidarity, prosperity, and territorial integrity of African states. It did not take long for reality to set in. Vast disparities in education and income made it hard to establish democracy in much of Africa. Expectations that independence would lead to stable political structures based on "one person, one vote" were soon disappointed as the initial phase of pluralistic governments gave way to a series of military regimes and one-party states. Between 1957 and 1982, more than seventy leaders of African countries were overthrown by violence, and the pace has not abated in recent years.

Hopes that independence would inaugurate an era of economic prosperity and equality were similarly dashed.

Manioc, Food for the Millions. Manioc, a tuber like the potato, was brought to Africa from South America soon after the voyages of Columbus. Although low in nutrient value, it can be cultivated in poor soil with little moisture and is reportedly the staple food for nearly one-third of the population of sub-Saharan Africa. Manioc is also widely grown in tropical parts of Asia and South America and is familiar to Westerners as the source of tapioca (it is also called cassava or yuca). In the photograph shown here, village women in Senegal rhythmically pound manioc to remove traces of naturally occurring cyanide that would otherwise poison those who rely on the tuber as a basic commodity.

Part of the problem could be (and was) ascribed to the lingering effects of colonialism. Most newly independent countries in Africa were dependent on the export of a single crop or natural resource. When prices fluctuated or dropped, they were at the mercy of the vagaries of the international market. In several cases, the resources were still controlled by foreigners, leading to the charge that colonialism had been succeeded by "neocolonialism," in which Western domination was maintained by economic rather than by political or military means. To make matters worse, most African states had to import technology and manufactured goods from the West, and the prices of those goods rose more rapidly than those of the export products.

World trade policies have often exacerbated these problems. While taking aggressive action to reduce tariff barriers on the flow of industrial goods worldwide, the advanced countries have provided massive subsidies to protect domestic producers of agricultural products, thereby preventing poor countries from improving their economic conditions through agricultural exports.

The new states also contributed to their own problems. Scarce national resources were squandered on military equipment or expensive consumer goods rather than used

Problems of Transport. The lack of efficient transportation is a serious problem in the developing world, especially in rural areas. In this painting by an artist from Zimbabwe, we see villagers trudging the long distance to the Weya Clinic. Some villagers travel to town on a pickup truck, while others watch the overcrowded bus pass them by. Although some artists in contemporary Africa continue to utilize traditional themes and techniques, this painting is an example of a new compositional African style, with painted figures resembling appliqué cutouts in bright colors. On the right side we see a typically overloaded bus in Senegal.

to build up their infrastructure to provide the foundation for an industrial economy. Corruption, a painful reality throughout the modern world, became almost a way of life in Africa, as bribery (known variously as *dash, chai,* or *bonsella*) became necessary to obtain even the most basic services. The Nigerian author Cyprian Ekwensi expressed his disillusionment with African politics in his novel *Jagua Nana.* When the heroine's boyfriend Freddie states, "I wan' money quick-quick; an' politics is de only hope," she replies, "No Freddie. I no wan' you to win. . . . Politics not for you, Freddie. You got education. You got culture. You're a gentleman an' proud. Politics be a game for dog. And in dis Lagos, is a rough game. De roughest game in de whole worl'. Is smell an' dirty an' you too clean an' sweet." [3]

Finally, population growth, which has hindered economic growth more severely than anything else in the new nations of Asia and Africa, became a serious problem and crippled efforts to build modern economies. By the mid-1980s, annual population growth averaged nearly 3 percent throughout Africa, the highest rate of any continent. Drought conditions and the inexorable spread of the Sahara (usually

known as desertification, a condition caused partly by overpopulation) have led to widespread hunger and starvation, first in West African countries such as Niger and Mali and then in Ethiopia, Somalia, and the Sudan. Despite global efforts to provide food, millions are in danger of starvation and malnutrition, and countless others have fled to neighboring countries in search of sustenance.

Predictions are that the population of Africa will increase by at least 200 million over the next ten years, but that estimate does not take into account the prevalence of AIDS, which has reached epidemic proportions in Africa in recent years. According to one estimate, one-third of the entire population of sub-Saharan Africa is infected with the virus, including a high percentage of the urban middle class. Over 75 percent of the AIDS cases reported around the world are on the continent of Africa. In some countries, AIDS is transmitted via the tradition that requires a widow to have sexual relations with one of her deceased husband's male relatives. Some observers estimate that without measures to curtail the effects of the disease, it will have a significant impact on several African countries by reducing population growth.

Poverty is endemic in Africa, particularly among the three-quarters of the population still living off the land. Urban areas have grown tremendously, but as in much of Asia, most are surrounded by massive squatter settlements of rural peoples who fled to the cities in search of a better life. The expansion of the cities has overwhelmed fragile transportation and sanitation systems and led to rising pollution and perpetual traffic jams, while millions live without water and electricity. Meanwhile, the fortunate few (all too often government officials on the take) live the high life and emulate the consumerism of the West (in a particularly expressive phrase, the rich in many East African countries are know as *wabenzi,* or "Mercedes-Benz people").

The Search for Solutions

Although all of the emerging African states have had to cope with the impact of Western civilization to one degree or another, each has dealt with the challenge in its own way, sometimes with strikingly different consequences. Despite all of the shared difficulties, Africa today remains one of the most diverse regions in the world.

Tanzania: An African Route to Socialism Concern over the dangers of economic inequality inspired a number of African leaders—including Nkrumah in Ghana, Nyerere in Tanzania, and Samora Michel in Mozambique—to restrict foreign investment and nationalize the major industries and utilities while promoting social ideals and values. Nyerere was the most consistent, promoting the ideals of socialism and self-reliance through his Arusha Declaration of 1967. Taking advantage of his powerful political influence, Nyerere imposed limits on income and established village collectives to avoid the corrosive effects of economic inequality and government corruption. Sympathetic foreign countries provided considerable economic aid to assist the experiment, and many observers noted that levels of corruption, political instability, and ethnic strife were lower in Tanzania than in many other African countries. Unfortunately, corruption has increased in recent years, while political elements on the island of Zanzibar, citing the stagnation brought by decades of socialism, are agitating for autonomy or even total separation from the mainland. Tanzania also has poor soil, inadequate rainfall, and limited resources, all of which have contributed to its slow growth and continuing rural and urban poverty.

In 1985, Nyerere voluntarily retired from the presidency. In his farewell speech, he confessed that he had failed to achieve many of his ambitious goals to create a socialist society in Africa. In particular, he admitted that his plan to collectivize the traditional private farm (*shamba*) had run into strong resistance from conservative peasants. "You can socialize what is not traditional," he remarked. "The *shamba*

can't be socialized." But Nyerere insisted that many of his policies had succeeded in improving social and economic conditions, and he argued that the only real solution was to consolidate the multitude of small countries in the region into a larger East African Federation.[4]

Kenya: The Perils of Capitalism The countries that opted for capitalism faced their own dilemmas. Neighboring Kenya, blessed with better soil in the highlands, a local tradition of aggressive commerce, and a residue of European settlers, welcomed foreign investment and profit incentives. The results have been mixed. Kenya has a strong current of indigenous African capitalism and a substantial middle class, mostly based in the capital, Nairobi. But landlessness, unemployment, and income inequities are high, even by African standards (almost one-fifth of the country's 34 million people are squatters, and unemployment is currently estimated at 45 percent). The rate of population growth—more than 4 percent annually—is one of the highest in the world. Eighty percent of the population remains rural, and 40 percent live below the poverty line. The result has been widespread unrest in a country formerly admired for its successful development.

Kenya's problems have been exacerbated by chronic disputes between disparate ethnic groups and simmering tensions between farmers and pastoralists. For many years, the country maintained a fragile political stability under the dictatorial rule of President Daniel arap Moi, one of the most authoritiarian of African leaders. Plagued by charges of corruption, Moi finally agreed to retire in 2002, but under his successor, Mwai Kibaki, the twin problems of political instability and widespread poverty continue to afflict the country.

South Africa: An End to Apartheid Perhaps Africa's greatest success story is in South Africa, where the white government—which long maintained a policy of racial segregation (apartheid) and restricted black sovereignty to a series of small "Bantustans" in relatively infertile areas of the country—finally accepted the inevitability of African involvement in the political process and the national economy. In 1990, the government of President F. W. de Klerk (b. 1936) released African National Congress leader Nelson Mandela (b. 1918) from prison, where he had been held since 1964. In 1993, the two leaders agreed to hold democratic national elections the following spring. In the meantime, ANC representatives agreed to take part in a transitional coalition government with de Klerk's National Party. Those elections resulted in a substantial majority for the ANC, and Mandela became president. In May 1996, a new constitution that called for a multiracial state was approved.

In 1999, a major step toward political stability was taken when Nelson Mandela stepped down from the presidency,

Cape Town: A Tale of Two Cities. First settled by the Dutch in the seventeenth century, Cape Town is the most modern city in Africa, as well as one of its most beautiful. Situated at the foot of scenic Table Mountain, its business and financial center has long been dominated by Europeans (see the left photo). Despite the abolition of apartheid in the 1990s, much of Cape Town's black population still resides in the crowded "townships" located along the fringes of the city, as shown in the right photo.

to be replaced by his long-time disciple Thabo Mbeki. The new president faced a number of intimidating problems, including rising unemployment, widespread lawlessness, chronic corruption, and an ominous flight of capital and professional personnel from the country. Mbeki's administration has been criticized for not doing enough to help the poor black population. The government's failure to carry out a promised land reform program—which was to provide farmland to the nation's 40 million black farmers—provoked some squatters to seize unused private lands near Johannesburg.

Still, South Africa remains the wealthiest and most industrialized state in Africa and the best hope that a multiracial society can succeed on the continent. The country's black elite now number nearly one-quarter of its wealthiest households, compared with only 9 percent in 1991.

Nigeria: A Nation Divided If the situation in South Africa provides grounds for modest optimism, the situation in Nigeria provides reason for serious concern. Africa's largest country in terms of population, and one of its wealthiest because of substantial oil reserves, Nigeria had for many years been in the grip of military strongmen. During his rule, General Sani Abacha ruthlessly suppressed all opposition and in late 1995 ordered the execution of a writer despite widespread protests from human rights groups abroad. Abacha died in 1998, and national elections led to the creation of a civilian government under Olusegun Obasanjo. Civilian leadership has not been a panacea for Nigeria's problems, however. In early 2000, religious riots between Christians and Muslims broke out in several northern cities as a result of the decision by provincial officials to apply Islamic law throughout their jurisdiction.

The dispute between Muslims and Christians in Nigeria is a contemporary variant of the traditional tensions that have existed between farmers and pastoralists throughout recorded history. Muslim cattle herders, migrating southward to escape the increasing desiccation of the grasslands south of the Sahara, compete for precious land with indigenous—primarily Christian—farmers. Often the confrontation leads to outbreaks of violence with strong religious and ethnic overtones. Although President Obasanjo has sought to defuse the crisis, the dispute threatens the fragile unity of Africa's most populous country.

The religious tensions that erupted in Nigeria have spilled over into neighboring states. In the Ivory Coast, the death of President Houphouet-Boigny in 1993 led to an outbreak of long-simmering resentment between Christians in the south and recently arrived Muslim immigrants in the north. National elections held in the fall of 2000, resulting in the election of a Christian president, were marked by sporadic violence and widespread charges of voting irregularities.

A similar fault line between farmers and pastoralists has been at the root of the lengthy civil war that has been raging in the Sudan. Conflict between Muslim pastoralists—supported by the central government in Khartoum—and predominantly Christian black farmers in the southern part of the country was finally brought to an end in 2004, but new outbreaks of violence have erupted in western Darfur province, leading to reports of widespread starvation among the local villagers.

Central Africa: Cauldron of Conflict The most tragic situation is in the central African states of Rwanda and

Burundi, where a chronic conflict between the minority Tutsis and the Hutu majority has led to a bitter civil war, with thousands of refugees fleeing to the neighboring Congo. In another classic example of conflict between pastoral and farming peoples, the nomadic Tutsis, supported by the colonial Belgian government, had long dominated the sedentary Hutu population. It was the attempt of the Bantu-speaking Hutus to bring an end to Tutsi domination that initiated the most recent conflicts, marked by massacres on both sides. In the meantime, the presence of large numbers of foreign troops and refugees intensified centrifugal forces inside Zaire, where General Mobutu Sese Seko had long ruled with an iron hand. In 1997, military forces led by Mobutu's longtime opponent Lauren Kabila managed to topple the general's corrupt government. Once in power, Kabila renamed the country the Democratic Republic of the Congo and promised a return to democratic practices. The new government systematically suppressed political dissent, however, and in January 2001, Kabila was assassinated, to be succeeded by his son. Peace talks are now under way.

Sowing Seeds of Democracy Not all the news in Africa has been bad. Stagnant economies have led to the collapse of one-party regimes and the emergence of fragile democracies in several countries. Dictatorships were brought to an end in Ethiopia, Liberia, and Somalia, although in each case the fall of the regime was later followed by political instability or civil war. In Senegal, national elections held in the summer of 2000 brought an end to four decades of rule by the once-dominant Socialist Party. The new president, Abdoulaye Wade, is a staunch advocate of promoting development on the capitalist model throughout Africa. Perhaps the most notorious dicter was Idi Amin of Uganda, who led a military coup against Prime Minister Milton Obote in 1971. After ruling by terror and brutal repression of dissident elements, he was finally deposed in 1979. In recent years, stability has returned to the country, which in May 1996 held its first presidential election in more than fifteen years.

The African Union: A Glimmer of Hope It is clear that African societies have not yet begun to surmount the challenges they have faced since independence. Most African states are still poor and their populations illiterate. Moreover, African concerns continue to carry little weight in the international community. A recent agreement by the World Trade Organization (WTO) on the need to reduce agricultural subsidies in the advanced nations has been widely ignored. In 2000, the General Assembly of the United Nations passed a Millennium Declaration calling for a dramatic reduction in the incidence of poverty, hunger, and illiteracy worldwide by the year 2015. So far,

however, little has been done to realize these ambitious goals. At a conference on the subject held in September 2005, the participants squabbled over how best to fund the effort. Some delegations, including that of the United States, argued that external assistance cannot succeed unless the nations of Africa adopt measures to bring about good government and sound economic policies.

Certainly, part of the solution to the continent's multiple problems must come from within. Although there are gratifying signs of progress toward political stability in some countries, including Senegal, Uganda, and South Africa, other nations like Sudan, Somalia, and Zimbabwe are still racked by civil war or ruled by brutal dictatorships. Conflicts between Muslims and Christians in West Africa threaten to spread throughout the region. To alleviate such problems, UN peacekeeping forces have been sent to several African countries including the Democratic Republic of the Congo, Eritrea, the Ivory Coast, and Sierra Leone.

A significant part of the problem is that the nation-state system is not particularly well suited to the African continent. Africans must find better ways to cooperate with each other and to protect and promote their own interests. A first step in that direction was taken in 1991, when the OAU agreed to establish the African Economic Community (AEC). In 2001, the OAU was replaced by the African Union, which is intended to provide greater political and economic integration throughout the continent on the pattern of the European Union (see Chapter 10). The new organization has already sought to mediate several of the conflicts in the region.

As Africa evolves, it is useful to remember that economic and political change is often an agonizingly slow and painful process. Introduced to industrialization and concepts of Western democracy only a century ago, African societies are still groping for ways to graft Western political institutions and economic practices onto a native structure still significantly influenced by traditional values and attitudes.

Continuity and Change in Modern African Societies

In general, the impact of the West has been greater on urban and educated Africans and more limited on their rural and illiterate compatriots. After all, the colonial presence was first and most firmly established in the cities. Many cities, including Dakar, Lagos, Johannesburg, Cape Town, Brazzaville, and Nairobi, are direct products of the colonial experience. Most African cities today look like their counterparts elsewhere in the world. They have high-rise buildings, blocks of residential apartments, wide boulevards, neon lights, movie theaters, and traffic jams.

Education

The educational system has been the primary means of introducing Western values and culture. In the precolonial era, formal schools did not really exist in Africa except for parochial schools in Christian Ethiopia and academies to train young males in Islamic doctrine and law in Muslim societies in North and West Africa. For the average African, education took place at home or in the village courtyard and stressed socialization and vocational training. Traditional education in Africa was not necessarily inferior to that in Europe. Social values and customs were transmitted to the young by storytellers, often village elders, who could gain considerable prestige through their performance. Among the Luo people in Kenya, for example, children were taught in a *siwindhe,* or the house of a widowed grandmother. Here they would be instructed in the ways and thinking of their people. A favorite saying for those who behaved stupidly was "you are uneducated, like one who never slept in a *siwindhe.*"[5]

Europeans introduced modern Western education into Africa in the nineteenth century, although some Africans had already become literate in one or more Western languages by taking part in commerce. The French set up the first state-run schools in Senegal in 1818. In British colonies and protectorates, the earliest schools were established by missionaries. At first, these schools concentrated on vocational training with some instruction in European languages and Western civilization. Most courses were taught in the vernacular, although many schools later switched to English or French. Eventually, pressure from Africans led to the introduction of professional training, and the first institutes of higher learning were established in the early twentieth century. Most college-educated Africans, called "been-to's," however, received their higher training abroad.

With independence, African countries established their own state-run schools. The emphasis was on the primary level, but high schools and universities were established in major cities. The basic objectives have been to introduce vocational training and improve literacy rates. Unfortunately, both funding and trained teachers are scarce in most countries, and few rural areas have schools. As a result, illiteracy remains high, estimated at about 70 percent of the population across the continent. There has been a perceptible shift toward education in the vernacular languages. In West Africa, only about one in four adults is conversant in a Western language.

Urban and Rural Life

The cities are where the African elites live and work. Affluent Africans, like their contemporaries in other developing countries, have been strongly attracted to the glittering material aspects of Western culture. They live in Western-style homes or apartments and eat Western foods stored in Western refrigerators, and those who can afford it drive Western cars. It has been said, not wholly in praise, that there are more Mercedes-Benzes in Nigeria than in Germany, where they are manufactured.

Outside the major cities, where about three-quarters of the continent's inhabitants live, Western influence has had less impact. Millions of people throughout Africa (as in Asia) live much as their ancestors did, in thatch huts without modern plumbing and electricity; they farm or hunt by traditional methods, practice time-honored family rituals, and believe in the traditional deities. Even here, however, change is taking place. Slavery has been eliminated, for the most part, although there have been persistent reports of raids by slave traders on defenseless villages in the southern Sudan. Economic need, though, has brought about massive migrations as some leave to work on plantations, others move to the cities, and still others flee to refugee camps to escape starvation. Migration itself is a wrenching experience, disrupting familiar family and village ties and enforcing new social relationships.

Nowhere, in fact, is the dichotomy between old and new, native and foreign, rural and urban so clear and painful as in Africa. Urban dwellers regard the village as the repository of all that is backward in the African past, while rural peoples view the growing urban areas as a source of corruption, prostitution, hedonism, and the destruction of communal customs and values. The tension between traditional ways and Western culture is particularly strong among African intellectuals, many of whom are torn between their admiration for things Western and their desire to retain an African identity. "Here we stand," wrote one Nigerian,

> *infants overblown*
> *poised between two civilizations*
> *finding the balancing irksome,*
> *itching for something to happen,*
> *to tip us one way or the other,*
> *groping in the dark for a helping hand*
> *and finding none.*[6]

African Women

As we have seen (see Chapter 2), one of the consequences of colonialism in Africa was a change in the relationship between men and women. Some of these changes could be described as beneficial, but others were not. Women were often introduced to Western education and given legal rights denied to them in the precolonial era. But they also

Building His Dream House. In Africa, the houses of rural people are often constructed with a wood frame, known as wattle, daubed with mud, and then covered with a thatch roof. Such houses are inexpensive to build and remain cool in the hot tropical climate. In this Kenyan village not far from the Indian Ocean, a young man is applying mud to the wall of his future home. Houses are built in a similar fashion throughout the continent, as well as in much of southern Asia.

Courtesy of William J. Duiker

became a labor resource and were sometimes recruited as forced labor on construction projects.

Independence also had a significant impact on gender roles in African society. Almost without exception, the new governments established the principle of sexual equality and permitted women to vote and run for political office. Yet as elsewhere, women continue to operate at a disability in a world dominated by males. Politics remains a male preserve, and although a few professions, such as teaching, child care, and clerical work, are dominated by women, most African women are employed in menial positions such as agricultural labor, factory work, and retail trade or as domestics. Education is open to all at the elementary level, but women comprise less than 20 percent of students at the upper levels in most African societies today.

Not surprisingly, women have made the greatest strides in the cities. Most urban women, like men, now marry on the basis of personal choice, although a significant minority are still willing to accept their parents' choice. After marriage, African women appear to occupy a more equal position than their counterparts in most Asian countries. Each marriage partner tends to maintain a separate income, and women often have the right to possess property separate from their husbands. Though many wives still defer to their husbands in the traditional manner, others are like the woman in Abioseh Nicol's story "A Truly Married Woman," who,

after years as living as a common-law wife with her husband, is finally able to provide the price and finalize the marriage. After the wedding, she declares, "For twelve years I have got up every morning at five to make tea for you and breakfast. Now I am a truly married woman [and] you must treat me with a little more respect. You are now my husband and not a lover. Get up and make yourself a cup of tea."

There is a growing feminist movement in Africa, but it is firmly based on conditions in the local environment. Many African women writers, for example, refuse to be defined by Western dogma and opt instead for a brand of African feminism much like that of Ama Ata Aidoo (b. 1942), a Ghanaian novelist, whose ultimate objective is to free African society as a whole, not just its female inhabitants.

In general, then, women in urban areas in contemporary Africa have been able to hold their own. Although they are still sometimes held to different standards than men (African men often expect their wives to be both modern and traditional, fashionable and demure, wage earners and housekeepers) and do not possess the full range of career opportunities that men do, they are manifestly better off than women in many Asian societies.

The same cannot necessarily be said about women in rural areas, where traditional attitudes continue to exert a strong influence and individuals may still be subordinated

Courtesy of William J. Duiker

Salt of the Earth. During the precolonial era, many West African societies were forced to import salt from Mediterranean countries in exchange for tropical products and gold. Today, the people of Senegal satisfy their domestic needs by mining salt deposits contained in lakes like this one in the interior of the country. These lakes are the remnants of vast seas that covered the region of the Sahara in prehistoric times. Note that women are doing much of the heavy labor, while men occupy the managerial positions.

to communalism. In some societies, clitoridectomy is still widely practiced. Polygamy is also not uncommon, and arranged marriages are still the rule rather than the exception. In some Muslim societies, efforts to apply *Shari'a* law have led to greater restrictions on the freedom of women. In northern Nigeria, a woman was recently sentenced to death for committing the act of adultery. The sentence was later reversed on appeal.

To a villager in Africa as elsewhere, an African city often looks like the fount of evil, decadence, and corruption. Women in particular have suffered from the tension between the pull of the city and the village. As men are drawn to the cities in search of employment and excitement, their wives and girlfriends are left behind, both literally and figuratively, in the native village, yet there are signs of change. In 2006, Ellen Johnson-Sirleaf was elected president of Liberia—the first woman to be elected president of a country on the African continent.

African Culture

Inevitably, the tension between traditional and modern, native and foreign, and individual and communal that has permeated contemporary African society has spilled over into culture. In general, in the visual arts and music, utility and ritual have given way to pleasure and decoration.

In the process, Africans have been affected to a certain extent by foreign influences but have retained their distinctive characteristics. Wood carving, metalwork, painting, and sculpture, for example, have preserved their traditional forms but are now increasingly adapted to serve the tourist industry and the export market.

Literature

No area of African culture has been so strongly affected by political and social events as literature. Except for Muslim areas in North and East Africa, precolonial Africans did not have a written literature, although their tradition of oral storytelling served as a rich repository of history, custom, and folk culture. The absence of written languages, of course, means a lack of a traditional African literature. The first written literature in the vernacular or in European languages emerged during the nineteenth century in the form of novels, poetry, and drama.

Angry at the negative portrayal of Africa in Western literature (see the box on p. 288), African authors initially wrote primarily for a European audience as a means of establishing black dignity and purpose. Embracing the ideals of *négritude,* many glorified the emotional and communal aspects of the traditional African experience.

One of the first was Guinean author Camara Laye (1928–1980), who in 1953 published *The Dark Child,* a touching and intimate initiation into village life in precolonial Africa. In the novel, which admitted the reader to the secret rituals and practices of daily life behind the protective hedges of an African village compound, the author openly regretted the lost ways of the African past while conceding that they were not appropriate to the Guinea of tomorrow.

Chinua Achebe of Nigeria was the first major African novelist to write in the English language. In his writings, he attempts to interpret African history from a native perspective and to forge a new sense of African identity. In his most famous novel, *Things Fall Apart* (1958), he recounts the story of a Nigerian who refuses to submit to the new British order and eventually commits suicide. Criticizing those of his contemporaries who have accepted foreign rule, the protagonist laments that the white man "has put a knife on the things that held us together and we have fallen apart."

After 1965, the African novel took a dramatic turn, shifting its focus from the brutality of the foreign oppressor to the shortcomings of the new native leadership. Having gained independence, African politicians were now portrayed as mimicking and even outdoing the injustices committed by their colonial predecessors. A prominent example of this genre is the work of Kenyan Ngugi Wa Thiong'o (b. 1938). His first novel, *A Grain of Wheat,* takes place on the eve of *uhuru,* or independence. Although it

AFRICA: DARK OR RADIANT CONTINENT?

Colonialism camouflaged its economic objectives under the cloak of a "civilizing mission," which in Africa was aimed at illuminating the so-called Dark Continent with Europe's brilliant civilization. In 1899, the Polish-born English author Joseph Conrad (1857–1924) fictionalized his harrowing journey up the Congo River in the novella *Heart of Darkness*. Expressing views from his Victorian perspective, he portrayed an Africa that was incomprehensible, irrational, sensual, and therefore threatening. Conrad, however, was shocked by the horrific exploitation of the peoples of the Belgian Congo, presenting them with a compassion rarely seen during the heyday of imperialism.

Over the years, Conrad's work has provoked much debate, and many African writers have been prompted to counter his vision by reaffirming the dignity and purpose of the African people. One of the first to do so was the Guinean author Camara Laye (1928–1980), who in 1954 composed a brilliant novel, *The Radiance of the King*, which can be viewed as the mirror image of Conrad's *Heart of Darkness*. In Laye's work, another European protagonist undertakes a journey into the impenetrable heart of Africa. This time, however, he is enlightened by the process, thereby obtaining self-knowledge and ultimately salvation.

Compare the depiction of the continent of Africa in these two passages. Is Laye responding to Conrad? If so, what is the response?

Joseph Conrad, *Heart of Darkness*

We penetrated deeper and deeper into the heart of darkness. It was very quiet there. At night sometimes the roll of drums behind the curtain of trees would run up the river and remain sustained faintly, as if hovering in the air high over our heads, till the first break of day. Whether it meant war, peace, or prayer we could not tell. . . . But suddenly, as we struggled round a bend, there would be a glimpse of rush walls, of peaked grass-roofs, a burst of yells, a whirl of black limbs, a mass of hands clapping, of feet stamping, of bodies swaying, of eyes rolling, under the droop of heavy and motionless foliage. The steamer toiled along slowly on the edge of a black and incomprehensible frenzy. The pre-historic man was cursing us, praying to us, welcoming us—who could tell? We were cut off from the comprehension of our surroundings; we glided past like phantoms, wondering and secretly appalled, as sane men would be before an enthusiastic outbreak in a madhouse. . . .

It was unearthly, and the men were No, they were not inhuman. Well, you know, that was the worst of it—this suspicion of their not being inhuman. It would come slowly to one. They howled and leaped, and spun, and made horrid faces; but what thrilled you was just the thought of their humanity—like yours—the thought of your remote kinship with this wild and passionate uproar. Ugly. Yes, it was ugly enough; but if you were man enough you would admit to yourself that there was in you just the faintest trace of a response to the terrible frankness of that noise, a dim suspicion of there being a meaning in it which you—you so remote from the night of first ages—could comprehend. And why not? The mind of man is capable of anything—because everything is in it, all the past as well as the future. What was there after all? Joy, fear, sorrow, devotion, valour, rage—who can tell?—but truth—stripped of its cloak of time.

Camara Laye, *The Radiance of the King*

"I enjoy life . . . ," thought Clarence. "If I filed my teeth like the people of Aziana, no one could see any difference between me and them." There was, of course, the difference in pigmentation in the skin. But what difference did that make? "It's the soul that matters," he kept telling himself. "And in that respect I am exactly as they are." . . .

But where was this radiance coming from? Clarence got up and went to the right-hand window, from which this radiance seemed to be streaming. . . .

He saw the king. And then he knew where the extraordinary radiance was coming from. . . .

And he had the feeling that all was lost. But had he not already lost everything? . . . He would remain for ever chained to the South, chained to his hut, chained to everything he had so thoughtlessly abandoned himself to. His solitude seemed to him so heavy, it burdened him with such a great weight of sorrow that his heart seemed about to break. . . .

But at that very moment the king turned his head, turned it imperceptibly, and his glance fell upon Clarence. . . .

"Yes, no one is as base as I, as naked as I," he thought. "And you, lord, you are willing to rest your eyes upon me!" Or was it because of his very nakedness? . . . "Because of your very nakedness!" the look seemed to say. "That terrifying void that is within you and which opens to receive me; your hunger which calls to my hunger; your very baseness which did not exist until I gave it leave; and the great shame you feel. . . ."

When he had come before the king, when he stood in the great radiance of the king, still ravaged by the tongue of fire, but alive still, and living only through the touch of that fire, Clarence fell upon his knees, for it seemed to him that he was finally at the end of his seeking, and at the end of all seekings.

SOURCES: From *Heart of Darkness* by Joseph Conrad. Penguin Books, 1991. From *The Radiance of the King* by Camara Laye, translated from the French by James Kirkup. New York: Vintage, 1989.

mocks local British society for its racism, snobbishness, and superficiality, its chief interest lies in its unsentimental and even unflattering portrayal of ordinary Kenyans in their daily struggle for survival.

Initially, Ngugi wrote in English for elite African and foreign readers, but he was determined to reach a broader audience and eventually decided to write in his native Kikuyu. For that reason, perhaps, in the late 1970s, he was placed under house arrest for writing subversive literature. From prison, he secretly wrote *Devil on the Cross,* which urged his compatriots to overthrow the government of Daniel arap Moi. Published in 1980, the book sold widely and was eventually read aloud by storytellers throughout Kenyan society. Fearing an attempt on his life, in recent years Ngugi has lived in exile.

Many of Ngugi's contemporaries have followed his lead and focused their frustration on the failure of the continent's new leadership to carry out the goals of independence. One of the most outstanding is Nigerian Wole Soyinka (b. 1934). His novel *The Interpreters* (1965) lambasted the corruption and hypocrisy of Nigerian politics. Succeeding novels and plays have continued that tradition, resulting in a Nobel Prize for literature in 1986. The winner of the Nobel Prize in 2003 was J. M. Coetzee (b. 1940), whose novels, such as *Disgrace* (1999), exposed the devastating social and psychological effects of apartheid on South Africans. His plea for tolerance and compassion echoed the moral commitment to human dignity on the part of many white African authors.

Some recent African authors, like the Somali writer Nuruddin Farah (b. 1945), argue that it is time for Africans to stop blaming their present political ills on either colonialism or their own dictators. In his writings, such as the novel *Sweet and Sour Milk*, Farah urges Africans to stop lamenting the contamination of African society by the West and take charge of their own destiny. In so doing, Farah joins other African writers in serving as the social conscience of a continent still seeking its own identity.

African women are also creating distinctive fiction today. Traditionally, African women were valued for their talents as storytellers, but writing was strongly discouraged by both traditional and colonial authorities on the grounds that women should occupy themselves with their domestic obligations. In recent years, however, a number of women have emerged as prominent writers of African fiction. Two examples are Buchi Emecheta (b. 1940) of Nigeria and Ama Ata Aidoo of Ghana, whose feminist perspective was mentioned earlier. Beginning with *Second Class Citizen* (1975), which chronicled the breakdown of her own marriage, Emecheta has published numerous works exploring the role of women in contemporary African society and decrying the practice of polygamy. In her own writings, Aidoo has focused on the identity of today's African women and the changing relations between men and women in society. Her novel *Changes: A Love Story* (1991) chronicles the lives of three women, none presented as a victim but all caught up in the struggle for survival and happiness. Sadly, the one who strays the furthest from traditional African values finds herself free but isolated and lonely.

One of the overriding concerns confronting African intellectuals since independence has been the problem of language. Unlike Asian societies, Africans have not inherited a long written tradition from the precolonial era. As a result, many intellectuals have written in the colonial language, a practice that sometimes results in guilt and anxiety. As we have seen, some have reacted by writing in their local languages to reach a native audience. The market for such work is limited, however, because of the high illiteracy rate and also because novels written in African languages have no market abroad. Moreover, because of the deep financial crisis throughout the continent, there is little money for the publication of serious books. Many of Africa's libraries and universities are almost literally without books. It is little wonder that many African authors, to their discomfort, continue to write and publish in foreign languages.

African Music

Contemporary African music also reflects a hybridization or fusion with Western culture. Having traveled to the Western Hemisphere via the slave trade centuries earlier, African drum beats evolved into North American jazz and Latin American dance rhythms, only to return to reenergize African music. In fact, today music is one of Africans' most effective weapons for social and political protest. Easily accessible to all, African music, whether Afro-beat in Nigeria, rai in Algeria, or reggae in Benin, represents the "weapon of the future," contemporary musicians say; it "helped free Nelson Mandela" and "will put Africa back on the map." Censored by all the African dictatorial regimes, these courageous musicians persist in their struggle against corruption, which one singer calls the second slavery, "the cancer that is eating away at the system." Their voices echo the chorus "Together we can build a nation,/Because Africa has brains, youth, knowledge."[8]

𝒩OWHERE IN THE DEVELOPING WORLD is the dilemma of continuity and change more agonizing than in contemporary Africa. Mesmerized by the spectacle of Western affluence yet repulsed by the bloody trail from slavery to World War II and the atomic bombs over Hiroshima and Nagasaki, African intellectuals have been torn between the dual images of Western materialism and African exceptionalism.

What is the destiny of Africa? Some Africans still yearn for the dreams embodied in the program of the OAU. Novelist Ngugi Wa Thiong'o argues that for his country, the starting point is a democratic Kenya. More broadly, he calls for "an internationalization of all the democratic and social struggles for human equality, justice, peace, and progress."[9] Some African political leaders, however, have apparently discarded the democratic ideal and turned their attention to what is sometimes called the "East Asian model," based on the Confucian tenet of subordination of the individual to the community as the guiding principle of national development. Whether African political culture today is well placed to imitate the strategy adopted by the fast-growing nations of East Asia is questionable, however Like all peoples, Africans must ultimately find their own solutions within the context of their own traditions and not by seeking to imitate the example of others.

For the average African, of course, such intellectual dilemmas pale before the daily challenge of survival. But the fundamental gap between the traditional village and the modern metropolis is perhaps wider in Africa than anywhere else in the world and may well be harder to bridge. The solution is not yet visible. In the meantime, writes Ghanaian author George Awoonor-Williams, all Africans are exiles:

> *The return is tedious*
> *And the exiled souls gathered at the beach*
>
> *Arguing and deciding their future*
> *Should they return home*
> *And face the fences the termites had eaten*
> *And see the dunghill that has mounted their*
> *   birthplace? . . .*
>
> *The final strokes will land them on forgotten*
> *   shores*
> *They committed to the impiety of self-deceit*
> *Slashed, cut and wounded their souls*
> *And left the mangled remainder in manacles.*
>
> *The moon, the moon is our father's spirit*
> *At the stars entrance the night revellers gather*
> *To sell their chatter and inhuman sweat to the*
> *   gateman*
> *And shuffle their feet in agonies of birth.*
> *Lost souls, lost souls, lost souls, that are*
> *   still at the gate.*[10]

TIMELINE

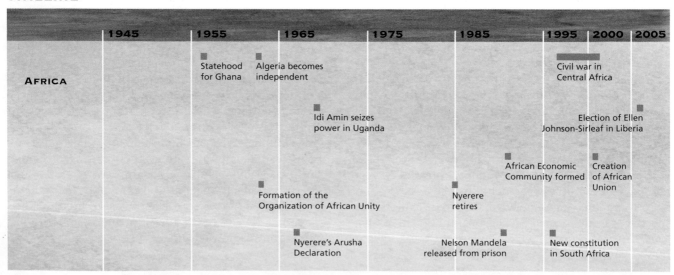

	1945	1955	1965	1975	1985	1995	2000	2005
AFRICA		Statehood for Ghana	Algeria becomes independent			Civil war in Central Africa		
			Idi Amin seizes power in Uganda					Election of Ellen Johnson-Sirleaf in Liberia
						African Economic Community formed	Creation of African Union	
			Formation of the Organization of African Unity		Nyerere retires			
			Nyerere's Arusha Declaration		Nelson Mandela released from prison	New constitution in South Africa		

CHAPTER NOTES

1. Quoted in G.-C. M. Mutiso, *Socio-Political Thought in African Literature* (New York, 1974), p. 117.

2. Aimé Césaire, *Cahier d'un retour du pays natal,* trans. John Berger and Anna Bostock (Harmondsworth, England, 1969), p. 10, quoted in Emmanuel N. Obiechina, *Language and Theme: Essays on African Literature* (Washington, D.C., 1990), pp. 78–79.

3. Cyprian Ekwensi, *Jagua Nana* (Greenwich, England, 1961), pp. 146–147.

4. *New York Times,* September 1, 1996.

5. Adrian Roscoe, *Uhuru's Fire: African Literature East to South* (Cambridge, England, 1977), p. 23.

6. Francis Ademola, *Reflections: Nigerian Prose and Verse* (Lagos, 1962), p. 65, quoted in Mutiso, *Socio-Political Thought in African Literature,* p. 117.

7. Abioseh Nicol, *A Truly Married Woman and Other Stories* (London, 1965), p. 12.

8. Gilles Médioni, "Stand Up, Africa!" *World Press Review,* July 2002, p. 34. Reprinted from *L'Express.*

9. Ngugi Wa Thiong'o, *Decolonising the Mind: The Politics of Language in African Literature* (Portsmouth, N.H., 1986), p. 103.

10. George Awoonor-Williams, *Rediscovery and Other Poems* (Ibadan, Nigeria, 1964), p. 11, quoted in Mutiso, *Socio-Political Thought in African Literature,* pp. 81–82.

WORLD HISTORY
RESOURCE CENTER

Visit the *Twentieth-Century World History* Book Companion website for resources specific to this textbook:

academic.cengage.com/history/duiker

The Wadsworth World History Resource Center at worldrc.wadsworth.com/ offers a variety of tools to help you succeed in this course, including access to quizzes; images; documents; interactive simulations, maps, and timelines; movie explorations; and a wealth of other sources.

15

FERMENT IN THE MIDDLE EAST

"𝒲E MUSLIMS ARE OF ONE FAMILY even though we live under different governments and in various regions."[1] So said Ayatollah Ruholla Khomeini, the Islamic religious figure and leader of the 1979 revolution that overthrew the shah in Iran. The ayatollah's remark was not just a pious wish by a religious mystic but an accurate reflection of one crucial aspect of the political dynamics in the region.

If the concept of African exceptionalism, or "blackness," represents an alternative to the system of nation-states in Africa, in the Middle East a similar role has been played by the forces of militant Islam. In both regions, a yearning for a sense of community beyond national borders tugs at the emotions and intellect of their inhabitants and counteracts the dynamic pull of nationalism that has provoked political turmoil and conflict in much of the rest of the world. ◆

Crescent of Conflict

A dramatic example of the powerful force of pan-Islamic sentiment took place on September 11, 2001, when Muslim militants hijacked four U.S. airliners and turned them into missiles aimed at the center of world capitalism. Although the headquarters of the terrorist network that carried out the attack—known as al-Qaeda—was located in Afghanistan, the militants themselves came from several different Muslim states. In the months that followed, popular support for al-Qaeda and its mysterious leader, Osama bin Laden, intensified throughout the Muslim world. To many observers, it appeared that the Islamic peoples were embarking on an era of direct confrontation with the entire Western world.

What were the sources of Muslim anger? In a speech released on videotape shortly after the attack, bin Laden declared that the attacks were a response to the "humiliation and disgrace" that have afflicted the Islamic world for over eighty years, a period dating back to the end of World War I.

For the Middle East, the period between the two world wars was an era of transition. With the fall of the Ottoman and Persian Empires, new modernizing regimes emerged in Turkey and Iran, and a more traditionalist but fiercely independent government was established in Saudi Arabia. Elsewhere, however, European influence was strong; the British and French had mandates in Syria, Lebanon, Jordan, and Palestine, and British influence persisted in Iraq and southern Arabia and throughout the Nile valley. Pan-Arabism was on the rise, but it lacked focus and coherence.

During World War II, the Middle East became the cockpit of European rivalries, as it had been during World War I. The region was more significant to the warring powers than previously because of the growing importance of oil and the Suez Canal's position as a vital sea route.

For a brief period, the Afrika Korps, under the command of the brilliant German general Erwin Rommel, threatened to seize Egypt and the Suez Canal, but British troops defeated the German forces at El Alamein, west of Alexandria, in 1942 and gradually drove them westward until their final defeat after the arrival of U.S. troops in Morocco under the field command of General George S. Patton. From that time until the end of the war, the entire region from the Mediterranean Sea eastward was under secure Allied occupation.

The Question of Palestine

As in other areas of Asia, the end of World Was II led to the emergence of a number of independent states. Jordan, Lebanon, and Syria, all European mandates before the war, became independent. Egypt, Iran, and Iraq, though still under a degree of Western influence, became increasingly autonomous. Sympathy for the idea of Arab unity led to the formation of the Arab League in 1945, but different points of view among its members prevented it from achieving anything of substance.

The one issue on which all Arab states in the area could agree was the question of Palestine. As tensions between Jews and Arabs in that mandate intensified during the 1930s, the British attempted to limit Jewish immigration into the area and firmly rejected proposals for independence. After World War II, the Zionists turned for support to the United States, and in March 1948, the Truman administration, with the support of the United Nations, approved the concept of an independent Jewish state, despite the fact that only about one-third of the local population were Jews. In May, the new state of Israel was formally established.

To its Arab neighbors, the new state of Israel represented a betrayal of the interests of the Palestinian people, most of whom were Muslim, and a flagrant disregard for the conditions set out in the Balfour Declaration of 1917. Outraged at the lack of Western support for Muslim interests in the area, several Arab countries invaded the new Jewish state. The invasion did not succeed because of internal divisions among the Arabs, but both sides remained bitter, and the Arab states refused to recognize Israel.

The war had other lasting consequences as well because it led to the exodus of thousands of Palestinian refugees into neighboring Muslim states. Jordan, which had become independent under its Hashemite ruler, was now flooded by the arrival of one million urban Palestinians in a country occupied by half a million Bedouins. To the north, the state of Lebanon had been created to provide the local Christian community with a country of its own, but the arrival of the Palestinian refugees upset the delicate balance between Christians and Muslims. In any event, the creation of Lebanon had angered the Syrians, who had lost it as well as other territories to Turkey as a result of European decisions before and after the war.

Nasser and Pan-Arabism

The dispute over Palestine placed Egypt in an uncomfortable position. Technically, Egypt was not an Arab state. King Farouk, who had acceded to power in 1936, had frequently declared support for the Arab cause, but the Egyptian people werc not Bedouins and shared little of the culture of the peoples across the Red Sea. Nevertheless, Farouk committed Egyptian armies to the disastrous war against Israel.

In 1952, King Farouk, whose corrupt habits had severely eroded his early popularity, was overthrown by a military coup engineered by young military officers ostensibly under the leadership of Colonel Muhammad Nagib. The real force behind the scenes was Colonel Gamal Abdul Nasser (1918–1970), the son of a minor government functionary who, like many of his fellow officers, had been angered by the army's inadequate preparation for the war against Israel four years earlier. In 1953, the monarchy was replaced by a republic.

In 1954, Nasser seized power in his own right and immediately instituted a land reform program. He also adopted a policy of neutrality in foreign affairs and expressed sympathy for the Arab cause. The British presence had rankled many Egyptians for years, for even after granting Egypt independence, Britain had retained control over the Suez Canal to protect its route to the Indian Ocean. In 1956, Nasser suddenly nationalized the Suez Canal Company, which had been under British and French administration. Seeing a threat to their route to the Indian Ocean, the British and the French launched a joint attack on Egypt to protect their investment. They were joined by Israel, whose leaders had grown exasperated at sporadic Arab commando raids on Israeli territory and now decided to strike back. But the Eisenhower administration in the United States, concerned that the attack smacked of a revival of colonialism, supported Nasser and brought about the withdrawal of foreign forces from Egypt and of Israeli troops from the Sinai peninsula.

The United Arab Republic Nasser now turned to pan-Arabism. In 1958, Egypt united with Syria in the United Arab Republic (UAR). The union had been proposed by the Ba'ath Party, which advocated the unity of all Arab states in a new socialist society. In 1957, the Ba'ath Party assumed power in Syria and opened talks with Egypt on a union between the two countries, which took place in March 1958 following a plebiscite. Nasser, despite his reported ambivalence about the union, was named president of the new state.

Egypt and Syria hoped that the union would eventually include all Arab states, but other Arab leaders, including young King Hussein of Jordan and the kings of Iraq and Saudi Arabia, were suspicious. The latter two in particular feared pan-Arabism on the assumption that they would be asked to share their vast oil revenues with the poorer states of the Middle East. Such fears were understandable.

Nasser opposed the existing situation, in which much of the wealth of the Middle East flowed into the treasuries of a handful of wealthy feudal states or, even worse, the pockets of foreign oil interests. In Nasser's view, through Arab unity, this wealth could be put to better use to improve the standard of living in the area. To achieve a more equitable division of the wealth of the region, natural resources and major industries would be nationalized; central planning would ensure that resources were exploited efficiently, but private enterprise would continue at the local level.

In the end, however, Nasser's determination to extend state control over the economy brought an end to the UAR. When the government announced the nationalization of a large number of industries and utilities in 1961, a military coup overthrew the Ba'ath leaders in Damascus, and the new authorities declared that Syria would end its relationship with Egypt.

The breakup of the UAR did not end Nasser's dream of pan-Arabism. In 1962, Algeria finally received its independence from France and, under its new president, Ahmad Ben Bella, established close relations with Egypt, as did a new republic in Yemen. During the mid-1960s, Egypt took the lead in promoting Arab unity against Israel. At a meeting of Arab leaders held in Jerusalem in 1964, the Palestine Liberation Organization (PLO) was set up under Egyptian sponsorship to represent the interests of the Palestinians. According to the charter of the PLO, only the Palestinian people (and thus not Jewish immigrants from abroad) had the right to form a state in the old British mandate. A guerrilla movement called al-Fatah, led by the dissident PLO figure Yasir Arafat (1929–2004), began to launch terrorist attacks on Israeli territory, prompting Israel to raid PLO bases in Jordan in 1966.

The Arab-Israeli Dispute

The growing Arab hostility was a constant threat to the security of Israel. In the years after independence, Israeli leaders dedicated themselves to creating a Jewish homeland. Aided by reparations paid by the postwar German government and private funds provided by Jews living abroad, notably in the United States, the government attempted to build a democratic and modern state that would be a magnet for Jews throughout the world and a symbol of Jewish achievement.

Ensuring the survival of the tiny state surrounded by antagonistic Arab neighbors was a considerable challenge, made more difficult by divisions within the Israeli population. Some were immigrants from Europe, while others came from countries of the Middle East. Some were secular and even socialist in their views, while others were politically conservative and stressed religious orthodoxy. There were also Christians as well as many Muslim Palestinians who had not fled to other countries. To balance these diverse interests, Israel established a parliament, called the Knesset, on the European model, with proportional representation based on the number of votes each party received in the general election. The parties were so numerous that none ever received a majority of votes, and all governments had to be formed from a coalition of several parties. As a result, moderate secular leaders such as longtime prime minister David Ben Gurion had to cater to more marginal parties composed of conservative religious groups.

The Six-Day War During the late 1950s and 1960s, the dispute between Israel and other states in the Middle East escalated in intensity. Essentially alone except for the sympathy of the United States and several Western European countries, Israel adopted a policy of determined resistance to and immediate retaliation against alleged PLO and Arab provocations. By the spring of 1967, relations between Israel and its Arab neighbors had deteriorated as Nasser attempted to improve his standing in the Arab world by intensifying military activities and imposing a blockade against Israeli commerce through the Gulf of Aqaba. Concerned that it might be isolated, and lacking firm support from Western powers (which had originally guaranteed Israel the freedom to use the Gulf of Aqaba), in June 1967 Israel suddenly launched air strikes against Egypt and several of its Arab neighbors. Israeli armies then broke the blockade at the head of the Gulf of Aqaba and occupied the Sinai peninsula. Other Israeli forces attacked Jordanian territory on the West Bank of the Jordan River (Jordan's King Hussein had recently signed an alliance with Egypt and placed his army under Egyptian command), occupied the whole of Jerusalem, and seized Syrian military positions in the Golan Heights along the Israeli-Syrian border.

Despite limited Soviet support for Egypt and Syria, in a brief six-day war, Israel had mocked Nasser's pretensions of Arab unity and tripled the size of its territory, thus enhancing its precarious security (see Map 15.1). Yet Israel had also aroused more bitter hostility among the Arabs and included an additional million Palestinians inside its borders, most of them living on the West Bank.

During the next few years, the focus of the Arab-Israeli dispute shifted as Arab states demanded the return of the occupied territories. Meanwhile, many Israelis argued that

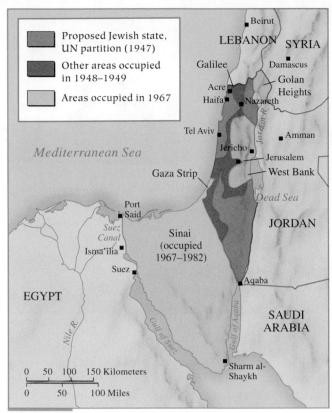

MAP 15.1 **Israel and Its Neighbors.** This map shows the evolution of the state of Israel since its founding in 1948. Areas occupied by Israel after the Six-Day War in 1967 are indicated in green. ❓ What is the significance of the West Bank? 🌐 View an animated version of this map or related maps at the World History Resource Center, at worldrc.wadsworth.com/

the new lands improved the security of the beleaguered state and should be retained. Concerned that the dispute might lead to a confrontation between the superpowers, the Nixon administration tried to achieve a peace settlement. The peace effort received a mild stimulus when Nasser died of a heart attack in September 1970 and was succeeded by his vice president, ex-general Anwar al-Sadat (1918–1981). Sadat soon showed himself to be more pragmatic than his predecessor, dropping the now irrelevant name United Arab Republic in favor of the Arab Republic of Egypt and replacing Nasser's socialist policies with a new strategy based on free enterprise and encouragement of Western investment. He also agreed to sign a peace treaty with Israel on the condition that Israel retire to its pre-1967 frontiers. Concerned that other Arab countries would refuse to make peace and take advantage of its presumed weakness, Israel refused.

Rebuffed in his offer of peace, smarting from criticism of his moderate stand from other Arab leaders, and increasingly concerned over Israeli plans to build permanent Jewish settlements in the occupied territories, Sadat attempted once again to renew Arab unity through a new confrontation with Israel. In 1973, on Yom Kippur (the Jewish Day of Atonement), an Israeli national holiday, Egyptian forces suddenly launched an air and artillery attack on Israeli positions in the Sinai just east of the Suez Canal. Syrian armies attacked Israeli positions in the Golan Heights. After early Arab successes, the Israelis managed to recoup some of their losses on both fronts. As a superpower confrontation between the United States and the Soviet Union loomed, a cease-fire was finally reached.

In the next years, a fragile peace was maintained, marked by U.S. "shuttle diplomacy" (carried out by U.S. Secretary of State Henry Kissinger) and the rise to power in Israel of the militant Likud Party under Prime Minister Menachem Begin (1913–1992). The conflict now spread to Lebanon, where many Palestinians had found refuge and the PLO had set up its headquarters. Rising tension along the border was compounded by increasingly hostile disputes between Christians and Muslims over control of the capital, Beirut.

The Camp David Agreement After his election as U.S. president in 1976, Jimmy Carter began to press for a compromise peace based on Israel's return of occupied Arab territories and Arab recognition of the state of Israel (an idea originally proposed by Kissinger). By now, Sadat was anxious to reduce his military expenses and announced his willingness to visit Jerusalem to seek peace. The meeting took place in November 1977, with no concrete results, but Sadat persisted. In September 1978, he and Begin met with Carter at Camp David in the United States. Israel agreed to withdraw from the Sinai, but not from other occupied territories unless it was recognized by other Arab countries.

The promise of the Camp David agreement was not fulfilled. One reason was the assassination of Sadat by Islamic militants in October 1981. But there were deeper causes, including the continued unwillingness of many Arab governments to recognize Israel and the Israeli government's encouragement of Jewish settlements in the occupied West Bank.

The PLO and the *Intifada* During the early 1980s, the militancy of the Palestinians increased, leading to rising unrest, popularly labeled the *intifada* (uprising) among PLO supporters living inside Israel. To control the situation, a new Israeli government under Prime Minister Itzhak Shamir invaded southern Lebanon to destroy PLO commando bases near the Israeli border. The invasion provoked international condemnation and further destabilized the perilous balance between Muslims and Christians in Lebanon. As the 1990s began, U.S.-sponsored peace talks opened between Israel and a number of its neighbors. The first

The Temple Mount at Jerusalem. The Temple Mount is one of the most sacred spots in the city of Jerusalem. Originally, it was the site of a temple built during the reign of Solomon, king of the Jews, about 1000 B.C.E. The Western Wall of the temple is shown in the foreground. Beyond the wall is the Dome of the Rock complex, built on the place from which Muslims believe that Muhammad ascended to heaven. Sacred to both religions, the Temple Mount is now a major bone of contention between Muslims and Jews and a prime obstacle to a final settlement of the Arab-Israeli dispute.

major breakthrough came in 1993, when Israel and the PLO reached an agreement calling for Palestinian autonomy in selected areas of Israel in return for PLO recognition of the legitimacy of the Israeli state.

Progress in implementing the agreement, however, was slow. Terrorist attacks by Palestinian militants resulted in heavy casualties and shook the confidence of many Jewish citizens that their security needs could be protected under the agreement. At the same time, Jewish residents of the West Bank resisted the extension of Palestinian authority in the area. In November 1995, Prime Minister Yitzhak Rabin was assassinated by an Israeli opponent of the accords. National elections held a few months later led to the formation of a new government under Benjamin Netanyahu (b. 1949), which adopted a tougher stance in negotiations with the Palestinian Authority under Yasir Arafat.

When Netanyahu was replaced by a new Labour government under Prime Minister Ehud Barak (b. 1942), the latter promised to revitalize the peace process. Negotiations continued with the PLO and also got under way with Syria over a peace settlement in Lebanon and the possible return of the Golan Heights. But in late 2000, peace talks broke down over the future of the city of Jerusalem, leading to massive riots by Palestinians, an Israeli crackdown, and the election of a new and more hard-line Israeli prime minister, the former defense minister Ariel Sharon (b. 1928). Sharon's ascent to leadership was accompanied by a rash of suicide attacks by Palestinians against Israeli targets, an intensive Israeli military crackdown on suspected terrorist sites inside Palestinian territory, and a dramatic increase in bloodshed on both sides.

The death of Yasir Arafat in 2004 and his replacement by the Palestinian moderate Mahmoud Abbas, followed by the unilateral evacuation of Israeli settlers from the Gaza Strip a year later, raised modest hopes for progress in peace talks (key issues that remain unresolved include the future status of Jerusalem and the presence of Jewish settlements in the occupied territories). But the incapacitation of Prime Minister Ariel Sharon by a stroke and the victory of Hamas, a militant organization that calls for the destruction of the state of Israel, in Palestinian elections held in late 2005 undermined the search for peace. In 2006, rocket attacks launched by Shi'ite Hezbollah guerrillas provoked an Israeli invasion of southern Lebanon to wipe out the source of the assault, thereby raising the specter of a wider conflict.

Revolution in Iran

The Arab-Israeli dispute also provoked an international oil crisis. In 1960, a number of oil-producing states formed the Organization of Petroleum Exporting Countries (OPEC) to gain control over oil prices, but the organization was not recognized by the foreign oil companies. In the 1970s, a group of Arab oil states established the Organization of Arab Petroleum Exporting Countries (OAPEC) to use as a weapon to force Western governments to abandon pro-Israeli policies. During the 1973 Yom Kippur War, some OPEC nations announced significant increases in the price of oil to foreign countries. The price hikes were accompanied by an apparent oil shortage and created serious economic problems in the United States and Europe as well as in the Third World. They also proved to be a boon to oil-exporting countries, such as Libya, now under the leadership of the militantly anti-Western Colonel Muammar Qadhafi (b. 1942).

One of the key oil-exporting countries was Iran. Under the leadership of Shah Mohammad Reza Pahlavi (1919–1980), who had taken over from his father in 1941, Iran had become one of the richest countries in the Middle East. Although relations with the West had occasionally been fragile (especially after Prime Minister Mossadeq had briefly attempted to nationalize the oil industry in 1951), during the next twenty years, Iran became a prime ally of the United States in the Middle East. With encouragement from the United States, which hoped that Iran could become a force for stability in the Persian Gulf, the shah attempted to carry through a series of social and economic reforms to transform the country into the most advanced in the region.

Iran

Statistical evidence suggests that his efforts were succeeding. Per capita income increased dramatically, literacy rates improved, a modern communications infrastructure took shape, and an affluent middle class emerged in the capital of Tehran. Under the surface, however, trouble was brewing. Despite an ambitious land reform program, many peasants were still landless, unemployment among intellectuals was dangerously high, and the urban middle class was squeezed by high inflation. Housing costs had skyrocketed, provoked in part by the massive influx of foreigners attracted by oil money.

Some of the unrest took the form of religious discontent as millions of devout Shi'ite Muslims looked with distaste at a new Iranian civilization based on greed, sexual license, and material accumulation. Conservative *ulama* (Muslim scholars) opposed rampant government corruption, the ostentation of the shah's court, and the extension of voting rights to women. Some opposition elements took to terrorism against wealthy Iranians or foreign residents in an attempt to provoke social and political disorder. In response, the shah's U.S.-trained security police, the *Savak,* imprisoned and sometimes tortured thousands of dissidents.

The Fall of the Shah Leading the opposition was Ayatollah Ruholla Khomeini (1900–1989), an austere Shi'ite cleric who had been exiled to Iraq and then to France because of his outspoken opposition to the shah's regime. From Paris, Khomeini continued his attacks in print, on television, and in radio broadcasts. By the late 1970s, large numbers of Iranians began to respond to Khomeini's diatribes against the "satanic regime," and demonstrations by his supporters were repressed with ferocity by the police.

But workers' strikes (some of them in the oil fields, which reduced government revenue) grew in intensity. In January 1979, the shah appointed a moderate, Shapur Bakhtiar, as prime minister and then left the country for medical treatment.

Bakhtiar attempted to conciliate the rising opposition and permitted Khomeini to return to Iran, where he demanded the government's resignation. With rising public unrest and incipient revolt within the army, the government collapsed and was replaced by a hastily formed Islamic republic. The new government, which was dominated by Shi'ite *ulama* under the guidance of Ayatollah Khomeini, immediately began to introduce traditional Islamic law. A new reign of terror ensued as supporters of the shah were rounded up and executed.

Though much of the outside world focused on the U.S. embassy in Tehran, where militants held a number of foreign hostages, the Iranian Revolution involved much more. In the eyes of the ayatollah and his followers, the United States was "the great Satan," the powerful protector of Israel, and the enemy of Muslim peoples everywhere. Furthermore, it was responsible for the corruption of Iranian society under the shah. Now Khomeini demanded that the shah be returned to Iran for trial and that the United States apologize for its acts against the Iranian people. In response, the Carter administration stopped buying Iranian oil and froze Iranian assets in the United States.

The effects of the disturbances in Iran quickly spread beyond its borders. Sunni militants briefly seized the holy places in Mecca and began to appeal to their brothers to launch similar revolutions in Islamic countries around the world, including far-off Malaysia and Indonesia. At the same time, ethnic unrest emerged among the Kurdish minorities along the border. In July 1980, the shah died of cancer in Cairo. With economic conditions in Iran rapidly deteriorating, the Islamic revolutionary government finally agreed to free the hostages in return for the release of Iranian assets in the United States. During the next few years, the intensity of the Iranian Revolution moderated slightly, as the government displayed a modest tolerance for a loosening of clerical control over freedom of expression and social activities. But rising criticism of rampant official corruption and a high rate of inflation sparked a new wave of government repression in the mid-1990s; newspapers were censored, the universities were purged of disloyal or "un-Islamic" elements, and religious militants raided private homes in search of blasphemous activities.

Iranian Woman Playing Soccer. Despite the restriction of having to cover their bodies in public, young Iranian women play soccer and other sports, attend schools and universities, and partake in other activities of the modern world. Here we see a female Iranian soccer player, fully covered compared to her Syrian opponent and wearing a traditional black hood. Although they rarely did so before the Islamic Revolution, today about two million Iranian women take part in sports.

In 1997, the moderate Islamic cleric Mohammad Khatemi was elected president of Iran. Khatemi, whose surprising victory reflected a growing desire among many Iranians for a more pluralistic society open to the outside world, signaled the tantalizing possibility that Iran might wish to improve relations with the United States. During the next few years, press censorship was relaxed, leading to the emergence of several reformist newspapers and magazines, and restrictions on women's activities were relaxed. But the new president faced severe pressures from conservative elements to maintain the purity of Islamic laws, and in April 2000, the judiciary ordered several reformist publications to close because they had printed materials that "disparaged Islam." Although student protests erupted into the streets in 2003, hard-liners continued to reject proposals to expand civil rights and limit the power of the clerics.

In 2004, new presidential elections brought a new leader, Mahmoud Ahmadinejad, to power in Tehran. He immediately inflamed the situation by calling publicly for the destruction of the state of Israel, while his government aroused unease throughout the world by indicating its determination to develop a peaceful nuclear energy program.

Crisis in the Gulf

Although much of the Iranians' anger was directed against the United States during the early phases of the revolution, Iran had equally hated enemies closer to home. To the north, the immense power of the Soviet Union, driven by atheistic communism, was viewed as a modern-day version of the Russian threat of previous centuries. To the west was a militant and hostile Iraq, now under the leadership of the ambitious Saddam Hussein (b. 1937). Problems from both directions appeared shortly after Khomeini's rise to power. Soviet military forces occupied Afghanistan to prop up a weak Marxist regime there. The following year, Iraqi forces suddenly attacked along the Iranian border.

Iraq and Iran had long had an uneasy relationship, fueled by religious differences (Iranian Islam is predominantly Shi'ite, while the ruling class in Iraq was Sunni) and a perennial dispute over borderlands adjacent to the Persian Gulf, the vital waterway for the export of oil from both countries (see Map 15.2). Like several of its neighbors, Iraq had long dreamed of unifying the Arabs but had been hindered by internal factions and suspicion among its neighbors.

During the mid-1970s, Iran gave some support to a Kurdish rebellion in the mountains of Iraq. In 1975, the government of the shah agreed to stop aiding the rebels in return for territorial concessions at the head of the gulf. Five years later, however, the Kurdish revolt had been suppressed, and President Saddam Hussein, who had assumed power in Baghdad in 1979, accused Iran of violating the territorial agreement and launched an attack on his neighbor. The war was a bloody one, with poison gas used against civilians and children sent out to clear minefields. Other countries, including the two superpowers, watched nervously in case the conflict should spread throughout the region. Finally, after nearly ten years, with both sides virtually exhausted, a cease-fire was arranged in the fall of 1988.

The Vision of Saddam Hussein The bitter conflict with Iran had not slaked Saddam Hussein's appetite for territorial

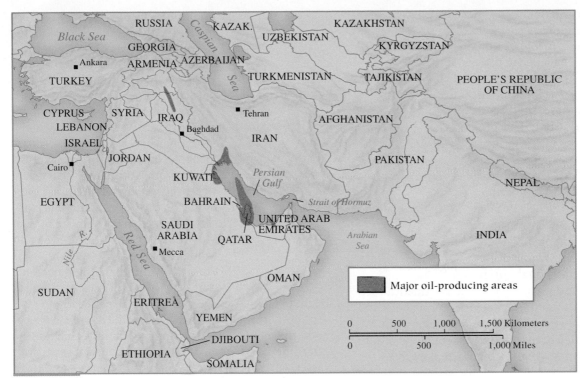

MAP 15.2 **The Modern Middle East.** Shown here are the boundaries dividing the independent states in the contemporary Middle East. ❓ Which are the major oil-producing countries? 🌐 **View an animated version of this map or related maps at the World History Resource Center, at** worldrc.wadsworth.com/.

expansion. In early August 1990, Iraqi military forces suddenly moved across the border and occupied the small neighboring country of Kuwait at the head of the gulf. The immediate pretext was the claim that Kuwait was pumping oil from fields inside Iraqi territory. Baghdad was also angry over the Kuwaiti government's demand for repayment of loans it had made to Iraq during the war with Iran. But the underlying reason was Iraq's contention that Kuwait was legally a part of Iraq. Kuwait had been part of the Ottoman Empire until the opening of the twentieth century, when the local prince had agreed to place his patrimony under British protection. When Iraq became independent in 1932, it claimed the area on the grounds that the state of Kuwait had been created by British imperialism, but opposition from major Western powers and other countries in the region, which feared the consequences of a "greater Iraq," prevented an Iraqi takeover.

Operation Desert Storm The Iraqi invasion of Kuwait in 1990 sparked an international outcry, and the United States amassed an international force that liberated the country and destroyed a substantial part of Iraq's armed forces. President George H. W. Bush had promised the American people that U.S. troops would not fight with one hand tied behind their backs (a clear reference to the Vietnam War),

but the allied forces did not occupy Baghdad at the end of the war because the allies feared that doing so would cause a total breakup of the country, an eventuality that would operate to the benefit of Iran. The allies hoped instead that the Hussein regime would be ousted by an internal revolt. In the meantime, harsh economic sanctions were imposed on the Iraqi government as the condition for peace. The anticipated overthrow of Saddam Hussein did not materialize, however, and his tireless efforts to evade the conditions of the cease-fire continued to bedevil the administrations of Presidents Bill Clinton and George W. Bush.

Conflicts in Afghanistan and Iraq The terrorist attacks launched against U.S. cities in September 2001 added a new dimension to the Middle Eastern equation. After the failure of the Soviet Union to quell the rebellion in Afghanistan during the 1980s, a fundamentalist Muslim group known as the Taliban, supported covertly by the United States, seized power in Kabul and ruled the country with a fanaticism reminiscent of the Cultural Revolution in China. Backed by conservative religious forces in Pakistan, the Taliban provided a base of operations for Osama bin Laden's al-Queda terrorist network. After the attacks of September 11, a coalition of forces led by the United States overthrew the Taliban and attempted to build a new and moderate government. But the country's history of bitter internecine warfare among various tribal groups represents a severe challenge to those efforts.

In the meantime, the Bush administration, charging that Iraqi dictator Saddam Hussein not only had provided support to bin Laden's terrorist organization but also sought to develop weapons of mass destruction, threatened to invade Iraq and remove him from power. The plan, widely debated in the media and opposed by many of the United States' traditional allies, disquieted Arab leaders and fanned anti-American sentiment throughout the Muslim world. Nevertheless, in March 2003, American-led forces once again attacked Iraq (in Operation Shock and Awe) and overthrew Saddam Hussein's regime. In the months that followed, occupation forces sought to restore stability to the country while setting forth plans to lay the foundations of a future democratic society. But although Saddam Hussein was later captured by U.S. troops, armed resistance by militant Muslim elements continues.

Efforts are under way to train an Iraqi military force capable of defeating the insurgents, and a provisional government has been formed, the embryo of a future pro-Western state that could serve as an emblem of democracy in the Middle East. Squabbling, marked by growing civic violence, among Sunni, Shi'ite, and Kurdish elements within the country, however, is a vivid reminder that a similar effort by the British eighty years earlier ended without success.

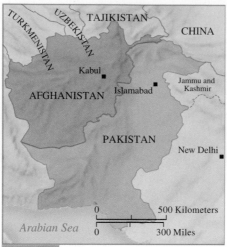
Afghanistan

Politics and Society in the Contemporary Middle East

To many seasoned observers, U.S. plans in Iraq seem unrealistic, since democratic values are not deeply rooted in the region. Feudal rulers remain in power, notably on the Arabian peninsula. The kings of Saudi Arabia, for example, continue to rule by traditional precepts and, citing the distinctive character of Muslim political institutions, have been reluctant to establish representative political institutions. As a general rule, these rulers maintain and even enforce the strict observance of

Predominantly Sunni areas
Predominantly Shi'ite areas
Predominantly Kurdish areas

Iraq

traditional customs. Religious police in Saudi Arabia are responsible for enforcing the Muslim dress code, maintaining the prohibition against alcohol, and making sure offices close during the time for prayer.

In other societies, traditional authority has been replaced by charismatic one-party rule or military dictatorships. Nasser's regime in Egypt is a good example of a single-party state where the leader won political power by the force of his presence or personality. The Ayatollah Khomeini in Iran, Muammar Qadhafi in Libya, and Saddam Hussein in Iraq are other examples. Although their personal characteristics and images differ, all sought to take advantage of their popular appeal.

In other instances, charismatic rule has given way to modernizing bureaucratic regimes. Examples include the governments of Syria, Yemen, Turkey, and Egypt since Nasser, where Anwar al-Sadat and his successor, Hosni Mubarak, have avoided dramatic personal appeal in favor of a regime focused on performance. Sometimes the authoritarian character of the regimes has been modified by some democratic tendencies, especially in Turkey, where free elections and the sharing of power have become more prevalent in recent years. A few Arab nations, such as Bahrain, Kuwait, and Jordan, have even engaged in limited forms of democratic experimentation (see the box on p. 302).

In Syria, the death of longtime president Hafez al-Assad in 2000 led to a referendum that elevated his son Bashar al-Assad to the office. The new president indicated that he would not seek to continue the personality cult that had arisen during the reign of his father but warned that he would not encourage political reforms that might threaten the domination of the country's one-party political system. Noting that he would tolerate only "positive criticism" of government policies, he declared that "we have to have our own democracy to match our history and culture, arising from the needs of our people and our reality."[2]

Only in Israel are democratic institutions firmly established. The Israeli system suffers from the proliferation of minor parties, some of which are able to dictate policy because their support is essential to keeping a government in power. In recent

Hosni Mubarak of Egypt. Hosni Mubarak (b. 1929) has been president of Egypt since the death of his predecessor Anwar al-Sadat in 1981. One of the most prominent political figures in the contemporary Middle East, Mubarak personifies the dilemmas of a Muslim leader in seeking to bring about democratic reforms in his society. Although Egypt has historically been one of the most tolerant of Muslim societies, in recent years traditionalist elements have energetically sought to impose their values, sometimes by the use of violence. To preserve the social order, Mubarak has catered to pressures from conservative Muslim elements while cracking down harshly on terrorist activities.

years, divisions between religious conservatives and secular elements within the Jewish community have become increasingly sharp, resulting in bitter disagreements over social policy and the negotiating process with the Palestinians. Nevertheless, the government generally reflects the popular will, and power is transferred by peaceful and constitutional means.

The Economics of Oil

Few areas exhibit a greater disparity of individual and national wealth than the Middle East. Although millions live in abject poverty, a fortunate few rank among the wealthiest people in the world. The annual per capita income in Egypt is about $4,000 (in U.S. dollars), but in the tiny states of Kuwait and United Arab Emirates, it is about $20,000 and $43,000, respectively. Some of that disparity can be explained by the uneven distribution of fertile and barren land, but the primary reason, of course, is oil. Unfortunately for most of the peoples of the region, oil reserves are distributed unevenly and all too often are located in areas where the population density is low. Egypt and Turkey, with more than 70 million inhabitants apiece, have almost no oil reserves. The combined population of Kuwait, the United Arab Emirates, and Saudi Arabia is less than 35 million people. This disparity in wealth inspired Nasser's quest for Arab unity (and perhaps Saddam Hussein's as well), but it has also posed a major obstacle to that unity.

The growing importance of petroleum has obviously been a boon to several of the states in the region, but it has

been an unreliable one. Because of the violent fluctuations in the price of oil during the past thirty years, the income of the oil-producing states has varied considerably. The spectacular increase in oil prices during the 1970s, when members of OPEC were able to raise the price of a barrel of oil from about $3 to $30, could not be sustained, forcing a number of oil-producing countries to scale back their economic development plans. The recent spike in oil prices is predicted to be longer lasting because the demand for liquid energy is currently growing faster than the supply.

Not surprisingly, considering their different resources and political systems, the states of the Middle East have adopted diverse approaches to the problem of developing strong and stable economies. Some, like Nasser in Egypt and the leaders of the Ba'ath Party in Syria, attempted to create a form of Arab socialism, favoring a high level of government involvement in the economy to relieve the inequities of the free enterprise system. Others turned to the Western capitalist model to maximize growth, while using taxes or massive development projects to build a modern infrastructure, redistribute wealth, and maintain political stability and economic opportunity for all.

Whatever their approach, all the states have attempted to develop their economies in accordance with Islamic beliefs. Although the Qur'an has little to say about economics and can be variously understood as capitalist or socialist, it is clear in its opposition to charging interest and in its concern for the material welfare of the Muslim community, the *umma*. How these goals are to be achieved, however, is a matter of interpretation.

ISLAM AND DEMOCRACY

One of George W. Bush's key objectives in launching the invasion of Iraq in 2003 was to promote the emergence of democratic states throughout the Middle East. According to U.S. officials, one of the ultimate causes of the formation of terrorist movements in Muslim societies is the prevalence in such countries of dictatorial governments that do not serve the interests of their citizens. According to the Pakistani author of this editorial, the problem lies as much with the actions of Western countries as it does with political attitudes in the Muslim world.

How does the author answer the charge that democracy and Islam are incompatible? To what degree is the West responsible for problems in the Middle East?

M. J. Akbar, "Linking Islam to Dictatorship"

Let us examine a central canard, that Islam and democracy are incompatible. This is an absurdity. There is nothing Islamic or un-Islamic about democracy. Democracy is the outcome of a political process, not a religious process.

It is glibly suggested that "every" Muslim country is a dictatorship, but the four largest Muslim populations of the world—in Indonesia, India, Bangladesh, and Turkey—vote to change governments. Pakistan could easily have been on this list.

Voting does not make these Muslims less or more religious. There are dictators among Muslims just as there are dictators among Christians, Buddhists, and Hindus (check out Nepal). . . . Christian Latin America has seen ugly forms of dictatorship, as has Christian Africa.

What is unique to the Muslim world is not the absence of democracy but the fact that in 1918, after the defeat of the Ottoman Empire, every single Muslim in the world lived under foreign subjugation.

Every single one, from Indonesia to Morocco via Turkey. The Turks threw out their invaders within a few years under the great leadership of Kemal Atatürk, but the transition to self-rule in other Muslim countries was slow, uncertain, and full of traps planted by the world's preeminent powers.

The West, in the shape of Britain, France, or America, was never interested in democracy when a helpful dictator or king would serve. When people got a chance to express their wish, it was only logical that they would ask for popular rule. It was the street that brought Mossadegh to power in Iran and drove the shah of Iran to tearful exile in Rome. Who brought the shah of Iran and autocracy back to Iran? The CIA.

If Iranian democracy had been permitted a chance in 1953, there would have been no uprising led by Ayatollah Khomeini in 1979. In other countries, where the struggle for independence was long and brutal, as in Algeria and Indonesia, the militias who had fought the war institutionalized army authority. In other instances, civilian heroes confused their own well-being with national health. They became regressive dictators. Once again, there was nothing Islamic about it.

Muslim countries will become democracies, too, because it is the finest form of modern governance. But it will be a process interrupted by bloody experience as the street wrenches power from usurpers.

Democracy has happened in Turkey. It has happened in Bangladesh. It is happening in Indonesia. It almost happened in Pakistan, and the opportunity will return. Democracy takes time in the most encouraging environments.

Democracy has become the latest rationale for the occupation of Iraq. . . . Granted, democracy is always preferable to tyranny no matter how it comes. But Iraqis are not dupes. They will take democracy and place it at the service of nationalism. A decade ago, America was careless about the definition of victory. Today it is careless about the definition of democracy.

There is uncertainty and apprehension across the Muslim nations: uncertainty about where they stand, and apprehension about both American power and the repugnant use of terrorism that in turn invites the exercise of American power. There is also anger that a legitimate cause like that of Palestine can get buried in the debris of confusion. Muslims do not see Palestinians as terrorists.

SOURCE: From M. J. Akbar, "Linking Islam to Dictatorship" in _World Press Review_, May 2004. Reprinted by permission.

Socialist theories of economic development such as Nasser's were often suggested as a way to promote economic growth while meeting the requirements of Islamic doctrine. State intervention in the economic sector would bring about rapid development, while land redistribution and the nationalization or regulation of industry would prevent or minimize the harsh inequities of the marketplace. In general, however, the socialist approach has had little success, and most governments, including those of Egypt and Syria, have shifted to a more free enterprise approach while encouraging foreign investment to compensate for a lack of capital or technology.

Although the amount of arable land is relatively small, most countries in the Middle East rely to a certain degree on farming to supply food for their growing populations. In some cases, as in Egypt, Iran, Iraq, and Turkey, farmers have until recently been a majority of the population. Often much of the fertile land was owned by wealthy absentee landlords, but land reform programs in several countries have attempted to alleviate this problem.

The most comprehensive and probably the most successful land reform program was instituted in Egypt, where Nasser and his successors managed to reassign nearly a quarter of all cultivable lands by limiting the amount a single individual could hold. Similar programs in Iran, Iraq, Libya, and Syria had less effect. In Iran, large landlords at the local and national level managed to limit the effects of the shah's reform program. After the 1979 revolution, many farmers seized lands forcibly from the landlords, giving rise to questions of ownership that the revolutionary government has tried with minimal success to resolve.

Agricultural productivity throughout the region has been plagued by the lack of water resources. With populations growing at more than 2 percent annually on average in the Middle East (more than 3 percent in some countries), several governments have tried to increase the amount of water available for irrigation. Many attempts have been sabotaged by government ineptitude, political disagreements, and territorial conflicts, however. The best-known example is the Aswan Dam, which was built by Soviet engineers in the 1950s. The project was designed to control the flow of water throughout the Nile valley, but it has had a number of undesirable environmental consequences. Today, the dearth of water is reaching crisis proportions and is having a political impact as governments squabble over access to scarce water resources in the region. For example, disputes between Israel and its neighbors over water rights and between Iraq and its neighbors over the exploitation of the Tigris and the Euphrates have caused serious tensions in recent years.

Another way in which governments have attempted to deal with rapid population growth is to encourage emigration. Oil-producing states with small populations, such as Saudi Arabia and the United Arab Emirates, have imported labor from other countries in the region, mostly to work in the oil fields. By the mid-1980s, more than 40 percent of the population in those states was composed of foreign nationals, who often sent the bulk of their salaries back to their families in their home countries. The decline in oil revenues after the mid-1980s, however, forced several governments to take measures to stabilize or reduce the migrant population. After the Iraqi invasion, Kuwait, for example, expelled all Palestinians and restricted migrant workers from other countries to three-year stays.

The Islamic Revival

In recent years, many developments in the Middle East have been described in terms of a resurgence of traditional values and customs in response to the pressure of Western influence.

Indeed, some conservative religious forces in the area have consciously attempted to replace foreign culture and values with allegedly "pure" Islamic forms of belief and behavior.

But the Islamic revival that has taken place in the contemporary Middle East is not a simple dichotomy between traditional and modern, native and foreign, or irrational and rational. In the first place, many Muslims in the Middle East believe that Islamic values and modern ways are not incompatible and may even be mutually reinforcing in some ways. Second, the resurgence of what are sometimes called "fundamentalist" Islamic groups may, in a Middle Eastern context, appear to be a rational and practical response to self-destructive practices, such as corruption and hedonism, drunkenness, prostitution, and the use of drugs. Finally, the reassertion of Islamic values can be a means of establishing cultural identity and fighting off the overwhelming impact of Western ideas.

Modernist Islam Initially, many Muslim intellectuals responded to Western influence by trying to reconcile the perceived differences between tradition and modernity and by creating an "updated" set of Islamic beliefs and practices that would not clash with the demands of the modern world. This process took place in most Islamic societies, but it was especially prevalent in Turkey, Egypt, and Iran. Mustafa Kemal Atatürk embraced the strategy when he attempted to secularize the Islamic religion in the new Turkish republic. The Turkish model was followed by Shah Reza Khan and his son Mohammad Reza Pahlavi in Iran and then by Nasser in postwar Egypt, all of whom attempted to make use of Islamic values while asserting the primacy of other issues such as political and economic development. Religion, in effect, had become the handmaiden of political power, national identity, and economic prosperity.

For obvious reasons, these secularizing trends were particularly noticeable among the political, intellectual, and economic elites in urban areas. They had less influence in the countryside, among the poor, and among devout elements within the *ulama*. Many of the latter believed that Western secular trends in the major cities had given birth to regrettable and even repugnant social attitudes and behavioral patterns, such as political and economic corruption, sexual promiscuity, individualism, and the prevalence of alcohol, pornography, and drugs. Although such practices had long existed in the Middle East, they were now far more visible and socially acceptable.

This reaction began early in the century and intensified after World War I, when the Western presence increased. In 1928, devout Muslims in Egypt formed the Muslim Brotherhood as a means of promoting personal piety. Later, the movement began to take a more activist approach, including the eventual use of terrorism by a radical minority. Despite Nasser's surface commitment to Islamic ideals

Answering the Call of the *Muezzin*. With the renewed fervor of Muslims in the world today, scenes such as this one in Kuwait exemplify the adherents' humble submission to God. Required to pray five times a day—at dawn, noon, mid-afternoon, sunset, and early evening—a Muslim, after ritual ablutions, prostrates himself facing Mecca to proclaim, "There is no god but Allah, and Muhammad is his prophet." Responding to the call of the *muezzin,* which today is often a recorded message from the minaret of a mosque, the faithful can perform their prayers in a few minutes, wherever they are, at home or in any public place. There are an estimated 1.3 billion Muslims in the world today, 175 million of whom are in Indonesia, 105 million in India, and 15 million in Europe.

© Patrick Robert/Sygma/CORBIS

and Arab unity, some Egyptians were fiercely opposed to his policies and regarded his vision of Arab socialism as a betrayal of Islamic principles. Nasser reacted harshly and executed a number of his leading opponents.

Return to Tradition The movement to return to traditional practices strengthened after World War II and reached its zenith in Iran. It is not surprising that Iran took the lead in light of its long tradition of ideological purity within the Shi'ite sect as well as the uncompromisingly secular character of the shah's reforms in the postwar era. In revolutionary Iran, traditional Islamic beliefs are all-pervasive and extend to education, clothing styles, social practices, and the legal system.

While the political aspects of the Iranian Revolution inspired distrust and suspicion among political elites elsewhere in the region, its cultural and social effects were profound. Although no other state in the Middle East adopted the violent approach to cultural reform applied in Iran, Iranian ideas have spread throughout the area and affected social and cultural behavior in many ways. In Algeria, the political influence of fundamentalist Islamic groups has grown substantially and enabled them to win a stunning victory in the national elections in 1992. When the military stepped in to cancel the second round of elections and crack down on the militants, the latter responded with a campaign of terrorism against moderates that has claimed thousands of lives.

A similar trend has emerged in Egypt, where militant groups such as the Muslim Brotherhood have engaged in

terrorism, including the assassination of Sadat and more recent attacks on foreign tourists, who are considered carriers of corrupt Western influence. In 1994, the prominent novelist Naguib Mahfouz was stabbed outside his home, apparently in response to earlier writings that were deemed blasphemous of Muslim belief.

Even in Turkey, generally considered the most secular of Islamic societies, a militant political group, known as the Islamic Welfare Party, took power in a coalition government formed in 1996. Worried moderates voiced their concern that the secular legacy of Kemal Atatürk was being eroded, and eventually, the new prime minister, Necmettin Erbakan, agreed to resign under heavy pressure from the military. Uncomfortable with the militancy of Arab neighbors, Turkey maintains close ties with the United States and is currently adopting reforms to extend human rights and freedom of expression in the hope of gaining entry into the European Union. But religious and economic discontent simmers beneath the surface.

Women and Islam

Nowhere have the fault lines between tradition and modernity in Muslim societies in the Middle East been so sharp as in the ongoing debate over the role of women. At the beginning of the twentieth century, women's place in Middle Eastern society had changed little since the days of the Prophet Muhammad. Women were secluded in their homes and had few legal, political, or social rights.

Early in the twentieth century, inspired in part by the Western presence, a "modernist" movement arose in several countries in the Middle East with the aim of bringing Islamic social values and legal doctrine into line with Western values and attitudes. Advocates of modernist views contended that Islamic doctrine was not inherently opposed to women's rights and that the teachings of Muhammad and his successors had actually broadened them in significant ways. To modernists, Islamic traditions such as female seclusion, wearing the veil, and even polygamy were pre-Islamic folk traditions that had been tolerated in the early Islamic era and continued to be practiced in later centuries.

During the first decades of the twentieth century, such views had considerable impact on a number of Middle Eastern societies, including Turkey and Iran. As we have seen, greater rights for women were a crucial element in the social revolution promoted by Mustafa Kemal Atatürk in Turkey. In Iran, Shah Reza Khan and his son granted female suffrage and encouraged the education of women. In Egypt, a vocal feminist movement arose in educated women's circles in Cairo as early as the 1920s.

Modernist views had somewhat less effect in other Islamic states, such as Iraq, Jordan, Morocco, and Algeria, where traditional views of women continued to prevail in varying degrees. Particularly in rural areas, notions of women's liberation made little headway. Most conservative by far was Saudi Arabia, where women were not only segregated and expected to wear the veil in public but were also restricted in education and forbidden to drive automobiles (see the box on p. 306).

Until recently, the general trend in urban areas of the Middle East was toward a greater role for women. This was particularly the case in Egypt and in Iran, where the liberal policies of the shah encouraged Western attitudes toward sexual equality. With the exception of conservative religious communities, women in Israel have achieved substantial equality with men and are active in politics, the professions, and even the armed forces. Golda Meir (1898–1978), prime minister of Israel from 1969 to 1974, became an international symbol of the ability of women to be world leaders.

Beginning in the 1970s, however, there was a shift toward a more traditional approach to gender roles in many Middle Eastern societies. It was accompanied by intense criticism of the growing Western influence within the media and on the social habits of young people. The reactions were especially strong in Iran, where attacks by religious conservatives on the growing role of women contributed to the emotions underlying the Iranian Revolution of 1979. Iranian women were instructed to wear the veil and to dress modestly in public. Films produced in postrevolutionary Iran expressed the new morality. They rarely featured women, and when they did, physical contact between men and women was prohibited. The events in Iran helped promote a revival of traditional attitudes toward women in other Islamic societies. Women in secular countries such as Egypt, Turkey, and far-off Malaysia have begun to dress more modestly in public, and open sexuality in the media has come under increased attacks.

Nevertheless, women have won some small victories in their struggle for equal rights in the Middle East. A woman in Kuwait now has the same right as her husband to obtain a divorce. In 1999, a governmental edict declared that women would be granted the right to vote in Kuwait, and finally, in the spring of 2006, women participated for the first time in municipal elections in that country. Even in Iran, women have many freedoms that they lacked before the twentieth century; for example, they can attend a university, receive military training, vote, practice birth control, and write fiction.

Contemporary Literature and Art in the Middle East

As in other areas of Asia and Africa, the encounter with the West in the nineteenth and twentieth centuries stimulated a cultural renaissance in the Middle East. Muslim authors translated Western works into Arabic and Persian and began to experiment with new literary forms. The advent of modern newspapers and magazines eliminated the traditional differences between the oral and written languages. The resulting fused language included colloquial speech, borrowed Western words, and ancient words resurrected from indigenous languages.

The new literature dealt with a number of new themes. The rise in national consciousness stimulated interest in historical traditions. Writers also switched from religious to secular themes and addressed the problems of this world and the means of rectifying them. Furthermore, literature was no longer the exclusive domain of the elite but was increasingly written for the broader mass of the population.

Iran has produced one of the most prominent national literatures in the contemporary Middle East. Since World War II, Iranian literature has been hampered somewhat by political considerations, since it has been expected to serve first the Pahlavi monarchy and more recently the Islamic Republic. Nevertheless, Iranian writers are among the most prolific in the region and often write in prose, which has finally been accepted as the equal of poetry. Perhaps the most outstanding Iranian author of the twentieth century was short story writer Sadeq Hedayat (1903–1951). Hedayat was obsessed with the frailty and absurdity of life and wrote with compassion about the problems of ordinary human beings. Frustrated and disillusioned by the government's suppression of individual liberties, he committed suicide in 1951. Like Japan's Mishima Yukio, Hedayat later became a cult figure among his country's youth.

KEEPING THE CAMEL OUT OF THE TENT

"Almighty God created sexual desire in ten parts; then he gave nine parts to women and one to men." So pronounced Ali, Muhammad's son-in-law, as he explained why women are held morally responsible as the instigators of sexual intercourse. Consequently, over the centuries Islamic women have been secluded, veiled, and in many cases genitally mutilated to safeguard male virtue. Women are forbidden to look directly at, speak to, or touch a man prior to marriage. Even today, they are often sequestered at home or limited to strictly segregated areas away from all male contact. Women normally pray at home or in an enclosed antechamber of the mosque so that their physical presence will not disturb men's spiritual concentration.

Especially limiting today are the laws governing women's behavior in Saudi Arabia. Schooling for girls has never been compulsory because fathers believe that "educating women is like allowing the nose of the camel into the tent; eventually the beast will edge in and take up all the room inside." The country did not establish its first girls' school until 1956. The following description of Saudi women is from *Nine Parts of Desire: The Hidden World of Islamic Women*, by journalist Geraldine Brooks.

According to the author, do women in Saudi Arabia have an opportunity to receive an education? What kinds of subjects are open to women?

Geraldine Brooks, *Nine Parts of Desire*

Women were first admitted to university in Saudi Arabia in 1962, and all women's colleges remain strictly segregated. Lecture rooms come equipped with closed-circuit TVs and telephones, so women students can listen to a male professor and question him by phone, without having to contaminate themselves by being seen by him. When the first dozen women graduated from university in 1973, they were devastated to find that their names hadn't been printed on the commencement program. The old tradition, that it dishonors women to mention them, was depriving them of recognition they believed they'd earned. The women and their families protested, so a separate program was printed and a segregated graduation ceremony was held for the students' female relatives. . . .

But while opening of women's universities widened access to higher learning for women, it also made the educational experience much shallower. Before 1962, many progressive Saudi families had sent their daughters abroad for education. They had returned to the kingdom not only with a degree but with experience of the outside world. . . . Now a whole generation of Saudi women have completed their education entirely within the country. . . .

Lack of opportunity for education abroad means that Saudi women are trapped in the confines of an education system that still lags men's. Subjects such as geology and petroleum engineering—tickets to influential jobs in Saudi Arabia's oil economy—remain closed to women. . . . Few women's colleges have their own libraries, and libraries shared with men's schools are either entirely off limits to women or open to them only one day per week. . . .

But women and men [take] the same degree examinations. Professors quietly acknowledge the women's scores routinely outstrip the men's. "It's no surprise," said one woman professor. "Look at their lives. The boys have their cars, they can spend the evenings cruising the streets with their friends, sitting in cafés, buying black-market alcohol and drinking all night. What do the girls have? Four walls and their books. For them, education is everything."

SOURCE: Geraldine Brooks, *Nine Parts of Desire: The Hidden World of Islamic Women* (New York: Doubleday, 1996).

Despite the male-oriented nature of Iranian society, many of the new writers were women. Since the revolution, the veil and the chador, an all-enveloping cloak, have become the central metaphor in Iranian women's writing. Advocates praise the veil and the chador as the last bastion of defense against Western cultural imperialism. Behind the veil, the Islamic woman can breathe freely, unpolluted by foreign exploitation and moral corruption. They see these garments as the courageous woman's weapon against Western efforts to dominate the Iranian soul. Other Iranian women, however, consider the veil and chador a "mobile prison" or an oppressive anachronism from the Dark Ages. A few use the pen as a weapon in a crusade to liberate their sisters and enable them to make their own choices. As one writer, Sousan Azadi, expressed it, "As I pulled the chador over me, I felt a heaviness descending over me. I was hidden and in hiding. There was nothing visible left of Sousan Azadi."[3]

Like Iran, Egypt in the twentieth century experienced a flowering of literature accelerated by the establishment of the Egyptian republic in the early 1950s. The most illustrious contemporary Egyptian writer was Naguib Mahfouz (1911–2006), who won the Nobel Prize for literature in 1988. His *Cairo Trilogy*, published in 1952, chronicled three generations of a merchant family in Cairo during the tumultuous years between the two world wars. Mahfouz was particularly adept at blending panoramic historical events with the intimate lives of ordinary human beings with great compassion and energy. Unlike many other modern writers, his message was essentially optimistic and reflected his hope that religion and science could work together for the overall betterment of humankind.

No women writer has played a more active role in exposing the physical and psychological grievances of Egyptian women than Nawal el-Saadawi (b. 1931). For decades, she has battled against the injustices of religious fundamentalism and a male-dominated society—even enduring imprisonment for promoting her cause. In *Two Women in One* (1985), el-Saadawi follows the struggle of a young university student as she rebels against the life her father has programmed for her, striking out instead on an unchartered independent destiny.

The emergence of a modern Turkish literature can be traced to the establishment of the republic in 1923. The most popular contemporary writer is Orhan Pamuk (b. 1952), whose novels attempt to capture Turkey's unique blend of cultures. "I am living in a culture," he writes, "where the clash of East and West, or the harmony of East and West, is the lifestyle. That is Turkey."[4] His novel *Snow* (2002) dramatizes the conflict between secularism and radical Islam in contemporary Turkey. Like the Japanese author Kenzaburo Oe (see Chapter 12), Pamuk, who won the Nobel Prize for literature in 2006, has been attacked by extremist compatriots for urging a reexamination of the national past.

Although Israeli literature arises from a totally different tradition from that of its neighbors, it shares with them certain contemporary characteristics and a concern for ordinary human beings. Early writers identified with the aspirations of the new nation, trying to find a sense of order in the new reality, voicing terrors from the past and hope for the future. Some contemporary Israeli authors, however, have refused to serve as promoters for Zionism and are speaking out on sensitive national issues. The internationally renowned novelist Amos Oz (b. 1939), for example, is a vocal supporter of peace with the Palestinians. Oz is a member of Peace Now and the author of a political tract titled *Israel, Palestine, and Peace.* With the Arabs feeling victimized by colonialism and the Jews by Nazi Germany, he says, each side believes that it alone is the rightful proprietor of ancient Palestine. For Oz, the only solution is compromise, which, however unsatisfactory for both sides, is preferable to mutual self-destruction.

Like literature, the art of the modern Middle East has been profoundly influenced by its exposure to Western culture. Reflecting their hopes for the new nation, Israeli painters sought to bring to life the sentiments of pioneers arriving in a promised land. Many attempted to capture the longing for community expressed in the Israeli commune, or kibbutz. Others searched for the roots of Israeli culture in the history of the Jewish people or in the horrors of the Holocaust. The experience of the Holocaust has attracted particular attention from sculptors, who work in wood and metal as well as stone.

The popular music of the contemporary Middle East has also been strongly influenced by that of the modern West, but to different degrees in different countries. In Israel, many contemporary young rock stars voice lyrics as irreverent toward the traditions of their elders as those of Europe and the United States. One idol of many Israeli young people, rock star Aviv Ghefen, declares himself to be "a person of no values," and his music carries a shock value that attacks the country's political and social shibboleths with abandon. The rock music popular among Palestinians, on the other hand, makes greater use of Arab musical motifs and is closely tied to a political message. One recording, "The Song of the Engineer," lauds Yehia Ayash, a Palestinian accused of manufacturing many of the explosive devices used in terrorist attacks on Israeli citizens. The lyrics have their own shock value: "Spread the flame of revolution. Your explosive will wipe the enemy out, like a volcano, a torch, a banner." When one Palestinian rock star from the Gaza Strip was asked why his group employed a musical style that originated in the West, he explained, "For us, this is a tool like any other. Young people in Gaza like our music, they listen to us, they buy our cassettes, and so they spread our message."

CONCLUSION

𝒯HE MIDDLE EAST IS ONE OF the most unstable regions in the world today. In part, this turbulence is due to the continued interference of outsiders attracted by the massive oil reserves under the parched wastes of the Arabian peninsula and in the vicinity of the Persian Gulf. Oil is both a blessing and a curse to the peoples of the region.

Another factor contributing to the volatility of the Middle East is the tug-of-war between the sense of ethnic identity in the form of nationalism and the intense longing to be part of a broader Islamic community, a dream that dates back to the time of the Prophet Muhammad. The desire to create that community—a vision threatened by the presence of the alien state of Israel—inspired Gamal Abdul Nasser in the 1950s and Ayatollah Khomeini in the 1970s and 1980s and probably motivated many of the actions of Saddam Hussein in Iraq.

A final reason for the turmoil in the Middle East is the intense debate over the role of religion in civil society. It has been customary in recent years for Western commentators to label Muslim efforts to return to a purer form of Islam as fanatical and extremist, reflecting a misguided attempt to reverse the course of history, and there is no doubt that many of the legal and social restrictions now being enforced in various Muslim countries in the Middle East appear excessively harsh to outside observers. But it is important to remember that Muslim societies are not alone in deploring the sense of moral decline that is perceived to be occurring in societies throughout the world. Nor are they alone in advocating a restoration of traditional religious values as a means of reversing the trend. Movements dedicated to such purposes are appearing in many other societies (including Israel and the United States) and can be viewed as an understandable reaction to the rapid and often bewildering changes that are taking place in the contemporary world. Not infrequently, members of such groups turn to violence as a means of making their point.

Whatever the reasons, it is clear that a deep-seated sense of anger is surging through much of the Islamic world today, an anger that transcends specific issues like the situation in Iraq or the Arab-Israeli dispute. Although economic privation and political oppression are undoubtedly important factors, the roots of Muslim resentment, as historian Bernard Lewis has pointed out, lie in a historical sense of humiliation that first emerged centuries ago, when Arab hegemony in the Mediterranean region was replaced by European domination. Today, the world is reaping the harvest of that long-cultivated bitterness, and the consequences cannot be foreseen.

TIMELINE

	1955	1965	1975	1985	1995	2005
MIDDLE EAST	Egypt nationalizes the Suez Canal		First oil crisis	Iranian Revolution	Iraqi invasion of Kuwait	U.S. invasion of Iraq
	Formation of the state of Israel	Wars between Israel and Egypt and other Arab states	Camp David accords		Moderates gain political influence in Iran	
		Founding of the Palestine Liberation Organization			Agreement on Palestinian autonomy	Election of Hamas in Palestine

CHAPTER NOTES

1. Quoted in R. R. Andersen, R. F. Seibert, and J. G. Wagner, *Politics and Change in the Middle East: Sources of Conflict and Accommodation*, 4th ed. (Englewood Cliffs, N.J., 1982), p. 51.
2. *New York Times*, July 18, 2000.
3. S. Azadi, with A. Ferrante, *Out of Iran* (London, 1987), p. 223, quoted in *Stories by Iranian Women Since the Revolution*, ed. S. Sullivan (Austin, Tex., 1991), p. 13.
4. *New York Times*, August 27, 2003.

REFLECTION PART IV

*I*N THE ATLANTIC CHARTER, issued after their meeting near the coast of Newfoundland in August 1941, Franklin Roosevelt and Winston Churchill set forth a joint declaration of their peace aims calling for the self-determination of all peoples and self-government and sovereign rights for all nations that had been deprived of them. Although Churchill later disavowed the assumption that he had meant these conditions to apply to colonial areas, Roosevelt on frequent occasions during the war voiced his own intention to bring about the end of colonial domination throughout the world at the close of the conflict.

It took many years to complete the process, but the promise contained in the Atlantic Charter was eventually fulfilled. Although some powers were reluctant to divest themselves of their colonies, World War II had severely undermined the stability of the colonial order, and by the end of the 1940s, most colonies in Asia had received their independence. Africa followed a decade or two later. In a few instances—notably in Algeria, Indonesia, and Vietnam—the transition to independence was a violent one, but for the most part, it was realized by peaceful means.

In their own writings and public statements, the leaders of these newly liberated countries set forth three broad goals at the outset of independence: to throw off the shackles of Western economic domination and ensure material prosperity for all their citizens, to introduce new political institutions that would enhance the right of self-determination of their peoples, and to develop a sense of nationhood and establish secure territorial boundaries. Most of them opted to follow a capitalist or moderately socialist path toward economic development. Only in a few cases—North Korea and Vietnam being the most notable examples—did revolutionary leaders decide to pursue the Communist model of development.

Within a few years of the restoration of independence, however, reality had set in, as most of the new governments in Asia and Africa fell short of their ambitious goals. Virtually all remained economically dependent on the advanced industrial nations. Several faced severe problems of urban and rural poverty. At the same time, fledgling democratic governments were gradually replaced by military dictatorships or one-party regimes that dismantled representative institutions and oppressed dissident elements and ethnic minorities within their borders.

What had happened to tarnish the bright dreams of affluence and political self-determination? During the 1950s and 1960s, one school of thought was dominant among scholars and government officials in the United States. Modernization theory adopted the view that the problems faced by the newly independent countries were a consequence of the difficult transition from a traditional agrarian to a modern industrial society. Advocates were convinced that the countries of Asia, Africa, and Latin America were destined to follow the path of the West toward the creation of modern industrial societies but would need time as well as substantial amounts of economic and technological assistance to complete the journey. In their view, it was the duty of the United States and other advanced capitalist nations to provide such assistance while encouraging the leaders of these states to follow the path already adopted by the West. Some countries going through this difficult period were especially vulnerable to Communist-led insurgent movements. In such cases, it was in the interests of the United States and its allies to intervene, with military power if necessary, to hasten the transition and put the country on the path to self-sustaining growth.

Modernization theory soon began to come under attack from a generation of younger scholars, many of whom had reached maturity during the Vietnam War and had growing doubts about the roots of the problem and the efficacy of the modernization approach. In their view, the responsibility for continued economic underdevelopment in the developing world lay not with the countries themselves but with their continued domination by the former colonial powers. In this view, known as dependency theory, the countries of Asia, Africa, and Latin America were the victims of the international marketplace, which charged high prices for the manufactured goods of the West while paying low prices for the raw material exports of preindustrial countries. Efforts by these countries to build up their own industrial sectors and move into the stage of self-sustaining growth were hampered by foreign control—through European- and American-owned corporations—of many of their resources. To end this "neocolonial" relationship, dependency theory advocates argued, developing societies should reduce their economic ties with the West and adopt a policy of economic self-reliance, thereby taking control of their own destinies. They should also ignore urgings that they adopt the Western model of capitalist democracy, which had little relevance to conditions in their parts of the world.

Both of these approaches, of course, were directly linked to the ideological divisions of the Cold War and reflected the political bias of their advocates. Although modernization theorists were certainly correct in pointing out some of the key factors involved in economic development and in suggesting that some traditional attitudes and practices were incompatible with economic change, they were too quick to see the Western model of development as the only relevant one and too ready to identify economic development in the developing world with the interests of the United States and its allies.

By the same token, the advocates of dependency theory alluded correctly to the unfair and often disadvantageous relationship that continued to exist between the former colonies and the industrialized nations of the world and to the impact that this relationship had on the efforts of developing countries to overcome their economic difficulties. But they often rationalized many of the mistakes made by the leaders of developing countries while assigning all of the blame for their plight on the evil and self-serving practices of the industrialized world. At the same time, the recommendation by some dependency theorists of a policy of self-reliance was not only naive but sometimes disastrous, depriving the new nations of badly needed technology and capital resources.

Many observers today would agree that there are important truths on both sides of this debate and that no one model fits all contingencies. Although the recent success of the Little Tigers in East Asia has aroused confidence that the capitalist model can be transplanted outside the boundaries of Western civilization, it has proved less effective in other parts of the world. History has shown that there are different roads to development and that the international marketplace can have both beneficial and harmful effects. Such has certainly been the case with the spread of free trade agreements in recent years. While the reduction of tariff barriers has undoubtedly spurred an increase in the exchange of goods worldwide, its disruptive effects within individual countries have often been severe, with unforeseen consequences.

What explains the failure of newly independent countries to establish stable democracies in the post–World War II era? It seems evident that many observers badly underestimated the difficulties in building pluralistic political systems in societies that lacked experience with Western democratic values. Many of these new states were composed of a wide variety of ethnic, religious, and linguistic groups that found it difficult to agree on common symbols of nationalism and forms of governance. As a result, African and Asian leaders soon began to experiment with political systems that appeared more relevant to local conditions. Although there have been tantalizing signs of a revival of interest in the Western democratic model in recent years, in many countries democratic institutions remain fragile. Influential voices in Asia and Africa argue that institutions such as free elections and freedom of the press can be both destabilizing and destructive of other national objectives. It is still not clear that Western-style democratic values have universal relevance in our rapidly changing world.

Future trends in the developing world, then, remain obscure as the impact of global interconnectedness provokes widespread resistance. Under the surface, however, the influence of the West continues unabated as changing economic circumstances have led to more secular attitudes, a decline in traditional hierarchical relationships, and a more open attitude toward sexual practices. In part, this change has been a consequence of the influence of Western music, movies, and television. But it is also a product of the growth of an affluent middle class in many societies of Asia and Africa. This middle class is often strongly influenced by Western ways, and its sons and daughters ape the behavior, dress, and lifestyles of their counterparts in Europe and North America. When Reebok sneakers are worn and coveted in Lagos and Nairobi, Mumbai (Bombay) and Islamabad, Beijing and Hanoi, it is clear that the impact of modern Western civilization has been universalized.

PART

V

THE NEW MILLENNIUM

The Guggenheim Museum in Bilbao, Spain

Photograph by David Heald © Solomon R. Guggenheim Foundation, NY

16

CONSTRUCTING A NEW WORLD ORDER

HE DECLINE OF COMMUNISM in the final decades of the twentieth century brought an end to an era, not only in the Soviet Union but in much of the rest of the world as well. For more than a generation, thousands of intellectuals and political elites throughout the world had viewed Marxism-Leninism as an appealing developmental ideology that could alleviate the evils of the capitalist system and rush preindustrial societies through the modernization process without the painful economic and social inequities associated with capitalism. Communism, many thought, could make more effective use of scarce capital and resources while carrying out the reforms needed to bring an end to centuries of political and social inequality.

The results, however, were much less than advertised. Although such diverse societies as China, Vietnam, and Cuba got off to an impressive start under Communist regimes, after a generation of party rule all were increasingly characterized by economic stagnation, low productivity, and underemployment. Even before the collapse of the Soviet Union, prominent Communist states such as China and Vietnam had begun to adopt reforms that broke with ideological orthodoxy and borrowed liberally from the capitalist model.

To many historians, the disintegration of the Soviet Union signaled the end of communism as a competitive force in the global environment. In some parts of the world, however, it has survived in the form of Communist parties presiding over a mixed economy combining components of both socialism and capitalism. Why have Communist political systems survived in some areas while the Marxist-Leninist economic model in its classic form has not? In the first place, it is obvious that one of the consequences of long-term Communist rule was the suffocation of alternative political forces and ideas. As the situation in Eastern Europe has demonstrated, even after the passing of communism itself, Communist parties often appeared to be the only political force with the experience, discipline, and self-confidence to govern complex and changing societies.

That monopoly of political experience, of course, is no accident. In its Leninist incarnation, modern communism is preeminently a strategy for seizing and retaining power. The first duty of a Communist Party on seizing control is to determine "who defeats whom" and to establish a dictatorship of the proletariat. As a result, even when perceptive party leaders recognize the failure of the Marxist model to promote the creation of a technologically advanced industrial society, they view the Leninist paradigm as a useful means of maintaining political stability while undergoing the difficult transition through the early stages of the Industrial Revolution. In such countries as China and Vietnam today, Marxism-Leninism has thus become primarily a political technique—a Marxist variant of the single-party or military regimes that arose in the Third World during the immediate postwar era. It is still too early to predict how successful such regimes will ultimately be or what kind of political culture will succeed them, but there is modest reason to hope that as their economic reform programs begin to succeed, they will eventually evolve into pluralistic societies such as are now taking shape elsewhere around the world. ◆

After the Cold War: The End of History?

With the end of superpower rivalry and the collapse of the Soviet Union in 1991, the attention of the world shifted to the new post–Cold War era. For many observers, the prognosis was excellent, U.S. President George H. W. Bush looked forward to a new era of peace and international cooperation that he labeled the "new world order," while pundits predicted the advent of a new "American century," marked by the victory of liberal democratic values and free enterprise capitalism.

The wave of optimism that accompanied the end of the Cold War was all too brief. After a short period of euphoria, it soon became clear that forces were now being released that had long been held in check by the ideological rigidities of the Cold War. The era of conflict that had long characterized the twentieth century was not at an end; it was simply in the process of taking a different form.

Nowhere was this trend more immediately apparent than in Southeast Asia, where even before the end of the Cold War, erstwhile allies in China, Vietnam, and Cambodia turned on each other in a fratricidal conflict that combined territorial ambitions with geopolitical concerns and deep-seated historical suspicions based on the memory of past conflicts (see Chapter 7). Ideology, it was clear, was no barrier to historical and cultural rivalries. The pattern was repeated elsewhere: in Africa, where several nations erupted into civil war during the late 1980s and 1990s; in the Balkans, where the Yugoslavian Federation broke apart in a bitter conflict that has yet to be fully resolved; and, of course, in the Middle East, where the historical disputes in Palestine and the Persian Gulf have grown in intensity and erupted repeatedly into open war. The irony of this explosion of national, ethnic, and religious sentiment is that it has taken place at a time when it is becoming increasingly evident that the main problems in today's society—such as environmental pollution, overpopulation, and unequal distribution of resources—are shared to one degree or another by all humanity. In a world that is increasingly characterized by global interdependence, how can it be that the world is increasingly being pulled apart?

Contemporary Capitalism and Its Discontents

The problems are by no means limited to the developing world. After a generation of rapid growth, in the late 1980s most of the capitalist states in Europe and North America began to suffer through a general slowdown in economic performance. This slowdown has in turn given rise to a number of related problems, several with serious social and political implications. These problems include an increase in the level of unemployment; government belt-tightening policies to reduce social services and welfare and retirement benefits; and in many countries, an accompanying growth in popular resentment against minority groups or recent immigrants, who are blamed for deteriorating economic prospects.

Europe: Speed Bumps on the Road to Unity

The problem of economic stagnation has been especially prevalent in Western Europe, where in the early 2000s unemployment reached its highest level since the 1930s and economic growth averaged less than 1 percent annually until a modest recovery in the mid-2000s. Conditions were exacerbated by the need for individual governments to set their financial houses in order so as to comply with the requirements for economic unification established by the Maastricht Treaty of 1991 (see Chapter 10). For an individual nation to take part in the process, government deficits could not greatly exceed 3 percent of gross domestic product, nor could the national debt greatly exceed 60 percent of total output. Inflation rates also had to be cut to minimal levels.

Many countries, however, have encountered difficulties first in adopting the severe economic measures needed to qualify for the transition to economic unity and then in continuing to comply with the standards. France, concerned at the potential impact on its own fragile economy, threatened not to carry out the necessary reforms. In Italy, the refusal of the Communist Party to agree to belt-tightening measures almost led to the fall of the government. Even in Germany, long the healthiest of all major Western European states, reductions in social benefits sharpened tensions between the eastern and western zones and undermined public support for the government.

But perhaps the most ominous consequence of the new economic austerity has been a rise in antiforeign sentiment. In Germany, attacks against foreign residents—mainly Turks, many of whom have lived in the country for years—have increased substantially. Conservative forces have used the idea of preserving "German culture" as a rallying cry to win the support of Germans concerned about the rapid change. In France, hostility to immigrants from North Africa has led to rising support for Jean-Marie Le Pen's National Front, which advocates strict limits on immigration and the ejection of many foreigners currently living in the country. The massive riots that erupted in Islamic neighborhoods outside Paris in 2006 were a vivid demonstration of the resentment within the Muslim community over its marginal role in French society.

By no means, though, do all Europeans believe that economic unity has been too costly. Official sources argue that it has increased the region's ability to compete with economic powerhouses such as the United States and Japan. But fear of change and a strong legacy of nationalist sentiment have promoted public fears that economic unification could still have disastrous consequences. This is true not only in Great Britain, which did not join the monetary union, but also France and Germany, where many see little benefit and much risk from joining a larger Europe.

Beyond the question of European unity is the equally controversial issue of how to preserve the European welfare state in a time of declining government revenues and increasing global competition. Proposals to trim social benefits have been soundly rejected in many countries, and recent legislation to reduce job security in France provoked massive student riots in Paris.

The United States: Capitalism Ascendant

In some respects, the United States has fared better than other capitalist states as the economic revival that took place in the 1990s enabled the Clinton administration to reduce budget deficits without having to engage in substantial tax increases or a massive reduction in welfare spending. Even there, however, continued increases in social spending provoked the passage of new legislation to reduce welfare and health care benefits. Nor has the steady growth in the gross domestic product led to increased prosperity for all Americans. Although the rich have been getting richer, the poorest 20 percent of the population has so far seen little benefit. The lack of sustained growth in consumer demand may be a major reason for the economic slowdown that occurred early in the new century and brought unemployment levels to the highest rate in recent years.

The United States has not yet witnessed the emergence of significant antiforeign sentiment on the scale of some countries in Europe, perhaps partly because of the salutary effect of a steadily growing economy. Recent history suggests that tolerance toward immigrants tends to decrease during periods of economic malaise, and vice versa. But there are indications that anger against the growing presence of foreign-born residents—especially those who have arrived illegally—is growing. Legislation to limit social benefits to noncitizens and to expel illegal aliens has been proposed at the state level and introduced in Congress. In the 1990s, American workers, with the support of labor unions, vocally opposed the enactment of the North American Free Trade Agreement (NAFTA) on the grounds that it would lead to a loss of jobs as U.S. corporations moved their plants to Mexico to take advantage of the cheaper labor. More recently, the "outsourcing" of service jobs to developing countries like India and China has aroused increasing concern about a mass outflow of middle-class jobs from the United States. Opponents of globalization have become increasingly vocal, leading to violent protest demonstrations at meetings of the World Trade Organization, the World Bank, and the International Monetary Fund.

Yet, as in the case of European unity, there is solid economic logic in pursuing the goal of increasing globalization of trade. Both the Republican president George W. Bush and his Democratic predecessor, Bill Clinton, for example, have supported the concept, including the creation of a free trade zone incorporating all of the nations of the Western Hemisphere. The U.S. industrial machine is increasingly dependent on the importation of raw materials from abroad, and corporate profits depend heavily on sales of U.S. goods in overseas markets. Although foreign competition can sometimes lead to a loss of jobs—or entire industries—in the United States, the overall effect is likely to be a growing market for U.S. goods in the international marketplace. Moreover, as the U.S. automobile industry has demonstrated, increased competition is crucial for maintaining and enhancing the quality of American products. Yet the social costs of globalization will inevitably be severe and require significant efforts by the government to alleviate the pain.

It is hardly surprising that the main proponent of the global economic marketplace is the United States, a country well placed to take full advantage of the technological revolution and turn it to its own advantage. Its large market relatively unfettered by onerous government regulations, generous amounts of capital, a tradition of political stability, and an outstanding system of higher education all combine to give the United States an edge over most of its rivals in the relentless drive to achieve a dominant position in the world economy. As Washington applies pressure on other governments to open up their economies to the competition of the international marketplace and to adopt concepts of human rights that accord with those in the United States, resentment of the U.S. behemoth and fears of U.S. global domination are once again on the rise, as they were during the immediate postwar era.

Asian Miracle or Asian Myth?

Until the late 1990s, the one area in the capitalist world that seemed to be in a strong position to advance rapidly in the economic sphere without suffering the social and political strains experienced in the West was East Asia, where Japan and the so-called Little Tigers appeared to combine rapid economic growth with a minimum of social problems and a considerable degree of political stability. Pundits in the region and abroad opined that the "East Asian miracle" was a product of the amalgamation of capitalist economic techniques and a value system inherited from Confucius that stressed hard work, frugality, and the subordination of the individual to the community—all reminiscent of the "Puritan ethic" of the early capitalist era in the West.

There is indeed some similarity between the recent performance of many East Asian societies and early capitalism in the West. Some commentators in East Asia have pointed with pride to their traditional values and remarked that in the West such values as hard work and a habit of saving have been replaced by a certain hedonism that values individual over community interests and prizes immediate gratification over future needs. Some observers in the West have agreed with this assessment and lamented the complacency and rampant materialism of Western culture.

The financial crisis of 1997 (see Chapter 12), however, demonstrated that the Pacific nations were not immune to the vicissitudes of capitalism and that overconfidence and lack of attention to fundamentals could be as destructive on one side of the ocean as the other. Mesmerized by the rhetorical vision of the Confucian work ethic and less experienced in riding the choppy waves of the capitalist business cycle, Asian governments and entrepreneurs alike became too complacent in thinking that the bull market in the region would never end. Banks extended loans on shaky projects, and governments invested heavily in expensive infrastructure improvements that exploded budget deficits but promised few financial returns until the distant future. When foreign investors grew wary and began withdrawing their funds, the bubble burst. It was a sobering experience. As one commentator put it, "It was all too Disneyland; so much glass that was too shiny. Now they are going through a cultural crisis triggered by the economic crisis. These countries have to become more pragmatic."[1]

The fiscal crisis of the late 1990s serves as a warning signal that success—in East Asia as in the West—is the product of hard work and can never be assumed. The economic fundamentals in many East Asian countries are essentially sound, however, and by the beginning of the new millennium, the region had recovered from the slowdown and resumed the steady growth that had characterized its performance during the last quarter of the twentieth century. Indeed, all signs indicate that, with the emergence of China and India as major players, the Asian region is poised to become an even more important component in the international marketplace.

China in particular has become a major force in the global economy, replacing Japan as the largest source of U.S. imports and supplanting the United States as Southeast Asia's biggest trading partner. Many observers see China, with its growing industrial base and abundant supply of cheap labor, as the most serious threat to the U.S. economic hegemony. More important in the long run, perhaps, is that China has become a leading oil importer, helping to drive up the price of oil on world markets and contributing to the threat of global warming.

Eliminating Poverty

The greatest failure of the global economy in the new millennium is the continued high level of poverty in many parts of the world. According to recent figures, more than one billion people—almost one-fifth of the entire world population—live on an income of less than one U.S. dollar a day. An equal number are illiterate, while hundreds of thousands die annually from malnutrition, hunger, or disease. At a Millennium Summit held in the year 2000, the United Nations adopted a plan calling for the advanced nations to double their financial assistance to poorer countries, while taking measures to equalize the playing field in the realm of trade to assist the developing countries in working their way out of debt. The declared goal was to reduce the number of those suffering extreme poverty and hunger by half by the year 2015, while reducing infant mortality and ensuring basic education for all the world's children.

Five years later, the UN General Assembly returned to the issue, approving a broad list of goals to carry through on the basic commitment. But the acrimony of the debate demonstrated how difficult the task would be to achieve, and the final results were disappointing to delegates of the poor countries. Disagreements on how to fight terrorism and protect human rights, combined with the unwillingness of industrial countries to open their markets to agricultural imports, prevented the delegates from implementing a plan. The U.S. delegation refused to make a specific financial commitment, pointing out that without honest and efficient governments in the poorer countries, foreign assistance would be squandered or fall into the hands of corrupt local officials. Once again, the failure to achieve concrete results demonstrated that ending widespread poverty is among the most tenacious problems facing the global community today.

From the Industrial to the Technological Revolution

As many observers have noted, the world economy as a whole is in the process of transition to what has been called a "postindustrial age," characterized by the emergence of a system that is not only increasingly global in scope but also increasingly technology-intensive. This process, which futurologist Alvin Toffler has dubbed the Third Wave (the first two being the Agricultural and Industrial Revolutions), has caused difficulties for people in many walks of life— for blue-collar workers, whose high wages price them out of the market as firms begin to move their factories abroad; for the poor and uneducated, who lack the technical skills to handle complex tasks in the contemporary economy; and even for members of the middle class, who have been

China Calling. In the new century, the entire world is becoming wired, as developing nations realize that economic success depends on information technology. Shown here is a young Chinese reporting to his family on a visit to the Great Wall. It is estimated that by 2007 China will be the world's largest user of the Internet, with 300 million individuals online. By then, an equal number of Chinese will possess cell phones.

AP Images/Greg Baker

fired or forced into retirement as their employers seek to slim down to compete in the global marketplace.[2]

It is now increasingly clear that the Technological Revolution, like the Industrial Revolution that preceded it, will entail enormous consequences and may ultimately give birth to a level of social and political instability that has not been seen in the developed world since the Great Depression of the 1930s. The success of advanced capitalist states in the second half of the twentieth century was built on the foundations of a broad consensus on several propositions: (1) the importance of limiting income inequities to reduce the threat of political instability while maximizing domestic consumer demand; (2) the need for high levels of government investment in infrastructure projects such as education, communications, and transportation as a means of meeting the challenges of continued economic growth and technological innovation; and (3) the desirability of cooperative efforts in the international arena as a means of maintaining open markets for the free exchange of goods.

As the twenty-first century gains momentum, all of these assumptions are increasingly coming under attack. Citizens are reacting with growing hostility to the high tax rates needed to maintain the welfare state, refusing to support education and infrastructure development, and opposing the formation of trading alliances to promote the free movement of goods and labor across national borders. Such attitudes are being expressed by individuals and groups on all sides of the political spectrum, making the

traditional designations of left-wing and right-wing politics increasingly meaningless. Although most governments and political elites have continued to support most of the programs that underpin the welfare state and the global marketplace, they are increasingly attacked by groups in society that feel they have been victimized by the system. The breakdown of the public consensus that brought modern capitalism to a pinnacle of achievement raises serious questions about the likelihood that the coming challenge of the Third Wave can be successfully met without increasing political and social tensions in both the domestic and international arenas.

A Transvaluation of Values

Of course, not all the problems facing the advanced human societies around the world can be ascribed directly to economic factors. It is one of the paradoxes of the modern world that at a time of almost unsurpassed political stability and economic prosperity for the majority of the population in the advanced capitalist states, public cynicism about the system is increasingly widespread. Alienation and drug use among young people in many Western societies are at dangerously high levels, and although crime rates have dropped slightly in some areas, the rate of criminal activities remains much higher than in the immediate postwar era.

The Family

The reasons advanced to explain this paradox vary widely. Some observers place the responsibility for many contemporary social problems on the decline of the traditional family system. The statistics are indeed disquieting. There has been a steady rise in the percentage of illegitimate births and single-parent families in countries throughout the Western world. In the United States, approximately half of all marriages will end in divorce. Even in two-parent families, more and more parents work full time, thus leaving the children to fend for themselves on their return from school.

Observers point to several factors as an explanation for these conditions: the growing emphasis in advanced capitalist states on an individualistic lifestyle devoted to instant gratification—a phenomenon that is promoted vigorously by the advertising media—the rise of the feminist movement, which has freed women from the servitude imposed on their predecessors, but at the expense of removing them from full-time responsibility for the care and nurturing of the next generation; and the increasing mobility of contemporary life, which disrupts traditional family ties and creates a sense of rootlessness and impersonality in the individual's relationship to the surrounding environment.

What is worth noting here is that to one degree or another, the traditional nuclear family is under attack in societies around the world, not just in the West. Even in East Asia, where the Confucian tradition of filial piety and family solidarity has been endlessly touted as a major factor in the region's economic success, the incidence of divorce and illegitimate births is on the rise, as is the percentage of women in the workforce. Older citizens frequently complain that the Asian youth of today are too materialistic, faddish, and steeped in the individualistic values of the West. Such criticisms are now voiced in mainland China as well as in the capitalist societies around its perimeter. Public opinion surveys, however, suggest that some of the generational differences in Asian societies are only skin deep. When queried about their views, most young Asians express support for the same conservative values of family, hard work, and care for the elderly as their parents. Still, the evidence suggests that the trend away from the traditional family is a worldwide phenomenon.

Religion

While some analysts cite the reduced role of the traditional family as a major factor in the widespread sense of malaise in the contemporary world, others point to the decline in religion and the increasing secularization of world society. It seems indisputable that one of the causes of the widespread feeling of alienation in many societies is the absence of any sense of underlying meaning and purpose in life, which religious faith often provides. Historical experience suggests, however, that while intensity of religious fervor may enhance the sense of community among believers, it can also have a highly divisive impact on society as a whole, as the examples of Northern Ireland, Yugoslavia, and the Middle East vividly attest. Religion, by itself, cannot serve as a panacea for the problems of the contemporary world.

In any event, the issue of religion and its implications for social policy is complicated. Although the percentage of people attending church on a regular basis or professing firm religious convictions has been dropping steadily in many Western countries, the intensity of religious belief appears to be growing in many communities. This phenomenon is especially apparent in the United States, where the evangelical movement has become a significant force in politics and an influential factor in defining many social issues. But it has also occurred in Latin America, where a drop in membership in the Roman Catholic Church has been offset by significant increases in the popularity of evangelical Protestant sects. There are significant differences between the two cases, however. Whereas the evangelical movement in the United States tends to adopt conservative positions on social issues such as abortion rights, divorce, and sexual freedom, in Brazil one of the reasons advanced for the popularity of evangelical sects is the stand taken by the Vatican on issues such as divorce and abortion. In Brazil, even the vast majority of Catholics surveyed support the right to abortion in cases of rape or danger to the mother and believe in the importance of birth control to limit population growth and achieve smaller families.

For many evangelical Christians in the United States, the revival of religious convictions and the adoption of a Christian lifestyle are viewed as necessary prerequisites for resolving the problems of crime, drugs, and social alienation. Some evidence does suggest that children who attend church in the United States are less likely to be involved in crime and that they perform better in their schoolwork. Some in the evangelical movement, however, not only support a conservative social agenda but also express a growing suspicion of the role of technology and science in the contemporary world. Some Christian groups have opposed the teaching of evolutionary theory in the classroom or have demanded that public schools present the biblical interpretation of the creation of the earth. Although fear over the impact of science on contemporary life is widespread and understandable, efforts to turn the clock back to a mythical golden age are not likely to succeed in the face of powerful forces for change set in motion by advances in scientific knowledge.

Technology

Concern about the impact of technology on contemporary life is by no means limited to evangelicals. Voices across the political and social spectrum have begun to suggest that scientific advances are at least partly responsible for the psychological malaise now so prevalent in much of the modern world. The criticism dates back at least to the advent of television. Television, in the eyes of its critics, has contributed to a decline in human communication and turned viewers from active participants in the experience of life into passive observers. With the advent of the computer, the process has accelerated as recent generations of young people raised on video games and surfing the World Wide Web find less and less time for personal relationships or creative activities. At the same time, however, the Internet provides an avenue for lonely individuals to communicate with the outside world and seek out others with common interests. The most that can be said at the present time is that such innovations provide both an opportunity and a danger—an opportunity to explore new avenues of communication and a danger that in the process, the nature of the human experience will be irrevocably changed.

Capitalism

Some theorists argue that the party most responsible for the hedonism and materialism of contemporary life is the capitalist system, which has raised narcissism and conspicuous consumerism to unprecedented heights in modern consciousness. It is no doubt true that by promoting material consumption as perhaps the supreme good, modern capitalism has encouraged the acquisitive side of human nature and undermined the traditional virtues of frugality and self-denial and the life of the spirit. As Karl Marx perceptively noted more than a century ago, under capitalism money is "the universal self-constituted value of all things. It has therefore robbed the whole world, human as well as natural, of its own values."[3]

Perhaps, however, it is more accurate to state that capitalism simply recognizes the acquisitive side of human nature and sets out to make a profit from it. Recent events around the world suggest that efforts to suppress the acquisitive instinct are ultimately doomed to fail, no matter how stringently they are applied. It is thus left to individual human beings, families, and communities to decide how to supplement material aspirations with the higher values traditionally associated with the human experience. Perhaps it is worth observing that more than once, capitalism has demonstrated the ability to rectify its shortcomings when they threaten the survival of the system. It remains to be seen whether it can successfully deal with the corrosive effects of contemporary materialism on the traditional spiritual longings of humankind.

One World, One Environment

Another crucial factor that is affecting the evolution of society and the global economy is growing concern over the impact of industrialization on the earth's environment. There is nothing new about human beings causing damage to their natural surroundings. It may first have occurred when Neolithic peoples began to practice slash-and-burn agriculture or when excessive hunting thinned out the herds of bison and caribou in the Western Hemisphere. It almost certainly played a major role in the decline of the ancient civilizations in the Persian Gulf region and later of the Roman Empire.

Never before, however, has the danger of significant ecological damage been as extensive as during the past century. The effects of chemicals introduced into the atmosphere or into rivers, lakes, and oceans have increasingly threatened the health and well-being of all living species. For many years, the main focus of environmental concern was in the developed countries of the West, where industrial effluents, automobile exhausts, and the use of artificial fertilizers and insecticides led to urban smog, extensive damage to crops and wildlife, and a major reduction of the ozone layer in the upper atmosphere. In recent decades, however, it has become clear that the problem is now global in scope and demands vigorous action in the international arena.

The opening of Eastern Europe after the revolutions of 1989 brought to the world's attention the incredible environmental destruction in that region caused by unfettered industrial pollution. Communist governments had obviously operated under the assumption that production quotas were much more important than environmental protection. The nuclear power disaster at Chernobyl in the Ukraine in 1986 made Europeans acutely aware of potential environmental hazards, and 1987 was touted as the "year of the environment." In response, many European states implemented new regulations to protect the environment and established government ministries to oversee environmental issues.

For some, such official actions were insufficient, and beginning in the 1980s, a number of new political parties were established to focus exclusively on environmental issues. Although these so-called Green movements and parties have played an important role in making people aware of ecological problems, they have by no means been able to control the debate. Too often, environmental issues come out second in clashes with economic issues. Still, during the 1990s, more and more European governments were beginning to sponsor projects to safeguard the environment and clean up the worst sources of pollution.

In recent years, the problem has spread elsewhere. China's headlong rush to industrialization has resulted in major ecological damage in that country. Industrial smog has created almost unlivable conditions in many cities, and hillsides denuded of their forests have caused severe problems of erosion and destruction of farmlands. Some environmentalists believe that levels of pollution in China are already higher than in the fully developed industrial societies of the West, a reality that raises serious questions about Beijing's ability to re-create the automotive culture of the modern West in China.

Destruction of the rain forest is a growing problem in many parts of the world, notably in Brazil and in the Indonesian archipelago. With the forest cover throughout the earth rapidly declining, there is less plant life to perform the crucial process of reducing carbon dioxide levels in the atmosphere. In 1997, forest fires on the Indonesian islands of Sumatra and Borneo created a blanket of smoke over the entire region, forcing schools and offices to close and causing thousands of respiratory ailments. Some of the damage could be attributed to the traditional slash-and-burn techniques used by subsistence farmers to clear forest cover for their farmlands, but the primary cause was the clearing of forestland to create or expand palm oil plantations, one of the region's major sources of export revenue.

The Issue of Global Warming

One of the few salutary consequences of such incidents has been a growing international consensus that environmental concerns have taken on a truly global character. Although the danger of global warming—allegedly caused by the release, as a result of industrialization, of certain gases into the atmosphere—has not yet been definitively proved, it had become a source of sufficient concern to bring about an international conference on the subject in Kyoto in December 1997. If, as many scientists predict, worldwide temperatures should increase, the rise in sea levels could pose a significant threat to low-lying islands and coastal areas throughout the world, while climatic change could lead to severe droughts or excessive rainfall in cultivated areas.

It is one thing to recognize a problem, however, and quite another to resolve it. So far, cooperative efforts among nations to alleviate environmental problems have all too often been hindered by economic forces or by political, ethnic, and religious disputes. The 1997 conference on global warming, for example, was marked by bitter disagreement over the degree to which developing countries should share the burden of cleaning up the environment. As a result, it achieved few concrete results. The fact is that few nations have been willing to take unilateral action that might pose an obstacle to economic development plans or lead to a rise in unemployment. India, Pakistan, and Bangladesh have squabbled over the use of the waters of the Ganges and Indus rivers, as have Israel and its neighbors over the scarce water resources of the Middle East.

Pollution of the Rhine River by factories along its banks provokes angry disputes among European nations, and the United States and Canada have argued about the effects of acid rain on Canadian forests.

Today, such disputes represent a major obstacle to the challenge of meeting the threat of global warming. Measures to reduce the release of harmful gases into the atmosphere will be costly and could have significant negative effects on economic growth. Politicians who embrace such measures, then, are risking political suicide. As President Bill Clinton remarked about a proposal to reduce the danger of global warming by raising energy prices, such a measure "either won't pass the Senate or it won't pass muster with the American people." In any event, what is most needed is a degree of international cooperation that would bring about major efforts to reduce pollution levels throughout the world. So far, there is little indication that advanced and developing nations are close to agreement on how the sacrifice is to be divided. International meetings convened to discuss how to implement the agreement hammered out at the Kyoto conference have been mired in dispute, and in 2001, President George W. Bush declared that the United States would not sign the treaty as it stands. Yet, as evidence of the severity of the problem continues to accumulate, the need for a global effort to deal with the challenge is becoming increasingly clear.

The Population Debate

At the root of much of the concern about the environment is the worry that the global population could eventually outstrip the capacity of the world to feed itself. Concern over excessive population growth, of course, dates back to the early nineteenth century, when the British economist Thomas Malthus worried that the population would increase more rapidly than the food supply. Such fears peaked in the decades immediately following World War II, when a rise in world birthrates and a decline in infant mortality combined to fuel a dramatic increase in population in much of the Third World. The concern was set aside for a period after the 1970s, when the Green Revolution improved crop yields and statistical evidence appeared to suggest that the rate of population growth was declining in many countries of Asia and Latin America.

Yet some experts question whether increases in food production through technological innovation (in recent years, the Green Revolution has been supplemented by a "Blue Revolution" to increase food yields from the world's oceans, seas, and rivers) can keep up indefinitely with world population growth, which continues today, though at a slightly reduced rate from earlier levels. From a total of 2.5 billion people in 1950, world population rose to 6.5 billion in 2006 and is predicted to exceed 9 billion by the middle of this century. Today, many eyes are focused on India, where the population recently surpassed one billion, and on China, where family planning programs have lost effectiveness in recent years and where precious rice lands have been turned to industrial or commercial use.

Many European countries (notably France, Italy, and Russia) have the opposite problem, as low fertility rates among European-born women raise the prospect of lower population levels in the near future. A decrease in population not only would lead to labor shortages, thereby increasing the need for "guest workers" from Africa and the Middle East, but also would reduce the number of employed workers paying taxes, making it difficult to maintain expensive welfare programs. Some European countries are now providing financial incentives to encourage young citizens to have larger families.

Global Village or Clash of Civilizations?

For four decades, such global challenges were all too frequently submerged in the public consciousness as the two major power blocs competed for advantage. The collapse of the Soviet Union brought an end to the Cold War but left world leaders almost totally unprepared to face the consequences. Statesmen, scholars, and political pundits began to forecast the emergence of a "new world order." Few, however, had any real idea of what it would entail. With the division of the world into two squabbling ideological power blocs suddenly at an end, there was little certainty, and much speculation, about what was going to take its place.

One hypothesis that won support in some quarters was that the decline of communism signaled that the industrial capitalist democracies of the West had triumphed in the war of ideas and would now proceed to remake the rest of the world in their own image. Some people cited a widely discussed book, *The End of History and the Last Man,* in which the American scholar Francis Fukuyama argued that capitalism and the Western concept of liberal democracy, while hardly ideal in their capacity to satisfy all human aspirations, are at least more effective than rival doctrines in achieving those longings and therefore deserve consideration as the best available ideology to be applied universally throughout the globe.[4]

Fukuyama's thesis provoked a firestorm of debate. Many critics pointed out the absence of any religious component in the liberal democratic model and argued the need for a return to religious faith, with its emphasis on the life of the spirit and traditional moral values. Others, noting that greater human freedom and increasing material prosperity have led not to a heightened sense of human achievement and emotional satisfaction but rather to increasing alienation

and a crass pursuit of hedonistic pleasures, argued that a new and perhaps "postmodernist" paradigm for the human experience must be found.

Whether or not Fukuyama's proposition is true, it is much too early to assume (as he would no doubt admit) that the liberal democratic model has in fact triumphed in the clash of ideas that dominated the twentieth century. Although it is no doubt true that much of the world is now linked together in the economic marketplace created by the Western industrial nations, it seems clear from the discussion of contemporary issues in this chapter that, despite their current dominating position as a result of the decline of communism, the future hegemony of Western political ideas and institutions is by no means assured.

For one thing, in much of the world today, Western values are threatened or are under direct attack. Such views are most prevalent in the Middle East, where the efforts of the administration of George W. Bush to promote democracy in the region have met with widespread resistance. But even in East Asia, where pluralistic societies have begun to appear in a number of industrializing countries, leading political figures have expressed serious reservations about Western concepts of democracy and individualism and openly questioned their relevance to their societies. The issue was raised at a meeting of the ASEAN states in July 1997, when feisty Malaysian Prime Minister Mahathir Mohamad declared that the Universal Declaration of Human Rights, passed after World War II at the behest of the victorious Western nations, was not appropriate to the needs of poorer non-Western countries and should be reviewed. The reaction was immediate. One U.S. official attending the conference retorted that the sentiments contained in the Universal Declaration were "shared by all peoples and all cultures" and had not been imposed by the West. Nevertheless, a number of political leaders in the region echoed Mahathir's views and insisted on the need for a review.

At the same conference, some argued that in defining human rights almost exclusively in terms of individual freedom, Western commentators have ignored the importance of providing adequate food and shelter for all members of society. Such comments were quickly seconded by Chinese president Jiang Zemin, who declared during a visit to the United States later in the year that human rights were not a matter that could be dictated by the powerful nations of the world but rather were an issue to be determined by individual societies on the basis of their own traditions and course of development.

It is possible, of course, that the liberal democratic model will become more acceptable in parts of Africa and Asia to the degree that societies in those regions proceed successfully through the advanced stages of the Industrial and Technological Revolutions, thus giving birth to the middle-class values that underlie modern civilization in the

West. There is no guarantee, however, that current conditions, which have been relatively favorable to that process, will continue indefinitely, or that all peoples and all societies will share equally in the benefits. The fact is that just as the Industrial Revolution exacerbated existing tensions in and among the nations of Europe, globalization and the Technological Revolution are imposing their own strains on human societies today. Should such strains become increasingly intense, they could trigger political and social conflict.

In *The Clash of Civilizations and the Remaking of the World Order,* Samuel P. Huntington has responded to these concerns by suggesting that the post–Cold War era, far from marking the triumph of Western ideas, will be characterized by increased global fragmentation and a "clash of civilizations" based on ethnic, cultural, or religious differences. According to Huntington, cultural identity has replaced shared ideology as the dominant force in world affairs. As a result, he argues, the coming decades may see the world dominated by disputing cultural blocs in East Asia, Western Europe and the United States, Eurasia, and the Middle East, with the societies in each region coalescing around common cultural features against perceived threats from rival forces elsewhere around the globe. The dream of a universal order dominated by Western values, he concludes, is a fantasy.[5]

Events in recent years have provided some support for Huntington's hypothesis. The collapse of the Soviet Union led to the emergence of several squabbling new nations and a general atmosphere of conflict and tension in the Balkans and at other points along the perimeter of the old Soviet Empire. Even more dramatically, the terrorist attack in September 2001 appeared to have set the advanced nations of the West and the Muslim world on a collision course.

In fact, the phenomenon is worldwide in scope and growing in importance. Even as the world becomes more global in culture and interdependent in its mutual relations, forces have been at work attempting to redefine the political, cultural, and ethnic ways in which it is divided. This process is taking place not only in developing countries but also in the West, where fear of the Technological Revolution and public anger at the impact of globalization and foreign competition have reached disturbing levels. Such views are often dismissed by sophisticated commentators as atavistic attempts by uninformed people seeking to return to a mythical past. But perhaps they should more accurately be interpreted as an inevitable consequence of the rising thirst for self-protection and group identity in an impersonal and rapidly changing world. Shared culture is one defense against the impersonal world around us.

Huntington's thesis serves as a useful corrective to the complacent tendency of many observers in Europe and the United States to see Western civilization as the zenith and the final destination of human achievement. In Western leaders' efforts to promote the concepts of universal human rights and a global marketplace, there is a recognizable element of the cultural arrogance that was reflected in the doctrine of social Darwinism at the end of the nineteenth century. Both views take as their starting point the assumption that the Western conceptualization of the human experience is universal in scope and will ultimately, inexorably spread to the rest of the world. Neither gives much credence to the view that other civilizations might have seized on a corner of the truth and thus have something to offer.

That is not to say, however, that Huntington's vision of clashing civilizations is necessarily the most persuasive characterization of the probable state of the world in the twenty-first century. In dividing the world into competing cultural blocs, Huntington has probably underestimated the centrifugal forces at work in the various regions of the world. As many critics have noted, deep-rooted cultural and historical rivalries exist among the various nations in southern and eastern Asia and in the Middle East, as well as in Africa, preventing any meaningful degree of mutual cooperation against allegedly hostile forces in the outside world. Differences between the United States and leading European nations over the decision to invade Iraq demonstrate that fissures are growing even within the Western alliance.

Huntington also tends to ignore the transformative effect of the Industrial Revolution and the emerging global information network. As the Industrial and Technological Revolutions spread across the face of the earth, their impact is measurably stronger in some societies than in others, intensifying political, economic, and cultural distinctions in a given region while establishing links between individual societies in that region and their counterparts undergoing similar experiences in other parts of the world. Whereas the parallel drive to global industrial hegemony encouraged Japan and the United States to cooperate on a variety of issues, for example, it has intensified tensions between Japan and its competitor South Korea and weakened the political and cultural ties that have historically existed between Japan and China.

The most likely scenario for the next few decades, then, is more complex than either the global village hypothesis or its conceptual rival, the clash of civilizations. The world of the twenty-first century will be characterized by simultaneous trends toward globalization and fragmentation, as the inexorable thrust of technology and information transforms societies and gives rise to counterreactions among individuals and communities seeking to preserve a group identity and a sense of meaning and purpose in a confusing world.

Under such conditions, how can world leaders hope to resolve localized conflicts and prevent them from spreading into neighboring regions, with consequences that could bring an end to the current period of economic expansion and usher in a new era of global impoverishment? To some analysts, the answer lies in strengthening the ability of the

United Nations and various regional security organizations to deal effectively with local conflicts. In recent years, the UN has dispatched peacekeeping missions to nearly twenty different nations on five continents, with a total troop commitment of more than 40,000 military personnel. Nearly 100,000 NATO troops are currently attempting to preserve a fragile cease-fire in the Balkans. The challenge is not only to bring about an end to a particular conflict but also to resolve the problems that gave rise to the dispute in the first place.

Some observers argue that the UN and similar multinational organizations are not the answer. The administration of George W. Bush, for example, has preferred to place its faith in unilateral strategies such as the construction of an antimissile defense system (a successor of the "Star Wars" project of the 1980s), combined with a policy of disengagement from conflicts that arise in areas deemed not vital to U.S. national security. One drawback to such an approach is that conflicts in isolated parts of the world often have the potential to spread, thus affecting issues of vital concern such as the oil supply in the Middle East or the safety of trade routes in Southeast Asia.

The U.S. decision to launch a preemptive invasion of Iraq in 2003 has also sparked controversy, arousing misgivings among its allies in Europe, who fear that unilateral actions not sanctioned by the UN could undermine global stability and spark a wave of anti-U.S. sentiment in various parts of the world.

The Arts: Mirror of the Age

If, as the Spanish tenor Placido Domingo once observed, the arts are the signature of their age, what has been happening in literature, art, music, and architecture in recent decades is a reflection of the evolving global response to the rapid changes taking place in human society today. This reaction has sometimes been described as Postmodernism, although today's developments are much too diverse to be placed under a single label. Some of the arts are still experimenting with the modernist quest for the new and the radical. Others have begun to return to more traditional styles as a reaction against globalization and a response to the search for national and cultural identity in a bewildering world.

The most appropriate label for the contemporary cultural scene, in fact, is probably pluralism. The arts today are an eclectic hybrid, combining different movements, genres, and media, as well as incorporating different ethnic or national characteristics. There is no doubt that Western culture has strongly influenced the development of the arts throughout the world in recent decades. In fact, the process has gone in both directions as art forms from Africa and Asia have profoundly enriched the cultural scene in the West. One ironic illustration is that some of the best literature in the English and French languages today is being written in the nations that were once under British or French colonial rule. Today, global interchange in the arts is playing the same creative role that the exchange of technology between different regions played in stimulating the Industrial Revolution. As one Japanese composer declared not long ago, "I would like to develop in two directions at once: as a Japanese with respect to tradition, and as a Westerner with respect to innovation. . . . In that way I can avoid isolation from the tradition and yet also push toward the future in each new work."[6]

Such a globalization of culture, however, has its price. Because of the popularity of Western culture throughout the developing world, local cultural forms are being eroded and destroyed as a result of contamination by Western music, mass television, and commercial hype. Although what has been called the "McWorld culture" of Coca-Cola, jeans, and rock is considered merely cosmetic by some, others see it as cultural neoimperialism and a real cause for alarm. How does a society preserve its traditional culture when the young prefer to spend their evenings at a Hard Rock Café rather than attend a traditional folk opera or *wayang* puppet theater? World conferences have been convened to safeguard traditional cultures from extinction, but is there sufficient time, money, or inclination to reverse the tide?

What do contemporary trends in the art world have to say about the changes that have occurred since the beginning of the twentieth century? One reply is that the euphoric optimism of artists during the age of Picasso and Stravinsky has been seriously tempered a century later. Naiveté has been replaced by cynicism or irony as protection against the underlying pessimism of the current age.

One dominant characteristic of the new art is its reticence—its reserve in expressing the dissonance and disillusioning events of the past century. It would appear that we entered the twentieth century with too many expectations, hopes that had been fueled by the promise of revolution and scientific discoveries. Yet however extraordinary the recent advances in medicine, genetics, telecommunications, computer technology, and space exploration have been, humankind seems to remain as befuddled as ever. It is no wonder that despite the impressive recent advances in science, human beings entered the new millennium a little worn and subdued.

What, then, are the prospects for the coming years? One critic has complained that Postmodernism, "with its sad air of the parades gone by,"[7] is spent and exhausted. Others suggest that there is nothing new left to say that has not been expressed previously and more effectively. The public itself appears satiated and desensitized after a century of "shocking" art and, as in the case of world events, almost incapable of being shocked any further. Human sensibilities have been irrevocably altered by the media, by technology,

Photograph by David Heald © Solomon R. Guggenheim Foundation, NY

The Shape of the Future? The Guggenheim Museum in Bilbao, Spain, is one of the most outstanding buildings of the twentieth century. Completed in 1997 by the American architect Frank Gehry, its curvilinear form stands in sharp contrast to the square and rectangular buildings long favored by his Modernist counterparts. The museum hugs the Nervión River in northern Spain like a graceful sailing ship, its billowing sails of titanium glistening in the sun.

and especially by the cataclysmic events that have taken place in our times. Perhaps the twentieth century was the age of revolt, representing "freedom from," while the next hundred years will be an era seeking "freedom for."

What is comforting is that no matter how pessimistic and disillusioned people claim to be, hope springs eternal as young writers, artists, and composers continue to grapple with their craft, searching for new ways to express the human condition. How can one not be astonished by architect Frank Gehry's Guggenheim Museum in Bilbao, Spain (see the photo above), with its thrusting turrets and billowing sails of titanium? Such exuberance can only testify to humanity's indomitable spirit and ceaseless imagination—characteristics that are badly needed in the world today.

CHAPTER NOTES

1. Henny Sender, "Now for the Hard Part," *Far Eastern Economic Review,* September 25, 1997.
2. Alvin Toffler and Heidi Toffler, *Creating a New Civilization: The Politics of the Third Wave* (Atlanta, 1995).
3. Quoted in John Cassidy, "The Return of Karl Marx," *New Yorker,* October 20, 1997, p. 250.
4. Fukuyama's original thesis was expressed in "The End of History," *National Interest,* Summer 1989. He has defended his views in Timothy Burns, ed., *After History? Francis Fukuyama and His Critics* (Lanham, Md., 1994). Fukuyama contends—rightly in my view—that his concept of the "end of history" has been widely misinterpreted. I hope I have not done so in these comments.
5. Samuel P. Huntington, *The Clash of Civilizations and the Remaking of the World Order* (New York, 1996). An earlier version was published under the title "The Clash of Civilizations?" in *Foreign Affairs,* Summer 1993.
6. The composer was Toru Takemitsu. See Robert P. Moran, *Twentieth-Century Music* (New York, 1991), p. 422.
7. Herbert Muschamp, "The Miracle in Bilbao," *New York Times Magazine,* September 7, 1997, p. 72.

Chapter 1. The Rise of Industrial Society in the West

For a useful introduction to the Industrial Revolution, see D. Landes, *The Unbound Prometheus: Technological Change and Industrial Development in Western Europe from 1750 to the Present* (Cambridge, 1969). More technical but also of value is P. Mathias and J. A. David (eds.), *The First Industrial Revolution* (Oxford, 1989). A provocative analysis of the roots of industrialization is D. Landes, *The Wealth and Poverty of Nations: Why Some Are So Rich and Some So Poor* (New York, 1997).

On the phenomenon of population growth in the West, see T. McKeown, *The Rise of Population* (London, 1976). Housing reform is discussed in N. Bullock and J. Read, *The Movement for Housing Reform in Germany and France, 1840–1914* (Cambridge, 1985), and E. Gauldie, *Cruel Habitations: A History of Working-Class Housing, 1790–1918* (London, 1974). On Karl Marx, the standard work is D. McLellan, *Karl Marx: His Life and Thought* (New York, 1974). On Freud, see P. Gay, *Freud: A Life for Our Time* (New York, 1988).

For a reinterpretation of Victorian society, see P. Gay, *Pleasure Wars: The Bourgeois Experience, Victoria to Freud* (New York, 1998). Changing social mores are examined in J. Flanders, *Inside the Victorian Home* (New York, 2004). On the intellectual scene, see William R. Everdell, *The First Moderns: Profiles in the Origins of Twentieth Century Thought* (Chicago, 1997), and J. W. Barrow, *The Crisis of Reason: European Thought, 1848–1914* (New Haven, 2000). On trends in modern art, see Robert Hughes, *The Shock of the New* (New York, 1991).

Chapter 2. The High Tide of Imperialism: Africa and Asia in an Era of Western Dominance

There are a number of recent works on the subject of imperialism and colonialism. For a study that focuses on the complex interaction between the colonial powers and the subject peoples, see D. K. Fieldhouse, *The West and the Third World: Trade, Colonialism, Dependence, and Development* (Oxford,

1999). In *Ornamentalism: How the British Saw Their Empire* (Oxford, 2000), D. Cannadine argues that it was class, not race, that motivated British policy in its colonies. For a carefully reasoned critique of the colonial experience, see D. Abernathy, *The Dynamics of Global Dominance: European Overseas Empires, 1415–1980* (New Haven, 2000). A spirited defense of the British colonial experience is presented in N. Ferguson, *Empire: The Rise and Demise of the British World Order and the Lessons for Global Power* (Basic Books, 2002). On the new technology, see D. R. Headrick, *The Tentacles of Progress: Technology Transfer in the Age of Imperialism, 1850–1940* (Oxford, 1988).

On the imperialist age in Africa, see T. Pakenham, *The Scramble for Africa* (New York, 1991) and B. Vandervoort, *Wars of Imperial Conquest in Africa, 1830–1914* (Bloomington, Ind., 1998). For India, see C. A. Bayly, *Indian Society and the Making of the British Empire* (Cambridge, 1988).

Chapter 3. Shadows over the Pacific: East Asia Under Challenge

The classic general overview of the era is J. K. Fairbank, A. M. Craig, and E. O. Reischauer, *East Asia: Tradition and Transformation* (Boston, 1973). Highly stimulating is J. Spence, *The Search for Modern China* (New York, 1990). On the Western intrusion, see F. Wakeman, *Strangers at the Gate: Social Disorder in South China, 1839–1861* (Berkeley, Calif., 1966), and P. W. Fay, *The Opium War, 1840–1842* (Chapel Hill, N.C., 1975). On the Taiping Rebellion, a good recent account is J. Spence, *God's Chinese Son: The Taiping Heavenly Kingdom of Hong Xiuquan* (New York, 1996).

For an overview of the final decades of the Chinese Empire, see F. Wakeman Jr., *The Fall of Imperial China* (New York, 1975). A stimulating comparison between Western and Chinese experiences with industrialization is K. Pomeranz, *The Great Divergence: China, Europe, and the Making of the Modern World Economy* (Princeton, N.J., 2000). For a recent biography of the Chinese revolutionary Sun Yat-sen, see Marie-Claire Bergère, *Sun Yat-sen* (Stanford, Calif., 1998).

On Japan, see M. B. Jansen (ed.), *The Emergence of Meiji Japan* (Cambridge, 1995), and C. Gluck, *Japan's Modern*

Myths: Ideology in the Late Meiji Period (Princeton, N.J., 1985). Its rise as an imperialist power is discussed in M. R. Peattie and R. Myers, *The Japanese Colonial Empire, 1895–1945* (Princeton, N.J., 1984). Also see D. Keene, *Emperor of Japan: Meiji and his world, 1852–1912* (New York, 2000).

Chapter 4. War and Revolution: World War I and Its Aftermath

A good starting point for the causes of World War I is J. Joll, *The Origins of the First World War* (London, 1984). Two good recent accounts on the war are M. Gilbert, *The First World War* (New York, 1994), and J. M. Winter's lavishly illustrated *Experience of World War I* (New York, 1989). A good overview by a renowned military historian is J. Keegan, *The First World War* (New York, 2000). For the making of the peace, see M. MacMillan, *Paris 1919: Six Months that Changed the World* (New York, 2003). On the Great Depression, see C. P. Kindleberger, *The World in Depression, 1929–1939*, rev. ed. (Berkeley, Calif., 1986), and P. Brenden, *The Dark Valley: A Panorama of the 1930s* (New York, 2000). For the revolution in musical composition, see R. P. Morgan, *Twentieth-Century Music: A History of Musical Style in Modern Europe and America* (New York, 1991). For an introduction to modern art, see N. Stangos, *Concepts of Modern Art: From Fauvism to Postmodernism* (London, 1994), and J.-L. Forrier (ed.), *Art of the Twentieth Century: The History of Art Year by Year from 1900 to 1999* (Paris, 2002).

A good introduction to the Russian Revolution can be found in S. Fitzpatrick, *The Russian Revolution, 1917–1932* (New York, 1982), and R. V. Daniels, *Red October* (New York, 1967). On Lenin, see R. Service, *Lenin: A Biography* (Cambridge, Mass., 2001), and R. Pipes, *The Unknown Lenin: From the Soviet Archives* (New Haven, 1997).

Chapter 5. Nationalism, Revolution, and Dictatorship: Africa, Asia, and Latin America from 1919 to 1939

The classic study of nationalism in the non-Western world is R. Emerson, *From Empire to Nation* (Boston, 1960). For an inquiry into the origins of the concept of nationalism, see B. Anderson, *Imagined Communities* (London, 1983), and P. Chatterjee, *The Nation and Its Fragments: Colonial and Postcolonial Histories* (Princeton, N.J., 1993).

There have been a number of interesting studies of Mahatma Gandhi and his ideas. For example, see S. Wolpert, *Gandhi's Passion: The Life and Legacy of Mahatma Gandhi* (Oxford, 1999).

For a general survey of events in the Middle East, see E. C. Bogle, *The Modern Middle East: From Imperialism to Freedom, 1800–1958* (Upper Saddle River, N.J., 1996). A more specialized treatment is H. M. Sachar, *The Emergence of the Middle East, 1914–1924* (New York, 1969). On the early Chinese republic, a good study is J. Fitzgerald, *Awakening China: Politics, Culture, and Class in the Nationalist Revolution* (Stanford, 1996). The rise of the Chinese Communist Party is discussed in A. Dirlik, *The Origins of Chinese Communism* (Oxford, 1989). Also see J. Fenby, *Chiang Kai-shek: China's Generalissimo and the Nation He Lost* (New York, 2003). For an overview of Latin American history in the interwar period, see E. Williamson, *The Penguin History of Latin America* (Harmondsworth, England, 1992). Also see J. Franco, *The Modern Culture of Latin America: Society and the Artist* (Harmondsworth, England, 1970).

Chapter 6. The Crisis Deepens: The Outbreak of World War II

For a general study of fascism, see S. G. Payne, *A History of Fascism* (Madison, Wis., 1996). The best biography of Mussolini is D. Mack Smith, *Mussolini* (New York, 1982). Two brief but sound surveys of Nazi Germany are J. Spielvogel, *Hitler and Nazi Germany: A History,* 3d ed. (Englewood Cliffs, N.J., 1996), and J. Bendersky, *A History of Nazi Germany* (Chicago, 1985). On Hitler, see A. Bullock, *Hitler: A Study in Tyranny* (New York, 1964), and Bullock's recent *Hitler, 1889–1936: Hubris* (New York, 1999). For an analysis of how Hitler changed Germany, see J. Lucas, *The Hitler of History* (New York, 1997).

General works on World War II include M. K. Dziewanowski, *War at Any Price: World War II in Europe, 1939–1945,* 2d ed. (Englewood Cliffs, N.J., 1991), and G. Weinberg, *A World at Arms: A Global History of World War II* (Cambridge, 1994). On the Holocaust, see R. Hilberg, *The Destruction of the European Jews,* rev. ed., 3 vols. (New York, 1985), and L. Yahil, *The Holocaust* (New York, 1990). On the war in the Pacific, see R. Spector, *The Eagle Against the Sun: The American War with Japan* (New York, 1991), and H. Cook and T. Cook, *Japan at War: An Oral History* (New York, 1992). Allied strategy is examined in. M. Beschloss, *The Conquerors: Roosevelt, Truman, and the Destruction of Hitler's Germany* (New York, 2002).

Chapter 7. East and West in the Grip of the Cold War

There is a substantial literature on the Cold War. Two general accounts are R. B. Levering, *The Cold War, 1945–1972* (Arlington Heights, Ill., 1982), and B. A. Weisberger, *Cold War, Cold Peace: The United States and Russia Since 1945* (New York, 1984). For a balanced treatment of the Cold War in retrospect, see J. L. Gaddis, *The Cold War: A New History* (New York, 2005). Also see M. Frankel, *High Noon in the Cold War: Kennedy, Khrushchev, and the Cuban Missile Crisis* (New York, 2004). On the end of the Cold War, see W. G. Hyland, *The Cold War Is Over* (New York, 1990), and B. Denitch, *The End of the Cold War* (Minneapolis, 1990).

Recent studies on the Cold War in Asia include O. A. Westad, *Cold War and Revolution: Soviet-American Rivalry and the Origins of the Chinese Civil War* (New York, 1993), D. A. Mayers, *Cracking the Monolith: U.S. Policy Against the Sino-Soviet Alliance, 1949–1955* (Baton Rouge, La., 1986), and S. Goncharov, J. W. Lewis, and Xue Litai, *Uncertain Partners: Stalin, Mao, and the Korean War* (Stanford, Calif., 1993). For a retrospective account, see J. L. Gaddis, *We Now Know: Rethinking Cold War History* (Oxford, 1997). On the role of Vietnam in the Cold War, see F. Logevall, *Choosing War: The Lost Chance for Peace and the Escalation of the War in Vietnam* (Berkeley, Calif., 1999), W. J. Duiker, *U.S. Containment Policy and the Conflict in Indochina* (Stanford, Calif., 1995), and M. Lind, *Vietnam: The Necessary War* (New York, 1999).

Chapter 8. The United States, Canada, and Latin America

For a general survey of American history, see S. Thernstrom, *A History of the American People*, 2d ed. (San Diego, Calif., 1989). The Truman administration is covered in R. J. Donovan, *Tumultuous Years: The Presidency of Harry S. Truman* (New York, 1997). Also see David McCullough's prize-winning biography, *Truman* (New York, 1992). On Eisenhower, see S. Ambrose, *Eisenhower: The President* (New York, 1984). For an account of the Kennedy years, see R. Dallek, *An Unfinished Life: John F. Kennedy, 1917–1963* (Boston, 2002). On the Johnson administration, see Robert Caro's multi-volume biography, *The Years of Lyndon Johnson* (New York, 1981–). On Nixon and Watergate, see J. A. Lukas, *Nightmare: The Underside of the Nixon Years* (New York, 1976). Other insightful works include B. Glad, *Jimmy Carter: From Plains to the White House* (New York, 1980), and G. Wills, *Reagan's America: Innocents at Home* (New York, 1987).

On postwar Canadian history, see R. Bothwell, I. Drummond, and J. English, *Canada Since 1945* (Toronto, 1981).

On social issues, see W. Nugent, *The Structure of American Social History* (Bloomington, Ind., 1981). Popular culture is treated in R. Maltby (ed.), *Passing Parade: A History of Popular Culture in the Twentieth Century* (New York, 1989). On the women's liberation movement, see D. Bouchier, *The Feminist Challenge: The Movement for Women's Liberation in Britain and the United States* (New York, 1983), and A. Cherlin, *Marriage, Divorce, Remarriage* (Cambridge, Mass., 1981). D. J. Garrow, *Martin Luther King Jr. and the Southern Christian Leadership Conference* (New York, 1986), discusses the emergence of the civil rights movement. For the most accessible introduction to American literature, consult *The Norton Anthology of American Literature*, shorter 4th ed. (New York, 1995). For an overview of American art since the 1960s, see I. Sandler's fascinating *Art of the Postmodern Era* (New York, 1996).

For general surveys of Latin American history, see E. B. Burns, *Latin America: A Concise Interpretive Survey*, 4th ed. (Englewood Cliffs, N.J., 1986), and E. Williamson, *The Penguin History of Latin America* (London, 1992). Also see T. E. Skidmore and P. H. Smith, *Modern Latin America*, 3d ed. (New York, 1992). On the role of the military, see A. Rouquié, *The Military and the State in Latin America* (Berkeley, Calif., 1987). U.S.-Latin American relations are examined in B. Wood, *The Dismantling of the Good Neighbor Policy* (Austin, Tex., 1985). For individual countries examined in this chapter, see L. A. Pérez, *Cuba: Between Reform and Revolution* (New York, 1988), B. Loveman, *Chile: The Legacy of Hispanic Capitalism*, 2d ed. (New York, 1988); J. A. Booth, *The End and the Beginning: The Nicaraguan Revolution* (Boulder, Colo., 1985); J. A. Page, *Perón: A Biography* (New York, 1983); D. Rock, *Argentina, 1516–1987: From Spanish Colonization to Alfonsín*, 2d ed. (New York, 1987); R. Da Matta, *Carnivals, Rogues, and Heroes: An Interpretation of the Brazilian Dilemma* (Notre Dame, Ind., 1991); and M. C. Meyer and W. L. Sherman, *The Course of Mexican History*, 4th ed. (New York, 1991). On Latin American literature, see N. Lindstrom, *Twentieth-Century Spanish American Fiction* (Austin, Tex., 1994).

Chapter 9. Brave New World: The Rise and Fall of Communism in the Soviet Union and Eastern Europe

For a general overview of Soviet society, see D. K. Shipler, *Russia: Broken Idols, Solemn Dreams* (New York, 1983). On the Khrushchev years, see W. Taubman, *Khrushchev: The Man and His Era* (New York, 2002). Also see S. F. Cohen,

Rethinking the Soviet Experience (New York, 1985). For an internal view, see V. Zubok and K. Pleshakov, *Inside the Kremlin's Cold War: From Stalin to Khrushchev* (Cambridge, 1996). For an inquiry into the reasons for the Soviet collapse, see R. Strayer, *Why Did the Soviet Union Collapse? Understanding Historical Change* (New York, 1998).

A number of books have appeared on the post-Soviet era in Russia. See, for example, R. Service, *Russia: Experiment with a People* (Cambridge, Mass., 2003), and C. Freeland, *Sale of the Century: Russia's Wild Ride from Communism to Capitalism* (New York, 2000).

For a general study of the Soviet satellites in Eastern Europe, see A. Brown and J. Gary, *Culture and Political Changes in Communist States* (London, 1977), and S. Fischer-Galati, *Eastern Europe in the 1980s* (London, 1981). On Yugoslavia, see L. J. Cohen and P. Warwick, *Political Cohesion in a Fragile Mosaic* (Boulder, Colo., 1983). For an account of the collapse of the satellite system, see T. G. Ash, *The Magic Lantern: The Revolution of '89 Witnessed in Warsaw, Budapest, Berlin, and Prague* (New York, 1990).

Chapter 10. Postwar Europe: On the Path to Unity?

For a general survey of postwar European history, see W. Laqueur, *Europe in Our Time* (New York, 1990) and T. Judt, *Postwar: A History of Europe Since 1945* (New York, 2005). The rebuilding of Europe after World War II is examined in A. Milward, *The Reconstruction of Western Europe, 1945–1951* (Berkeley, Calif., 1984), and M. Hogan, *The Marshall Plan: America, Britain, and the Reconstruction of Western Europe, 1947–1952* (New York, 1987). On the building of common institutions in Western Europe, see S. Henig, *The Uniting of Europe: From Discord to Concord* (London, 1997).

For a survey of West Germany, see H. A. Turner, *Germany from Partition to Reunification* (New Haven, Conn., 1992). On Adenauer, see C. Williams, *Adenauer: The Father of the New Germany* (New York, 2001). France under de Gaulle is examined in A. Shennan, *De Gaulle* (New York, 1993). On Britain, see K. O. Morgan, *The People's Peace: British History, 1945–1990* (Oxford, 1992). On the recent history of Europe, see E. J. Evans, *Thatcher and Thatcherism* (New York, 1997); S. Baumann-Reynolds, *François Mitterrand* (Westport, Conn., 1995), and K. Jarausch, *The Rush to German Unity* (New York, 1994).

On social conditions in Europe, see T. G. Ash, *A History of the Present: Essays, Sketches, and Dispatches from Europe in the 1990s* (New York, 1999). The problems of guest workers and immigrants are examined in J. Miller, *Foreign Workers in Western Europe* (London, 1981). On the development of the environmental movement, see M. O'Neill, *Green Parties and Political Change in Contemporary Europe* (Aldershot, England, 1997).

On the changing role of women in European society, see D. Meyer, *Sex and Power: The Rise of Women in America, Russia, Sweden and Italy* (Middletown, Conn., 1987), and C. Duchen, *Women's Rights and Women's Lives in France, 1944–1968* (New York, 1994). A broader historical view is presented in B. G. Smith, *Changing Lives: Women in European History Since 1700* (Lexington, Mass., 1989). Also see T. Keefe, *Simone de Beauvoir* (New York, 1998).

For a general view of postwar thought, see R. N. Stromberg, *European Intellectual History Since 1789*, 5th ed. (Englewood Cliffs, N.J., 1990). On contemporary art, consult R. Lambert, *Cambridge Introduction to the History of Art: The Twentieth Century* (Cambridge, 1981). Also see the bibliography in Chapter 1.

Chapter 11. The East Is Red: China Under Communism

There are a large number of useful studies on postwar China. The most comprehensive treatment of the Communist period is M. Meisner, *Mao's China, and After: A History of the People's Republic* (New York, 1986). For documents, see M. Selden, *The People's Republic of China: A Documentary History of Revolutionary Change* (New York, 1978).

There are many studies on various aspects of the Communist period in China. For a detailed analysis of economic and social issues, see F. Schurmann, *Ideology and Organization in Communist China* (Berkeley, Calif., 1968). The Cultural Revolution is treated dramatically in S. Karnow, *Mao and China: Inside China's Cultural Revolution* (New York, 1972). For an individual account, see the celebrated book by Nien Cheng, *Life and Death in Shanghai* (New York, 1986), and also Liang Heng and J. Shapiro, *After the Revolution* (New York, 1986). For the early post-Mao period, see O. Schell, *To Get Rich Is Glorious* (New York, 1986). On the Tiananmen incident, see L. Feigon's eyewitness account, *China Rising: The Meaning of Tiananmen* (Chicago, 1990). On China's dissident movement, see Liu Binyan, *China's Crisis, China's Hope* (Cambridge, 1990), and A. Nathan, *China's Transition* (New York, 1999).

On economic and political conditions in post-Mao China, see J. Gittings, *The Changing Face of China: From Mao to Market* (Oxford, 2005), T. Saioh, *Governance and Politics in China* (New York, 2002), and R. MacFarquahar (ed.), *The Politics of China: The Eras of Mao and Deng*, 2d ed. (Cambridge, 1993). Also see Bruce Gilley, *Tiger on the Brink: Jiang Zemin and China's New Elite* (Berkeley, Calif., 1998) and his more recent *China's Democratic Future: How It Will Happen and Where It Will Lead* (New York, 2004). Social conditions are considered in G. Barmée, *In the Red: On Contemporary Chinese Culture* (New York, 2000). On the controversial issue of Tibet, see T. Shakya, *The Dragon in the Land of Snows: The History of Modern Tibet Since 1947* (New York, 1999). China's changing relationship with the United States is dealt with provocatively in R. Bernstein and R. Munro, *The Coming Conflict with China* (New York, 1997).

For the most comprehensive introduction to twentieth-century Chinese art, consult M. Sullivan, *Arts and Artists of Twentieth-Century China* (Berkeley, Calif., 1996). On literature, see the chapters on Ding Ling and her contemporaries in J. Spence, *The Gate of Heavenly Peace* (New York, 1981). Also see E. Widmer and D. D. Wang (eds.), *From May Fourth to June Fourth: Fiction and Film in Twentieth-Century China* (Cambridge, 1993), and J. Lou and H. Goldblatt, *The Columbia Anthology of Modern Chinese Literature* (New York, 1995).

Chapter 12. Toward the Pacific Century? Japan and the Little Tigers

The number of books in English on modern Japan has increased in direct proportion to Japan's rise as a major industrial power. The immediate postwar era is dealt with in J. W. Dower, *Embracing Defeat: Japan in the Wake of World War II* (New York, 1999). For a topical approach with a strong emphasis on social matters, J. E. Hunter, *The Emergence of Modern Japan: An Introductory History Since 1853* (London, 1989), is excellent. General studies of modern Japan include J. McLain, *Japan: A Modern History* (New York, 2001), which debunks the myth of Japanese uniqueness, and Ian Buruma's interpretative study *Inventing Japan* (New York, 2002), which emphasizes the fragility of the country's democratic institutions.

Relatively little has been written on Japanese politics and government. Political dissent and its consequences are dealt with in N. Fields, *In the Realm of the Dying Emperor* (New York, 1991). For a contemporary treatment of economic conditions in Japan, see D. Flath, *The Japanese Economy* (Oxford, 2000). Japanese social issues are treated in R. J. Hendry, *Understanding Japanese Society* (London, 1987), and T. C. Bestor, *Neighborhood Tokyo* (Stanford, Calif., 1989). On the role of women in modern Japan, see S. Buckley, *Broken Silence: Voices of Japanese Feminism* (Berkeley, Calif., 1996), N. Bornoff, *Pink Samurai: Love, Marriage, and Sex in Contemporary Japan* (New York, 1991), and K. Fujimura-Fanselow and A. Kameda (eds.), *Japanese Women* (New York, 1995).

Books attempting to explain Japanese economic issues have become a growth industry. The classic account of the Japanese miracle is E. F. Vogel, *Japan as Number One: Lessons for America* (Cambridge, Mass., 1979). For a provocative response providing insight into Japan's current economic weakness, see J. Woronoff, *Japan as—Anything but—Number One* (Armonk, N.Y., 1991). On the role of government in promoting business in Japan, see C. Johnson, *MITI and the Japanese Miracle* (Stanford, Calif., 1982). J. Nathon's *Japan Unbound* (New York, 2004) examines the growth of social discontent in Japan since the 1990s.

On Japanese literature after World War II, see D. Keene, *Dawn to the West: Japanese Literature in the Modern Era* (New York, 1984), and A. Birnbaum, *Monkey Brain Sushi: New Tastes in Japanese Fiction* (Tokyo, 1991). For Japanese fiction, see K. Oe, *Teach Us to Outgrow Our Madness* (New York, 1977) and *The Silent Cry* (Tokyo, 1974). See also H. Murakami, *The Wind-Up Bird Chronicle* (New York, 1997).

On the four Little Tigers and their economic development, see E. F. Vogel, *The Four Little Dragons: The Spread of Industrialization in East Asia* (Cambridge, Mass., 1991), J. W. Morley (ed.), *Driven by Growth: Political Change in the Asia-Pacific Region* (Armonk, N.Y., 1992), and J. Woronoff, *Asia's Miracle Economies* (New York, 1986). For individual treatments of the Little Tigers, see H. Sohn, *Authoritarianism and Opposition in South Korea* (London, 1989), L. Chao and R. Myers, *The First Chinese Democracy* (Baltimore, 1998) Lee Kuan-yew, *From Third World to First: The Singapore Story, 1965–2000* (New York, 2000), and K. Rafferty, *City on the Rocks: Hong Kong's Uncertain Future* (London, 1991).

Chapter 13. Nationalism Triumphant: The Emergence of Independent States in South and Southeast Asia

For a recent survey of contemporary Indian history, see S. Wolpert, *A New History of India*, rev. ed. (New York, 1989). For two interesting accounts written for nonspecialists, see B. Crossette, *India: Facing the Twenty-First Century* (Bloomington, Ind., 1993), and S. Tharoor, *India: From Midnight to the Millennium* (New York, 1997). Also see P. Brass, *The New Cambridge History of India: The Politics of India Since Independence* (Cambridge, England, 1990), O. B. Jones, *Pakistan: Eye of the Storm* (New Haven, Conn., 2002), and C. Baxter, *Bangladesh: From a Nation to a State* (Boulder, Colo., 1997). A recent overview, packed with interesting ideas, is S. Khilnani, *The Idea of India* (New York, 1998).

On the period surrounding independence, see the dramatic account by L. Collins and D. Lapierre, *Freedom at Midnight* (New York, 1975). On Indira Gandhi, see K. Frank, *Indira: The Life of Indira Nehru Gandhi* (New York, 2000).

For a useful anthology of Indian fiction since independence, see S. Rushdie and E. West (eds.), *Mirror Work* (New York, 1997), and S. Tharu and K. Lalita (eds.), *Women Writing in India*, vol. 2 (New York, 1993).

For an introductory survey of modern Southeast Asia, see N. Tarling, *Nations and States in Southeast Asia* (Cambridge, 1998). For a more scholarly approach, see D. J. Steinberg (ed.), *In Search of Southeast Asia*, 2d ed. (New York, 1985). On Thailand, see P. Phongpaichit and C. Baker, *Thailand's Crisis* (Singapore, 2001). The best overall survey of the Philippines is D. J. Steinberg, *The Philippines: A Singular and a Plural Place* (Boulder, Colo., 1994). For a recent treatment of politics in Singapore, see R. Vasil, *Governing Singapore: A History of National Development and Democracy* (Singapore, 2000).

There is a rich selection of materials on modern Indonesia. On the Sukarno era, see J. Legge, *Sukarno* (New York, 1972). On the Suharto era and its origins, see M. Vatikiotis, *Indonesian Politics Under Suharto* (London, 1993). The most up-to-date treatment of Indonesia in its present state of crisis is G. Lloyd and S. Smith (eds.), *Indonesia Today: Challenges of History* (Singapore, 2001). Also see the thoughtful overview by T. Friend, *Indonesian Destinies* (Cambridge, Mass., 2003). Most of the literature on Indochina in recent decades has dealt with the Vietnam War and related conflicts in Laos and Cambodia. On conditions in Vietnam since the end of the war, see W. J. Duiker, *Vietnam: Revolution in Transition*, 2d ed. (Boulder, Colo., 1995).

The rise of terrorism in the region is examined in Z. Abuza, *Militant Islam is Southeast Asia* (Boulder, Colo., 2003).

Chapter 14. Emerging Africa

For a general survey of African history, see J. Reader, *Africa: A Biography of the Continent* (New York, 1998), M. Meredith, *The Fate of Africa: A History of 50 Years of Independence* (Washington, D.C., 2005) and K. Shillington, *History of Africa* (New York, 1989), which takes a chronological and geographical approach and includes excellent maps and illustrations. Also of interest is H. French, *A Continent for the Taking: The Tragedy and Hope of Africa* (New York, 2004).

On nationalist movements, see P. Gifford and W. R. Louis (eds.), *The Transfer of Power in Africa* (New Haven, Conn., 1982). For a poignant analysis of the hidden costs of nation building, see N. F. Mostert, *The Epic of South Africa's Creation and the Tragedy of the Xhosa People* (London, 1992). For a survey of economic conditions, see *Sub-Saharan Africa: From Crisis to Sustainable Growth* (Washington, D.C., 1989), issued by the World Bank. Also

see J. Illiffe, *The African Poor* (Cambridge, England, 1983). On political events, see S. Decalo, *Coups and Army Rule in Africa* (New Haven, Conn., 1990).

On African literature, see D. Wright, *New Directions in African Fiction* (New York, 1997), L. S. Klein (ed.), *African Literatures in the Twentieth Century: A Guide* (New York, 1986), and C. H. Bruner (ed.), *African Women's Writing* (Oxford, 1993).

Chapter 15. Ferment in the Middle East

Good general surveys of the modern Middle East include A. Goldschmidt Jr., *A Concise History of the Middle East* (Boulder, Colo., 2001), and G. E. Perry, *The Middle East: Fourteen Islamic Centuries* (Elizabeth, N.J., 1992).

On Israel and the Palestinian question, see D. Ross, *The Missing Peace: The Inside Story of the Fight for Middle East Peace* (New York, 2004), and B. Wasserstein, *Divided Jerusalem: The Struggle for the Holy City* (New Haven, Conn., 2000). On U.S.-Israeli relations, see S. Green, *Living by the Sword: America and Israel in the Middle East, 1968–1997* (London, 1998).

For historical perspective on the invasion of Iraq, see J. Kendell, *Iraq's Unruly Century* (New York, 2003). R. Khalidi's *Resurrecting Empire: Western Footprints and America's Perilous Path in the Middle East* (Boston, 2003), is a critical look at U.S. policy in the region.

On the politics of the Middle East, see J. A. Bill and R. Springborg, *Politics in the Middle East* (London, 1990), and R. R. Anderson, R. F. Seibert, and J. G. Wagner, *Politics and Change in the Middle East: Sources of Conflict and Accommodation* (Englewood Cliffs, N. J., 1993). For expert analysis on the current situation in the region, see B. Lewis, *What Went Wrong? Western Impact and Middle Eastern Response* (Oxford, 2001), and P. L. Bergen, *Holy War, Inc.: Inside the Secret World of Osama bin Laden* (New York, 2001).

Two excellent surveys of women in Islam from pre-Islamic society to the present are L. Ahmed, *Women and Gender in Islam: Historical Roots of a Modern Debate* (New Haven, Conn., 1993), and G. Nashat and J. E. Tucker, *Women in the Middle East and North Africa* (Bloomington, Ind., 1999). Also consult M. Afkhami and E. Friedl, *In the Eye of the Storm: Women in Post-Revolutionary Iran* (Syracuse, N.Y., 1994), and W. Wiebke, *Women in Islam* (Princeton, N.J., 1995).

For a scholarly but accessible overview of Arabic literature, see M. M. Badawi, *A Short History of Modern Arab Literature* (Oxford, 1993).

Chapter 16. Constructing a New World Order

For divergent visions of the future world order (or disorder), see S. P. Huntington, *The Clash of Civilizations and the Remaking of World Order* (New York, 1996), and F. Fukuyama, *The End of History and the Last Man* (New York, 1992). Also of interest is J. Scott, *Seeing like a State: How Certain Schemes to Improve the Human Condition Have Failed* (New Haven, Conn., 1998). An account of the impact of the fall of communism is contained in R. Skidelsky, *The Road from Serfdom: The Economic and Political Consequences of the End of Communism* (New York, 1996). Also see F. Furet, *The Passing of an Illusion: The Idea of Communism in the Twentieth Century* (Chicago, 1999).

On the Technological Revolution and its impact, see A. Toffler and H. Toffler, *Creating a New Civilization: The Politics of the Third Wave* (Atlanta, 1997). On the dangers of globalization, see J. E. Stiglitz, *Globalism and Its Discontents* (New York, 2002). For a stimulating discussion of the impact of globalization on our time, see T. Friedman, *The World Is Flat: A Brief History of the Twenty-First Century* (New York, 2005).

On current trends in the cultural field, see B. Nettl et al., *Excursions in World Music,* 2d ed. (Upper Saddle River, N.J., 1997), P. Geyh et al. (eds.), *Postmodern American Fiction: A Norton Anthology* (New York, 1998), and D. Damrosch, *What Is World Literature?* (Princeton, N.J., 2003).

INDEX

Page numbers followed by "p" indicate photographs; by "m" indicate maps; by "b" indicate shadedboxes.

nationalism as reaction to, 90–92
in Southeast Asia, 31–36
system and philosophy of, 7–8, 27–28
see also Western imperialism
Comintern (Communist International), 99
Common Market (European Economic Community), 207–08, **210m**
Communism
in Asia and Africa, 98–100
in China, 219–21, 224–25, 232
in decline, 194, 196, 310, 318
Eurocommunism and, 200–201
Great Depression and, 79
Islam and, 96
Marx definition of, 80
McCarthyism and the "Red Scare" of, 161
in Nazi Germany, 114, 118
Stalinism vs., 141
western containment of, 141–42, 146–47, 156, 189, 207, 240, 258
The Communist Manifesto (Marx & Engels), 18–**19b**
Communist Party
creating the "dictatorship of the proletariat," 84
formation in Soviet Russia, 77, 85
in Germany, 82
in Vietnam, 99–100
Concentration camps
British introduction of, 39
in Nazi Germany, 116, 125
in Soviet Union, 85, 183–84, 190
Confessions of a Mask (Mishima), 247
Confucianism
in China, 42–48, 51, 99–105
in Japan, 56, 243, 246
in Korea, 248
Mao rejection of, 220, 224
post-Mao China return to, 223
in Southeast Asia, 272
in Taiwan, 250
traditions and values, 52, 229, 232, 255, 312–15
Congress of Vienna (1815), 66
Conrad, Joseph, **288b**
Containment
ofcommunist expansion, 146–47, 156, 189, 207, 240, 258
Truman Doctrine and, 141–42
as U.S. policy, 143, 145
Contraception. *see* Abortion; Birthcontrol
Costa Rica, 173
Council for Mutual Economic Assistance (COMECON), 143–**44m**
Crimean War, 15
Croatia, 209–10
Cry, the Peacock (Desai), 265
Cuba
Castro and revolution in, 176–78
Soviet alliance with, 152
as Soviet model, 172–73
Spanish-American War (1898), 33
Cuban Missile Crisis (1962), 152
Cultural identity
in Africa, 278–79, 285, 287, 289
China and, 53
in Europe, **206B, 208b**
globalization impact on, 319
India and, 93, 263, 266
Indonesia and, 267

Islam and, 303
Japan and, 53, 58, 247
Latin America and, 110
in literature and the arts, 169, 320
nationalism and, 12, 90
Russia and, 319
totalitarianism and, 113
Culture
antiforeign sentiment in preservation of, 203, 211, 311
under Communism in China, 230–32
Eastern Europe suppression of, 191
the globalization of, 320–21
Industrial Revolution and, 62
nationalism giving rise to, 90–92
post-WWI developments in, 87
in post-WWII Japan, 246–48
sciences in the transformation of, 20–22, 170
Soviet Bloc repression of, 189–92
in Third Wave economic development, 313–14
trends in Africa, 287
trends in Latin American, 179–80
trends in post-war Europe, 214–15
trends in Southeast Asia, 272–73
trends in U.S., 169–70
U.S.-Soviet exchanges, 151–**52p**, 156
western influence in Africa, 285
Western influence on Chinese, 104–05
see also Literature, arts andmusic
Czech Republic, 209–11
Czechoslovakia
alliance with France, 117
Communist takeover, 141
end of Soviet control over, 194
German occupation of, 118–19
spread of authoritarianism to, 116
unrest over Soviet domination in, 189
Versailles Peace Conference and, 79
as Warsaw Pact member, 143
women's right to vote in, 213

daSilva, Luiz Inacio ("Lula"), 175
Dalí, Salvadore, 86
The Dark Child (Laye), 287
Darwin, Charles, 21
Das Kapital (Marx), 18
de Beauvoir, Simone, 213
de Gaulle, Charles, 202, 276
de Klerk, F. W., 282
Deconstruction, 214
Dei-Anang, Michael Francis, 275
Dekker, E. Douwes, **34b**
Democracy
inAfrica, 280–82, 284
Atlantic Charter (1941) and, 322
in China, 217, 221
colonialism as introduction to, 137
failures in Southeast Asia, 267
and the global village, 318–20
in India, 258, 261, 266
in Indonesia under Sukarno, 267–68, **269b**
Islam compatibility with, **302b**
in Isreal, 300–301
Japanese experiment with, 105, 116–17
in Latin America, 173
Middle East experiments in, 300
in the "new world order," 311–13
in post-Soviet Eastern Europe, 209–10
post-WWI dictatorships and, 112–13

rise of post-WWI dictatorships and, 116
in South Korea, 249
Three People's Principles of Sun Yat-sen, 51, 103
WWI "to make the world safe for," 81–82
. *see also* Right to vote
Democratic Republic of the Congo, 278, 284
Democratic Republic of Vietnam (DRV) *see* Vietnam
Deng Xiaoping, 220–22
Denmark, 121, 124, 143–**44m,** 208
Dependency theory, 40, 107–09, 172–73, 229, 322–23
Desai, Anita, 265
The Descent of Man (Darwin), **21b**
Devi, Phoolan, 264
Deweu, John, 100
Dewey, George, 33
Diaghilev, Sergei, 23
Díaz, Porfirio, 18, 109
Dickens, Charles, 3
Dictatorships, 112–13, 114–15, **302b**
Diefenbaker, John, 171
Diem, Ngo Dinh, 154–55, 267
Ding Ling, 230–31
Disgrace (Coetzee), 289
Divorce
in China, **228b**–29
in Europe, 212
feminism and, 12
in Japan, 56, 244–45
in Kuwait, 305
in Russia, 197
in the United States, 166, 315
see also Marriage
Djugashvili, Joseph *see* Stalin, Joseph (Joseph Djugashvili)
Doctor Zhivago (Pasternak), 190
Doctrine of natural rights, 12
A Doll House (Ibsen), **11b**
Domingo, Placido, 320
Don Segundo Sombra (Guiraldes), 110
Dona Barbara (Gallegos), 110
Dreiser, Theodore, 87
Drug use/abuse
inChina, 231
colonialism and, 22
in Europe, 212
Islam and, 272, 303
in Japan, 244, 247
societal values and, 313, 315
in U.S., 166
Dubcek, Alexander, 189
Duchamp, Marcel, 86
Dutch East India Company (VOC) *see* Indonesia; Southeast Asia
Dutch Republic
abolishment of slave trade by, 36
colonial expansion and, 4, 26
colonialism and the Dutch East Company, 31–36
political ideologies of change in, 13
South African Cape Colony, 39–40
Dzerzhinsky, Felix, **183p**

East Africa Federation, 282
East Germany
Berlin Blockade (1948), 143
Berlin crisis (1958), 150–51
Berlin occupation zones, **143m**

women's right to vote in, 213
in WWI, 66, 73
in WWII, 123
see also Fascist Italy
Ivory Coast, 283–84

Jagua Nana (Ekwensi), 281
Japan
alliance with Germany, 120
alliance with Nazi Germany, 118
in China, 101
as closed society, 55–56, 90
as colonial power, 27, 58–60, 62, 106, 242
experiment in democracy, 105
industrialization of, 57–58
Meiji Constitution (1889), 56–57, 240–41
in the "new world order," 313
rise of militarism, 116–17
rise of nationalism, 107
Shidehara diplomacy, 106–07
Soviet Union declaration of war on, 145
timelines in history, **61b, 134, 256b**
war with China, 49, 120–21
war with Imperial Russia, 59–60, 74, 145
in WWI, 72
in WWII, 125–29, **130p,** 131
WWII, events leading to, 120–**22b**
WWII mobilization, 131–32
WWII surrender of, 130–31
see also Manchuria
Japan, post-WWII
adapting traditional political culture to, 241–42
Allied occupation, 239
constitution and government, 240–41
in the "Pacific Century," 238
retention of the Emperor, **239b**
wartime atrocities and remilitarization, 242
Japanese-American internment, 132
Jews/Jewish people
anti-Semitism and, 114
depicted in literature, 169, 307
Hitler's rise to power and, 115–16
the Holocaust, 124–25
Isreal as homeland, 294
Palestine and, 98, 293
in Soviet Union, 183, 185
Jiang Quing, 220
Jiang Zemin, 223–24, 318
Jinnah, Mohammed Ali, 257, 261
Johnson, Lyndon B., **154b**–55, 160–63
Johnson-Sirleaf, Ellen, 287
Jordan, 98, 292–94, 300, 305
Joyce, James, 87

Kabila, Lauren, 284
Kádár, János, 188–89, 194
Kahlo, Frida, 110
Kandinsky, Wassily, 86
Kanehara, Hitomi, 247
Kapoor, Karisma, 264
Kashmir dispute, 258, **260m,** 261, 266
Kellogg, Frank B., 81
Kellogg-Briand Pact (1928), 81
Kemal, Mustafa ("Atatürk"), 95–**96b, 302b,** 303–05
Kennan, George, 143, 145
Kennedy, John F., 151–52, 160–61, 173, 176
Kenya, 277–78, 282, 285
Kenyatta, Jomo, 277, 279

Kerensky, Alexander, 75
Kerry, John F., 165
Khatemi, Mohammad, 298
Khomeini, Ruholla (Ayatollah), 164, 266, 292, 297, 300, **302b**
Khrushchev, Nikita, 150–52, **153b,** 156, 177, 183–84, **185b**
Kibaki, Mwai, 282
Kim Dae Jung, 249
Kim Il Sung, 248
Kim Jong Il, 249
Kim Young Sam, 249
King, Martin Luther, 161–**62b**
Kingoro, Hashimoto, **122b**
Kipling, Rudyard, 28, **29b**
Kirchner, Nestor, 173–74
Kissinger, Henry, 155, 295
Klee, Paul, 86
Kohl, Helmut, 204–05
Koizumi, Junichiro, 241–42
Korea
Chinese influence over, 49, 101, 148
Chinese intervention in, 149
Japanese annexation of, 58–60, 148
Japanese seizure of, 106
timelines in history, **256b**
in WWII, 127
see also South Korea
Korean War (1950–1952), 148–49, 161, 170, 248
Kornilov, Lavr, 75
Kosovo, 209–10
Kosygin, Alexei, 156, 184
Kuwait, 299, 300–301, 305
Kwasniewski, Aleksander, 209

Labor
19th Century discipline for, **10b**
Japanese use of forced, 126–28, 132
Middle East guest worker programs, 303
Nazi use of forced, 124–25
"outscourcing" and, 165, 262, 312
population growth as source of, 3, 8, 318
in post-war Europe, 212–13
socialist movements, 18
Soviet Bloc inequalities in, 191–92
in Soviet Union, 181–82
see also Child labor; Workingclass
Labor movements, 16–18
Laissez-faire economics, 12–13
Landed aristocracy, 9
Laos, 32, 149
Latin America
Alliance for Progress, 173
cultural tradition and political change in, 17–18
economic weaknesses, 171–72
illegal immigration to U.S., 166
Monroe Doctrine in, 33
nationalism and dictatorship in, 107–09
post-WWI dictatorships in, 112–13
religion and cultural values in, 315
role of the Catholic Church in, 172
Soviet expansion in, 152
timelines in history, **24b, 111b, 180b**
in the U.S. shadow, 172–73
Latvia, 79, 210
Laurier, Wilfrid, 17
Lawrence, T. E. (Lawrence of Arabia), 71–72

Laye, Camara, 287–**88b**
Le Corbusier, 87
League of Nations, 79–82, 112, 132
Leary, Timothy, 212
Lebanon, 98, 292–93, 295
Ledendorff, Erich von, 78
Lee Hsien-luong, 253
Lee Kuan-yew, 252
Lee Teng-hui, 251
Lend-Lease Program, 129
Lenin, Vladimir, 75–78, **77p,** 84, 98, 118, **153b**
Les Demoiselles D'avignon (Picasso), **23p**
Lesseps, Ferdinand de, 37
Lévesque, René, 171
Lewis, Sinclair, 87
Liang Hang, 220
Liberalism, as ideology of change, 12–18
Liberia, 284, 287
Libya, 16, 37, 297
Literature, arts and music
Africa, 286–89
American transformations in, 167–70
under Communism in China, 230–32
contemporary trends in 20th Century, 22–23, 320–21
India, 265–66
Japanese, 105, 246–48
Latin America, 179–80
Mexico, 110
Middle East, 305–07
post-war Europe, 214–15
post-WWI developments in, 85–87
Southeast Asia, 272–73
Soviet Bloc repression of, 189–92
Soviet Union, 183, **193p**
see also Culture; Movieindustry
Lithuania, 79, 210
Little Red Book (Mao), 220, 225, **230p**
"Little Tigers"
"East Asian miracle" of, 312–13, 323
Hong Kong, 251–54
in the "Pacific Century," 238
Singapore, 251–54
South Korea, 248–49
Taiwan, 249–51
see also specific country byname
Liu Shaoqi, 220
Livingstone, David, 38
Llosa, Mario Vargas, 179
Louis Philippe (king of France), 13
Luxembourg, 143–**44m,** 207–08

Maastricht Treaty (Treaty on European Union), 208–09
MacArthur, Douglas, 126, 148–49, **239b**–40
Macaulay, Thomas Babington, **31b**
Madagascar Plan for relocation of Jews, 125
Madero, Francisco, 109
Magellan, Ferdinand, 8
Mahathir Mohamad, 318
Mahatma ("Great Soul") *see* Gandhi, Mohandas
Mahfouz, Naguib, 304, 306
Major, John, 207
Makota, Saito, 117
Malamud, Bernard, 169
Malaysia, **252m**
as ASEAN member, 271
communism in, 99
end of colonial rule in, 266
Muslim tensions in, 269, 297

in Vietnam, 154–56, 163
in WWI, 72–73, 78–79
in WWII, 120–21, 125–26, 129–32
see also Cold War
United States colonialism
ascolonial power, 27, 62
Hawaiian Islands and, 33
Open Door policy, 48, 60
slave trade and, 36
Universal Declaration of Human Rights, 318
Universal health care, 160
Universal suffrage, 81–82
see also Right to vote
Urbanization, Industrial Revolution and, 8–9,
16, 18
Uruguay, 172

V (Pynchon), 169
Values *see* Family structureand values; Religion;
Society and social structures
Van Gogh, Vincent, 22
Vanderbilt, Consuelo, 9
Vargas, Getúlio, 108, 174
Venezuela, 17, 173, 178–79
Versailles Peace Conference *see* Treaty of
Versailles (1919)
Vichy France, 121
Victor Emmanuel III (king of Italy), 113
Victoria (queen of England), 9
Vietminh Front, 149, 267
Vietnam
as ASEAN member, 271
colonialism in, 32, 90
communism in, 268
failure of democracy in, 267
Franco-Vietminh War (1946–1954),
149, 267
Geneva Accords (1954), 149, 154, 267–68
reunification of North and South, 270
role of China in, 155–56
role of Soviet Union in, 155
status of women in, 272
U.S. war (1963–1975), 154–56, 163
"Vietnam syndrome," 156
Villa, Pancho, 109
Vo Nguyen Giap, **150p**

Wade, Abdoulaye, 284
Waiting for Godot (Beckett), 214
Wales, 206
Walesa, Lech, 194
Wallachia, 15
Wang Shuo, 231
War crimes, 204, 210, 239
War reparations
inestablishment of Isreal, 294
post-WWI, 81
post-WWII, 132–33, 143, 181
Warfare
antimissile defense, 320
Blitzkrieg ("lightningwar"), 121
computers, 170
concentration camps, 39, 85, 116, 125
cruise missiles, 157
ICBMs, 150, 152, 156
internal combustion engine, 6
internment camps, 132
Kellogg-Briand Pact renouncing, 81
propaganda use, 74
radar, 122, 170

submarines, 73
tanks, 71, 130
see also Technology development; World
War I
Warhol, Andy, 167
Warren, Earl, 161
Warsaw Pact (1955), 143–**44m**, 188, 234
Wealth
colonialism and creation of, 62
creation of consumer, 7–8, 161, 165–66
Industrial Revolution impact on, 3
inequalities in the concentration of, 106
oil and Middle East, 301–03
oil exploration and, 97–98
in post-WWII Japan, 244
post-WWII U.S., 160–61
socialist movement and distribution of,
18–20
The Wealth and Poverty of Nations
(Landes), 62
Weapons of mass destruction (WMD), 300
Weimar Republic, 82, 114–15, 117
Welfare state
in Canada, 171
creation in the U.S., 79–80, 160–61
dismantling the U.S., 164
in Europe, 201–02, 212
model of France as, 202–03
model of Great Britain as, 205–07
model of West Germany as, 203–05
shrinking the future, 212
West Germany
Common Market and, 207–08
as NATO member, 143–**44m,** 203
reunification with East Germany,
204–**06b**
unification of occupation zones, 143, 203
as welfare state, 203–05
West Side Story (Bernstein), 151
Western imperialism
benefits vs. negatives of, 136–37
competition for Africa, 38, 63
depicted in literature, **288b**
Industrial Revolution and, 26–27
Latin America and, 17–18, 33
Marxism and, 98–100
opening China to, 47–50, 53–55, 63
opening Japan to, 55–56, 63
in Southeast Asia, 31–36, 63
U.S. war in Vietnam as, **154b**
the veil and chador as defense from, 306
as "white man's burden," **29b**
see also Colonialism
White Teeth (Smith), 215
"The White Man's Burden" (Kipling), **29b**
Whither Bound Africa (Dei-Anang), 275
William II (Emperor of Germany), 66, **69b,**
73, 78
Wilson, Woodrow, 16, 73, 78–79, 81
The Wind-Up Bird Chronicle (Murakami), 247
Women's Social and Political Union, 12
Women/women's rights/equality of
in Africa, 285–87
in Argentina, 173
in China, 54–55, 104, **228b**–29
in colonial Africa, 42
in Cuba, 177
depicted in art, 179
depicted in literature, 247, 289
in fascist Italy, 113

gender roles and sexual equality, 179, 228,
244, 286, 305
in Great Britain, 15
in India, 263–65
Industrial Revolution impact on, 10–12
in Islam, 304–05
in Japan, 58, 105
Japanese forced prostitution of, 127
in literature, 265–66, 306–07
in Nazi Germany, 116
in post-war Europe, 212–13
in post-WWII Japan, 243–45
in Southeast Asia, 272
Soviet Bloc inequalities in, 192
in Soviet Union, 181–82
trends in literature, 169
in Turkey, 96
in the United States, 166
in WWI, 74
in WWII, 131–32
see also Abortion; Birthcontrol; Marriage
Working class, 9, 18–**19b**
see also Labor
Works Progress Administration (WPA), 83
World Bank, 312
World Disarmament Conference
(1932), 81
World economy, Industrial Revolution
impact on, 8
The World of Yesterday (Zweig), **72b**
World Trade Organization (WTO), 227,
284, 312
see also Globalization
World War I, **71p**
actions leading up to, 66–68
conduct of, 68–72
entry of U.S., 72–73
League of Nations and, 79
post-war peace failure, 80–82
society and social structure in, 73–74
Versailles Peace Conference, 78–79
women's equality following, 12, 81–82
see also principal countriesinvolved
World War II
Battle of Britain (1940–1941), 122–23
events leading to, 112, 117–18, 120–21
Japanese occupation policies in, 126–29
mobilization for global war in, 131–32
Munich Conference and, 118–**19b**
Nazi occupation policies in, 124–25
peace settlement of, 132–33
Soviet Union in, 124, 129–30
U.S. entry into, 129–31
the war in Europe (1939–1941), 121–24
see also principal countries involved
World Wide Web *see* Internet, computers
and the
Wright, Frank Lloyd, 23
Wright, Wilbur & Orville, 7

Xinjiang (Chinese Turkestan), 148
Xu Mangyao, 231

Yalta Conference, 132
The Yellow Arrow (Pelevin), 197
Yeltsin, Boris, 195–96
Yemen, 294, 300
Yom Kippur War (1973), 295–96
Yuan Shikai, 100–101
Yudhyono, Susilo, 270